Contemporary Finance

for Aviva and Benjamin

Contemporary Finance

Money, Risk, and Public Policy

Allan M. Malz

Published by John Wiley & Sons, Inc., Hoboken, New Jersey.
Published simultaneously in Canada.

For general information on our other products and services or for technical support, please contact our Customer Care Department within the United States at (800) 762-2974, outside the United States at (317) 572-3993 or fax (317) 572-4002.

Wiley also publishes its books in a variety of electronic formats. Some content that appears in print may not be available in electronic formats. For more information about Wiley products, visit our web site at www.wiley.com.

Library of Congress Cataloging-in-Publication Data:

Names: Malz, Allan M., author.
Title: Contemporary finance : money, risk, and public policy / Allan M.
   Malz.
Description: Hoboken, New Jersey : Wiley, [2024] | Includes index.
Identifiers: LCCN 2024019680 (print) | LCCN 2024019681 (ebook) | ISBN
   9781394179626 (hardback) | ISBN 9781394179640 (adobe pdf) | ISBN
   9781394179633 (epub)
Subjects: LCSH: Finance.
Classification: LCC HG173 .M276 2024 (print) | LCC HG173 (ebook) | DDC
   332—dc23/eng/20240516
LC record available at https://lccn.loc.gov/2024019680
LC ebook record available at https://lccn.loc.gov/2024019681

Cover Design: Wiley
Cover Image: Courtesy of Julia Zimbalist and Allan Malz

Set in 10/12pt TimesLTStd by Straive, Chennai, India

SKY10084836_091724

Contents

List of Figures

List of Tables

Preface

Finance is a noble discipline that has been pursued in something like its present form since the early Renaissance. It has been an integral part of the world's emergence from privation over the past few centuries.

This book aims to help students and professionals understand today's financial world. It tries to soften the distinction in university teaching between economics and finance, which may be useful in designing curricula but sets up a misleading dichotomy. Today, after the global financial crisis, the era of low interest rates that led up to it, Covid, and the inflation and banking turmoil that followed, monetary policy has changed drastically. It was always simplistic to think about how monetary policy works without reference to the financial system, but today it would entirely miss the point.

One goal of the book is to integrate what is needed to understand the crisis world we've experienced and the public policy responses it led to. To understand crises and capital regulation, for example, you need to understand credit risk and securitization, and to understand those, you need some option pricing theory and the CAPM. This book avoids treating risk analysis and management as a distinct specialization, somehow separate from the rest of finance. Economics and finance study one unitary world, risk analysis is embedded in all decision making, and you need insights from all these disciplines to make sense of things.

Another goal is to make some of these models more comprehensible for a general finance and economics audience. There was an unavoidable trade-off between doing that for more topics and limiting the length of the book. For sufferers through the chapter on option pricing, for example, there are fine alternative presentations, cited at the end.

The book is US-centric, with US financial institutions spelled out in more detail than those of other advanced market economies. Because the details of regulation can be mind-numbing, some readers may breathe a sigh of relief that it's kept largely to one country.

In economics and finance, unrealistic simplified starting points are often a good way to gain insight into the complicated workings of the real world. Examples include assuming that markets clear perfectly all the time, that asset price changes are normally distributed, or that households can achieve through their own borrowing and lending anything corporate managers leave undone in firms' financial management. In explaining how finance works, we'll therefore often start with a clear, simple sketch and then bring in some of the messy reality.

In many places in the book, I summarize the empirical evidence on an issue. I've done my best to be fair, but we come to things with a perspective, and I'm not aware of a controversy in economics or finance in which statistical evidence hasn't been brought in support of opposing points of view. I've cited sources that present or survey empirical work, and the graphs display and cite a tiny fraction of the plethora of easily available data from many public and private sources. Readers are urged to look at controversies, arguments and data, and form their own view.

Most of the book is organized analytically but presents more recent developments chronologically. The contemporary reality can't be understood except against the background of historically low interest rates over the past three decades and more and the global financial crisis. Some of the changes in financial institutions and public policies are so recent and so intertwined that the clearest way to describe them is in the context of the succession of stress events in the financial system.

I'd like to thank Flavio Bartmann, Aaron Brown, Richard Cantor, Don Chew, Rich Clarida, Kevin Dowd, Louis Geser, Fumio Hayashi, Ali Hirsa, and Bill Nelson for carefully reading part or all of the manuscript, and helping me organize the presentation and avoid numerous errors. I've had the fortune and privilege, at the New York Fed, the RiskMetrics Group, and a few hedge funds, to work with and learn from the smartest, funniest, and most annoying people I've ever encountered. (I may have annoyed a few myself.) I continue to learn from and enjoy the company of my colleagues at Columbia University. I'd also like to thank Mick Jagger, the former London School of Economics student who long ago taught me everything I know.

About the Author

Allan M. Malz has been chief risk officer at several multi-strategy hedge fund management firms. He began his career at the Federal Reserve Bank of New York as a researcher and foreign exchange trader, before heading the research effort at the RiskMetrics Group. Returning to the New York Fed from 2009 to 2014 as a vice president in the Markets Group, Malz helped implement the Term Asset-Backed Securities Lending Facility (TALF), a Fed emergency liquidity program addressing the financial crisis.

Malz is an investment consultant and adjunct professor at Columbia University. His work on predicting financial crises and risk measurement for options has been published in industry and academic journals, and he is the author of *Financial Risk Management: Models, History, and Institutions* (Wiley, 2011). Malz holds a Ph.D. from Columbia and a *Diplom* from Ludwig-Maximilians-Universität München.

Part I: Finance in the Economic System

1

Functions and Structure of the Financial System

1.1 Functions of the Financial System

Finance is a human activity that deals with planning for the future. The financial sector of the economy is made up of markets in which promises of future payment are issued and assets are traded, the people and the firms making and assisting with these claims and exchanges, and the specialized facilities through which trading and other functions are carried out. It is embedded in a larger economic system shaped in part by how law and institutions, ranging from corporate organization to government regulations, have emerged historically. Finance is an important contributor to overall economic efficiency. Regions with developed and well-functioning financial systems tend to have higher economic growth.

The financial system carries out a number of functions aimed at improving the allocation of resources over time, between firms, and geographically, under conditions of constant change and profound uncertainty. It gathers resources from savers or lenders and transfers them to investors or borrowers, enabling people to defer consumption into the future and move resources to other places. Savers include households or firms with a surplus or resources; investors are households or firms using the resources to add to society's capital stock, including machines, supply chain organization, education, and consumer durables. The financial system helps people plan for the future, identify risks, and insure against adverse outcomes.

An **asset** is a good that provides value over time, rather than being consumed and disappearing in a moment. Assets include **financial instruments**, contracts, such as equity, debt, and derivatives contracts, as well as **real assets,** such as real estate and commodities.

Risk is the possibility of an unwanted event, encompassing the many ways in which people or companies become poorer or worse off, ranging from adverse price changes to bankruptcy to losing a lawsuit. The financial system facilitates managing, reducing, and sharing of risk, via forms of financing, providing insurance, and pooling and diversification of assets. For example, it is sometimes possible to **hedge** against a risk, that is, isolate it and offset its effects.

Assets have value or payoffs in an uncertain future, so their values today are influenced by how much time will pass before the future value is realized, what people think the future payoffs and their probabilities might be, and how they feel about the risks posed by that range of possibilities. If asset prices are set in more or less **efficient** financial markets, they will roughly reflect people's expectations, desires and fears about the future. The most important asset price is the, **interest rate,** which is the rate paid for borrowing money, expressed as a percent of the **principal, par value,** or **notional amount** of money borrowed per unit of time, generally annually.

Mechanisms to facilitate exchange of goods and services and for trading include the creation and use of **money** and other **media of exchange**, and more generally, of **liquid** assets. **Payment systems** also facilitate carrying out exchanges.

Many risks come bundled with benefits or with other risks. Forms of organization, such as the corporation and partnerships, and contracts, such as debt and equity, reduce risk and facilitate investment by pooling and sharing ownership and other claims on resources. Institutional structure is determined to a large extent by historical development.

In carrying out these functions of resource allocation, risk management, and facilitation of exchange, households and firms gather and create information. They identify opportunities for productive investment or allocation of capital. **Financial innovation** includes the discovery and implementation of new assets, such as securitization, derivatives, cryptocurrencies, and new techniques for disseminating information about prices and trading activity.

1.2   Market Participants, Intermediaries, and Governments

A number of terms are used to describe the variety of market participants, ultimately human beings, with all their disparate goals. Final consumers of financial services are called households, individuals, or investors. The term "agent" is used in two different senses: generally as a synonym for market participant and more specifically for one acting on behalf of another.

Firms that specialize in financial functions, such as banks, insurance companies, and investment managers, are called **financial intermediaries**. Their value added is nearly 8 percent of US gross domestic product (GDP).[1] Many are parts of large holding companies with subsidiaries operating internationally in widely varying functions. Most intermediaries carry out multiple functions and can be classified from both an institutional perspective, by type of firms, and from a functional perspective, by product or service, e.g. lending or facilitating transactions.

Many of these functions are carried out by financial firms "using their balance sheets" to transform assets and change their characteristics, by acquiring assets with one set of characteristics, and issuing liabilities with different characteristics that become the assets of other market participants. Intermediaries can separate and redistribute those characteristics in a way that better suits market participants at lower cost.

Maturity transformation changes the term to maturity of a debt contract by borrowing short-term and lending at longer term. In **credit transformation**, the credit quality of a debt contract is changed (and not necessarily raised). Monitoring, using **collateralization**, by which the borrower puts assets under the control of the lender, and using guarantees, may raise credit quality. **Risk distribution** and **transfer**, such as securitization, may create some securities with lower credit quality. The liquidity transformation carried out by banks and **money market mutual funds** (MMMFs) makes debt contracts function more like money and goes hand-in-hand with maturity transformation.

"What do banks do?" is a perennial question, with no universally accepted definitions. Older forms of banking, dating back to the medieval era, are referred to as **merchant banks**, which connect investors to investment possibilities, and generally also take an ownership stake. Modern **commercial banks** lend directly to households and companies and monitor their creditworthiness.

---

[1] The GDP share of the industry group Finance and Insurance was 7.8 percent in Q3 of 2022.

Banks may engage in **proprietary trading** of assets for their own accounts. **Investment banks** facilitate **market intermediation**, including securities issuance by companies, through **syndication**—arranging the securities' initial sale—and **underwriting**—assuming at least part of the price risk. The share of market compared to bank intermediation is higher in the United States than in continental Europe. Some banks also provide **custodial services** for clients, including custody of their customers' securities and cash balances, record keeping, and managing cash flows such as dividends and interest from investments.

Broker-dealers trade and invest in securities. **Dealers, market makers,** or **liquidity providers** take principal positions, using equity and borrowed funds to finance and execute securities trading. They take long or short positions and bear the market and credit risk of securities inventories, and are compensated through trading profits and interest. **Brokers** act as agents, facilitating trades and provide trading infrastructure without taking principal positions. They are compensated through fees, commissions, and may earn net interest by lending customer cash balances to other intermediaries at a higher rate than the broker pays.

Specialized intermediaries and mechanisms facilitate pooling investments. **Investment managers** and **management companies** manage investments on behalf of clients, whose portfolios remain in separate accounts. In the United States, **investment companies** are a legal form of pooled investment portfolio of securities and other assets in which investors own equity shares. **Open-end mutual funds**, the largest category of investment company, must calculate a **net asset value** (NAV) at the end of each day at which it issues or redeems shares at investors' initiative, adding or selling assets in its portfolio to match. The volume of investment in the fund is not limited, in contrast to **closed-end funds** trading in markets. **Money market mutual funds** (MMMFs) are a specialized type of mutual fund that invest in high credit quality, short-term money market instruments. **Exchange-traded funds** (ETFs) were introduced in the 1990s and differ from mutual funds in that investors buy and sell shares in the market, rather than in transactions with the fund itself. Large intermediaries act as **authorized participants**, buying and selling the constituent assets of an ETF and redeeming or issuing shares.

Institutional investors are large pools of assets that manage investments on behalf of others. They include investment management companies, pension funds, insurance companies, family offices, foundations, and endowments. Many are advised by consultants, such as McKinsey and Callan, that play a large role in their decision making. **Defined benefit pension funds** or plans are a form of employer-provided retirement benefit common in many countries. They provide for payments of a specified annual amount over the life of the retiree that is related to the years of work, average salary earned, and age at retirement. Many such plans are indexed for inflation. The benefits are disbursed out of funds that are financed by a combination of employer and employee payments and are invested. In a **defined contribution plan**, employees have an ownership claim on a portion of the fund, and future benefits depend on the fund's returns.

The financial system has evolved together with systems of government. In most of the world, government involvement with the financial system is carried out through the state itself and through **central banks,** which resemble commercial banks in some ways but are under some form of public ownership and government control. **Monetary policy** influences economic outcomes through interest rates, money markets, and control over the issuance of money. The legal structure within which financial intermediation is carried out is shaped by **regulatory policy**, the set of rules governing permitted, required, and prohibited actions and forms of organization.

Though these domains of state action are referred to as policy, suggesting a dispassionate process of evaluation and formulation, they are generally part of a larger political process. Historically, through their evolution, and institutionally, through legal and corporate arrangements, central banks in many countries, including the United States, are not purely government-owned agencies but have some private-sector participation in their governance. Some regulatory powers, such as standard setting and licensing, are delegated to private-sector entities.

1.3   Assets and Markets

1.3.1   Money and Money Markets

Money encompasses a wide range of commonly accepted assets with stability of exchange value that provide money services, including:[2]

Payment services: can be exchanged for other goods or assets, or in settlement of debts.
Liquidity services: relative certainty as a **store of value**.
Nominal unit of account: prices and values that are most often measured in money units.

Money has its origins in a past so remote that there is little definitive evidence for its earliest forms. In one view, state sanction is needed for a **medium of exchange** to be widely accepted, for example, because it must be used to pay taxes or because the state distributes it widely. More likely, money is emergent, evolving gradually during prehistory as market participants gravitated to particular commodities as convenient means of exchange.

Money can take the form of a physical or digital object or **token**, based on its intrinsic value or confidence in its wide acceptance. In the historical era, until the Middle Ages, most money was in the form of coins or **specie** issued by governments. For most of the past millennium, money has also been account-based, meaning a liability of a government, central banks, financial intermediaries carrying out liquidity transformation, or even a nonfinancial business, its value dependent on the trustworthiness of the claim issuer. New forms of money have emerged recently, for example MMMF shares in the 1970s and cryptocurrencies in the current century.

Banks have historically been the largest issuers of claims used as money. The owner of an account with a positive balance could instruct a bank to transfer funds to another person's account at the same or at a different bank. A large part of the liabilities of central banks and commercial banks consist of **deposits**, book-entry liabilities that correspond to assets their owners can use to make payments or settle debts. Typically, commercial banks, government-owned enterprises, and a few other intermediaries that are allowed to issue deposits are authorized—and in many jurisdictions required—to hold deposits at a central bank, called **reserve balances**. In the United States, **federal funds**, or fed funds, are reserve balances at Federal Reserve (Fed) district banks that are traded or used to settle payments among banks.

Cash and close substitutes for cash, or **narrow money**, include currency and short-term central bank and commercial bank deposits that can be used for immediate payment. Some liquid short-term claims—**broad** or **near-money** and **money substitutes**—bear interest, including shorter-term government debt and bank deposits such as **certificates of deposit** (CDs). They are used less frequently as means of payment but may be readily sold for cash or used as collateral to borrow cash or other assets at reliably foreseeable values.

---

[2] Tobin (1958) defines it as " ... a species we may call monetary assets—marketable, fixed in money value, free of default risk."

Many forms of money trade in money markets, which are among the highest-volume and the most active financial markets. They include **interbank lending**, **commercial paper**, and perhaps most importantly, **repo** markets.

1.3.2   Foreign Exchange

A **foreign exchange rate** is the price of currency issued in one jurisdiction in terms of another. Foreign exchange markets are among the largest financial markets in the world by many measures with, daily trading volume of $7.5 trillion.[3]

Appreciation (depreciation) of a foreign currency is a rise (fall) of its price in home or local currency units. Long positions in foreign currency and investments in foreign assets are exposed to appreciation of the home currency and depreciation of foreign currency. Short positions in foreign currency, such as future payment obligations for imported goods or repayment of borrowing in foreign currency, are exposed to depreciation of the home currency or appreciation of foreign currency.

1.3.3   Digital Currencies

Digital currencies are a relatively recent innovation in money and payments systems made possible by advances in technology and the rapidly declining cost of computers. They currently take several forms. A **cryptocurrency** is a means of exchange that relies on algorithms to preserve limited supply and scarcity and to maintain the ledger that documents ownership. Cryptocurrencies are different from most privately created forms of money used in the past in that they are not inside money, that is claims on a private issuer, but are added to the total stock of assets.

Stablecoins are digital assets with values pegged to that of another form of money. Some, such as Tether, are tied to the US dollar; others are tied to the value of a cryptocurrency. The values are promised by the issuer to be maintained either by issuing the stablecoin as a liability supported by asset reserves or through an algorithm asserted to maintain the pegged value.

Central bank digital currencies (CBDCs) are digital currencies issued by central banks or governments. They have not yet become widespread but are being widely considered. Benefits claimed for introducing CBDCs include reducing crimes committed using physical cash, such as tax evasion, money laundering, and dealing in contraband, and providing banking services to poor people.

The disadvantages include the potential for surveillance and government control of people's transactions. Substitution of CBDCs for bank deposits raises monetary policy implementation concerns and competitive concerns for commercial banks. Public acceptance of CBDCs is also not assured in countries with weak currencies, for example, the 2023 attempt by the Nigerian central bank to introduce a digital currency.

1.3.4   Equity, Loans, and Bonds

Equity is an ownership stake in a firm, a **residual claim** that pays or is worth the remaining value of the firm's assets after other claims have been met in full. Under the legal structure of firm organization prevailing since the 19th century, equity investors, or **shareholders**, enjoy **limited liability**, owing external claimants no more than the value of their investment.

---

[3] As of April 2022.

Money can be invested or lent for shorter or longer periods of time. The lender receives a claim in return, part of a larger category of **fixed-income debt instruments**. Some short-term claims are used as money to carry out transactions.

Debt instruments are highly diverse. **Loans** are bilateral contracts between a lender, often a single bank or nonbank loan originator, and the borrower. Many equity claims and most bonds are **securities**, subject to a body of law and regulation. The legal design of **debt securities** including **bonds** facilitates offering them to many potential lenders at issuance. Bonds are generally issued by larger corporations and by governments. The largest bond markets are those for sovereign debt, that of central governments, such as the market for US government bonds, or Treasurys.

Some longer-term claims can be bought and sold in **capital markets**. Loans and bonds differ primarily in how readily they trade. Loans are usually retained by the originator; bonds are designed to be traded. Large loans may be **syndicated**, with several lenders extending credit under a uniform agreement. Regulatory policy distinguishes between **public capital markets** subjected to more stringent requirements regarding accounting and disclosure, and accessible to the general public and **private markets** open only to **qualified**—institutional or wealthy—**investors**.

Securities are initially sold to investors by the issuers of the claims, directly or through intermediaries, in **primary markets**. In the stock market, a firm enters the public markets and opens ownership of its shares to a wider range of investors through an **initial public offering** (IPO). Once issued, investors trade them in **secondary markets**. Secondary markets also exist for syndicated and some other large loans.

In the US Treasury market, the benchmark 10-year note and other bonds, bills, and notes issued by the US federal government are initially sold on regular schedules through an auction process to a small set of **primary dealers**. Secondary market trading is carried out by a much wider set of dealers.

Corporations and the legal treatment of their funding sources took on their modern forms as the result of a long historical evolution of law and corporate institutions. Corporations began emerging in the Middle Ages and, by the 16th century, were structured to outlast a specific project, such as an overseas trading voyage. Among the important features of the modern corporation is permanence: in contrast to simple family businesses and partnerships, a corporation can survive even if the partners pass away, and owners' stakes can be sold to new owners.

Equity and debt claims began, as part of this evolution, to trade in secondary markets. Corporate forms of organization are capable of coordinating a much wider scope and greater complexity of operations and of distribution and pooling of risks, for example, the development of insurance. These institutional innovations then create a need for incentive alignment mechanisms, information generation, and **corporate control** to facilitate the vetting, selection, and monitoring of borrowers, managers, and other agents working on behalf of others.

Figures 1.1 and 1.2 illustrate recent developments in US loan and debt markets, with an outstanding value of $98.4 trillion in 2023. Federal, state, and local government are the largest category of borrowers, with over one-third of the total. Financial sector borrowing increased steadily until the global financial crisis, but its share has declined since. Until the **disintermediation** of the 1970s, banks and investment banks had been the predominant lenders but have been displaced by a combination of investment funds, the public sector, primarily through government-guaranteed residential mortgage loans, and, for a time, securitization.

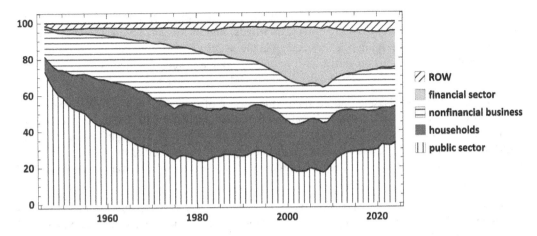

Figure 1.1 Who's borrowing in the United States, 1945–2023

Share in the total of each sector's outstanding borrowing in US markets via loans and debt securities, annual, percent. *Data source*: Federal Reserve Board, Financial Accounts of the United States (Z.1), Table D.3.

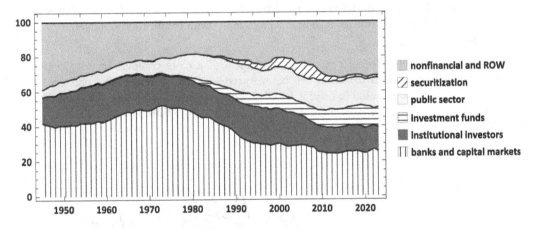

Figure 1.2 Who's lending in the United States, 1945–2023

Share of each sector in total lending via loans and debt securities in US markets, annual, percent. Banks and capital markets includes finance companies, brokers, and dealers. Institutional investors include insurance companies and private and public pension funds. Public sector includes assets held by the Federal Reserve and are held or guaranteed by government-sponsored enterprises (GSEs). Securitization includes nongovernment-guaranteed asset-backed securities (ABS). *Data source*: Federal Reserve Board, Financial Accounts of the United States (Z.1), Tables L.208 and L.214.

1.3.5   Spot and Derivative Assets

Spot markets involve an exchange of assets now and create no future obligation apart from fulfilling the terms of the exchange. A **derivative** is a financial instrument or contract agreed now but involving an exchange of assets in the future. A derivative's value and the counterparties' returns depend on the as-yet unknown future prices of another asset, called the **underlying asset**. Derivatives are widely used to establish a desired exposure to an underlying asset or to hedge an exposure.

One way to categorize the great variety of derivatives is by how their values are related to those of their underlying asset. The values of **futures, forwards, and swaps** have a linear and symmetric relation to that of the underlying price. A change in the underlying price has a proportional impact on the derivative's value. **Option** values have a nonlinear and asymmetric relation to the underlying price, depending on its current level and the direction and size of changes.

There are futures, forwards, and options on a wide variety of assets, including foreign exchange, stocks and stock indexes, bonds, and commodities. Fixed-income derivatives include **credit default swaps** (CDS). Derivatives can be classified by how they are traded, on an organized exchange or **over-the-counter** (OTC) and can be classified by underlying asset, a stock or stock index, a bond or interest rate, a commodity or a currency. Futures are traded on exchanges; forwards are traded OTC between dealers or their customers.

Measuring the size of derivatives markets is problematic because the aggregate and its composition by underlying asset differ greatly depending on the metric. The **notional** or **nominal principal amount outstanding** is the par value of existing contracts, generally a far larger number than the aggregate **net present value** (NPV) that accounts for offsetting payments. The **gross** notional outstanding includes many offsetting trades between pairs of counterparties and is much larger than the **net** amount.

As seen in Figure 1.3, by far the largest share of the OTC derivatives markets is that of interest rate swaps. Foreign exchange derivatives also have a large share, with credit, equity, and others making up the remainder.

Derivatives may be built into other assets as an element of a more complex security or portfolio. For example, **structured products** can be analyzed as a set of derivatives contracts on an underlying set of assets. A **callable** bond is bundled with a short call option on the bond through which the issuer can repay the bond prior to maturity. A **convertible** bond is bundled with a long out-of-the-money call; the bond can be exchanged for equity in the issuing firm if the stock price rises.

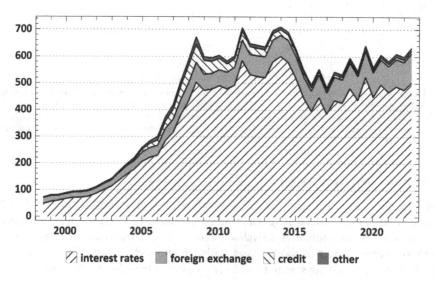

Figure 1.3 OTC derivatives markets 1998–2022

Notional amounts outstanding, G10 countries including Switzerland, trillions of US dollars, semiannual, H1 1998 to H1 2022. *Source*: BIS, Semiannual OTC derivatives statistics, Table D5, www.bis.org/statistics/derstats.htm.

1.3.6 Alternative Investments

The largest categories of alternative investments, which are outside the public stock and bond markets, are private funds: **hedge funds** and **private equity**. Both are usually organized as limited partnerships, with a general partner making investment decisions. Mergers and acquisitions of firms are often financed in large part by borrowing from banks and through bond issuance. More recently, a portion of this credit has been extended by **private credit** funds, which extend credit to private companies often owned by private equity funds, without taking ownership. Alternative investments also include funds investing in **real assets**, such as real estate, commodities, and forests. US private funds, according to regulatory data, managed $20.9 trillion in gross assets and $14.0 trillion in net assets in Q2 2023.

Most alternative investments are highly illiquid and have high investment fees and other costs compared to public-market and traditional investments. Institutional investors are the largest investors in alternatives. In recent years, **liquid alternatives**, mutual funds and ETFs employing typical alternative investment strategies, have been marketed to households.

Hedge funds are a loosely defined group of investment companies that are open, due to regulatory constraints, only to institutional investors and wealthy households but not to the general public. US hedge funds managed $5051.6 billion of gross assets at the end of 2023, more than three times as much as in 2012.[4] They are not subject to many restrictions on investment style and technique constraining other funds' ability to trade derivatives, take short positions, and borrow. This permits hedge funds to take more risk than other funds and to engage in strategies that cannot be carried out without these tools.

Hedge funds are an old form of investment company, dating back (at least anecdotally) to the late 1940s. For tax reasons, they are often organized in an onshore-offshore structure, in which several accounts have nearly identical investments. The offshore account is organized as a corporation and domiciled in a tax haven, a country that does not tax profits. The investors are then responsible for paying taxes where they reside. The onshore account, typically organized as a limited partnership, is domiciled in a developed country.[5] Its investors are entities, such as pension funds that are not obliged to pay profit taxes. Both accounts are managed in parallel by a hedge fund management company. Investors can withdraw funds but only on specified dates, and the manager may be permitted to limit withdrawals.

The hedge fund manager is compensated through a "2 and 20" structure. The management company organizes the fund and receives an annual management fee, often 2 percent of the fund's net asset value (NAV), the value of the investor assets it manages. A general partner, the owner of the management company, makes the investment decisions and receives a performance fee, typically 20 percent of the return, if the fund has positive returns as measured by the excess over the previous maximum value or "high water mark" of an investor's shares. In recent years, a number of hedge funds have accepted lower fees.

Most hedge funds are classified as following one of these strategies:

Equity funds take views on specific equity prices rising or falling.
Relative value seeks to exploit arbitrage opportunities in and between markets in all asset classes.

---

[4] The data are from the 2023 Securities and Exchange Commission Form PF annual report (https://www.sec.gov/files/2023-pf-report-congress.pdf) and from data provider BarclayHedge (https://www.barclayhedge.com/solutions/assets-under-management/hedge-fund-assets-under-management/).

[5] Some hedge funds are organized as limited liability corporations.

Macro strategies are based on views on central bank policy, foreign exchange rates, and other macroeconomic and political developments.

Event-driven strategies express views through stock and bond positions on events such as corporate mergers and acquisitions, defaults, and bankruptcies. They include activist funds, which attempt to directly influence corporate decisions.

The portfolios can be very concentrated or diversified, depending on the strategy. Many hedge funds are highly reliant on large broker-dealers for **prime brokerage** services including execution and financing of trades, safekeeping of securities, information and technology, and **capital introduction** to potential investors.

Private equity funds have grown rapidly since their origins in the 1970s and fall into two major categories: investing in **leveraged buyouts** (LBOs) and **venture capital**. Leveraged buyout funds acquire all or a controlling stake in the equity of publicly traded firms they identify as undervalued due to mismanagement, corporate structure, or other reasons. The equity purchase is funded largely by borrowing. Venture capital funds invest in new startup firms, with a view to eventually taking the firm public or selling their stakes at higher values.

Private equity funds are intended to be relatively short-lived compared to hedge funds, which are in principle perpetual. The private equity fund raises investor money in the form of immediate payments and commitments to make further investments up to some limit over the next few years, when called upon by the general partner. In the initial years of the fund, the general partner seeks investment opportunities and deploys the invested cash, and in later years, as the investments reach fruition, they are sold or taken public and cash is returned to investors. The fund is expected to last 10 to 12 years. The general partner is compensated with a share of the return, and the fund is structured so it can be treated for tax purposes as **carried interest** or capital gain rather than fee income.

The rise in assets of private equity funds has coincided with a sharp decline in the number of publicly traded companies and of IPOs in the United States, from a peak of 677 in 1997, to just 38 in 2022.[6] A number of explanations for this shift have been put forward. Technological change may have increased the economies of scale and scope that make a smaller firm more valuable as part of a larger one. Changes in regulation have increased the cost of entering public markets and of complying with public-market accounting and audit rules. Low interest rates have made private equity funds, which employ a large volume of debt to fund acquisitions, more attractive to some institutional investors.

1.4   Mechanics of Trading

1.4.1   Asset Positions and Risk Exposures

People hold assets because they anticipate some benefit over time. The expected benefit can be the cash flows the asset throws off (e.g. a stock or bond), its usefulness in a production process (crude oil), the ease with which it can be exchanged for goods or other assets (money), the consumable services it provides (a house), or from expected appreciation in value over time (bitcoin). Those expectations may all be disappointed, making assets risky.

---

[6] Statistics on IPO activity are available at https://site.warrington.ufl.edu/ritter/files/IPO-Statistics.pdf.

A **position** in an asset is a holding of x units of the asset. We'll denote its time-t price by S_t, its next-period (one day, week, month ...) price by S_{t+1}, and so on. The current value of the position is xS_t.

There are different ways to understand an asset's value that may diverge from one another. It can be:

- an estimate of its "real" value, the **fundamental**, **intrinsic**, or **fair value**, possibly based on mathematical modeling,
- the market value, the price at which it can be bought or sold, or
- an accounting or book value, as ordained by recognized practices or law.

A **short position** in an asset, with $x < 0$, expresses the view that S_t will decline. A short position risks a loss if the price rises. Unlike a long position, a short position inherently involves borrowing. It is generally established by borrowing x units of the asset and selling it in the spot market, with the intent to buy an equal number of units and returning them to the lender at a future date. Short positions can also be expressed through derivatives trades, for example, selling a forward or futures, a long put or short call option on the asset, or a swap.

The cash flows of short positions are complex. The lender of an asset generally retains the right to interest and dividends. The short seller receives interest on the cash proceeds from the sale. The transaction is usually intermediated by a broker-dealer or custodial bank, which can obtain a fee for locating the asset. Its owner and lender may also receive a fee. There are different legal structures and mechanics for lending stocks and bonds, as well as across countries.

Portfolios are combinations of asset positions. With x_i denoting the number of units of asset i and S_{it} its time-t price, the value of each constituent position is $x_i S_{it}$ and the value of the portfolio is $\sum_i x_i S_{it}$. For example, with two positions, the portfolio value is $x_1 S_{1t} + x_2 S_{2t}$. For a portfolio consisting of long positions only, $x_i > 0$ for all i, asset i's **weight** in the portfolio is

$$w_i = \frac{x_i S_{it}}{\sum_i x_i S_{it}},$$

with $w_i > 0$ for all i, and $\sum_i w_i = 1$.

The definition of constituent weights is more complicated for a short and for a long-short portfolio. For a long-short portfolio with a zero net market value, $x_i \gtrless 0$ and $\sum_i x_i S_{it} = 0$, such weights can lead to potentially misleading understatements of the portfolio's risk. Weights may be defined in alternative ways to avoid division by zero, e.g. using absolute values:

$$w_i = \frac{|x_i| S_{it}}{\sum_i |x_i| S_{it}}.$$

In many cases, risk is assumed not by deliberately putting on a position but in the course of business, such as operating an airline or refining petroleum, in which case one may refer to a **risk exposure**. Airlines have a short risk exposure to the highly volatile price of gasoline: a rise in the price increases operating costs. An oil refiner's position is more complex, most often a long exposure to the price of gasoline and a short exposure to the price of crude oil because the difference between their prices, the **crack spread**, is directly related to its profit margin.

Not every risk exposure can be expressed in terms of the price of a specific asset. Rather, exposures may be to one or more **risk factors**, drivers of return derived from modeling and observation that don't coincide with prices of investible or identifiable assets, these exposures including macroeconomic factors. Analysis and measurement in finance, including market and credit risk modeling, is often conducted using risk factors. Modeling is more tractable with a limited number of risk factors rather than myriad assets.

Hedging is the process of ridding a portfolio or business or household of exposures to risk factors that it doesn't desire or target. It is closely related to **insurance**, a contract in which one party agrees to compensate another for specified types of losses.

Market participants may have offsetting hedging needs, and forward and futures markets have grown to facilitate this redistribution of risk. An oil refiner, for example, may wish to focus on the efficiency of its refining process and rid itself of exposure to the prices of its main input and output. An oil producer is focused on discovering and extracting the resource, and an airline on safety and scheduling. If the oil refiner buys and and oil producer sells oil, and the oil refiner sells and the airline buys jet fuel for future delivery at agreed prices, all have reduced risk.

For an exposure taken on in the course of business, hedging decisions involve forecasts not only of the impact of changes in risk factor prices but also of the size of the exposure. For example, airlines found that they had put on too-large long positions in fuel when the Covid pandemic curtailed air travel, resulting in large losses from the direction of fuel prices and the collapse in revenue.[7]

1.4.2   Market Microstructure

Market microstructure describes the institutional arrangements that assist in overcoming frictions and using information efficiently to complete searches and execute trading. Very different mechanisms are used to effect transactions in different markets.

Most market participants are **price takers**, entering the market to buy or sell at the prevailing market-clearing price. Dealers, brokers, and many other market participants are **price makers**, specifying the prices at which they are willing to transact and the quantities they are willing to buy or sell at those prices.

Quote-driven trading systems rely on dealers or market makers, who maintain inventories of the asset, currencies, bonds or commodities, as well as money balances and stand ready to buy or sell given amounts at a given price. The **quote** consists of the **bid** price, at which dealers are prepared to buy, and the **offer** or **asking** price, at which they are prepared to sell. Both are stated for a specific amount. The difference between bid and offer prices is the **bid-ask spread**. The dealer may post the quote publicly or disclose it only upon inquiry to an established customer.

An **order-driven** system resembles an auction. In it, market participants declare or enter into the system a **limit order**, an amount of the good they wish to buy or sell and the price at which they are prepared to do so. At any point in time, buy and sell limit orders can be ranked from low to high price. Transactions take place when orders can be matched, with an offer to sell at a price no higher than the highest order to buy. The transaction is then effected for the smaller of the two amounts specified.

Quote-driven trading is prevalent in **over-the-counter** (OTC) markets, which include foreign exchange, bond, and many derivatives markets. Order-driven markets include most stock and futures markets. Stock trading in the United States and other advanced economies was once heavily concentrated in a few exchanges, but today it is highly fragmented. Stocks and some other assets

---

[7] Chong Koh Ping, "'Overhedging' Oil Prices Lands Some Coronavirus-Battered Global Airlines in Further Trouble," *Wall Street Journal*, May 15, 2020, https://www.wsj.com/articles/overhedging-oil-prices-lands-some-coronavirus-battered-global-airlines-in-further-trouble-11589555843.

have historically traded primarily though no longer exclusively on **exchanges**, which are centralized loci of trading. Most trading in securities, commodities, and derivatives contracts was executed by people on exchanges or using telephones in OTC markets, but that is now becoming a relic.

With the advent of **electronic** and **algorithmic trading systems**, the distinction between OTC and exchange trading has blurred. Algorithmic trading is conducted automatically, as instructed by a computer program. Brokers and exchanges may use a **central limit order book** (CLOB), a standard market structure for electronic trading systems, to match trades. It consolidates orders from different sources and applies a set of rules to match trades. **Alternative Trading Systems** (ATS) is a regulatory term for non-exchange trading platforms. ATS, or "dark pools," have been used primarily for trading between dealers but are increasingly used for trades between dealers and customers as well.

Exchanges and ATS are registered with the **Securities and Exchange Commission** (SEC) and report executed stock trade data, but are regulated differently. Exchanges are obliged to make bids and offers public through the **National Best Bid and Offer** (NBBO) system. Under the SEC's 2005 **Regulation NMS** (RegNMS), they must send arriving orders to the exchange displaying the best price. ATS and other market makers are only required to report trades after execution.

Nonprofessional investing has also grown as a share of trading volume. Regulatory changes permitting fee competition contributed to the growth of retail trading, primarily of stocks and stock options. Discount brokerages such as Charles Schwab, E*Trade, and Ameritrade arose in the 1970s to serve the retail market. As brokerage volumes grew, low- and eventually zero-commission online stock trading became feasible. Index funds, which first appeared in the 1970s, were particularly cost efficient. The introduction and widespread adoption of electronic trading further massively cheapened trading. Zero-fee mutual funds and exchange traded funds (ETFs) followed, and brokerages began offering zero-commission stock trading.

The move to zero-fee and zero-commission trading has also been enabled by a shift in the sources of brokerage revenue. The decline in trading fees and commissions is offset by net interest on customers' cash balances, stock lending fees, and **payment for order flow** (PFOF) by wholesale market makers that execute the trades.

Electronic trading has been prevalent in foreign exchange markets for many years, and accounts for about 75 percent of trading volume. It is now also becoming more prominent in bond markets as information technology becomes cheaper and knowledge of how best to design and implement the systems grows. Bond markets are still heavily reliant on human traders, but the volume of trades on systems, such as BrokerTec, TradeWeb, and MarketAxess, has been growing rapidly.

ATS and CLOBs have become particularly important for the most recently issued and heavily traded US Treasury securities. These markets could soon more closely resemble the stock market, in which trade orders, including those from non-intermediaries, may be routed for execution to many places within the larger trading system rather than within one platform. Disruptions to the Treasury market in recent years may accelerate the push toward ATS.[8] Some firms that operate ATS platforms, such as Citadel Securities, have also entered the corporate bond market.

1.4.3 Payment Systems

Money is part of a larger set of ways in which exchanges are effected. People and firms routinely transfer money among one another for myriad reasons, including exchanges of goods for money

---

[8] See Chapter 20 below.

and for settling securities trades and debt obligations. These transfers are often made via retail and wholesale payment systems, which help market participants economize on the stock of money they hold to conduct transactions.

Payment systems generally don't function instantaneously although there has been progress in that direction. In the past, only hand-to-hand cash payments were completed close to instantly. Most payments are made at a distance and require time and a series of verification steps. The imperfect simultaneity of payments by the two parties leads to a type of short-term credit extension by at least one. The introduction of cryptocurrencies, and particularly CBDCs, are sometimes viewed as paths to speeding up and improving payments systems, conflating two sets of issues.

Like most aspects of finance, payments systems have been evolving and speeding up with communication and information technology. More time-consuming, but well-established means include checks to effect bank transfers and credit cards, introduced in the mid-20th century. Credit card operators extend short-term credit to purchasers and pay vendors and merchants almost immediately. An electronic network connects merchants to the card operator. In an **electronic bank transfer** (EBT), no written instruction is needed. Checks, EBTs, and credit cards were originally used primarily by businesses and wealthy people but are now routine in retail transactions.

Large-value or **wholesale payments systems** are used to move money among banks. Most operate during normal business hours and on trading days. Many of these systems are operated by central banks, since payments are ultimately settled by transfers of balances at central banks. The Fed provides payments services to approved banks and other financial institutions, most prominently **Fedwire Securities Service** (Fedwire), a system for intraday US dollar funds and securities transfers between banks. The **Clearing House Interbank Payments System** (CHIPS) is a similar, privately operated system for intraday payments. These wholesale systems permit bank transfers to be completed within a day. The **Automated Clearing House** (ACH) system is an older and slower system operated by banks and the Fed, and efforts are underway to speed up its settlement times. The **Society for Worldwide Interbank Financial Telecommunication** (SWIFT) messaging service opens these and other national systems up to international transactions.

An increasing volume of payments are being completed within one day, or even nearly instantaneously. PayPal introduced direct **person-to-person** (P2P) payment systems used primarily for exchanges among households and small businesses. Alipay and Zelle also provide same-day payments to nonbank users. Most are ultimately settled through commercial banks, which still takes a discrete amount of time.

1.4.4   Clearing and Settlement

Once payments, trades, and exchanges have been agreed upon by market participants, they have to be completed; the handshake has to be followed by the exchange of an asset or a good for money or for another asset. There are several steps involved, intertwined with the operation of money markets and requiring specialized procedures, systems, and personnel. This post-trade processing is sometimes called the back-office operations or "plumbing" of the financial system.

The initial step is **clearing** in which the counterparties to a trade confirm its terms. The counterparties match trade records with one another, each entering the trade onto the firm's books and records. In payment systems, it is the step in which payment instructions are conveyed between the banks or other intermediaries involved. The final step is **settlement**, transferring securities, money, or other assets and making final payments between market participants and intermediaries.

Trades generally settle some time after the **trade date**. The time to settlement varies across markets and jurisdictions.

In markets with a great deal of activity, there may an additional step between clearing and settlement: **netting**, or cancelling offsetting trades. **Gross settlement** occurs via transfer of the gross amounts due, without netting, and **net settlement** occurs at specific times, such as end of day, via the transfer of the net amount of money or asset due. Netting is easier if money or traded assets are fungible, meaning it is irrelevant which units of the asset you own.

Most settlement and netting occurs via large-scale systems. For example, the **Depository Trust and Clearing Corporation** (DTCC) operates settlement systems or platforms for securities and some derivatives. Obligations vis-à-vis the clearing platform replace bilateral contracts, a process called **central clearing**. DTCC and similar platforms employ **delivery versus payment** (DVP) settlement, in which it is ensured that delivery occurs if and only if payment occurs. In derivatives markets, efforts at **trade compression** and central clearing, accelerated in recent years by regulatory **mandatory clearing**, have reduced the disparity between gross and net notional volumes of derivatives outstanding.

Fedwire, in which the Fed settles payments between banks, and TARGET, a similar large-value interbank funds transfer system operated by the European Central Bank (ECB), are **real-time gross settlement** (RTGS) systems. Final settlement of payments is effected continuously without netting. CHIPS, the private payments platform operated by US banks, in contrast, computes a net amount due or owed by each participating institution and makes a corresponding transfer at the end of each business day. FedNow is a payment system introduced by the Fed that plans to work through banks to offer same-day payments to retail and small business clients.

Even short settlement times introduce risk and are potentially costly. Most electronic retail and business payments settle through the ACH system for transmitting and carrying out payment instructions, with a few days between the time one account is debited and the receiving account credited. Most foreign exchange spot trades settle two business days after the trade date ("T+2"), as do most bond trades.[9] US government bond trades are settled one day after the trade date ("T+1"). The settlement cycle for securities is subject to regulation, and in the United States, the standard time for stock settlement was shortened to T+1 as of mid-2024.

In some markets, the settlement cycle for a trade may not be completed because one party is unable to deliver securities it has sold, events called **failures to deliver**, or **fails**. In US Treasury markets, where fails are more common, they may arise for a number of reasons related to the way in which US debt is distributed to investors and to the mechanisms by which they are used as collateral. Fails may also occur because of the failure of an intermediary. In stock markets, a **naked short** is a less common form of short position in which the asset is sold without first borrowing it. A fail may occur if a naked short position cannot be covered by borrowing the stock by the settlement date.

Further Reading

On the link between financial and economic development, see Levine (2005), recently updated in Levine (2021). A functional approach to analysis and regulation of the financial system was introduced by Merton (1995). Tobin (2018) provides an overview of financial intermediation.

---

[9] USD trades against the Canadian dollar settle in one day.

Goetzmann (2016) is a history of monetary and financial institutions. Baskin and Miranti (1997) describe the evolution of the modern corporation since its emergence in the medieval era. Harris (2020) focuses on the evolution of limited liability.

Adrian and Mancini-Griffoli (2021) and Makarov and Schoar (2022) provide overviews of digital currencies, and Prasad (2021) places them in the larger context of the functions of money in the financial system. See Chen and Siklos (2022), Dowd (2024), and Genc and Takagi (2024) on CBDCs.

Chaboud et al. (2023) and McGuire et al. (2022) provide up-to-date overviews of the foreign exchange and related derivatives markets, relying in part on the Bank for International Settlement's Triennial Central Bank Survey.

Chambers et al. (2018) is a nontechnical overview of alternative investments. Ivashina and Lerner (2019) is an introduction to private equity. Cai and Haque (2024) discuss private credit.

Kahn and Roberds (2009) is an introduction to payment systems, and Kahn and Roberds (2001) to settlement risk and the CLS system.

Asset Returns and Risk

Yesterday I read in the *Wall Street Journal* about the melancholy of affluence. "Not in all the five millenia of man's recorded history have so many been so affluent." Minds formed by five millenia of scarcity are distorted. The heart can't take this sort of change. Sometimes it just refuses to accept it.

Saul Bellow, *Humboldt's Gift*. Viking Press, 1975

2.1 Asset Returns and Interest Rates

2.1.1 Measuring Asset Returns

Financial analysis usually focuses on asset **returns**, or changes in the value of a position or portfolio, rather than price levels. The change in position value in currency units, or **capital gain** on a position of x units of an asset currently priced at S_t, over the time interval $[t, t+1]$, is $x(S_{t+1} - S_t)$, and is part of the **profit and loss** (P&L) over the interval. The P&L may be **realized**, based on an actual purchase or sale that unwinds the position or a **mark-to-market** (MTM) gain or loss, based on an estimate of value.

A common measure of return is the **arithmetic**, **simple**, or **linear return** over a discrete interval

$$r_{t,t+1}^{\text{arith}} = \frac{S_{t+1} - S_t}{S_t} = \frac{S_{t+1}}{S_t} - 1.$$

The **gross return** is $1 + r_{t,t+1}^{\text{arith}}$. The **logarithmic, geometric,** or **continuously compounded return** is the change in the logarithm of price:

$$r_{t,t+1} = \ln\left(\frac{S_{t+1}}{S_t}\right) = \ln(S_{t+1}) - \ln(S_t),$$

with $\ln(x)$ representing the natural logarithm of x.

Arithmetic and logarithmic returns are related by (see Figure 2.1)

$$r_{t,t+1}^{\text{arith}} = e^{r_{t,t+1}} - 1$$

$$r_{t,t+1} = \ln(1 + r_{t,t+1}^{\text{arith}}).$$

Arithmetic returns are greater than logarithmic:

$$r_{t,t+1}^{\text{arith}} \geq r_{t,t+1},$$

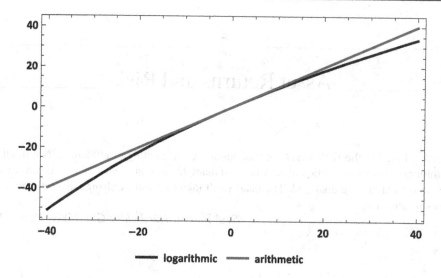

Figure 2.1 Comparing arithmetic and logarithmic returns

Arithmetic and logarithmic returns, percent. The vertical distance is the difference between the two return definitions for a given initial level and change in asset prices.

apart from the trivial case in which both are zero. As long as $r_{t,t+1}$ and $r_{t,t+1}^{\text{arith}}$ are relatively small, the difference is small: $r_{t,t+1}^{\text{arith}} \approx r_{t,t+1}$. Over longer periods, returns are larger in magnitude and arithmetic returns diverge more from logarithmic.

Logarithmic returns are convenient when measuring returns over multiple periods, when computing returns from several sources, such as total or real returns, and are also commonly used in computing standard measures of risk such as volatility (see Chapter 4). Arithmetic returns are most convenient when measuring portfolio returns.

Logarithmic returns aggregate nicely across time, a property related to their nature as the mathematical limit of an arithmetic return as the length of the interval over which they are measured becomes smaller. Logarithmic, but not arithmetic return, is defined for variables that unfold continuously over time rather than being measured at discrete moments. Financial models are, therefore, generally framed in terms of logarithmic rather than arithmetic returns.

The τ-period **cumulative logarithmic return** is the sum of the shorter-term log returns encompassed. With τ the number of periods,

$$\ln\left(\frac{S_{t+\tau}}{S_t}\right) = \ln\left(\frac{S_{t+1}}{S_t}\cdots\frac{S_{t+\tau}}{S_{t+\tau-1}}\right) = \sum_{\theta=1}^{\tau} r_{t+\theta-1,t+\theta}.$$

With t measured in months, for example, annual is related to monthly return by $\ln\left(\frac{S_{t+12}}{S_t}\right) = \sum_{\theta=1}^{12} r_{t+\theta-1,t+\theta}$. With t measured in years, the logarithmic annual **compound** τ-year return is the simple average of yearly log rates $\frac{1}{\tau}\sum_{\theta=1}^{\tau} r_{t+\theta-1,t+\theta}$.

Arithmetic returns don't aggregate so nicely across time, making them inconvenient in modeling or working with return time series. The τ-period **cumulative arithmetic return** is

$$\frac{S_{t+\tau}}{S_t} - 1 = \frac{S_{t+1}}{S_t} \cdots \frac{S_{t+\tau-1}}{S_{t+\tau-2}} \cdot \frac{S_{t+\tau}}{S_{t+\tau-1}} - 1$$

$$= \prod_{\theta=1}^{\tau} \frac{S_{t+\theta}}{S_{t+\theta-1}} - 1 = \prod_{\theta=1}^{\tau} (1 + r^{\text{arith}}_{t+\theta-1,t+\theta}) - 1,$$

so the compound τ-year arithmetic return at an annual rate is related to a geometric rather than a simple average:

$$\left[\prod_{\theta=1}^{\tau} (1 + r^{\text{arith}}_{t+\theta-1,t+\theta}) \right]^{\frac{1}{\tau}} - 1 = \left(\frac{S_{t+\tau}}{S_t} \right)^{\frac{1}{\tau}} - 1.$$

The realized cumulative return from time 0 to time τ can be expressed as an index, using historical short-term returns and setting $S_0 = 100$:

$$S_t = 100 \prod_{\theta=1}^{\tau} (1 + r^{\text{arith}}_{\theta-1,\theta}) = 100 \, e^{\sum_{\theta=1}^{\tau} r_{\theta-1,\theta}}.$$

These aggregation properties of logarithmic and arithmetic returns have an important role in measuring long-term returns. Investors' actual outcomes are determined by compounding. The rate at which an asset's value grows or shrinks over several years is most accurately measured by the annual logarithmic return. The simple average annual arithmetic return over the period can be much higher or lower. The timing of episodes of unusually high or low returns makes a difference in real-life outcomes that logarithmic calculations capture but is missed in many arithmetic return calculations. This mathematical property is important in risk management, in the price behavior of some ETFs, and is central to the gambler's ruin problem.[1]

Arithmetic returns, however, aggregate nicely across assets. The portfolio arithmetic return $r^{\text{arith}}_{p,t,t+1}$ is a weighted average of the constituent returns $r^{\text{arith}}_{i,t,t+1}$, using the portfolio weights:

$$r^{\text{arith}}_{p,t,t+1} \equiv \frac{\sum_i x_i S_{i,t+1} - \sum_i x_i S_{it}}{\sum_i x_i S_{it}}$$

$$= \frac{\sum_i x_i (1 + r^{\text{arith}}_{i,t,t+1}) S_{it} - \sum_i x_i S_{it}}{\sum_i x_i S_{it}}$$

$$= \sum_i w_i r^{\text{arith}}_{i,t,t+1}.$$

---

[1] See Chapter 4.

Portfolio P&L is equal to the arithmetic portfolio return times the initial portfolio value $r_{p,t,t+1}^{\text{arith}} \sum_i x_i S_{it}$. Logarithmic returns don't aggregate so nicely across assets:

$$r_{p,t,t+1} = \ln\left(\frac{\sum_i x_i S_{i,t+1}}{\sum_i x_i S_{it}}\right) = \ln\left(1 + \sum_i w_i r_{i,t,t+1}\right).$$

2.1.2 Interest Rates and Yield Curves

The **term** or **time to maturity** of debt is specified contractually and may be flexible. Rates on **fixed rate** debt are set at a particular value for all or part of the term, and those on **floating rate** debt vary over the term, generally as a fixed spread to a market-based index.

Interest rates, risk-free or for a given obligor, are not a single risk factor but vary with the term of the loan. The **term structure of interest rates**, or **yield curve**, describes how rates of a specific type vary as a function of maturity. There is a distinct yield curve for each type of debt issue, e.g., liquid US Treasury issues or euro-denominated bank obligations. Figure 2.2 displays the US Treasury yield curve on different dates.

Debt securities may make **coupon** payments, contactually stipulated cash flows, over their term. The simplest debt instrument is a **discount** or **zero-coupon bond** or **bill**. The difference, almost always positive, between the par value and current price, or **discount**, implies an interest rate. The bond isn't necessarily free of default risk; that as well as **time value**, the compensation purely for temporarily parting with resources, will be reflected in the price and yield.

Debt instruments can be treated like any other asset in computing returns. Let S_t denote the time-t price of a one-period zero-coupon bond that pays 1 dollar at time $t + 1$. Its **yield-to-maturity** can be

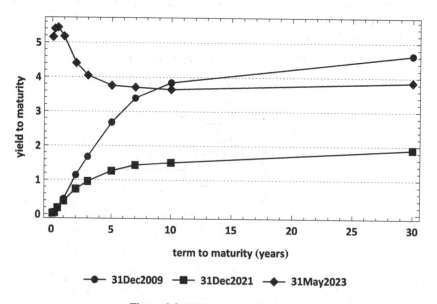

Figure 2.2 US Treasury yield curve

US on-the-run Treasury benchmark yield curve (1-month T-bill to 30-year bond), percent. *Source*: Bloomberg.

expressed as the rate at which the initial investment S_t must grow to reach par. The arithmetic yield over the interval $[t, t+1]$ is

$$r_{t,t+1}^{\text{arith}} = \frac{1 - S_t}{S_t} = \frac{1}{S_t} - 1$$

and **discount rate**, or **discount factor**, is $\frac{1}{1+r_{t,t+1}^{\text{arith}}}$. The logarithmic yield is

$$r_{t,t+1} = \ln\left(\frac{1}{S_t}\right) = -\ln(S_t),$$

and the logarithmic discount factor is $e^{-r_{t,t+1}}$.

There are several equivalent ways of representing the term structure, each useful in particular contexts. The yield-to-maturity as a function of term is the most directly observable yield curve but is a slightly ambiguous metric because the results vary with coupon size, pay frequency, and day count conventions as well as price.

Spot or **zero-coupon rates** eliminate this ambiguity. They state the yield on money lent now and repaid at a single future point in time. **Forward rates** state the yields on loans of a specified term to maturity commencing at different **settlement dates** in the future, for example, rates on 3-month loans settling immediately, in 1 month, in 3 months, etc. The spot and forward yield curves are derived from prices or yields-to-maturity.

The bond price S_t of a t-year bond with coupon c_t, assuming an annual payment frequency and compounding, is related to its yield y_t by[2]

$$S_t = c_t \left[\frac{1}{1 + y_t} + \frac{1}{(1 + y_t)^2} + \cdots + \frac{1}{(1 + y_t)^t} \right] + \frac{1}{(1 + y_t)^t}.$$

The bond price is also related to spot rates $r_1, r_2, \ldots, r_t$, with r_τ the yield of a t-year discount bond at an annual rate, by

$$S_t = c_t \left[\frac{1}{1 + r_1} + \frac{1}{(1 + r_2)^2} + \cdots + \frac{1}{(1 + r_t)^t} \right] + \frac{1}{(1 + r_t)^t}.$$

There are equivalent ways of expressing the spot curve. The **discount curve** or series of discount factors expresses the **present values** of discount bonds corresponding to spot rates: the discount factor corresponding to r_1 is $(1 + r_1)^{-1}$, corresponding to r_2 is $(1 + r_2)^{-2}$, and so on. The **par yield curve** is composed of yields on hypothetical bonds with coupons equal to those yields. It is computed from the spot curve by setting the price to par and solving for the coupon rate. Both curves match observed market quotes.

Forward curves are calculated from the spot curve and vice versa. Their consistency facilitates pricing, valuation, and risk analysis. The forward rate $f_{0,1}$ settling immediately is identical to the shortest-term spot rate. The 1-period forward rate $f_{t,t+1}$ from t to $t+1$ is related to the spot rates r_t and r_{t+1} by

$$f_{t,t+1} = \frac{(1 + r_{t+1})^{t+1}}{(1 + r_t)^t} - 1.$$

---

[2] The formulas here are simplified by assuming the payment frequency, compounding, and the rate at which the rates are expressed are all the same, namely, annual. We're using arithmetic rates and simplifying the notation by dropping the current time subscript and "arith" superscript.

The forward curve is higher than the spot curve if the spot curve is positively sloped. The forward curve is negatively sloped if the spot curve is concave, for example, its slope is positive but declining.

Bootstrapping is a technique for obtaining the generally unobservable spot curve from observed price or yield quote data.[3] It starts with the shortest maturity security and uses each successively longer-term security to capture a longer-term spot rate. For each bond maturity, the technique assumes we have either a price or a yield and the coupon rate.

Example 2.1   Bond prices, yield to maturity and spot rates

To illustrate, imagine a simple term structure, with the shortest-term issue a 1-year bill and bonds with annual coupons maturing in 2, 3, and 4 years. The assumed coupons, current prices, and corresponding annualized yields-to-maturity are[4]

term	coupon	price	yield
1 year	0.00	98.6923	1.32500
2 years	1.75	100.1039	1.69674
3 years	2.00	100.2368	1.91804
4 years	2.00	100.0286	1.99249

To obtain the spot curve by bootstrapping, note that the 1-year bond has no coupon ($c_0 = 0$), so S_1 and r_1 satisfy

$$S_1 = 0.986923 = \frac{1}{1 + r_1} = \frac{1}{1.01325}.$$

Next, solve for $r_2 = 0.0170$ from

$$S_2 = 1.001039 = c_2 \left[\frac{1}{1 + r_1} + \frac{1}{(1 + r_2)^2} \right] + \frac{1}{(1 + r_2)^2}$$

$$= \frac{0.0175}{1.01325} + \frac{0.0175 + 1}{(1 + r_2)^2}.$$

Solve the same type of equation to get $r_3 = 0.01925$:

$$S_3 = 1.002368 = c_2 \left[\frac{1}{1 + r_1} + \frac{1}{(1 + r_2)^2} + \frac{1}{(1 + r_3)^3} \right] + \frac{1}{(1 + r_3)^3}$$

$$= 0.02 \times 1.95377 + \frac{0.02 + 1}{(1 + r_3)^3}.$$

And, finally, $r_4 = 0.02$ (left to the reader).

---

[3] Other techniques include spline interpolation or least-squares fitting.
[4] Interest rates are expressed in percent and prices in percent of par value.

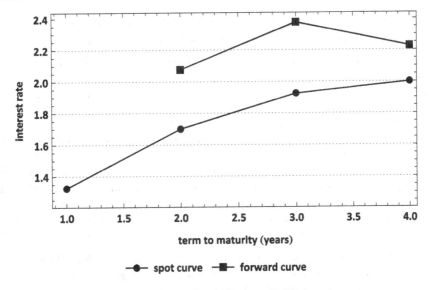

Figure 2.3 Spot and forward curves in the example

Derived spot and forward curves, percent.

The discount, par yield, and spot and forward curves for the example (illustrated in Figure 2.3) are

term	discount factor	par yield	spot	forward
1 year	0.98692	1.32500	1.325	
2 years	0.96685	1.69683	1.700	2.07639
3 years	0.94440	1.91831	1.925	2.37649
4 years	0.92385	1.99252	2.000	2.22533

2.1.3 Total Returns and Asset Values

Asset owners may receive payments of cash, other assets, or other positive and negative gains that flow over time. These encompass pecuniary gains, such as interest, dividends, stock dividends, or rent and include hard-to-measure nonpecuniary benefits, such as housing services. Refiners may gain a **convenience yield** from having readily available physical inventory of crude oil. An owner of real estate and commodities may incur costs or negative cash flows, such as physical storage and maintenance costs.[5] The **total return** includes these in addition to the capital gain or loss.

---

[5] Convenience yields of commodities are not directly observable. They are related to the difference between actual spot prices and those that would be expected based solely on futures prices and money market rates and estimated using spot and futures prices and an estimate of storage costs. The shelter value or housing services of a residence can be estimated as the **owners equivalent rent**, the cost per period of renting a residence of comparable location, size, and quality. There are nonpecuniary housing services as well; homeowners enjoy their homes.

If time-$t+1$ cash flows are denoted $q_{t+1} \gtrless 0$, the arithmetic total return over the past period is $\frac{S_{t+1}+q_{t+1}}{S_t} - 1$ and the logarithmic total return is $\ln\left(\frac{S_{t+1}+q_{t+1}}{S_t}\right)$. If q_{t+1} is a dividend payment and the period is one year, then $\frac{q_{t+1}}{S_t}$ is the stock's cash **dividend yield**. **Trailing** dividend yields are reported based on recent past dividend payments, and **forward** dividend yields are based on projected future dividends. If q_{t+1} is a coupon payment, then $\frac{q_{t+1}}{S_t}$ will be the bond's **current yield**.

The present value of a cash flow 1 periods in the future, given a discount factor r_1 is $q_{t+1}(1+r_1)^{-1}$, A common way to value stocks illustrates the simplifications typical of a tractable yet useful asset valuation model. A **required return** measures the return or discount curve investors would demand to make an investment worthwhile given its risk or that justifies an observable asset price. The **dividend growth**, or **Gordon, model** assumes that discount rates are constant over all future horizons and dividends grow at a constant rate. Letting r_t represent the required return or cost of equity, the risk-adjusted discount rate that is consistent with the share price, and letting g represent the dividend growth rate, we assume $r_t = r$ and $q_t = q_0(1+g)^t$ for all t.

The model implicitly assumes that the distant future price of the stock doesn't grow so fast that it outpaces the effect of discounting: $S_t(1+r)^{-t}$ goes to zero as t grows very large.[6] The stock is priced by its future cash flows, with no additional discounting to compensate for risk, or at least risk compensation is constant over time. After all, the model has assumed the future cash flows are known with certainty. Dividend growth g is also assumed to be at least somewhat smaller than the discount rate r. The result of the model is a stock value

$$S_t = q_t \sum_{\tau=1}^{\infty} \left(\frac{1+g}{1+r}\right)^{\tau} = q_{t+1}\frac{1}{r-g}.$$

We can also use the algebra of discounting and compounding to define return indexes. If we let an initial sum of \$100 compound over time, reinvesting discrete cash flows, the balance at the end of τ periods is an index of the cumulative total return in currency units:

$$100 \prod_{\theta=1}^{\tau} \left(1 + \frac{S_{t+\theta}+q_{t+\theta}}{S_t}\right).$$

Over longer periods of time, with reinvestment of cash flows and compounding, the differences between total return and capital gains alone can be very large. As seen in Figure 2.4, for example, dividend cash flows, if reinvested, multiply the half century cumulative total return on the S&P 500 basket of stocks approximately fourfold compared to the cumulative price return.[7]

2.1.4   Inflation and Real Returns

Asset prices are generally expressed in **nominal** terms, i.e., in units of money. **Inflation**, a rise in the general price level, erodes the purchasing power of money—the amount of goods, services, or assets obtainable with a unit of currency—thus the **real** values of assets, expressed in units of goods or purchasing power.

---

[6] This assumption is also important in ruling out bubbles, unlimited speculative price increases. See Chapter 7.

[7] Looking at the past half century may seem too long a period to be relevant. In fact, it's quite short compared to the entire history of stock and bond markets, even just in the United States. Looking at shorter periods may miss sustained above- or below-average returns that can have lifetime impact on investors.

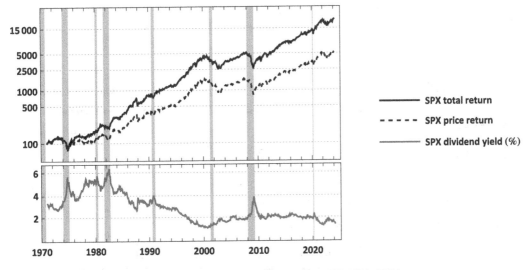

Figure 2.4 Price and total return of S&P 500 1971–2024

Index of cumulative price and total return, month-end, logarithmic scale, Jan. 1971 (=100) to Feb. 2024. Trailing 12-month dividend yield, percent. Vertically shaded intervals denote recessions, as determined by the National Bureau of Economic Research (NBER). *Data source*: Bloomberg.

Real asset price levels and returns are computed by applying a **price index** or **deflator**. There are widely used price indexes for many currencies, typically including goods and services, but not asset prices. In the United States, the two widely used price indexes differ in what goods are included and how they are computed. The **Consumer Price Index for All Urban Consumers** (CPI-U) is used in indexing Social Security and many other pension payments. The **Price Index for Personal Consumption Expenditures** (PCE) is based on a wider range of goods and services than the CPI-U, and is used to define the Federal Reserve's inflation goal (see Chapter 17). Both have "core" subindexes that exclude the especially volatile prices of food and energy.

If P_t represents the price index level at time t, the real asset price is $\frac{S_t}{P_t}$. If P_t is rising over time, the inflation rate is positive and real returns are lower than nominal returns. The logarithmic real return is

$$\ln\left[\frac{S_{t+1}}{P_{t+1}}\left(\frac{S_t}{P_t}\right)^{-1}\right] = \ln\left[\frac{S_{t+1}}{S_t}\right] - \ln\left[\left(\frac{P_{t+1}}{P_t}\right)\right] = r_{t,t+1} - \pi_{t,t+1},$$

with $\pi_{t,t+1}$ the logarithmic inflation rate from t to $t+1$. The definition can also include asset cash flows q_{t+1}, leading to the **total real return**. The arithmetic real return is a slightly more complicated expression, but as in the case of nominal returns, the difference between the arithmetic and logarithmic measures is typically small over short periods:

$$\frac{\frac{S_{t+1}}{P_{t+1}}}{\frac{S_t}{P_t}} - 1 = \frac{S_{t+1}}{P_{t+1}}\frac{P_t}{S_t} - 1 = \frac{S_{t+1}}{S_t}\frac{P_t}{P_{t+1}} - 1 = \frac{1 + r_{t,t+1}^{\text{arith}}}{1 + \pi_{t,t+1}^{\text{arith}}} - 1$$

$$\approx r_{t,t+1}^{\text{arith}} - \pi_{t,t+1}^{\text{arith}}.$$

A real interest rate subtracts the inflation rate from the nominal interest rate expressed in money units.

Figure 2.5 displays nominal and real returns on US T-bills over the past half century. Much of the divergence happened early in the period, during the 1970s inflation that peaked around 1980 with

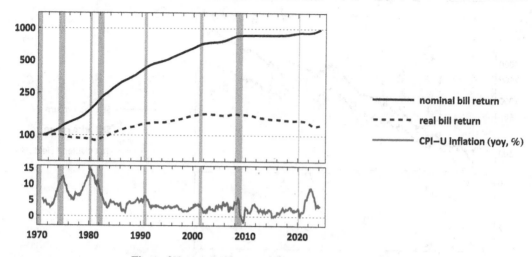

Figure 2.5 Nominal and real return of T-bills 1971–2024

Index of cumulative total nominal and real returns, month-end, logarithmic scale, Jan. 1971 (=100) to Feb. 2024. Real returns computed by subtracting year-over-year change in CPI-U, calculated as geometric average of monthly rates. This slightly smooths the month-to-month effect of inflation. Vertical shading represents NBER recession dates. *Data source*: Bloomberg.

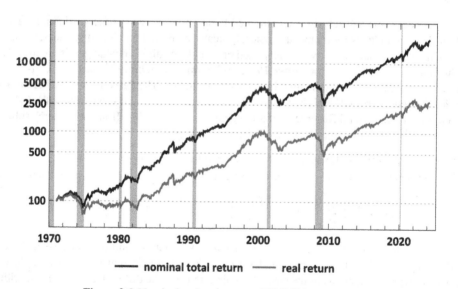

Figure 2.6 Nominal and real return of S&P 500 1971–2024

Index of cumulative total nominal and real returns, month-end, logarithmic scale, Jan. 1971 (=100) to Feb. 2024. Real returns computed by subtracting year-over-year change in CPI-U at a monthly rate. This slightly smooths the month-to-month effect of inflation. Vertical shading represents NBER recession dates. *Data source*: Bloomberg.

the tightening of monetary policy. Figure 2.6 shows nominal and real returns on the S&P 500 index. Much of the cumulative price return on the S&P 500 index—an over 40-fold increase—and the 160-fold total return are nominal, less than meets the eye once inflation is accounted for. Adjusted for inflation, money invested in 1970 and continuously reinvested grew about 25-fold over the subsequent half century.

2.1.5   Excess Returns

Analysis may stipulate the availability of a **risk-free**, or **riskless asset**, as part of the set of available investment choices. The risk-free return is often used as a benchmark or conventional standard to which other returns can be compared. A risk-free asset can also serve as a tool in valuation models based on macroeconomic fundamentals and household time and risk preferences. It is intended to represent the pure rate of interest compensating the lender for the use of funds over time.[8]

Assets conventionally classified as riskless include cash or money balances because they are legal tender, or redeemable on very short notice at par value, interbank money market loans and par interest rate swaps, and government debt issues of advanced market economies with low or negligible credit risk such as the US Treasury curve. Their yields define a **risk-free curve** or set of risk-free rates with different terms to maturity.

A **benchmark** is an asset price or return that serves as a uniform and conventionally accepted representative of a broader category or as a point of comparison for other prices or returns. For example, Brent crude or West Texas Intermediate (WTI) are specific grades or blends of crude oil, but their prices are used as benchmarks for the general level of crude oil prices.

In some asset classes, the benchmark is an **index**, an average of the prices of a well defined group of assets. Examples of long-standing equity market indexes include the Dow Jones Industrial Average (DJIA), a simple average of the prices of 30 large-company US stocks, and the S&P 500 (SPX), a market-value weighted average of the prices of 500 large-company US stocks. Widely used indexes of bond prices include the ICE BofA Merrill Lynch group of indexes, currently managed by exchange operator Intercontinental Exchange (ICE).

The **excess return** on an asset is defined as the difference between the return (usually measured as total return) on an asset or portfolio and a benchmark. In some contexts, such as assessing the skill of an investment manager, the relevant benchmark may be an index of the returns of an asset class. In

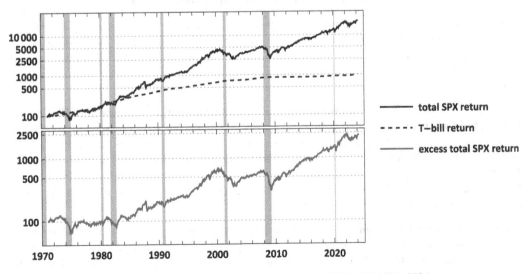

Figure 2.7 Cumulative total and excess return of S&P 500 1971–2024

Index of cumulative total nominal S&P 500, 3-month US T-bill yield, and excess returns over T-bills, month-end, logarithmic scale, Jan. 1971 (=100) to Feb. 2024. Vertical shading represents NBER recession dates. *Data source*: Bloomberg.

---

[8] We discuss risk-free rates further in the next chapter.

other contexts, such as understanding the risk and return of a portfolio or asset class, the comparison may be to a proxy for the risk-free return.

The risk-free return is ideally known at the start of, and its term matched to, the interval over which the return comparison is made. For some purposes, such as measuring long-term investment performance, a proxy, such as a long-term government bond, may be appropriate but is subject to greater price fluctuations within the comparison period.

Over long periods of time with compounding, excess return can be quite large. Figure 2.7, shows, for example, that the cumulative total return of the risky stock index was almost $2\frac{1}{2}$ times that of the "riskless" 3-month T-bill.[9]

Our S&P 500 return data are summarized in Table 2.1:

Table 2.1   Return experience of the S&P 500 1971–2024

	Annual	*Cumulative*
Price return	7.84	5 530
Total return	10.81	23 458
Bill return	4.40	988
Excess total return	6.15	2 384
Inflation	3.96	790
Real total return	6.59	2 973
Real bill return	0.42	125

In percent, using monthly returns Jan. 1971 to Feb. 2024. *Data source*: Bloomberg.

2.2   Asset Return Probability Distributions

Most financial analysis relies on quantitative or qualitative assessments of the probability distribution of future asset prices or returns and how they behave over time. A formal hypothesis about the distribution may be expressed as the **stochastic process** of an asset price, which is a mathematical model of how the price moves over time, or a less formal statistical estimate of the return frequency distribution.

The results of a process unfolding over time may differ from the results of a repeated random event. In the **gambler's ruin** problem, a gambler with a given initial stake and targeting a given amount of winnings plays a repeated game, such as tossing a fair coin. The coin should come up heads 50 percent of the time. Now consider the results of gamblers, starting with an initial stake of $2, betting $1 repeatedly on the results of the coin toss, with the goal of increasing their stake to $100. On each toss, they either loses the $1, or receives $2 back, a gain of $1. The probability of losing the entire $2 initial stake is 0.98, close to 100 percent.

Such a process is said to be **non-ergodic**: The expected value over time for one agent differs from the **ensemble** average for one coin toss across many agents at a point in time. The outcome varies with initial conditions: the probability of ruin would be lower with a larger initial stake or the ability to borrow if ruined.

Expectations of future prices may be understood as market participants' ideas or as the "real-life" distribution. When treated as a statement of fact about future return behavior from a point of view

---

[9] With negative risk-free rates, as observed in recent years in Europe and Japan, the excess return can exceed the return itself.

of superior knowledge, a distributional hypothesis is called the **actuarial**, **physical**, or real-world distribution. **Subjective** distributions, those in the minds of market participants, are unobservable and can only be inferred from data, models, and surveys. **Risk-neutral** estimates of the return distribution are those implied by market prices of assets and may or may not coincide with anyone's expectations. They are derived from prices of derivatives contracts—futures, forwards, and options—in markets where these trade alongside cash assets.

The payoffs and risks of asset returns can be captured by the characteristics, primarily **moments**, of their frequency or probability distribution:

Expected, or **mean return**, is the average or central tendency of returns, or a forecast of its future realization;

Volatility, or **standard deviation**, of returns is a measure of how large in magnitude returns tend to be or how far future returns might stray from recent or expected returns;

Correlations of returns are parameters of **multivariate** return distributions. Payoffs depend on the joint behavior of returns; do values of different assets tend to move in lockstep, in opposite directions, or appear to have no relation?

Extreme events, or **tail risks**, are events in the "tails" of an asset return distribution occur, that is extremely large returns, clusters of defaults, or drastic changes in correlations. Higher moments of distributions are one rough measure of tail risk.

Models may assume distributions and their moments are invariant over time, or more realistically, are time-varying. Figure 2.8 compares time series of the daily returns of low-volatility Coca-Cola Co. and high-volatility Meta Platforms, Inc. stock. The typical magnitudes of returns are visibly different and also vary over time with relatively calm periods succeeded by more volatile ones. Both time series display unusually large-magnitude returns, but those of Meta are more frequent and larger.

Even though not every random phenomenon in the world follows the bell-shaped normal distribution, a remarkable number of phenomena do. The **central limit theorem** in statistics states that averages

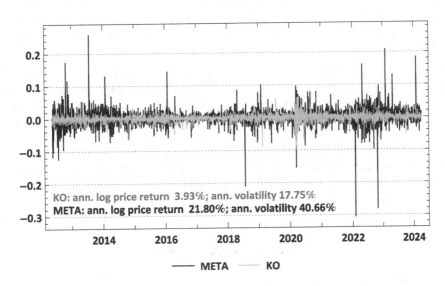

KO: ann. log price return 3.93%; ann. volatility 17.75%
META: ann. log price return 21.80%; ann. volatility 40.66%

Figure 2.8 Comparison of more and less volatile stocks

Daily logarithmic stock price returns of Coca-Cola Co. (KO) and Meta Platforms, Inc. (ticker META), 18May2012 to 03Apr2024. *Data source*: Bloomberg.

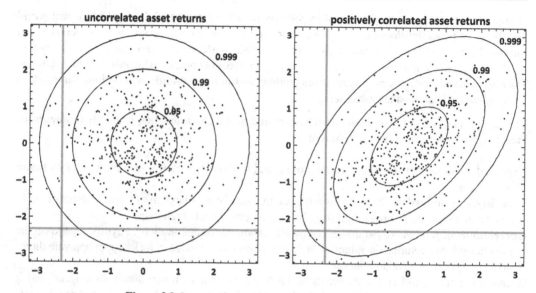

Figure 2.9 Impact of correlation on joint return distributions

Constant probability density contours of a bivariate standard normal distribution and random sample of 500 realizations. Realizations of the joint normal pair **x** fall within each contour with the indicated probability. The grid lines indicate the 0.01-quantiles of each marginal distribution. Left panel: correlation coefficient $\rho = 0$. Right panel: correlation coefficient $\rho = 0.50$.

behave like normals even if the underlying data are non-normal. The normal distribution is tractable, easy to estimate, and has few parameters.

Distributional hypotheses are useful but highly restrictive. Models often assume logarithmic returns are normally distributed, an assumption drastically wrong and often a reasonable first approximation. Empirically, many asset and factor returns are distributed very roughly normally. Monthly asset returns are often much closer to normally distributed than daily returns. No alternative model is unambiguously better. But the normal hypothesis underestimates the likelihood of tail events, and its assumption of symmetry between large positive and negative returns doesn't usually prevail in the real world.

The joint behavior of returns on several assets can be described by a multivariate normal distribution. Returns on two assets or factors are modeled as a bivariate (two-variable) standard normal distribution with a given return correlation. Constant probability density contours are two-dimensional confidence intervals identifying the range of values of a pair of random variables occurring with a given probability. We can use visualizations of joint distributions, such as Figure 2.9, to compare the potential impact of correlation on the risk of a portfolio. In simulations of a pair of returns with positive correlation, there are more results with large losses or gains. The distribution has more extremes in either direction that fall within the contours for any probability. Positive correlations in a long-only portfolio increase the likelihood of large losses and large gains.

2.3 Financial Risks

2.3.1 Market Risk

Market risk is the risk of loss from changes in market prices or risk factors. The most direct form is **price risk**, the risk that asset prices go the wrong way. But it also affects efforts to transact.

Execution risk is the risk that one cannot execute trades quickly or skillfully enough to avoid a loss. A **stop-loss order** is an instruction to a dealer to exit a position if the worst price the customer is willing to accept is reached, and **stop-loss risk** is the risk the dealer cannot execute it when prices are changing rapidly.

Market risk events include irrevocable, realized losses resulting from unwinding positions. **Mark-to-market (MTM) risk** is the risk of losses "on paper," based on changes in market valuation, but not realized through transactions. They may be recorded in a firm's accounts or publicly reported. These losses can be reversed or amplified by later asset price moves.

Market risk can be categorized by asset class, including equity, interest rates, foreign exchange, and physical assets, such as commodities and real estate. Most positions and portfolios are exposed to several market risks. Commodity futures prices, for example, fluctuate with commodity prices and short-term interest rates.

Foreign exchange, or **currency, risk** is the risk of loss from fluctuations in foreign exchange rates. An exposure is created by a long or short position in an asset denominated in a currency different from that of the investor's domicile or funding the position. Foreign exchange risk is usually bundled with other risks. Stocks are valued in local currency, for example, and their value to a foreign investor depends on foreign exchange and equity risk factors.

Sovereign debt has a great deal of convertibility risk. Even sovereign debt with low default risk may have the risk of redenomination at an unfavorable exchange rate, for example, if a eurozone member leaves the single currency and converts its debt to a new local currency.

Foreign exchange risk can also be part of economic or business risks, potential losses on assets, liabilities, and future cash flows denominated in foreign currencies. **Translation risk** refers to accounting losses for firms with foreign subsidiaries and revenues if the home currency appreciates. For example, the US dollar's appreciation against most other major currencies in 2022 led to significant foreign exchange losses for many nonfinancial companies. Procter & Gamble's 2022 net earnings were reduced by about 9 percent—a loss of nearly $1.5 billion—due to foreign currency translation apart from the significant impact of higher sales prices in local currency on its exports and, therefore, sales growth.[10]

Inflation risk is the risk of loss from a rise in the general price level. It directly affects debt securities with payoffs defined in nominal terms and indirectly affects all assets via macroeconomic conditions. Changes in expected inflation influence the yield curve. Inflation is difficult to hedge, increasing the risk compensation for nominal securities.

2.3.2 Credit Risk

Credit risk is the risk that the creditworthiness of a debt obligation deteriorates. It encompasses **default risk** events in which a debtor becomes insolvent, i.e. unable to pay timely and in full, as well as the **credit migration** risk that a default becomes more likely or that an issuer or security receives a lower **credit rating**.

It's not just whom you lend to but also who you trade with. **Counterparty risk** is the risk that a trading counterparty does not fulfill an obligation to pay or to deliver a security or collateral. Derivatives contracts, for example, a long option or a swap, generate exposure to credit risk that fluctuates with

---

[10] See Procter & Gamble's 2022 Annual Report at https://www.pginvestor.com/financial-reporting/annual-reports/.

market prices. Counterparty risk arises from market and credit risks, and it is challenging to disentangle them.

Credit quality depends in part on macroeconomic and market conditions. Interactions between market and credit risk include **wrong-way risk**, a credit exposure correlated with a market risk. The creditworthiness of a bank borrowing in foreign currency to lend it locally will deteriorate if the local currency depreciates. Counterparty risk is greater under market conditions that puts a counterparty at risk of default.

Liquidity risk falls between market and credit risks and has several meanings. **Market liquidity risk** occurs when the market is not deep enough, at the time you have to buy or sell, to trade without pushing the price against you. **Funding liquidity risk** events occur when credit becomes unavailable, or is offered only on more stringent terms. It can lead to forced unwinding and losses.

2.3.3   Operational Risks

A number of other firm-killers are grouped unter the heading **operational risk**, a major source of risk and regulatory capital component, alongside market and credit risks. The Basel Committee defines it as the " … risk of loss resulting from inadequate or failed internal processes, people and systems or from external events."[11]

Operational risks include **model risk**, the potential loss arising from incorrect models or their use in valuing illiquid or infrequently traded assets. Among the harder-to-measure operational risks are **reputational risk**, with potential for damage to a firm's goodwill or brand, and the **legal risk** that they may be sued for financial practices or that a valuable contract cannot be enforced. **Business** and **strategic risks** are risks to the firm's ability to deliver expected outcomes. Some operational risk events are difficult to classify. Squirrels have chewed through power lines and caused trading interruptions on the Nasdaq stock exchange on two occasions: December 9, 1987, and August 1, 1994.

Trading and investment management face important operational risks. **Clearing risk** includes failure to record trades accurately in the firm's books and records. Example include unauthorized trading by Nick Leeson at Barings Bank, leading to the centuries-old bank's failure in 1995, and by Jérôme

---

[11] See Basel Committee on Banking Supervision (2021).

Kerviel at Société Générale in 2008, resulting in a €4.9 billion loss. **Custodial risk** events result from commingling of customer securities or cash with the custodian's assets and becoming unavailable in the event of insolvency. Examples include Lehman Brothers' UK subsidiary in 2007 and MF Global in 2011.

Settlement risk occurs when one party to a trade irrevocably fulfills its obligation, delivering cash or an asset, but the counterparty fails to complete settlement. It has been important in foreign exchange markets where it is known as **Herstatt risk**. The Herstatt Bank, a large German correspondent bank, had been closed by local regulators during the New York trading day after its US counterparties had delivered Deutschmarks to it in anticipation of receiving dollars, leading to large losses. Subsequent reforms, in particular the Continuous Linked Settlement (CLS) system, aimed to introduce greater simultaneity into the process while shielding counterparties from liquidity and credit risks.

Settlement risk also played a role in the GameStop stock volatility episode. Robinhood Securities, the clearing subsidiary responsible for delivering cash for shares to settle a large volume of GameStop stock purchases, was subjected to a large margin call it could not readily meet.[12]

Market Episode: The Knight Capital error

One operational risk event illustrates many different facets. On August 1, 2012, market making firm Knight Capital erroneously executed over four million orders in the first 45 minutes four of the trading day. The resulting trades led to losses of about $460 million and the eventual forced sale of the firm. According to the SEC cease and desist order, the trigger was an "… error in the operation of its automated routing system," driving the erroneous orders.

The event constituted business risk in that speedy code changes were motivated as a competitive response to the New York Stock Exchange's Retail Liquidity Program (RLP), permitting sub-penny pricing for retail investors. An existing algorithm had been revised and a new one introduced to implement the RLP, an example of model risk. As a regulatory risk event, apart from the firm's payment of a $12 million SEC fine for risk management failure, the RLP was a response to Regulation NMS (RegNMS) eliminating sub-penny pricing. Reputational risk was reflected in the sudden cessation of large customers trading with Knight. It was also a market risk event in that losses were generated by changes in the value of the unintended positions taken.

Further Reading

Dimson et al. (2002) summarize the long-term behavior of equity and fixed income markets in the United States and other countries and have regularly updated their work in a series of *Global Investment Returns Yearbooks* now published by UBS. Ibbotson and Harrington (2021) focus on US equity and fixed income. Bodie (1995), using option pricing theory, and McQuarrie (2024), using US return data since the 18th century, cast doubt on the inevitability of equity outperforming bond returns.

More detail on probability distributions and their properties is provided in Appendix A.

Hull (2023), Christoffersen (2012), and Malz (2011) are general overviews of financial risk management. Brown (2016) and Coleman (2011) are less technical introductions.

---

[12] See Malz (2021).

3

Information, Preferences, and Asset Prices

3.1 Information and the Quantification of Risk

The practical difference between the two categories, risk and uncertainty, is that in the former the distribution of the outcome in a group of instances is known (either through calculation *a priori* or from statistics of past experience), while in the case of uncertainty this is not true, the reason being in general that it is impossible to form a group of instances, because the situation dealt with is in a high degree unique.

Knight, *Risk, Uncertainty, and Profit* [1921], p. 233

Markets are the process by which households and firms, with disparate goals and fragmentary, dispersed, uncertain, and partial information, meet and exchange goods and services for mutual benefit. Financial intermediation can be viewed as intermediation of information and facilitation of cooperation. The merchant banker connecting equity investors to ventures is intermediating between new to ideas/techniques and information about savings available to invest. Asset prices are among the most important information sources in this process because they signal to market participants what assets are more and less sought after or shunned and, through those signals, what changes might be occurring and how other market participants view them.

Financial models simplify the world along a number of analytically useful but potentialy misleading dimensions: thinning out the range of possible outcomes among which market participants choose, treating information gathering as a mere cost, and defining equilibrium as a state rather than an evolving process. The approach assumes that outcomes can be summarized quantitatively and have well-defined probability distributions, and people's ability to unambiguously rank outcomes by desirability. Models have low dimensionality, a lack of richness, ignore fine-grained, qualitative information, and focus on the limited number of things about which quantitative information is available and would be useful.

3.1.1 Conceptions of Equilibrium

Knowledge is incomplete and dispersed among many people, neither concentrated in the minds of a few nor shared uniformly by all. More importantly, most useful information is not yet known by anyone and must first be discovered. Market participants act on the basis of incomplete knowledge, even about current prices and with possibly hazy expectations about future prices. Investor and firm decisions are about a range of possible outcomes in the future, many of which can't yet be identified, rather than a set of known alternatives. **Search** is the costly process by which buyers and sellers locate and identify one another, and agree on a price and amount.

Even with well-defined probability distributions of outcomes, there are difficulties in obtaining an unambiguous preference ranking and a useful definition of **risk aversion**, the extent to which people shun risk. Different approaches may contradict one another or may fail to provide an unambiguous ranking of choices.

Analysis generally assumes **time preference** in **intertemporal choice** or **substitution** between consumption now and later. People are impatient, preferring consumption earlier rather than later. Alternatively, agents maximize the expected value of their future wealth, using all the information at their disposal. Analysis also assumes people are risk averse, preferring less risk to more, and that they are particularly leery of low or negative payoffs occuring just when times are bad. Assets that are considered safe are in high demand.

The choice problem is further simplified to maximization of **expected utility** and specification of a **utility function**, which is the theoretical vehicle used to map from consumption or wealth into satisfaction. The **intertemporal utility function** is an elaborated version that maps from future consumption in different states of the world into satisfaction. To capture time preference, it is set up so future consumption is discounted, less valued than present. Low-probability payoffs are less salient than high-probability ones. To capture risk aversion, utility functions generally assume diminishing marginal utility; more is better, but the more you have, the less the next increment adds to happiness. This implies that a large payoff that coincides with bad times is more highly valued.

In a simplified world, exchange is easily accomplished through markets, with contracts concluded now between all households for all goods for all future states and times. Households and firms plan their activities now—time 0—for a sequence of future dates $t = 1, \ldots, T$. Uncertainty is captured by imagining a finite set of possible realizations of the future $1, \ldots, N$. In this **Arrow-Debreu model** of equilibrium, there is a market for each good, and market-clearing prices at which it will be exchanged for other good at each time in the future, in each state of the world.

In the simplified Arrow-Debreu world, prices are determined now and households and firms trade just once at the beginning of history. There is uncertainty, but all the insurance against all the contingencies is in place, however expensive it may be. History after time 0 just consists of fulfilling contracts. In such a world of **complete markets**, financial intermediation is superfluous. Rather than a state toward which the economy is gravitating as change takes place, equilibrium is treated as a static, final point of rest.

In the real world, markets are incomplete; only a tiny fraction of the necessary **contingent claims** actually exist, and there are no **complete contracts** that take account of all possible future states of the world. Financial intermediation is an important part of how planning, allocation, and execution of future-oriented activities actually get done in an uncertain world. Equilibrium is never reached, but in general, the market-clearing process gradually approaches it even as the equilibrium itself is changing.

In models incorporating **rational expectations**, agents make decisions sequentially, in real time, rather than only once at the beginning of history. They base these decisions on their preferences and available information. As new information accretes over time, the information set becomes larger.[1] The concept of equilibrium focuses on the absence of surprise, which comes only from newly found information.

The rational expectations hypothesis presumes that at any point in time, learning has ceased and that market participants have " … somehow come to possess fantastic knowledge."[2] The rational expectations model has the virtue of excluding systematic error but is far from how even rational agents

---

[1] This view of progressively unfolding knowledge is known as the **law of iterated expectations**.
[2] Phelps (2018), p. 3859.

use information. In a world of undiscovered, dispersed, and costly information, learning is continuous, and there is disagreement; not everyone will share an identical "correct" model.

The economist Frank H. Knight used the term "risk" to describe situations or problems that are quantifiable and which one can reasonably describe with a probability distribution. Uncertainty refers to situations in which no quantitative estimates can be made and the outcomes are unknown or can only be guessed at. Knight viewed entrepreneurial profit as compensation for bearing uncertainty, not risk. Knightian uncertainty rather than risk is predominant in most real-world situations.

Another approach to recognizing limited knowledge and information costs is the concept of **bounded rationality**, which posits that agents make decisions based on a subset of all available knowledge. Life is short, time and effort are valuable, and people don't go about their lives calculating the likelihoods of outcomes and the costs of achieving them for every decision they make. The bounds on the use of information are themselves set rationally.

People are aware of the limits of their knowledge, and take that into account by developing **heuristics**, or rules of thumb, that enable them to make decisions with limited knowledge. Part of the cost of information is the time needed to gather and process it. Heuristics help reduce the delay of acting with incomplete but valid information. Not all knowledge is explicit or can be stated clearly. Apart from explicit knowledge, or "knowing that," there are tacit knowledge and skill, or "knowing how," much of it intuitive.

Behavioral finance is an alternative approach to explaining choices and prices focusing on psychological factors said to limit understanding of the world or inhibit rational action rather than on the limits of knowledge and reasoning. These **cognitive biases** might be found in the evaluation of information, for example, **overconfidence**, or might be found in the ranking of outcomes, for example, **loss aversion**. Market price behavior and choices can be attributed to preferences as well as to irrationality, so biases are generally identified through psychological research tools, such as questionnaires and tests. In contrast to the bounded rationality approach, which identifies constructive adaptations to the limits of knowledge, behavioral finance identifies irrationality and defects in our interactions with the world that may need to be corrected by an external authority.

3.1.2   Technical Progress

Technical progress in the past half century has increased the capacity, speed, and security of computing, data transmission, and communication. Two innovations played a crucial role in the development of finance: the introduction of money and **double-entry accounting**, a system for managing firms' financial information first introduced in medieval Italy.

Double-entry accounting is most familiar in analyzing the condition of businesses and households but has also proven invaluable in understanding how a country's or region's economy is faring and in understanding international financial transactions. It relies on a **ledger**, a complete record of a firm's transactions, distinguishing and reconciling **stocks** and **flows**. A stock is an amount of a good or an asset at a point in time. Flows have a time dimension, measuring the rate at which a stock is changing. Wealth measured in dollars or the number of barrels of oil in a storage facility are stock measures. Income or the rate of oil production are flows.

Firm and household accounting ensure the value of the entity's assets is matched by a set of identified **liabilities** of equal value. Liabilities are the entity's obligations and the sources of funding for the assets. Matching assets and liabilities constrains firms and households from exaggerating the values of assets. The accounting ledger ensures that the record of transactions—flows of revenue and expenditures—are consistent with changes in the balance sheet, which states assets and liabilities, and can be compared with other entities' records of the same transactions.

The ledger relates double-entry accounting to money. Applied to cryptocurrencies, although challenging to implement, the ledger approach ensures transactions are recorded identically in buyers' and sellers' accounts, the ledger is publicly accessible, and the overall amount created of a cryptocurrency is matched by ownership of the outstanding volume. This form of ledger enables **decentralized finance** (DeFi), which includes applications, such as **bitcoin** as well as **smart contracts**.

3.1.3 Frictions and Transaction Costs

> That inscrutable thing is chiefly what I hate; and be the white whale agent, or be the white whale principal, I will wreak that hate upon him.
>
> Ahab, in Melville, *Moby-Dick or, the Whale*

Financial intermediation is difficult and costly because it has to overcome many unavoidable impediments in the real world. The cost of information is a chief contributor to **transaction costs** or **trading frictions**. Sometimes invidiously characterized as **market failures**, in many cases costs stem from a regulatory constraint. They include several sources:

Limited or **asymmetric information**: Apart from information costs, market participants have access to different information. Conflicts of interest can be difficult to resolve through simple exchange.

Imperfect competition: Firms have pricing or monopoly power, or there are barriers to entry of new competitors.

Externalities and **public goods**: For some goods, such as the atmosphere, use by one person doesn't limit use by others, nor is it possible to exclude people from using it. In other cases, a good imposes costs, such as pollution, on people not involved in its production, or it provides them with free benefits, such as new knowledge.

Promises of future actions are hard to enforce, so financial transactions, whether immediate or involving a future claim, require some level of **trust** between the parties. Trading and lending are information- and trust-intensive. Lenders try to distinguish good from bad borrowers and must **monitor** their financial condition over the terms of the loans.

Intermediation displays **economies of scale**, **economies of scope**, and **network effects**, which are a type of positive externality. All present opportunities for specialization, such as mortgage servicing or factoring. These economies may also introduce competitive issues.

Asymmetric information is prevalent. Counterparties to a trade, borrowers, and lenders generally have different information sets from one another. Borrowers, for example, have more information about their own ability to repay than lenders. This asymmetry can be mitigated through costly monitoring. Insurance or guarantees diminish beneficiaries' incentives to monitor, perform due diligence, and mitigate risks, generating **moral hazard**.

Information gathering itself is subject to this problem. It's difficult to establish a market for information because the purchaser can't be sure of its value before buying it.[3] Information channels

---

[3] A phenomenon known as the **Arrow information paradox**.

also differ regionally. Banks have a comparative advantage in gathering granular, often confidential, information on borrowers, while capital markets are more reliant on public information.

Trade and credit are also impeded by another consequence of asymmetric information, **adverse selection**, also known as the "lemons problem." A seller and current owner is more likely to know of the defects of any good than a prospective buyer. Potential buyers of a used car, the classic example, can't know as much about its true condition as the seller. The risk that some sellers will fail to disclose known defects lowers the market-clearing price of all used cars. In debt markets, a market maker must widen the bid-ask spread to offset the risk of encountering better-informed traders. A similar problem arises in the originate-to-distribute model in securitization.

The imperfect alignment of interests is a perpetual dilemma and limitation in designing contracts and public policy. Intermediaries function as **agents** of **principals**, the owners of funds being lent or invested. The principal lacks complete information on the nature or behavior of the agent, the party paid to act on behalf of the principal. For example, an investment manager may maximize fee and trading income rather than investor returns. Complete contracts between the parties that would account for all possible future developments can't be written. Bankruptcy is costly, influencing the behavior of lenders and borrowers. The resulting **principal-agent problem** generates **agency costs** of better aligning incentives.

An asymmetry of risks and rewards can create option-like payoffs for parties to a contract or institutional arrangement and incentives to **risk shifting**. Equity investors, who enjoy unlimited potential returns, have an incentive to take more asset risk than lenders with a fixed return. Owners of a troubled business are likelier to fund it through borrowing than with their own resources. Banks benefiting from the Too Big to Fail policy may shift downside risk to the public.

Financial markets are susceptible to externalities; actions by one market participant may impose costs or provide benefits to others that can't be readily compensated through market mechanisms because those costs and benefits are nonexcludable or because of information asymmetries. Externalities may lead to **coordination failures** or **collective action problems**. Parties may not be able to agree on actions that benefit all but may be costly for each, for example holdouts in bankruptcy restructuring and depositors in bank runs.

3.1.4   Institutions

Economic activity is carried out through forms of voluntary cooperation and decentralized coordination other than market transactions in a legal, contractual, and regulatory framework. **Institutions** include arrangements, such as property rights, corporate forms of organization, bankruptcy law, and many types of financial contracts. Frictions, such as information costs and conflicts of interest, generate an institution-forming response to resolve or mitigate them and shape what actions are carried out through markets or within households and firms. Institutions vary widely across regions.

Though externalities have been viewed as an insuperable challenge that can only be addressed through legal and regulatory measures, voluntary cooperation and social organization have frequently found solutions. If the overall benefit is large enough, there will be a net benefit for all parties even after compensation of those negatively affected by those who gain. Historical examples abound of private action to provide public goods or to manage **commons**, which are nonexcludable resources, such as fisheries shared by a group.[4]

---

[4] Ronald Coase has shown how some externalities can be "internalized" contractually, and Elinor Ostrom has provided examples of non-state social organizations managing commons.

Money is perhaps the most important mechanism helping economize on information and overcome trading frictions. A widely accepted medium of exchange solves two fundamental limitations of barter in a market economy. There are myriad agents and commodities, desired at many points in time. The likelihood of a **double coincidence of wants**—a pair of trading partners meeting, each preferring the good offered by the other—is low. Maintaining a stock of money or close substitutes for money enables market participants to carry out desired exchanges when the opportunity arises. Money has network effects. The more people use a particular means of exchange, the lower the search costs and the higher the reliability.

An IOU, or promise to "pay" later, with a counterparty's desired good once located (indirect barter), isn't credible. A complete, accurate, and credible ledger or record of each transaction and of all claims doesn't exist. Money can facilitate each agent's desired transaction separately and requires less trust. In earlier times, rare, nonperishable commodities with high intrinsic value that were relatively convenient to transport, divide, and assay served the purpose. As a physical or digital mechanism for maintaining a ledger, money is a historical record of past actions and commitments. Money is, thus, a substitute for both trust and **memory**.[5]

Institutions are emergent and can, therefore, be entrenched and costly to alter, one of many examples of **path dependence** in economics and finance. History matters, and the state of any set of institutions, such as markets or financial firms, depends in part on their past.

Many early banks, such as the public banks of Venice and Amsterdam and the Bank of England, were created as a hybrid of private and government activity. Cities or states had a motivation to foster liquid markets for their debts or to grant legal privileges supporting efforts by local merchants to create liquid markets for commercial paper and foreign exchange. Other markets, such as the New York Stock Exchange (NYSE), created by the Buttonwood Agreement in 1792, were established by agreements entirely among market participants.

Capital markets are historically a later development than banks. They facilitate types of investment and lending that bump up against the limitations of banks: longer maturities, a wider investor base, the ability to trade the claims in secondary markets, and better pricing for issuers. Capital markets, therefore, require greater reliability of legal institutions and property rights than banks.

3.2   Risk Premiums

3.2.1   The Convention of the Risk-Free Rate and Reference Rates

Real-world investment choices can include only low-risk, not truly risk-free, assets. An authentically riskless asset would be free of default, price, currency, and inflation risks. Its actual return would equal its expected return with certainty. Conventionally defined riskless assets are subject to several risks, and those on nongovernment claims are, therefore, called **nearly risk-free** rates. Bank obligations, even short-term, contain credit, counterparty, and other risks. Risk-free rates are vulnerable to liquidity risks, such as a decline in collateral values, and to sudden yield changes due to changes in risk preferences, such as "risk-on" bond selloffs. Since the 2007 crisis, interbank and government curves have displayed anomalous behaviors related to these risks.[6] Interbank and most government debt are nominal issues, exposed to inflation risk and to currency appreciation or depreciation if held by nonresidents.

---

[5] See Kocherlakota (1998).

[6] See Chapters 15 and 18.

Sovereign credit risk is often low for bonds issued in local currency but only because alternatives to default—inflation, devaluation, or suspension of currency convertibility—are available to the issuer. Foreign currency-denominated emerging-market issues are subject to sovereign default risk.

Cash in the form of currency and deposit balances has significant risks and costs as well, sometimes referred to by the shipping industry term **demurrage**. Cash is exposed to theft, physical destruction, disruption of payment or settlement systems, and currency reforms or unannounced changes in the currency system. An example of a risk event affecting central bank money is the demonetization of large-denomination banknotes in India on November 8, 2016, intended to thwart tax evasion. Costs may also be deliberately imposed on holding cash as a matter of policy, such as negative interest rates on some advanced economy central bank deposits from 2009 onward. Proposals have also been made for the public sector to avert disinflation or discourage the use of cash by issuing moneys that expire or lose value over time, forcing its holders to spend it rapidly.

Risk-free rates are the inspiration for **reference rates** used as benchmarks in setting prices and rates of risky fixed-income securities and derivatives, such as floating-rate debt and interest rate swaps. Like other financial benchmarks, reference rates have been calculated by private-sector organizations, based on recent yields on different types of money market instruments, and found wide acceptance. Reference rates are employed primarily for financial contracts between private entities, so short-term government rates, which don't reflect the counterparty and other risks of private contracts, are used less frequently as major currency reference rates. For some countries at some times, the possibility of a dearth of sovereign issuance may also arise, so any benchmark would potentially be based on few, illiquid government issues.

For the most widely used currency, the US dollar, by far the most important set of reference rate has rate has been the **London Interbank Offered Rate** (LIBOR) curve. It was based on the interbank rates at which large banks lend to one another at short term and which are generally higher than those on US Treasury bills, reflecting their credit risk. Similar curves were set for other major currencies. The reference rates were based on representative rates submitted by a panel of large banks and published by their trade association. The **LIBOR manipulation scandal** revealed that some submitted rates were off-market, manipulated by the traders submitting them to affect the banks' MTM valuations, or to avoid the potential stigma of a high submitted rate, which might be interpreted as indicating that the bank faces reluctance to lend to it.

Central banks often operate to keep very short-term interbank rates close to the policy rates they set and publish reference rates based on representative averages of overnight interbank loans to monitor and communicate monetary policy. They are also used in money market derivatives contracts. The **effective federal funds rate** (EFFR) is a representative US dollar rate published by the New York Fed, and the euro short-term rate (€STR) is the euro equivalent.

3.2.2   Expected Returns and Risk Premiums

Asset prices are driven by two realities: the uncertain future payoffs of an asset and how market participants value them. To better understand that subjective valuation component, we'll imagine people know more than is possible in reality about the potential payoffs themselves. The **expected returns** of an asset can be understood as the statistical mean of the future asset price or as the price a market participant subjectively expects. Expected returns are not directly observable but must be estimated. Only realized returns are observable, and they are but one realization from an entire *ex ante* return distribution.

Suppose there are only two periods, t and $t + 1$, and only a finite number N of well-defined future states of the world, each with a probability $\pi_1, \ldots, \pi_N$ and understood as subjective or "true" probabilities. Each state is a unique combination of all the things that contribute to well-being, such as the economy, productivity, abundance, and high demand for labor, or their absence, or war and conflict. Suppose that asset i has a set of contingent future payoffs $p_{i,1,t+1}, \ldots, p_{i,N,t+1}$ in each future state. The expected value of the future payoffs is

$$\mathbf{E}[p_{i,n,t+1}] = \sum_{n=1}^{N} \pi_n p_{i,n,t+1}.$$

The value we assign to $\mathbf{E}[p_{i,n,t+1}]$, and thus, the current value of the asset, depends on how we evaluate the $p_{i,n,t+1}$ and the probabilities π_i.

Imagine that we know or can guess the contingent payoffs and their probabilities. We also observe a current price S_{it} of this asset. We can then calculate a discount rate or factor r_{it}, the return on the asset that aligns the observed price with the expected value of the payoffs:

$$S_{it} = \frac{1}{1 + r_{it}} \mathbf{E}[p_{i,n,t+1}] = \frac{1}{1 + r_{it}} \sum_{n=1}^{N} \pi_n p_{i,n,t+1}.$$

The excess of the expected value of the future return over the risk-free rate r_t^f is the asset's expected excess return, or **risk premium**, $r_{it} - r_t^f$. It is the risk compensation component of the required return. The market discounts risky income streams at the risk-free rate plus this risk premium. Expected returns on risky assets are higher than the risk-free rate to compensate for the risk borne. Risk premiums help us understand how asset values are related to risk by linking the expected value of the future payoffs to an observed price.

Risky assets are cheaper than safer ones with similar anticipated cash flows. An asset with a much wider range of future payoffs, or with their worst payoffs more likely coinciding with the worst future states—recession, declining asset prices, unemployment, or war—will likely be cheap and have a high risk premium. If market participants are risk averse and so crave insurance, then assets with reliable payoffs or high payoffs in bad times will be dear.

A **certainty equivalent** is a certain return that has a utility equal to the expected value of the utility of a set of uncertain payoffs. The asset price can be viewed as the present value of a certainty equivalent, discounted at the risk-free rate rather than a discount factor that includes a risk premium.

Expectations and views on the probability distribution of future outcomes are entangled with risk preferences. An asset's risk premium is as unobservable as the expected return or underlying probability estimates and can only be intuited or estimated via a theory of how agents value uncertain future payoffs. Conversely, current prices embed information about what might happen in the future, inextricably blended with how people feel about those possibilities. A **stochastic discount factor**, or **pricing kernel**, captures this idea, assigning specific values or **state prices** $\phi_1, \ldots, \phi_N$ to a \$1 payoff in different states of the world. It can account for time preference as well as specific models of risk aversion that have been coded into the intertemporal utility function. The stochastic discount factor reflects how much people value a higher payoff that arrives in bad times. In contrast to the risk premium, the stochastic discount factor is not unique to one asset but can be used to value or explain the price of any asset.

Suppose people's preferences show a positive correlation between ϕ_n and the payoff $p_{i,n,t+1}$ in the corresponding state n. A state price ϕ_n might then be high because state n is a particularly bad one, so an asset with a high payoff in state n is valued as insurance, as a type of hedge against bad times. The price of the asset today will be higher, that is, its risk premium will be low.

The observed price can again be written as a function of the probabilities π_n but valuing each state's payoff $p_{i,n,t+1}$ at ϕ_n rather than discounting the expected value of the $p_{i,n,t+1}$ using a risk premium:

$$S_{it} = \mathbf{E}[\phi_n p_{i,n,t+1}] = \sum_{n=1}^{N} \pi_n \phi_n p_{i,n,t+1}.$$

The stochastic discount factor involves vectors of two unobservable parameters: the subjective probabilities of each state and the stochastic discount factor that values a payoff in that state. A simpler way of applying the stochastic discount factor is to blend the probabilities and state prices in a set of **risk-neutral probabilities** π_n^* for each state: $\pi_n^* = (1 + r^f)\pi_n \phi_n$. These look like probabilities in that they are normalized to all fall between 0 and 1. Each risk-neutral probability equals the future value of the payoff received in a state times its probability. Like the pricing kernel, and unlike a risk premium, they are not unique to a specific asset but apply to all assets. Each can be interpreted as the present value of an **Arrow security** that pays $1 in state n and zero otherwise and has a value $\pi_n \phi_n$ now. A claim on $1 in good times with a low probability, for example, will be cheap. A portfolio of Arrow securities for every state guarantees a payoff of $1 in the future, so its present value is $(1 + r^f)^{-1}$ and the risk-neutral probabilities sum to 1.

The present value of the expected value of the future asset payoffs, treating these as authentic probabilities and discounted at the risk-free rate, gives us the current asset value:

$$S_{it} = \mathbf{E}^*[p_{i,n,t+1}] = \frac{1}{1 + r^f} \sum_{n=1}^{N} \pi_n^* p_{i,n,t+1}.$$

This procedure is called a **change of measure**, replacing the π_n by the π_n^*. The term "risk-neutral" comes from discounting by the risk-free rate rather than using an asset-specific risk premium. We can use current market prices of derivatives to estimate risk-neutral probabilities. These estimates provide information on market thinking about future asset prices and about the likelihoods and valuation of different outcomes.[7]

Risk premiums, the pricing kernel, and risk-neutral probabilities are different ways of expressing the relationships among people's preferences and attitudes to risk, their views about what outcomes are more and less likely, and the resulting asset prices. But preferences and probabilities are inextricably bundled in all three. Because of this bundling, risk premiums are difficult to estimate empirically. Efforts to do so have more often than not resulted in high estimates of risk premiums, sometimes referred to as "puzzles," that are hard to justify based on the behavior of returns. For example, historical excess returns on stocks have been high compared to its return volatility, and spreads on credit-risky bonds have been wide relative to realized credit losses. Both are well beyond what a range of models of investor preferences can readily explain unless a high degree of risk aversion or of aversion to large, sudden losses is assumed.

---

[7] See Chapter 6.

3.2.3   Interest Rate Spreads

A **spread** is the difference between any two interest rates. With myriad fixed-income instruments, there are myriad spreads between maturities on a yield curve, between rates in different currencies, and between credit-risky and "safe" securities. Many are narrow but persistent because they arise out of subtle differences between similar instruments.

The risk-free curve is a base or benchmark relative to which risky yield curves are measured. Interest rates can be decomposed into the unobservable risk-free rate of interest and spreads over the risk-free rate that compensate primarily for credit, liquidity, and other risks. **Credit spreads** are the market-clearing difference between risk-free and default-risky interest rates of corporate and government bonds. They compensate for bearing default risks, including the expected value of losses from default, uncertainty of the timing and extent of recovery, potential extreme loss in the event of default, and for liquidity risk. Credit spreads vary by obligor credit quality, bond tenor or maturity, and liquidity. There are often differences in spreads among obligors of similar credit quality. Corporate bond spreads are also affected by a bond's position in the issuer's capital structure and whether it enjoys third-party guarantees or is supported by collateral. Spreads can be measured for similar fixed-income securities across currencies.

There are several conventional measures of credit spread, some used by traders as units for price quotes, usually measured relative to swaps, Treasurys, or other government bonds with similar maturity. All attempt to distinguish the part of the security's interest rate that is compensation for credit and liquidity risk from compensation for the time value of money:

Yield spread: the difference between the yield to maturity of a credit-risky bond and a benchmark government bond with approximately the same maturity.

i-**spread:** The benchmark government bond, or a freshly initiated plain-vanilla interest rate swap, almost never have the same maturity as a particular credit-risky bond. Sometimes, the maturities can be quite different. The *i*- (or interpolated) spread is the difference between the yield of the credit-risky bond and the linearly interpolated yield between the two benchmark government bonds or swap rates with maturities flanking that of the credit-risky bond.

z-**spread:** The *z*- (or zero-coupon) spread builds on the zero-coupon swap curve derived from money market and par swap rates. It is generally defined as the spread that must be added to the zero-coupon swap curve to price the bond but may also be measured relative to a government bond curve.

Asset-swap spread: the spread or quoted margin on the floating leg of an asset swap on a bond, a transaction in which investors exchange coupons of a credit-risky bond for a nearly risk-free money market rate plus a fixed spread, gaining exposure to credit risk without exposure to interest rate risk.

Credit default swap spread: the market premium, expressed in basis points, on a CDS.

Option-adjusted spread (OAS) is a version of the *z*-spread that takes account of call options often embedded in corporate bonds. If the bond contains no options, the OAS is identical to the *z*-spread.

Figure 3.1 displays an example of the decomposition of a curve into a risk-free and spread curve. Figures 3.2 and 3.3 display historical data on US and European corporate bond spreads.

Another set of spreads arising out of the US Treasury market are **swap-Treasury spreads** between Treasury bonds and notes, and par interest rate swaps with the same maturity. Similar spreads are traded for other currencies as well.

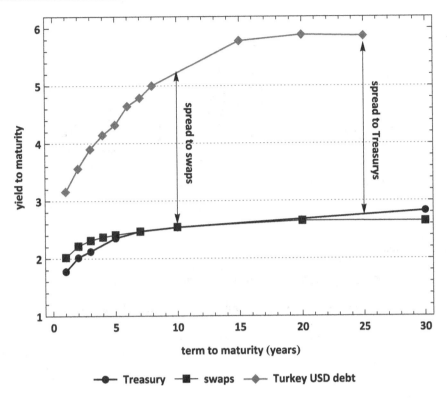

Figure 3.1 US and Turkish dollar-denominated sovereign yield curves

US on-the-run Treasury, par swap, and Republic of Turkey US dollar-denominated yield curves, 16Jan2018. *Source*: Bloomberg.

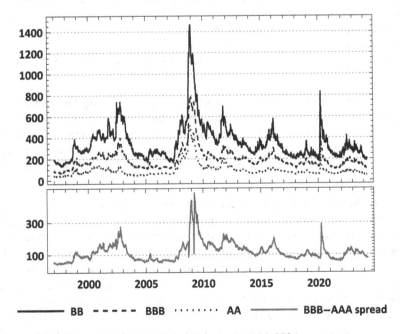

Figure 3.2 US credit spreads 1996–2024

ICE BofA Merrill Lynch US indexes of option-adjusted spreads (OAS) to the Treasury curve for corporate securities rated AA (C0A2), BBB (C0A4) and BB (H0A1), daily, in basis points, 31Dec1996 to 19Apr2024. The BBB-AAA quality spread is the difference between the BBB and AAA (C0A1) indexes. *Source*: FRED.

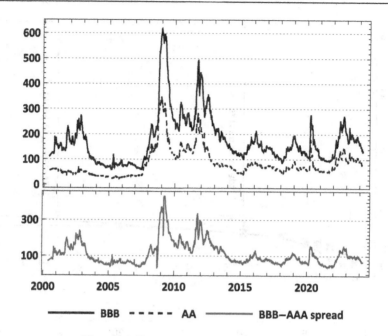

Figure 3.3 European credit spreads 1999–2024

Bloomberg Euro Corporate Bond Index option-adjusted spread (OAS) for securities rated AAA, and BBB, in basis points. Daily, 31May2000 to 01Apr2024. *Data source*: Bloomberg.

3.3   An Era of Low Interest Rates and Slowing Growth

Yesterday I read in the *Wall Street Journal* about the melancholy of affluence. "Not in all the five millenia of man's recorded history have so many been so affluent." Minds formed by five millenia of scarcity are distorted. The heart can't take this sort of change. Sometimes it just refuses to accept it.

Saul Bellow, *Humboldt's Gift*. Viking Press, 1975

It's impossible to understand today's financial world except against the backdrop of the low level of interest rates of recent decades. Assets have multi-period lives by definition, whether a physical investment, a loan, or a business, and their valuation depends in part on interest rates. Interest rates are in some respects the most important prices in the economy, with a role in valuation of anything involving the passing of time and determining the attractiveness of borrowing to fund investment or consumption.

Until the rapid worldwide post-Covid rise in interest rates, nominal and real interest rates had been unusually low for several decades. Figure 3.4 displays the behavior of shorter- and longer-term US nominal rates over the past 50 years. Low risk-free rates result in a lower absolute level of yields regardless of expected returns and risk premiums though these may be lower as well. The decline in rates set in following the inflation episode that ended in the 1980s. It occurred in several phases, with an initial large drop due to disinflation and a subsequent steady decline. The fall in interest rates went even further, to zero and even negative values in some countries, after the 2007 onset of the global financial crisis and the introduction of highly accommodative monetary policies.[8] Data from the 14th to the 21st century suggest a long-term trend of declining real interest rates, but levels the past quarter century have been below that trend, even after their recent rise.

---

[8] See Chapter 18.

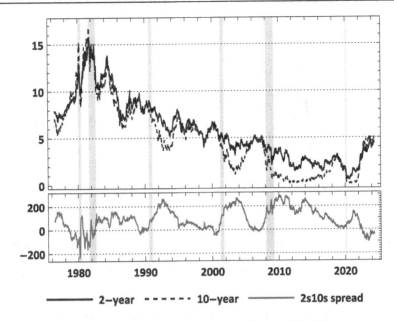

Figure 3.4 US 2- and 10-year nominal rates 1976–2024

Upper panel: US Treasury note yields, percent. Lower panel: 2s-10s spread (10- minus 2-year rate), basis points. Vertical shading represents NBER recession dates. Weekly, 04Jun1976 to 05Jan2024. *Data source*: Bloomberg.

Zero or negative real interest rates had an early manifestation in Japan from the mid-1980s and have occurred across regions and currencies. Japanese bond yields have been exceptionally low and economic growth stagnated following a sharp stock market decline in 1990. Figure 3.5 shows nominal yields of Germany's and Japan's 10-year government bonds, which fell to negative levels after 2007 alongside those of the United States.

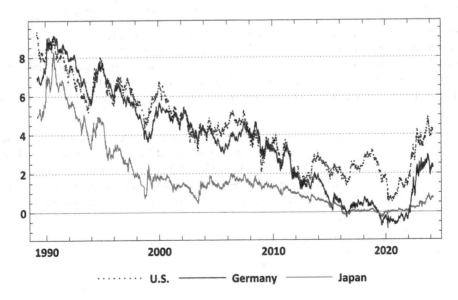

Figure 3.5 US, German, and Japanese 10-year nominal rates 1976–2023

10-year benchmark yields of US Treasury notes, German bunds, and Japanese government bonds (JGBs), percent, daily, 03Apr1989 to 29Mar2024. *Data*: Bloomberg.

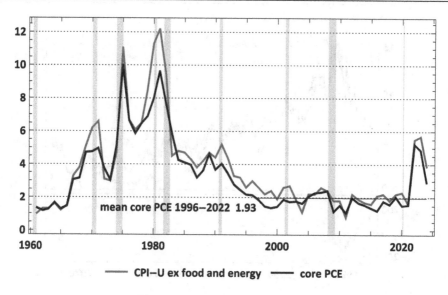

Figure 3.6 US inflation 1960–2023

Annual percent change in the consumer price index–all urban consumers (CPI-U), all items less food and energy (*Source*: US Bureau of Labor Statistics, series CUUR0000SA0L1E), and core Personal Consumption Expenditures price index (PCE) (*Source*: US Bureau of Economic Analysis). The core PCE is a broader index and has different weights from the CPI-U. Vertical shading represents NBER recession dates.

For a long time, the unusually low level of rates seemed to be a benign phenomenon as it coincided with a sharp and then sustained decline in inflation. As seen in Figure 3.6, US inflation, as measured by the two predominant indexes, fell from a peak near 10 or 12 percent in 1980 to an average below 2 percent annually between 1996 and 2020.

Figure 3.7 shows the behavior of real US interest rates over the past 50 years. Real interest rates cannot be directly observed, so Figure 3.7 displays two very different estimates, applying macroeconomic modeling and inferring them from market prices. Both approaches are imprecise due either to the imprecision of the models or to the presence of unidentifiable risk premiums in bond yields.

The growth of national income has also displayed unusual behavior in recent decades. Coinciding with the decline in interest rates and inflation, the variability of gross domestic product (GDP) growth dropped after 1980 as seen in Figure 3.8. This meant fewer, less sharp surprise disappointments and rebounds in economic growth. Together with the fall in rates, this added to the sense of a benign era, a Great Moderation, following the inflation and economic stagnation of the 1970s and the costly disinflation of the 1980s.

However, real economic growth and productivity have also declined in recent decades. One simple if narrow productivity measure, the growth of output per hour of labor input, fluctuates widely over time but is significantly lower than during the post-1945 decades and the recovery from the decline in the 1970s (Figure 3.9).[9] Similar declines can also be seen in nonresidential investment spending and the pace at which new businesses are formed. The low growth of productivity, business formation,

---

[9] A preferable, but more difficult measure of productivity to estimate, is **total factor productivity**, the part of output growth that can't be explained by higher inputs of capital and labor and, therefore, can be attributed to greater technological mastery and invention of new techniques.

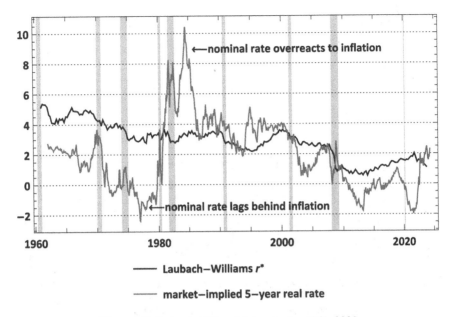

Figure 3.7 Estimated US real interest rates 1961–2023

Estimates of the short-term natural rate r^*: based on Laubach and Williams (2003) Mar. 1961–Oct. 2023, quarterly. Market-implied real rate: 5-year US TIPS yield July 1997–Dec. 2023 (Bloomberg ticker USGGT05Y) and 5-year nominal yield (Bloomberg ticker USGG10YR) minus a 10-year moving average of annual CPI-U All Items inflation rates centered on the current month Jan. 1967–June 1997, monthly. Vertical shading represents NBER recession dates. *Source*: https://www.newyorkfed.org/research/policy/rstar, Bloomberg.

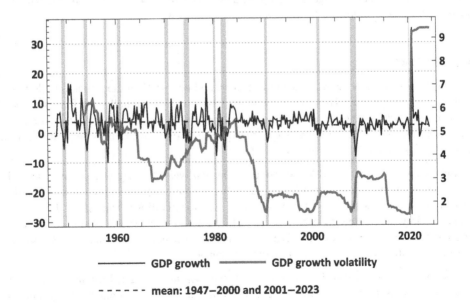

Figure 3.8 US GDP growth rate and its volatility 1947–2023

Percent change from preceding period in real gross domestic product, US GDP growth, seasonally adjusted at an annual rate (left axis), Q2 1947 to Q3 2023, and rolling standard deviation of the past 5 years' quarterly growth rates in percent (right axis), Q2 1952 to Q3 2023, quarterly, percent. Mean growth rates were 3.64 from Q2 1947 to Q4 2000 and 2.17 from Q1 2001 to Q3 2023. Vertical shading represents NBER recession dates. *Data source*: US Bureau of Economic Analysis.

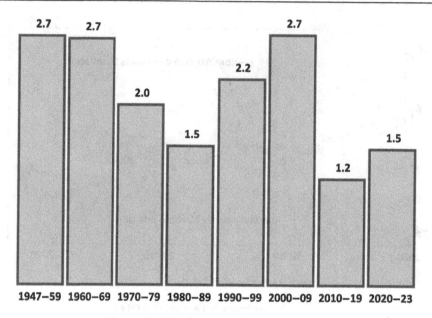

Figure 3.9 US labor productivity 1947–2023

Percent change in nonfarm business output per hour at an annual rate, quarterly Q2 1947 to Q3 2023. *Source*: US Bureau of Labor Statistics, series PRS85006092.

and private investment are consistent with low real interest rates. Low investment might also reflect the impact of technological change, reducing the demand for inputs of physical capital, but then low productivity growth is somewhat anomalous.

3.3.1 Safe Assets

The term **safe assets** has been introduced to describe and help explain the remarkably low interest rates of the past few decades. They overlap with longer-term conventionally risk-free assets, such as government debt but also include other types of debt perceived as relatively low in credit, inflation, and currency risks with high liquidity. They are expected also to have returns negatively correlated with those of risky assets such as stocks.

Safe assets are also characterized as **information-insensitive**, relatively free of asymmetric information problems, requiring little or no credit analysis or research to be accepted in transactions or that can be treated as low-risk by relying on legally sanctioned ratings. The assets, therefore, don't need to be underwritten anew by each market participant taking ownership and have low monitoring costs, permitting them to circulate freely. Information-insensitive debt and safe assets underpin forms of lending that create assets that function as money.

Few bonds exist that meet this definition and are issued in large quantities relative to worldwide demand, so US Treasury notes and bonds have by far the most prominent place. The **global savings glut hypothesis** states that the supply of safe assets has lagged behind demand as world wealth and longevity grows. The shortfall is said to have played a key role in depressing interest rates over the past few decades, exacerbated by the disappearance or disqualification of previously "safe" assets following the global financial crisis, such as the not exactly riskless senior tranches of mortgage-backed securities (MBS). Since the onset of the crisis, the safe asset category has narrowed to include primarily advanced-economy government and government-guaranteed issues. German Bunds, for example, fit the description, but the issuer's economy and the volume of Germany's deficit financing are too small to satisfy demand except at an extremely low interest rate.

An important source of demand for safe assets, particularly US government issues, are aging populations outside the United States, including many developing countries with weaker property and other legal protections that have fewer alternatives to advanced-economy government debt. The world has grown wealthier and is living longer than a century ago. Though hasn't happened uniformly across countries over time, but over long periods, there has been great progress. World per capita income is roughly 15 times what it was two centuries ago. Though income doubled during the century between 1820 and 1920, it is estimated to have increased nearly sevenfold in the past century (Figure 3.10). Life expectancy has also increased dramatically over the past 250 years (Figure 3.11).[10]

People with greater wealth can afford to increase savings and buy safety for their future, and rising longevity motivates them to do so. In a seeming paradox, ownership of risky assets has widened at the same time that the demand for safe assets has grown. Before 1970, individuals and households that weren't wealthy invested in stocks mainly via pension claims and insurance products rather than direct ownership of stocks and mutual funds. From the mid-1970s, changes in regulation, technical progress, rising wealth, and better understanding of long-term investing brought about a shift. Ownership of stocks has risen rapidly, equity mutual fund ownership even faster. Though home ownership remains the largest constituent of household wealth, in the United States especially, equity is a much higher share than in the past.

Low consumption growth and investment demand, coupled with slowing technical progress and productivity gains, are also referred to as **secular stagnation**, a term introduced in the 1930s to express Keynesian concerns that prosperity might be held back by low aggregate demand and must be countered by public expenditure programs. The term applies equally well to concerns that proliferating

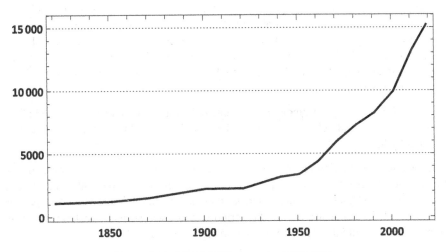

Figure 3.10 World GDP per capita 1820–2018

Real GDP per capita in 2011 US dollars. *Source*: Maddison Project Database, https://www.rug.nl/ggdc/historicaldevelopment/maddison/releases/maddison-project-database-2020.

---

[10] The declines in life expectancy in 1959–60 and 2020–21 are attributable to the Great Leap Forward in China and the Covid pandemic.

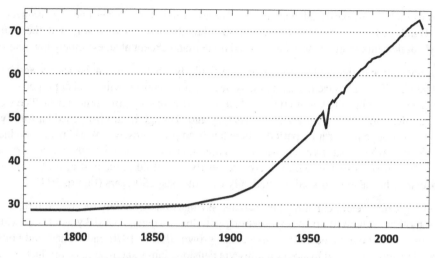

Figure 3.11 Life expectancy 1770–2021

Average number of years a newborn would live if age-specific mortality rates in the current year were to stay the same throughout its life. *Source*: Our World in Data.

regulatory constraints and a complex system of taxation and subsidization of specific sectors thwart productivity-enhancing investment and suppress income growth.

3.3.2   Rising Debt

During this period of low interest rates, private and public debt has increased dramatically. Low interest rates encourage higher levels of borrowing relative to assets or income. A simple measure is the ratio of aggregate debt to income, represented by GDP. For the United States as a whole and by sector, the upward trend is summarized in Figure 3.12. Overall, the ratio of debt to GDP has more than doubled since 1980 after several decades of little change. Up until the global financial crisis, the financial sector accounted for most of the growth though households and nonfinancial companies also increased borrowing.

Since 2008, the US federal government has accounted for much of the continued rise in borrowing. From 1980 to 2006, federal debt as a share of GDP doubled from 31 to 64 percent, and then again to 120 percent by late 2023.[11]

The Bank for International Settlements (BIS) reports similar data for a large number of countries. The ratio to GDP of credit to nonfinancial sectors has risen from 191.7 percent at the end of 2001 to 242.8 percent in Q3 2023, a less dramatic increase than in the United States over the same period, but large nonetheless.[12] The increase during the period of low interest rates accelerated a longer-term postwar trend of financial intermediaries taking on higher levels of debt.

---

[11] US Office of Management and Budget and Federal Reserve Bank of St. Louis, Federal Debt: Total Public Debt as Percent of Gross Domestic Product, https://fred.stlouisfed.org/series/GFDEGDQ188S retrieved from FRED. The data displayed in Figure 3.12 exclude Treasury debt held by the Social Security Trust Funds and are closer to the more frequently cited measure, federal debt held by the public. The 2020 spike in the debt-to-GDP ratio is accounted for by the drop in GDP, the denominator, during the lockdown phase of Covid.

[12] Table F1, "Credit to non-financial sector" (https://data.bis.org/topics/TOTAL_CREDIT/data), series key Q.5A.C.A.M.770.A.

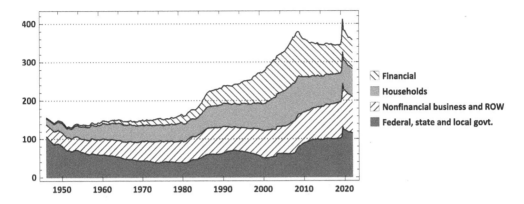

Figure 3.12 US debt-to-GDP ratio by sector 1946–2022

	Q4 1980	Q2 2020	Q4 2022
Total	162	412	358
Financial	21	86	76
Households	48	83	73
Nonfinancial business and ROW	55	112	94
Federal, state, and local govt.	39	131	115

Ratio of total debt outstanding (debt securities and loans) to GDP, current dollars, percent, quarterly, Q4 1946 to Q4 2022. *Source*: Federal Reserve Board, Financial Accounts of the United States (Z.1), Tables D.3 and F.2.

Further Reading

Hayek (1945) and Kirzner (1997) discuss the role of knowledge, discovery, and their diffusion through the market process. The concept of bounded rationality is explained in Simon (1990) and the use of intuition and heuristics in Gigerenzer (2007). Michael Polanyi discusses tacit and explicit knowledge in Polanyi (1964 [1958]) and other works. Rebonato (2007) discusses the complexities of applying probability models in finance.

Arrow (1973) and Williamson (1985) discuss limited information and transactions costs in markets. The latter work also focuses on the role of institutions. Coase (1974) provides an example of a private solution of an externality problem. Ostrom (2010) and Ostrom et al. (2012) summarize the author's work on the management of common resources.

On reference rates, see Schrimpf and Sushko (2019) and Huang and Todorov (2022) for analysis and a survey covering several countries.

Ross (2005) and Rosenberg and Engle (2002) discuss pricing kernels and risk-neutral probabilities. Abel (1991) and Amato and Remolona (2003) discuss the puzzles of sustained high equity excess returns and credit spreads.

Rogoff et al. (2024) estimate long-term interest rates since the medieval era. Phelps et al. (2023) try to explain the decline in interest rates and growth rates.

Gorton (2017) and Caballero et al. (2017) describe the characteristics of safe assets and their role in the financial system.

Part II: Markets, Uncertainty, and Risk

4

The Behavior of Asset Returns over Time

All models are wrong but some are useful.

G. E. P. Box[1]

4.1 Standard Model of Asset Price Behavior and Reality

Quantitative understanding of asset risk and return for investment, trading, and risk management involves **asset price dynamics**, the behavior of asset prices over time, discussed in this chapter, and **equilibrium asset prices**, the configuration of asset prices at a point in time, which we discuss in the next.

The geometric Brownian motion model, a continuous stochastic process based on the discrete random walk, is the baseline for asset price dynamics in financial modeling. In it, asset prices have a tendency to move up or down at random. Proportional changes in the prices i.e., logarithmic returns, are normally distributed. The **martingale property** states that successive and nonoverlapping changes in an asset price are independent of one another and of its initial position S_t; knowing what the price was last week adds no useful information to knowing what it is now. It can include a drift, or tendency to move up or down gradually over time with certainty, overlaid on the short-term fluctuations. Figure 4.1 displays simulated paths of a discrete process similar to a geometric Brownian motion.[2]

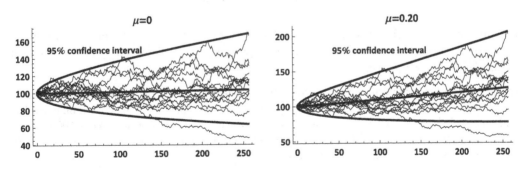

Figure 4.1 Sample paths of a geometric Brownian motion

Simulations of the path of the daily price over one year of an asset following a process similar to a geometric Brownian motion with annualized volatility 25 percent and initial asset price 100. The time series of daily logarithmic asset returns are based on a 256×15 array of independent random draws from a standard normal distribution, a particular case of the martingale property. The levels of the paths are lognormally distributed. Each increment of each sample path is equal to $\exp\left[\left(0.15 + \frac{1}{2}0.25^2\right)\frac{1}{256} + 0.25\sqrt{\frac{1}{256}}\epsilon\right]$, with ϵ a random normal variate. Rays and hyperbolas plot the mean paths and 95 percent confidence intervals over time.

---

[1] 1979, p. 202.

[2] There's some background on these and other statistical concepts in Appendix A.

Geometric Brownian motion has a number of useful properties for modeling asset price behavior. It's more realistic than the random walk because the asset price S_t is always positive. The variation properties of Brownian motion are oddly intuitive:

- It is imagined as continuous but not smooth, consisting of uncountably many immeasurably small jumps, creating noise even if the process has no drift. Therefore, it travels infinitely far to arrive a finite distance from its initial level.
- Any sample path of a geometric Brownian motion has a propensity to wander away from its starting point. The further into the future we look, the likelier it is that the asset price will be far from its current level.
- But the confidence level of the change in price from a given starting point increases with the square root of the time elapsed, rather than with time, limiting how far the price is likely to move. The propensity to wander is parameterized by its volatility. The higher the volatility, the likelier it is that the asset price will be far from its current level within a short time.

The normality of logarithmic returns implies that the price level "compounds down" due to noise. A decrease moves it to a lower base for the next move up or down. An increase does the opposite. Random fluctuations therefore, lower the price slightly over time relative to the path it would take based just on a zero or positive drift. This Jensen's inequality effect, the **volatility drain** or **drag**, is larger if volatility is higher and over longer periods. Apart from the Jensen's inequality effect, a geometric Brownian motion process with zero drift is equally likely to move up or down (see Appendix A).

Because of volatility drain, mean arithmetic will exceed logarithmic rates of return over time. For example, consider a process that begins at a value of 1, increasing by 1 percent in period 1 and decreasing by 1 percent in the next. The outcomes form a sequence $[1, 1 + 0.01(-1)^0, 1 + 0.01(-1)^1, 1 + 0.01(-1)^2, 1 + 0.01(-1)^3, \dots]$. It has a mean arithmetic return over two consecutive periods of zero and a slightly negative mean logarithmic return of

$$\frac{1}{2}[\ln(1.01) + \ln(0.99)] = -0.0000500025.$$

The difference, in this discrete example, is slightly bigger than the Jensen's inequality term. If we take 0.01, the absolute value of the average return, as a measure of the volatility of the process it equals $\frac{0.01^2}{2} = 0.00005$ per period.

The average arithmetic return exceeds the logarithmic return per period, and it's the latter that counts for longer-term returns. The higher the volatility, the higher the gap. Over time, the cumulative arithmetic return $\prod_{t=0}^{T}[1 + 0.01(-1)^t] - 1$ slowly sinks further below 0 as T grows. After 100 periods, the return is -0.49878 percent.[3] Portfolio managers reporting their average annual arithmetic return overstate the long-term results for their investors.

The geometric Brownian motion model restricts return behavior in several ways. It assumes that logarithmic asset returns are normally distributed, implying that very large-magnitude returns are rare. In its basic version, it assumes the parameters of the return distribution are constant over time, including correlations of returns on different assets. For a single asset with constant drift μ and volatility parameter σ, the τ-period log return is:

$$r_{t,t+\tau} = \ln(S_{t+\tau}) - \ln(S_t) \sim \mathcal{N}(\mu\tau, \sigma^2\tau).$$

---

[3] The same result is obtained using the cumulative log return $\sum_{t=0}^{T} \ln[1 + 0.01(-1)^t]$, -0.500025 percent.

The mean of $S_{t+\tau}$ includes the Jensen's inequality term $\frac{1}{2}\sigma^2\tau$: $\mathbf{E}[S_{t+\tau}] = S_t e^{\left(\mu + \frac{1}{2}\sigma^2\right)\tau}$. More complex models of time series behavior permit both parameters to vary, make those changes a function of volatility or of the asset price level, or add randomly occurring discontinuous jumps.

In reality, asset returns are far from normally distributed. Very large returns are rare but not extremely so. Surprisingly, even shockingly high-magnitude returns are recurrent. Negative large-magnitude and extreme returns predominate for many assets, positive ones for others. The standard model is a baseline rather than an accepted model. Nobody believes it, but it's a starting point for thinking about risk and return, and some conventional and regulatory risk measures are based on it.

Much effort is devoted to identifying and modeling real-world departures from the standard model. The similarities and differences between it and observed return behavior are summarized as the "stylized facts" because they at least roughly describe properties of the time series of a wide range of returns on different assets. These patterns over time describe the behavior of returns, the behavior of volatility, the prevalence and patterns of extreme returns, and relationships between returns on different assets.

4.2   Return, Volatility, and Correlation Behavior

4.2.1   Return Predictability

The standard model's feature of lack of return predictability is largely but not entirely borne out. The **autocorrelations** of returns are parameters describing relationships between returns in successive time periods. First-order autocorrelations or **serial correlations** are the relationships between today's and subsequent price returns. Higher-order return correlations are those between squared or higher powers of returns and subsequent ones.

First-order return autocorrelations tell us something about return predictability, second-order autocorrelations about future volatility given current volatility, and higher-order autocorrelations about the prevalence of extreme returns and whether they are likelier to be positive or negative. In the geometric Brownian motion model of asset prices with constant volatility and drift, the first-order as well as all higher-order return autocorrelations are zero. There is no statistical relationship between current returns and volatility and future returns and volatility. This implication is consistent with the efficient markets hypothesis.[4]

Autocorrelations of daily and lower-frequency returns are generally close to but not exactly zero; there is some measurable dependency in an asset's successive price changes. In the short term, there is often a detectable positive autocorrelation of returns, a phenomenon often referred to as **momentum**. Positive or negative returns are often, though not very reliably, immediately followed by returns of the same sign. A good or bad day in the stock market is, sometimes, just a bit more likely to be followed by another good than a bad day. The pattern is most detectable in high-frequency, intraday returns. There are also regularities in stock returns around earnings announcements.

Over longer periods such as quarters and years, and more robustly verified, one observes **mean reversion of returns**, a negative autocorrelation. When returns have recently been unusually high for some time, there is a tendency for them to be somewhat lower in the future, and vice versa. If an asset is badly sold off, there is a higher likelihood that it will recover at least somewhat in the future.

---

[4] See Chapter 7 below.

This also implies **long-range dependence**, or **long memory**, a long-term characteristic rate of return to which each asset will eventually gravitate. A selloff in stocks is likely to be followed within a few years by a recovery. Longer-term mean reversion has been related to persistent yet not permanent changes in investors' risk aversion.

A related property is **aggregational Gaussianity** or normality. Over longer periods, such as weeks or months, returns look closer to normally distributed than daily and intraday returns. Like most financial market phenomena, these patterns are hard to state precisely and verify because they apply more or less strongly to different assets and to individual stocks as opposed to indexes, because they depend on data frequency and because the meaning of "low returns recently" and "higher than usual" is ambiguous.

4.2.2   Time Variation in Return Volatility

In contrast to returns themselves, recent past and long-term return volatility help predict future volatility; second-order is stronger than first-order autocorrelation. Volatility behavior over time displays some typical patterns:

Persistence: The magnitudes or squares of returns display positive autocorrelation, leading to return volatility persistence. Volatility tends to stay near its current level; periods of high or low volatility tend to be enduring.

Abrupt changes in volatility—**volatility of volatility**—are nonetheless not unusual. Together with persistence, they lead to **volatility clustering**, or **volatility regimes**. A large-magnitude return shocks volatility higher; volatility then tends to persist at its higher level. Markets can almost as suddenly become calm. Shifts from low to high volatility are more abrupt, and shifts from high to low volatility are more gradual.

Long-term mean reversion: An asset's return volatility tends to gravitate to a long-term level. This in turn implies a **term structure of volatility**: current estimates of volatility for different time horizons will be different. If short-term volatility is unusually low compared to the long-term experience for as asset, volatility will be expected to rise.

Figure 4.2 illustrates these patterns with an estimate of the volatility of oil prices in recent decades, and Figure 2.8 shows the relatively placid Coca-Cola and volatile Meta.

4.2.3   Time Variation in Return Correlation

Like volatility, correlations vary over time. Abrupt increases in correlation are frequently observed during periods of financial stress, leading to a diminution of diversification benefits and the failure of some hedging strategies. Even the sign of the correlation can change persistently over time.

Stock returns and bond yields in the United States since the inflation of the 1970s (Figure 4.3) are an example. Their correlation is determined by inflation expectations, the robustness of the economy, investors' risk appetites, and expectations about monetary policy, among other factors.[5] From the 1960s to the 1990s, during a major inflation and disinflation, it was generally negative. Rising rates were driven primarily by rising inflation expectations and were associated with an adverse impact on economic growth and stock prices from higher-than-expected inflation and the anticipated policy response. Once a low-inflation monetary policy became fully credible in the early 1990s, rising

---

[5] A positive correlation of equity returns and yield changes corresponds to negative correlation of stock and bond returns.

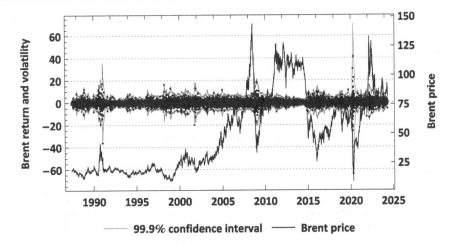

Figure 4.2 Volatility of crude oil prices 1987–2024

Prices (USD per barrel) and returns (points, in percent) of Brent Europe crude oil; 99.9 percent confidence interval calculated using EWMA volatility (estimated daily with decay factor $\lambda = 0.94$), daily, 20May1987 to 13May2024. *Data source*: U.S. Energy Information Administration via FRED (series DCOILBRENTEU).

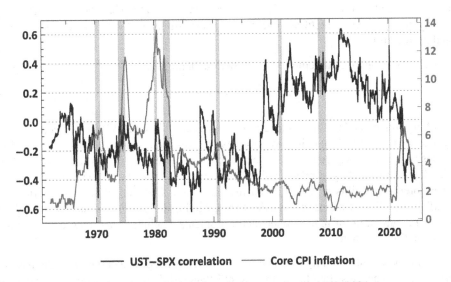

Figure 4.3 Correlation of stock returns and rates 1962–2024

Correlation (estimated via EWMA with decay factor $\lambda = 0.97$) of weekly log S&P price return and weekly changes in constant-maturity yield of 10-year US Treasury note, 05Jan1962 to 17May2024 (left y-axis); year-over-year core CPI-U inflation, monthly, percent, Jan. 1962 to Apr. 2024 (right y-axis). Vertical shading represents NBER recession dates. *Data source*: Bloomberg.

long-term rates were more often driven by positive expectations about economic growth, and the correlation shifted from strongly negative to mildly positive. The correlation of equity returns and yields turned negative again in 2022, during the post-Covid rise in inflation, which was associated with expectations of restrictive monetary policy and slower economic growth.

Since the global financial crisis, a short-term pattern of "risk-on, risk-off" behavior has been noted. Investors eagerly embrace risky assets and shed less risky ones, or the opposite. This leads to a tendency for correlations across risky assets such as stocks to rise in stress periods when risk appetites decline. The risk-on, risk-off pattern also raises the correlation between equity returns and Treasury yields, as investors reduce allocations to risky in favor of safe assets and vice versa. For example, during the 2011 tensions over European and US public debt, and in the early phase of Covid in 2020, yields and stock markets fell sharply as investors fled risky assets, leading to upward spikes in correlation.

4.3   Volatility Forecasting

4.3.1   Simple Approaches to Volatility Estimation

Persistence and mean reversion to a long-term "forever" level of volatility make volatility at least somewhat predictable. Conditional or short-term volatility forecasts can be updated with fresh information based on the magnitude of recent returns. Volatility tends to rise when it is currently low relative to its long-term average level. The term structure of volatility, e.g., whether weekly volatility is higher or lower than daily, is also informative. Predictability is limited by the abruptness of changes in volatility.

Volatility, unlike return, is not directly observable but must be estimated. We'll denote by σ_t the current estimate of future return volatility based on a model and on information through time t. That estimate is then used as a forecast of volatility over some reasonably short horizon. The magnitude and possibly the sign of recent returns, together with past estimates of volatility, drive changes in the estimated σ_t over time.

Let r_t represent the logarithmic return over one period ending at t:

$$r_t \equiv r_{t-1,t} \equiv \ln(S_t) - \ln(S_{t-1}).$$

When working with daily data, this is the return from yesterday's to today's close. Short-term volatility is typically calculated using daily close-to-close returns though other frequencies are also used in estimates, such as weekly and intraday. At the close of each day t, we use r_t, possibly together with other inputs, to update yesterday's volatility estimate σ_{t-1}. We use the new estimate σ_t to measure risk or forecast volatility over the next business day $t+1$. Over longer periods, return frequency doesn't affect volatility estimates as much due to aggregational normality, mean reversion of returns, and lower autocorrelation of higher-order return moments, leading to less day-to-day variation in long-term volatility estimates.

The simplest conditional volatility estimator uses a moving window incorporating the past m trading days' returns. The most familiar is the sample standard deviation, the bias-corrected average magnitude of return deviations from the mean return $\bar{r}_t = \frac{1}{m} \sum_{\tau=1}^{m} r_{t-m+\tau}$:

$$\sigma_t = \sqrt{\frac{1}{m-1} \sum_{\tau=1}^{m} (r_{t-m+\tau} - \bar{r}_t)^2}.$$

In the geometric Brownian model, one often assumes the drift $\mu = 0$, implying[6]

$$r_{t,t+\tau} = \ln(S_{t+\tau}) - \ln(S_t) \sim \mathcal{N}(0, \sigma^2 \tau).$$

---

[6] Discrete returns will have a slightly negative mean due to the Jensen's inequality term.

Why assume zero-mean returns? In part because we can: the mean return has only a small impact on volatility over short intervals. In the example of Meta Platforms, Inc. and Coca-Cola Co., the daily expected return on a 50-50 portfolio is just 5.13 basis points, but the daily volatility—the magnitude of a return one would, in a lognormal world, expect to see exceeded 1 day out of 3—is 1.410 percent, $27\frac{1}{2}$ times as large.

In the lognormal model, the mean and variance of price changes are proportional to the time elapsed, and volatility is proportional to the square root of time as seen in Figure 4.1. Over longer periods, therefore, the mean has a larger impact on returns than volatility.

But we also assume a zero-mean return because we must. Volatility is easier to estimate than expected return, introducing an additional source of statistical error. Imagine an asset return time series approximately following a geometric Brownian motion process with constant parameters. You can only observe one sample path in real history. Therefore, the only information on the mean return or drift is the single observation on return over the entire period. But finer intervals—daily rather than weekly, every five minutes instead of daily—provide more information on volatility and the price's tendency to wander away from any starting point. The confidence interval of the volatility estimate tends toward zero as the intervals become shorter but not that of the mean estimate.[7] In practice, market participants disagree far more about their return forecasts than about whether volatility is currently high or low.

Incorporating the typical volatility modeling choice to estimate the return volatility, but assuming the mean return is zero, the standard deviation reduces to the sample root mean square (RMS) or average magnitude of returns:

$$RMS_t = \sqrt{\frac{1}{m}\sum_{\tau=1}^{m} r_{t-m+\tau}^2}.$$

It is also closer to the conventional use of the term "volatility" in practice.

The assumption of lognormal returns has an additional convenience, a rule of thumb called the **square-root-of-time rule**. To apply the rule, note that a typical year includes about 250–260 trading days, depending on the market and its location.[8] The volatility forecast horizon includes trading days only, not calendar time. Prices can change only when the market is open, even if the holding period and cash flows accrue every calendar day. Assuming there are $256 = 16^2$ trading days, an annualized volatility is about 16 times the daily volatility. The long-term average annual volatility of US stock indexes has been about 16–20 percent, for example, a daily vol of about 1–1.25 percent. A ±2 percent logarithmic daily return thus roughly corresponds to $(-1.96, 1.96)$, the 95 percent confidence interval of a standard normal. One shouldn't be surprised, in a roughly normal world, to see a return of around 2 percent in magnitude about once per month.

The square-root-of-time rule should be used cautiously because it assumes a constant return volatility, i.e., a flat term structure of volatility. It is also at odds with changes in volatility over time and with long-term mean reversion. The rule is nonetheless practically useful even if returns are only approximately lognormal.

---

[7] See Merton (1980).

[8] The number also depends on the year because holidays may fall on weekends. National stock markets are typically open a little more than 250 days. Foreign exchange markets, which can operate simultaneously in many jurisdictions, are open on more days.

4.3.2 The GARCH Model

The inscrutably named but widely used **generalized autoregressive conditional heteroscedasticity** (GARCH) model incorporates the recurrent patterns in volatility we've identified. In it, volatility is tied to recent volatility, recent returns, and a long-term volatility $\bar{\sigma}$. In **GARCH(1,1)**, the simplest variant, the model looks back one period, incorporating the long-term level of volatility, yesterday's vol estimate, and the most recent return. The estimate σ_t at today's close updates yesterday's estimate σ_{t-1} with the latest return r_t, while anchoring it to $\bar{\sigma}$:

$$\sigma_t^2 = \alpha r_t^2 + \beta \sigma_{t-1}^2 + \gamma \bar{\sigma}^2.$$

Today's return r_t is the only pertinent new information on date t. The model specifies that it is determined by a shock or innovation ϵ_t together with the current volatility σ_{t-1}:

$$r_t = \epsilon_t \sigma_{t-1},$$

with ϵ_t assumed to have mean 0 and variance 1 and to be identically and independently distributed (i.i.d.). The stronger assumption of normality is sometimes made. Thus r_t is random but not "free"; rather it is set by the current vol and the random shock ϵ_t.

If α is relatively high, a large r_t causes a larger immediate change in the new estimate of return volatility σ_t. As fresh return observations come in, it leads to a wider range of variation of σ_t over time. High volatility will fade more quickly if return magnitudes decrease. The volatility of volatility will be higher. A relatively high β leads to less variation and more persistence in σ_t over time and to more persistent deviations from $\bar{\sigma}$. The presence of $\bar{\sigma}$ generates a term structure of volatility, as volatility will be expected to gravitate to its long-term level. A relatively high γ implies faster mean reversion and a flatter term structure.

The parameters or weights in the GARCH(1,1) model satisfy $\alpha, \beta, \gamma > 0$ and $\alpha + \beta + \gamma = 1$. This imposes a trade-off between the influence of long-term variance and that of the most recent volatility estimate and return. Estimates of β are generally not very far from 1, and $\alpha + \beta$ quite close to 1.

The GARCH(1,1) formula can be recast in terms of the t most recent and past squared returns and a starting value σ_0 (setting $\omega \equiv \gamma \bar{\sigma}^2$):

$$\sigma_1^2 = \alpha r_1^2 + \beta \sigma_0^2 + \omega$$
$$\sigma_2^2 = \alpha r_2^2 + \beta \sigma_1^2 + \omega = \alpha r_2^2 + \beta(\alpha r_1^2 + \beta \sigma_0^2 + \omega) + \omega$$
$$= \alpha r_2^2 + \alpha \beta r_1^2 + \beta^2 \sigma_0^2 + (1 + \beta)\omega$$
$$\vdots$$
$$\sigma_t^2 = \alpha \Sigma_{\tau=1}^{t} \beta^{t-\tau} r_\tau^2 + \Sigma_{\tau=1}^{t} \beta^{t-\tau} \omega + \beta^t \sigma_0^2$$
$$\approx \alpha \Sigma_{\tau=1}^{t} \beta^{t-\tau} r_\tau^2 + \frac{1}{1-\beta}\omega$$

Because $\alpha < 1$ and $\beta < 1$, more remote past returns and any starting value σ_0 have only a small influence on σ_t. We can use a numerical search procedure to find the parameters, with $\omega \equiv \gamma \bar{\sigma}^2$ treated as a single parameter and γ then recovered as $1 - \alpha - \beta$. We also get an estimate of the long-term volatility from

$$\bar{\sigma} = \sqrt{\frac{\omega}{1 - \alpha - \beta}}.$$

The numerical search procedure can be sensitive to the initial trial guess. In practical applications, one may estimate parameters infrequently but use the estimated model regularly to forecast volatility.

Example 4.1   GARCH(1,1) model estimation

We'll apply the model to the S&P 500 index, using $m + 1 = 3651$ closing-price observations from 30Jun2005 to 31Dec2019, and using r_1^2 as the starting value σ_0. The results are:

	Parameter estimates		
α	0.12174	β	0.85620
ω	2.41317×10^{-6}	$\bar{\sigma}\,(\%)$	1.04606
γ	0.02205		

4.3.3   The Exponentially Weighted Moving Average Model

The **exponentially weighted moving average** (EWMA), or **RiskMetrics model**, is much simpler to estimate. In it, variance is a weighted average of past returns. The weights decline for more remote past returns at a rate governed by a single parameter, called the **decay factor** $0 < \lambda < 1$. A low λ drives rapid adaptation and a high λ slow adaptation to recent returns.

The current volatility estimate σ_t uses the m most recent observed returns $r_{t-m+1}, \cdots, r_t$:

$$\sigma_t^2 = \frac{1-\lambda}{1-\lambda^m} \sum_{\tau=1}^{m} \lambda^{m-\tau} r_{t-m+\tau}^2 \approx (1-\lambda) \sum_{\tau=1}^{m} \lambda^{m-\tau} r_{t-m+\tau}^2.$$

The formula differs from the simple RMS formula in that the weight on each squared return observation $\tau = 1, \dots, m$ is $\frac{1-\lambda}{1-\lambda^m} \lambda^{m-\tau}$, rather than $\frac{1}{m}$. For the most recent (time t) return, $\lambda^{m-m} = 1$, and for the most remote (time $t - m + 1$) return, $\lambda^{m-1} \approx 0$. The number of observations m doesn't have to be large; $m \approx 100$ is adequate unless λ is quite close to 1.

The decay factor λ can be estimated using various criteria, such as minimizing forecast errors. Often, it is chosen judgmentally. Widely adopted standard settings for the decay factor are $\lambda = 0.94$ for short-term (e.g. one-day) forecasts and $\lambda = 0.97$ for medium-term (e.g. 1-month) forecasts. Figure 4.4 compares the effect of these two values as the dates of the observed returns recede into the past. The lower value generates much higher volatility of volatility.

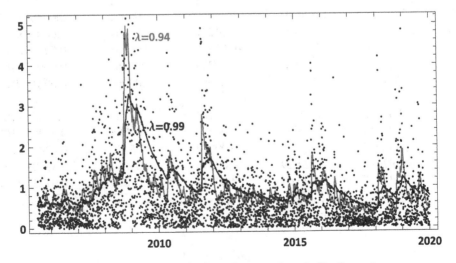

Figure 4.4 Effect of the decay factor on the volatility forecast

EWMA estimates of the volatility of daily S&P 500 index returns 01Jul2005 to 31Dec2019, at a daily rate in percent, using decay factors of $\lambda = 0.94$ and $\lambda = 0.99$. Points represent the absolute value of daily return observations.

An even simpler alternative for estimating EWMA volatility is to use a recursive formula. It updates the most recent volatility estimate with new data on return magnitude:

$$\sigma_t^2 = \lambda \sigma_{t-1}^2 + (1 - \lambda) r_t^2.$$

Example 4.2   Volatility estimation with EWMA

Table 4.1 shows how the data might be laid out to compute volatility with the EWMA model. Table 4.2 displays the data layout for computing volatility using the recursive EWMA formula. The starter value is not crucial as it converges quickly, especially for a smaller λ.

The recursive formula shows the similarity of EWMA to a "one-parameter" GARCH(1,1) model, with $1 - \lambda$ analogous to α and λ analogous to β, but with the parameter of long-term volatility $\gamma = 0$ so that $\alpha + \beta = 1$. Framed as a GARCH specification, it is also known as the **integrated GARCH**, or IGARCH(1,1), model. The EWMA model thus implies a flat term structure of volatility and follows the square-root-of-time rule. Volatility itself behaves as a random walk, subject to shocks that put it on a new path permanently, with no long-term "forever" vol.

The EWMA estimate is usually quite close to the unrestricted GARCH(1,1) estimate. Figure 4.5 compares the two models. The most notable difference is seen during periods of very low volatility. The absence of the long-term volatility term permits the EWMA forecast to sink visibly lower than the GARCH(1,1) estimate.

Table 4.1   Estimating volatility with the EWMA model

τ	Date	$S_{t+\tau-m}$	$r_{t+\tau-m}$	$\frac{1-\lambda}{1-\lambda^m}\lambda^{m-\tau}$	$\frac{1-\lambda}{1-\lambda^m}\lambda^{m-\tau}r_{t+\tau-m}^2$
0	21Jul2014	1973.63	NA	NA	NA
1	22Jul2014	1983.53	0.00500	0.00000	0.00000×10^{-6}
2	23Jul2014	1987.01	0.00175	0.00000	0.00000×10^{-6}
3	24Jul2014	1987.98	0.00049	0.00000	0.00000×10^{-6}
4	25Jul2014	1978.34	−0.00486	0.00000	0.00000×10^{-6}
⋮	⋮	⋮	⋮	⋮	⋮
173	27Mar2015	2061.02	0.00237	0.00051	0.00286×10^{-6}
174	30Mar2015	2086.24	0.01216	0.00054	0.08052×10^{-6}
175	31Mar2015	2067.89	−0.00883	0.00058	0.04520×10^{-6}
176	01Apr2015	2059.69	−0.00397	0.00062	0.00973×10^{-6}
177	02Apr2015	2066.96	0.00352	0.00066	0.00814×10^{-6}
⋮	⋮	⋮	⋮	⋮	⋮
246	13Jul2015	2099.60	0.01101	0.04684	5.67368×10^{-6}
247	14Jul2015	2108.95	0.00444	0.04984	0.98391×10^{-6}
248	15Jul2015	2107.40	−0.00074	0.05302	0.02866×10^{-6}
249	16Jul2015	2124.29	0.00798	0.05640	3.59398×10^{-6}
250	17Jul2015	2126.64	0.00111	0.06000	0.07335×10^{-6}

Return vol of the S&P 500 index, estimated after the close on 17Jul2015 (date t), with $m = 250$, $\lambda = 0.94$. Return (4th column) expressed as a decimal. Add the 250 values in the last column to get the estimated variance σ_t^2.

The Behavior of Asset Returns over Time **69**

Table 4.2 Recursive formula for EWMA volatility estimates

t	Date	S_t	r_t (%)	$\lambda\sigma_{t-1}^2$	$(1-\lambda)r_t^2$	σ_t (%)
1	30Jun2005	1191.33	NA	NA	NA	0.55583
2	01Jul2005	1194.44	0.2607	0.29041×10^{-4}	0.40783×10^{-6}	0.54267
3	05Jul2005	1204.99	0.8794	0.27682×10^{-4}	4.63987×10^{-6}	0.56853
4	06Jul2005	1194.94	−0.8375	0.30383×10^{-4}	4.20873×10^{-6}	0.58815
5	07Jul2005	1197.87	0.2449	0.32516×10^{-4}	0.35986×10^{-6}	0.57338
6	08Jul2005	1211.86	1.1611	0.30903×10^{-4}	8.08946×10^{-6}	0.62444
7	11Jul2005	1219.44	0.6235	0.36653×10^{-4}	2.33279×10^{-6}	0.62439
⋮	⋮	⋮	⋮	⋮	⋮	⋮
3644	19Dec2019	3205.37	0.4449	0.24206×10^{-4}	1.18778×10^{-6}	0.50392
3645	20Dec2019	3221.22	0.4933	0.23870×10^{-4}	1.45986×10^{-6}	0.50329
3646	23Dec2019	3224.01	0.0866	0.23810×10^{-4}	0.04497×10^{-6}	0.48842
3647	24Dec2019	3223.38	−0.0195	0.22424×10^{-4}	0.00229×10^{-6}	0.47356
3648	26Dec2019	3239.91	0.5115	0.21080×10^{-4}	1.56983×10^{-6}	0.47592
3649	27Dec2019	3240.02	0.0034	0.21291×10^{-4}	0.00007×10^{-6}	0.46142
3650	30Dec2019	3221.29	−0.5798	0.20014×10^{-4}	2.01673×10^{-6}	0.46937
3651	31Dec2019	3230.78	0.2942	0.20709×10^{-4}	0.51921×10^{-6}	0.46074

Return vol of the S&P 500 index, estimated daily using the recursive formula, with $\lambda = 0.94$. Initial vol estimate: RMS of the 20 daily returns 01Jul2005–29Jul2005. The starter value 0.55583 is the RMS using the first 21 days of data.

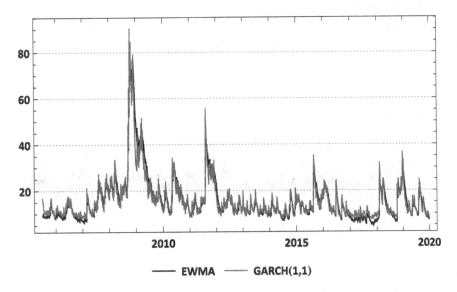

Figure 4.5 GARCH(1,1) and EWMA volatility estimates

Daily estimates of S&P 500 index's annualized return volatility, 30Jun2005 to 31Dec2019. EWMA estimates use $\lambda = 0.94$ and GARCH(1,1) estimates use parameters $\alpha = 0.12195$, $\beta = 0.85609$, $\gamma\bar{\sigma}^2 = 2.40805 \times 10^{-6}$. The annual realized return volatility was 15.69 percent over the period.

4.4 Tail Risk: the Prevalence of Extremes

Volatility is not identical to risk. Focusing exclusively on volatility estimates, which only imperfectly capture one characteristic of real-world return distributions, can lead to ignoring important elements of risk. Tail risk describes losses arising from extreme events that are entirely outside the range of experience the lognormal model would lead one to expect. The recurrence of these extremes is important in understanding asset pricing phenomena, such as puzzlingly high equity market returns and in measuring risk.

4.4.1 Extreme Asset Returns

Figures 4.6 and 4.7 display the longer-term return behavior of two important asset classes: the US stock market, represented by the S&P 500 index, and the US government bond market, represented by the 10-year Treasury yield. Table 4.3 tabulates departures from the standard model for the S&P 500. Confidence intervals on returns are computed two ways: one assuming returns are lognormal while using the entire sample to compute a single volatility estimate and the other treating volatility as time-varying and using a daily EWMA conditional volatility estimate.

Tail risk can be seen in the number of days on which the magnitude of the return far exceeds the volatility estimate. Exceedances are less frequent using conditional volatility, which widens the confidence interval during high-volatility regimes, capturing a smaller set of larger-magnitude returns, but the exceedances are nonetheless far more frequent than is consistent with normality. Table 4.3 shows, for example, 12 occurrences in 24,060 trials (about 1 in 2000) of returns that, if they were normally distributed with a volatility equal to the EWMA estimate of the prior day, would have a one-in-a-billion probability.

Another illustration of extremes in returns and volatility is drawn from foreign exchange rates. Figure 4.8 plots returns on representative exchange rates against the dollar. It illustrates the

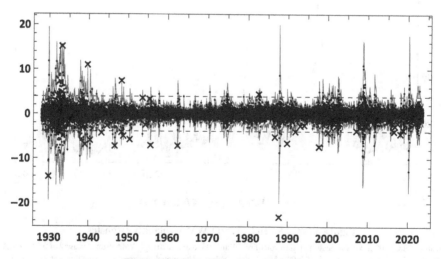

Figure 4.6 S&P 500 returns 1927–2023

Points: realized change in yield (bps). Solid lines: 99.9% confidence interval (±3.3 vols) based on EWMA return volatility estimate, daily, 02Jan1928 to 11Oct2023. Horizontal dashed grid lines: 99.9% confidence interval using standard deviation of entire series. ✗: returns outside the EWMA 99.9999% confidence interval (one in a million). *Data source*: Bloomberg.

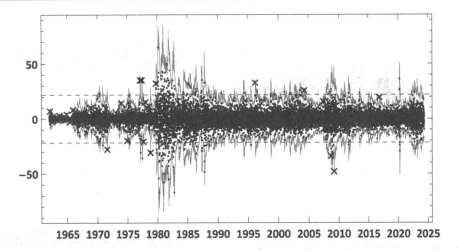

Figure 4.7 10-year Treasury Note yield fluctuations 1962–2024

Points: realized change in yield (bps). Solid lines: 99.9% confidence interval (±3.3 vols) based on EWMA normal yield volatility estimate, daily, 05Jan1962 to 11Jan2024. Horizontal dashed grid lines: 99.9% confidence interval using standard deviation of entire series of yield changes. ×: yield changes outside the EWMA 99.9999% confidence interval (one in a million). *Data source*: Bloomberg.

Table 4.3   Extreme moves in the S&P 500 1928–2023

Confidence level (%)	99.9	99.99	99.9999	99.9999999
Odds: one in …	1,000	10,000	1,000,000	1,000,000,000
Number of std dev	± 3.291	± 3.891	± 4.892	± 6.109
Expected no. exceedances	24.1	2.4	0.0	0.0
Unconditional volatility				
No. exceedances	332	201	106	49
No. negative	181	111	58	24
No. positive	151	90	48	25
Ratio negative/positive	1.2	1.2	1.2	1.0
Conditional (EWMA) volatility				
No. exceedances	183	94	33	12
No. negative	140	76	26	10
No. positive	43	18	7	2
Ratio negative/positive	3.3	4.2	3.7	5.0

Based on 24,060 observations of daily S&P 500 returns 02Jan1928 to 11Oct2023.

similarities as well as the differences between major currencies and those of middle-income countries.

Historically, many countries have adopted fixed or pegged exchange rates, setting the exchange rate of their local currency to a fixed price in terms of another, enforced by sales and purchases of foreign currency. This doesn't eliminate foreign exchange risk and may exacerbate rate volatility. Many episodes of extreme volatility are associated with the collapse or sudden abandonment of formal or informal exchange rate pegs and associated with currency crises. As seen in Figure 4.8, the Turkish lira and Mexican peso have experienced repeated large-magnitude returns, many of which are related

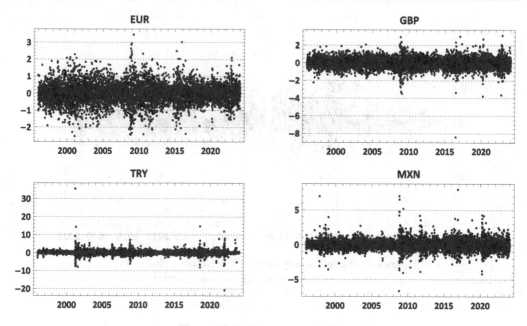

Figure 4.8 Exchange rate volatility

Daily returns in percent of the euro (EUR), British pound (GBP), Turkish lira (TRY), and Mexican peso (MXN) against USD, 02Jan1996 to 11Jan2024. EUR and GBP are conventionally stated as USD price per currency unit, so positive returns represent *appreciation* against USD; TRY and MXN are conventionally stated as the currency price of US$1, so positive returns represent *depreciation* against USD. *Source*: Bloomberg.

to abrupt changes in exchange rate policy. The unusual large depreciation of sterling in early 2016 is related to the Brexit referendum.[9]

4.4.2   Skewness and Kurtosis

There are two major departures from normality in the shape of distributions of asset returns over long periods: skewness and kurtosis. **Skewness** is the property that large-magnitude returns of one sign are more frequent than the other. The degree of return skewness may vary over time, depending on current volatility, a characteristic described as **conditional skewness**. Asset returns also display **kurtosis**, fat tails, or **leptokurtosis**; large-magnitude returns occur more frequently than if returns followed a normal distribution. Skewed and kurtotic return distributions may be **multimodal**, with histograms or density functions exhibiting multiple modes or peaks. Figure 4.9 displays examples of skewed and kurtotic return distributions.

The skewness of the distribution of S&P 500 returns is clear in Table 4.3. It is particularly pronounced using conditional volatility; among the largest-magnitude returns, negative ones dominate. Exchange rates returns are typically skewed; extreme returns tend to be either appreciations or depreciations. The largest-magnitude changes in emerging market exchange rates against major currencies are generally depreciations. Treasury yields display somewhat less skewness.

---

[9] See Chapter 15 below.

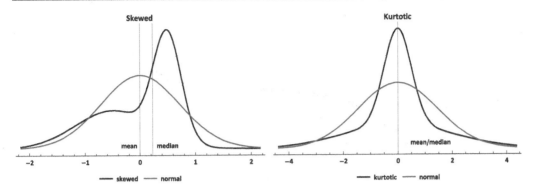

Figure 4.9 Normal and non-normal distributions

Left: skewed and normal distributions with the same mean of 0 and the same variance. The skewed distribution is a mixture of two normals, with distributions $\mathcal{N}(-0.5, 0.6861125)$ and $\mathcal{N}(0.5, 0.25)$, each with a probability of 50 percent of being realized. Right: kurtotic and normal distributions with the same mean of 0 and the same variance. The kurtotic distribution is a mixture of two normals, with distributions $\mathcal{N}(0, 2.0)$ and $\mathcal{N}(0, 0.5)$, each with a probability of 50 percent of being realized. The characteristics of the distributions are:

	skewed	kurtotic
Mean	0	0
Median	0.232938	0.
Variance	0.516625	2.125
Kurtosis excess	3.0	5.33564
Skewness	−0.824564	0

A **quantile-quantile**, or **quantile**, or **q-q plot** is a useful visual tool for comparing two empirical or theoretical distributions: Each point in the plot is the pair consisting of corresponding quantiles of the two distributions. Differences in the distributions are highlighted by drawing a reference line along points corresponding to a comparison distribution. The contrasts between the distributions are reflected in the shape and location of the plot. If the two distributions are similar, the plot will lie close to the reference line.

Figure 4.10 compares quantiles of the S&P 500 return distribution to those of a standard normal distribution. The kurtosis in the S&P 500 returns leads to an S-shape, with the q-q plot below (above) the reference line for low (high) quantiles. Skewness leads to an asymmetric shape with the lower tail particularly far from the reference line.

4.4.3   Clues to Financial Puzzles in the Behavior of Volatility

Volatility varies remarkably widely over time and is correlated with other return characteristics, phenomena closely connected to the question of market efficiency and the prevalence of opportunities to achieve excess returns that are unusually high for their risk.[10] **Volatility asymmetry** describes the fact that returns on some assets are negatively correlated with increases in volatility. When markets decline, volatility tends to rise, and when prices are buoyant, volatility tends to abate. The phenomenon is asymmetric, often more pronounced on the downside, with declines in price associated with larger changes in volatility than increases. It is a prominent feature of equity returns, leading to different hypotheses regarding its nature and causes. Figure 4.11 shows the correlation between sharp declines in the S&P 500 and increases in its volatility.

---

[10] See Chapter 7.

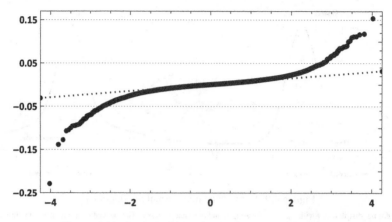

Figure 4.10 Quantile plot of S&P 500 returns 1928–2020

Quantiles of daily returns (as decimals) of the S&P 500 index 02Jan1928 to 11Oct2023, plotted against quantiles of a standard normal distribution. The axes are expressed in units of return (as decimals) against quantiles (z values) of the standard normal. Each point represents a pair consisting of a quantile of the standard normal and the corresponding quantile of the set of return observations. *Data source*: Bloomberg.

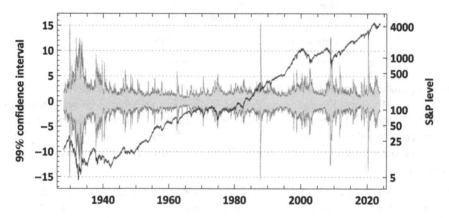

Figure 4.11 Volatility asymmetry in the US stock market 1927–2023

99 percent confidence interval using EWMA estimate of S&P 500 index return volatility with decay factor 0.94 (grey area, left y-axis), and log of S&P 500 index closing price (black plot, right y-axis), daily, 30Dec1927 to 11Oct2023. *Data source*: Bloomberg.

Volatility asymmetry is sometimes called the **leverage effect**. When stock prices fall, leverage rises, increasing the riskiness volatility of equity.[11] Alternatively, the phenomenon is also termed **volatility feedback** on a hypothesis that reverses the direction of causality. Higher volatility makes the asset less attractive to investors. Equilibrium is restored by a fall in price that increases its expected return. Volatility feedback is related to time-varying expected returns or risk premiums: periods of lower stock prices and higher volatility are associated with higher perceived risk or risk aversion.

The asymmetric volatility pattern has been noted for individual stocks and broad indexes. It is consistent with the observation of **negative coskewness**: sharp negative return surprises in some individual stocks coincide with bad S&P 500 days, making those stocks less effective diversifiers and requiring

---

[11] See the discussion of the Merton model in Chapter 9.

higher excess returns in equilibrium. It can be rationalized by household aversion to skewness in portfolio returns.[12]

Asymmetric volatility is part of a more general phenomenon of returns behaving differently in rising and falling markets. **Tail dependence** is the association of a higher probability of extreme returns in one asset with extreme returns in other assets. It is related to coskewness through **asymmetric correlations**; cross-sectional correlations increase in bear markets. It may be hard to distinguish this regularity from the effect of high time-varying volatility on sample correlations.

Further Reading

Barro (2006) discusses the impact of rare extreme losses on asset prices. Andersen et al. (2010) and Engle and Patton (2001) survey techniques of volatility estimation. The topic is also covered in the risk management texts cited in Chapters 2 and 8.

See Cont (2001) on patterns of asset return behavior. Schwert (1989) and 1990 discusses patterns in US stock market volatility and its relationship to macroeconomic conditions, leverage, and other factors. See Bekaert and Wu (2000), Ang and Chen (2006), and Ang et al. (2006) on volatility asymmetry, correlation asymmetries, and other deviations from the standard model in return behavior.

[12] The next chapter discusses investor decisions.

5

Capital Markets: How Asset Prices Are Determined

The market-clearing process determines asset prices and prospective returns by finding momentary equilibrium prices, given the supply and demand for securities. Equilibrium asset prices express current "consensus" risk preferences, possible payoffs in the future, and investors' information and expectations about them. Why do market prices end up where they do in equilibrium? The steps in the explanation are:

1. Take the menu of available assets, the prospective returns, and their risks as given and identify among the range of possible investment choices the portfolios that just waste opportunities.
2. Specify investor preferences and explain how people choose among the remaining, efficient portfolios.
3. Once we know how individuals make their choices, how does the market clear and establish asset prices at a point in time and thus, the prospective returns we take as given in the first step?

5.1 Portfolios, Diversification, and Investor Choice

5.1.1 Portfolio Risk

Diversification refers to combining assets in portfolios. Investors can not only mix the characteristics of the constituent assets but also expand the investment choices available to them. Diversification is powerful; it can lead to a reduction of risk without sacrificing return.

Investment choices can be summarized by identifying the available combinations of **portfolio expected return** and **portfolio return variance** or **volatility**, based on the expected returns, volatilities, and correlations of the constituent assets, parameters that we assume are known to investors. Some combinations may be clearly superior or inferior to others. Once we identify a menu of choices that are available and reasonable, we can analyze which ones investors prefer.

The portfolio expected return μ_p is a simple weighted average of the constituent assets' expected returns μ_i. In the case of a long-only portfolio with two risky constituents and no borrowing,

$$\mu_p = w\mu_1 + (1-w)\mu_2,$$

with w representing the asset 1 weight. The portfolio expected return changes in proportion to a change in each constituent's expected return.

The portfolio return variance σ_p^2 also incorporates the return correlation ρ_{12}:

$$\sigma_p^2 = w^2\sigma_1^2 + (1-w)^2\sigma_2^2 + 2w(1-w)\sigma_1\sigma_2\rho_{12}.$$

The **portfolio volatility** is its square root: $\sigma_p = \sqrt{\sigma_p^2}$. Portfolio variance and volatility don't change in proportion to a change in constituent volatility, and the portfolio variance can be strongly influenced up or down by the return correlation ρ_{12}.

Mixing risky assets can reduce portfolio return volatility even if constituent volatility is high and correlation is positive. Adding a small amount of even a high-volatility asset can reduce portfolio volatility though the effect is more limited if the return correlation is strongly positive. Lower correlation enables the investor to achieve lower portfolio volatility for any given expected returns. Negative correlation provides the strongest volatility reduction.

Example 5.1   Portfolio return variance and volatility

The characteristics of Meta Platforms, Inc. (ticker META) and Coca-Cola Co. (KO), estimated using daily logarithmic return data from May 18, 2012, to September 24, 2020, are:

	META	KO
Mean daily logarithmic return (%)	0.090177	0.012446
Standard deviation of daily returns (%)	2.346570	1.141170
Correlation coefficient	0.21290	

The expected return of a 50-50 META-KO portfolio is:

$$\mu_p = 0.5 \cdot 0.00090177 + 0.5 \cdot 0.00012446 = 0.00051311,$$

or 5.13 basis points per day.

The return variance of a 50-50 META-KO portfolio is:

$$\sigma_p^2 = 0.5^2 \cdot 0.0234657^2 + 0.5^2 \cdot 0.0114117^2$$
$$+ 2 \cdot 0.5 \cdot 0.5 \cdot 0.0234657 \cdot 0.0114117 \cdot 0.2129 = 0.000199,$$

and the portfolio volatility is $\sqrt{0.000199} = 0.01409690$, or 1.410 percent daily.

Figure 5.1 illustrates the impact of constituent volatility and correlation on portfolio return volatility. In the left panel, we see that combining a small amount of higher-volatility META to a portfolio initially consisting solely of low-volatility KO reduces the portfolio volatility up to a point. The diversification effect is muted if we combine KO with an even higher-volatility stock than META such as KB Home (KBH). In the right panel, at the maximum correlation of 1, the portfolio behaves as a linear combination of its constituents. At a minimum correlation of −1 each is a perfect hedge of the other, with a zero-volatility point available.

The set of **feasible** or **attainable portfolios**, or the **investment opportunity set**, are all the portfolios we can form by varying the asset 1 weight w from 0 to 1. Not every feasible portfolio is **efficient**, though. A portfolio is efficient if all the feasible portfolios with higher return also have higher volatility and all the feasible portfolios with lower volatility also have lower return. A portfolio with the same volatility but a lower return than some other portfolio, or the same return but a higher volatility, is inefficient. A mean-variance investor would be making no trade-off, only gaining, with that other portfolio.

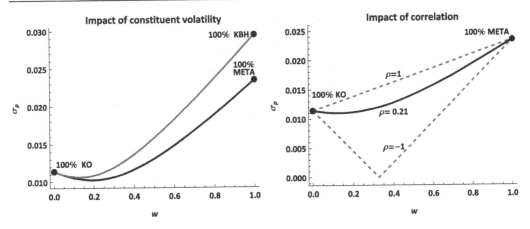

Figure 5.1 Impact of diversification on portfolio return volatility

Left panel: volatility (*y*-axis) of portfolios combining long positions in KO stock with long positions in META or KB Home (KBH), assuming a daily return correlation of 0, both plotted as a function of the META or KBH portfolio weight (*x*-axis). KBH had a volatility of close to 30 percent annually over the 2012–2020 observation period. Right panel: volatility of portfolios combining long positions in KO stock with long positions in META assuming different nonzero return correlations. The plot in the middle uses the estimated return correlation of 0.2129.

The **efficient frontier** is the set of return and volatility pairs of efficient portfolios. The **global minimum variance portfolio** has the lowest return and volatility among the efficient portfolios.[1] With more than two risky assets, some of the assets may lie in the interior of the efficient frontier, that is, have a lower return and higher volatility than portfolios on the efficient frontier but form part of some efficient portfolios.

The high-return/high-volatility asset is always on the efficient frontier because a portfolio consisting entirely of it is the only way to get that high expected return. The low-return/low-volatility asset is not on the efficient frontier if the two assets are not perfectly correlated because you can achieve the same low return with lower volatility by including some of the high-return/high-volatility asset in the portfolio. The global minimum variance portfolio typically has lower volatility and higher return than the low-return/low-volatility asset.

Example 5.2   Feasible and efficient portfolios

In our META-KO example, a portfolio consisting of all or almost entirely low-return and low-volatility KO is not efficient. Adding some high-return and high-volatility META lowers the portfolio volatility and raises portfolio return. Such a portfolio is unambiguously more desirable to all investors than KO alone.

Figure 5.2 displays the feasible portfolios and the efficient frontier. It's related to Figure 5.1 by plotting the portfolio returns against the portfolio volatilities. Table 5.1 displays the numbers for a few of the portfolios, including the global minimum variance portfolio.

The plot using the estimated return correlation of 0.2129 is the same as that in the right panel in Figure 5.1. The inflection point in the plots occur at the same META weight in both. If the correlation were instead −0.25, life would be better, and the investor could attain higher return or lower volatility portfolios.

---

[1] The global minimum variance portfolio can be found mathematically by minimizing σ_p^2 with respect to w.

Table 5.1 Feasible and efficient portfolios

META wt. (%)	KO wt. (%)	return (%)	volatility (%)
0	100	0.012446	1.141170
10	90	0.020219	1.101140
12.92	87.08	0.022486	1.098950
20	80	0.027992	1.111820
50	50	0.051311	1.409690
90	10	0.082404	2.139120
100	0	0.090177	2.346570

In percent. The global minimum variance portfolio is highlighted.

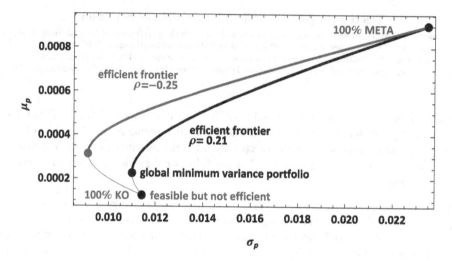

Figure 5.2 The risk-return trade-off

Volatility (x-axis) and mean (y-axis) of portfolios combining long positions in KO and META stock, estimated using the historical return correlation of 0.2129 and if the return correlation were −0.25. The heavy part of the plot is the efficient frontier.

5.1.2   Optimal Investor Choice

So far, we've described the choices available to an investor. The next step in explaining market outcomes is to take investor choice into account. In the **mean-variance optimization** model, individuals value risky assets and portfolios based only on their expected return and return volatility, and don't care about other distributional characteristics, such as the potential for very large losses or for losses to occur when the investor might face unemployment on top of bad returns.

Preferences are represented by a utility function, increasing with portfolio mean return and decreasing with variance, with k expressing the strength of investor's risk aversion. If k is high, higher volatility diminishes utility more:

$$V(\mu_p, \sigma_p) = \mu_p - \frac{1}{2}k\sigma_p^2.$$

Indifference curves express the trade-off between mean and volatility. They are defined by fixing utility at a specific level $V°$ and differentiating the utility function to find the combinations of μ_p and

σ_p that result in utility of V°. Along an indifference curve,

$$\left.\frac{d\mu_p}{d\sigma_p}\right|_{V=V^\circ} = k\sigma_p.$$

Its slope is positive: the investor must be compensated with additional expected return if risk increases. Indifference curves are also convex to the origin: slope is increasing in σ_p. Investors optimizes by choosing the efficient portfolio that just touches the highest indifference curve they can achieve.[2]

A risk-free asset, which has zero volatility and a certain return r^f, usually but not always positive, may also be available. Suppose investors are able to freely lend, that is, invest in the risk-free asset or borrow to finance leveraged positions in additional risky assets at the risk-free rate.[3] Additional portfolios can be formed that include the risk-free asset, and some of these additional portfolios are more desirable to any mean-variance investor than some lower-return portfolios that are efficient only when there's no riskless asset. The efficient frontier is now a ray from $(0, r^f)$ through the **tangency portfolio**, which is the risky asset portfolio at which the ray from $(0, r^f)$ is tangent to the old efficient frontier.

A remarkable result emerges when a riskless asset is available to investors: the **two-fund separation**, or **mutual fund, theorem**. All investors choose the same portfolio of risky assets, the tangency portfolio, with the same constituents and same weights for everyone, but different allocations to that risky portfolio and to the risk-free asset. Investors optimize by mixing the risk-free asset and the tangency portfolio, the mix depending on her risk preferences. The more risk averse choose a smaller allocation to the tangency portfolio. Investors face a simple, linear trade-off between return and risk, summarized by portfolio volatility.

The expected excess return or risk premium of asset i is the difference $\mu_i - r^f$ between its expected return and the risk-free rate. Its **Sharpe ratio** is the ratio $\frac{\mu_i - r^f}{\sigma_i}$ of its risk premium to volatility or the expected excess return per unit of risk, represented by volatility. The slope of the efficient frontier at any point is the highest attainable Sharpe ratio for the given return. If there is a risk-free asset, the tangency portfolio has the highest Sharpe ratio attainable.

Reported Sharpe ratios, used for example in investment marketing, are usually *ex post* measures based on realized or historical returns. They may be quite different from the unobservable ratio of expected excess return to expected volatility. An asset that has had a recent runup in price may have a high reported Sharpe ratio using its recent excess returns but reduced expected excess return and a low unobservable true Sharpe ratio, reflected in its high price apart from possibly higher expected volatility.

Example 5.3   Optimal investor choice among portfolios

Figure 5.3 illustrates mean-variance optimization for a more and for a less risk-averse investor in the absence of a riskless asset. The thick indifference curve of the risk-averse investor is tangent to the efficient frontier. The thinner indifference curve of the risk-averse investor is at a higher but unobtainable utility level. The risk-friendly investor chooses a higher allocation to

---

[2] Mathematically, substitute the expressions for μ_p and σ_p^2 into the utility function and differentiate with respect to w, the investor's choice variable. The resulting first-order condition can be solved for the optimal w.

[3] Many households can buy assets, such as housing and common stock on a secured basis at relatively narrow spreads over risk-free proxy rates, but in general, this is a somewhat unrealistic assumption. The Black version of the CAPM assumes that investors can only lend, not borrow, at r^f.

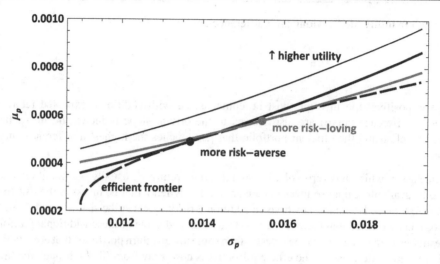

Figure 5.3 Optimal portfolios

Indifference curves for utility function $V(\mu_p, \sigma_p) = \mu_p - \frac{1}{2}k\sigma_p^2$ with $k = 4$ and $k = 2$ (solid plots), and the efficient frontier of portfolios combining long positions in KO stock and META stock (dashed plot).

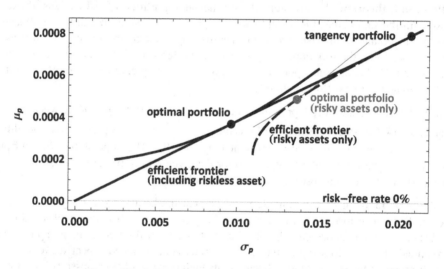

Figure 5.4 Optimal investor choice with a risk-free asset

Efficient frontier of portfolios combining only long positions in KO stock and META stock, and of portfolios that also include a risk-free asset, with $r^f = 0$, and the indifference curves for $V(\mu_p, \sigma_p) = \mu_p - \frac{1}{2}k\sigma_p^2$ with $k = 4$ at the optimal portfolios. The tangency portfolio, a line through $(0, r^f)$, is the point on the efficient frontier of portfolios combining risky assets only that is tangent to the efficient frontier.

the riskier asset. Figure 5.4 illustrates mean-variance optimization in the presence of a riskless asset. The risk-averse investor can lower risk with less sacrifice of return. Table 5.2 summarizes the optimal allocations.

5.2   The Capital Asset Pricing Model

We've assumed the risk premiums $\mu_i - r^f$ are givens, but in the real world, they are unobservable outcomes of market clearing. They can be explained and estimated with a model of how the market finds equilibrium asset prices based on investor preferences and the assets' return characteristics.

Table 5.2   Summary of optimal investor choice

Weight	No risk-free asset		Including risk-free asset		
	$k = 3$	$k = 4$	tangency	$k = 3$	$k = 4$
Risk-free	NA	NA	NA	0.379	0.535
META	0.586	0.472	0.866	0.537	0.403
KO	0.414	0.528	0.134	0.083	0.063

Weights (adding up to 1) in the optimal portfolio of a mean-variance investor with utility function $V(\mu_p, \sigma_p) = \mu_p - \frac{1}{2}k\sigma_p^2$ for $k = 3,4$. Optimization is over portfolios combining long positions in KO stock and META stock only, and portfolios that also include a risk-free asset.

5.2.1   The Efficiency of the Market Portfolio

The **capital asset pricing model** (CAPM) builds on the mean-variance picture of investor choice to explain how asset risk is priced in the market in equilibrium. In it, risk premiums are driven by risk appetites and a single common source of risk, the **systematic**, or **market, risk**, which is the risk stemming from the **market factor**. Systematic risk is understood as the return volatility of the **value-weighted market portfolio** of all risky assets, their market capitalization with each asset weighted by its share of the total value at market prices. The market portfolio is conventionally proxied by a broad stock index, such as the S&P 500, but is conceived in the model as including all assets.

The CAPM assumes that agents are mean-variance optimizers, they have complete information, and are in agreement on the expected means and variances of future security returns. They are not, however, identical in their risk preferences and degree of risk aversion. There is a risk-free asset at which all agents can freely borrow or lend. The mutual fund theorem holds, and all investors engage in two-fund separation, each choosing the same portfolio of risky assets but with different combinations of the market portfolio and the risk-free asset. All markets clear, with no frictions due to trading costs or taxes.

The key result of the CAPM can be summarized in a simple statement with layers of meaning: the market portfolio is a mean-variance efficient portfolio, a tangency portfolio. The market portfolio is the only source of risk. The CAPM models the prices and risk of specific assets relative to the market factor and thus, to one another. Diversification enables market participants to shed all **nonsystematic**, or **idiosyncratic, risk**, with return fluctuations due to the vagaries of an individual firm's or asset's returns alone and which are therefore, uncompensated by any risk premium in equilibrium. The model implies absence of arbitrage opportunities and can be understood as a simple way of incorporating the stochastic discount factor (Chapter 3), with the market factor governing the distribution of future states and mean-variance optimization their value to investors.

The CAPM states a linear relation in equilibrium among the market factor, the market portfolio's excess return, and the return on a specific asset, quantified by its **beta**. Asset i's risk premium $\mu_i - r^f$ is related via its beta to its co-movement with that of the market portfolio $\mu_m - r^f$:

$$\mu_i - r^f = \beta_i(\mu_m - r^f).$$

Most equities have positive estimated betas most of the time. A high positive beta indicates the security price typically moves with the market, and a low positive beta indicates the comovements are in the same direction, but smaller than the market's. A negative beta indicates that the security is a possible hedge for market returns.

The **security market line** is the linear relationship of the $(\beta_i, \mu_i - r^f)$ across firms. There's no intercept term; α_i is zero in the CAPM. The market portfolio, with a beta of 1, lies at the point $(1, \mu_m - r^f)$. For given values of μ_m and r^f and for any individual asset's β_i, the security market line states its μ_i.

An asset i's beta can be calculated from its excess return volatility σ_i, the market portfolio's excess return volatility σ_m, and their correlation $\rho_{i,m}$:

$$\beta_i = \rho_{i,m}\frac{\sigma_i}{\sigma_m}.$$

Beta is high if asset i's risk is high, as measured by σ_i, relative to that of the market factor, or if its returns are highly correlated to market factor returns. Its risk premium will then also be higher in equilibrium.

Asset i's total risk, as measured by its excess return variance σ_i^2, can be decomposed into a systematic risk component $\beta_i^2\sigma_m^2$, the part of σ_i^2 that is related to fluctuations in market returns, and idiosyncratic risk, the remainder $\sigma_i^2 - \beta_i^2\sigma_m^2$. Systematic and idiosyncratic risk can be expressed as shares of total risk:

$$\frac{\beta_i^2\sigma_m^2}{\sigma_i^2} + \frac{\sigma_i^2 - \beta_i^2\sigma_m^2}{\sigma_i^2} = 1.$$

The systematic risk share of an asset can be stated in terms of its excess return correlation $\rho_{i,m}$ to that of the market:

$$\frac{\beta_i^2\sigma_m^2}{\sigma_i^2} = \rho_{i,m}^2\frac{\sigma_i^2}{\sigma_m^2}\frac{\sigma_m^2}{\sigma_i^2} = \rho_{i,m}^2.$$

An asset's Sharpe ratio is related to that of the market portfolio by

$$\frac{\mu_i - r^f}{\sigma_i} = \rho_{i,m}\frac{\mu_m - r^f}{\sigma_m}.$$

Because $0 \le \rho \le 1$, no asset can have a higher Sharpe ratio in equilibrium than the market portfolio, another way of seeing the efficiency of the market portfolio.

5.2.2   Estimating Systematic and Nonsystematic Risk

To assess the value or risk of an asset using the CAPM, beta must be estimated. The CAPM is framed as a forward-looking model of expected returns and variance, but practitioners and information services routinely do so via a simple linear regression model of security i's on the market portfolio's excess return using historical data. If recent realized excess returns differ substantially from expected excess returns, these estimates can be misleading in the same way as a Sharpe ratio estimated from historical data.

Using T daily, weekly, or monthly observations,

$$r_{it} - r_t^f = \alpha_i + \beta_i(r_{mt} - r_t^f) + u_{it}, \qquad t = 1, \ldots, T,$$

leads to estimated parameters $\hat{\alpha}_i$ and $\hat{\beta}_i$. The u_{it} are treated as normally distributed and independent of one another over time, and of $r_{mt} - r_t^f$. The CAPM predicts $\hat{\alpha}_i = 0$. Figure 5.5 illustrates the technique

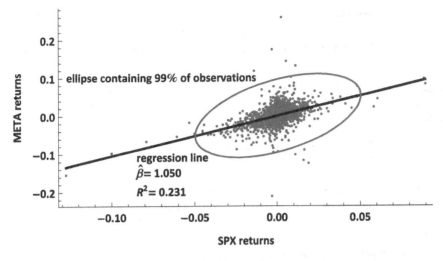

Figure 5.5 Computing beta via linear regression

Computation of beta of the META to S&P 500 via simple linear regression using 2087 unweighted daily excess return observations 18May2012 to 24Sep2020, relative to 3-month US T-bill yield at the beginning of the return period. Points mark daily excess return pairs, expressed as decimals.

with data on META stock prices, and Table 5.3 provides results for Coca-Cola (KO) and KB Home (KBH) as well.

The standard regression properties provide more intuition on the CAPM. The explanatory power of the regression is conventionally measured by the (unadjusted) **coefficient of determination** R^2:

$$R^2 = \hat{\beta}_i^2 \frac{\sum_t (r_{mt} - r_t^f)^2}{\sum_t (r_{it} - r_t^f)^2} = \hat{\beta}_i^2 \frac{s_{r_m - r^f}^2}{s_{r_i - r^f}^2},$$

Table 5.3 Systematic and nonsystematic risk: example

	META	KO	KBH
Parameter estimates:			
$\hat{\alpha}_i$	0.0004435	−0.0001763	0.0001699
$\hat{\beta}_i$	1.051	0.674	1.456
Goodness-of-fit and correlation:			
R^2 (unadjusted)	0.23068	0.40096	0.28040
Adjusted R^2	0.23032	0.40067	0.28006
Excess return correlation to S&P	0.48030	0.63321	0.52953
Risk decomposition:			
Variance of excess returns	0.0005507	0.0001302	0.0008689
Systematic variance	0.0001270	0.0000522	0.0002436
Nonsystematic variance	0.0004236	0.0000780	0.0006253
Risk decomposition (share of total variance):			
Systematic variance	0.23068	0.40096	0.28040
Nonsystematic variance	0.76932	0.59904	0.71960

Estimated using daily return data from 18May2012 to 24Sep2020. Variances are of excess returns relative to 3-month US T-bill yield expressed as decimals.

with $s^2_{r_m-rf}$ and $s^2_{r_i-rf}$ the sample variances of the market's and security i's excess returns and is equal to the square of the sample correlation between excess returns of security i and the market. It tends to be high if the estimated $\hat{\beta}_i$ is high, and if $r_{it} - r_t^f$ has a low variance compared to the explanatory variable $r_{mt} - r_t^f$.

We can identify the part of security i's return variance explained by the regression estimate with systematic risk and the residual variability with nonsystematic risk. Explained or systematic variance is

$$\hat{\beta}_i \sum_t (r_{it} - r_t^f)(r_{mt} - r_t^f) = \hat{\beta}_i^2 \sum_t (r_{mt} - r_t^f)^2 = R^2 \sum_t (r_{it} - r_t^f)^2 .$$

The share of systematic variance in the total variance of stock i's returns is R^2, and the share of residual or idiosyncratic variance is $1 - R^2$, the portion unexplained by beta.

5.2.3   More General Factor Models

The core conclusion of the CAPM is that the market portfolio is mean-variance efficient. To empirically test and validate the CAPM, we need data on the market portfolio that investors actually consider in their choices. The most problematic assumption of the CAPM is that the market portfolio is well-defined, has an identifiable, observable counterpart, and that non-traded assets are unimportant. In fact, there is no observable index of all traded assets. Conventional proxies, such as the S&P 500 index, omit important elements of wealth: infrequently traded, illiquid and non-traded assets, such as human capital and real estate. A world capital market and large cross-border investments are important determinants of investment behavior.

This likely insuperable problem is known as the **Roll critique** or **market proxy problem**. Whether they tend to validate or invalidate the CAPM, research conclusions are unreliable if the proxy used isn't the risky portfolio entering into people's choices. Evidence that the proxy we test is not efficient may not be evidence against the CAPM but just the result of testing the wrong proxy. We also encounter this **joint hypothesis problem** in testing market efficiency.

The CAPM, for instance, predicts $\alpha_i = 0$ in equilibrium, meaning the impact of risk on any particular security is completely captured by its beta to the market portfolio. If we find that, in general, $\alpha_i \neq 0$, this may be due to the limitations of the CAPM in explaining returns or to using the wrong proxy. The α test cannot discern which.

The CAPM does a remarkable job explaining historical asset returns but doesn't fit the data perfectly. The CAPM is a single factor model: it explains asset returns and cross-asset correlations by returns to the market portfolio alone. Each stock is priced exactly by its beta if we assume all the idiosyncratic risk can be diversified away. But the **cross-sectional variation** of realized excess returns across individual stocks we see in the market is somewhat off the security market line and not fully explained by beta.

The divergences from the security market line indicate there are additional systematic drivers of individual stock prices to which an apparently diversified portfolio may be exposed. One way to reconcile theory and observation is with additional **priced risk factors** that help explain individual securities' returns. There are many securities, and far fewer meaningfully independent influences on them. In the **arbitrage pricing theory** (APT), the myriad individual assets can be priced exactly as a linear function of this smaller number of distinct risk factors. Each risk factor has its own risk premium.

Factor models explain prices or values in terms of underlying and possibly unobservable variables. The **Fama-French three-factor model** includes these factors in addition to the market portfolio:

Small Minus Big (SMB): the difference between returns on stocks of small-cap and large-cap publicly traded firms.

High Minus Low (HML): the difference between the returns on value (high **book-to-market ratio**) and on growth (low book-to-market) portfolios. Well-established firms that pay regular and reliable dividends but also firms with stock prices that have fallen recently tend to be value firms.

A fourth factor is less robust but often included in analysis: The **momentum** factor quantifies the weak short-term tendency of some stocks' high recent returns to persist. Other factors related to measurable characteristics include profitability, investment expenditures of the firm, and liquidity. Additional factors potentially help explain either the behavior of stocks over time or cross-sectional variation in returns.

Priced factors are not necessarily intuitively associated with observable phenomena. A set of non-intuitive time series constructed from model residuals, similar to the factorization of a matrix, may further "explain" return variations. Traders and investment managers pursuing **smart beta** strategies target specific factors by estimating the exposure to each factor of the portfolio and reallocating to maintain the desired weights of each factor. The strategy also calls for continuously examining the residuals between returns and models to identify additional priced factors. The proliferation of hundreds of identified factors, often of fleeting significance and adding little to or even diminishing risk-adjusted returns, is referred to as the "factor zoo,"[4] and raises concerns about data mining.

Further Reading

Malkiel (2023) is a nontechnical overview of modern thinking about capital markets. Sharpe (1970) and Fama and French (2004) are accessible introductions to portfolio choice and the CAPM. Cochrane (2005) and Campbell (2018) provide more detail on the algebra of portfolio risk and return, portfolio choice, and the CAPM and more general factor models. The Roll critique was initially presented in Roll (1977). See also Ang (2014) on factor models and investing.

---

[4] The term was introduced by Cochrane (2011).

6

Derivatives Values and Risks

Derivative asset values are determined to a large extent by the benchmarks they are based on or by their underlying prices. They have payoffs in the future, so their values are also driven to some extent by interest rates.

Futures, forwards, and swaps have a linear, one-for-one response to changes in the values of the asset, index, or interest rate on which the contract is based and permit **static hedging** of an exposure. They can be hedged with a one-time trade in the underlying asset and can be used as a hedge with relatively straightforward management. Options, with their nonlinear changes in value, require **dynamic hedging**. Repeated trades are needed to stay hedged or keep an exposure within desired limits.

This implies other basic differences:

- The values of futures, forwards, and swaps are driven by the underlying price alone, not its volatility. The value of an option is driven by the volatility or tendency to fluctuate of the underlying, as well as its level.
- In any derivatives contract, the payments or assets each counterparty is bound to deliver in the future has a present value, and the difference is the net present value (NPV) of the derivative. Futures, forwards, and swaps can have an NPV of zero, at least initially, and no money necessarily changes hands at initiation. In an option, one party to the contract inevitably has a contingent, time-varying obligation to the other and has to be paid a **premium** at initiation.

Participants in forward, futures, and options contracts are said to be long if, at maturity, they will be receiving the asset, its value, or an uncertain difference between the future underlying and strike prices. They are short if they will be delivering that future value or if they received the premium and are obliged to pay if the option is exercised.

6.1 Futures, Forwards, and Swaps

Forwards and futures are claims on the future value of a stated amount of an asset. One party agrees to pay the other an agreed price, either for the asset itself or its future monetary value, delivered in the future. Forward and futures prices are related by arbitrage relations to spot or cash prices, money market rates, the underlying asset cash flows, and unobservable factors, such as storage cost and convenience yield.

If $F_{t,\tau}$ is the time-t futures or forward price for delivery τ years out, $r_{t,\tau}$ is the τ-year money market rate, and $q_{t,\tau}$ is the cash flow and other identifiable value from holding a spot position in the asset over the next τ years, then this relationship to the cash price S_t should hold fairly closely:

$$\frac{F_{t,\tau}}{S_t} = \left(\frac{1 + r_{t,\tau}}{1 + q_{t,\tau}}\right)^{\tau}.$$

If an asset had no cash flows, the cash price would be lower by the interest earned by going long in the forward market and keeping the amount of money S_t in a money market account. Positive cash flows reduce that difference. Stock index futures prices, for example, will be higher than the current value of the underlying index if the dividend yield is lower than the money market rate.

Swaps are contracts in which one counterparty pays the other the difference between a sequence of future prices or interest rates and some observable benchmark, index, or agreed level, in exchange for a fixed constant payment. Forwards and futures contracts stipulate one exchange in the future, and swap contracts call for several periodic exchanges.

A notional principal amount is stipulated at initiation but is not necessarily exchanged at the start and end of a swap contract. Multi-period swaps are structured so that one counterparty will **pay fixed** (the "fixed leg"), making fixed payments based on market pricing at initiation. The other will **receive fixed** (the "floating leg"), making floating payments based on realizations of an index or another uncertain future event, such as default. Most swaps are initiated **at-market**, with regular payments equal to the index and no positive or negative spread. Some counterparties may pay a positive or negative credit spread vis-à-vis the index due to their lower or higher credit quality than that of the typical counterparty.

Swaps have different structures for different underlying assets:

Foreign exchange swaps consist of the simultaneous spot purchase and future sale of one currency for another at an agreed **forward foreign exchange rate** and, unlike other swaps, involve just one future point in time.

Interest rate swaps have counterparties exchange fixed-rate for floating-rate interest payments on an agreed principal at set times (quarterly, semi-annually, or annually) until the maturity date. The most common is the **plain-vanilla interest rate swap**, initiated with an NPV of zero. The floating rate in the past has typically been LIBOR, but more recently, a central bank reference rate. They are generally done initially through a large bank or broker-dealer and governed by a standardized contract, an **ISDA Master Agreement** published by the **International Swaps and Derivatives Association**.

Currency swap counterparties exchange interest payments on an agreed principal in two different currencies. The principal amount is exchanged at the start and end of the swap. In a **cross-currency basis swap** counterparties exchange fixed-rate for floating-rate interest payments.

Credit default swaps provide protection against default risk. The purchaser makes fixed payments to a seller in exchange for a contingent payment, if a bond or firm defaults.

Asset swaps are portfolios consisting of a cash position in a credit-risky bond and an interest rate swap, for example, a long fixed-rate bond plus paying fixed rate in swap. The combination is intended to hedge the interest rate risk while retaining the exposure to credit spread risk.

Total return swaps (TRS) are contracts in which one counterparty receives the total return on an asset or basket of assets in exchange for a fixed fee. They are often used as a means of establishing a short position in a stock.

Foreign exchange and interest rate swaps have an allocative role. Most businesses have regular cash flows related to financing, such as receivables from customers and payables to suppliers, cash flows related to debt financing, capital expenditures, and returns on investments. These cash flows may be predictably and enduringly mismatched in some dimension that creates risk. For import and export businesses, the currency of inflows may not match that of outflows. Multinational firms may have a funding advantage in their home country but a large volume of business or investments abroad. Swaps are a mechanism for mitigating the problem.

Financial intermediaries borrow from providers of capital and lend to employers of capital. For banks, funding costs are usually closely tied to short-term interest rates, but interest income is more closely related to the longer-term rates on commercial and real estate loans, a motivation to pay fixed in a swap. Institutional investors, such as pension funds and life insurance companies, must meet long-term, fixed-rate commitments and are motivated to receive fixed.

A swap can be used to "transform" fixed into floating cash flows or vice versa. A market participant with a comparative advantage in longer-term funding markets, for example, a well-established firm that can issue bonds, can transform its cash flows via an interest rate swap so it instead pays a floating rate based on short-term rates. It faces the risk of collateral calls should long-term interest rates rise. Because it's harder for some borrowers to issue long-term, fixed-rate bonds, they face **rollover risk** on short-term credit.[1]

It may not always be possible to exactly match an exposure to a derivatives contract employed to mitigate it. There can also be differences in the exact definitions of the payoffs, introducing **basis risk**. For example, a floating-rate bond may stipulate a particular short-term interest rate. The bond issuer uses an interest rate swap to take on a fixed-rate obligation instead, but the floating-rate index of the swap is not identical to that of the bond.

6.1.1   Forward Foreign Exchange Markets

A **spot foreign exchange** transaction is a contract for immediate exchange of currencies and generally settled within two days. Foreign exchange hedging is closely integrated with local money markets via the forward foreign exchange markets, which are liquid for a range of standard times to maturity from overnight to a few years, depending on the currency pair and the state of development of its market. **Forward outright** transactions are contracts for the exchange of currencies at a future date, agreed at the current forward rate. Spot transactions are equivalent to a forward contract with zero time to settlement.

Foreign exchange markets are largely OTC, though with a significant and growing electronic trading component. **Foreign exchange futures** are similar to forwards but have fixed maturity dates rather than times to maturity and are traded on futures exchanges.

The difference between the spot and forward exchange rates with a given time to settlement is the **forward foreign exchange premium** or **discount**, expressed in percent or in **forward points** which are the number of currency units, times a standard multiple. If the τ-year forward premium is

$$\frac{F_{t,\tau}}{S_t} - 1,$$

with S_t and $F_{t,\tau}$ the spot and τ-year forward rates (the local price of one unit of the foreign currency), then the τ-year forward points are $F_{t,\tau} - S_t$ times a power of 10, such as 100 or 10,000.

A spot or forward foreign exchange position is an **open**, or **uncovered**, position and exposed to exchange rate risk. The market participant takes delivery of the currency, now or in the future, at a known exchange rate with the intent to sell later at the then-prevailing spot rate. It is profitable if the realized appreciation of foreign currency exceeds the forward premium.

For example, one might borrow or otherwise fund \$1 at a rate r_t, convert it to foreign currency at a spot rate S_t (foreign currency units per USD), and lend the foreign exchange proceeds at a rate r_t^*, the

---

[1] See Chapter 12.

foreign currency money market rate, with the intent to close the position in a year at an expected spot rate S_{t+1}. We can view the trade in terms of the USD or the foreign currency-denominated income statement:

	USD balance sheet		FX balance sheet	
	$ borrowing	FX transaction	FX transaction	FX lending
t	$+1$	-1	$+\dfrac{1}{S_t}$	$-\dfrac{1}{S_t}$
$t+1$	$-(1+r_t)$	$+\dfrac{S_{t+1}}{S_t}(1+r_t^*)$	$-\dfrac{1}{S_t}(1+r_t^*)$	$+\dfrac{1}{S_t}(1+r_t^*)$

The trade is profitable if the next-period foreign currency proceeds, once converted back to USD at S_{t+1}, exceed the USD debt obligation:

$$\frac{S_{t+1}}{S_t}(1+r_t^*) > 1+r_t.$$

Foreign-currency exposures are generally embedded in foreign money market, debt, equity, or other investments rather than in cash. A long (short) forward position can be used to hedge or cover or **close** a short (long) foreign exchange position. A foreign exchange swap pairs a spot and a forward foreign exchange transaction, or, less typically, two forward transactions with different settlement dates. A foreign exchange swap is a closed position; a foreign currency is bought and sold in advance at known exchange rates.

Forward foreign exchange transactions or money markets in different currencies can be used to replicate foreign exchange positions, creating an arbitrage relationship between interest rates and forward exchange rates. Assume for concreteness we're operating with the US dollar as the home currency. Two sets of transactions, with no net cash flow now, are equivalent:

Initiated in forward markets: Buy or sell foreign exchange in the spot and forward markets now, take delivery on the forward settlement date, or initiate a foreign exchange swap.
Initiated in money markets: Borrow—or deploy one's own capital—now in one money market, convert the proceeds in the spot market, and lend in the other money market.[2] Later, redeem the deposit and convert it back to the borrowed currency.

The equivalence between these sets of transactions, if it holds exactly, implies **covered** or **closed interest rate parity**. Differentials between equivalent—tenor, credit risk, etc.—short-term interest rates denominated in different currencies are then equal to the forward foreign exchange premium, and the costs of funding a currency position through the money markets and via foreign exchange swaps are equal. Spot and forward exchange rates of different maturities match up with the term structure of interest rates in both currencies.

The equivalence should be enforced by low-risk covered interest rate arbitrage in markets as liquid as the foreign exchange and money markets. The local currency is "priced to depreciate" by an amount equal to the forward premium $\dfrac{F_{t,\tau}}{S_t} - 1$ over τ years. The differential between the local ($r_{t,\tau}$) and

---

[2] The money market rate is an explicit cost if borrowing, or an opportunity cost if deploying one's own capital.

foreign ($r_{t,\tau}^*$) τ-year money market rates at an annual rate is

$$\frac{1 + r_{t,\tau}}{1 + r_{t,\tau}^*} - 1 \approx r_{t,\tau} - r_{t,\tau}^*.$$

The interest rate differential must also equal the annualized forward premium:

$$\left(\frac{F_{t,\tau}}{S_t}\right)^{\frac{1}{\tau}} = \frac{1 + r_{t,\tau}}{1 + r_{t,\tau}^*}.$$

If they aren't equal, the arbitrage consists of offsetting sets of transactions in the foreign exchange swap and the two money markets.

Example 6.1 Foreign exchange premium and covered interest-rate arbitrage

Suppose the spot pound sterling exchange rate (GBP-USD or "cable," conventionally measured as the US dollar price of £1) is $1.3000, and the three-month forward premium is 60 points (the standard multiple is 10,000). The forward outright rate is then $1.3060, so £1 deliverable 3 months hence is

$$\frac{1.3060}{1.30} - 1 = 0.004615,$$

or 0.46 percent costlier in dollars than in the spot market. The forward market is pricing in appreciation of sterling against the dollar.

Suppose the US and UK money market rates are $r_{t,\tau} = 0.0275$ and $r_{t,\tau}^* = 0.01$ for $\tau = \frac{3}{12}$. The no-arbitrage 3-month forward foreign exchange rate and premium are then $1.30559, or 55.9 forward points, and 0.004304 (0.43 percent):

$$F_{t,\tau} = S_t\left(\frac{1 + r_{t,\tau}}{1 + r_{t,\tau}^*}\right)^{\tau} = 1.3000\left(\frac{1 + 0.0275}{1 + 0.01}\right)^{\frac{3}{12}} = 1.3000 \times 1.004304$$

$$= 1.30559.$$

There is an arbitrage opportunity because the market forward rate is higher: borrow $1.30 at 2.75, buy £1, and deposit it at 1 percent. The trader owes $1.30885 and receives £1.00249 in 3 months. With $F_{t,\tau} = 1.3060 > 1.30559$, the trader can buy $1.30925 forward, deliver £1.00249 at settlement to close out the forward transaction, repay the initial USD money market loan of $1.30885, and clear 0.04 cents. The arbitrage profit is $400 on every £1,000,000 bought in the spot market and sold forward.

A forward foreign exchange market can facilitate local borrowing and lending where it is more developed, liquid, and accessible than money markets as is the case in some emerging-market and middle-income countries. If we assume covered parity holds, we can construct an implied local money market term structure from forward rate data.

Example 6.2 Deriving an interest rate curve from foreign exchange forwards

As of June 30, 2023, the closing level of the spot Turkish lira exchange rate (USD-TRY) was 26.0145 (TRY price of $1) and the 1-month TRY forward points were 1,965.34 (the standard multiple is 10,000 for USD-TRY), indicating an expected TRY depreciation of $\frac{0.196534}{26.0145} =$

Table 6.1   Deriving a foreign-currency interest rate curve from forwards

Term	1 month	3 months	1 year	5 years
USD spot interest rates	5.2950	5.5200	5.8838	4.2190
Forward points	1965.34	11406.37	72843.20	547324.50
Forward premium (% p.a.)	9.452	18.726	28.001	25.424
Forward exchange rates	26.211034	27.155137	33.298820	80.746950
TRY spot interest rates	15.247575	25.279740	35.532322	30.716085

Interest rates in percent. *Data source*: Bloomberg.

0.007555 or a bit over $\frac{3}{4}$ percent. The 1-month USD money market rate was 5.295 percent. The 1-month TRY forward rate should then equal

$$\left(1 + \frac{0.196534}{26.0145}\right)^{12} \cdot 1.05295 - 1 = 0.152476$$

or 15.2476 percent. With a range of maturities, we can infer a TRY money market curve.

6.1.2   Valuation of Interest Rate Swaps

The value of an interest rate swap is the NPV of its future payments or the difference between the values of a fixed rate bond with a coupon equal to the swap fixed rate and of a floating rate bond:

NPV of swap = PV of fixed payments − PV of floating payments.

The NPV of a swap fluctuates over its life as market interest rates fluctuate, and the terms of swap remain fixed, so a swap that has been in effect for some time generally has a nonzero NPV.

The **par swap rate** is the market-clearing fixed rate on a newly initiated plain-vanilla swap and sets its NPV to zero. The swap is at-market, with no additional credit risk or basis risk spread, at initiation, and arbitrage enforces equality of the present values of the swap's fixed and floating payments. The par swap rate is equal to the coupon rate at which a congruent fixed-rate bond, with the same credit and other risks, would price at par.

Example 6.3   Pricing an interest rate swap

The par swap rate is a maturity-weighted geometric average of spot rates. The spot curve example of Chapter 2 can be used to calculate it as the coupon of a fixed-rate bond priced at par:

	Zero-coupon rate assumptions			
Term	1 year	2 years	3 years	4 years
Spot rates	1.3250	1.7000	1.9250	2.0000
Forward rates		2.0764	2.3765	2.2253

Using these rate assumptions, for each $100 of par value,

$$100 = 100r \left(\frac{1}{1.01325} + \frac{1}{1.017^2} + \frac{1}{1.01925^3} + \frac{1}{1.02^4}\right) + \frac{100}{1.02^4},$$

which can be solved for a par swap rate $r = 0.0199252$, or 1.99252 percent, the fixed rate in a swap against 1-year LIBOR or its replacement reference rate "flat," i.e., at-market.

With low counterparty risk after collateralization, fixed-rate flows are close to risk-free. For a notional principal of 1,000,000, the cash flows in the interest rate swap example can be summarized in the table below. Cash flows that are uncertain at swap initiation are highlighted. The table gives one possible scenario for floating cash flows (italicized amounts): future 1-year rates happen to equal today's forward interest rates. An increase in short-term rates would increase them and vice versa.

Cash flows in interest rate swap				
Date	1 year	2 years	3 years	4 years
Fixed	19 925.20	19 925.20	19 925.20	19 925.20
Floating	13 250.00	20 763.90	23 764.90	22 253.30

This interest rate swap potentially provides risk mitigation for both counterparties. The receiver of floating/payer of fixed is protected against a rise in short-term interest rates. Gains on the swap offset at least some losses due to a rise in rates. The receiver of fixed/payer of floating is protected against a fall in long-term interest rates.

An **overnight index swap** (OIS) is similar to an interest rate swap in that it is an exchange at regular intervals of interest payments on a notional principal amount, with a term to maturity between a few weeks and several years. The payments are based on a market-clearing fixed rate determined at initiation, reflecting market expectations for the average overnight reference rate over the term, and a floating overnight reference rate. One party pays to the other the difference between the proceeds of an overnight investment rolled over daily at the fixed rate, and the proceeds of investing the notional amount at the reference rate and rolling it over continuously. The floating leg is thus equal to the notional amount multiplied by a geometric average of the reference rate.

OIS are less exposed to the credit and counterparty risk of commercial banks than interbank loans because, like most other swaps, they don't involve the exchange of notional payments at initiation and are typically collateralized. The fixed rates on OIS are therefore, generally lower than interbank rates with the same time to maturity. The gap tends to widen, sometimes dramatically, during periods of financial stress. The **LIBOR-OIS spread** (LOIS) had been a useful indicator of concern about the stability of the banking system.[3]

6.1.3 The LIBOR Transition

Following the LIBOR manipulation scandal, the Federal Reserve, along with other major central banks, initiated an effort to replace LIBOR with reference rates drawn from market data on secured overnight loans.[4] The effort took longer than expected, since LIBOR is embedded in a large volume of long-term private debt and derivatives contracts. It has also expanded beyond the initial objective of taking the business of publishing reference rates out of the hands of private-sector panels to also include replacing benchmarks and reference rates based on interbank loans with nearly risk-free rates drawn from liquid, observable overnight money markets. For the US dollar and the Swiss franc (CHF), they are based on secured money market rates. The main US reference rate, **Secured Overnight Financing Rate** (SOFR), is based on Treasury repo and is considered as free of credit risk as a nongovernment claim can be.[5]

---

[3] See Chapter 15.

[4] The review has included other regulators and encompassed privately published indexes such as the S&P 500 as well. See, for example, the principles for financial benchmarks published by securities regulators: https://www.iosco.org/library/pubdocs/pdf/IOSCOPD415.pdf.

[5] See Chapter 12.

These goals were initially advanced through suasion; in the United States particularly, the influence the Federal Reserve can bring to bear on primary dealers. The United Kingdom's Financial Conduct Authority has stopped LIBOR from being published after mid-2023. Under rules the Fed has issued implementing the Adjustable Interest Rate (LIBOR) Act of 2022, legacy contracts will replace LIBOR with newly developed reference rates. Outside the United States, similar interbank curves for other currencies are also being gradually phased out, and intermediaries are in the process of revising existing contracts that extend beyond the cessation dates. Nearly risk-free rates have been developed as benchmarks for non-dollar bonds, derivatives, and other contracts.

Though the transition is complex and costly for market participants, resistance to it has been muted, in part because the significant presence of credit risk in longer-term interbank rates impairs its use as a benchmark as seen in the wide LOIS spread during periods of stress. There has also been a sharp decline in the volume of interbank lending on which LIBOR curves are based since the global financial crisis, so reference rates based on transactions in these markets became less representative of short-term funding costs.

However, interest-rate swaps using SOFR or other nearly risk-free rates as a floating index are mismatched with the bank funding cost risk they may be used to hedge against. Interbank lending rates may rise sharply, while SOFR or T-bill rates driving swap payoffs do not, or even fall. Spread widening coupled with a nearly risk-free hedge can cause severe losses.

Swap markets have been transformed by the transition. The permanent discontinuation of LIBOR reference rates related to interbank loans requires not only new types of contracts but also revisions to a large volume of existing contracts. Newly originated swaps using SOFR or other nearly risk-free rates are priced, as in the past, so the NPV of the swap is zero. For existing swaps to be converted to a new reference rate, two adjustments are required, for the difference in credit risk and for the term to maturity of the legacy and new reference rates:

- A credit adjustment spread must be estimated to equalize the old and new rates. The level of this adjustment has been a source of controversy between banks and customers.
- The new reference rates are overnight rates, leaving the problem of how to obtain nearly risk-free rates for use in swaps and floating-rate bonds, with payment dates a calendar quarter or more apart. This can be done in a backward- or forward-looking fashion. One approach is to determine floating payments in arrears, by compounding the past quarter's or 180 days' daily SOFR rates. For US dollar instruments, the CME Group and Intercontinental Exchange (ICE), operators, of futures and options exchanges, have developed longer-term SOFR futures that can be used as forward-looking reference rates. SOFR futures are similar to OIS: they pay the difference between a fixed rate determined at the contract's initiation and the compounded return on SOFR over the term of the contract. Term SOFR and to a lesser extent SOFR in arrears are gradually replacing LIBOR in US dollar swaps and other fixed-income instruments.

The new reference rates are often used as the floating rates stipulated in OIS swaps. The overnight money market indexes on which OIS are based are calculated in different ways in different currencies, and are generally published by central banks. For US dollar-denominated OIS, that rate is the effective federal funds rate (EFFR) and, for the euro, the euro short-term rate (€STR). OIS using SOFR as a reference rate (SOFR OIS) are now also traded.

6.1.4 Credit Default Swaps

Exposures to the credit risk of larger companies are traded OTC through credit default swaps, derivatives that pay off in the event of the default of an entity or a security. The CDS contract is written on a specific **reference entity** or underlying issuer, typically a firm or a government, and specifies whether the contract protects its senior or subordinated debt. For companies that have issued senior and subordinated debt, there may be CDS contracts of both kinds.

CDS are used by a range of market participants for hedging or to establish open positions. Contracts on over 4,000 firms and indexes of CDS prices covering groups of firms by region and credit quality are traded.[6] The market has grown rapidly since 1999, when the ISDA first introduced a standard swap agreement and settlement procedures. It is a relatively small but important part of the overall OTC derivatives market.

In a CDS, the counterparty buying protection agrees to make a set of payments to the counterparty selling protection, called the **premium** or **fee leg**. In the event of default, the **contingent leg** of the CDS specifies how the protection seller is to compensate the protection buyer for the default loss on a specified notional amount of the underlying debt. The recurring fixed rate premium payer, or protection buyer, has a short credit risk position and is said to be long the CDS. The contingent payer in a credit event, the protection seller, has a long credit risk position and is said to be short the CDS.

As with interest rate swaps, the premium of the CDS is set through the market process to equate the expected present value of the fee leg to that of the contingent leg on the initiation date. The initial expected NPV of an at-market CDS contract is then zero.

The premium leg can be expressed as a **par spread** in basis points, a market-clearing spread over a risk-free curve. The protection buyer undertakes to make spread payments each quarter until the maturity date of the contract, until and unless there is a default event pertaining to the underlying name on which the CDS is written. For example, in a CDS with quarterly premium payments on a notional amount of $10 million and a CDS spread of 100 bps, the protection buyer's quarterly payments are $25,000.

Apart from recurrent future payments, there is in some cases also a one-time payment at the initiation of the contract. The par spread could be set at a level that would obviate the need for a one-time payment, but under the standard agreements prevailing for most CDS, the par spread is set at 100 or 500 basis points. A **points up front** payment is made by one counterparty to the other to equate the initial NPV of an at-market CDS to zero, given the expected default loss.

The contingent leg of the CDS specifies cash or physical settlement. With cash settlement, the protection seller pays the protection buyer an amount equal to the estimated loss given default, that is, the notional amount less the recovery on the underlying bond. The contingent payment is determined by an auction process, specified in the CDS agreement, that enforces arbitrage with prices of the defaulted entity's debt in the distressed debt market. Alternatively, the protection seller pays the protection buyer the par amount of a deliverable bond of the reference entity, and the protection buyer delivers in exchange a defaulted bond from a list of acceptable or "deliverable" bonds issued by the entity.

The ISDA swap agreements define nonpayment and other default events that trigger contingent payments. In some cases, the CDS may be triggered, or not, in surprising ways. For example, in 2018, the highly indebted construction firm Hovnanian Enterprises and credit-focused hedge fund GSO Capital Partners came to an agreement under which GSO would refinance part of Hovnanian's debt. It included an arrangement in which Hovnanian bought for its own account a portion of its existing debt on which GSO had bought CDS protection. Hovnanian would fail to pay interest on that debt, presumably triggering contingent payments on GSO's CDS protection, which would come not

---

[6] According to S&P Global, a vendor of market data, including CDS pricing data since its acquisition of IHS Markit in 2022.

at Hovnanian's expense but at the CDS protection sellers' expense. A large CDS protection seller brought suit against GSO, which eventually abandoned the deal.[7]

For many companies, CDS trades are conducted regularly in standardized maturities of 1, 3, 5, 7, and 10 years, with the 5-year point generally the most liquid. Standardization contributes to liquidity. When CDS on a company's bonds exist, they are generally more heavily traded and have a tighter bid-offer spread than bond issues, and the liquidity of CDS with different maturities differs less than that of bonds of a given issuer. The pricing of a CDS is a measure of the risk-adjusted expected present value the market assigns to future credit losses on the underlying firm's debt, similar to a credit spread.

CDS are exposed to credit and counterparty risk. If market prices change, the NPV becomes positive for one counterparty and negative for the other, that is, there is a MTM gain and loss. There are therefore, also generally exchanges of margin when a CDS trade is executed. **Double default risk** is the risk that the underlying credit and the CDS counterparty default.

6.2   Options

6.2.1   Option Values

Options are contracts in which the option seller promises to pay the buyer the difference between the future value of an asset and a **strike** or **exercise price** stipulated now. A **call** has a positive payoff and is therefore, exercised by the owner when the price is higher than the exercise price, and a **put** pays off when the price is lower. The price of the contract is the option premium.

There is a future payment only if the option is exercised. **European** options can be exercised only on the option's expiry date; **American** options can be exercised anytime up to expiry. The terminal payoff is $\max(S_T - X, 0)$ for a European call and $\max(X - S_T, 0)$ for a put struck at X and expiring at T.

Options are complicated to value and manage. Valuation requires evaluating a conditional payoff, an amount that depends not only on the underlying price but is also conditioned on its being higher or lower than the exercise price. At expiry, European option payoffs have the well-known "hockey stick" profile relative to the expiry-date underlying price. Before expiry they have highly nonlinear values relative to the underlying price that depend on how far and in what direction the underlying asset price wanders away from the exercise price. The current option value, therefore, depends also on how the market views the asset's return volatility.

Some statements about the values of options—for example, put-call parity—are based on arbitrage arguments; others are based on models that include assumptions about asset return behavior that don't hold precisely in reality. The **Black-Scholes-Merton model** was based on the recognition that options can be hedged by holding an offsetting position in the underlying asset and adjusting it over time. It simplifies the valuation problem by assuming the asset price S_t follows a geometric Brownian motion with a known return volatility σ. It also assumes the sort of perfect market environment in which continuous, exact and transaction-cost-free hedging is possible. The model doesn't assume we know the drift of the geometric Brownian process. Instead, it assumes we know that the volatility is known and that the option can be perfectly hedged.

---

[7] See Carruzzo et al. (2018) and Andrew Scurria, "Blackstone Stands Down on Hovnanian Swaps Wager," *Wall Street Journal*, May 30, 2018.

Under the seamless and costless hedging assumption, an option position can be immunized against the immeasurably tiny but frequent changes in the value of the underlying asset by holding and constantly adjusting a portfolio consisting of an offsetting asset position and an amount of money. This hedged portfolio is riskless and should earn only the risk-free rate in equilibrium. Perfect hedging and the absence of arbitrage opportunities imply risk-neutral valuation, meaning the option will be priced as if the drift were equal to the riskless rate r_t^f. To value the option, we don't need to know the drift rate of the asset, since we can replace it with r_t^f.

With those assumptions, call and put values are given by straightforward formulas. The Black-Scholes formula for the time-t value of a European call on one unit of an asset with a current price S_t, struck at X and with a tenor of $\tau = T - t$ is:

$$v(S_t, X, \tau, \sigma, r_t^f, q_t) = S_t e^{-q_t \tau} \Phi\left[\frac{\ln\left(\frac{S_t}{X}\right) + \left(r_t^f - q_t + \frac{\sigma^2}{2}\right)\tau}{\sigma\sqrt{\tau}}\right]$$
$$-Xe^{-r_t^f \tau}\Phi\left[\frac{\ln\left(\frac{S_t}{X}\right) + \left(r_t^f - q_t - \frac{\sigma^2}{2}\right)\tau}{\sigma\sqrt{\tau}}\right],$$

(6.1)

where σ is the asset's logarithmic return volatility and q_t is the continuously compounded rate of cash flow yielded by the underlying assets, known at time t. The Black-Scholes time-t model value of a European put struck at X is:

$$w(S_t, X, \tau, \sigma, r_t^f, q_t) = -S_t e^{-q_t \tau} \Phi\left[-\frac{\ln\left(\frac{S_t}{X}\right) + \left(r_t^f - q_t + \frac{\sigma^2}{2}\right)\tau}{\sigma\sqrt{\tau}}\right]$$
$$+Xe^{-r_t^f \tau}\Phi\left[-\frac{\ln\left(\frac{S_t}{X}\right) + \left(r_t^f - q_t - \frac{\sigma^2}{2}\right)\tau}{\sigma\sqrt{\tau}}\right].$$

(6.2)

Each Black-Scholes formula can be interpreted as the sum of two terms: the present value of the conditional expected future value of the exercise price and of the underlying asset, both conditional on the asset price finishing higher (lower) in the case of a call (put) than the strike. In the case of a call, the second term is the present value of the exercise price, multiplied by the risk-neutral probability of exercise, that is, the probability of a terminal underlying price S_T higher than X in the geometric Brownian model. The first term is the expected value of the underlying asset, conditional on it being higher than X.

Under the model assumptions, the log return $\ln(S_T) - \ln(S_t)$ is normally distributed. Once we've applied risk-neutral valuation by setting the unknown drift term to r_t^f, and taking account of the Jensen's inequality term $\frac{\sigma^2}{2}\tau$, the distribution of the log return is:

$$\ln(S_T) - \ln(S_t) \sim \mathcal{N}\left[\left(r_t^f - q_t - \frac{\sigma^2}{2}\right)\tau, \sigma^2\tau\right].$$

The log of the amount by which the future realized price exceeds the exercise price is then also normally distributed:

$$\ln(S_T) - \ln(X) \sim \mathcal{N}\left[\ln\left(\frac{S_t}{X}\right) + \left(r_t^f - q_t - \frac{\sigma^2}{2}\right)\tau, \sigma^2\tau\right],$$

and the quantity

$$d_2 \equiv \frac{\ln\left(\frac{S_t}{X}\right) + \left(r_t^f - q_t - \frac{\sigma^2}{2}\right)\tau}{\sigma\sqrt{\tau}}$$

is a standard normal quantile that measures in volatility units the mean-adjusted initial difference between the current and the exercise price. The probability of exercise, that the option ends in-the-money, with $S_T \geq X$, is:

$$P[S_T \geq X] = \Phi\left[\frac{\ln\left(\frac{S_t}{X}\right) + \left(r_t^f - q_t - \frac{\sigma^2}{2}\right)\tau}{\sigma\sqrt{\tau}}\right] \equiv \Phi(d_2).$$

The second term of the formula for the value of a European call option states the expected cost to the option owner of exercising it if it ends in-the-money. The exercise price X is not random, but a known part of the option contract, so this conditional expected cost is the probability of exercise times the present value of the exercise price $Xe^{-r_t^f\tau}$.

In the first term,

$$\Phi\left[\frac{\ln\left(\frac{S_t}{X}\right) + \left(r_t^f - q_t + \frac{\sigma^2}{2}\right)\tau}{\sigma\sqrt{\tau}}\right] = \Phi(d_2 + \sigma\sqrt{\tau}) \equiv \Phi(d_1) \tag{6.3}$$

is called the **delta** of the call option. The delta is a little larger than the risk-neutral probability of exercise $\Phi(d_2)$ because the Jensen's inequality term is added back in; if S_T ends up higher than X, positive returns will have predominated.

The expected present value of the future underlying price S_T, if it ends up higher than X, is $S_t e^{-q_t\tau}\Phi(d_1)$. The expected present value of S_T, conditional on $S_T > X$, is found by dividing that expected value by the probability of exercise:

$$S_t e^{-q_t\tau}\frac{\Phi(d_1)}{\Phi(d_2)}.$$

The value of a European call is the difference between this conditional expected value of the underlying and the cost of exercise, times the probability of exercise:

$$v(S_t, X, \tau, \sigma, r_t^f, q_t) = \left[S_t e^{-q_t\tau}\frac{\Phi(d_1)}{\Phi(d_2)} - Xe^{-r_t^f\tau}\right]\Phi(d_2). \tag{6.4}$$

For a European put, the interpretation of the Black-Scholes formula is analogous. The second term in the formula is the expected proceeds of exercising it by buying the underlying asset at the exercise price, and the first term is the expected present value of the amount by which the exercise price exceeds the underlying price, if the underlying asset price ends lower.

Example 6.4   Black-Scholes model

Let's evaluate at-the-money (ATM) 3-month European options on the S&P 500 index, as of May 31, 2023, using the Black-Scholes model. The market data as of that date are:

Underlying price	4179.83
3-month T-bill yield	5.4030
12-month trailing dividend yield	1.6569
3-month ATM option implied vol	16.0290

The results, once the yields have been expressed as logarithmic rates, are:

	Call	Put
Option value	152.0474	114.5577
Delta	0.5585	−0.4374
Probability of exercise	0.5290	0.4710

The probabilities of exercise sum to 1: either the index value in three months is exactly 4179.83 or one of the options will be exercised. The delta of an ATM call is somewhat higher than 0.5, and that of a put is somewhat higher than −0.5, so their absolute values sum to less than 1.

6.2.2   The Option-Implied Volatility Surface

Let's relate these valuation formulas to the market prices of options. Five of the six arguments in the functions $v(S_t, X, \tau, \sigma, r_t^f, q_t)$ and $w(S_t, X, \tau, \sigma, r_t^f, q_t)$ are known at time t: X and τ are part of the option contract's terms; S_t, r_t^f, and q_t are observable quantities. So, if the option prices are also observed—and the model assumptions of a known volatility and perfect markets with costless hedging are correct—we can use the formulas together with market prices to back out the value of σ they imply. We'll denote by $c(t, X, \tau)$ the time-t market value of a European call on one unit of an asset, struck at X and with a tenor of $\tau = T - t$, and that of a European put by $p(t, X, \tau)$. Either of these equations:

$$c(t, X, \tau) = v(S_t, X, \tau, \sigma, r_t^f, q_t)$$

$$p(t, X, \tau) = w(S_t, X, \tau, \sigma, r_t^f, q_t)$$

can be solved for one unknown σ, called the **Black-Scholes implied volatility**.

There's a one-to-one mapping between the implied vol and the option price. Implied volatilities are a metric for expressing the option price and contain the same information. The Black-Scholes implied volatility is a risk-neutral estimate and can be interpreted as the market's best guess at future realized volatility, adjusted for the market's willingness to bear return volatility risk. Option prices and implied volatilities will be higher if the market is more eager to buy protection against volatility.

If we assume either geometric Brownian motion or, more generally, a constant and known volatility, we confront an empirical puzzle. For any asset with a well-developed option market, option prices don't translate into a single, unique implied volatility. Rather, there are different implied volatilities at any point in time for options struck at different exercise prices or expiring at different maturity dates. The pattern of implied volatilities for any particular asset at any particular time is called its **volatility**

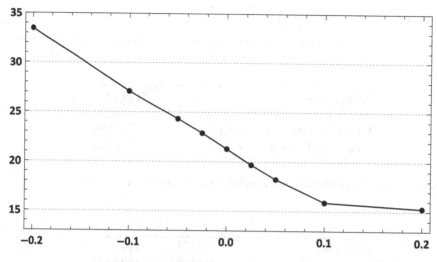

Figure 6.1 S&P 500 index volatility smile

Implied volatilities of 3-month European options on the S&P 500 index (SPX) on 20Mar2023, in percent at an annual rate, as a function of moneyness, expressed as distance in percent above or below current index level. *Source*: Bloomberg.

surface and can be represented graphically as a three-dimensional plot or function. The **volatility smile** is the pattern of implied volatilities for a specific time to maturity. The typical pattern, as the name indicates, is for out-of-the-money options to have higher implied volatilities than at-the-money (ATM). For some markets, such as equity prices, the smile is often a downward sloping line, a pattern called a **volatility smirk**. Figure 6.1 is an example of a volatility smile for 3-month options on the S&P 500 index.

Vols might rise or fall with option maturity, that is, there is **term structure of volatility**. Just as an upward sloping term structure of interest rates indicates a market expectation of rising short-term rates or at least a degree of eagerness to protect against that outcome, a rising volatility term structure indicates analogous expectations or concerns about rising vol.

The use of implied volatilities doesn't depend on or imply the validity of the Black-Scholes or any other model of option prices. In fact, the volatility smile implies a non-normal distribution of logarithmic asset returns. A flat volatility smile or surface would imply a market consensus that the lognormal model is correct. The wide variation of implied volatilities by strike and maturity, and over time, suggests market expectations of a different behavior of underlying asset prices. Each option might be priced as if the asset price followed a geometric Brownian motion with a volatility parameter equal to the implied vol. But the differences across the vol surface reveal different views about future prices, hedging needs, and risk. The patterns of implied volatility, in other words, imply a set of risk-neutral probabilities for future asset prices, providing a great deal of information on how far markets are expected, or feared, to depart from the simple standard model.

6.2.3   Option Risks

Option markets use the Black-Scholes model routinely without believing that it's perfectly accurate. Like the standard asset return model, it's useful for framing even though it's wrong in important ways. The model focuses traders on the key option risks, changes in the underlying price, and in the implied volatility, and the Black-Scholes formulas provide an important set of units for managing them.

If a put or call is in-the-money, the difference between the current underlying and the exercise prices is its **intrinsic value**. The intrinsic value of an out-of-the-money option is zero. The shorter the time to maturity of an option, the lower the likelihood that its intrinsic value will change drastically. Therefore, options have a **time value** that decays over time at a rate **theta**. It reflects the fact that an option is a "wasting asset" and is particularly high relative to option value for short-term options. Theta is not a risk but a deterministic quantity at any point in time, similar to fixed-income roll-down (Chapter 10), for which the Black-Scholes formulas and the terms of the option provide a precise value. But theta also fluctuates with changes in the underlying price, interest rates, and implied volatility.

The option risk stemming from the underlying asset price risk is summarized by option traders in two characteristics: the first and second derivatives of the option value with respect to underlying price. The option delta δ_t is the linear price risk of the underlying asset as measured by the rate at which option value changes with underlying asset price. For a European call, it is defined as:

$$\delta_t \equiv \frac{\partial c(S_t, X, \tau)}{\partial S_t},$$

and for a European put as:

$$\delta_t \equiv \frac{\partial p(S_t, X, \tau)}{\partial S_t}.$$

This linear response is never greater in magnitude than the price shock for a plain-vanilla European call option, $0 \leq \delta_t \leq 1$, and for a put, $-1 \leq \delta_t \leq 0$. In the Black-Scholes model, the call delta takes on the value in equation (6.3) above.

The risk management of option positions is the flip side of their value: their values depend on the underlying asset's behavior and is derived via an arbitrage argument, so their risks depend on how well the arbitrage holds up. The delta tells the trader carrying it out how much of the underlying asset to short given the current price S_t. Imagine the probability of exercise $\Phi(d_2)$ is 0.5. Those random fluctuations will not exactly balance each other out. Price rises threaten the trader more than drops because it will take a larger subsequent drop to offset them, so even though at this moment exercise is a coin toss, the trader should hedge by shorting just a bit more than 0.5 units of the asset.

The sensitivity of option value to the underlying price is greatest near the strike, and may fall off rapidly as the option goes in- or out-of-the-money. This nonlinearity of price risk is captured by the **gamma** γ_t, the rate at which the delta δ_t changes with the underlying asset price:

$$\gamma_t \equiv \frac{\partial}{\partial S_t}\delta_t = \frac{\partial^2 c(S_t, X, \tau)}{\partial S_t^2}$$

for a call. For a vanilla European put or call option, $\gamma_t \geq 0$ and like the delta it is greater the closer to the strike is the underlying price. In the replicating portfolio that hedges the option over time, the offsetting underlying asset position is related to the delta and the money balance to the gamma.

The change in an option's value in response to underlying shocks can be estimated using the **delta-gamma approximation**, a second order Taylor expansion. The approximate change in value of a European call option on one unit of the underlying asset if S_t changes by ΔS is:

$$c(S_t + \Delta S, X, \tau) - c(S_t, X, \tau) \approx \delta_t \Delta S + \frac{1}{2}\gamma_t \Delta S^2,$$

with the other market variables that might affect its price—volatility, risk-free rate, cash flow rate—held constant.

Options are also exposed to other risk factors. Because an option matures at a future date, it bears interest-rate risk, or **rho**, as does the value of any future payoff, even a contingent one. In the Black-Scholes formula, volatility is taken as a constant parameter, but because implied volatility is random, a number of risk sensitivities are related to its fluctuations. The sensitivity to changes in implied volatility is called the option **vega**. The risk from changes in volatility, which is vega risk, can be thought of as the options own-price risk apart from other drivers such as underlying price and interest rates.

Analogous to the gamma, an option's vega varies with the implied volatility itself. This second derivative with respect to volatility is called **volga**. Because, as summarized in the volatility smile, implied volatility can vary a great deal with price, options also have a cross-sensitivity **vanna**, the response of the option delta to a change in implied volatility.[8]

6.2.4   Put-Call Parity

If you put together a credit risk-free put and call on the same asset, maturing at the same time and with the same exercise price, the portfolio is equivalent to having a long or short position in the asset, deliverable at the maturity of the options. The parity relation for a long put and and short call position is:

$$c(t, X, \tau) - p(t, X, \tau) + Xe^{-r_t^f \tau} = S_t.$$

with r_t^f the τ-year risk-free rate. Buying a call and selling a put with the same exercise price X is equivalent to owning a forward position in the underlying asset itself and borrowing a sum X. Whatever the value of the asset at time τ, the options will permit (the call, with $S_\tau > X$) or oblige (the put, with $S_\tau < X$) the investor to buy the asset at a price X later on.

Put-call parity implies that puts and calls with the same time to maturity and exercise price on the same asset must have identical implied volatilities. Any difference would open up an arbitrage opportunity. Therefore, the volatility smile illustrated in Figure 6.1 doesn't distinguish between puts and calls but is a function solely of exercise prices.

6.2.5   Interest Rate Implied Volatility

There are two standard conventions in fixed-income option markets for expressing implied volatility. **Normal volatility** is the standard deviation of changes in yield $\sigma_{n,t}$ in basis points. This convention is followed, for example, in OTC swaption markets. **Yield** or **Black volatility** is the volatility of proportional changes in yield $\sigma_{y,t}$ in percent, or

$$\sigma_{y,t} = \frac{\sigma_{n,t}}{y_t}.$$

Black volatility measures yield changes, somewhat oddly, in percent rather than basis points but avoids negative yield scenarios.

---

[8] The sensitivities related to implied volatility are named after a star in the constellation Lyra, a river in Russia, and a television personality.

Fixed-income options have an additional dimension, the time to maturity of the underlying interest rate exposure, apart from the strike and the tenor of the option. Therefore, the analogue to the volatility surface has three dimensions and is referred to as the **volatility cube**.

6.3   Market-Implied Asset Price Forecasts

Asset prices are inherently forward-looking. To the extent markets are efficient, prices clear at levels consistent with risk appetites and expectations. In efficient markets, asset prices capture and summarize information and points of view widely dispersed among market participants about current and future conditions, asset prices, and cash flows. Viewing prices as forecasts provides an external, market-adjusted assessment of the future to compare with those generated by knowledge, intuition, or models.

Derivatives prices are particularly suited to expressing expectations because they have maturity and delivery dates in the future conveying information about prices or payoffs at those dates. Forwards and futures provide mean forecasts, that is, risk-neutral expectations of future prices. Credit spreads on corporate or sovereign debt imply a risk-neutral probability of default over their term to maturity. Options provide risk-neutral estimates of asset return volatility and of the entire probability distribution of future prices.

Futures and forward prices, as well as past returns, have very little efficacy in predicting future returns. Option markets do at least a less poor job forecasting return variance, a characteristic called **second-moment efficiency**. This is unsurprising given the finding for return autocorrelations that squared returns have greater predictive power for future volatility than past returns do for future returns. Though option-implied volatility and squared recent returns have some information value for future realized volatility, they often miss sharp changes in volatility. Different ways to measure historical volatility make this a difficult property to test.

The challenge in extracting information from current asset prices is that they are also determined by risk preferences. Asset prices embed risk-neutral expectations, the subjective probability distribution that would be imputed to a representative agent assumed to be indifferent to risk. It's a somewhat odd name because risk-neutral expectations express risk aversion. But if we imagine a representative agent who is indifferent to risk, each risk-neutral probability would equal a dispassionate estimate of the real world probability, and each element of the stochastic discount factor would equal the riskless present value of \$1.[9] To interpret these expectations in a world of risk-averse people, we have to keep in mind that a high probability ascribed to a future outcome can mean it is viewed with apprehension as well as that it is likely.

6.3.1   Risk-Neutral Mean Forecasts

Forward and futures prices, once adjusted for short-term rates, known future cash flows and estimated convenience yields, are risk-neutral estimates of future asset prices. Expectations theories state that they are also authentic forecasts of future prices. In some markets, such as stock index futures, the relationship to cash prices is tight enough, with new information affecting both synchronously, that an expectations view does not differ greatly from the random walk hypothesis.

In foreign exchange markets, uncovered interest rate parity is an expectations theory stating that the forward premium is not only a risk-neutral but also a true market forecast of the change in the spot

---

[9] See Chapter 3.

exchange rate over the term of the forward rate. Equivalently, interest rate differentials are equal to the expected appreciation or depreciation of one currency against another. Empirically, realized changes in exchange rates deviate greatly from forward-implied rates.

In fixed-income markets, the **expectations theory of the term structure** states that longer-term interest rates are determined by expected future short-term rates. The curve of forward short-term rates is the risk-neutral expectation of the sequence of future short-term rates. An upward sloping term structure, with longer-term rates higher than short-term, implies that the market expects short-term rates to rise.

Inflation compensation, or the **break-even inflation** rate, is measured as the difference between nominal and real rates on bonds with the same tenor and is used as an indicator of market views on future inflation. A common measure of break-even inflation is the rate implied by the difference between nominal government bond yields and those of inflation-protected bonds. The United States (since 1997) and a number of other countries issue **inflation-protected** or **inflation-linked bonds**. These include Treasury Inflation Protected Securities (TIPS) in the United States and "linkers" in the United Kingdom that protect the holder against inflation by increasing the nominal principal at specified intervals based on changes in a price index.

Forward break-even inflation rates are computed similarly to forward interest rates and provide information on market views regarding inflation in future years. The 5-year forward inflation expectation rate, the average inflation rate over a 5-year period starting in 5 years, is a widely used risk-neutral measure of long-term inflation drawn from yields on 5- and 10-year US Treasury notes and TIPS.

Inflation swaps are also used to hedge inflation risk. One party pays a fixed rate for the term of the swap and receives floating payments tied to the realized inflation rate. Their fixed rates are also a source of data on risk-neutral expected inflation. There is generally a gap between break-even inflation estimates drawn from swap rates and bond yields, likely due to higher risk premiums and lower convenience yields on inflation-protected bonds than on nominal government bonds.

Many futures contracts have features that create ambiguities when interpreting them as expectations of future prices. For example, an entire class of US notes or bonds with different maturities can be delivered against each Treasury note and bond futures contract on any trading day in the month ending with the futures contract's expiration. The **cheapest to deliver** bond is the cheapest at any point in time but can change with the term structure of interest rates.

Another example is fed funds futures, for which the payoff is defined as the average funds rate during the expiration month. Not until the last day of the delivery month is its payoff unambiguous. Fed funds futures prices can be used to derive a market-implied probability of a change in Fed monetary policy rates, but such estimates depend on assumptions about the size of any change in the target rate; will it be 25 or 50 basis points?[10]

Risk premiums of different types make it difficult to infer forecast prices accurately. In government bond markets and some other markets, central bank policies may further distort these premiums. Most importantly, in efficient markets, forward and futures prices add little information to that in current prices. Forward foreign exchange rates and stock index futures have little predictive power for future realized rates and index levels. Option-implied probability distributions are potentially

---

[10] A guide to these calculations can be found at https://www.cmegroup.com/articles/2023/understanding-the-cme-group-fedwatch-tool-methodology.html.

more interesting because they contain clues about market risk preferences beyond what is captured in forward prices.

6.3.2 Risk-Neutral Volatility and Correlation Forecasts

Broader indexes of implied volatility have been developed to summarize the information in the volatility smile or surface. Although they are generally dependent on at least some restrictions on the behavior of returns on the underlying asset, such as the absence of jumps, they have a looser connection to the Black-Scholes model and are referred to as **model-free implied volatilities**. Some have become widely used indicators of the state of markets, most prominently the CBOE Volatility Index (VIX), a measure of the 1-month implied volatility of the S&P 500 index based on the prices of 1-month options.

Interest-rate volatility estimates can also be used as a rough gauge of future volatility and how the market views it. For example, a swaption normal volatility of 80 basis points, using the square-root-of-time rule, implies a daily vol of 5 bps. A one-day rate change of 3 bps, less than a standard deviation, is routine by that metric, while a change of 12 bps over two standard deviations is noteworthy. The Merrill Lynch Option Volatility Estimate (MOVE) Index of short-term yield volatility is drawn from prices of options on US Treasury bonds.

Derivatives instruments have also been developed that let market participants take a view on future volatility, such as **variance swaps**, in which counterparties exchange payments depending on the difference between realized volatility over some period relative to a fixed rate determined at the initiation of the contract. Variance swaps are exposed to or hedge the volatility of volatility.

Implied correlations, the correlations between asset returns or credit events that are implied by prices of options, are analogous to implied volatilities. Index returns are a weighted average of the individual stock returns, and the volatility of index returns could be estimated using those weights together with estimates of the volatilities and pairwise correlations of the constituent stocks, the elements of their variance-covariance matrix. Implied correlations between stock price returns can be derived from observable option-implied volatilities on the individual stocks and on the equity indexes by assuming that all the pairwise correlations are the same. The implied correlation is the estimated uniform pairwise correlation found by equating the index implied volatility to that implied by the constituent weights.

Implied correlations can also be estimated in fixed income markets. Prices of credit default swaps on individual firms and on indexes imply a default correlation.[11] Implied volatilities of swaptions exercising into swaps of different maturities and of options on the spreads between swap rates of different maturities imply a probability of yield curve steepening or flattening.

6.3.3 Risk-Neutral Probability Distributions

Options embed expectations of future payoffs contingent on future prices, and their values imply a **risk-neutral probability distribution** of future prices. Risk-neutral distributions can be estimated for broad indexes and many other assets with relatively liquid options and forward or futures prices.

---

[11] See Chapter 14.

The difference between the prices of two options with different but closely spaced exercise prices is equal to the risk-neutral probability that the underlying price will end up in that interval when the option expires. In the Black-Scholes model, we can find the price of an option by assuming that the asset return follows a geometric Brownian motion with a known constant volatility. If we observe a dense enough set of option prices, we can reverse this logic, using the market prices of the options to draw inferences about the distribution rather than using a postulated distribution to find the option prices. We continue to assume that no arbitrage possibilities arise. Neighboring strike option prices then inform us as to the market's risk-neutral probability of ending between the two.

Example 6.5   Risk-neutral distribution of the EUR-USD exchange rate

Figure 6.2 displays the risk-neutral probability density of the EUR-USD exchange rate one month hence using prices of 1-month European options. Vols were much higher on March 15, 2023, than on May 10, 2021, leading to a more spread out distribution. The distribution has much thicker tails on the later date, that is, large-magnitude dollar appreciation as well as depreciation are viewed as more likely. On the earlier date, there is a skew to a weaker dollar, but on the later date, there is a skew to a stronger dollar.

Risk-neutral probabilities are valuable as a market-adjusted estimate of real-world probabilities but are a mix of unobservable expectations and risk preferences as filtered through the market. The price of an option can be high because it's expected to pay off handsomely or because there is expected to be a high correlation between high payoffs and bad economic outcomes. A high risk-neutral probability of a low future value of the S&P 500 could reflect the high state price of such an outcome rather than its likelihood. We can't discern directly empirically; the risk-neutral probabilities reflect both.

In principle, there is just one set of risk-neutral probabilities that applies to any asset and its future payoffs, just as does the stochastic discount factor. The risk-neutral probabilities are the same for all assets because they apply to future states of the world. In practice, estimated risk-neutral probabilities

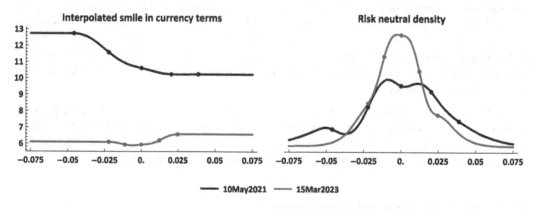

Figure 6.2 Risk-neutral distribution of the EUR-USD exchange rate

	≤ −5.0	≤ −2.5	≤ −1.0	≤ 0.0	≥ 1.0	≥ 2.5	≥ 5.0
15Mar2023	8.6	17.3	34.4	48.4	38.5	19.7	4.8
10May2021	0.2	8.0	27.5	51.5	25.1	9.3	0.5

Implied volatilities of 1-month European options on EUR-USD and risk-neutral probability density of 1-month changes in the EUR-USD exchange rate, in percent, as of 10May2021 and 15Mar2023. Points mark the option exercise prices, expressed as percent differences from the forward rate, and volatilities. Positive changes are EUR appreciation. *Data source*: Bloomberg.

pertain just to one asset. It's hard to identify the payoffs of any real-world observable asset with states of the world and therefore, hard to make the estimated probabilities uniform across assets: Is the event that the S&P 500 rises 3 percent over the next month identical to that in which the dollar rises 1 percent against the euro? Attempts to empirically measure the underlying stochastic discount factor therefore rely on risk-neutral distributions of broad stock indexes, so that states can be identified as total wealth or future consumption.

Further Reading

Introductions to derivatives markets and pricing include Neftci (2008) and Hull (2022). Derman and Miller (2016) and Taleb (1997) cover option pricing and trading. Demeterfi et al. (1999) explain variance swaps. Black et al. (1990) discuss pricing of interest rate options.

IHS Markit (2021) is an introduction to CDS and indices on them by IHS MarkIt, a CDS data provider now part of S&P Global. Boyarchenko et al. (2018b) describe the instruments and analyze the CDS-bond basis. Alternative Reference Rates Committee issued by a group of market participants advising the Federal Reserve, and Tuckman (2023) detail the issues involved in transitioning away from LIBOR reference rates in existing and new derivatives contracts.

Lloyd (2023) details the use of OIS to estimate market interest rate expectations. Fleckenstein et al. (2014) discuss the spread between bond- and swap-implied inflation expectations. Jackwerth (2004) surveys risk-neutral probability distributions. Malz (2014) provides a practical guide to estimation of risk-neutral distributions. Malz (2013) uses interest-rate implied correlations to assess the effect of central bank communication policy.

7

Capital Market Efficiency

Come, fill the South Sea goblet full;
The gods shall of our stock take care;
Europa pleased accepts the *Bull*,
And Jove with joy puts off the *Bear*.

Alexander Pope, "An Inscription upon a Punch-Bowl"[1]

Market efficiency is the proposition that observable asset prices are as close as possible to "correct," in the sense of incorporating all information or reflecting the asset's fundamental value. Efficiency implies a tendency for markets to diminish but not necessarily eliminate arbitrage opportunities. It is impossible to systematically earn "abnormal" returns—higher risk-adjusted returns than the market as a whole—without engaging in higher risk or bearing some cost. Information diffuses and influences market participants' buy and sell decisions fast enough that riskless arbitrage profits are unusual.

In the purist market efficiency viewpoint, held by precisely no one, markets clear smoothly and continuously and asset prices reflect all available information about the determinants of fundamental value at all times. But there are more nuanced views that allow for the messiness of markets in a friction-ridden real world. Nobody's view of the correct price is demonstrably superior to the market price. Prices act as signals even if they are not perfectly correct at any time. Information is partial, dispersed among many people, and constantly evolving. There is a tendency toward equilibrium, even if equilibrium is never actually reached as the world changes and knowledge grows.[2]

Correct price, like equilibrium, is a construct serving as a starting point for analysis of processes. In a less idealized formulation that can be tested empirically, the **efficient markets hypothesis** focuses on information rather than "correctness," maintaining that at any point in time, asset prices fully reflect all available information that is relevant to an asset's value.

7.1 Asset Price Behavior in an Efficient Market

Market efficiency has been a controversial topic for at least a century. The debate focuses on:

1. **Predictability:** Can future prices be forecast from past behavior?
2. **Active management:** Can investors consistently achieve above-market excess returns without taking on additional risk?

---

[1] Pope also provided this investment advice to a friend: "I was made acquainted late last night, that I might depend upon it as a certain gain, to Buy the South Sea-Stock at the present price, which will certainly rise in some weeks, or less. I can be as sure of this, as the nature of any such thing will allow, ..." See http://corsair.themorgan.org/vwebv/holdingsInfo?bibId=301686&v1=1.

[2] Black (1986) provides the rule of thumb that efficiency prevails if "price is within a factor of 2 of value."

A lot of trading is not required for prices to be informative. If new, adverse information surfaces implying a stock has a lower value than reflected in the current price, not many current owners of the stock have to sell. Potential buyers may instead step away from the market until there is a fall in the price that the market consensus views as adequate given the new information. Owners of the stock experience a fall in value. Some stock may change hands among a few market participants who have different views of what the new information implies, and a new transitory equilibrium is established.

7.1.1   Validating the Efficient Markets Hypothesis

Empirical evidence on market efficiency is drawn from many sources. Methodological difficulties are introduced by trading costs, return volatility, and changes in investors' expectations and risk appetite over time. Expectations theories are difficult to test because one can't observe expected future prices and rates. How fast market prices should adjust and how closely they should be to equilibrium to validate the efficient markets hypothesis isn't obvious.

Different definitions of "all information" are used in empirical tests. The **weak form** of the efficient markets hypothesis states that only clues offered by past prices are necessarily embedded in the current price. People involved in a business or an industry may, however, have information that isn't widely available and trade on it or share it with others. The **strong form** of the efficient markets hypothesis states that all public and private information influences prices.

Strong or weak form efficiency are used together with the rational expectations hypothesis to test for efficiency empirically. Among the measurable phenomena used in efficiency tests are:

Time series behavior of asset returns: past returns should contain no information that could help forecast future returns.

Return forecasts based on information variables: Do variables other than past returns—e.g., macroeconomic data or data on company fundamentals—help predict future returns?

Efficacy of active management by mutual and hedge funds: can managers systematically beat their benchmarks?

Event studies: new information coming to light, surprises, such as announcements of stock splits and mergers, should have a close to instantaneous and persistent impact on price and perhaps on volatility but not on subsequent returns.

Patterns of asset price behavior over time have a bearing on whether markets are efficient. The efficient markets hypothesis implies that returns are not predictable. Prices should have the martingale property and approximate a random walk, with return autocorrelations close to zero. The direction and magnitude of the next move must be a surprise. The current price is the best predictor of tomorrow's, and nothing is to be gained from trying to outguess it. Future prices will be based on the larger set of information available, but the additional information is unknowable now. Changes in the term structure don't help predict changes in rates, and today's bond yield is the best indicator of its likely return. A higher forward foreign exchange rate doesn't predict depreciation of the foreign currency.

Nonzero autocorrelations are more detectable at longer horizons. Returns themselves exhibit longer-term mean reversion. "Cheap" assets, those with unusually low recent returns, often have higher than normal returns over subsequent years. Prospective returns may be unusually high relative to measurable risk for some assets following overall market slumps or for heavily sold-off securities issued by some sectors and firms because macroeconomic conditions or recent price declines make them distasteful to many investors.

7.1.2   Market Efficiency, Preferences, and Knowledge

Market efficiency presumes rational decision making by market participants in some sense. The stronger assumption of rational expectations—that investors' subjective expectations of future asset values are equal to the best available statistical estimates—is a narrower interpretation of efficiency as well as of equilibrium. Even if expectations are formed rationally, investment choices and thus, asset prices are nonetheless determined by risk preferences and the entire distribution of outcomes and not just by their expected values. Aversion to large losses will make a stock with more downside risk cheaper. Market efficiency doesn't presume any patterns in preferences or that they are uniform across market participants.

Many deviations of price from fundamental value can be identified from the standpoint of particular asset pricing models or valuation approaches. In the behavioral finance approach, these **anomalies** (or "puzzles") are interpreted as departures from rationality and evidence against market efficiency rather than illustrating the often clumsy market adjustment process. Behavioral finance views market participants' choices as influenced by numerous cognitive and emotional biases.

As in other areas of finance and the social sciences generally, data mining is a pitfall. It is possible to sift through large amounts of data and find anomalies that pass statistical significance tests. But anomalies are not systematically exploitable for risk-adjusted excess returns, and many dissipate once discovered.

A persistent puzzle identified in behavioral finance as an anomaly is the **excess volatility** of asset prices compared to that of their fundamental determinants or cash flows. Stock returns have higher volatility than subsequent dividend yields, violating variance bound tests. Foreign exchange rates display higher volatility than money market rates and local price levels. Return volatility is hard to correlate empirically with the arrival of new information.

These anomalies don't, however, present arbitrage opportunities exploitable by simultaneously buying and selling near-identical assets at different prices, but involve risk-taking. A model of risk is required to adjudicate empirically whether excess return volatility is to be explained as a result of "irrational" fluctuations in sentiment or by changes in risk appetites. The source of equity volatility may be expected fluctuations in cash flows, such as dividends that fail to materialize or **time-varying risk premiums**, with people shunning or seeking risk based on their own prospects for steady employment or business. Both can drive fluctuations in asset prices seemingly unrelated to cash returned by assets.

A similar debate applies over the existence of **bubbles**, defined as a rapid appreciation in an asset price not justified by fundamental value. Because they culminate in a severe drop in price, they are also episodes of extreme volatility. In the view of behavioral finance, the phenomenon is recurrent and reflects market inefficiency or irrational behavior. Putative examples have been chronicled over the centuries but do not generally stand up to closer scrutiny.

The argument for bubbles as a real phenomenon is empirically weak. It requires that investors be able to identify bubbles while they are happening. But bubbles have not been detected *ex ante*, while asset prices are still high and rising, but only in hindsight after they've fallen. In many supposed bubbles, moreover, historical ones, such as the so-called tulip mania of the 17th century, John Law's Mississippi Company in the 18th century, and modern episodes of rapidly increasing stock prices such as GameStop in 2021, it's not clear that price rises were detached from fundamental value.

In some definitions of the phenomenon, at least some buyers are aware of the overvaluation but are confident that they can liquidate their positions at an even higher price. In such **rational bubbles**, price dynamics play out in which rational buyers planning to sell tomorrow drive up the price, retroactively validating their expectations, and permitting the bubble to continue for some finite period. An example are "crowded trades" of short-term investors in which an unusual fraction of the tradable volume of an asset is held by short-term investors aiming to liquidate at a higher price. Such positions have high risk of loss but may benefit from information about positioning in the market and are not evidence of self-validating price dynamics unconnected to fundamental value.

Testing for excess volatility and bubbles are examples of the joint hypothesis problem in empirical testing of return models. Tests of efficiency are also tests of the model that defines the "correct" price. Changes in prices must be compared with models that explain any time-varying risk premium based on changes in financial or macroeconomic conditions. Rejection of the joint hypothesis—market efficiency plus the pricing model—entails rejection of the efficiency model, the pricing model, or both. Finding abnormally high returns to a trading strategy may just reflect inadequacies of the model in capturing risk preferences.

Another anomaly is large trading volumes in financial markets, which are attributed in part to irrational investor behavior. Trading motivations are often classified into a simple dichotomy between informed and uninformed, with the latter labeled somewhat dismissively as **noise traders**. Others are termed **information traders**, well-informed because they're privy to investment research or inside information not yet filtered into prices. They have a view on value.[3]

What is viewed as noise trading, however, plays a role in efficient pricing. Retail and institutional investors may have no nonpublic information, but good reasons to trade, such as portfolio allocation, reallocation to or from cash, hedging, tax motivations, or mimicking an index. Still other retail traders may trade as a leisure activity or for emotional satisfaction and not just in response to information or "rationally." Their trading activity adds to market liquidity and facilitates price adjustment.

7.2   Apparent Violations of Market Efficiency

7.2.1   Slow Arbitrage

Markets clear but not instantaneously. Market frictions introduce a range of impediments to instantaneous, smooth arbitrage. The market process requires time, costly search, and information gathering, and it imposes transactions costs and risk on market participants. During that process, reality changes disruptively, and market participants gather information even as it is becoming outdated. What appears as inefficiency or anomalies is the market process at work reducing arbitrage opportunities.

The equilibrium price itself is not observable, changes over time, and can also be influenced by market participants through their own actions. These realities pose **limits to arbitrage** and make **slow arbitrage** rewarded with profits the rule. Constant change and slow arbitrage keep prices perpetually approaching but never reaching equilibrium.

Investors have distinct appetites for risk and time horizons over which they assess returns, different types of asset managers and institutional investors have distinct clienteles, and similar securities may be regulated in different ways, leading to **market segmentation**. For example, some investors, such as pension funds, may prefer long-term bonds (their "preferred habitat"), and equities may trade in markets with different market-clearing mechanisms. Risk premiums for some assets, anomalies in relative asset prices, and the responses to market shocks may then be larger and more persistent. "Patient capital" of investors with a long horizon and low propensity to change positions is

---

[3] Black (1995) distinguished between "news" and "nice" traders.

scarce, and portfolios with significant differences from benchmarks may capture such arbitrage profits. Some traders may be constrained by a limited ability to borrow to fund near-arbitrage trades.

In a theoretical perfectly efficient market, no one can be remunerated for the cost and effort of information gathering. The **Grossman-Stiglitz Paradox** concludes that markets cannot be perfectly efficient but rather exhibit gradual price adjustment and transitory deviations from equilibrium. Asset prices reflect available information to the extent that the profits from acting on it are greater than the cost of obtaining the information. In this view, however, information is treated as extant but costly to obtain rather than yet to be discovered.

7.2.2   Basis Spreads

A number of perceived anomalies in financial markets are differences in pricing between similar financial instruments. In more liquid markets, there may be a small price differential, a **basis**, or **basis spread**, between near-identical exposures. They seem more anomalous than spreads compensating for credit or term interest rate risk, which can be attributed to differences in risk. The distinction between a spread and a basis is imprecise, and the label on a price difference is in part a matter of convention. Some bases arise in futures markets and for securities that are issued on a regular schedule, generating assets that are not identical but close substitutes. The extent of the difference varies as issuance or maturity dates draw closer.

Examples abound:

Treasury basis: price difference between cash Treasurys and the typically slightly higher price of the futures contract. They typically converge over the life of the futures. The basis is partly explainable by uncertainty about exactly which Treasury note or bond will be cheapest to deliver among those eligible.

Commodity futures basis: the difference between spot and futures prices. For example, crude oil futures may be higher or lower than spot prices.

Cross-currency basis: In foreign exchange markets, spot rates and money market rates are generally consistent with covered interest rate parity, which states that international interest rate differentials are equal to the forward premium. But there are persistent deviations.

On-the-run/off-the-run spread: differences in yield between the most recent and earlier issues of Treasury notes. They result from the US Treasury's auction calendar for its debt securities. The most liquid bonds and notes (on-the-run) enjoy better market liquidity and therefore, slightly lower yields than very similar ones issued at earlier auctions (off-the-run).

CDS-bond basis: differences in a given firm's credit spread implied by its bond prices and by prices of CDS of the same maturity.

These gaps are kept small through **basis trades**, in which traders take a long position in the relatively expensive exposure and short the relatively cheap one, in the expectation that the gap is likelier to narrow than widen further. These trades are frequently highly leveraged. The Treasury basis trade, for example, involves taking a short position in the futures and a long position in the underlying Treasury notes, financed in large part in the repo market.

The persistence of a basis can best be understood as the result of transactions costs, the time it can take to gather information, place offsetting trades to take advantage of a basis, the potentially limited availability of funding for such trades, and the risk and uncertainty involved. Some financial instruments involved in a basis spread may be relatively illiquid, increasing the time and cost of arbitrage. Some assets, particularly physical commodities, may be in different geographical locations.

Basis trades have low return and low return volatility most of the time but are vulnerable to sudden extreme losses.

There are usually many traders actively searching for a basis spread large enough to be worth exploiting, so basis spreads are fairly small in most markets most of the time. Market segmentation and limitations on liquidity, however, may lead to a larger spread or basis vis-à-vis an index, for example, due to higher US dollar borrowing costs for non-US banks or dealers turning cautious.

In some cases, a basis may evolve into a spread. The LOIS spread—the difference, before the transition from LIBOR, between term interbank money market rates and prices of derivatives serving the same function of locking in a lending rate for one or three months—was narrow and apt to widen only sporadically before the global financial crisis. After 2007, it behaved more as a spread, persistently wide and understood to compensate for banks' default risk of which markets had become far more conscious.

7.2.3   Foreign Exchange Markets

Exchange rates are unpredictable in the short term. Exchange rate forecasts based on fundamental data are no more accurate than random walk forecasts, and persistently successful trading systems are rare. Foreign exchange markets are similar to other asset markets in displaying rough market efficiency. Nonetheless, there are some persistent anomalies in foreign exchange markets.

Uncovered or **open interest rate parity** states that interest rate differentials are equal to the expected appreciation or depreciation of one currency against another. The foreign exchange risk premium is assumed to be zero, the realized spot rate at maturity is expected to equal the current forward rate, and the expected change in the exchange rate over the next τ years is equal to the interest rate differential:

$$\frac{\mathbf{E}[S_{t,t+\tau}] - S_t}{S_t} = \frac{F_{t,\tau}}{S_t} = \left(\frac{1 + r_{t,\tau}}{1 + r_{t,\tau}^*}\right)^{\tau},$$

with S_t, $S_{t,t+\tau}$, and $F_{t,\tau}$ the spot and τ-year future spot and forward exchange rates, and $r_{t,\tau}$ and $r_{t,\tau}^*$ the local and foreign money market rates. If the local rate is higher, the local price of foreign currency should rise and the exchange rate depreciate.

Myriad empirical studies have concluded that uncovered parity does not hold. Currencies with higher interest rates often appreciate rather than depreciate against currencies with lower rates. This foreign exchange, or Fama, puzzle, includes exchange rates among developed as well as developing-market currencies.[4] The failure of uncovered parity supports the trade thesis of foreign exchange carry trades (see Chapter 11), that the interest rate differential captured through transactions in foreign exchange and money markets is unlikely to be be entirely offset by exchange rate depreciation.

Uncovered parity is difficult to test, even compared to other assets, due to the "peso problem." The sudden abandonment of fixed-exchange rate levels by monetary authorities leads to large, sudden, but infrequent jumps in exchange rates. Exchange rates are also subject to overshooting as a result of divergences between different countries' monetary policies. When a central bank raises interest rates, for example, a country's exchange rate tends to appreciate sharply initially and then depreciate

---

[4] See Fama (2014). Mussa (1979) concludes his survey of the failure of foreign exchange forecasting models, including uncovered parity: "A model that was able to explain more than 50 percent of quarter-to-quarter changes in exchange rates should either be rejected on the grounds that it is too good to be true or should be reported to the Vatican as a miracle justifying the canonization of a new saint."

gradually as domestic prices fall relative to those in other currencies and equilibrium is established at a higher real exchange rate than initially prevailed.

Covered interest rate parity (see Chapter 6) states that international interest rate differentials are equal to forward foreign exchange premiums. Market segmentation gives rise to the cross-currency basis, which is a recurrent violation of covered interest parity. The arbitrage requires access to money markets in both currencies, which banks and traders not domiciled in the United States may lack.[5]

7.3   Efficacy of Active Management

7.3.1   Passive and Active Investment Management

Much of the research on market efficiency compares active to passive investment management. **Passive management** or **investing** in a narrower sense refers to a strategy of holding the value-weighted market portfolio as the investor's only risky asset at all times, implemented by investing in a broad stock market index fund. In the CAPM, doing so diversifies away idiosyncratic risk. There is no source of returns to security-specific analysis. Like the CAPM, passive management also faces the problem of defining the market portfolio. The term "passive management" is also used more broadly to refer to strategies that deviate moderately from the value-weighted market portfolio by applying "tilts," such as value or growth, based on multi-factor models. It is applied even more broadly to mutual funds or ETFs that consistently follow a specific strategy.

Active management is an approach to investing that aims to achieve risk-adjusted excess returns after trading costs by holding a portfolio different from the market portfolio or from a specific benchmark. Active managers claim that, apart from compensation for taking risk ("beta"), they can, by dint of superior information and skill, exploit inefficiencies in capital markets and achieve above-market, risk-adjusted returns ("alpha"). An investment advisor may claim the ability to identify active managers capable of earning higher risk-adjusted excess returns than the market or benchmark. Predictive ability includes the ability to forecast relative asset prices based on security-specific analysis, or "stock picking," and **market timing**, meaning skill in forecasting returns.

Several trends have reduced the dominance of active management in advanced market economies while also leading to overall growth in the investment management business. With growing wealth and diversification away from residential housing, individual ownership of liquid assets, directly and through mutual and exchange-traded funds, has increased. The relative role of institutional investors such as insurance companies and defined benefit pension funds has declined. With the introduction of index mutual funds in the 1970s, passive investment strategies became more practicable for households and for professional investment managers. The volume of passive investment funds has grown enormously over recent decades, particularly those mimicking broad stock indexes.

A fund's returns can be measured **gross** or **net** of management fees and other costs borne by the investor, including the administrative, office, salary, and trading expenses of the manager. In a static world in which the market portfolio doesn't change and in which no investors need to buy or sell, **equilibrium accounting**, or the **arithmetic of active management**, prevails. It states that investors' gross returns in aggregate must equal those of the market portfolio.

Because passive investors by definition hold the market portfolio, active investors must on average at all times also hold the market portfolio. The gross return to active management before fees and costs is zero. The above-market returns of some active managers must be offset by below-market returns of others. In aggregate, passive investors earn the value-weighted return and pay very low management costs. Active managers' net returns, after fees, must be negative, and their investors on average must underperform the market portfolio and passive investors.

In the evolving real world, investors buy and sell assets to establish portfolios, reallocate, obtain liquidity, and consume in retirement. The market portfolio is changing as new assets emerge or others cease to exist. Firms distribute cash at discrete times through dividend payments and stock issuance and buybacks. A large portion of traded assets are illiquid investments readily available to investment managers, such as private equity funds, but not to investors at large. Investors cannot at every instant hold the value-weighted market portfolio.

Genuine opportunities to earn above-market returns after fees are then possible but limited. If they arise, such opportunities will eventually attract investors, most of whom will invest via an asset manager charging fees. The capacity of any trade thesis to yield excess returns is limited as market prices adjust toward equilibrium. As opportunities are exploited and more widely recognized, the returns diminish toward the market portfolio norm, and a higher proportion of the excess return is absorbed into the fees of the active manager. Skill-based risk-adjusted excess returns, if they exist, may accrue largely or entirely to the investment manager through fees. Any excess returns are limited and competed away over time, though new opportunities constantly arise.

Active managers with authentic skill likely exist but are a small subset of the active managers who believe they possess skill. The exercise of skill requires additional costs of information and analysis and requires time to come to fruition. Investors lack ability to identify managers with skill *ex ante*. Active departures from the market portfolio often involve exposure to additional risk factors and don't earn risk-adjusted excess return: "There is no 'alpha.' There is just beta you understand and beta you do not understand[.]"[6]

7.3.2   Empirical Validation of Active Management

There is little evidence that active professional management pays off for investors. Claims by active asset managers that they can "beat the market" are weak. There are several ways to assess these claims. One is to see whether active managers as a whole have achieved higher risk-adjusted returns than the market portfolio. Another is to identify successful trading rules, with systematic approaches that persistently yield risk-adjusted excess returns. In spite of evidence of some short- and longer-term predictability and the autocorrelation of functions of returns, few such trading rules have been identified, and whether they are authentically superior after adjusting for risk and trading costs is debatable. Managers may trade frequently solely to suggest they have superior information.

It is challenging to distinguish between persistent skill and luck because any set of active managers will have a range of outcomes over any past interval, including some with above-market returns, even if they underperform the market on average. Some active managers undoubtedly possess skill but are thinly dispersed among a much larger group of active managers without it.

Other empirical challenges to verifying the efficacy of active management include identifying the comparison market portfolio or benchmark, the time frame chosen, and **survivorship bias**, the fact that many underperforming funds close and may be removed from datasets. Large-scale studies of

---

[6] Cochrane (2011), p. 1087.

fund performance focus on mutual funds, which are more numerous and for which data are more readily available, rather than hedge funds or other managers.

Many studies over the course of decades indicate that the average actively managed mutual fund has lower net returns than market indexes. The degree of underperformance is generally found to be comparable to management expenses. These results are also confirmed by the annual S&P 500 Indices Versus Active (SPIVA) Scorecard, which finds that in most years, a majority of US large-cap domestic equity mutual funds underperforms the S&P 500 index. The underperformance tends to worsen as the time horizon lengthens from 1 to 5 years.[7] Over very long periods comparable to the investment horizons of most investors, the underperformance is dramatic. One study assesses the cost to US investors at over $1 trillion between 1991 and 2020.

A formal framework for measuring active management performance overall is to compare active managers' monthly or annual returns to the performance of a model or to a set of benchmarks of market return represented by a vector $\mathbf{x}$, the constituent variables of which can be thought of as factors or indexes. In the CAPM, $\mathbf{x}$ would be a single variable, the market portfolio and in the Fama-French three-factor model, the value and growth factors would also be included.

If a manager can predictably and reliably achieve higher excess returns than the market, then in a time series regression of manager j's excess returns $r_{jt} - r_t^f$ on the factors $\mathbf{x}$:

$$r_{jt} - r_t^f = \alpha_j + \mathbf{x}_t \boldsymbol{\beta}_j + u_{jt}, \qquad t = 1, \dots, T,$$

the estimated $\hat{\alpha}_j$ is likely to be positive. An active manager underperforms if $\hat{\alpha}_j < 0$. The excess return $r_{jt} - r_t^f$ can be measured gross or net.

There is a great deal of variability in managers' and market factor returns. We can't expect $\hat{\alpha}_j > 0$ for every manager j even if they are efficacious as a group. Rather, the result will be a distribution of estimated $\hat{\alpha}_j$. Observing $\hat{\alpha}_j > 0$ for a preponderance of managers would be inconsistent with efficiency.

To discern if a significant fraction of managers "beat the market," we focus on the t-statistic $t(\hat{\alpha}_j)$, which tells us whether the distribution of the measured alphas as a whole is skewed toward outperformance or not. The t-statistic is calculated by normalizing $\hat{\alpha}_j$, dividing it by its standard error $\sigma(\hat{\alpha}_j)$:

$$t(\hat{\alpha}_j) = \frac{\hat{\alpha}_j}{s(\hat{\alpha}_j)}.$$

If active manager performance typically matches the benchmark $\mathbf{x}$, then the distribution of manager t-statistics will closely resemble a standard normal variate $\mathcal{N}(0,1)$, with a mean of zero. If, however, active managers on the whole or a significant fraction outperform, the distribution of $t(\hat{\alpha}_j)$ will have a positive mean or at least be skewed to positive values. Positive skew would indicate that at least a fraction of managers substantially outperform the benchmark model, and a smaller fraction underperform the model.

The evidence is not favorable for active management outperformance. Figure 7.1 illustrates typical findings, comparing the actual distribution of active manager t-statistics to the distribution one would expect if the claims were true. The $t(\hat{\alpha}_j)$ don't generally look like a sample from a standard normal. The mean of the distribution of $t(\hat{\alpha}_j)$ using gross returns is close to zero. The mean of the distribution

---

[7] See, for example, S&P Dow Jones Indices (2023).

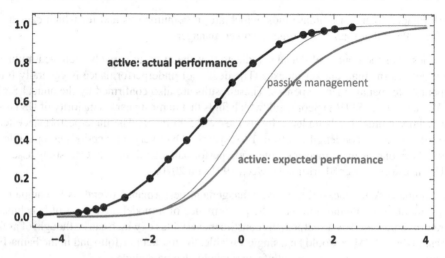

Figure 7.1 Evidence on active management outperformance

Stylized representation of the empirical results in the Jensen (1968) and other papers comparing active mutual fund returns to benchmark models. The data points are from Table III of Fama and French (2010) and displays percentiles of *t*-statistics for net returns of actively managed US equity mutual funds with assets under management (AUM) in excess of $ 1 bill. The plots represent the distribution functions of *t*-statistics of fund managers' returns. Returns are measured on the *x*-axis in standard deviations of managers' excess returns over returns on value-weighted market portfolio, with excess returns measured net of investment management costs. The **gray** plot displays the expected empirical result if active management results in outperformance: a positive mean or a skew to outperformance. The **black** plot displays the actual empirical result: active management has a *negative* mean and a skew to surprisingly large *underperformance*. The thin **gray** displays results for the benchmark, i.e., the broad indexers.

using net returns is negative. Even worse, the distribution of $t(\hat{\alpha}_j)$ using gross or net returns is skewed to large *negative* values, indicating an investor is more likely to end up with a very bad than a very good outcome.[8]

Active managers perform worse than if their performance relative to benchmarks were entirely random. The results indicate that the typical active manager doesn't outperform the market even before management costs are taken into account. From their clients' standpoint, the managers are well behind the market once management fees and cost are taken into account.[9] The overall cost to investors as a whole, the bulk of whom are retail mutual fund and institutional investors, has been estimated at about 67 basis points.

Another approach to validating the efficacy of active management focuses on long-term returns, which are closer to the investment approach of most households and institutional investors. The average longer-term underperformance of actively managed mutual funds compared to broad indexes appears to be even worse than for short-term returns apart from the impact of volatility drag on longer-term results compared to the average annual arithmetic return. However, managers' longer-term returns may have positive skewness brought about by skewness in the returns of individual stocks, leading to high excess returns of a relatively small handful of outperforming managers in the large pool. The effect of skewness in the returns of individual stocks is amplified by the effect of compounding, which is most pronounced for the highest-returning stocks.[10] The compounding effect grows with time, indicating that some managers' skill is aided by patient long-term investor funding.

---

[8] This result echoes Cowles (1933), 324, who tested to see if market forecasting works: "There is some evidence ... to indicate that the least successful records are worse than what could reasonably be attributed to chance."

[9] Fama and French (2010), from which Figure 7.1 is drawn, exclude load, other sales charges, or commissions that further reduce investor return, so these results are tilted in favor of active management.

[10] See, for example, Bessembinder et al. (2023).

The plausibility of any individual active manager's claim of abnormal returns is hard to validate, given how widely returns vary over time. Many years of observations are required to establish individual active manager efficacy with high confidence. Suppose a market index x is used as the benchmark, and a fund manager claims the ability to beat the market by an α of 3 percent annually. This would be a relatively modest claim on the part of the manager, as the excess over the market would barely cover typical active manager fees. The manager's return over the benchmark is then y, given by

$$y = \alpha + \beta x,$$

with β the beta of the manager's excess return relative to that of the benchmark. In a regression estimate endeavoring to validate the claim that $\alpha = 0.03$, the square of the standard error $s_{\hat{\alpha}}^2$ of $\hat{\alpha}$ is:[11]

$$s_{\hat{\alpha}}^2 = (1 - R^2)s_Y^2 \frac{1}{T}\left(1 + \frac{\bar{X}^2}{s_X^2}\right),$$

where $\bar{X}$ is the sample mean of the benchmark return, s_Y^2 and s_X^2 are the sample variances of the manager's and benchmark returns, and R^2 the square of their correlation. In any real-world case, it would take many observations over time to reduce $s_{\hat{\alpha}}^2$ enough to make the $\hat{\alpha}$ estimate useful.

Example 7.1   Validating the efficacy of an individual active manager

Suppose an individual mutual or hedge fund manager claims the ability to achieve an excess return greater than that of the market portfolio. Assume further that the manager is able to achieve this together with other desirable return characteristics: a relatively low correlation to the market portfolio of 0.5 and a return volatility that is no higher than that of the market. This is a generous starting point: any individual active manager likely has a higher s_Y^2 than the average.

Assume an annual market return of 6 percent and a market return volatility of about 20 percent. The assumptions regarding excess returns and return volatilities, expressed as decimals, are:

Claimed α (monthly)	0.0025
Active fund correlation to market	0.50
Active fund β to market	0.25
Active fund return volatility (monthly)	0.050
Market portfolio expected excess return (monthly)	0.0050
Market portfolio return volatility (monthly)	0.055

We want to test the hypothesis $\alpha = 3$ percent annually, or 25 bps/month, against a null hypothesis that $\alpha = 0$. To reject the null hypothesis at a 95 percent confidence level requires, given the parameters we've assumed, T years of time series data on the manager's performance, where T is the solution to

$$1.96 \leq \frac{\hat{\alpha}}{s(\hat{\alpha})} = \frac{0.0025}{\sqrt{\frac{0.5 \times 0.050^2}{12T}\left(1 + \frac{0.0050^2}{0.055^2}\right)}}.$$

---

[11] Ignoring the term $\frac{T-1}{T-2}$ for simplicity. See Appendix A for the exact expression and the derivation.

In our example, 96.8 years are needed to obtain a test statistic significant at a 95 percent confidence level. If the manager makes the less modest claim of a 6 percent excess return, or double that of the market, the time needed is reduced to $T = 24.2$ years.

Empirical data overwhelmingly indicate that observed mutual fund outperformance is not persistent. Investors in public and private investment funds that "chase returns," investing in vehicles that have shown recent above-market returns, are unlikely on that basis to successfully earn positive alpha. The "winners" in any period are generally not the winners in subsequent periods. Short-term outperformance tends to draw additional investors to a fund, who are more likely than not to underperform the market portfolio.

7.3.3   Alternative Investments

Alternative investment managers make two key claims for their services, neither entirely well founded empirically. One is the ability to achieve alpha, or to earn higher excess returns, on a risk-adjusted basis and after fees and management costs compared to other assets. Hedge funds may claim superior stock selection or market timing ability, the latter often framed as skill in "rotation" between sectors or strategies. Alternatives are also claimed to provide a diversification benefit, that is, a low correlation or beta to public stock markets, reducing portfolio volatility without sacrifice of return when combined up to some level with traditional investments.

Generalization about alternative investments is difficult due to data issues and the number and variety of funds. Fund return data exhibit survivorship bias and are inconsistent and error-prone due to self-reporting and other problems. Common excess return measures use broad equity indexes as a benchmark, but funds may have very different exposures to the market portfolio. Comparisons with public market returns must take account of the risk profile of alternative investments. Some measured alpha may only be apparent and more accurately attributable to other priced factors or to additional risk taken on in hard-to-detect ways that fall outside the CAPM framework used to measure alpha.

Alternative asset returns have to be assessed from an investor point of view, net of the high investment fees charged explicitly and other investment costs. Fees on alternative funds are particularly high and, for private equity, complex. A charge of 1 to 2 percent on the total invested or committed, and between 15 and 25 percent on any growth, is typical. Alternative funds' underlying investments are generally highly illiquid because the positions themselves have low market liquidity or because trading portfolios cannot be readily disassembled and liquidated. Investors in alternatives should therefore earn a liquidity premium.

Private equity investments are long-term, and data on private equity vehicles that have come to fruition are sparse. The typical lifespan of a private equity fund is 10 years. The cash flows are complex: investors commit to investing a sum of money, but much or all is not invested immediately. Rather, the investor agrees to have the full amount drawn sporadically over an interval which may span many years. Investors must maintain relatively liquid assets to meet these capital calls. The timing of returns is equally uncertain with some funds returning capital relatively quickly and others requiring much longer.

Much of the data on private equity pertain to vehicles still earning returns. Their performance can't be accurately assessed before enough time has elapsed since their "vintage year". Measurement issues may enable the reporting to magnify returns. The returns are not based on market prices but on valuations the managers themselves provide. This impact is exacerbated by the use of the internal rate of return (IRR) as a valuation measure, which permits managers to project growth in valuations early in a fund's life, long before the investments have had an opportunity to mature, into a distant future. IRR calculations assume that future cash flows before liquidation of an investment can be reinvested at the computed IRR. They tend to amplify the returns of short-lived funds and overstate the returns of funds that have long remaining cash flows. The **public market equivalent**, a valuation in which past and projected cash flows are assumed to be invested in public stock markets, typically shows lower returns.

Comparing public market and alternative returns is complicated and there is considerable variation in the conclusions drawn by different studies. Findings on the degree of hedge fund return correlation to public markets come to particularly divergent conclusions. The results depend on the dataset, the categories of hedge fund or private equity firm included, the time period studied, and the public market indexes with which their returns are compared.

Private equity and hedge fund returns appear to have experienced two phases since attaining significant size. In their first few decades, ending sometime around 2005, alternatives may have achieved significantly higher returns than public markets net of fees. Since then, they have had gross returns closer to those of the market and equal or possibly below those of public markets once fees are netted out.

Hedge funds and private equity returns may be due in part to their risk-taking and costly information gathering. Hedge funds as well as private equity firms add risk through leverage, directly or embedded via derivatives. Prime brokerage offices of broker dealers and banks extend credit to hedge funds, through short-term lending collateralized by the securities in which the funds are taking positions and as counterparties of derivatives transactions. Private equity leverage is taken on largely through syndicated bank loans to the firms in their portfolios.

Private equity engages in highly illiquid markets and carries out entrepreneurial functions. Part of private equity returns is attributable to entrepreneurial discovery that is particularly hard to quantify. Venture capital funds invest in new companies, and part of their return is a reward for successfully identifying, in aggregate, firms with high entrepreneurial profit opportunities. Merger and acquisition excess returns may reflect skill in identifying highly illiquid and misallocated corporate assets and managerial skill in organizing firms.

Especially since the global financial crisis and retrenchment by banks,[12] hedge funds have taken on a greater role in near-arbitrage involving basis spreads and in exploiting short-term predictable patterns in prices, that is, deviations from zero first-order autocorrelation. They also identify possible mispricing and align prices more accurately with fundamental value. Long-short strategies, for example, involve fundamental analysis that some market participants have to carry out if prices are to align with fundamental value.

Returns to hedge fund strategies often have highly nonlinear responses to observable prices, indexes, and factors, earning steady above-benchmark returns during normal times and suffering large and widespread losses during periods of market stress. The cross-section of hedge funds appears to have a very wide distribution of returns, with a good number having large losses at some point. This increases the risk to potential investors and makes historical return data, even over several years, less useful in assessing performance.

Private equity and hedge fund valuations may be deliberately smoothed or at least come out of a calculation process which is insulated from market fluctuations. If broad stock indexes decline by 1 percent, private equity and credit fund valuations are unlikely to decline by as much even if they are

---

[12] See Chapters 19 and 20.

equally exposed to the market factor. Therefore, they will display a low beta and a low volatility, an impact called **volatility laundering**.

A simple strategy that illustrates nonlinear exposures with embedded leverage and high downside risk is to invest the NAV of a fund in a broad stock market index while at the same time writing out-of-the-money puts and calls against the stock portfolio. The option premium will, in most measurement periods, add to return. In a small number of periods, however, the entire portfolio of stock index units and short puts will experience extreme losses. The fund is not exercising active management. Rather, it is carrying out a simple, well-known, rote strategy. For hedge funds and private equity, there is a strong finding that returns can be replicated by similar strategies employing options or leverage. Replication may be partly responsible for a general decline in hedge fund returns over the past two decades.[13]

Example 7.2   Juicing returns by writing options

Consider a fund in which investors initially place $100, with four different strategies for deploying the investments over time. All include investing $100 in the S&P 500 index, and three add a program of writing three-month 10 percent out-of-the-money European options on a notional amount of the S&P 500 index equal to the current value of the portfolio: puts alone, calls alone, or both puts and calls—a short strangle—with a notional underlying equal to the portfolio value. Assume for simplicity that the S&P 500 index position is sufficient margin for the strategies that include option writing.

At the beginning of the initial and each subsequent quarter, the option-writing strategies invest the option premium in additional S&P 500 units, and from the beginning of the second quarter onward, any losses incurred because the written options expire in-the-money are funded by selling S&P 500 units. The notional amount of the option strategies is limited to the number of S&P 500 index units held at the beginning of the period.

Table 7.1 displays the results, and Figure 7.2 plots the returns to the option writing strategies. The returns to the strategies combining put or put and call writing with a position in the

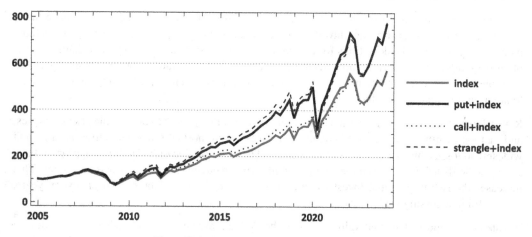

Figure 7.2 Returns to option writing strategies

Cumulative value of an initial $100 invested in the index and strategies combining the index with writing out-of-the-money call and puts, Q1 2005 to Q4 2023.

---

[13] Lo (2001) uses a similar replication strategy for his fictitious Decimation Partners LLP illustration. A similar exercise by He et al. (2015) has more positive results.

Table 7.1 Returns to option writing strategies

	index	put	call	straddle
Mean quarterly arithmetic return	2.68	3.33	2.64	3.29
Cumulative annualized arithmetic return	9.54	11.30	9.55	11.36
Mean quarterly logarithmic return	2.29	2.69	2.29	2.70
Mean quarterly arithmetic excess return	2.33	2.99	2.29	2.94
Standard deviation of quarterly arithmetic excess return	8.57	10.74	7.97	10.14
Sharpe ratio	0.83	0.90	0.84	0.90
Minimum return	−23.72	−37.41	−23.68	−37.37
Maximum return	26.73	33.80	14.91	21.99
0.05 quantile of returns	−15.51	−20.15	−15.32	−19.97
0.95 quantile of returns	14.71	16.29	12.09	15.46
Coefficient of skewness	−0.69	−1.08	−1.11	−1.51
Coefficient of kurtosis	4.29	6.18	4.15	6.41

Data from Q1 2005 to Q4 2023. Returns are expressed in percent. The Sharpe ratio is based on annualized quarterly returns and volatility. The option strategies all combine long positions in the S&P 500 index and 3-month out-of-the-money European options with a notional underlying value equal to the index position. The option prices are derived from Bloomberg implied volatility smile data. *Data source*: Bloomberg.

index have significantly higher excess returns than the index alone. But they also have higher volatility, larger extreme losses as well as gains, and a barely higher Sharpe ratio. All three of the option writing strategies have high correlations to the index and would provide little diversification benefit in an institutional investor portfolio.

Interestingly, the call writing and index strategy has slightly lower returns than those of the index alone. The call premiums are generally much lower than those of the put due to the volatility smirk. Bearish index implied volatilities and option prices are much higher than bullish ones. The call premiums don't suffice to make up for the occasional large increases in the S&P index level, which generally follow immediately on sharp losses in the index.

Market Episode: The Allianz Global Investors Structured Alpha strategies

Allianz Global Investors (Allianz GI) is a US subsidiary of German insurance company Allianz. It followed a strategy, marketed as "Structured Alpha," similar in structure to the index option positions described in the example above. The strategy involved even higher outright and embedded leverage than that of the example because it was not linked to a large underlying position in the underlying index itself. Apart from the sold option positions, Allianz GI also stated that it would maintain deeper in-the-money long put option positions to limit losses in the event of an extreme decline in the index. The funds' investors consisted largely of public defined benefit retirement funds.

In March 2020, the funds experienced losses estimated at over $5 billion. A note sent to clients in April indicates the funds had liquidated positions at a large loss rather than risk further losses. Its long put protection was close to 35 percent out-of-the-money. The put options were cheap, but losses would be extremely high well before the puts afforded effective protection. A number of the retirement funds that had invested in them brought lawsuits alleging fraud, in particular false reporting of P&L and misleading marketing descriptions of the strategy. The SEC also initiated proceedings against Allianz GI, which settled the lawsuits and with the SEC in May 2022, and pleaded guilty to having defrauded the pension funds.

The risk of sporadic, extreme losses, together with the wide dispersion of hedge fund returns, high investment fees, and questionable excess returns and diversification benefits vis-à-vis the market portfolio have implications for the **endowment model** adopted by many institutional investors. It calls for a substantial allocation to a number of different private equity and hedge fund managers. Investors have found it difficult and costly to assemble a portfolio of alternative investments with superior risk-adjusted net returns that mitigates the high idiosyncratic risk of large losses in any single fund.[14]

Further Reading

Fama (1970) introduced the concept of market efficiency and defend it empirically. Grossman and Stiglitz (1980) clarified the role of information costs, reflected in the later Fama (1991) presentation of efficient markets theory. Malkiel (2003) and Fama (2014) summarize the empirical evidence.

Market efficiency tests of future returns and volatility based on historical return data or on implied volatilities are described in Campbell et al. (1997), and Poon and Granger (2003) and 2005. A recent example is Liu and Xie (2023). Krasker (1980) was an early formulation of the "peso problem" in assessing foreign exchange market efficiency.

Kahneman et al. (1991), Barberis and Thaler (2003), Kahneman (2002), and Shiller (2003) are overviews of behavioral economics and financial market anomalies. Schwert (2003) finds many anomalies to be ephemeral, becoming less pronounced once identified and named.

The relationships and debates among bounded rationality and behavioral economics are set out in Gigerenzer (2018). Shleifer and Vishny (1997) and Black (1986) discuss limited, slow, and near-arbitrage in overall efficient markets. Mitchell et al. (2007) discuss several episodes illustrating the capital and liquidity constraints on speedy arbitrage.

Garber (1990) and Velde (2009) are skeptical reviews of earlier putative bubbles. The concept of a rational bubble was introduced in Blanchard and Watson (1982). DeRosa (2021) is a critical survey of the bubble literature. See Shleifer and Summers (1990) and Black (1995) on the distinction between noise and information trading and the role of noise trading in asset markets.

Berk and Green (2004) model the capture of limited opportunities for active management excess returns by managers rather than investors. Barth and Kahn (2020) discuss basis trades and their role in the March 2020 market turmoil.

---

[14] Chapter 15 further discusses institutional investment strategies.

Jensen (1968), Carhart (1997), Fama and French (2010), and Bessembinder et al. (2023) compare active equity mutual performance with passive index returns. French (2018) estimates the cost to investors of active management. Sharpe (1991) presents the arithmetic of active management, and Pedersen (2018) discusses why it can't be applied precisely. Cremers et al. (2019) offer some caveats to the overall conclusion that active management fails to earn superior risk-adjusted returns.

Fung and Hsieh (1999), Asness et al. (2001), Malkiel and Saha (2005), Stulz (2007), and Getmansky et al. (2023) survey the hedge fund sector, including risk-taking, returns and leverage. Coval and Stafford (2018) provide evidence that any hedge fund excess returns are compensation for high tail risk.

Shleifer and Vishny (1997) compare private equity performance with public market returns. Stafford (2022) provides evidence for replicability of private equity returns. Swensen (2009) presents and Ennis (2021) critiques the endowment model, including the role of alternative investments.

8
Market Risk

8.1 Definition of Value-at-Risk

8.1.1 Why Value-at-Risk?

Value-at-Risk (VaR) is a single number summarizing the risk of a position or a portfolio. Ahead, we'll define VaR and analyze its many drawbacks and limitations as a risk measure, but it's important to be aware of the virtues that led to its wide and long-standing adoption.

VaR can be computed for portfolios encompassing very different asset types. It can be roughly accurate for many portfolios. It is applicable even to large and complex portfolios and can be computed using a broad range of return models, estimation methods, and data sources.

The most salient criticism of VaR is that in most practical applications, if it is accurate at all, it is as a measure of the risk of unusual but recurrent losses. VaR loses all accuracy if used to estimate extreme losses. But this should be understood not as a criticism but as stating the appropriate use of VaR. Any asset portfolio will routinely display fluctuations in value, and VaR can be a reasonably accurate measure of them. A bank's trading desk, for example, may wish to estimate the size of the losses that it can expect to recur on a regular basis, say, monthly. But VaR will be a far less useful guide to the likelihood of losses large enough to endanger the bank, require public or regulatory reporting, or impel it to fundamentally reassess its trading business.

In large trading operations, **VaR limit systems** have been widely used to set position size limits based on VaR, rather than on nominal size, thus controlling risk while giving some discretion to individual trading desks. They are a form of **risk budgeting**, which endeavors to allocate the **economic capital** required for an activity, measured by its contribution to the firm's overall risk rather than allocating the balance-sheet funding it employs.

There are a number of common misconceptions about VaR. VaR is not wedded to the standard model in which returns or their logarithms are assumed normally distributed but can be employed with any distributional hypothesis. Nor is it attached to a particular way of using market data, e.g., a particular observation interval. VaR models typically employ some form of conditional volatility, with distributional parameters or quantiles reestimated periodically with recent data. In practice, however, reliance on normality is widespread as is the use of relatively short observation intervals, both to a large extent attributable to uniformity fostered by detailed regulatory prescriptions.

As limited as a single number measuring risk may appear, there are situations in which it's needed. A portfolio or risk manager can't refuse to answer when a valued client or the CEO of an investment management firm asks, "How much can we lose?" But in such situations, one must also avoid another misconception—or outright distortion—that VaR is "the most we can lose." Widely publicized losses at banks have been orders of magnitude larger than the VaR measures reported by their risk management.

As inaccurate as it may be, VaR can help portfolio and risk managers to form judgments about risk exposure. There are complex pros and cons for each decision in VaR modeling, but the need for judgment calls in risk modeling is not unique to VaR. Most importantly, we can learn a lot from criticizing VaR and understanding its limitations and pitfalls. In this respect, it resembles the standard lognormal model of asset returns and the CAPM, demonstrably flawed but providing a framework for thinking.

8.1.2   Value-at-Risk Is a Quantile

The loss of a position or portfolio over a given future horizon can be treated as a random variable, and the VaR is a quantile of the **loss distribution**. Loss and VaR are defined as positive numbers, in dollar or return units, so the loss distribution is -1 times the probability distribution of P&L. To define VaR, let X represent loss over a future interval τ, and the probability α the **confidence level** of the VaR estimate. The τ-period VaR at confidence level α is the α-quantile of the loss distribution. The loss quantile varies with the confidence level, the probability with which a corresponding loss level won't be exceeded.

The probability of losing no more than the VaR is α, say, 99 percent. The probability of suffering a loss worse than the VaR is then $1 - \alpha$, say, 1 percent. A 1-day VaR at a 95 percent confidence level should occur roughly once in 20 trading days, or once per month. A one-day VaR at a 99 percent confidence level should be exceeded roughly once in 100 days, about two or three times a year.

Example 8.1   Quantile and VaR

We'll take the 1-day VaR of a long S&P 500 position as of December 31, 2021, as an example. Suppose daily changes in the S&P 500 index are lognormally distributed, and we have an estimate of its mean return and return volatility as of December 31, 2021. The 1-day loss distribution of a long position in the S&P 500 depends on its closing level the next trading day (see Figure 8.1). Figure 8.2 shows how the one-day VaR might be estimated.

8.2   Computing Value-at-Risk for One Risk Factor

8.2.1   Modeling Approaches to Value-at-Risk Estimation

Estimating VaR requires an estimate of the loss distribution. The basic approaches are:

Parametric VaR relies on a hypothesized return distribution and estimates of its moments or other characteristics. For example, if returns are assumed to be lognormally distributed with mean zero and we have a volatility estimate, we can express it in a formula which we'll state below.

Monte Carlo simulation also relies on a distributional hypothesis but uses random draws based on it. It is particularly useful for portfolios that include derivatives or securities such as mortgage-backed securities, the values of which are functions of underlying risk factors such as stock prices or interest rates. Return scenarios are then an output of pricing models rather than direct observations.

Historical simulation is based on historical returns over some past observation period. No distributional hypothesis is put forward. Instead, the near-term future distribution is assumed to resemble that of the historical sample.

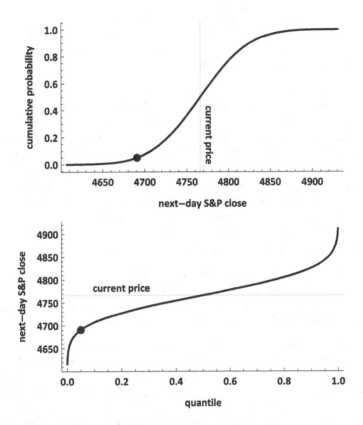

Figure 8.1 Distribution and quantile functions

The upper panel displays the distribution function of the next-day S&P 500 level under the assumption that log returns are normally distributed with mean zero. The lower panel is the corresponding quantile function. The point identifies the 0.01-quantile of the next-day price.

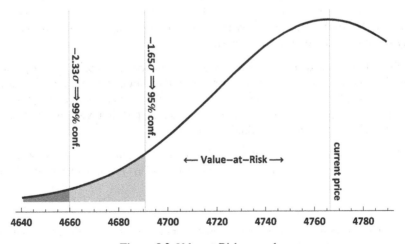

Figure 8.2 Value-at-Risk example

1-day VaR of a long S&P 500 index position on 31Dec2021. Volatility computed via EWMA with a decay factor of 0.94. Grid lines at VaR scenarios for confidence levels of 95 and 99 percent. VaR is the difference between its 31Dec2021 closing value 4766.18, and the index value in the VaR scenario 4659.88, times the number of index units held.

For the parametric and Monte Carlo approaches but not for historical simulation, the VaR user posits a distributional hypothesis or asset return model and chooses how to estimate its parameters, especially volatility. Model choices include the normal, lognormal, or other distributions, and parameter estimation might be carried out using GARCH or EWMA.

Apart from these fundamental modeling choices in VaR estimation, practitioners make judgment calls about the **risk factor mapping**. Market risk may be more accurately modeled as a function of a small number of risk factors compared to the number of positions in a portfolio. It's not computationally feasible, for example, to apply time series data on thousands of different prices to a large stock portfolio or to a portfolio that includes complex, illiquid, or non-traded assets valued using models. This requires assigning risk factors to positions, including a measure i.e., the **loading**, of the impact of each risk factor on each position. For example, equity risks may be modeled as a function of a broad index or Fama-French factors, and bond risks may be modeled as a function of key points on the interest-rate curve. Many assets may be exposed to a common risk factor, such as the euro-US dollar exchange rate, or a macroeconomic factor. Option risk may be crudely measured using the price of the underlying asset, with a loading based on the option delta.

There are many pitfalls in determining to which risk factors a portfolio is exposed. Omitting a key risk factor, such as option-implied volatility for an option portfolio, can lead to underestimation of risk. Before the 2007 crisis, for example, some banks mapped AAA subprime mortgage bond returns to those of AAA corporate bonds, vastly understating their risks.

Judgment calls about how much historical data to use determines how we incorporate conditionality. Is the VaR estimate aimed at capturing recurrent losses or extreme events? Using a longer observation period is likelier to include extreme return experiences that provide valuable information about how bad portfolio losses might be. But observations reaching further back into the past may be unrepresentative of the range of possible outcomes in the near future. The choice of observation period is also a decision on whether to include or exclude specific extreme and possibly "unique" events. How should we treat extreme stress periods such as 2008 and 2020?

VaR is less accurate at longer time horizons and higher confidence levels deep in the right tail of the loss distribution. This can be problematic if using VaR to estimate economic capital, which should be set high enough to cover rare, very large and costly, even existential losses. VaR is more accurate at predicting routine losses that can be seen as a recurrent cost of doing business and can be interpreted as the likely worst-case loss if an extreme event does *not* occur.

We'll describe with an extended example how VaR is estimated for a single position using the modeling approaches stated above. The data for our VaR computation example are as follows: The risk factor is the S&P 500 index, which closed at $S_t = 4766.18$ on the calculation date t, December 31, 2021. The exposure is assumed to be the equivalent of a long position with an initial value of $xS_t =$ \$1,000,000.[1] For a 1-day horizon, with time measured in days, $\tau = 1$.

For parametric and Monte Carlo estimates, we'll assume logarithmic asset or factor returns $r_{t,t+\tau} \equiv \ln(S_{t+\tau}) - \ln(S_t)$ over the future interval (t, τ) are normally distributed, with a mean of zero:

$$r_{t,t+\tau} \sim \mathcal{N}(0, \sigma_t^2 \tau).$$

This assumption is tractable and widespread in practice but belied by empirical asset return behavior. Alternative assumptions have their own drawbacks.

The volatility of the S&P 500 σ_t at a daily rate is used in computing VaR parametrically and via Monte Carlo but not via historical simulation. It is estimated via EWMA (Chapter 4), with $\lambda = 0.94$,

---

[1] The computation doesn't require the number of index units $x = \frac{1\,000\,000}{4766.18} = 209.812$, just the initial position value xS_t.

at 0.00969577, just below 1 percent, at the close on December 31, 2021. The annualized volatility is about 16 percent, close to the long-term average for the S&P 500 index. Our volatility estimate σ_t is based on information up to time t, but we'll assume it's a constant parameter over any future horizon τ, whether a day, a week, or a month. We can then use the square-root-of-time rule to apply this daily volatility estimate to longer horizons.

8.2.2 Parametric Normal Value-at-Risk

The first step in computing VaR for a single position parametrically is to find the VaR scenario—the quantile of loss corresponding to the confidence level α—in log return terms. For a long position in the risk factor or asset, it's the $1 - \alpha$ quantile of $r_{t,t+\tau}$. For a long position and assuming lognormality, we use $z_{1-\alpha}$, the $1 - \alpha$ quantile of the standard normal distribution, a negative number such as $z_{0.01} = -2.32635$. The log return in the VaR scenario is $z_{1-\alpha}\sigma_t\sqrt{\tau}$.

Note that we use $z_{1-\alpha}$ rather than $z_{1-\frac{\alpha}{2}}$, as we would in two-tailed hypothesis testing. VaR is a one-tailed test because a simple exposure generates losses only if prices go in the wrong direction. In more complex cases, such as option portfolios, underlying price fluctuations in either direction may generate losses, but we would still be using a high quantile of the portfolio's loss distribution.

The $1 - \alpha$ quantile of the change in the risk factor $S_{t+\tau} - S_t$ is

$$S_t e^{z_{1-\alpha}\sigma_t\sqrt{\tau}} - S_t = S_t \left(e^{z_{1-\alpha}\sigma_t\sqrt{\tau}} - 1\right).$$

The VaR scenario in P&L terms—the $1 - \alpha$-quantile of the change in position value—is $xS_t(e^{z_{1-\alpha}\sigma_t\sqrt{\tau}} - 1)$. The VaR at a confidence level α expresses it as positive number:

$$\text{VaR}_t(\alpha, \tau) = -xS_t\left(e^{z_{1-\alpha}\sigma_t\sqrt{\tau}} - 1\right) = xS_t\left(1 - e^{z_{1-\alpha}\sigma_t\sqrt{\tau}}\right).$$

A widely used approximation is in most cases very close, using the slightly larger-loss log return $z_{1-\alpha}\sigma_t\sqrt{\tau}$ in place of the arithmetic return $e^{z_{1-\alpha}\sigma_t\sqrt{\tau}} - 1$.[2]

Example 8.2 Parametric normal Value-at-Risk

Let's apply the theory to the 1-day VaR, at a 99 percent confidence level, of a $1,000,000 long position in the S&P 500 index. The VaR scenario in log return terms 1 is an index decline of about 2.25 percent:

$$z_{0.01}\sigma_t\sqrt{1} = -2.32635 \times 0.00969577 = -0.0225557.$$

The change in the risk factor is the 0.01-quantile of the 1-day change $S_{t+1} - S_t$:

$$S_t(e^{z_{0.01}\sigma_t} - 1) = 4766.18\left(e^{-0.0225557} - 1\right) = 4766.18 \times (-0.02230325)$$
$$= 4659.88 - 4766.18 = -106.301.$$

The VaR scenario in P&L terms is

$$xS_t(e^{z_{0.01}\sigma_t} - 1) = 1\,000\,000 \times -0.02230325 = -22\,303.25,$$

so the 1-day VaR at a 99 percent confidence level is $22,303.25.

---

[2] This is equivalent to assuming arithmetic, not log, returns are normally distributed.

The 1-week (five business days) VaR, using the square-root-of-time rule, is $49,185.36:

$$-1\,000\,000 \left(1 - e^{0.0225557\sqrt{5}} \right) = 1\,000\,000 \times 0.04918536.$$

The approximation is $-xS_t z_{0.01}\sigma_t = \$22,555.73$ for the 1-day VaR and $-xS_t z_{0.01}\sigma_t\sqrt{\tau} = \$50,436.15$ for the 5-day VaR at a 99 percent confidence level.

8.2.3   Computing Value-at-Risk via Monte Carlo Simulation

Like parametric, Monte Carlo computation of VaR proceeds from a hypothesis about the distribution of the risk factors, and requires estimates of volatility or other parameters. It is useful for complex portfolios involving options or other nonlinear assets for which the quantile can't be reduced to a simple formula. The simulated risk factor returns become inputs into pricing models that are used to revalue the positions for each simulated shock, and the securities are revalued in a set of random draws from the hypothesized distribution.

The steps in the algorithm for one risk factor are:

1. Generate a set of independent draws. If the lognormal model is assumed, multiplying, say, $\epsilon_i, i = 1, \ldots, 10{,}000$ realizations of a standard normal distribution by the estimated volatility σ_t gives us a random sample of simulations $r_i = \sigma_t\epsilon_i$ of $r_{t,t+1}$, the 1-day log return, the next-period price $S_i = S_t e^{r_i}$, and the P&L $x(S_i - S_t)$. We use the simulated risk factor returns but the current position size or portfolio weights.
2. Sort the realizations in ascending order to obtain the order statistics of the simulated returns $r_{(i)}$, next-period prices $S_{(i)} = S_t e^{r_{(i)}}$, position values $xS_{(i)}$, and of the P&L $x(S_{(i)} - S_t), i = 1, \ldots, 10{,}000$.
3. The 100th order statistic of the P&L, the $1 - \alpha$ quantile, times -1, is the VaR at a 99-percent confidence level. Scenarios near the quantile may be averaged or interpolated to reduce simulation noise.

Example 8.3   Monte Carlo computation of Value-at-Risk

Figure 8.3 compares the result, $22,254.19, with parametric VaR. Table 8.1 displays the data layout for the computation. In a simple portfolio consisting of a single position with a value responding linearly to changes in price, the histogram of simulated returns is almost identical to the assumed lognormal distribution with zero drift.

8.2.4   Computing Value-at-Risk via Historical Simulation

For historical simulation, the steps in the algorithm are similar to those for Monte Carlo. The main difference is in the first step; the sample of simulations is drawn from recent historical experience rather than from an assumed distribution:

1. Select a historical observation period, say, 2 years, and compute a time series of m daily log or arithmetic returns.
2. From here, the procedure is similar to Monte Carlo: Use the historical returns $r_{t-\tau+1}$ or $r^{\text{arith}}_{t-\tau+1}, \tau = 1, \ldots, m$ but the current position size x to compute simulated realizations of the next-period price and P&L

$$xS_t r^{\text{arith}}_{t-\tau+1} = xS_t(e^{r_{t-\tau+1}} - 1), \qquad \tau = 1, \ldots, m.$$

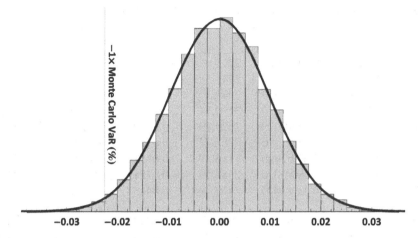

Figure 8.3 Monte Carlo computation of Value-at-Risk

Histogram of Monte Carlo return simulations and probability density function of $\mathcal{N}(0, \sigma_t^2)$, with $\sigma_t = 0.00969577$.

Table 8.1 Monte Carlo computation of Value-at-Risk

i	$r_{(i)}$	$S_{(i)}$	P&L
1	−0.03581	4598.53	−35,173.97
2	−0.03531	4600.83	−34,692.51
3	−0.03475	4603.38	−34,156.83
⋮	⋮	⋮	⋮
99	−0.02253	4660.01	−22,275.88
100	−0.02251	4660.11	−22,254.19
101	−0.02248	4660.24	−22,228.40
⋮	⋮	⋮	⋮
4999	0.00007	4766.52	70.74
5000	0.00008	4766.54	75.34
5001	0.00008	4766.56	80.14
⋮	⋮	⋮	⋮
9998	0.03288	4925.51	33,430.06
9999	0.03299	4926.05	33,542.21
10000	0.03378	4929.92	34,353.67

Entries in the second column are $r_{(i)} = \sigma_t \epsilon_{(i)}$, where the $\tilde{\epsilon}^{(i)}$ are the ordered draws from $\mathcal{N}(0, \sigma_t^2)$, with $\sigma_t = 0.00969577$. Entries in the second column are $S_{(i)} = S_t e^{r_{(i)}}$. The P&L realizations are $xS_t(e^{r_{(i)}} - 1)$, with $xS_t = 1,000,000$.

3. Sort the m historical return or P&L realizations in ascending order to obtain the order statistics of $r_{(i)}$, the next-period prices $S_{(i)} = S_t e^{r_{(i)}}$, position values $xS_{(i)}$, and P&L $x(S_{(i)} - S_t), i = 1, \ldots, m$.
4. The VaR of a long position at confidence level α is −1 times the $(1 - \alpha)$-quantile of the order statistics of P&L.

Example 8.4   Historical simulation Value-at-Risk

We'll apply historical simulation to a $1,000,000 long position in the S&P 500 index on December 31, 2021. Using 2 years of price data from December 31, 2019 yields

Table 8.2   Order statistics for historical simulation Value-at-Risk

i	t	S_t	date t	S_{t-1}	$r_{(i)}$	$r_{(i)}^{arith}$	P&L
1	51	2386.13	16Mar2020	2711.02	−0.12765	−0.11984	−119 840.50
2	49	2480.64	12Mar2020	2741.38	−0.09994	−0.09511	−95 112.68
3	46	2746.56	09Mar2020	2972.37	−0.07901	−0.07597	−75 969.68
4	112	3002.10	11Jun2020	3190.14	−0.06075	−0.05894	−58 944.12
5	53	2398.10	18Mar2020	2529.19	−0.05322	−0.05183	−51 830.82
6	48	2741.38	11Mar2020	2882.23	−0.05010	−0.04887	−48 868.41
7	39	2978.76	27Feb2020	3116.39	−0.04517	−0.04416	−44 163.28
8	63	2470.50	01Apr2020	2584.59	−0.04515	−0.04414	−44 142.40
9	55	2304.92	20Mar2020	2409.39	−0.04433	−0.04336	−43 359.52
⋮	⋮	⋮	⋮	⋮	⋮	⋮	⋮
23	290	3829.34	25Feb2021	3925.43	−0.02478	−0.02448	−24 478.85
24	123	3009.05	26Jun2020	3083.76	−0.02453	−0.02423	−24 226.92
25	184	3236.92	23Sep2020	3315.57	−0.02401	−0.02372	−23 721.41
26	481	4594.62	26Nov2021	4701.46	−0.02299	−0.02272	−22 724.86
27	72	2783.36	15Apr2020	2846.06	−0.02228	−0.02203	−22 030.46
28	343	4063.04	12May2021	4152.10	−0.02168	−0.02145	−21 449.39
29	91	2870.12	12May2020	2930.32	−0.02076	−0.02054	−20 543.83
⋮	⋮	⋮	⋮	⋮	⋮	⋮	⋮

The entries in the last three columns are the order statistics of the logarithmic and arithmetic historical return and P&L realizations: $\bar{r}^{(i)}$, $e^{\bar{r}^{(i)}} - 1$, and $xS_t(e^{\bar{r}^{(i)}} - 1)$, $i = 1, \ldots, m$ and $m = 505$. The VaR scenario for the 99.5-, 99-, and 95-percent confidence levels are highlighted.

$m = 505$ return observations January 2, 2020 to December 31, 2021, so $(1 - \alpha)m = 0.01 \cdot 505 = 5.05$.

The VaR scenario is the observation with a rank equal to the ceiling $\lceil 5.05 \rceil = 6$ of 5.05, using the most-common quantile definition. The 6th order statistic of arithmetic returns $\bar{r}^{arith,(i)}$, $i = 1, \ldots, m$ in the historical sample is −0.04887: at least 1 percent of the sample is even worse. The VaR at a 99-percent confidence level is \$48,868, much higher than parametric or Monte Carlo.[3]

Table 8.2 displays the data layout for the computation, and Figure 8.4 illustrates. During the observation period, the largest moves in the S&P 500 occurred during the early months of Covid, from late February 2020. Figure 8.5 shows how the VaR scenario is identified.

8.2.5   Value-at-Risk for Short Positions

The definition of VaR doesn't change for a short position, in which an asset is borrowed and sold, with the intent to purchase and return it to the lender. But VaR has a major drawback for short positions: it doesn't capture their unlimited downside. Asset prices are floored at zero but have no

---

[3] The α-quantile is unambiguous only for continuous distributions that are not flat at $1 - \alpha$ and for discrete distributions if $(1 - \alpha)m$ happens to be an integer. VaR could be reported as lying elsewhere on the interval $[\bar{r}^{(5)}, \bar{r}^{(6)}]$ if alternative quantile definitions were applied. There can be large differences among the handful of historical return observations in the tails. When using historical simulation with a short observation period, alternative quantile definitions potentially have a material influence on the VaR scenario.

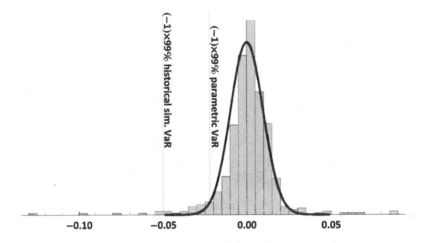

Figure 8.4 Computation of Value-at-Risk by historical simulation

Histogram of daily S&P 500 return 02Jan2020 to 31Dec2021 and probability density function of $\mathcal{N}(0, \sigma_t^2)$, with $\sigma_t = 0.00969577$.

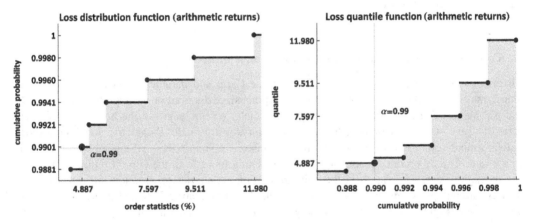

Figure 8.5 Historical simulation Value-at-Risk scenario

Points identify $(-1)\times$arithmetic return observations in the left tail. These are the magnitudes of the return observations leading to the largest observed losses in the historical sample. The larger point denotes the quantile using $\lceil(1-\alpha)m\rceil$-th order statistic. With $\alpha = 0.99$ and $m = 505$, $\lceil(1-\alpha)m\rceil = 6$, and the VaR scenario at a 99-percent confidence level in arithmetic return terms is -4.887 percent.

upper limit. The P&L of a long position can be no worse than a complete loss $-xS_t$. The P&L and risk of a short position have no upper limit as price rises.[4]

Example 8.5   Value-at-Risk for short positions

Applying historical simulation to the example of a short position in the S&P 500 index on December 31, 2021, we estimate the 99-percent 1-day VaR at $49,396.34, slightly larger than for a long position. While there was high kurtosis, apart from the very largest-magnitude returns, there was more moderate skewness or asymmetry between positive and negative price returns.

---

[4] The price of West Texas Intermediate (WTI) crude oil on April 20, 2020 is a rare exception. A sharp decline in demand and limited storage capacity drove spot and short-term futures prices below zero. Equivalently, the implied cost of storage skyrocketed and the implied convenience yield went sharply negative as holders of long oil futures positions sought to avoid taking delivery.

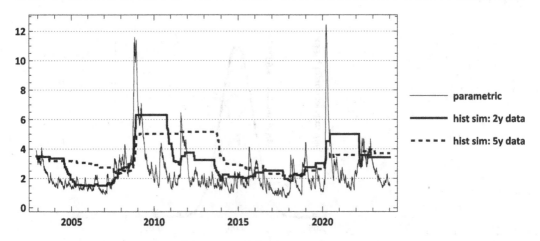

Figure 8.6 Value-at-Risk responsiveness to shocks

Time series of one-day, 99 percent VaR estimates for a long position in the S&P 500 index, daily, 29Nov2002 to 11Jan2024, expressed as returns in percent. Parametric estimates assume a lognormal return distribution using the contemporaneous EWMA volatility with a decay factor of 0.94. Historical simulation estimates use 2 or 5 years of daily return data.

8.2.6   Comparison of Value-at-Risk Computation Approaches

Historical simulation can differ greatly from Monte Carlo and parametric because the historical returns may have thicker or thinner tails than the hypothesized distribution underpinning Monte Carlo and parametric. These differences may depend crucially on the length of the historical look-back period and the state of markets at the time the estimates are made. Parametric and Monte Carlo VaR are more responsive to recent returns than historical simulation. A longer historical observation interval may produce inaccurate results deviating more from the current return distribution due to major events or changes in the volatility regime. A shorter observation interval may miss or overstate tail risk. This contributes to the difficulty of validating VaR and its susceptibility to manipulation. Figure 8.6 shows how widely the VaR scenario can vary over time, using accepted approaches.

Apart from estimation technique, VaR results depend heavily on the choice of confidence level and time horizon, based on the business or regulatory application. VaR computed via any technique increases with the confidence level α and is generally larger at longer time horizons. But if there has been a sharp recent increase in return volatility, VaR computed via historical simulation may be lower at a longer horizon.

8.3   Nonlinear Market Risks

8.3.1   Nonlinearity and Risk Measurement

Many portfolios exhibit **nonlinear market risk** or **convexity**, with returns varying nonlinearly rather than proportionally with risk factors, similarly to options. Their prices may barely budge or may change drastically, depending on the level of interest rates or underlying prices, on the magnitude of risk factor returns, and on other market conditions. Price changes in one direction may also have a larger P&L impact than changes in the opposite direction. Nonlinearity has the potential to quickly transform modest exposures into large ones, triggered by modest moves in risk factors, and occasionally has a large impact on markets generally.

Loss-amplifying **convexity risk** can be crucial for longer-term or callable coupon and zero-coupon bonds, and for MBS, and to to a lesser extent for shorter-term non-callable bonds. Options bear **gamma risk**, convexity risk with respect to the underlying price. The delta δ_t and gamma γ_t of a security, not necessarily an option, are defined as the derivatives of its value $f(S_t)$ with respect to a risk factor S_t. If a security has a payoff that is nonlinear with respect to a risk factor S_t, then its value $f(S_t)$ has nonzero second and possibly higher derivatives:

$$\delta_t \equiv f'(S_t) \equiv \frac{\partial f(S_t)}{\partial S_t}$$

$$\gamma_t \equiv f''(S_t) \equiv \frac{\partial^2 f(S_t)}{\partial S_t^2}.$$

Similarly to options, nonlinear securities can be described by a delta-gamma approximation:

$$f(S_t + \Delta S) - f(S_t) \approx \delta_t \Delta S + \frac{1}{2}\gamma_t \Delta S^2.$$

A widely-used application of the delta-gamma approximation, apart from options, is in managing the convexity risk of MBS hedged with Treasurys (see Chapter 10).

8.3.2 Applying Delta-Gamma Value-at-Risk to the Value of an Option

There are several VaR techniques for nonlinear positions. One is simulation with full repricing, using an asset valuation model, such as an MBS valuation model. Each position is revalued at each simulated set of factor returns to estimate its return distribution, possibly requiring time-consuming and costly large-scale computation. It is often more practical to apply **delta-gamma**, a variant of the parametric approach that assumes arithmetic returns are normally distributed with zero mean and applies a linear-quadratic approximation of P&L responses to risk factor returns. Delta-gamma trades accuracy for tractability and speed.

Nonlinearity has a large influence on option risk; underlying price moves amplify losses for a long call or short put. Delta-gamma can be used to estimate the VaR of an option position. Its value is represented by $xf(S_t)$, with x the number of options. Assume we have an estimate of the return volatility σ_t of the underlying price S_t, distinct from the implied volatility of the option, which is a metric of the option's own price. Positive and negative shocks in the underlying price are then estimated by their quantiles $z_\alpha \sigma_t \sqrt{\tau} S_t$ and $z_{1-\alpha} \sigma_t \sqrt{\tau} S_t$. The $(1-\alpha)$-quantile of the distribution of changes in option value, using the arithmetic returns approximation, is

$$\delta_t z_{1-\alpha} \sigma_t \sqrt{\tau} S_t + \frac{1}{2}\gamma_t \left(z_{1-\alpha}\sigma_t\sqrt{\tau}S_t\right)^2 \quad \text{with} \quad 0 < \delta_t < 1, \gamma_t \geq 0$$

for a long call option,

$$\delta_t z_\alpha \sigma_t \sqrt{\tau} S_t + \frac{1}{2}\gamma_t \left(z_\alpha\sigma_t\sqrt{\tau}S_t\right)^2 \quad \text{with} -1 < \delta_t < 0, \gamma_t \geq 0$$

for a long put option,

$$-\left[\delta_t z_\alpha \sigma_t \sqrt{\tau} S_t + \frac{1}{2}\gamma_t \left(z_\alpha\sigma_t\sqrt{\tau}S_t\right)^2\right] \quad \text{with} \quad 0 < \delta_t < 1, \gamma_t \geq 0$$

for a short call option,

$$-\left[\delta_t z_{1-\alpha} \sigma_t \sqrt{\tau} S_t + \frac{1}{2}\gamma_t \left(z_{1-\alpha}\sigma_t\sqrt{\tau}S_t\right)^2\right] \quad \text{with} -1 < \delta_t < 0, \gamma_t \geq 0$$

for a short put option.

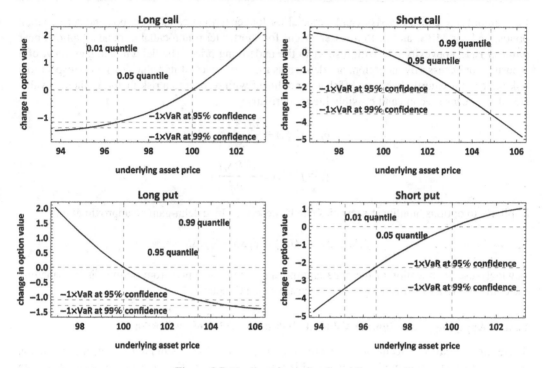

Figure 8.7 Nonlinearity and option risk

Each panel plots the P&L in currency units of an unhedged option position, using the Black-Scholes valuation formula.

An unhedged long call or short put has a long exposure to the underlying price and losses if S_t declines, as represented by a low quantile $z_{1-\alpha}$ of the underlying price. An unhedged short call or long put has a short underlying exposure, and losses prevail if a high quantile z_α of the underlying price S_t is realized. The delta of a long call is positive, that of a long put is negative, and for any option position, $\gamma_t \geq 0$. Gamma dampens P&L fluctuations for long option positions, reducing VaR, and amplifies P&L for short option positions, increasing VaR. Figure 8.7 illustrates for plain-vanilla European option values, estimated using the Black-Scholes model.

Example 8.6   Delta and gamma calculations

Consider a short position in an at-the-money (ATM) put with 1 month to expiry on one share of a non-dividend paying stock. The initial stock price is $S_t = 100$, the 1-month money market rate is 1 percent, and the option implied volatility is 15 percent per annum. Because this is a short position, a price decline will hurt the position through its negative δ_t, and the γ_t will amplify its negative effect on P&L. We'll use a volatility estimate or forecast of 15 percent, equal to the implied vol, for simplicity. In general, there is a variance risk premium; historical volatility estimates are typically somewhat lower than implied vols.[5] The weekly vol is about 2 percent: $\sigma_t \sqrt{\tau} = 0.15 \sqrt{\frac{1}{52}} = 0.0208$.

To compute the 1-week VaR $\left(\tau = \frac{1}{52} \right)$, we find the difference in the value of a 3-week option at the initial underlying price and its value in the VaR scenario. We'll compute the difference using a delta-only and a delta-gamma approximation and compare with the full repricing

---

[5] See Chapter 15.

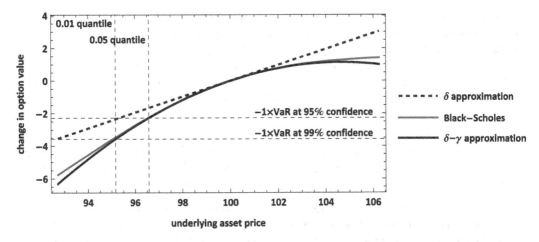

Figure 8.8 Delta and delta-gamma approximations

Short put option struck at 100, initial underlying asset price 100, money market rate 1 percent, model valuation using Black-Scholes formula.

difference computed via Black-Scholes. The Black-Scholes delta of a 3-week ATM put is −0.4857 and its gamma is 0.1050.[6] A short put has a delta equivalent of 48.57 worth of stock, and high gamma: delta declines to −0.3829 if the underlying price rises to 101. Quantiles of $S_{t+\tau}$ are:

		VaR estimates		
	VaR scenario	delta-only	delta-gamma	Black-Scholes
$\alpha = 0.95$	−3.422	1.662	2.276	2.250
$\alpha = 0.99$	−4.839	2.350	3.579	3.465

The VaR scenario is the 1-week change in the underlying stock price, in percent. The VaR estimates are quantiles of the change in option value corresponding to the VaR scenarios, computed using the three approaches.

Figure 8.8 illustrates the difference in the approaches. The delta-gamma approximation comes close to the Black-Scholes valuation and is more accurate than delta alone. But note that the delta-gamma approximation is downward sloping for large shocks to S_t, violating no-arbitrage constraints on option pricing.

8.3.3   Portfolio Value-at-Risk

Most real-world VaR applications involve portfolios, with multiple risk factors and multiple positions. Even portfolios with relatively few line items are exposed to several risk factors. For instance, hedged positions, relative value trades such as spread trades, long-short trades, and portfolio products such as structured credit, for instance, require a portfolio approach to risk analysis.

---

[6] The delta of 1-month ATM put is a bit larger.

To estimate the VaR for a portfolio, we need to take account of correlations as well as volatilities of risk factor returns. **Delta-normal**, like delta-gamma, treats arithmetic, not log returns, as normally distributed, but applies a linear rather than a linear-quadratic approximation. The sensitivities of the portfolio value to a set of risk factors are represented by their deltas. The **delta equivalent** of a position is $x\delta_t S_t$, a measure of exposure that plays a crucial role in hedging option risk. The delta-normal VaR for a single position exposed to single risk factor at a confidence level α is

$$\mathrm{VaR}_t(\alpha, \tau)(x) = -z_{1-\alpha}\sigma\sqrt{\tau}x\delta_t S_t,$$

identical to the approximation for the parametric VaR of a linear long position. Delta-normal portfolio VaR builds on the algebra of portfolio returns (see Chapter 5). For two positions or a portfolio with two risk factors, there are three parameters to estimate, including the return correlation.

Delta-normal may be drastically inaccurate for some portfolios. Payoffs with respect to some risk factor returns may be **nonmonotone** as well as convex: the sign of $f'(S_t)$ may change for different values of S_t. Examples of nonmonotonicity include delta-hedged plain-vanilla options, which are highly exposed to gamma risk. A hedged short call or put has large losses for positive as well as negative underlying returns.

8.4   Incorporating Extreme Events Into Risk Measurement

8.4.1   Why Not Value-at-Risk?

The financial regulatory regime has encouraged the use of VaR and risk measures closely related to it, and it is prevalent in practice. But VaR has serious limitations as a risk measure. For many assets, over many observation intervals, and using a variety of models and simulation approaches, VaR can vastly over- or underestimate loss at a given confidence level. For example, losses exceeding a daily VaR at a 99 percent confidence level may occur significantly more or less often than once in 100 trading days. This is the case even when not relying on the standard model, but the typical normality assumption worsens matters.

VaR provides an inadequate treatment of the frequency and size of tail risk events and performs poorly during crises or in the face of large losses. VaR doesn't tell a risk manager how large the loss might be if the VaR were to be exceeded. There is an enormous practical difference between having a loss 10 percent greater versus 10 times greater than the VaR on those occasions. These limitations are even more serious in portfolios containing options or other nonlinear risks. The London Whale episode (Chapter 14) is one of many examples of reported losses far greater than VaR.

The accuracy of VaR is difficult to test statistically. The standard approach to **backtesting** is to compare the frequency with which losses exceed the VaR with its confidence level. Exceedances occurring too often or too infrequently indicate the VaR model is inaccurate. This approach has limited usefulness because it doesn't examine, for example, how bad losses are in the event VaR is exceeded or how likely an exceedance is to be followed immediately by others.

The tests also have low power. If the VaR model is not accurate, even in the narrow sense of the frequency with which the VaR is exceeded, it takes far more observations to reject its accuracy statistically than are generally available. There is a material probability that the VaR model is inaccurate, but one hasn't been able to demonstrate it.

VaR is a market risk measure focusing on asset risk. It doesn't reveal capital structure risk: both sides of the balance sheet are important in assessing risk. High leverage induces greater vulnerability to a surprise asset price decline. VaR must be compared to equity to fully capture the effect of asset risk on firm viability.[7]

The widespread use of VaR drives **procyclicality**. It can amplify price fluctuations by inducing similar buy or sell behavior of market participants in response to fluctuations in volatility. This impact is especially powerful if it is used to set trading desks' or traders' position size limits.

VaR is also relatively easy to manipulate by traders seeking to avoid risk management constraints or by financial firms seeking to avoid regulatory limits. One way is to exploit its neglect of tail risk. As we have seen, option strategies can produce steady low returns with low volatility most of the time but extreme losses rarely and unpredictably. A credit portfolio with a low default probability may have a low credit VaR if hard-to-measure default correlation is underestimated. This characteristic is shared by many structured products as well.

The use of VaR as a risk measure encourages such strategies. VaR is not **coherent** and specifically not **subadditive**. The VaR of a portfolio may be larger than the sum of the VaR measures of its constituents. A simple example is a short straddle, a portfolio of a short call and a short put, both with the same exercise price and the same expiry. The probability of a loss below a given threshold may be greater than, say, 99 percent, for either a short put or a short call position. If the two are joined in a straddle, however, the resulting portfolio may have a probability greater than 99 percent of losing an above-threshold amount because a price move in either direction triggers losses.

This property of VaR may lead to dividing up components of a strategy in such a way as to evade being flagged. This can happen on a small scale, such as a portfolio manager who oversees several trading desks and distributes positions so each stays within a VaR limit, or on a large scale, such as separating activities into subsidiaries to lower aggregate regulatory capital funding requirements for the holding company.[8]

VaR can also be manipulated through the user settings. The devil in the details. Subtle and not-so-subtle differences in how VaR is computed can lead to large differences in results.

Example 8.7   Getting whatever answer you want from Value-at-Risk

Consider an estimate of the 10-day (2-week) VaR of an S&P 500 index exposure, computed four different ways, two applying parametric normal and two via historical simulation. One parametric estimate uses the 10-day volatility, computed via the EWMA model, using nonoverlapping observations, and the other applies the square-root-of-time rule, multiplying the 1-day EWMA volatility estimate by $\sqrt{10}$. The historical simulation estimates both use nonoverlapping observations of 10-day returns, one with 2 years and the other 5 years of data.

The results show large differences among the approaches. Table 8.3 displays the estimates as they would have been computed on two different dates, one during a very low-volatility period, the other during the global financial crisis. On the latter date, the highest VaR estimate is double the lowest.

8.4.2   Stress Testing and Scenario Analysis

The standard model doesn't match well with experience in the way that matters most to market participants, capturing the extremes in asset returns. To address this failing, one can seek an alternative

---

[7] See Chapter 11.
[8] We'll provide a credit portfolio example in Chapter 13.

Table 8.3   Comparison of Value-at-Risk techniques

Technique	12Mar2003	26Nov2008
Parametric: 10-day volatility	9.90	14.43
Parametric: 1-day volatility $\times \sqrt{10}$	9.03	28.75
Historical simulation: 2 years of data	8.15	24.60
Historical simulation: 5 years of data	9.66	20.15

model of asset return behavior or simulation approach that better fits the data, for example, a different distributional hypothesis regarding returns or observation interval for historical simulation. None have proven clearly superior in practice.

One can also use **scenario analysis** and **stress testing**. These apply heuristic portfolio analysis, a combination of analysis and judgment, to estimate P&L or other performance metrics under extreme loss scenarios. To carry out scenario analysis and stress testing, we determine appropriate scenarios, estimate the shocks to the risk factors in each scenario, and value the portfolio in each scenario.[9] In **reverse stress testing**, the starting point is a large loss, and scenarios are found that lead to a loss of that size.

Scenario analysis applies more moderate shocks and takes a wider range of risk factors into account; stress testing addresses tail risk with more extreme shocks to a smaller number of key risk factors. Both are intended to reduce model risk. In practice, banks and other intermediaries continue to rely heavily on scenario analysis to quantify risk. Because of the recognized drawbacks of formal risk measurement, the regulatory framework for banks and other intermediaries is heavily reliant on stress testing and has become more so during the succession of financial crises since 2007. Regulators have adopted stress testing as a core element of its supervision regime for banks.[10]

Stress tests can reveal vulnerabilities in specific positions or groups of positions. Stress scenarios are easier to communicate than VaR or other formal risk measures, so they also help portfolio and risk managers "know the book." They can take into account some risk drivers that can't be readily captured by time series of prices or risk factors. Price dynamics such as fire sales or abrupt changes in the correlation between bond yields and equity returns are empirically difficult to predict. The role of overall financial conditions, such as liquidity, in driving risk is better expressed as a constellation of substantial price, rate, and spread changes.

Appropriate stress scenarios are tailored to the firm's specific key vulnerabilities. This is largely judgmental, with unavoidable arbitrariness in scenario design, but a set of scenarios omitting, for example, credit spread widening or option-implied volatility would be inappropriate for an investment fund with large long positions in corporate bonds or option portfolios. Stress tests should also avoid assumptions that favor the firm, for example, the competitive advantages the firm would putatively gain in a crisis. Stress scenarios should be extreme but not implausible. This, too, is a matter of judgment in the absence of reliable probability estimates for scenarios. Events that truly are impossible needn't be considered, but events that are improbable, extreme yet distinctly possible, should be.

Historical scenarios are based on actual past events but have a number of issues that also apply to other risk measures based on historical data: the time frame used and the potential for omitting a key risk factor. Hypothetical what-if scenarios are based on a judgmental assessment of potential large

---

[9] Examples in this book include interest-rate risk (see Chapter 10), carry trades (see Chapter 11), and structured product risk (see Chapter 14).
[10] See Chapter 19.

market and credit events, calibrated so as to achieve the appropriate severity. They may be based on macroeconomic models or scenarios and must then be translated into asset returns.

8.4.3 Expected Shortfall

Expected shortfall[11] is an alternative or supplementary risk measure to VaR, widely adopted largely because it has become more central to regulatory bank capital requirements. It is defined as the expected value of losses, conditional on the VaR loss being exceeded. VaR is a quantile of the loss distribution; expected shortfall is a conditional first moment of the truncated loss distribution. As seen in Figure 8.9, representing portfolio losses (as a positive number) by X, the expected shortfall is the expected value of realizations of X in the tail of the distribution to the right of the VaR scenario:[12]

$$\mathrm{E}[X|X \geq \mathrm{VaR}(t, \alpha, \tau)].$$

Expected shortfall for a single position can be estimated employing the same basic approaches and distributional hypotheses as VaR. Parametric expected shortfall using the lognormal model can be computed analytically. In the lognormal model, a closed-form expression for expected shortfall can be computed using the formula for a normal distribution truncated at the VaR. The ratio of expected shortfall to the VaR is:

$$-\frac{\phi(z_{1-\alpha})}{(1-\alpha)z_{1-\alpha}}, \tag{8.1}$$

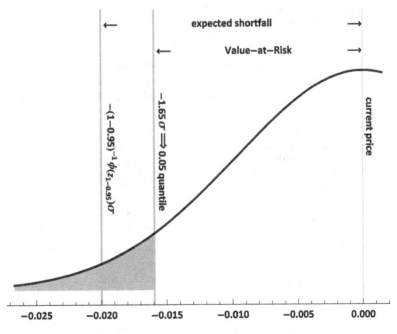

Figure 8.9 Definition of expected shortfall

Expected shortfall at a 95 percent confidence level is the area under the density function to the left of the VaR, divided by the probability (0.05) that the VaR is breached.

---

[11] Or **conditional Value-at-Risk**, or **tail Value-at-Risk**, or **expected tail loss**.
[12] Some presentations employ a strict inequality, which can change the results for discrete data.

where $\phi(\cdot)$ represents the standard normal density function, for example $\phi(z_{0.05}) = \phi(-1.645) = 0.103136$. The Monte Carlo and historical simulation approaches employ the same set of simulated values as VaR. The time-t estimate of the τ-day expected shortfall at a confidence level α is calculated as the average of the simulated losses in excess of $\text{VaR}_t(\alpha, \tau)$.

Example 8.8   Parametric normal and historical simulation estimates of expected shortfall

The example continues the analysis of a long position in the S&P 500 index with an initial value $1,000,000 as of the close on December 31, 2021. Assume returns are lognormally distributed, and apply the EWMA estimate of daily volatility 0.00969577. The 1-day expected shortfall is computed by multiplying the VaR computed above by the ratio given in equation (8.1), as seen in Table 8.4 for different VaR confidence levels.

Using 2 years ($T = 505$) of return observations up to December 31, 2021, we get the historical simulation results summarized in Table 8.5. In this table, the expected shortfall is computed first, and then the ratio of the expected shortfall to the historical simulation VaR from Table 8.2 is computed so it can be compared with the formulaic ratio for parametric normal. Table 8.6 details how the results for expected shortfall are obtained.

Expected shortfall is the average of loss levels greater than the VaR, so it is always at least as great as the VaR. It can be much larger than the VaR if the return distribution is heavy-tailed and skewed. The normal distribution is thin-tailed. Parametric normal estimates of the ratio of expected shortfall to VaR are therefore relatively low at lower confidence levels. This is another way of seeing the main disadvantage of the standard model: it implies that the risk of very large losses is relatively low. Real-life asset return distributions are generally very heavy-tailed, as seen in Figure 8.4, which displays the data underpinning the estimates in the example.

Historical simulation estimates of expected shortfall are generally high relative to VaR. There are more outsize observations beyond the VaR at lower confidence levels, so the disparity shrinks as the confidence level rises and fewer extremes remain in the tail beyond (see Figure 8.10). As with VaR,

Table 8.4   Parametric normal estimate of expected shortfall

conf. level	VaR	exp. shortfall	ratio
0.900	12 348.75	16 910.63	1.3694
0.950	15 821.62	19 840.95	1.2540
0.975	18 823.93	22 452.78	1.1928
0.990	22 303.25	25 552.05	1.1457

Parametric estimates of 1-day VaR and expected shortfall in dollars of $1,000,000 long position in S&P 500 on 31Dec2021.

Table 8.5   Historical simulation estimates of expected shortfall

conf. level	rank	VaR	exp. shortfall	ratio
0.900	50	12 985.88	29 654.64	2.2836
0.950	25	22 724.86	42 076.01	1.8515
0.975	12	33 687.32	57 213.93	1.6984
0.990	5	48 868.41	80 339.56	1.6440

Historical simulation estimates of 1-day VaR and expected shortfall in dollars of $1,000,000 long position in S&P 500 on 31Dec2021. The rank stated in the table is that of the smallest loss included in expected shortfall and is one less than that of the VaR scenario.

Table 8.6 Computation of expected shortfall by historical simulation

i	t	S_t	date t	S_{t-1}	$\tilde{r}^{(i)}$	$\tilde{r}^{arith,(i)}$	P&L
1	51	2386.13	16Mar2020	2711.02	−0.12765	−0.11984	−119 840.50
2	49	2480.64	12Mar2020	2741.38	−0.09994	−0.09511	−95 112.68
3	46	2746.56	09Mar2020	2972.37	−0.07901	−0.07597	−75 969.68
4	112	3002.10	11Jun2020	3190.14	−0.06075	−0.05894	−58 944.12
5	53	2398.10	18Mar2020	2529.19	−0.05322	−0.05183	−51 830.82
6	48	2741.38	11Mar2020	2882.23	−0.05010	−0.04887	−48 868.41
⋮	⋮	⋮	⋮	⋮	⋮	⋮	⋮

The entries in the sixth column are the ordered arithmetic historical returns $\tilde{r}^{(i)}, i = 1, \ldots, T$ and $T = 505$. The P&L realizations are $x(\tilde{S}_{(i)} - S_t)$.

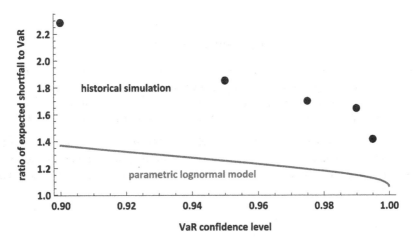

Figure 8.10 Relationship of expected shortfall to Value-at-Risk

Ratio of expected shortfall to VaR as a function of confidence level.

expected shortfall estimates via historical simulation may vary widely with the historical look-back period.

Expected shortfall has the advantage over VaR, in principle, in that it is oriented toward tail risk measurement and more appropriate, say, for setting economic capital. But it is unlikely *per se* to provide significant improvement, as it is an additional statistic within the VaR framework rather than an alternative to VaR. If the data and the model do not provide good tail risk estimates, expected shortfall is unlikely to help.

Expected shortfall has the additional disadvantage in that it is even more difficult than VaR to backtest because extremes are less frequent than observations in the body of the distribution. VaR backtesting involves counting episodes in which a quantile is exceeded. At any useful confidence level, there are relatively few exceedances of VaR, and each provides one observation on exceedance size. But you need many for statistically robust evidence that your estimate of the size of the mean outlier occuring with a certain frequency is too low. This difficulty is added to all the limitations of VaR backtesting.

The difficulty of backtesting expected shortfall is an example of the **elicitability** problem that can arise for risk measures. Elicitability is a desirable property of a statistic of a random variable, such as P&L. Elicitable statistics permit a **scoring function** to be devised by which forecasts can be tracked day by day to see how close they are to their realizations. For VaR, such a scoring function might be:

- Each day, measure the absolute value of the difference between VaR and the realized P&L.
- The observation's weight is α if there is an exceedance, and otherwise $1 - \alpha$.

A low score indicates few exceedances, thus validating VaR.[13] Expected shortfall is not elicitable, that is, no such scoring function can be formulated.

The revised Basel standards place expected shortfall at the core of model-based capital requirements for market risk. But they call for backtesting the VaR underlying the expected shortfall estimate at 97.5- and 99 percent confidence levels as an internal model check, rather than a requirement to test the expected shortfall estimate itself.

Further Reading

Dowd (2005) provides an overview of market risk measurement techniques. Klugman et al. (2019) is a clear exposition of many of these techniques, oriented toward the insurance industry. See also Linsmeier and Pearson (2000). The financial risk texts cited in Chapter 2 also cover market risk. See McNeil et al. (2015) for precise definitions of coherence, subadditivity, and expected shortfall.

Daníelsson (2002) is a critical view of VaR. Jorion (2000) uses the failure of the hedge fund Long-Term Capital Management in 1998 to illustrate misleading interpretations and uses of VaR. Beder (1995) discusses the variability of VaR results with assumptions about parameters and data.

---

[13] Note that a zero score would indicate P&L has no variability at all and is always a loss equal to VaR.

9

Credit and Counterparty Risk

9.1 Default, Bankruptcy, and Resolution

9.1.1 Equity, Debt, and Leverage

Credit analysis begins with a firm's or household's balance sheet. A firm acquires assets with a view to making a positive net return, funded by issuing claims, in two contractually distinct ways. **Equity** in its simplest form are the funds directly invested by owners of the firm, including **paid-in capital** and **retained earnings**. More broadly, equity can be shareholder or partner equity, the down payment on a house, or the part of a position funded by the trader rather than a dealer.

Equity is a residual claim on earnings; any revenues not owed to other parties flow to the equity investors. **Debt** is a contract providing fixed obligations in exchange for the funds. Debt holders have claims only to contractually stipulated returns. If the debt exceeds the asset value, limited liability law precludes **recourse** to other property of owners. Therefore, equity has characteristics in common with options.

These funding contracts are ultimately traceable to the distinct investment roles of those taking on a limited part or the brunt of the uncertainty pervading any enterprise. Investors looking to limit their risk will prefer a contractually guaranteed income, while the more venturesome will prefer the potential high return of a residual income. Equity stakes and ownership of firms are also linked to control over firm management. As firm organization and its legal framework have evolved, this relationship has become more complicated and problematic. Management may not always act strictly in owners' interests.

Taking on the corporate form was once a special privilege requiring permission from a sovereign or parliament and brought with it the right to conduct businesses not open to all. Today, in advanced economies, it is open to any individual or group meeting simple criteria although licensing and other requirements still restrict entry to many economic activities, including finance.

A firm's **capital structure** is the composition of its funding among different types of equity and debt. It can be represented by the schematic **balance sheet** displayed in Figure 9.1. The assets and funding can be measured in market, accounting, or theoretical, fundamental analysis-based, fair value terms. The balance sheet is subject to the accounting identity

$$A_t = E_t + D_t.$$

Leverage is the ratio of assets to equity:

$$L_t = \frac{A_t}{E_t},$$

Assets	Liabilities
Value of assets (A_t)	Equity (E_t)
	Debt (D_t)

Figure 9.1 Schematic company or household balance sheet

a multiple referred to as "turns" of leverage. It must exceed 1 for a solvent firm. Leverage enhances returns or losses on equity capital. Each turn of leverage increases **return on equity** (RoE) by the difference between the return on assets and cost of debt, an important incentive as well as risk (discussed further in Chapter 11).

9.1.2   Information Costs in Credit Intermediation

Lending is an information-intensive business. **Underwriting** is the initial assessment of a potential borrower, and **monitoring** is the ongoing process of assessing creditworthiness.

Apart from the direct cost of gathering and assessing information about potential and actual obligors, credit intermediation faces special costs that stem from information challenges in markets identified in Chapter 3:

Asymmetric information is prevalent in credit markets. Borrowers have much more information about their condition, their prospects, and their ability to repay than lenders. Intermediaries underwrite and monitor loans, introducing a principal-agent problem and consequent agency costs.

Risk shifting arises from the asymmetry of risks and rewards between debt and equity, and among different forms of debt, leading to option-like payoffs. Equity investors, with limited downside and unlimited potential returns, may favor riskier assets. Lenders will be acutely aware of this.

Adverse selection: In bond markets, asymmetric information can lead to an adverse selection problem, given even a small likelihood a seller but not the buyer knows of defects of a security. This can lead to higher borrowing costs and a wider bid-ask spread in secondary markets.

Externalities arise in credit intermediation when actions by one market participant impose costs or provide benefits to others that can't be compensated through market mechanisms without additional costs or institutional arrangements. Risk taking by one intermediary can increase the risks of others that own the liabilities of risky lenders or because the public is made suspicious of lenders generally.

Lenders may engage advisory services to assess and monitor obligors' creditworthiness, reduce information costs, and mitigate the information problems in credit assessment described above. Such services are particularly economical for bonds and other marketable credit-risky securities. **Credit rating agencies** (CRAs) have existed since the 19th century, providing alphanumerical **credit ratings** and detailed reports on the creditworthiness of borrowers or securities. Consumer credit reporting and single-number **credit scores** have been developed for household lending. Securities ratings may be **investment grade** (higher-rated) or **speculative grade** (lower-rated).

The asymmetric information problem can only by partly mitigated through ratings, just as the used-car "lemons" problem can be only partially mitigated through certification by trusted dealers.

Rating firms may err in their assessments or have conflicting incentives that skew them. CRAs originally operated on a **subscriber-pays** business model, with bond investors paying for the information. It was superseded by the current **issuer-pays** model, prompted by advances in copying technology from the 1970s.

9.1.3   Default and Migration

Default or a **default event** is the failure of the borrower or **obligor** to fulfill the terms of a debt contract. The most frequent type of default is failure to pay contractually agreed interest or principal when due. Default events also include attempts at fraud or **breach of representations and warranties**: lenders may have the right to cancel a debt contract if borrowers can be shown to have lied about their financial condition or prospects.

Insolvency is the inability to pay debts, a state of existence of the borrower as opposed to an actual event of nonpayment. **Cash flow insolvency** is a state in which cash is insufficient to meet imminent or near-term debt obligations. **Balance-sheet insolvency** is a state in which, from an accounting or economic standpoint, debt exceeds assets and the borrower has negative capital or **net worth**. An insurance company, for example, that has sold underpriced long-term policies may continue in existence for years before the inadequacy of the premiums and the investments they fund to pay future claims render the company unviable. **Bankruptcy** is a legal procedure in which a defaulting or insolvent debtor "seeks relief" from creditors, and the conflicts among owners and lenders are resolved.

Figure 9.2 displays one measure of default frequency, its rate of occurrence in US bond markets over the past century. Defaults are a fairly unusual occurrence, with many years in which no investment-grade bond defaults occur. Defaults cluster over time: when defaults rise, they often spike sharply. Measuring this propensity to cluster is one of the chief challenges in modeling credit portfolio risk.

Credit events other than default occur regularly. Any credit exposes the lender to a deterioration in the creditworthiness of the borrower, regardless of whether a rating is involved. **Credit rating**

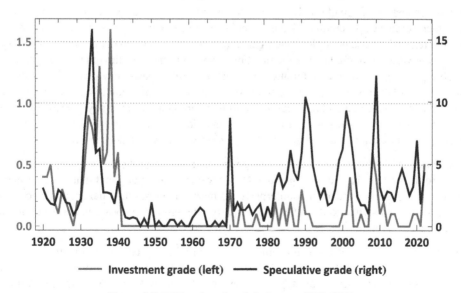

Figure 9.2 US bond market default rates 1920–2022

Annual issuer-weighted corporate default rates by letter rating, percent. 2022 data include Russian defaults. *Source*: Moody's Investors Service.

Table 9.1 Rating migration rates, 1920–2022

From/To:	Aaa	Aa	A	Baa	Ba	B	Caa	Ca–C	WR	Def
Aaa	87.1	7.5	0.8	0.2	0.0	0.0	0.0	0.0	4.4	0.0
Aa	1.0	84.5	7.6	0.7	0.1	0.0	0.0	0.0	6.0	0.1
A	0.1	2.6	85.8	5.2	0.6	0.1	0.0	0.0	5.5	0.1
Baa	0.0	0.2	3.9	84.1	4.1	0.6	0.1	0.0	6.7	0.2
Ba	0.0	0.1	0.4	6.0	74.6	6.6	0.7	0.1	10.4	1.1
B	0.0	0.0	0.1	0.6	5.5	72.2	6.3	0.4	11.8	3.0
Caa	0.0	0.0	0.0	0.1	0.4	6.0	69.9	2.8	14.0	6.8
Ca–C	0.0	0.0	0.1	0.1	0.4	2.5	9.6	45.2	17.2	25.0

Average 1-year letter rating migration rates, 1920–2022, percent. Each row shows the probability of starting the year with the rating in the row heading and ending with the rating in the column heading. "WR" denotes withdrawn rating. 2022 data include Russian defaults. *Source*: Moody's Investor Service.

migration refers to a change in credit rating, an **upgrade** or **downgrade**. Migration is a credit and a market risk event because it can affect the pricing of the borrower's debt and can influence the market's readiness to extend credit in the future.

Ratings correspond to estimated default and migration rates or frequencies that can be presented in a corporate ratings **transition matrix** such as Table 9.1. It displays the estimated probability of an obligor or security having a given rating at end of a year, conditional on its rating at the beginning of the year. Investment-grade are likelier than speculative-grade firms to see no change in rating. If there is a change of rating, firms with high ratings are likelier to be downgraded; the lowest-rated firms are likelier to either default or be upgraded.

9.1.4   Counterparty Risk and Collateral

Counterparty risk is a form of credit risk that arises in OTC derivatives markets, such as those for options, interest rate swaps, credit derivatives, and short-term financing markets. It is not an obligor but the counterparty whose possible default generates the risk. Counterparty credit exposure is not a fixed value but varies with market risk factors. For swaps and forwards, though not for options, cash flows subsequent to the contract's initiation are bilateral. Either party may owe value to the other, depending on market conditions. The credit exposure at the time of default is, therefore, uncertain. OTC options don't have bilateral risk, but the contingent amount the seller pays varies over time, so the purchaser faces a time-varying credit exposure that depends on market prices. Derivatives can have large gross notional amounts and, therefore, a high volatility of net exposure.

Suppose, for example, two counterparties engage in a plain-vanilla interest rate swap with an initial NPV of zero. It can later have a large positive NPV for one counterparty, but that good news brings with it a credit exposure to the other counterparty. As market interest rates change, the exposure may grow, shrink, or even switch to the other counterparty. Though the exposure is known at any point in time, the risk is bilateral.

Counterparty risk can be managed and mitigated by monitoring and diversification of counterparties, setting exposure limits, **collateral**, and netting of transactions. For swaps and other OTC derivatives, collateral and netting are typically governed by ISDA Master Agreements. Among the terms of these agreements are **cross-default provisions** automatically defaulting a counterparty on all its similar derivatives contracts with other counterparties if it defaults against any counterparty.

This prevents counterparties from strategically cherry-picking counterparties against which to default.

Many credit and derivatives transactions are supported by collateral or **secured**. Assets are **pledged** to repay the debt if the borrower fails to meet specific obligations. Assets typically pledged as collateral include cash, securities, future cash flows or revenues, and specific factories or corporate subsidiaries. The borrower retains ownership of the collateral, but it is held by the lender, who is permitted by the debt contract to sell it should the borrower default. Most central bank monetary operations rely on markets that use securities as collateral.

External forms of **credit support** include **guarantees**. Credit default swaps in which one party promises to make the other whole in the event of a default, are a mechanism of external credit support. CDS are exposed to a specific form of counterparty risk, double default risk, the risk that both the underlying credit and the counterparty selling protection default.

9.1.5 Bankruptcy, Capital Structure, and Resolution

Bankruptcy is the legal process of adjudicating the conflicting claims of creditors and shareholders. It unfolds under a bankruptcy court's supervision and is subject to bankruptcy rules as well as negotiation and efforts at risk shifting among stakeholders. Impaired debt holders become residual claimants but gain control rights from shareholders. **Resolution** is a part of broader mechanisms of debt enforcement, the ability of creditors to enforce contracts with debtors. In recent years, the view that bankruptcy law ought to take account of a wider circle of non-owner stakeholders, for example, employees, customers and suppliers, and even the public at large, has gained traction in the United States.

Debt contracts differ in many respects, including the strength of their claim to repayment. **Debt priority** describes the order in which debts have to be repaid and the credit risk ranking of lenders; the last in line bears the greatest risk. Though debt priority may be modified during bankruptcy and is therefore, somewhat malleable, it is largely determined by law and by the terms and characteristics of all the firm's liabilities, such as:

Security: debt secured by collateral is to be paid in full before unsecured debt. Debt that is not secured is backed only by the firm's assets and cash flows. In the United States, a **debenture** is a bond backed by a firm's general credit. **General obligation** bonds are those issued by municipalities backed only by its general revenues and ability to tax.

Seniority: a debt contract may itself provide for **subordination** to senior debt in return for a higher yield. The senior debt may also contain contractual limitations on issuance of additional debt with the same or higher priority. The top of the "capital stack" generally consists of bank loans and **senior secured debt**. **Hybrid securities**, such as junior, subordinated and convertible debt, and preferred stock, have characteristics of debt and equity and have priority over dividend payments to equity owners.

Corporate structure: holding company obligations are generally subordinate to those of **operating subsidiaries**.

Short-term maturity also effectively confers priority over long-term debt because lenders can periodically reassess their willingness to lend.

At the opening of a bankruptcy proceeding, an **automatic stay** or injunction stops unilateral creditor actions to recover debt, such as separate lawsuits, seizure of debtor property, or netting of debts. The stay is intended to prevent a value-destroying race to grab assets by creditors. Bankruptcy culminates in resolution, followed by **bankruptcy discharge**. Resolution takes two forms under Title 11 of the United States Code. In a **liquidation** (US Chapter 7), the firm goes out of business, with an equitable distribution of its remaining assets to creditors. Aggregate **recovery** is often greater than zero because the bankrupt firm likely still has valuable assets, so creditors don't all lose the entire amount of debt. Debt claims receive proceeds from the liquidation in priority order.

In a **reorganization** (US Chapter 11), the firm survives and is rehabilitated by restructuring its balance sheet and operations. Firms and their creditors embark on the Chapter 11 route only if they are confident that the firm can emerge as a going concern. Part or all of its debt may be converted to equity in the newly reorganized firm. The firm's capital structure, negotiations, and the judicial system determine the **fulcrum security**, the senior most claim that is converted to new-firm equity. Senior creditors may get a larger equity stake than subordinated creditors, or senior creditors may get newly issued bonds while subordinated creditors get an equity stake.

Senior and secured creditors are often biased toward liquidation. They have less interest in the realization of the full potential value of the failing firm because they have a better chance of high recovery on their own claims than more junior creditors, even if aggregate recovery is low. Junior creditors and equity owners, in contrast, are biased toward reorganization. They have an acute interest in the realization of full value because it may be their only avenue to realizing any value for their securities. Any plan must adhere to the **absolute priority rule**: if a senior class is impaired, any more junior class equity, for example, must be wiped out. Senior and secured creditors may get full recovery, and subordinated debt is likely to get a "haircut," or reduction in the value of its claim. A **cram-down** is a plan agreed by a majority of creditors and gaining judicial approval, but forced upon a dissenting class of holdout creditors.

Bankruptcy incurs administrative costs and the costs of reallocating resources. There are more consensual alternatives to resolution in bankruptcy court by which a better outcome can be achieved at lower cost. In a **voluntary restructuring**, the liabilities of the firm are restructured by renegotiating the debt contract terms, and the assets may be restructured through sales. Part of such a restructuring may be a **distressed debt exchange** in which creditors receive securities or cash with worse terms or reduced par value in exchange for the original debt. The creditors accept these terms to avoid the potentially larger risk, delay, and cost of resolution in court.

An example of such a restructuring is the reorganization of CIT Group, a trade-finance lender with $75 billion in assets in October 2009. It simultaneously presented proposals for an exchange and a restructuring to its creditors, who approved the latter. Another example is the restructuring of Greece's sovereign debt in 2012.

New financing generally has a senior claim to existing debt. Internationally, loans by supranational organizations such as the International Monetary Fund (IMF) to distressed sovereigns have had higher priority than existing debt. For example, during the European sovereign debt crisis of 2010–2012, central bank and supranational purchases of apparently insolvent countries' debt subordinated private holdings of earlier issues.

A form of legal risk for all stakeholders is **latent subordination**, or subordination of claims after the fact, with new creditors getting in front of the old. One path by which this occurs is **debtor-in-possession** (DIP) financing in Chapter 11 proceedings, in which the management of the bankrupt firm remains in court-supervised control during reorganization. Latent subordination doesn't necessarily induce losses to the holder of older debt because it may improve the borrower's financial condition enough to compensate.

The **resolution regime** is the set of legal processes and institutions applied in the event of firm insolvency or default. Procedures for corporate insolvency are related to several efficiency objectives. Resolution mitigates coordination and collective action problems among creditors. By facilitating a fair distribution among claimants, it prevents a "race to the courthouse." Reorganization improves recovery to the benefit of creditors and possibly owners. Resolution in or out of the courts preserves the going-concern value of the bankruptcy estate if it is larger than the liquidation value of the possibly quite illiquid assets.

International differences in resolution regimes are related to overall economic efficiency and growth. The cost of resolution, the structure of the financial system, and the speed, efficiency, and certainty of legal institutions and governance differ across countries. Governments may be reluctant to permit bankruptcies or wish to explicitly subsidize firms. Banks may be reluctant to recognize loan losses, and, instead, receive tacit support from governments for subsidized lending to insolvent **zombie firms**. Examples include Japan, since the post-1989 "lost decades," and Italy, where bankruptcies take very long to resolve. Both have experienced unusually slow economic growth, even by European and developed-country standards.

9.2   Quantifying Credit Risk

Lenders and investors use quantitative models to estimate potential losses due to credit risk, while regulators use them to formulate rules for the behavior of banks, insurance companies, and other firms. Many of these models share a basic set of metrics and a common framework for conceptualizing credit risk.

9.2.1   Credit Risk Metrics

The typical horizon of a credit risk assessment is much longer than for market risk, typically on the order of 1 year rather than 1 day. Credit risk events are rare: for most firms, most of the time passes without a default, up- or downgrade, or other credit event. Asset returns large enough in magnitude to deserve attention occur much more frequently.

Several key metrics appear in credit risk models as parameters or results. The **probability of default** π is defined over a specified time horizon. The **exposure at default** is the amount the lender can lose in a default event. For a loan or bond, it is straightforward: the par value of the debt plus any accrued interest. For derivatives, counterparty risk complicates matters because the exposure is driven also by changes in the market value of the underlying asset. When a default occurs, the assets available to settle bankruptcy claims may have enough value to pay at least part of the debt. Creditors then lose less than 100 percent of their exposure. **Recovery** is the fraction $r \leq 1$ ultimately recouped, and the **loss given default** (LGD) equals the exposure minus recovery $(1 - r)$.

The **expected loss** (EL) equals the default probability times the LGD, $\pi \times (1 - r)$. Expected losses are estimated in advance through underwriting and credit analysis and kept up-to-date through monitoring. They are treated as a normal cost of a lending business, analogous to an input to a manufacturing process. Commercial banks account for these losses in advance by diverting part of loans' initial asset value to a balance sheet position, the reserve for losses.[1] Lenders are compensated for predictable credit losses and other costs through credit spreads. Expected losses, with adjustments

---

[1] See Chapter 19.

for risk, can also be indirectly measured by the market spread over the risk-free rate or cost of funds on loans to a category of obligor.

Credit risk management focuses on **unexpected loss**. **Credit Value-at-Risk** (credit VaR) is defined, analogously to market risk measurement, as a quantile of the credit loss distribution of a portfolio of credits. In the case of market VaR, we assume that the mean, or expected value, of the asset return is zero. Expected asset returns are hard to estimate with any accuracy, and risk is generally measured for shorter horizons over which the contribution of expected return is small compared to the dispersion of the distribution. Credit VaR, in contrast, is measured over longer horizons during which the expected credit loss can be significant even relative to the overall uncertainty about credit losses. Therefore, we measure credit VaR as a quantile of the unexpected loss distribution, excluding the expected value of losses. The credit VaR at a confidence level α defined as

$$\alpha\text{-quantile of credit loss distribution} - \text{EL}.$$

A standard measure of counterparty risk, incorporated into international regulatory standards, is the accounting position **credit valuation adjustment** (CVA). It is defined as the difference between the market value of the derivatives contract, net of collateral, and its market value if it were free of credit risk. CVA represents the expected loss due to counterparty default, the market value of counterparty risk, or the hedging cost. Ideally, measurement would take into account the possible future values of the derivatives exposure, if positive, the probability of the counterparty defaulting and the LGD in each of those states, and the discount factor to be applied for each time and state. It is conventionally measured using estimates of exposure and credit risk parameters, such as default probability and recovery.

CVA has an odd counterpart, the **debit valuation adjustment** (DVA), an accounting position that measures the reduction in CVA resulting from the firm's own default risk. DVA, if positive, reduces a counterparty's liabilities stemming from a negative NPV on a swap or from a sold in-the-money put position. It reflects the fact that, if a less creditworthy firm sells, say, an option, or the firm's creditworthiness deteriorates after the option is sold, it will be worth less to any option purchaser. During the global financial crisis, an increase in the CVA of lightly collateralized in-the-money puts it had sold enabled Berkshire Hathaway to negotiate a restructuring of the option positions that avoided large losses.[2]

9.2.2   Default Modeling

Default probabilities are estimated in a number of ways. Physical default probabilities are based on fundamental analysis of a borrower's balance sheet and business, its mix of assets and debt, historical default frequencies, scenario analyses, or a formal credit model. Credit ratings are also based on fundamental analysis and associated with default probability estimates.

Risk-neutral default probabilities are based on market prices, such as credit spreads on credit-risky securities or the prices of credit default swaps. The credit spread is a risk-neutral measure of expected loss. To estimate a default probability from a credit spread, an estimate of LGD is therefore, also required. Risk-neutral probabilities may be higher than physical probabilities due to risk premiums compensating investors over and above expected credit losses. Credit spreads reflect the judgment of many market participants and, in a liquid market, leave no predictable return that is not compensation

---

[2] See Triana (2015).

for risk, but the presence of risk premiums is nonetheless problematic in risk measurement, which aims for actuarial accuracy rather than market equivalence.

Credit models differ in whether they focus on estimating default probabilities or use them as inputs to estimate other risk metrics. **Structural**, or **fundamental, models** derive measures of credit risk from analysis of a firm's condition and creditworthiness, and of the industry it belongs to. **Reduced form**, or **intensity, models** take estimates of default probability and LGD as inputs to simulate default times as one step in portfolio credit risk modeling. **Factor models** incorporate company, industry, or economy-wide fundamentals in a schematized fashion. Most models employed in practice fall into several of these categories. Models are said to operate in **migration mode** if they take into account credit rating migration or a change in creditworthiness as well as default. A model taking only default into account is said to operate in **default mode**.

9.2.3 Intensity Models and Default Time Analytics

Although the vast majority don't default, any borrower could conceivably at any time. In discrete time models, the occurrence of a default event for a single company over a given discrete time horizon t is modeled as a Bernoulli distribution, with a probability π of occurrence and $1 - \pi$ of not occurring. In a continuous time **default intensity model**, default is conceptualized as an event that can at occur at any time in the future and modeled as a jump or Poisson process, with at most one jump possible. The point in time τ at which default occurs is a random variable. Default is an **absorbing state**; it can happen only once to an individual borrower, and if it does, there is no returning. The probability of default between now and time t is $\mathbf{P}[0 \leq \tau < t]$. The **survival probability**—the likelihood the obligor remains solvent until at least time t—is $1 - \mathbf{P}[0 \leq \tau < t]$.

The default probability increases as the horizon t grows longer. Every firm defaults eventually:

$$\lim_{t \to \infty} \mathbf{P}[0 \leq \tau < t] = 1.$$

Over a tiny time interval dt, the probability of default is λdt, where λ is the **hazard rate**, or **default intensity**.[3] The parameter λ can be modeled as a constant or as changing over time. Default probabilities can be expressed through the **cumulative default time distribution function**. With a constant hazard rate, this takes the simple form

$$\mathbf{P}[0 \leq \tau < t] = 1 - e^{-\lambda t}.$$

The survival probability is $e^{-\lambda t}$. If t is expressed in years, the 1-year default probability is $1 - e^{-\lambda}$. Default of any obligor can only occur once, so probabilities of default in successive periods are not independent events. The **conditional probability of default** is the probability of default over a future time interval $[t, t + \Delta t)$, conditional on no default having occurred up until time t. In the intensity model, the parameter λ is the instantaneous conditional default probability, the probability of default over the next instant, given no prior default.

---

[3] In insurance, it is called the **force of mortality**, the probability of death of a population member over the next short time interval.

Table 9.2   Default probability analytics: example

Hazard rate	λ	0.15
1-yr. default probability	$1 - e^{-\lambda}$	0.1393
2-yr. default probability	$1 - e^{-2\lambda}$	0.2592
1-yr. survival probability	$e^{-\lambda}$	0.8607
1-yr. conditional default probability	$1 - e^{-\lambda}$	0.1393

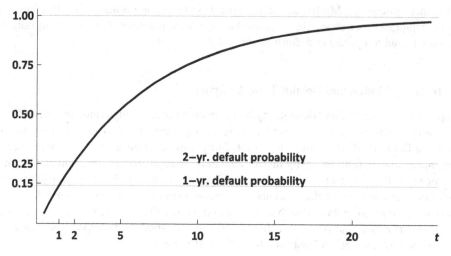

Figure 9.3 Default time distribution with a constant hazard rate

Cumulative default time distribution function π_t, constant hazard rate $\lambda = 0.15$, t measured in years, π_t and λ at an annual rate.

With a constant hazard rate, the conditional probability of default over a discrete interval starting in the future is

$$\mathbf{P}[t \le \tau < t + \Delta t \mid t < \tau] = \frac{\mathbf{P}[t \le \tau < t + \Delta t \cup t < \tau]}{\mathbf{P}[t < \tau]}$$

$$= \frac{(1 - e^{-\lambda \Delta t})e^{-\lambda t}}{e^{-\lambda t}} = 1 - e^{-\lambda \Delta t}.$$

The unconditional 1-year default probability is lower for more remote years. From the point of view of time 0, default is less likely in year 10 than in year 1 because there is some likelihood of it having occured before year 10. But the time to default is memoryless; if we posit that no default occurs next year, the probability of default over the subsequent year is $1 - e^{-\lambda}$, the same as next year's. Table 9.2 and Figure 9.3 provide an example.

9.3   Single-Obligor Credit Risk Models

The **Merton default model** is a widely used structural model of default probability and debt valuation based on fluctuations in the value of a debt-issuing firm's assets. It applies option pricing theory[4],

---
[4] See Chapter 6.

treating the debt and equity as positions involving options on the firm's assets. Equity claims have an unlimited upside, once all debt obligations have been met, but limited liability. Losses cannot exceed the equity value. Therefore, equity can be viewed as an implicit long call on any upside from the firm's assets, with a strike price equal to the par value of the debt, plus any interest.

The debt receives a fixed return as long as its value is less than that of the firm's assets, so it can be viewed as a portfolio of a riskless bond with the same current value as the debt, plus an implicit short put on the firm's assets. This **default put** also has a strike price equal to the par value plus accrued interest of the debt. The lender would be immunized against credit risk by buying back the short put, so the implicit put value is a measure of credit risk that allows us to derive the probability of default. The model assumes default has no legal or other costs.

In applying the model, the put is assumed to be out-of-the-money and the call in-the-money; the common exercise price is the cash due to lenders in the future from the debt. The exercise price has to be less than the asset value for the funds to have been advanced in the first place. Default occurs if the asset value falls below a **default threshold**, at which its equity value is extremely low or zero and its asset value is equal to or near the value of debt.

With the assumption that the asset value follows a geometric Brownian motion process with a known drift and volatility, the options can be valued using the Black-Scholes model. Figure 9.4 displays an example of asset price behavior and the resulting probability distribution of asset value.[5] Only the endpoints of each path matter: if the asset value dips below the default threshold before debt maturity but then recovers, no default occurs. The model implies a physical or actuarial default probability, the likelihood of the terminal asset value falling below the default threshold. But it also can be used to value the debt.

Suppose the equity pays no dividends, and the implicit options have a one-period time to maturity. The firm's debt is a 1-period zero-coupon bond with a nominal face value at maturity of B.

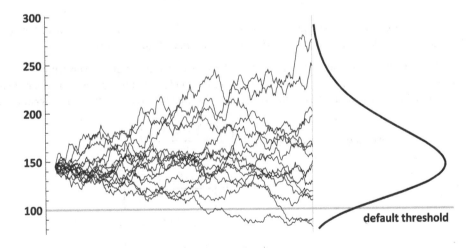

Figure 9.4 Merton default model

Left: 15 daily-frequency sample paths of the geometric Brownian motion process of the firm's assets with a drift of 10 percent and an annual volatility of 25 percent, starting from a current value of 145. Right: probability density of the firm's asset value on the maturity date, 1 year hence, of the debt, a zero-coupon bond with a par value of 100. The grid line represents the debt's par value.

---

[5] Compare with Figure 4.1.

The firm could be liquidated at the end of the period and the assets sold to pay off the debt with the residual value paid to the equity owners. If the asset value is below the debt par value, the firm is in default. If the firm is still viable, it could instead continue doing business.

The Merton default model states that the market value of the equity is equal to the Black-Scholes value $v(A_0, B, 1, \sigma, r_f, 0)$ of a 1-period call option on the firm's assets at their current value A_0, struck at B, with r_f the continuously compounded riskless rate. The market value of the debt is equal to the value $Be^{-r_f\tau}$ of a risk-free bond minus the Black-Scholes put value: $Be^{-r_f\tau} - w(A_0, B, 1, \sigma, r_f, 0)$.

The values of these implicit options on the assets are bound by arbitrage relations. Substituting the model's debt and equity values D_0 and E_0 into the balance sheet constraint, we have:

$$A_0 = E_0 + D_0 = v(A_0, B, 1, \sigma, r_f, 0) - w(A_0, B, 1, \sigma, r_f, 0) + Be^{-r_f}.$$

This is a statement of put-call parity, consistent with the Merton default model and the balance sheet accounting constraint.[6]

The equity owners' call option can be viewed, via put-call parity, as a portfolio: they own the risky firm assets and the default put, with debt financed at the risk-free rate. The put is the limited liability component, insuring any loss due to default. The vega of a long call or put option is positive, so an immediate consequence of the model is that higher volatility, i.e., higher asset risk, benefits equity owners at the expense of debtholders.

Given the values of the equity, assets, debt, risk-free rate, and asset volatility, we can use the option valuation model to estimate the actuarial and the risk-neutral probability of default. The market value of the debt D_0 and the firm's continuously compounded credit-risky borrowing rate r are given by:

$$D_0 = Be^{-r} = Be^{-r_f} - w(A_0, B, 1, \sigma, r_f, 0)$$
$$\Rightarrow \quad B(e^{-r_f} - e^{-r}) = w(A_0, B, 1, \sigma, r_f, 0).$$

The present value of the additional financing cost over the riskless rate equals the value of the default put. This equation can be solved for the bond yield r or evaluated numerically.

Analogously to the interpretation of the value of a call as the expected value of exercising the option, conditional on ending in-the-money (equation 6.4), we can understand the Black-Scholes put value as the conditional expected value of default losses, the value that would insure the bond owner against default:

$$w(A_0, B, 1, \sigma, r_f, 0) = -A_0 \Phi\left[-\frac{\ln\left(\frac{A_0}{B}\right) + r_f + \frac{\sigma^2}{2}}{\sigma}\right]$$

$$+ Be^{-r_f}\Phi\left[-\frac{\ln\left(\frac{A_0}{B}\right) + r_f - \frac{\sigma^2}{2}}{\sigma}\right] \tag{9.1}$$

$$= -A_0\Phi(-d_1) + Be^{-r_f}\Phi(-d_1-\sigma)$$

$$= \Phi(-d_1-\sigma)\left[Be^{-r_f} - A_0\frac{\Phi(-d_1)}{\Phi(-d_1-\sigma)}\right],$$

with

$$d_1 \equiv \frac{\ln\left(\frac{A_0}{B}\right) + r_f + \frac{\sigma^2}{2}}{\sigma}.$$

---

[6] It is also consistent with its stronger economic version, Modigliani-Miller irrelevancy, discussed below in Chapter 11.

The risk-neutral default probability is $\Phi(-d_1-\sigma)$, the likelihood of $A_0 < B$. The actuarial default probability is obtained by substituting an estimate of the expected return on the firm's assets for the riskless rate in this expression.

The first term inside the square brackets on the last line of equation (9.1) is the present value of a riskless bond with the same par value as the firm's debt. The second term is the expected present value of the assets, conditional on default occurring and the put expiring in-the-money, i.e., the expected present value of recovery on the debt. The difference between terms inside the brackets is the loss given default (LGD), discounted to its present value at the risk-free rate. The default put option's value is this expected loss, the present value of the LGD, times the probability of the loss occurring. If the put expires out of the money, it's because the corporate bond was repaid at par.

For a traded firm, the equity and debt face values can be obtained from public markets and reports. In the real world, in which Modigliani-Miller holds only loosely, the book values of the assets can be misleading, and the asset fair value, asset volatility, the firm's leverage, and default threshold must be be estimated. Practitioner applications such as Moody's KMV provide estimates for specific firms based on the model and fundamental analysis. With estimates of asset value and observations on a traded firm's equity volatility, we can infer the asset volatility, using the Black-Scholes call option delta:

$$\frac{\Delta E}{E} \approx \frac{\partial E}{\partial A} \frac{A}{E} \frac{\Delta A}{A}$$

$$\Rightarrow \qquad \sigma_E = \Phi \left[\frac{\ln\left(\frac{A_0}{B}\right) + \left(r + \frac{\sigma^2}{2}\right)}{\sigma} \right] L\sigma,$$

with σ_E the equity volatility. Using the model together with historical data on similar firms, default frequencies can be estimated.

The firm's asset value is stochastic in the Merton model, so all its results also have to be treated as instantaneous. The model's relationship between equity and asset volatility, such as leverage and other variables, changes with the asset value. The Black-Scholes assumptions can be applied as approximations at each moment, but not over time.

Treating the asset volatility as an implied volatility links the model to market prices. The call might be more valuable because some market participants value the asymmetric payoff profile and bid up the price, and puts might be costly and the credit spread wider because other market participants have to be compensated for owning defaultable bonds.

Example 9.1   Merton default model

Suppose a firm has assets with a current value $A_0 = 145$. The asset value fluctuates as a geometric Brownian motion process, with a volatility $\sigma = 0.25$, a drift $\mu = 0.10$ and a continuously compounded risk-free rate $r_f = 0.05$, measured at an annual rate. The firm finances itself by issuing a 1-year zero-coupon bond with a face value at maturity of $B = 100$.

The fair value of the equity in the Merton default model can be assessed as the value of a 1 year call option on the firm's assets struck at \$100, applying a volatility parameter of 0.25. The value of the bond is equal to that of a portfolio consisting of a riskless discount bond with a face value of \$100 and a short 1-year put option struck at \$100. Applying the Black-Scholes model to evaluate the options, we have the results in Table 9.3.

Table 9.3   Merton model valuation of firm liabilities

Physical default probability	3.910
Risk-neutral default probability	5.980
Firm's equity value	50.321
Present value of a riskless bond	95.238
Firm's debt value	94.679
Debt yield	5.467
Credit spread (bps)	58.8
Risk-neutral PV of loss given default	9.344
Value of the default put	0.559
Firm initial leverage	2.9

Probabilities and continuously compounded yields in percent.

Further Reading

Knight (1921), ch. IX explains the emergence of equity and debt funding by the prevalence of uncertainty and differences in risk appetites. Weiss and Wruck (1998) use the example of Eastern Airlines to illustrate the complexities and conflicts of interest in corporate bankruptcy procedures. Griffiths (2010) describes the CIT restructuring.

Introductions to counterparty risk include Canabarro and Duffie (2003), Gregory (2012), and Singh and Segoviano (2008).

Chatterjee (2015) is a basic introduction to credit risk models. The financial risk texts cited in Chapter 2 also cover credit risk. Sundaresan (2013) and chapter 9 of Crouhy et al. (2000b) provide introductions to the Merton credit risk model.

Part III: Market Institutions and Risk Assessment

10

Interest Rate Risk

10.1 Sources of Interest Rate Risk

The values of loans and debt securities vary as interest rates change. The broad sources of yield curve uncertainty are

Expected future rates: the current risk-free curve fluctuates with expected future rates;
Liquidity risk: the cost and risk of exiting, adjusting, or maintaining an investment position;
Inflation risk: the risk of loss from a rise in the general price level;
Credit spreads: the risk of default and credit migration losses or the market-clearing compensation
  for credit risk may change.

Each source of volatility is compensated through a component of the risk premium of the loan or security. Risk premiums are generally positive, making bonds cheaper and increasing prospective future returns, but may be negative for the most sought-after safe assets.

Longer-term rates along a risk-free curve can be decomposed into the short-term rates expected to prevail up to maturity or the expected return from rolling over short-term debt, and a **term premium**, the additional yield compensating lenders for bearing the interest-rate risk of a longer-term security. The term premium is sometimes defined simply as the observable spread between longer- and shorter-term government bond yields but more generally as the unobservable spread between the long-term nominal rate and the rate implied by the expected path of short-term risk-free nominal rates.

The term premium as well as expected short-term rates fluctuate; aversion to term risk may change without a material change in expected future interest rates. The term premium can be negative if investors are eager to lock in the current level of longer-term rates and avoid the possibility that short-term rates decline more than expected. Estimates of US Treasury term premiums have ranged between 5 percent at the height of the early 1980s disinflation effort, when investors were wary of holding long-term nominal securities, and low negative levels during the global financial crisis when investors craved safe assets.[1]

The term structure is generally, but by no means invariably, upward sloping, with longer-term risk-free interest rates and credit spreads higher than short-term. The yield curve may be downward sloping—displaying **yield curve inversion**—overall or in some segments. Inversion at the short end of the curve, while unusual, can occur if short-term rates spike, and are not expected to persist at the higher levels. This may happen, for example, for interest rates on debt denominated in emerging-market currencies that come under devaluation pressure, for individual obligors whose creditworthiness is suddenly called into question, or if monetary policy has tightened sharply and

---

[1] US term premiums are estimated regularly by the Federal Reserve Board (available at https://fred.stlouisfed.org/series/THREEFYTP10) and the New York Fed (https://www.newyorkfed.org/research/data_indicators/term-premia-tabs#/overview)

markets expect some reversal. Inversion can also occur at the long end of the yield curve, brought about by the expectation that shorter-term rates will eventually decline, or by high demand for safe long-term bonds equivalent to negative risk premiums.

Examples in US Treasury markets include the 2005 "Greenspan conundrum," and the 2023 monetary tightening. During the 2005 conundrum episode, low long-term interest rates indicated that policy might not yet be tight enough although short-term rates had already been increased substantially. In the rapid 2022–2023 tightening, as seen in Figure 2.2, long-term rates eventually rose enough to indicate that markets expected higher short-term rates to persist but not to the level of the short-term rates themselves. In both episodes, uncertainty about term and risk premium behavior clouded interpretation.

A positive **liquidity premium** expresses an aversion to the risk of holding less liquid, generally longer-term securities. A relatively easy to observe, but narrow, set of liquidity premiums arises from the US Treasury's auction calendar for its debt securities, measured by the on-the-run/off-the-run spread. Liquidity premiums vary across maturities for a given issuer and across issuers. Many long-term, credit-risky bonds are infrequently traded or have small issuance volume, exposing them to market liquidity risk. High liquidity premiums are therefore, more likely for corporate bond and sovereign bonds issued outside advanced market economies.

Liquidity risk can have a disparate effect on yields: Financial stress is likely to impair general liquidity conditions and induce a **flight to quality**, increasing yields and widening many spreads to risk-free rates. Sovereign issues of advanced market economies may have negative liquidity risk premiums because they are considered safe assets to which investors may flee in stressed markets. Yields on the most liquid sovereign bonds tend to decline sharply during these episodes.

Shorter-term safe assets enjoy a negative **money premium**, raising their prices and lowering their yields because they provide money services. Short-term US Treasuries, for example, are close substitutes for cash balances and bear lower yields in compensation for the money services they provide. Therefore, the very short end of the Treasury yield curve is likely steeper than it otherwise would be. In Figure 2.2, even on the sharply inverted yield curve of May 31, 2023, the 1-month bill has a slightly lower yield than the 3- and 6-month.

Nominal interest rates have declined as sharply as they have from the 1980s because not only the inflation compensation component but also because real interest rates declined. The **Fisher equation** or **identity** relates expected inflation to nominal interest rates. It defines the real rate $\tilde{r}_t$ as the difference between the (observable) nominal interest rate (defined for convenience as the discount yield of a t-year bond) and (unobservable) expected future inflation:

$$\tilde{r}_t \equiv r_t - \mathbf{E}[\pi],$$

with π denoting inflation over the life of the bond. Although an identity, it is also taken as a statement about the long-term relationship of real and nominal rates. We can combine the Fisher and term premium decompositions to see the yield on a longer-term bond as the sum of the expected future path of inflation, the expected path of real short-term interest rates, and a set of risk premiums. The yields on inflation-protected bonds are a market-adjusted measure of real rates that may be lower than the unobservable expected real rate by a positive inflation risk premium.[2]

Investors in bonds also take **spread risk** into account, closely related to credit risk, but itself the market risk of credit exposures. An example of a pure credit risk event would be a deterioration of a firm's credit quality without credit spreads generally widening. If reflected in a change in rating,

---

[2] See Chapter 6.

for example, a AA-rated company might be downgraded to A with no change in AA or A spreads generally, or in risk-free rates. The formerly AA-rated firm's spread would widen consistently with its new A rating. A pure market risk event would be a spread widening, a decline in risky bond prices, due to a shift in investor sentiment. One might, for example, see a widening spread between AA yields and risk-free rates without widespread downgrades, other credit events, or changes in credit quality.

Also, deterministic sources of fixed-income return are realized even with no change in market interest rates. These include the cash flows of the security, and the **roll down** or **theta**. As time passes, and the time to maturity of the investment shortens, each future cash flow has drawn closer. It is priced differently even with an unchanged yield curve. Typically, yield curves are upward sloping, so the now more-proximate cash flows will be discounted at lower spot rates, and the value of the security will rise. For example, a 3-year bond held for 1 year becomes a 2-year bond, with a typically lower yield and higher market value.

10.2   Interest Rate Risk Measurement

There are several ways to measure interest rate risk. Scenario analysis analyzes exposure to specified changes in the yield curve. Another is formulaic, closed-form measures of sensitivity to yield curve changes. Value-at-Risk (VaR) can also be computed for bonds and bond portfolios.

10.2.1   Measuring Bond Price Sensitivity to Rates

A scenario analysis measures the impact of a specified change in the yield curve on the price S_t of a bond. The scenario result is a price change $\tilde{S}_t - S_t$. Some commonly encountered scenario analyses include:

Parallel shifts: the price change if all spot interest rates or yields to maturity rise, say, 25 basis points.
Curve steepening: longer-term, risk-free rates rise as short-term rates or credit spreads remain unchanged.
Roll-down return: the bond "ages" by, say, 1 year, while rates along the yield curve remain unchanged.
Credit spread widening: credit spreads increase, and risk-free rates remain unchanged. The change in price is the same for an equal change in the risk-free rate or the spread.

Example 10.1   Scenario analysis

To illustrate, we'll use the yield curve Example 2.1 of Chapter 2. The price impact of each scenario can be computed from the present values of the cash flows, discounted at the shocked rates, expressing rates as decimals.

Parallel shift: Suppose all spot rates rise 25 basis points (0.25 percent). The new bond values are found from

$$\tilde{S}_t = c_t \left[\frac{1}{1 + r_1 + 0.0025} + \cdots + \frac{1}{(1 + r_t + 0.0025)^t} \right]$$
$$+ \frac{1}{(1 + r_t + 0.0025)^t}, \qquad t = 1, \dots, 4.$$

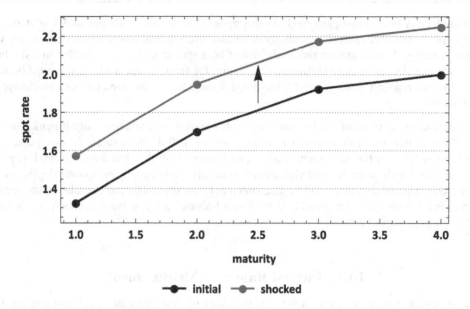

Figure 10.1 Yield curve scenario analysis: parallel shift

All bond prices fall, but longer-term bond prices fall the most, by close to 1 percent (Figure 10.1).

term	initial S_t	shocked $\tilde{S}_t$	$\tilde{S}_t - S_t$
1 year	98.692	98.449	−0.246
2 years	100.104	99.618	−0.486
3 years	100.237	99.517	−0.718
4 years	100.029	99.082	−0.946

Curve steepening: 1- and 2-year spot rates are unchanged, and 3- and 4-year spot rates rise by 15 and 25 basis points, respectively. Short-term bond prices are unchanged, but longer-term bond prices fall (Figure 10.2).

term	initial	shocked	Δ price (%)
1 year	98.692	98.692	0.000
2 years	100.104	100.104	0.000
3 years	100.237	99.813	−0.423
4 years	100.029	99.102	−0.926

Roll down effect: Assume the spot curve is unchanged and calculate the bond values one year in the future. The 1-year bond will converge to par and return exactly its initial yield to maturity. If the yield curve is upward sloping, then as maturities shorten, the other bonds' cash flows are

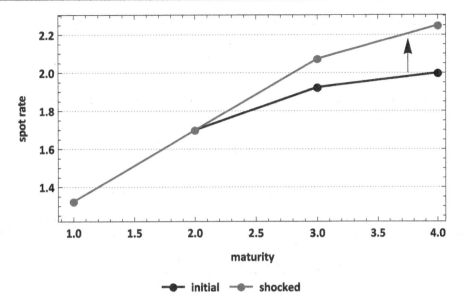

Figure 10.2 Yield curve scenario analysis: curve steepening

discounted at lower spot rates. All the bonds will experience a positive return over and above the yield:

term	initial S_t	1 year hence	Δ price
Initially 1 year	98.692	100.000	1.325
Initially 2 years	100.104	100.419	0.315
Initially 3 years	100.237	100.592	0.355
Initially 4 years	100.029	100.237	0.208

The roll down return is positive and higher because the yield curve is upward sloping than if it were flat.

10.2.2   Duration and Convexity

Rate sensitivity can be measured using **duration** and **convexity**, approximate measures of the impact of small changes in yield y_t or small parallel shifts on the bond price S_t. They are related to the first and second derivatives of the bond value with respect to yield or the level of the spot curve and provide parameters by which scenarios on yield can be evaluated.

The first derivative $\frac{dS_t}{dy_t}$ is the **DV01**, the change in price. The **modified duration** of the bond, denoted mdur_t, converts the DV01 to a relative change, and is defined as

$$\mathrm{mdur}_t \equiv -\frac{1}{S_t}\frac{dS_t}{dy_t}.$$

Modified duration states the proportional or percent change in bond price as the yield or level of the yield curve rises 1 percent. Because of the negative relation between price and yield, the convention is to express it as a positive number.

Convexity, denoted conv_t, is defined as the change in duration as the yield changes:

$$\text{conv}_t \equiv \frac{1}{S_t}\frac{d^2 S_t}{dy_t^2}.$$

The effect on price of a Δy increase in yield can then be estimated using the delta-gamma approach (see Chapter 8) with the linear-quadratic approximation:

$$\frac{\Delta S_t}{S_t} \approx -\text{mdur}_t \Delta y + \frac{1}{2}\text{conv}_t \Delta y^2. \tag{10.1}$$

A back-of-the-envelope approximation might omit the convexity term if it is known to be small.

Effective duration is a common method for approximating the linear impact of yield curve changes on bond prices. It is the average $\frac{dS_t}{dy_t}$ resulting from shifting the spot curve up and down by 1 basis point:

$$\frac{dS_t}{dy_t} \approx -\frac{S_t(\text{shifted up}) - S_t(\text{shifted down})}{2 \times 0.0001}.$$

Effective convexity is estimated analogously.

Example 10.2   Calculating effective duration

In the simple yield curve we've been working with, the effective durations of the bonds are:

term	initial	+1bp shock	−1bp shock	duration
1 year	98.692	98.683	98.702	0.987
2 years	100.104	100.084	100.123	1.950
3 years	100.237	100.208	100.266	2.886
4 years	100.029	99.991	100.067	3.807

Example 10.3   Rate sensitivity of the US 10-year note

The US on-the-run 10-year note on January 17, 2017, with expiration November 15, 2026, (term to maturity 9 year 10 months), bore a 2 percent coupon. As seen in the Bloomberg screen shot in Figure 10.3, the price quote is $97 - 01+$. The units are dollars, 32nds, and 64ths of a dollar per $100 of par value:

$$97\text{–}01+ \equiv 97 + \frac{1}{32} + \frac{1}{64} = 97.0468750.$$

The quote includes 01 32nds, and the $+$ indicates an additional 64th of one percent of par. The Bloomberg estimate of the modified duration is $\text{mdur}_t = 8.8160$. If the yield were to fall by 1 bp, the price would rise by 0.088160 percent to 97.1324:

$$97.0468750 \times (1 + 0.088160) = 97.1324$$

The Bloomberg estimate of convexity is $\text{conv}_t = 0.8713$. The bond has **positive convexity**: duration declines slightly as the yield rises, attenuating the price decline.[3]

The bond price impact of a 25 bps increase in rates can be computed as follows:

Duration: $-\text{mdur}_t \Delta y = -8.816 \cdot 0.0025 = -0.0220$ (-2.20 percent).

---

[3] The Bloomberg divides the more common conventional measure of convexity by 100.

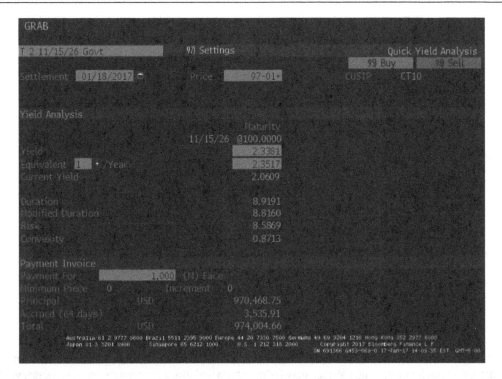

Figure 10.3 Duration and convexity of US 10-year note

Screen capture of Bloomberg Quick Yield Analysis for US on-the-run 10-year note on 17Jan2017.

Convexity: $\frac{1}{2}\text{conv}_t\Delta y^2 = 87.13 \cdot 0.0025^2 = 0.00027$ (0.027 percent).

Total: $-8.816 \cdot 0.0025 + 87.13 \cdot 0.0025^2 = -0.0217$ (−2.17 percent).

The duration and the duration-convexity approximations are illustrated in Figure 10.4. For a plain-vanilla coupon bond, the effect of convexity is small.

For credit risky bonds, the **credit spread01**, or CS01, is a common metric of spread risk, analogous to the DV01. It measures the change in the price or value of a credit-risky bond for a 1 basis point change in its credit spread, as represented, say, by the z-spread—the spread to an estimated zero-coupon riskless yield curve—and stated as the change in value per $100 or $1,000,000 notional underlying amount or bond par value. We can compute the CS01 the same way we do the DV01: increase and decrease the z-spread by 0.5 basis points, reprice the bond for each of these shocks, and compute the difference. Analogous to the duration measure of the proportional impact of a change in yield on bond value, **spread duration**, defined as the ratio of the CS01 to the bond price, is the proportional impact of a spread change on the price of a credit-risky bond.

A typical CS01 for a 5-year bond (or CDS) is about $400 per $1,000,000 of par value. At high spread levels, however, the CS01 can be substantially lower. As the spread increases and the bond price decreases, the discount factor applied to cash flows further in the future declines. Therefore, any increase or decrease in spread has a smaller impact on the bond's value when spreads are higher and discount factors lower.

10.2.3   Convexity and the Mortgage-Backed Securities Markets

Convexity has a moderate impact on the returns of plain-vanilla bonds, including most nominal advanced-economy central government issues, but a potentially large impact on securities with cash

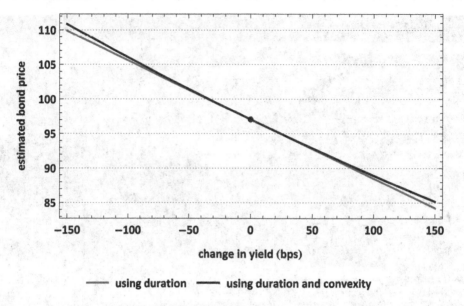

Figure 10.4 Response of US 10-year note to shocks

flows that themselves depend on interest rates. Examples include **mortgage-backed securities** (MBS), for which interest rate changes may induce sharp variations in prepayments, and bonds with embedded options. All bonds exhibit some convexity, but MBS are unusual in the high **negative convexity** they exhibit. Convexity is similar to the gamma of options in that even small moves in interest rates can have a large impact on bond prices; increases in interest rates may have a much greater or smaller effect than decreases. Negative convexity behaves like negative option gamma, increasing the market risk of long bond exposures.

Agency MBS constitute a large part of the US bond market. They are secured by pools of mortgage loans that are in turn secured by residential properties.[4] Payment of the bonds' principal and interest is guaranteed by the **government-sponsored enterprises** (GSEs), the **Federal National Mortgage Association**, (Fannie Mae) and the **Federal Home Loan Mortgage Corporation** (Freddie Mac), which are understood to enjoy an implicit US federal government solvency guarantee.[5] Constituent Federal Home Loan Banks (FHLBs) of another GSE, the **Federal Home Loan Bank System**, are owned by their member banks and insurance companies, to which the FHLBs make loans, called "advances," collateralized by residential mortgage loans, Treasurys, or agency MBS.

If the underlying mortgages meet certain credit quality and maximum size criteria, they are deemed **conformable** by the GSEs and the federal regulatory authorities, and can be sold by the banks and other intermediaries originating them into the pools securing agency MBS. Prepayment penalties are limited or prohibited for most conventional US residential mortgages under regulations at the state and federal level that were tightened as part of the 2010 Dodd-Frank Act. The resulting **prepayment option** allows homeowners to refinance their mortgages at a lower rate and with minimal transactions costs if mortgage interest rates fall. Essentially an interest rate option written by the lender, it induces high negative convexity in agency MBS. Most mortgages originated in the United States, and most of those securing agency MBS are fixed-rate 30-year mortgages, a preponderance attributable primarily to the implicit federal government guarantee of agency MBS and the

---

[4] See Chapter 14 on the mechanics and risk assessment of securitizations.

[5] The **Government National Mortgage Association** (Ginnie Mae) serves the same objectives, but is directly owned by the US government.

mandatory prepayment option. Until the global financial crisis, privately issued residential mortgage securitizations had a substantial share of the market as well.

The interest rate risk of MBS differs greatly from that of Treasury securities. Embedded in the underlying mortgages is the **prepayment risk** that pool loans will be repaid earlier than anticipated, ahead of the contractually stipulated amortization schedule. When mortgages prepay, a portion of the long-term agency MBS they support will also be prepaid from mortgage pools. When interest rates fall, more homeowners refinance their existing loans into new lower-rate mortgages. Cash flows to securitization investors occur earlier and can only be reinvested in bonds with lower yields, reducing the bond's value and shortening its duration. However, when rates rise, refinancing activity tends to decline and prepayments fall. Mortgage borrowers are not apt to repay their existing mortgage and borrow at a higher rate unless motivated by life circumstances, such as a new job in a different region. The mortgage bonds' duration lengthens, extending the period of time investors receive below-market rate returns on their investment. This is known as extension risk in MBS markets.

A fall in yields shortens the bonds' duration, and a rise in yields lengthens it, hence the negative convexity. When rates fall, MBS prices rise much less than Treasury securities because of their shortening duration. When rates rise, MBS prices fall much faster than Treasury securities because of their lengthening duration. Many market participants, particularly dealers in MBS, hedge negative convexity using short positions in US Treasurys. The appropriate hedge ratios and estimates of risk are based on duration estimates calculated using prepayment models of homeowner behavior that attempt to measure the labor market and demographic determinants of prepayment behavior and distinguish their impact from that of interest rates and the prepayment option.

Most agency MBS trading and hedging transactions are in to-be-announced (TBA) 30-year agency MBS, a type of forward contract for delivery of an agency MBS. It is analogous to **when-issued** (WI) Treasury securities, bonds for which a coupon maturity and auction date have been announced but which have not yet been delivered to auction purchasers. The class of securities—issuing agency, coupon, and principal amount—supporting a TBA will have been announced but not the exact list of its constituent pools. TBAs have a longer horizon to delivery than WIs but are the most liquid agency MBS market.

Example 10.4   Example of MBS convexity

We use the to-be-announced (TBA) 30-year agency MBS as of August 26, 2013, to illustrate agency MBS convexity. The scenario analysis in Table 10.1 is drawn from the Bloomberg TRA function, which contains a prepay model, and is applied to the TBA MBS on that date. Each line shows the impact on the yield and price of the on-the-run 10 year note and TBA of the specified changes in the Treasury yield curve. The Treasury note yield and price responses are based on duration and convexity. The yield and price responses of the TBA MBS are based on discounting and yield formulas, and on the prepayment model's estimates of the intensity of prepayments of the MBS at different interest rates.

The effective duration of the 10-year Treasury can be estimated from these data as the $\frac{dS_t}{dy_t}$ resulting from shifting the curve up and down by 50 basis points:

$$\frac{dS_{\text{UST},t}}{dy_{\text{UST},t}} \approx -100\frac{93.612 - 101.770}{0.01} = 8.158.$$

The duration of the TBA is lower than that of the 10-year note. The sensitivity of the TBA MBS to the US 10-year yield can also be estimated as

$$\frac{dS_{\text{TBA},t}}{dy_{\text{UST},t}} \approx -100\frac{105.406 - 99.681}{0.01} = 5.7254.$$

Table 10.1   TBA convexity calculations

T shift	T yield	T price	TBA yield	TBA price
−150	1.291	110.740	1.305	106.370
−100	1.791	106.150	1.943	106.321
−50	2.291	101.770	2.656	105.406
0	2.791	97.595	3.391	103.149
50	3.291	93.612	4.042	99.681
100	3.791	89.812	4.597	96.082
150	4.291	86.186	5.133	92.539

T shift: the specified shift in Treasury yields; T yield: the resulting Treasury note yield; T price: the resulting Treasury note price; T yield: the resulting TBA yield; TBA price: the resulting TBA price. The on-the-run 10-year Treasury note yield was 2.791 percent on August 26, 2013.

This gives us a hedge ratio of $0.701814 = \frac{5.7254}{8.158}$. A rise in rates that leads to a decline in the value of the US 10-year note by \$1 will also lead to a decline in the value of the TBA of \$0.701814, so to hedge the value of the TBA MBS against a rise in interest rates, the dealer should short a market value of 10-year notes equal to a bit over 70 percent of that of the TBA MBS position.

If interest rates were to drop sharply, prepayments would be expected to increase and the duration of the MBS to fall. The sensitivity of the TBA MBS to further declines in rates would rapidly fall away, calling for a reduction in the short Treasury position to near zero. But if rates were to rise sharply, the MBS duration would extend, calling for an increase in the Treasury short position to stay hedged. Figure 10.5 illustrates these analytics and the sharp negative convexity of the MBS.

The need by dealers to hedge agency MBS portfolios has a large impact on fixed-income markets. Dealers and other market participants with hedged positions are obliged to increase their hedge

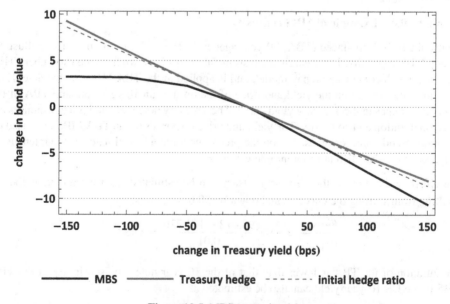

Figure 10.5 MBS convexity risk

ratios by increasing their short positions in Treasurys. With the large volume of agency MBS out-standing, the convexity in these and other widely held securities and derivatives positions can greatly amplify shocks originating elsewhere and have episodically affected US rates markets. In these **convexity events**, a type of fire sale, an increase in interest rates forces some market participants out of rate-sensitive positions because they encounter loss, VaR, or other trading limits or because they are unable to continue financing positions. Though the impact of rising rates on dealer behavior can't be observed directly, convexity events can be identified through the behavior of the repo rates at which dealer finance their inventories, futures market activity, and market participants' anecdotes.[6]

The liquidation of these positions drives interest rates higher and accelerates the selling pressure, just as an option dealer exposed to gamma risk might be forced to sell into a falling market. The rapid rise in interest rates can have a large impact on the economy as a whole. The volatility in rates is ultimately driven by two indirect subsidies of the US residential mortgage market: The regulatory requirement to incorporate a prepayment option increases the demand for 30-year mortgages. The implied guarantee of the agencies' solvency permits them in turn to guarantee the mortgages and securitize them on a large scale, expanding the market for their risks beyond banks and other mort-gage lenders. In this originate-to-distribute model, banks can originate 30-year mortgages without having to bear the interest and prepayment risk.[7]

Market Episode: The 1994 convexity event

In early 1994, the Federal Reserve (Fed) aggressively increased short-term interest rates. Even though the tightening was not a surprise—the yield curve had been steeping for some time—the rapid pace was. Long-term rates rose sharply, inducing large losses and consider-able turmoil in markets. The first money market fund ever to "break the buck," the Community Bankers US Government Fund, had a quarter of its NAV invested in adjustable-rate derivative securities, which had severe losses. Another large casualty of the convexity event was Orange County's investment fund.[8]

The increase in US rates also affected long-term rates in other countries, with sharp selloffs in the large government bond markets of the United Kingdom and Germany. The increase in rates also triggered a currency crisis in Mexico (the so-called "tequila crisis").

10.2.4   Measuring Value-at-Risk for a Bond Position

Value-at-Risk (VaR) can be measured for fixed-income exposures via the parametric approach, using yields to maturity and an estimate of interest rate volatility.[9] Assuming yields are lognor-mally distributed, as in the Black interest-rate option pricing model, proportional yield changes are normally distributed. Quantiles of the probability distribution of future yields over a time hori-zon τ can be identified from estimates of yield volatility via generalized autoregressive condition-ally heteroscedastic (GARCH) or exponentially weighted moving average (EWMA) or by using fixed-income, option-implied volatilities. We use the upper (lower) tail of the yield distribution for a long (short) bond position because bond values decline as rates rise. If the model is accurate, the

---

[6] See Chapter 15 on fire sales and Chapter 20 for examples of such events and their impact on repo rates since the global financial crisis.

[7] See Chapter 14. The subsidies also encourage households to purchase rather than rent housing, and to purchase larger homes.

[8] Described in Chapter 12.

[9] See Chapters 4 and 8.

probability is α that yield will rise (fall) no more than $100z_\alpha\sigma_{y,t}$ ($100z_{1-\alpha}\sigma_{y,t}$) percent, with $\sigma_{y,t}$ the estimated yield volatility. The estimated α-quantile of the proportional change in yield from t to $t+\tau$ is the simple arithmetic approximation $z_\alpha\sigma_{y,t}\sqrt{\tau}$. Multiplying that quantile by the current yield gives us the yield change in basis points $z_\alpha\sigma_{y,t}\sqrt{\tau}y_t$, equivalent to using the normal volatility $z_\alpha\sigma_{n,t}\sqrt{\tau}$.

To measure VaR at a confidence level α over a horizon τ for a long bond position, we can apply the delta-gamma approach using duration and convexity estimates. Setting Δy to the VaR quantile of the change in yield in basis points, the time-t VaR of a long position—in percent of value—is measured as:

$$\text{VaR}_t(\alpha, \tau) = \text{mdur}_t z_\alpha\sigma_{y,t}y_t\sqrt{\tau} - \frac{1}{2}\text{conv}_t(z_\alpha\sigma_{y,t}y_t\sqrt{\tau})^2.$$

Reversing the signs from those in equation (10.0) converts the negative impact of a rise in yield to a positive number representing loss.

Example 10.5   VaR of long US 10-year note position

Assume the yield, 2.3381 percent in the Bloomberg screen example 10.3 above, has lognormally and proportional yield changes normally distributed, and that normal volatilities for at-the-money (ATM) short- to medium-term swaptions on 10-year US dollar swaps are about 90 bps at an annual rate. We can use the volatility together with the duration and convexity estimates for the US on-the-run 10-year note on January 17, 2017, to estimate the 1-day VaR at a confidence level of 99 percent of a \$1,000,000 position in the bond.

Using the ballpark estimate of normal volatility drawn from option markets implies a yield volatility $\frac{0.0090}{0.023381} = 0.384928$, or 38.5 percent at an annual rate. Dividing the annual volatility by $\sqrt{256} = 16$ and multiplying by $z_\alpha = -2.32635$ to obtain the 0.01 quantile (99 percent confidence level) of the 1-day return, we have

$$2.32635\frac{0.384928}{16} = 0.0559673,$$

or a 5.6 percent change in yield.

The VaR scenario in basis points is

$$2.32635\frac{0.384928}{16}0.023381 = 0.0559673 \cdot 0.023381 = 0.00130857.$$

The VaR in dollars, \$11,123.30, is the initial bond value times the proportional change in value using this estimate of the pertinent yield change quantile, together with the duration and convexity estimates from the Bloomberg screen:

$$\text{VaR}_t(\alpha, \tau) = \left(8.816 \cdot 0.00131 - \frac{1}{2}87.13 \cdot 0.00131^2\right) \times 970\,468.75$$
$$= 11\,123.30.$$

Further Reading

Tuckman and Serrat (2022) is a standard overview of fixed-income markets. See Vickery and Wright (2013) and Kish (2022) on the structure of MBS markets, and Hanson (2014) and Malz et al. (2014) on the market impact of mortgage convexity. Bank of England (2010), 22f. describes the 1994 convexity event and its international impact.

11

Leverage

11.1 Defining and Measuring Leverage

11.1.1 Company Financing

Financial leverage is used extensively in banking, trading, investment, and by nonfinancial firms and takes many institutional forms. For a firm, leverage measures the funding of assets by issuance of debt relative to shareholders' equity, the firm owners' own resources. A thinner equity share increases default risk, the likelihood that asset value falls sharply enough to deplete it entirely.

Most nonfinancial firms fund themselves at least partly through debt. Even small firms routinely have some short-term debt to suppliers and other business outstanding. Financial firms typically employ more leverage than nonfinancial firms as an essential aspect of how they carry out intermediation, and as part of a larger system for distributing leverage and liquidity risks through the financial system. Banks and other financial intermediaries are highly exposed to credit risk because of the extensive leverage they employ. Some form of leverage and collateralization is involved in derivatives transactions, such as futures, swaps and options, and in establishing short positions. Other markets and financial instruments, such as the collateralized securities lending and structured product markets, have been developed in large part to facilitate secured borrowing.

We defined leverage L in Chapter 9 as the ratio of assets to equity:

$$L = \frac{A}{E} = \frac{E + D}{E} = 1 + \frac{D}{E}.$$

There are common alternative definitions, for example, the ratio of debt to assets $\frac{D}{A}$, sometimes called the **capitalization ratio** or **debt burden**. The economic definition of leverage is also distinct from the regulatory leverage ratio for banks, defined as the ratio of regulatory capital funding to a measure of assets, with detailed definitions of numerator and denominator. These definitions are also distinct from **operating leverage**, the rate at which a firm's operating income grows as its sales grows. Operating leverage is high, for example, when net revenue increases rapidly with output and sales revenue due to low variable and high fixed production costs.

We'll think of leverage in terms of a firm's or agent's economic balance sheet because accounting or regulatory standards may not fully reflect economic reality. Some exposures and obligations may not be recorded on the balance sheet, some assets and liabilities may be presented at inaccurate historical values, and the standards may permit the use of possibly inaccurate valuation models. These differences exist for a host of valid and less-valid business, regulatory, and taxation reasons.

11.1.2   Corporate Finance Policy

Corporate finance policy describes the firm's decisions about its capital structure: the extent and forms of debt and equity issuance and **capital distributions**, the ways in which equity can be returned to the firm's owners and removed from the firm's balance sheet, most importantly dividends and share repurchases.

The risks of leverage stem in part from frictions and information costs. In a simplified world without frictions, the **Modigliani-Miller theorem**, or **irrelevancy**, holds:[1] The firm's market value—the sum of its equity and debt values—equals the market assessment of its asset value and is independent of its capital structure. Only the firm's asset choices, investments in productive capital, matter for firm value. The economic values of debt and equity conform to balance sheet constraints and add up to the value of the assets.[2]

The proposition doesn't preclude that debt is risky. It does require a strong assumption of perfect capital markets, including perfect arbitrage, no taxes, and no default costs, such as the bankruptcy process, apart from loss given default (LGD). With perfect markets and absent any frictions, investors can borrow or lend freely at prevailing rates to offset corporate financial decisions that expose them to more or less asset risk and to achieve the degree of leverage they desire.

Modigliani-Miller irrelevancy can be stated in terms of the **weighted average cost of capital** (WACC), the cost of funding the firm's assets. The proposition holds that in market equilibrium, the firm's WACC equals the rate of return on its assets. Denoting by r^a the rate of return on assets, the equilibrium WACC can be expressed as

$$r^a = \frac{1}{L}r^e + \left(1 - \frac{1}{L}\right)r,$$

with r the blended cost of the firm's debt financing and r^e the expected or market-clearing rate of return on the firm's equity (RoE).

In the messy real world, corporate finance decisions are intertwined with decisions about assets. What investments, businesses, and projects to pursue is decided in tandem with how to finance them. Asset choices are determined in light of the firm's current cost of debt financing, the expected or required return on equity it attributes to potential and actual shareholders, and how a change in the funding or business mix will influence returns and funding costs.

The pecking order theory of corporate finance notes that external finance comes with asymmetric information problems, for which outsiders to the firm require an additional layer of risk premium. It recommends that firms raising funds do so through retained earnings to the extent possible, and otherwise through debt, which is less susceptible to asymmetric information problems, rather than new issuance of equity.

Apart from default risk risk, leverage is related to systematic risk, the undiversifiable risk stemming from fluctuations in overall market and economic conditions. Modigliani-Miller Proposition I, the independence of WACC and leverage, implies the firm's asset value equals that of the portfolio of equity and debt financing them. Proposition II states that higher leverage increases the required equity return in equilibrium. Assume that debt has no systematic risk (although possibly considerable

---

[1] This is their Proposition I.

[2] In the Tobin's q theory of investment decisions, if the market value of equity is significantly greater than the book value, investment is stimulated until a new equilibrium prevails.

idiosyncratic risk). Then the equity return's systematic risk is a linear function of the asset return:

$$\beta^a = \frac{1}{L}\beta^e \Leftrightarrow \beta^e = L\beta^a.$$

11.1.3   Margin and Haircuts

Most leverage is supported by some form of security or collateral. The full value of the collateral is rarely lent, and the amount of collateral may be frequently adjusted, with different mechanisms in various markets. **Overcollateralization**, the excess of the collateral value over the amount lent, protects the lender by providing equity or a buffer against variation in the value of the collateral itself. It is employed in secured bond and loan issuance, OTC and exchange-traded derivatives, collateralized securities lending, and securitization.

Two equivalent conventions have emerged for expressing overcollateralization and for monitoring and controlling leverage. **Margin** expresses overcollateralization as the ratio of the market value of the collateral to the cash, the notional amount of the swap, or the value of the securities borrowed. The **haircut** is expressed as the amount by which the maximum that can be borrowed is reduced from the market value of collateral. For example, a loan of $100 in cash supported by collateral worth $105 implies margin of 105 or 5 percent and a haircut of 4.76 percent.[3] Expressing the relationship in terms of margin is standard in derivatives markets and margin lending. Both are equal or about equal to the reciprocal $\frac{1}{L}$ of the leverage in the transaction.

The agreements underpinning these transactions and detailed regulatory or self-regulatory organization rules set out the levels and adjustment procedures for margin and haircuts as collateral or underlying asset values vary over time. **Initial margin** is the margin agreed when a transaction is initiated. To preserve overcollateralization as collateral value fluctuates, counterparties exchange **variation margin**. Declines in value require borrowers to post additional collateral or trim their borrowing. Large moves in asset prices can bring about both large increases in margin and greater reluctance of lenders to extend credit, leading to forced or fire sales.

11.2   Attractiveness of Leverage and Reaching for Yield

Leverage is attractive because it amplifies the return on equity. We can rearrange the WACC definition as

$$r^e = Lr^a - (L-1)r = L(r^a - r) + r,$$

implying

$$\frac{\partial r^e}{\partial L} = r^a - r.$$

If the anticipated asset return is greater than the debt cost ($r^a > r$), there's no upper limit on r^e as leverage rises. But if the opposite prevails ($r^a < r$), losses are amplified as leverage rises.[4] Losses

---

[3] $1 - \frac{100}{105} = 0.0476190.$

[4] Two degenerate cases to note: If the asset return equals the debt cost ($r^a = r$), then it must also equal the return on equity ($r^e = r^a$), and leverage has no effect on return. If there is no debt financing (leverage equals 1), then the asset return will equal the return on equity $r^e = r^a$: equity owners earn exactly the asset return.

are more difficult to deal with for highly indebted firms. A firm with five turns of leverage must sell roughly 5 percent of its remaining assets to restore its previous leverage if its asset value declines by 1 percent. A firm with 20 turns of leverage must sell roughly 20 percent of its assets to do the same.

Equity is an asymmetric, option-like asset, and more so with high leverage, generating incentives to take risk. A decline in r relative to asset returns makes leverage more attractive. Periods of low interest rates are associated with higher leverage, as seen in Figure 3.12.

Banks, other firms, and portfolio managers set **hurdle** or **target rates of return**, minimum rates of return that an investment or portfolio must meet to satisfy goals. In the context of corporate planning hurdle rates serve as a criterion by which projects are selected. A defined benefit pension plan may require a high rate of return to make promised payments in the future. A fund manager may set L so as to achieve a return target:

$$\text{required leverage} = \frac{\text{target } r^e - r}{r^a - r}.$$

For example, if a fund's target return is $\bar{r}^e = 25$ percent, its expected asset return will be $r^a = 4$ percent and $r = 2$ percent; therefore, it sets $L = 11.5$. If, as was the case during the low-yield decades, expected asset returns are declining, but the hurdle rate is unchanged, the fund may simply increase leverage, an important driver of the reaching for yield phenomenon observed during the long period of low rates.[5]

11.3   Leveraged Trades

Certain types of trades, with relatively low risk over long periods of time and relatively low returns, are reliant on leverage. They are profitable enough to attract investors only if they employ extensive leverage, raising the return on the trade to the hurdle rate investors seek. Basis trades and similar near-arbitrage trades, which identify small pricing discrepancies between similar assets and are positioned to profit as prices converge, are among those reliant on high leverage for profitability.[6] **Carry trades** rely on cash flows from an asset that exceed the cost of funding and on no significant adverse change in prices occurring. They are a staple of many hedge fund portfolios.

The extent of hedge fund leverage varies with the markets in which they operate, lower, for example, in equity markets than in futures, fixed income, and foreign exchange markets. Traders can also put on leverage through the use of short positions and derivatives. Long-short equity funds may use both, paying fixed in total return swaps (TRS) on stocks they are long, while receiving fixed on stocks they wish to sell short. Archegos Capital Management, for example, used TRS to establish stock exposures which eventually led to its failure in 2021 as well as that of Credit Suisse in 2023 (see Chapter 20).

Though basis trades have low risk in the long run, because the price convergence patterns are very reliable, the leverage used exposes them to high risk. On rare occasions, generally due to a liquidity risk event, for example, the on-the-run/off-the-run spread widens beyond its normal bounds. The large hedge fund Long-Term Capital Management L.P. (LTCM) collapsed in 1998 after a trade with the thesis that the spread would return to its normal range suffered large losses. In this trade, the fund at times had leverage approaching 100. Similarly, illiquidity and selling pressure in Treasury markets in March 2020 drove the basis between bond and futures prices wider, leading to losses and forced liquidations.

[5] See Chapter 15.
[6] See Chapter 7.

11.3.1 Carry Trades

We can decompose r^a into asset appreciation $\frac{\Delta S}{S} = \frac{S_{t+1} - S_t}{S_t}$ and cash flow q, representing bond coupon, foreign currency-denominated interest, dividends, or, if $q < 0$, storage or maintenance costs:

$$r^e = L\left(\frac{\Delta S}{S} + q\right) - (L-1)r = L\left(\frac{\Delta S}{S} + q - r\right) + r,$$

with $\frac{\Delta S}{S}, q$, and r defined as per-period rates. The difference between incoming cash flow and outgoing financing rates $q - r$ is called the **carry**.[7] The unlevered return on a carry trade can be viewed as its excess return and leverage as a mechanism for amplifying it if it's positive.

The asset appreciation $\frac{\Delta S}{S}$ can be decomposed into the expected asset appreciation $\mathbf{E}\left[\frac{\Delta S}{S}\right]$ and a surprise component $\frac{\Delta S}{S} - \mathbf{E}\left[\frac{\Delta S}{S}\right]$, representing much of the market risk in leveraged trading and investing. The risk is higher if equity in the trade is thinner or if the carry is lower, or if an adverse surprise occurs over a shorter time horizon. Leverage also amplifies funding liquidity risks. Carry trades are vulnerable to rollover risk and forced unwinding if r rises sharply, there is a margin call, or if lenders decline to extend credit any longer.[8]

Carry trades are generally expected to have positive carry while avoiding surprises $\frac{\Delta S}{S} - \mathbf{E}\left[\frac{\Delta S}{S}\right]$ sufficiently adverse to exceed the carry. Many institutional and retail investors are reluctant to or cannot bear sustained negative carry, adding to the attractiveness of the strategies to investment managers. The cash flow q, known at the time the trade is initiated and paid over its lifetime, is often fairly reliable. Carry trade financing is typically collateralized in some fashion and provided by a broker-dealer, so r will represent a short-term nearly risk-free rate. It is generally less reliable than q, as short-term rates or credit conditions may change abruptly.

These market and liquidity risks can be analyzed using scenario analysis. We establish a set of baseline assumptions, formulate scenarios that differ from the baseline, and determine the impact on the equity return r^e. For example, we can find the decline in asset price $\frac{\Delta S}{S}$ sharp enough to drive the equity return to zero:

$$r^e = 0 \Leftrightarrow \frac{\Delta S}{S} = -\left(q - r + \frac{r}{L}\right).$$

A decline in asset price sufficient to wipe out the equity ($r^e = -100$ percent) is found from

$$r^e = -1 \Leftrightarrow \frac{\Delta S}{S} = -\left[(q - r) + \frac{1}{L}(1 + r)\right],$$

exceeding that in the $r^e = 0$ scenario by the margin $\frac{1}{L}$. The analysis is a form of reverse stress testing in which the scenario is found that results in a given loss.

A fixed-income carry trade typically buys a higher-yielding bond, for example, a longer-term or credit-risky bond, financed in large part by short-term borrowing, often in the repo market. The carry is the difference between the yield and the financing cost and assumes the yield curve, credit spreads, and hence the bond price won't change materially.

The audience for these trades includes hedge funds and bank prop desks. The key risks are a bond price decline ($\frac{\Delta S}{S} < 0$) and a loss of funding or rise in funding cost. The maturity of the bond is

---

[7] The stand-alone r arises from the equity funding, the fraction on which r is not paid.

[8] See Chapter 12.

shorter at the unwinding of trade, so the roll down can also have an impact on P&L for fixed-rate securities, adding to or diminishing the carry.

Some variants may have negative carry but appeal to a narrower set of investors. Examples include the "big short" of the mid-2000s in which traders assumed short positions in subprime residential mortgage bonds, usually via derivatives. These trades involved a monthly net loss on the cost of the derivatives protection but had a large positive payout once the bonds' prices collapsed in 2007–2008. The common "2s-10s" trade takes positions in 2- and 10-year Treasury notes, one long and one short, but with little or no net exposure to the level of interest rates, only to the slope of the yield curve. It may have positive or negative carry.

Example 11.1   Fixed-income carry trade

As an example of a fixed-income carry trade, consider a long position in a floating-rate AAA asset-backed securities (ABS). The trader faces market parameters:

Expected change in bond price	$\mathbf{E}\left[\frac{\Delta S}{S}\right]$	0
Leverage	L	25
Repo rate	r	0.025
Coupon rate	q	0.035

The risk scenarios (at an annual rate, but to be monitored daily) are

Scenario	$\frac{\Delta S}{S}(\%)$	$q - r(\%)$	$r^e(\%)$
Baseline: zero bond price change	0.00	1.00	27.50
Break-even bond price change	−1.10	1.00	0.00
Bond price change→100% loss	−5.10	1.00	−100.00
Funding rate ↑100 bps	0.00	0.00	3.50

We can use these scenarios to do back-of-the-envelope risk calculations, informal assessments of risk based on rough approximations or assumptions. How large a spread widening would lead to a 100 percent loss? Suppose the CS01 is 400, that is, an increase of 1 bp would be associated with a $\frac{\Delta S}{S} = -0.04$ percent decline in the bond's value. Then a widening of 127.5 bps would lead to a decline of $\frac{\Delta S}{S} = -5.1$ percent in price and wipe out the trade.

How likely is that to occur? If the option-implied normal volatility is around 80 or 90 bps annually, then a widening of 127.5 bps, in the market's assessment, will be a $1\frac{1}{2}$ standard deviation event, with a 6.67 percent or 1-in-15 likelihood of occurring. The high leveraged return in the baseline is the anticipated reward for the risk.

The term "carry trade" originated in foreign exchange, where they are common. To initiate a currency carry trade, essentially an open position, the trader buys S_t^{-1} units of a higher-yielding **target currency**, multiplied by the desired size of the trade, at the time-t exchange rate S_t, and invests it in the foreign money market at a rate q. The currency purchase is financed by borrowing in a lower-yielding **funding currency**. The amount of the funding currency borrowed is the leverage in the trade. The trade is often implemented via foreign exchange swaps, but is equivalent, if covered interest rate parity holds to a bank deposit denominated in the target currency, funded by a short-term, funding-currency bank loan. It earns the difference between money market rates in the target and funding currencies.

At time $t+1$, if the trade is unwound, the trader sells the target currency proceeds at a rate S_{t+1} obtaining an excess return

$$(1+q)\left(1+\frac{\Delta S}{S}\right) - (1+r) = (1+q)\frac{\Delta S}{S} + q - r.$$

If leverage is applied, the return on equity is

$$r^e = L\left[(1+q)\frac{\Delta S}{S} + q - r\right] + r.$$

The key risk is target currency depreciation $\frac{\Delta S}{S} < 0$, with S representing the funding currency price of the target currency. The proceeds of the target currency may then not suffice to repay the borrowed funding currency.

Part of the underlying thesis of a foreign exchange carry trades is the empirical finding that open interest rate parity doesn't hold. A differential between interest rates in two different currencies is not reliably offset by a subsequent depreciation of the higher-yielding currency. The Australian dollar (AUD) and many emerging-markets currencies are long-standing examples of currencies persistently at odds with open interest parity, with relatively high money market rates relative to subsequent depreciation. Conversely, the Swiss franc (CHF) and particularly the Japanese yen (JPY) have not appreciated in line with their low money market rates over many years. We'll provide a simple example here, and explore the phenomenon further in the context of international financial imbalances.[9]

Example 11.2   Foreign exchange carry trade

Consider a carry trade long AUD against the Japanese yen as the funding currency, with these market parameters:

Expected exchange rate appreciation	$E\left[\frac{\Delta S}{S}\right]$	0
Leverage	L	25
¥ money-market rate	r	0.005
AUD money-market rate	q	0.025

Some risk scenarios include:

Scenario	$\frac{\Delta S}{S}(\%)$	$r^e(\%)$
Baseline: zero ¥ appreciation	0.000	50.500
Break-even ¥ appreciation	−1.971	0.000
¥ appreciation→100% loss	−5.873	−100.000

We can do a back-of-envelope risk calculation of the probability of the trade being wiped out over one year if held with unchanged size and leverage. Suppose the implied or historical volatility of the AUD-JPY exchange rate is about 6 percent per annum and that the AUD-JPY exchange rate is approximately normally distributed. Yen appreciation of at least 6 percent is then a 1 standard deviation event, so the probability is about 16 percent that a 100 percent loss occurs.

11.3.2   Leveraged Investment Funds

Leverage has been introduced in a wide range of investment products. So-called liquid alternatives investing in private equity and hedge funds are available to retail investors in the form of open-end mutual funds. **Exchange traded products** (ETPs) are similar to ETFs but create more complex exposures to the constituent asset prices. Among the relatively new types of ETPs are **leveraged ETFs**, which provide the returns of a leveraged position in an asset or index, and **inverse ETFs**, which provide the returns of a short position. They are essentially claims on the authorized participants, which manage the risks using hedging techniques or offset the risk using total return swaps.

Leveraged ETFs have a quirk related to the difference between geometric and arithmetic returns discussed in Chapter 4. The ETF return is defined in arithmetic terms, and a succession of offsetting arithmetic returns brings the leveraged ETF to a lower value, rather than back to its initial value. The volatility drag results in successive +10 percent and −10 percent changes in an index that starts at 100 leaving it at 99. The higher the volatility, the greater the drag on the leveraged ETF value.

Systematic funds are another type of leveraged investment fund. **Commodity Trading Advisor** (CTA) or **managed futures** funds take positions in futures markets. The motivation of **risk parity** funds can be explained using the portfolio optimization model outlined in Chapter 5. In the risk parity approach, rather than maximizing the Sharpe ratio, the focus is on risk contributions, measured by the volatility of the constituent assets. A relatively low volatility asset, such as bonds, may contribute a relatively small amount to the overall portfolio volatility even if its share of the value of the portfolio is high. Risk parity addresses this by adding enough of the low volatility asset, financed through borrowing, to equalize the risk contributions. This results in investors holding a riskier portfolio and, in the portfolio optimization model, a nonoptimal allocation.

Volatility control funds target a level of realized return volatility, taking advantage of the modest short-term predictability of volatility. When volatility has been low, the strategy assumes it will remain low for the next trading day and increases position sizes through borrowing. When volatility rises, it reverts closer to an unlevered position. Overall, the intention is to keep fund volatility constant. Risk parity and volatility control funds are an artifact of the low volatility–low return environment of recent decades and are vulnerable to adverse price declines in low volatility asset classes, such as the bond market decline in 2022, and to sudden increases in return volatility and correlations.

11.4   Incentive Alignment and Capital Structure

11.4.1   Leverage and Incentives to Risk Shifting

The limited liability default option, in tandem with information limitations, provides an incentive to equity owners to engage in risk shifting to the firm's lenders through leverage and **asset substitution**, investing in riskier projects or loans. Risk shifting is an agency problem, and the resulting inefficiencies and perverse incentives cannot be completely and costlessly mitigated through contract design. Over time, a "leverage ratchet effect" may present incentives to owners of highly leveraged firms to further increase rather than reduce leverage. The prospect of public-sector support exacerbates the effect by increasing debtholders' risk tolerance, particularly those funding large financial firms.

Taxation and regulation encourage leverage and risk shifting. The tax systems of most advanced economies exhibit strong **debt bias**, privileging debt over equity funding. Cash returned to investors in the form of interest on bonds and loans is treated as a deductible expense for calculating corporate taxes, but cash returned to owners is not. Funding in the form of equity is subject to both corporate taxes when net income is realized and income or capital gains taxation when paid out. For households, tax deductibility of interest on mortgage debt and bank regulation in some countries create strong incentives toward debt-financed home ownership. US residential mortgages financed with minimal equity and poor underwriting were a major contributing factor to the global financial crisis.

Debt bias locks capital into existing firms. In the typical life cycle of an investment or firm, cash initially flows out to acquire assets, and later flows in as investments come to fruition. Mature firms may have larger cash inflows than they can invest in projects with positive NPV or offering higher expected returns than the cost of capital. The appropriate action is then for these firms to return funds for their owners to redeploy. Instead, firms are motivated to retain earnings to invest in lower-NPV projects or in liquid assets.

Incentives are particularly strong for financial intermediaries to employ leverage, and amplify the effects of public-sector guarantees on risk taking. The current structure of capital regulation and government guarantees such as deposit insurance and too big to fail add inducements for equity owners to increase risk and to creditor complacency.[10] These mechanisms are intensified in financial crises by a decline in asset values, leading to efforts to buy time rather than deleverage, or to investments in riskier loans and socially negative NPV projects. At the extreme, a distressed bank's owners may engage in **gambling for resurrection** or **redemption**, additional high-risk activities financed by borrowing, to obtain a small probability that their equity stakes will have a positive value in the future.

Dividends and **stock repurchases**, or **buybacks**, are the most common forms in which cash distributions are carried out. Both increase leverage, reducing cash balances, offset by reducing an equity account by the amount of stock outstanding or retained earnings. Dividends are recurring scheduled payments and are valued for their predictability and regularity, although they may be changed at any time by the firm's managers, but are more heavily taxed than cash distributions via repurchases. Shareholders prefer to receive cash returned to them in the form of capital gains that are income-tax deferred if unrealized and may be taxed at a lower rate if realized, rather than dividends taxed at a higher rate.

Repurchases have increased relative to dividends since the 1980s, likely related to rapidly falling interest rates, which increase the asymmetrical rewards to leverage. Banks, which enjoy implicit and explicit government guarantees, engaged in large repurchases in the years immediately preceding the global financial crisis. The trend, which coincides with the decline in initial public offerings (IPOs) (see Chapter 7), has been met with objections grounded in skepticism about the ability of corporate managers to accurately assess potential positive NPV, and their motivation to do so given pervasive conflicts of interest. These conflicts are embedded in larger ones between the interests of managers and shareholders, claims that positive NPV is a misleading metric for whether a project is socially valuable, and that repurchases are partly responsible for slowing wage growth and an increase in income inequality.

---

[10] See Chapter 18.

11.4.2 Debt Overhang

High leverage can disincentivize investment. **Debt overhang** stemming from a high default probability can lead equity owners to shun low-risk projects if a project's positive NPV has a larger impact on the recovery and current market value of existing senior debt than on equity. Any gains from the new investment would benefit senior creditors rather than owners or junior debt. The impact on current owners may even be negative due to dilution or funding via new junior debt.

Example 11.3 Debt overhang

Assume a firm's existing capital structure consists of senior debt with a par value of 100 and a yield (for simplicity) of $r = 0$ and that debt covenants prevent increased issuance of senior debt or subordination to new debt. Assume two possible outcomes: the firm's asset value falls to 80 and it defaults, with a probability of π, or, in the nondefault event, its asset value is 110. The recovery value of the debt is then $\min[80,100] = 80$ and LGD is 20. The firm's current asset value is the default probability-weighted average of the two outcomes:

$$\text{asset value} = \pi \times 80 + (1 - \pi) \times 110.$$

The debt value is the probability-weighted average of recovery and par:

$$\text{debt value} = \pi \times \min[80,100] + (1 - \pi) \times \min[110,100]$$

$$= \pi \times 80 + (1 - \pi) \times 100.$$

The equity value is the probability-weighted average of the residual:

$$\text{equity value} = \pi \times \max[80 - 100,0] + (1 - \pi) \times \max[110 - 100,0]$$

$$= (1 - \pi) \times 10.$$

Suppose a new investment opportunity arises to invest 5 dollars, with a certain future value of 15 dollars. There is no uncertainty about the results of the new investment, only about the firm's survival in its absence. (In reality, of course, the profitability of any new investment is uncertain.) Due to the debt covenant, financing must be through issuance of new shares or junior debt. Current shareholders could buy the new securities. If the investment is made, the firm value and the recovery value of the senior debt rise by 15, regardless of state. The debt and equity values become:

$$\text{debt value} = \pi \times \min[95,100] + (1 - \pi) \times \min[125,100]$$

$$= 100 - 5\pi$$

$$\text{equity value} = \pi \times \max[95 - 100,0] + (1 - \pi) \times \max[125 - 100,0]$$

$$= (1 - \pi) \times 25.$$

Table 11.1 shows the possible outcomes for the firm's investors of making the new investment with different assumptions on the firm's default probability.

If the default probability is low, senior debt recovery is little changed, and owners have ample incentive to invest. If the default probability is high, much or all of the future value of new investment goes to senior debt holders in the form of an increase in recovery value. Little is left over after the cost of investment to incentivize current or new equity and junior debt investors. Current owners may even be worse off.

Table 11.1 Debt overhang example

Default probability	1.000	0.500	0.005
	Before new investment		
Firm value	80.000	95.000	109.850
Debt value	80.000	90.000	99.900
Equity value	0.000	5.000	9.950
	After new investment		
Firm value	95.000	110.000	124.850
Debt value	95.000	97.500	99.975
Equity and junior debt value	0.000	12.500	24.875
Equity gain net of funding cost	−5.000	2.500	9.925

Debt overhang is difficult to identify empirically. As is the case for so many phenomena relating to credit, distressed firms are unusual, so there are few cases from which to draw inferences. The term "debt overhang" is also used to describe a situation in which sovereign borrowers cannot obtain new credits because their current debt burden and likelihood of default are viewed as extremely high. It affects appropriate debt relief policy of both borrowers and lenders.[11]

The phenomenon of debt overhang is similar to that of a zombie company or bank. In both cases, investment and economic growth are weakened because projects with positive NPV are not carried out. A zombie firm is insolvent but kept in existence through bank lending subsidized or guaranteed by the public sector, and the zombie firm's assets have positive NPV internally only because its cost of capital is below that prevailing in the market. Its subsidized borrowing rate encourages it to take greater risks than would a market-clearing cost of capital. Because capital is tied up in socially negative NPV projects, the cost of capital to new or solvent existing firms is higher, so some new socially positive NPV projects are not carried out.

Further Reading

Myers (2001) discusses firm capital structure. The irrelevancy propositions were first presented in Modigliani and Miller (1958).

Koijen et al. (2018) discuss carry trades. Melvin and Shand (2017) focus on foreign exchange carry.

Ang et al. (2011) provide several definitions of leverage for hedge funds, estimate leverage for different types of funds, and relate changes in leverage to individual fund characteristics such as return volatility and to market developments.

International Monetary Fund (2016) surveys countries' tax code bias favoring debt funding. Stock repurchases are analyzed in Shoven (1987) and Bagwell and Shoven (1989), and recent data can be found in Aramonte (2020). See Lazonick (2008) for the broader critique of stock repurchases. Ewens and Farre-Mensa (2020) discuss reasons for the decline in US IPOs over the past quarter century.

Myers (1977) discusses debt overhang, and Admati et al. (2018) model the leverage ratchet effect. Caballero et al. (2008) applied the term "zombie lending" to Japan's lost-decade experience. Acharya et al. (2023) is a survey of the empirical and theoretical literature on the phenomenon.

---

[11] The term is also used simply to describe a debt burden that exceeds a given fraction of annual GDP, say, 100 percent.

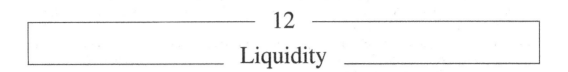

12

Liquidity

Why should anyone outside a lunatic asylum wish to use money as a store of wealth?

Keynes, "The General Theory of Employment"[1]

12.1 Funding and Market Liquidity Risk

The term "liquidity" has several closely related meanings. **Funding**, or **balance-sheet**, **liquidity** describes the ability to maintain debt-financed asset positions and meet immediate cash obligations. A market participant is liquid in this sense. **Market, transactions**, or **liquidity** describes a market participant's ability to buy or sell an asset without influencing prices adversely, pushing them up if buying or down if selling. A market or a financial instrument is liquid in this sense.

Liquidity is also used to describe a stock of assets available to carry out exchanges. The different meanings of liquidity are linked by different ways to use an asset to raise funds. An asset can function as money directly, as a means of payment, or indirectly because it can be readily sold to obtain money or used as collateral to borrow money. Funding liquidity reflects the ability to borrow against an asset, and market liquidity is defined by the ease with which an asset can be exchanged for money.

Both are rooted in two transformations that lead to the creation of assets that resemble or can be used as money, carried out on financial intermediaries' balance sheets, historically, primarily by banks. Intermediaries effect a **maturity, duration transformation** of a longer- into a shorter-term asset by borrowing short-term and lending long-term. Banks carry out maturity transformation by using equity, short-term deposits, and other borrowing to fund longer-term lending.

Short-term borrowers and lenders gain. The lenders, such as depositors, have a short-term asset that can be readily used as or converted to cash, compensating them for earning reduced or no interest. Borrowers, such as banks, pay a lower interest rate than earned on their longer-term interest earning assets. In this way, maturity transformation is linked to **liquidity transformation**, making an asset more readily exchangeable for goods or other assets.

12.1.1 Market Liquidity

Market liquidity is determined by information, search and trade processing costs, and by information asymmetries. Price, timing, and size of a trade are uncertain prior to execution. Like funding liquidity, market liquidity is difficult to measure but has identifiable characteristics:

Tightness is the cost of a round-trip transaction: buying and then selling, or vice versa. It is typically measured by the bid-ask spread.

---

[1] Keynes (1937), p. 216.

Depth describes how large an order it takes to move the market. **Adverse price impact** is the effect on market price of an order. A large sell order will tend to depress the price transitorily, while a large buy order will support the price.

Resiliency is the speed with which adverse price impact fades away after a large order moves the market. **Slippage** is the cumulative loss from adverse price impact over the time it takes to get a large trade done in a moving market.

In practice, measures of liquidity only fuzzily capture these characteristics. With market participants continuously responding to change, the current price cannot be observed directly with precision, but only with a lag, even if measured in nanoseconds. Data on market liquidity includes bid-ask spreads, transactions or turnover volume, the outstanding amounts of securities, and the size of order books. Market size can be measured in terms of transactions flow volume, the value that changes hands on a particular day or in a typical day, or in terms of outstanding amount, the value of the stock of the asset. The expected transactions cost is the **half-spread** or **mid-to-bid spread**. The volatility of the half-spread is a measure of transaction cost risk.

Market depth in the US Treasury market can be calculated using data from the central limit order book (CLOB) of a large electronic trading platform. The Federal Reserve Bank of New York, for example, employs the total par amount of executable orders at the price levels closest to execution for a specific on-the-run Treasury security as a measure of market depth. The data are obtained from BrokerTec, among the largest platforms in the Treasury market, and averaged over the trading day. This measure of depth doesn't itself reveal price impact, which can be roughly estimated by regressions of price changes on changes in the volume of buy and sell orders.[2]

Dealers play a layered role in intermediating between buyers and sellers. In stating bid and ask prices for assets, they help disseminate price information while facilitating exchanges of assets among willing buyers and sellers. Dealers are the most direct observers of variations in order flow and occasional temporary imbalances between potential buyers and sellers. Once identified, they stand ready to add or sell securities out of their inventories and to assume asset risks from customers for short periods. This important function, sometimes referred to as "front-running," helps equilibrate markets and reduce price volatility and is also profitable. It is limited by the size of the imbalance, but also by dealers' ability, for risk management, funding and regulatory reasons, to expand and contract inventory.

Adverse selection increases transaction costs. Dealers are wary of information traders and the possibility that the counterparty has better information on the security's value. Bid-ask spreads have to be wider in the presence of informed traders to compensate for the risk of adverse selection. Information-insensitive assets can therefore trade at narrower bid-ask spreads.

The opportunity to front-run is one incentive to market makers to scale up their order books, permitting overall trading costs to decline for all market participants, as they have over the past few decades. If market makers are to minimize principal risk and commissions are zero, then the cost of providing liquidity has to come primarily from bid-ask spreads. Spreads have to be wider in the presence of informed traders to compensate for the risk of adverse selection. The presence of less informed traders who can be "picked off" by the market makers and information on order flows helps narrow spreads. The market makers are intermediating; trading gains go to the well informed at the expense of the less informed as the market is kept at a limited arbitrage price near that which a perfect market would find.

---

[2] The data are published as part of the regular meeting materials of the Treasury Market Practices Group (TMPG) at https://www.newyorkfed.org/TMPG/meetings.html.

Market microstructure has changed and asset trading volumes have grown tremendously in recent decades, with rising wealth, technological development, and regulation the predominant drivers. A large share of trading volume in many markets is algorithmic, carrying out automatically functions that used to require a human agent, such as dynamically adjusting the pace of execution of a large buy or sell order to market conditions that change by the moment. Its growth has coincided with, and may be partly responsible for, a decline in trading costs and bid-ask spreads so far as these can be measured.

Market liquidity risk measures have limited usefulness. The **liquidity-adjusted VaR** is a market VaR estimate adjusted for the "time to escape" a position. It starts from an estimate of the number of days T needed to liquidate the position without adverse price impact and of the position's 1-day VaR. Assume the position is liquidated in equal parts each day. Applying the square-root-of-time rule, multiplying the VaR by $\sqrt{T}$, overestimates risk. The trader faces a 1-day holding period on the entire position, a 2-day holding period on a fraction $\frac{T-1}{T}$ of the position, and so on. The sequence of position sizes during the process of liquidation is the original position size times $1, \frac{T-1}{T}, \frac{1}{T}, \dots, \frac{T-2}{T}$. So, the VaR is adjusted by

$$\sqrt{1 + \left(\frac{T-1}{T}\right)^2 + \cdots + \left(\frac{1}{T}\right)^2} = \sqrt{\frac{(1+T)(1+2T)}{6T}}.$$

For example, if $T = 5$ days, multiply the VaR at a daily rate by 1.48.

12.1.2   Market Liquidity Stress Events

Since the global financial crisis, liquidity in specific markets has suddenly become not just impaired but has nearly disappeared for short periods. These flash crashes, relatively brief but extreme market liquidity risk events, are a sporadically recurring phenomenon even in more liquid markets. In a flash crash, prices decline extremely sharply before recovering within a few minutes. They differ from fire sales, in which a price decline initiated by one or a few market participants' selling forces selling by others, in the speed of the price move and aren't set off by market participants' loss of funding. Although flash crashes are brief, there is concern they can lead to enduring effects on price discovery and the capacity of market makers.

Market Episode: The May 2010 US stock market flash crash

The brief May 6, 2010, drop in US stock prices was one of the earliest and most dramatic examples of a flash crash. It occurred during the European debt crisis, a time of elevated market volatility and risk aversion. The event was triggered by a large mutual fund's algorithmic order to sell a type of S&P 500 futures contract, the E-mini, programmed to pace offers by market volume alone, not taking prices or speed of change into account. Within a few minutes, the selling pressure had been transmitted to other S&P 500 futures and cash markets as market maker capacity was exhausted and the index fell about 9 percent, compared to a typical daily price range of about 1.5 percent.

Though the chronology of the crash is clear, the underlying causes remain controversial. The increased role of high-frequency traders, with less willingness and balance-sheet capacity to quickly absorb market imbalances than exchange and desk market makers, may have played a role. Market makers may have withdrawn for a time because they hit risk limits or because of the perceived increased risk of adverse selection by well informed traders. One futures trader pleaded guilty in a US court to fraud and spoofing, a prohibited trading practice in which orders are entered into the market and quickly withdrawn to suggest higher trading volume or a direction of price change.

Overall trading volume on the day more than doubled compared to the prior trading days, as fundamental traders entered the market to take advantage of the price dislocation. After about 30 minutes, prices recovered to their initial level as buy orders entered the market. Similar episodes have occurred in the US Treasury market on October 15, 2014, the German government bond market on January 15, 2015, sterling on October 7, 2016, the market for cryptocurrency Ethereum on June 21, 2017, and silver futures on July 6, 2017.

Exchanges may impose **trading halts**, or **curbs** that temporarily pause trading in specified or all stocks, on one or all exchanges and platforms. Some curbs on trading are imposed on individual stocks in anticipation of news with potential to strongly impact trading and pricing, such as earnings reports. One type of market-wide halt is a **circuit breaker** in which trading is halted for a period of time in response to high volatility, generally defined as a price decline exceeding a trigger magnitude within a stated time interval. In 2010, US rules were altered to permit volatility-induced halts on trading of individual stocks. Market-wide circuit breakers were first introduced following the October 19, 1987, US stock market crash. They are regarded as a potential mitigant of flash crashes, but rarely imposed. The pandemic-related stock market decline of March 9, 2020, was a recent trigger.

The efficacy of circuit breakers in reducing volatility is unclear. The regulatory argument in favor, rooted in behavioral finance, is that they reduce panic among investors. By impairing market liquidity, however, they may instead increase volatility.

12.1.3 Funding Liquidity

Market participants engaged in maturity transformation expose themselves to the market risk of a **duration**, or **maturity**, **mismatch** on their balance sheets with longer-term assets financed by short-term debt. Borrowers lower their funding costs at the cost of higher liquidity risk. Even if the market participant is able to roll over borrowing today, there is uncertainty about tomorrow. If debt can't be retained or can be refinanced only on highly disadvantageous terms, positions become unprofitable or may have to be unwound.

Funding liquidity, rollover, or **balance sheet risk** arises through the use of leverage. It is the risk that creditors decline to continue extending short-term credit, or change the terms on which it is granted, before the investment or trades being funded can come to fruition. Funding liquidity is adequate if market participants own ample stocks of liquid assets or are less reliant on **volatile liabilities**, unstable sources of short-term funding. Financial intermediaries are particularly likely to be exposed to funding liquidity risk. Banks, for example, may be overly reliant on wholesale short-term funding or nonoperating deposits.[3] Insurance firms may be overly reliant on **guaranteed investment contracts** (GICs), or on policyholder deposits that are apt to be surrendered.

---

[3] See Chapter 19.

Asset-liability management (ALM) in the bank and insurance sectors monitors metrics of funding liquidity based on stocks or flows of liquid assets:

Stock measures compare liquid asset holdings to short-term liabilities. There may be a **liquidity gap**, with liquid assets less than volatile liabilities.

Flow measures include projections of outflows and inflows of cash and other liquid assets over a specified time horizon and can be combined with stock measures. A cash flow mismatch is a difference between estimated inflows and outflows of cash over a future horizon. The **liquidity coverage ratio** (LCR), the stock of liquid assets relative to an estimate of net cash outflow, is a key ratio for Basel liquidity regulation.

Funding and market liquidity risks are closely tied to one another and to the use of leverage. Position sizes financed through debt are larger and more exposed to market liquidity risk. A loss of funding liquidity can force a market participant to unwind a position at a bad moment, or in a size the market can't easily cope with, leading to a market liquidity risk event. Lenders are exposed indirectly to the liquidity risks of borrowers, who may default if the positions being financed can only be unwound at a substantial loss. A funding liquidity risk event can lead to widespread asset liquidations, and to a wider market liquidity risk event.

Funding illiquidity is distinct from insolvency, but the two can be difficult to distinguish in practice. The risk of insolvency arises if firms fund assets primarily through debt liabilities relative to equity. The risk of funding illiquidity arises if firms maintain inadequate reserves of liquid assets given their asset risk, the maturities of their debt liabilities and other cash obligations.

12.2 Private Liquidity Creation: Commercial Banking

12.2.1 Historical Emergence of Banks

Money issued by a government or central bank is the most unquestionably liquid asset in the financial system but forms of liquidity created privately by banks and through markets are close substitutes. Public and private liquidity creation are linked to mechanisms that enable market participants to establish leveraged positions funded at short term.

For much of recorded history, monetary systems were based almost entirely on commodity money, usually gold. Payments were made and accounts settled by transfers of coin or specie. Commercial banking and capital markets began taking their modern forms during the late medieval era, emerging to address the need for credit financing of local and long-distance trade and to mitigate the inconvenience and insecurity of settling debts in specie.

Goldsmiths, originally in the business of exchanging, assaying, and safekeeping of specie and precious metals, issued receipts acknowledging deposits of gold and silver. Deposit balances could be transferred from a payor's to a recipient's bank. Claims on deposits with trusted goldsmiths became fungible claims, not claims on specific precious metal deposited, and could be used to settle transactions and circulate in place of specie. These early forms of paper money significantly lowered the transactions costs of assaying, weighing and moving metal. Early banks discovered that not all precious metal deposits were redeemed simultaneously, freeing up some, or even the bulk, of deposits for lending. They could issue receipts for more gold than had been deposited. **Fractional-reserve banking** is the practice of creating deposit liabilities in excess of the amount of cash and highly liquid assets a bank holds.

Larger merchants evolved into banks by financing long-distance transactions in which they were not directly involved as importers or exporters. The **bill of exchange** evolved as a negotiable debt instrument that further reduced the need to settle exchanges in specie. With the advent of merchant and commercial banking, payments and settlement could be effected by bills, deposit certificates, and other documented promises to pay, facilitated by the introduction of double-entry accounting.

12.2.2   Commercial Bank Liquidity Creation

Bank lending is inherently deposit creation. Banks issue loans by creating a deposit liability and crediting it to the borrower. To make use of the funds, the borrower can withdraw cash, write checks, or transfer the deposit. Banks also carry out a liquidity transformation by creating deposits that are transferable and for the most part redeemable on demand. Both transformations are effected by "using balance sheet" as if it were a manufacturing process. Banks also effect the settlement and clearing of payments by offsetting debts, repaying one debt with others. Banks can thereby not only transfer liquidity among market participants as part of their payments and settlements role but also enhance liquidity.

Apart from the usefulness of deposits as a means of payments, a primary motivation for household depositors to hold liquid but lower-yielding assets is to insure the value of stored wealth if consumption is desired earlier than planned. Similarly, corporate treasuries keep liquid assets to insure against contingencies. **Liquidity risk sharing** has historically been a primary function of banks. Banks lend in large part to finance projects or assets requiring a long time to pay off. Early liquidation is often possible only at a loss. Banks are a vehicle for depositors to coinsure against liquidity risk by pooling with others. Pooling of deposits smooths out random fluctuations in withdrawals and makes them more predictable for banks. Interbank money markets provide similar coinsurance to banks themselves. All accept lower interest rates because deposits also provide money services.

The bank can offer a better return to short-term depositors than projects' early liquidation value, and deposit accounts provide money services to depositors in exchange for low-interest financing of their assets, but it is viable only if the bank accurately predicts the timing of withdrawals. In a fractional-reserve banking system, banks cannot meet simultaneous withdrawals by all or even a large number of depositors. Banks estimate the size and likelihood of a low-probability, but plausible, cluster of simultaneous withdrawals. Banks hold **reserves**, a buffer stock of liquid assets, to meet unexpected cash withdrawals by depositors.

Liquidity transformation is viable if the bank can accurately predict the distribution of the timing of withdrawals and holds sufficient reserves but can nonetheless offer a better return to short-term depositors than the projects' early liquidation value. The trade-off of the risk of an underestimate of withdrawals against the opportunity cost of holding low-yield reserves instead of higher-yielding but less liquid loans or securities is at the heart of the phenomenon of bank runs.[4]

Reserves can consist of a wide range of assets. The most liquid and, therefore, most closely matching the deposit liabilities are cash and reserve deposits with the central bank. Readily marketable, low credit risk securities, such as high-quality short-term commercial paper and government debt, don't provide same-day liquidity but must first be sold and converted into means of payment. Some forms of liquidity, such as deposit accounts with other commercial banks, contribute less to a credible liquidity reserve and are exposed to credit risk. Though highly liquid in normal times, depositor and obligor banks may be eager to reduce these balances when financial conditions tighten.

---

[4] See Chapter 15.

Assets	Liabilities
Liquidity reserve: cash and government bonds $15	Capital: common equity $10
Loans and debt securities $85	Deposits $80
	Longer-term borrowing $10

Figure 12.1 Schematic balance sheet of a commercial bank

Deposits are relatively short-term. **Demand** or **sight deposits** are those redeemable instantly without delay. **Time deposits** have a fixed term to maturity ranging from a few days to a few years and generally pay a higher interest rate. Many deposit accounts are small, particularly those belonging to households, but those owned by companies can be quite large. Some are insured by the public sector.

Figure 12.1 displays the balance sheet of a simple commercial bank. It relies primarily on deposits for funding and has 10-to-1 leverage, high by long-term historical, though not by current standards. But it also has a high reserve ratio of 18.75 percent.

Banks earn fees for **loan commitments** or **credit lines** to companies, providing for loans up to a specified amount at an agreed interest rate, at the initiative of the borrower. Lines of credit can be drawn upon immediately by corporate customers, serving as a liquidity substitute for deposits. Fees are lower than loan rates, reducing customers' liquidity risk management costs relative to borrowing or liquid reserves. Credit lines are a contingent use of banks' liquidity reserves.

There are synergies between banks' activities, one activity leading to economies in another. Deposit taking, maintenance of a ledger of debits and credits, and a key role in payments and settlements rely on the same systems. Lending and loan commitments rely on underwriting and liquidity risk pooling. Deposits and loan commitments are supported by the bank's stock of liquid assets.

In addition to loans, portfolios of marketable as well as illiquid securities are a large and growing share of banks' interest-earning assets. For most banks historically, particularly in the United States, asset risk mainly arose from the credit risk of their loan portfolios. Figure 12.2 shows the composition of US commercial banks' balance sheets over the past three decades. Securities have become a far larger share of assets. Funding sources have also shifted. Though deposits remain the mainstay of bank funding, issuance of debt securities has become much more important.

12.2.3   Commercial Bank Risks

Banks are primarily exposed to credit, liquidity, and interest rate risk. **Nonperforming loans** (NPLs) are bank loans on which borrowers are delinquent, failing to pay interest or principal due. When banks recognize losses on the loans, they are charged off or recognized in banks' accounting statements. Figure 12.3 plots US banks' **charge-off** and **delinquency rates** over the past few decades.

Universal banks that combine commercial banking with investment activities and commercial banks increasingly in recent decades are exposed to interest rate and other market risks. A commercial bank's primary source of earnings is **net interest margin** (NIM), which is the difference between

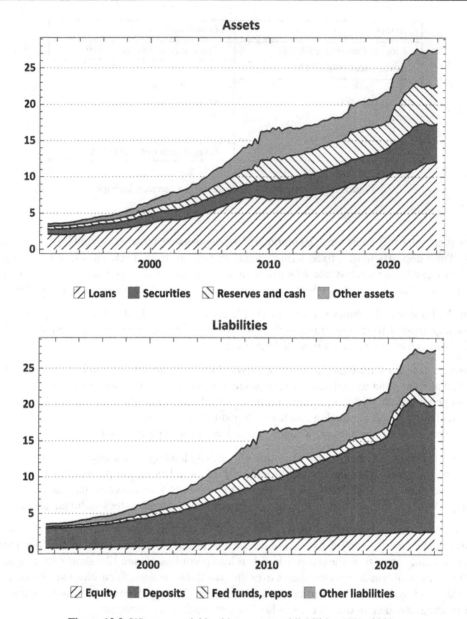

Figure 12.2 US commercial banking assets and liabilities 1991–2023

Securities includes available for sale (AFS), held to maturity (HTM), and trading assets. Other liabilities consist largely of debt securities issued by banks and bank holding companies (BHCs).

The data are based on call reports and other filings of US commercial banks and BHCs, including nonbank subsidiaries of BHCs and not including assets and liabilities of foreign bank organizations (FBOs). USD trillions, quarterly Q1 1991 to Q4 2023. *Source*: Federal Reserve Bank of New York, Quarterly Trends for Consolidated US Banking Organizations, Table 1: Balance Sheet Composition.

interest earned and interest paid:

$$\text{NIM} = \frac{\text{net interest income}}{\text{interest earning assets}} = \frac{\text{interest income} - \text{interest expense}}{\text{interest earning assets}}.$$

Net interest margin is generally substantially positive because banks fund a large part of their assets with deposits. The yield curve tends to be particularly steeply upward sloping at the very short end

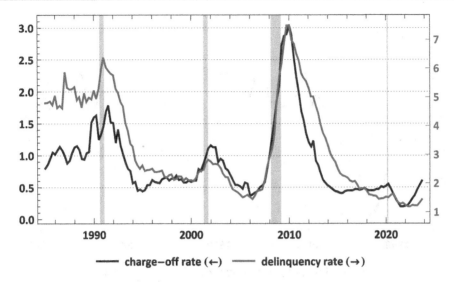

Figure 12.3 Bank charge-off and delinquency rates 1985–2022

All commercial banks, all loans. Percent of aggregate loan balances, seasonally adjusted at annual rate, Q1 1985–Q3 2022. Charge-offs are the value of loans removed from the books and charged against loss reserves, net of recoveries. Delinquent loans are those past due 30 days or more and still accruing interest as well as those in nonaccrual status. Vertical shading represents NBER recession dates. *Source*: Federal Reserve Board and FRED.

because the shortest-term deposits provide money services and thus bear a negative risk premium; the interest rate on sight deposits is often zero.

But Figure 12.4 shows how widely this source of banks' net income has fluctuated over the past century for US banks as interest rates change. NIM was at its lowest when Treasury and Federal Reserve policy deliberately aimed at keeping rates low and the yield curve flat, during the Second World War and its aftermath to facilitate war financing and during the global financial crisis in an effort to lower the hurdle rates to investment and keep asset prices buoyant.

High market interest rates generally lead to higher NIM and benefit banks, but the transition, during periods of rising rates, can be difficult. For example, during the "conundrum" period of rising short-term rates from 2004 to 2007, long-term rates were unusually sluggish in moving higher, resulting in a very flat yield curve and a lower NIM. A more complex set of difficulties for banks marked the rising rate environment from mid-2022.[5]

Larger banks enjoy implicit and explicit government guarantees and can offer lower deposit rates in exchange for the additional safety, a competitive advantage over smaller ones. But because they also fund through higher-cost means, such as bond issuance, their overall cost of funding may be higher. Large depositors may be concentrated geographically or by sector, increasing a bank's funding liquidity risk. NIM is generally higher for smaller banks with a stable deposit base that can rely on a lower-cost funding source compared to larger banks.

Loan-to-deposit ratios are a measure of liquidity risk for banks. A low ratio indicates a bank is reliant on a stable funding source or has liquid assets it could sell to meet withdrawals. Loan-to-deposit ratios should be interpreted cautiously as a risk metric because they tend to be

---

[5] See Chapter 20.

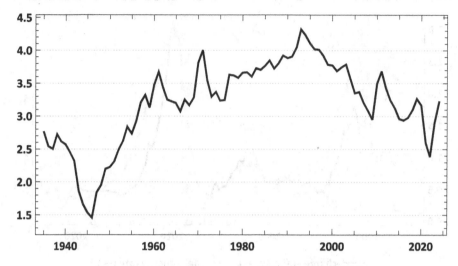

Figure 12.4 Net interest margin of US banks 1934–2023

Ratio of net interest income (series NIM) to total interest earning assets (series INTBAST), all FDIC-insured commercial banks, annual, percent. *Source*: Federal Deposit Insurance Corporation (FDIC), Historical Statistics on Banking (https://banks.data.fdic.gov/bankfind-suite/historical).

different for different types of banks. They are generally higher for smaller banks more reliant on deposits and with limited access to public debt markets for funding.

Like other intermediaries, banks are agents of their principals: shareholders, depositors, and other lenders seek reliable mechanisms to monitor bank management. Several characteristics of banks make this more complicated. Banks are generally more leveraged than nonfinancial firms, with much of its senior funding provided by small, dispersed deposits. Banks are opaque and their corporate structure often complex. It can be difficult for outsiders, or even insiders, to understand their risks. Higher leverage shifts risk to the banks' lenders, strengthening the need for monitoring, and the dispersion of deposits and their senior position in the banks' capital structure weakens individual depositors' incentive to monitor.

It has in contrast, been argued that banks are more disciplined in their underwriting and liquidity risk management because they are carefully watched by jittery depositors, making banks more stable rather than less. Large depositors are especially motivated to carefully monitor their banks' asset and funding risks. Banks have been important money market creditors of other banks and in monitoring other banks' soundness.

The argument that banks' leverage enhances their stability by providing incentives to closer scrutiny is highly controversial. It is at odds with the argument that bank opacity facilitates the use of deposits as money by limiting the flow of potentially adverse information. Sudden widening of the LIBOR-OIS (LOIS) spread during crises indicates that banks have limited confidence in their own ability to monitor one other (see Chapter 15). The prevalence of deposit insurance, a government guarantee of deposits against losses, and expectations that all depositors will be made whole in the event of bank failures weaken protected depositors' incentives to monitor banks.

12.3   Private Liquidity Creation: Short-Term Funding

Even though bank deposits, banker's acceptances, commercial paper, and bills of exchange have been used for centuries, much short-term credit today is in relatively new forms. Leverage collateralized by securities, predominantly stocks and bonds, has grown enormously in advanced economies in the past few decades. **Collateralized securities lending**, often called **market-based** or **short-term wholesale financing** (SWTF), or **securities financing transactions** (SFTs) by regulators, are loans used to take long or short positions in securities in which either the securities or the cash in the transaction serve as collateral. The mechanisms by which the financial system establishes and finances bond and equity positions and supplies liquidity to markets and large intermediaries rely on information-insensitive assets that can be readily used as collateral to borrow money. Money market mutual funds (MMMFs) are an important distribution channel through which short-term credit is funded by retail and nonfinancial corporate investors as well as by other intermediaries and central banks.

12.3.1 Structure of Collateralized Securities Lending Markets

Collateralized securities lending is largely conducted wholesale. Participants are predominantly intermediaries on both sides of transactions, with a broker-dealer ("sell side") on at least one side. They enable borrowers to finance long positions in securities collateralized by the securities themselves. Short sellers can borrow securities to establish positions, with cash from the short sales serving as collateral. Lenders of securities or cash can earn additional interest through collateralized loans. Almost of this lending is short-term and accounts for a large share of money market activity.

The collateral markets can be thought of as consisting of an "outer market" of investors deploying cash or securities, with larger banks and broker-dealers intermediating between lenders and borrowers of cash and securities, and an "inner market" of dealers. Cash lenders include money market funds, corporate treasuries, and institutional investors deploying the cash collateral posted by borrowers of their securities. Cash borrowers include hedge funds taking leveraged positions in securities. The demand for and supply of cash also varies with institutional investors' hedging activities. Some outer-market participants come to the market primarily to lend securities perhaps because they have large portfolios of assets that can be used as collateral. In the inner market, dealers trade with one another to manage and finance their inventories and to support market making.

The legal mechanics of collateralized security loans have been refined in recent decades, building on the general treatment of collateral. Securities are **pledged**, meaning used as collateral, to obtain secured loans of cash or of other securities. The lender of cash has custody of the pledged securities, which are said to be **encumbered**. The full value of the collateral is not lent. Overcollateralization, expressed as margin or a haircut, provides a buffer against price variation of the collateral.

Two types of arrangement have evolved for holding collateral, and they are legally distinct but economically similar. In one, a **security interest** in the collateral is transferred to the lender of cash. Alternatively, title is transfered to the lender, with an obligation to return **equivalent collateral**. The holder of pledged securities must remit dividend and coupon payments. Voting rights are a tricky issue, with arrangements in US equity markets for lenders of stock to exercise voting rights in spite of a contract transferring ownership rights. Netting has also become more prevalent.

Collateral is frequently **rehypothecated** or repledged by the lender. Dealers reuse collateral to refinance loans of cash they've extended or to borrow securities in high demand. Rehypothecation deepens the liquidity of collateral markets in normal times but can cause impairment of markets in stress events. It exposes owners to **rehypothecation risk**, the risk that their collateral is seized by a downstream lender exercising that right against a downstream borrower of cash.

Rehypothecation chains can be long as the repo market distributes collateral within the network of dealers. In doing so, it distributes the credit risk and liquidity benefits of safe assets among market participants who may value them in different ways. But rehypothecation chains are hard to track in a large and complex market, so the overall extent of collateral reuse and which dealers may be reliant on collateral that is not unquestionably safe are an additional source of uncertainty for market participants. In financial stress events, concern can suddenly surface about collateral quality or about the soundness of the intermediaries in possession. In 2007, skepticism about the credit quality of subprime mortgage debt triggered flights from the asset class and the intermediaries thought to be exposed.

There are three major types of collateralized securities lending:

Margin loans finance security transactions in which the loan of a security, usually traded equity, is collateralized by cash. In a short sale financed by margin, the securities borrower obtains cash by selling the securities. There is a wide range of participants in margin lending: short sellers, such as long-short equity hedge funds, retail investors, and institutional investors. Figure 12.5 shows the growth in margin lending over the past few decades.

Securities lending is the loan of a security, collateralized by cash which can be invested elsewhere for a fee. The lenders are most often institutional investors, which maintain portfolios of long-term high-quality collateral to meet their investment objectives and don't actively trade them. They earn additional return from the lending fees and investing the cash collateral. It is administered on a large scale by major **custodian banks**, e.g., Bank of New York Mellon (BNYM), State Street, and JPMorgan Chase.

Repurchase agreements, or repo, consists of the matched spot sale and forward repurchase of security. The spot price is the market price of the security, and the forward price is set at initiation to imply a secured lending rate collateralized by the security. Repo is legally structured as a pair of sales but economically equivalent to lending.

Margin and securities loans are collateralized by cash of which part may be returned to the securities borrower in the form of a **rebate**. If demand to borrow a particular stock is high, because the shares

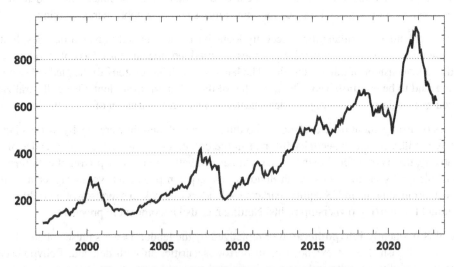

Figure 12.5 US stock market margin debt 1997–2023

Debit balances in customers' securities margin accounts at Financial Industry Regulatory Authority (FINRA) member firms, month-end, Jan. 1997 to—Feb. 2023, $ billions *Source*: FINRA.

available for trading are limited and it is sought after by short sellers, the securities lender may receive a negative rebate, in addition to returns on the cash collateral. Repo lenders of particularly sought-after securities temporarily in high demand, such as when-issued (WI) Treasurys trading special, can borrow cash at a lower rate.

12.3.2   Repo Markets

The repo market is the largest set of collateralized securities financing markets and an important part of US Treasury markets generally. Central banks conduct monetary policy to a large extent through repo transactions, and the Federal Reserve has deepened its participation as part of its post-crisis monetary policy. Repo markets are at the heart of regulatory efforts to replace privately calculated with government-calculated reference rates for money markets and derivatives (see Chapter 6).

A cash borrower lends the securities and is said to have entered a repo transaction or "repo out" the securities, and a cash lender borrows the securities, engaging in a **reverse repo** or "reversing in" the securities. It is a secured loan rather than a purchase and sale because the cash borrower, though formally having sold rather than lent the securities, has the obligation to repurchase them. The cash borrower also bears the market risk of the transaction because the repurchase price is determined at initiation and the cash price at maturity may have fallen.

In dealer **matched-book repo**, dealers simultaneously enter repo and reverse repo trades with different counterparties earning a spread or truing up their inventories. The dealer raises cash from the reverse-repo counterparty and lends it to a repo counterparty. At the same time, the dealer may rehypothecate a repo counterparty's collateral to a reverse-repo counterparty. This inner market also interfaces with the banks and broker-dealers carrying out end-user transactions.

The repo market has segments addressing different objectives. Most repo consists of **general collateral** GC transactions. They can be collateralized by any securities within a class, such as Treasurys or agency debt, and specific securities can be substituted for one another as long as the total value of the collateral is sufficient. The repo purchaser (cash lender) may return fungible or "equivalent" securities. A relatively small volume of repo transactions are collateralized by specific securities identified by CUSIP.[6] Most repo is **Treasury repo** collateralized by Treasurys. There is also a smaller volume of repo using agency MBS and other securities as collateral. Treasury and agency repo transactions can be settled via Fedwire.

Repo is operationally complex. There are several platforms for carrying out repo, depending on the participants, purpose, and the collateral. In **tri-party repo**, a third party keeps track of collateral, values it, compares it to the terms of the repo agreement to make sure the transaction is adequately secured, provides custodial services, and settles trades via transfers of cash and securities between participants' accounts.[7] Rehypothecation is not practiced in tri-party repo; the custodian's credible guarantee of collateral delivery is an important structural element.

Triparty is used by larger participants in repo markets and has become the primary trading venue, accounting for about two-thirds of US transaction volume. In the United States, BNYM is currently the sole tri-party custodian, JPMorgan chase having exited the business in 2019. **GCF Repo** is similar to tri-party repo but is open to smaller dealers and executed though the **Fixed Income Clearing Corporation** (FICC), a DTCC subsidiary, and cleared through the BNYM tri-party platform.

---

[6] A CUSIP (Committee on Uniform Securities Identification Procedures) number is an identifier used for most North American securities.

[7] Third-party valuation became standard in the wake of the Drysdale Securities failure in 1982. Drysdale had used internal valuations ignoring accrued interest to engage in matched-book repo transactions that netted cash. Losses to the securities portfolio in which the cash was invested rendered Drysdale insolvent.

Delivery versus payment (DVP) or **bilateral repo** are direct transactions, generally between dealers. Much DVP repo, called **cleared** or **sponsored** repo, is cleared through the FICC. In a sponsored matched book repo, the dealer executes the repo and reverse repo transactions through the FICC. Doing so enables the dealer to conduct a larger volume of repo with the same amount of margin, enabling additional leverage compared to holding the matched-book repo trades on its balance sheet. DVP counterparties may be able to simply exchange the cash and securities directly or through a securities dealer rather than relying on clearing through a custodian or on a clearing platform. The motivation for DVP trades, particularly of hedge funds, is often positioning in specific securities not eligible for clearing about which the trader has a view. Some general collateral repo is also executed via DVP.

On occasion, securities trade **special** for a time. They are particularly desired by market participants because they are obligated to deliver those specific bonds as part of a sale or to unwind a short position. Treasury bonds can trade special when dealers have committed to deliver to a customer a when-issued (WI) bond they don't own for which auction demand has proven surprisingly strong. Failures to deliver, or fails, are costly, so a dealer will pay up to borrow a security and avoid a fail. Owners of those bonds can then repo them out in the bilateral market to borrow cash at a below-market **special repo rate**. They receive the "rent" for the use of their temporarily precious collateral in the form of a low cost of funding and an opportunity to earn an above-market carry.

Repo is the largest by far in terms of volume of the collateralized securities lending markets, with about $7 trillion in outstanding liabilities and assets. The outstanding volume of tri-party repo was $4.0 trillion as of October 2023 (Figure 12.6).[8]

Repo transactions are generally governed by standardized documentation, the **Master Repurchase Agreement**, which also provides for some netting. Most repo transactions are overnight but are often rolled over continuously for longer periods. **Term repo** has a longer initial maturity than overnight.

The growth of the repo markets has been encouraged by their exemption from the automatic stay that is the norm in bankruptcy but an important difference between a repo transaction and a collateralized loan. Instead, the cash lender can seize and sell collateral without delay. Most derivatives are also exempt from the stay. The exemption, or "safe harbor," privileges counterparties of a defaulting firm by comparison with its other creditors, substantially reducing counterparty risk by at least reducing delay in recovery. It also reduces the risk that a nondefaulting counterparty's solvency or liquidity suffers in consequence.[9]

The New York Fed is the administrator of several reference rates based on Treasury repo rates. The most widely used is the Secured Overnight Financing Rate (SOFR), based on data from three sources: tri-party GC Treasury repo transactions, provided by the custodian BNYM, GCF repo, provided by FICC, and DVP Treasury repo cleared through FICC.[10]

[8] See Federal Reserve Board, Financial Accounts of the United States (Z.1), Table L.207 for totals and Table L.130 for broker-dealer outstandings. Fed funds liabilities are a small part of the totals stated for recent years. The Federal Reserve Bank of New York provides data on triparty repo market volume and transactions, and the US Financial Accounts on the outstanding and transactions volumes of broker-dealer repo.
[9] Repo had long been structured as a matched purchase and sale in part to avoid the stay. The exemption was clarified under legislation passed in 1984.
[10] There are also two subindexes based on the constituent marketplaces: The **Broad General Collateral Rate** (BGCR) doesn't include the DVP transactions and the **Tri-Party General Collateral Rate** (TGCR) includes only the BNYM transactions.

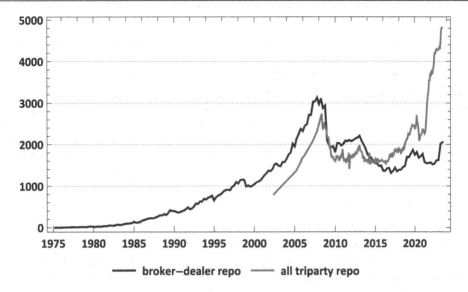

Figure 12.6 US broker-dealer and triparty repo 1975–2023

Net liabilities (borrowed cash) under security repurchase agreements of US broker-dealers, $ billions, quarterly, Q1 1975 to Q2 2023. *Source*: Federal Reserve Board, Financial Accounts of the United States (Z.1), Table L.130. Total volume of tri-party repo (market value of the collateral), all collateral classes, $ billions, monthly, 31May2002 to 31Oct2023. *Source*: Federal Reserve Bank of New York.

Market Episode: The Orange County bankruptcy

In late 1994, Orange County, California, was obliged to declare bankruptcy after a loss of $1.6 billion, at the time the largest municipal bankruptcy in US history and an exceedingly rare event by comparison with personal and corporate bankruptcies. Its treasury had managed its own investment fund and on behalf of a number of other California local public agencies, drawn by Orange County's apparent success in achieving higher returns than other state funds.

Orange County had been highly leveraged, primarily through the use of reverse-repo transactions in which the fund used its initial equity capital to borrow a larger amount of bonds. The county also invested in its fund the proceeds of bonds it issued. It is estimated that the fund was leveraged 3-to-1, apart from considerable additional embedded leverage through the use of derivatives.

Orange County's portfolio was highly exposed to interest rate and liquidity risk. Its interest rate exposure was achieved in large part through derivatives that paid off if interest rates remained low or fell and through the use of **inverse floating-rate bonds**, a type of structured product that pays the difference between a high fixed rate and a floating rate that is lower at initiation. If interest rates rise, that gap is narrowed, reducing the value of the security.

The Orange County fund's liquidity risk was inherent in its technique for establishing leverage. It borrowed at short term in repo markets and invested in longer-term securities. The borrowing could be terminated or its terms changed at short notice, and its investments could be liquidated only over a longer time without adverse price impact. The strategy unraveled and the bankruptcy ensued at the end of a year of rising interest rates that had been disrupting financial markets in the United States and abroad.

12.3.3 Money Market Mutual Funds

Money market mutual funds (MMMFs) play a large role in pooling and distributing short-term claims, including repo exposures, to a wide set of nonfinancial corporate and household investors. Most MMMFs globally are domiciled in the United States and invest in dollar-denominated assets.[11] MMMFs are a close money substitute for bank deposits and cash; in the United States, some MMMF holdings are a component of the broadly defined money supply. They emerged in the 1970s, a time of rapidly rising interest rates and regulatory interest rate ceilings on bank deposit accounts. Their wide yield gap vis-à-vis other money market instruments and liquidity made them attractive and they have grown rapidly. US MMMFs are subject to specific regulations that limit their assets to low credit risk short-term instruments, diversified by issuer, and permit them to maintain a constant share price of $1.00 as long as the market value of its investments remains within a tight range.[12]

Their growth has seen some major interruptions: During the so-called conundrum of 2004–2005, as the Fed raised rates steadily with little impact on longer-term rates, the money fund yield advantage of pooling investments with terms to maturity of a few weeks or months compared to deposit rates was lost. The financial crisis of 2008 included a run on money market funds and a 25 percent fall in their assets. Another run took place as part of a larger liquidity stress event at the onset of Covid in March 2020.[13]

Money fund investors at first were almost exclusively households, but their investor base has shifted substantially to businesses. Ownership by non-households has grown to nearly half the total, roughly evenly divided between nonfinancial business and a wide range of financial entities, such as pension funds, other institutional investors, and investment funds (Figure 12.7). European money market funds have an even lower share of household investors. This has affected their functioning during periods of stress. Similarly to bank deposits, households fled somewhat less readily than other investors during the 2008 and 2020 outflows. A shift toward government-issued assets could offset the higher vulnerability to runs induced by a shift away from households.

Initially, MMMFs invested almost entirely in liabilities of the private sector: commercial paper, time deposits at banks, and corporate bonds with short remaining maturities. Short-term Treasury, agency, and municipal securities accounted for a small share of MMMF assets. Later on, as the repo market developed in the 1980s, they invested also in reverse repos with bank and dealer counterparties. In recent years, money funds have at times been the largest category of counterparty of the Federal Reserve's crisis-era overnight reverse repo (ON RRP) program. Federal Reserve liabilities accounted by 2023 for nearly half of MMMF assets, and for nearly all of MMMF reverse repo assets but have fallen since (see Chapter 20). Money funds have become a key intermediary transforming government liabilities into forms of money (Figure 12.8).

---

[11] International Organization of Securities Commissions (2020), p. 11, citing the Investment Company Institute.

[12] See Chapters 18.

[13] See Chapter 20.

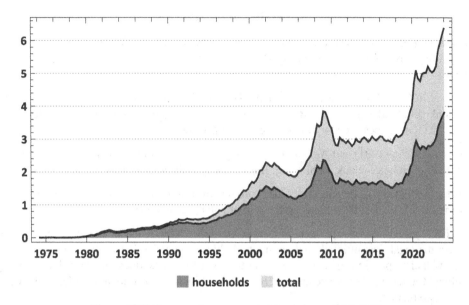

Figure 12.7 Owners of money market fund shares 1974–2023

Value of households' and nonprofit organizations' MMMF shares and total value of MMMF shares, $ trillions, quarterly, Q1 1974 to Q4 2023. *Source*: Federal Reserve Board, Financial Accounts of the United States (Z.1), Table L.206.

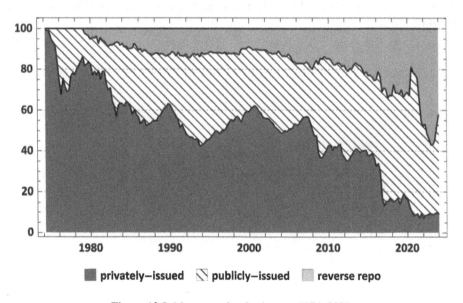

Figure 12.8 Money market fund assets 1974–2023

Share of each asset type in total assets of US money market mutual funds, percent, Q1 1974 to Q4 2023. *Source*: Federal Reserve Board, Financial Accounts of the United States (Z.1), Table L.121.

Further Reading

Foucault et al. (2023) and Hasbrouck (2023) provide detail on market liquidity and trading mechanisms in different markets. McLeay et al. (2014a and 2014b) describe the creation of deposits through lending.

Adrian et al. (2017) illustrate a number of market liquidity measures. Hendershott et al. (2011) and Kirilenko et al. (2017) discuss algorithmic trading and its impact on the cost of trading stocks. Fleming (2023) describes Treasury market liquidity measures.

Calomiris and Kahn (1991) and Admati and Hellwig (2024a) provide contrasting views on whether deposit funding enhances bank monitoring. Bank opacity is discussed in Gorton (2014).

Lipson et al. (2012) and Copeland et al. (2012) provide overviews of secured lending markets. Singh (2014) and Infante et al. (2020) focus on the role of collateral and its reuse.

Munyan (2023) is an overview of the repo market. Garbade (2006) and Menand and Younger (2023) summarize the legal, institutional, and contractual changes contributing to the emergence of repo markets and their expansion since the 1980s. Barth et al. (2021) describes the cleared repo segment. International Capital Market Association (2019 and 2023) detail institutional practice in the US and European repo markets.

The Orange County bankruptcy is analyzed in Jorion (1996) and Baldassare (1998).

Agapova (2015) is an overview of money market funds. The SEC summarizes its data on US money funds in "Money Market Fund Statistics" at https://www.sec.gov/divisions/investment/mmf-statistics.

13

Portfolio Credit Risk

Chapter 9 summarized the legal and institutional nature of credit risk and introduced models of the timing and probability of default of a single borrower. In practice, credit risk is concerned with losses in portfolios of loan or bonds with many different obligors. A US regional bank will have a loan book on the order of $100 billion outstanding, and banks and investment managers can easily have have bond investment portfolios that size or much larger.

The most important elements of credit risk can only be understood in a portfolio framework. Credit risk is driven not only by the likelihood of default but also by the likelihood that a surprising number of defaults will coincide. The average loan in a credit portfolio could have a relatively low default rate, but the portfolio can experience greater than expected losses if many loans default simultaneously.

A common metric for portfolio credit risk is its credit Value-at-Risk (VaR). For a given confidence level α, it is the α-quantile of the portfolio's unexpected credit loss distribution over a given time horizon, the loss the manager can plausibly state will be exceeded with a probability of only $1 - \alpha$. Credit VaR is based on the distribution of credit losses in excess of the expected loss (EL). Lenders take account of expected losses in reserving and capital planning and regard them as a regular cost of doing business. The bank, investor, or asset manager focuses on averting large, surprising clusters of credit losses.

Credit VaR is generally defined for longer horizons such as a year, while market VaR is defined for shorter periods, days or weeks. Significant fluctuations in asset prices can occur over short periods of time, but changes in creditworthiness or its assessment are slower. Credit VaR also generally employs a higher confidence level, more often 99 than 95 percent, related to the need to capture low-probability losses that are disastrous, that is, the heavy left tail of credit loss distributions.

13.1 Credit Portfolios and Default Correlation

13.1.1 Challenges in Portfolio Credit Risk Modeling

Portfolio credit risk modeling faces two core difficulties. First, relevant data are scarce. Default is infrequent relative to the large number of obligors. Observations on joint default, the near-simultaneous default of several borrowers, are even less frequent. In many years, for example, the number of investment-grade defaults is zero, and in some years, even the speculative-grade default rate is zero. Observations of many defaults in a year are recurrent but rare and sporadic (Figure 9.2).

The probability of default can be estimated at least roughly through underwriting, monitoring, and the experience of the past. The propensity of many loans or bonds to default simultaneously is more difficult to assess. The sparseness of default data is similar to a difficulty shared with market risk measurement, the paucity of extremely large-magnitude return observations. It leads to a similar dilemma, the difficulty of estimating the size and likelihood of very large losses that are unlikely but could occur and have occurred in the past.

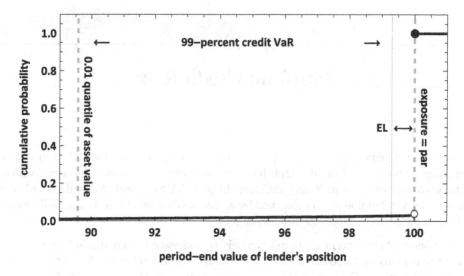

Figure 13.1 Skewness of credit risk

Probability distribution of bond value one year hence in the Merton model. Firm initial asset value is 145, the asset drift rate 10 percent, and volatility 25 percent at annual rates, debt consists of a zero-coupon bond with a par value of 100 and 8 percent. Actuarial default probability is 3.91 percent (from Table 9.3), so 96.09 percent of the probability mass is located at a single point.

A second basic challenge in credit risk modeling is the pronounced skewness of credit loss distributions. Credit risk outcomes of a single obligor and even some portfolios are close to binary: either a return close to expectation or a large loss. Many structured credit products are also close to binary in return.

Figure 13.1, illustrates using the example of the basic Merton default model introduced in Chapter 9. It displays the real-world, actuarial cumulative probability distribution of payoffs to the holder of debt issued by the firm in the example. The likeliest event, with a probability just over 96 percent, is that the firm doesn't default in which case the return will be the bond par value. The distribution is discontinuous, jumping to a probability of 100 percent at par, which is the maximum creditors can receive. In the event the firm defaults, a range of values below par has a positive probability, depending on the debt's recovery value, which in turn depends on the firm's asset value in one year. Most asset return distributions also have fat left tails but are more continuous.[1]

With these caveats, we can describe the key factors in the credit risk of a portfolio of debt instruments. **Granularity** or diversification describes whether the portfolio contains debt obligations of many different obligors, relative to its total size. Granularity generally makes credit portfolios less risky. Concentration in a small handful of borrowers leaves the portfolio more exposed to default by one or just a few. It is often measured via the **Herfindahl index** of the portfolio, the sum of squares of the shares of the individual obligors in the portfolio.[2]

The other key determinant of portfolio credit risk is **default correlation**, a measure of the likelihood that two firms will default at the same time, and a distinct concept from that of default probability. The typical loan or bond in a credit portfolio may have a relatively low default probability, but the obligors may nonetheless have a high propensity to default simultaneously, for example, if their businesses are

---

[1] Currencies with fixed exchange rates are an important counterexample.

[2] The index, also known as the Herfindahl–Hirschman index, is used to measure firm concentration in an industry.

exposed to the same low-probability risks. Default correlation is closely related to financial system **contagion**, the impact of one intermediary's financial distress or insolvency on others.

High correlation leads to a portfolio credit loss distribution with a heavier left tail. Portfolio lenders are averse to even a low likelihood of such a cluster of defaults, which can cause extreme losses even for portfolios with high granularity and low default probability. Structured product investors may accept high default correlation risk but only if offered high expected returns to compensate.

13.1.2   Default Correlation

Default correlation is more difficult than granularity to capture in a portfolio credit risk model. It differs conceptually from the return correlation of two assets in that it is an event correlation, measuring the propensity of firms' default events to coincide. An asset return correlation, in contrast, is a measure of the linear relationship between the returns: What size fluctuation in one asset price is associated with a fluctuation in the other? The statistical measures of the two types correlation, however, are similar.

Consider a fixed time horizon of τ years, and two obligors—households, firms, or countries—for which the event of default over the next τ years is Bernoulli distributed and possibly correlated.[3] The Bernoulli variates x_1 and x_2 take on the value 1 if default occurs and zero otherwise. Default occurs with probabilities π_1 and π_2. The joint default probability, the probability both obligors default, is π_{12}. The joint default distribution is that of the product $x_1 x_2$ of the Bernoulli variates:

Outcome	x_1	x_2	$x_1 x_2$	Probability
Both firms default	1	1	1	π_{12}
Firm 1 only defaults	1	0	0	$\pi_1 - \pi_{12}$
Firm 2 only defaults	0	1	0	$\pi_2 - \pi_{12}$
No default	0	0	0	$1 - \pi_1 - \pi_2 + \pi_{12}$

The default correlation is measured by the correlation coefficient of x_1 and x_2:

$$\rho_{12} = \frac{\pi_{12} - \pi_1 \pi_2}{\sqrt{\pi_1(1 - \pi_1)}\sqrt{\pi_2(1 - \pi_2)}}. \tag{13.1}$$

The default correlation is zero if the firms' default events are independent. The joint default probability is then equal to the probability of two independent events both occurring: $\pi_{12} = \pi_1 \pi_2$.

If the firms are identical, with $\pi_1 = \pi_2 = \pi$, their default events are not necessarily independent. The correlation simplifies to:

$$\rho_{12} = \frac{\pi_{12} - \pi^2}{\pi(1 - \pi)}.$$

Joint default probability and default correlation are generally small numbers because default is infrequent and joint default therefore even more so. For example,

$$\pi_1 = \pi_2 = 0.01, \pi_{12} = 0.0005 \Rightarrow \rho_{12} = 0.040404$$

$$\pi_1 = \pi_2 = 0.10, \pi_{12} = 0.0250 \Rightarrow \rho_{12} = 0.166667.$$

---

[3] See Appendix A.

13.1.3   Granularity and Uncorrelated Portfolios

In a simple credit portfolio of n identical loans or bonds, each with a default probability π and with all pairwise default correlations zero, the number of defaults follows a binomial distribution with parameters n and π. The expected number of defaults, the expected value of the default count, is πn. To analyze the credit risk of the portfolio, we can use probabilities and quantiles of the default count together with loan par values and recovery rates to determine the credit loss distribution.

Example 13.1   Loss distribution of an uncorrelated credit portfolio

Consider a portfolio of $n = 100$ identical uncorrelated loans, each with a default probability $\pi = 0.025$. The default count follows the binomial distribution displayed in Figure 13.2 and partially tabulated below. The 0.99-quantile of the default count is 7: the lowest number of defaults such that the probability of ending with a higher count is no more than 1 percent.

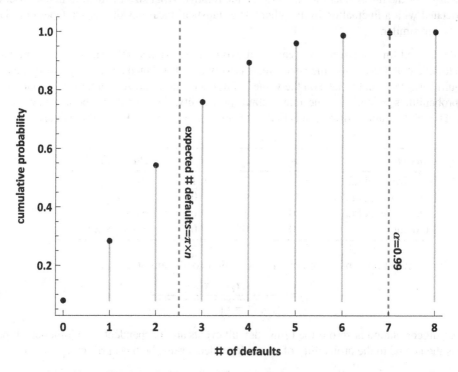

Figure 13.2 Uncorrelated default count distribution

Binomial probability distribution with $n = 100$ and $\pi = 0.025$. Grid lines placed at the expected default count and 0.99-quantile of the default count. The x-axis is truncated at 8 defaults.

# defaults	cumulative probability
0	0.0795
1	0.2834
2	0.5422
3	0.7590
4	0.8937
5	0.9601
6	0.9870
7	0.9963
8	0.9991

With additional assumptions on the term and size of the n loans, we can determine the distribution of credit loss. Assume 1-year loans that have no interim cash flows, so default occurs only at maturity. The loan size is equal to a fraction n^{-1} of the portfolio par value. If the expected recovery is equal to zero (the LGD is 100 percent), the credit loss will be equal to the default count times the loan size. The expected loss is the expected value of credit loss, that is, the default probability $\pi = 0.025$ times the total par value of the portfolio. The 1-year credit VaR is a high quantile of the default count times the loan size, minus the expected loss.

Suppose the portfolio total par value is $1,000,000 and there $n = 100$ loans to uncorrelated borrowers, each with $\pi = 0.025$. The size of each loan is $10\,000$, and we have

	$\alpha = 0.95$	$\alpha = 0.99$
Loss quantile (no. loans)	5	7
Loss quantile ($)	50 000	70 000
Credit VaR ($)	25 000	45 000

Let's extend this example to a range of default probabilities and degrees of granularity. We set the number of 1-year zero-coupon loans to $n \in \{1, 50, 1000\}$ and the default probability to $\pi \in \{0.005, 0.025, 0.05\}$. Granularity is absent for $n = 1$ and very high for $n = 1000$. Figure 13.3 displays a grid of the credit loss distributions for each pair of assumptions on n and π, and Table 13.1 displays the exact results, including an extremely granular case, $n = 50\,000$.

A portfolio with low granularity has binary risk. It behaves like a lottery, a single trial with a high probability of no loss and a small but material probability π of a complete loss. If the probability of default is less than $1 - \alpha$, low granularity coupled with a low default probability can even lead to a negative credit VaR. For $n = 1$, for instance,

$$\text{credit VaR} = \left\{ \begin{array}{c} -\text{EL} \\ 1 - \text{EL} \end{array} \right\} \quad \text{for} \quad \pi \left\{ \begin{array}{c} < \\ \geq \end{array} \right\} 1 - \alpha.$$

A portfolio with high granularity is likely to experience a loss rate in a narrow range near the expected loss π. High granularity thus reduces credit loss variance, eliminating risk and turning default losses into a predictable cost. In Figure 13.3, the credit loss distribution converges to a right-angled S-shape in the bottom panels. High granularity is similar in economic effect to a low default correlation and reduces credit risk to near zero in credit portfolios with low default probabilities. But the risk reduction effect of granularity is lower in a portfolio with high correlation, for example, a granular

Table 13.1 Granularity and credit Value-at-Risk

n		$\pi = 0.005$	$\pi = 0.025$	$\pi = 0.05$
1	0.99-quantile of credit losses	0.00000	1.00000	1.00000
	Credit VaR at 99% confidence	−0.00500	0.97500	0.95000
50	0.99-quantile of credit losses	0.04000	0.08000	0.14000
	Credit VaR at 99% confidence	0.03500	0.05500	0.09000
1000	0.99-quantile of credit losses	0.01100	0.03700	0.06700
	Credit VaR at 99% confidence	0.00600	0.01200	0.01700
50000	0.99-quantile of credit losses	0.00574	0.02664	0.05228
	Credit VaR at 99% confidence	0.00074	0.00164	0.00228

Expressed as a fraction of portfolio par value.

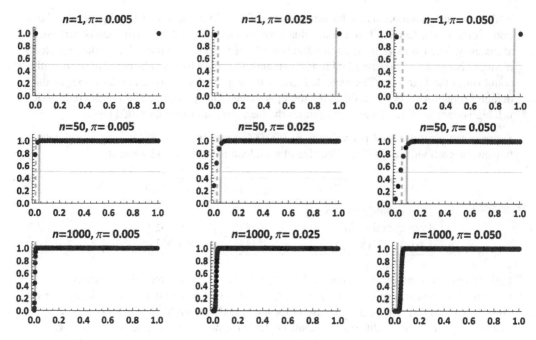

Figure 13.3 Uncorrelated default count distribution and granularity

Cumulative probability distribution function of losses for n equally-sized loans and default probabilities π, as a fraction of portfolio value. The x-axis measures the loss rate in the portfolio as a fraction of the portfolio's total par value; the y-axis measures probability. Each point marks the probability of a realized loss of that magnitude or less. Solid vertical grid lines are placed at the 99 percent credit VaR. Dashed vertical grid lines are placed at the expected loss at the same position in each column.

mortgage pool, but regionally concentrated and with high-risk borrowers. A portfolio with moderate granularity has a wider range of likely outcomes and thus a greater probability of material unexpected loss but a low probability of a complete or near-complete loss.

13.1.4   Granularity, Subadditivity, and Credit Value-at-Risk

In some cases, a concentrated portfolio may have a credit VaR higher than the sum of the VaRs of its constituent securities. This is a violation of a desirable property of risk measures known as **subadditivity**.[4] Violations of subadditivity provide an incentive to portfolio managers in VaR-based limit systems, or whose credit VaR is monitored regularly, to separate low-probability but high loss credits into distinct portfolios.

Example 13.2   Violations of subadditivity

Suppose a portfolio consists of equal amounts of two ($n = 2$) identical uncorrelated loans, both with zero recovery and default probability π. The portfolio default count and credit loss probability distribution is

event	loss (%)	probability
No default	0.0	$(1 - \pi)^2 = 1 - 2\pi + \pi^2$
One defaults	0.5	$2(\pi - \pi^2) = 2\pi(1 - \pi)$
Both default	1.0	π^2

---

[4] See Chapter 8.

Table 13.2   Violations of subadditivity

	portfolio credit loss distribution	
Loss (%)	$\pi = 0.005$	$\pi = 0.00525$
0.0	0.990025	0.9895275625
0.5	0.00995	0.0104449
1.0	0.000025	0.0000275625
Expected credit loss	0.005	0.00525
0.99-quantile of credit loss	0.0	0.5
Credit VaR at 99% confidence	−0.005	0.49475

Losses in a portfolio of two uncorrelated loans with the stated probabilities, expressed as a fraction of portfolio par value.

The portfolio credit VaR is negative for a default probability, so low that the likelihood of no default occurring is greater than the VaR confidence level α:

$$(1 - \pi)^2 > \alpha \quad \Leftrightarrow \quad \pi < 1 - \sqrt{\alpha}.$$

For example, for $\alpha = 0.99$, $\pi < 1 - \sqrt{0.99} = 0.0050126$ and a default probability of 0.5 percent lead to a negative VaR. The credit VaR for each loan taken individually is negative for any $\pi < 1 - \alpha = 0.01$ or 1 percent.

The subadditivity property is violated for $1 - \sqrt{\alpha} \leq \pi < 1 - \alpha$. With $\alpha = 0.99$, a 2-loan portfolio violates subadditivity for any $1 - \sqrt{0.99} < \pi < 0.01$. If, for example, $\pi = 0.00525$, the credit VaR of each loan individually is negative, and the portfolio consisting of both is positive (Table 13.2). A highly granular portfolio of uncorrelated loans with $\pi = 0.00525$ would have a 0.99-quantile of credit losses slightly higher than 0.00525 and a credit VaR of 0.00025, or 0.025 percent, close to zero, but still positive.

13.2   Measuring Portfolio Credit Risk

13.2.1   Single Factor Credit Risk Model

The single factor model is widely used in the risk management of portfolios exposed to credit risk and by policymakers setting bank capital standards. Conceptually related to the Merton default and CAPM asset pricing models, it provides a simple way of estimating portfolio credit loss distributions with just a few parameters.[5]

In the single factor model, as in the Merton model, default occurs when a firm's asset value falls below a default threshold. The single factor model introduces two uncorrelated random variables that drive asset returns and thus defaults:

Market risk factor m affecting all firms' asset returns though not equally. The market risk factor can be thought of as the influence of general business conditions or the state of the economy on the firm's creditworthiness. It is a latent factor, not directly observed but influencing results indirectly via the model parameters.

---

[5] The single factor credit risk model is also known as the **Vasicek model**, after one if its originators, and as the **asymptotic single factor model**.

Idiosyncratic risk factor ϵ_i affecting just the asset returns of firm i and expressing the influence of an individual firm's fortunes on its default risk.

A combination of sufficiently adverse market and idiosyncratic shocks will push the borrower into default. Returns and shocks are measured as deviations from expectations or from a neutral state in which there are neither happy nor adverse surprises. For the market risk factor, this neutral state is a "Goldilocks economy," running neither hotter nor colder than expected, and for the idiosyncratic risk factor, a state in which the firm's strategy is playing out just as planned.

The single factor model has two parameters:

Default probability π_i or, equivalently, the default threshold k_i of firm i, reached if the firm's asset return r_i is sufficiently negative.

Correlation β_i of the asset return of firm i to the market risk factor m, which drives default correlation.

In the Merton model, the focus is on how asset return volatility impacts default probability. In the single factor model, the focus is on how firms' asset return correlations affect their propensity to default simultaneously. The correlation parameter β_i governs the influence of general business conditions on the individual firm's default risk and drives default correlation.

The model is

$$r_i = \beta_i m + \sqrt{1 - \beta_i^2}\, \epsilon_i, \qquad i = 1, 2, \dots ,$$

and assumes that m and ϵ_i are uncorrelated standard normal variates:

$$m \sim \mathcal{N}(0,1)$$

$$\epsilon_i \sim \mathcal{N}(0,1)$$

$$\mathrm{Cov}[m, \epsilon_i] \quad = 0, \qquad i = 1, 2, \dots .$$

The oddly complicated parameter $\sqrt{1 - \beta_i^2}$ of the idiosyncratic risk factor ensures that r_i is also a standard normal variate:

$$\mathbf{E}[r_i] = 0$$

$$\mathrm{Var}[r_i] = \beta_i^2 + 1 - \beta_i^2 = 1,$$

and, $r_i \sim \mathcal{N}(0,1), i = 1, 2, \dots .$ Asset return r_i and its drivers m and ϵ_i are expressed in normalized units as deviations from a neutral state of the business cycle and corporate plan fulfilment.

Default occurs if r_i is negative and large enough to wipe out the equity, so the default threshold k_i is a negative number:

$$r_i = \beta_i m + \sqrt{1 - \beta_i^2}\, \epsilon_i \leq k_i.$$

The default threshold is the standard normal quantile corresponding to the default probability:

$$\pi_i = \mathbf{P}[r_i \leq k_i] \Leftrightarrow k_i = \Phi^{-1}(\pi_i),$$

where $\Phi(\cdot)$ is the standard normal cumulative distribution function (CDF). The **distance-to-default** $-k_i = |-k_i|$ expresses it as a positive number. In contrast to the Merton model, the default probability is an input in the single factor model, a stipulated parameter rather than an output.

Example 13.3   Default probability and asset correlation in the single factor model

Default probability π_i	0.01	0.10
Distance-to-default $-k_i$	2.33	1.28

As seen in Figure 13.4, the asset return distribution is the same for both, but a firm with a high default probability has a higher default threshold and lower distance-to-default.

Figure 13.5 illustrates the relationships between correlation, market shocks, the firm's asset returns, and default. The default threshold is the same for both firms displayed, an asset return -1.645 standard deviations below normal, corresponding to a default probability of 5 percent. In a sequence of simulations of the 1-period model, the propensity to dip below the default threshold is the same for both. But the low-correlation firm's asset returns track those of the market much less closely than those of the high-correlation firm. The low-correlation firm has relatively high idiosyncratic risk because in the model the squares of the parameters add up to 1.

In both the single factor model and the CAPM model, returns are driven by a general, market-wide factor, and a firm-specific, idiosyncratic factor. In the single factor model, with the convenient

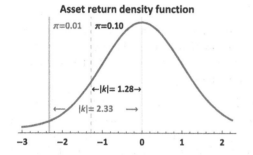 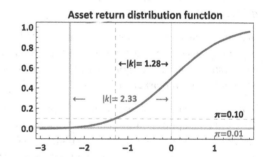

Figure 13.4 Default probability in the single factor model

Vertical grid lines mark the default thresholds corresponding to default probabilities of 0.01 and 0.10.

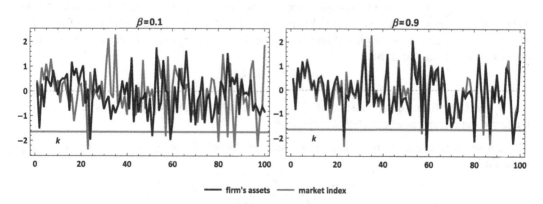

Figure 13.5 Asset and market returns in the single factor model

Each panel shows a sequence of 100 simulations of a sequence of results from the 1-period single factor model. The simulated returns on the market index m are the same in both panels, and the associated returns for each firm's assets are $r_i = \beta_i m + \sqrt{1 - \beta_i^2}\,\epsilon_i$, with the specified β_i to the market. Plots are generated by simulating m and ϵ_i as a pair of uncorrelated $\mathcal{N}(0,1)$ variates, using the same random seed for both panels.

assumption that $\text{Var}[r_i] = \text{Var}[m] = 1$, the β_i is the correlation of the latent market factor and firm returns and is the analogue of the CAPM beta. As in the CAPM, we can measure the contributions to the firm's asset return variability of the market and idiosyncratic factors. The share of the market risk factor is β^2, and that of the idiosyncratic risk factor is $1 - \beta_i^2$.

Example 13.4   Market and idiosyncratic credit risk

	$\beta = 0.40$	$\beta = 0.90$
Market factor β^2	0.16	0.81
Idiosyncratic factor $1 - \beta^2$	0.84	0.19

13.2.2   Single Factor Model for Portfolios

The correlations of two individual firms' asset returns are used to estimate their default correlation. The model assumes zero correlation between the idiosyncratic risks of different firms, permitting a key feature, **conditional independence**. Once a realization of the market factor m is stipulated, firms' returns are independent because the remaining drivers of returns, the idiosyncratic factors, are independent.

In a sufficiently granular credit portfolio, this lets us invoke the law of large numbers. Idiosyncratic risk disappears. We can then model the probability distribution of portfolio credit *losses* as if it were that of a single obligor's *default*, conditional on a particular value of m. Default correlation, in conjunction with market shocks, still affects the loss distribution.

In laying out the model, we begin by explaining how default correlation is generated. We then introduce the concept of conditional independence of firms' returns and defaults and use the concept to derive the portfolio credit loss distribution. To simplify, we assume all obligors are identical, with the same default probability for all credits and the same default correlation for all pairs of credits. In practice, risk measurement systems will recognize different categories of risk among obligors.

Default correlation is closely related to asset return. The asset return correlation of two firms i and j is given by $\beta_i\beta_j$.[6] The joint distribution of the asset returns of the ith and jth firms is given by the joint CDF $\Phi_{\beta_i\beta_j}(r_i, r_j)$ of the two standard normal variates r_i and r_j with a correlation of $\beta_i\beta_j$. The joint default probability of the ith and jth firms is the probability π_{ij} that both firms' returns fall by at least their distances-to-default:

$$\pi_{ij} = \Phi_{\beta_i\beta_j}(k_i, k_j),$$

with k_i and k_j the firms' default thresholds. The joint default probability π_{ij} can thus be found from the firms' default and asset correlation parameters.

The default correlation ρ_{ij} is related to π_{ij} and the firms' default probabilities by (applying equation 13.1):

$$\rho_{ij} = \frac{\pi_{ij} - \pi_i\pi_j}{\sqrt{\pi_i(1 - \pi_i)}\sqrt{\pi_j(1 - \pi_j)}},$$

---

[6] From $\text{Cov}[r_i, r_j] = \beta_i\beta_j\text{E}[m^2]$.

with π_i, π_j the firm's individual default probabilities. The asset return correlation and default correlation are thus related by

$$\Phi_{\beta_i\beta_j}(k_i, k_j) = \pi_i\pi_j + \rho_{ij}\sqrt{\pi_i(1 - \pi_i)}\sqrt{\pi_j(1 - \pi_j)}.$$

Example 13.5   Impact of a market shock

Suppose we have two identical firms, with a common beta to the market factor β, default threshold k, and default probability $\pi = 0.01$. Their asset return correlation and default correlation are related by

$$\Phi_{\beta^2}(k, k) = \pi^2 + \rho\pi(1 - \pi).$$

We can use this relationship to solve for the default correlation ρ, given β:

Market return correlation β	0.5251	$\sqrt{0.25}$
Asset return correlation β^2	0.2757	0.25
Default correlation ρ	0.04	0.0341
Joint default probability $\Phi_{\beta^2}(k, k)$	4.9600×10^{-4}	4.3752×10^{-4}

We can see the relationships between asset return and default correlation on the one hand and credit tail risks on the other in Figure 13.6. It displays a set of simulations from the distribution of an uncorrelated and a correlated pair of standard normals and is identical to Figure 2.9. In the simulated results, a high asset return correlation does not affect the likelihood of either firm defaulting because that is governed solely by the default threshold and probability. But it does result in more cases of both firms defaulting and more cases of neither defaulting.

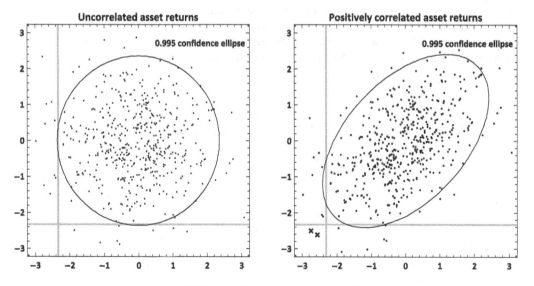

Figure 13.6 Correlated and uncorrelated defaults

Simulation of defaults applying the single factor model in a portfolio of two credits, both with $\pi = 0.01$. Left panel: correlation coefficient $\rho = 0$. Right panel: correlation coefficient $\rho = 0.50$. The grid lines are placed at default thresholds. Simulated return pairs marked by points if they result in default of at most one credit and by x's if they result in default for both. Realizations of the asset return pair have a 99.5 percent probability of falling within the density contour.

Suppose we know the state of the economy, a particular realization $\bar{m}$ of m. Asset return r_i then has only one random driver, the idiosyncratic factor ϵ_i:

$$r_i = \beta_i \bar{m} + \sqrt{1 - \beta_i^2}\, \epsilon_i, \qquad i = 1, 2, \dots .$$

Conditional on a specific value of the market factor $m = \bar{m}$:

- The mean of the asset return distribution changes from zero to $\beta_i \bar{m}$.
- The variance of the return distribution is reduced from 1 to $1 - \beta_i^2$, because we have excluded the market factor as a source of variation.
- The default threshold k_i itself hasn't changed, but the distance-to-default—the magnitude of a default-triggering idiosyncratic shock—becomes $-k_i + \beta_i \bar{m}$, or in standard units $-\frac{k_i + \beta_i \bar{m}}{\sqrt{1 - \beta_i^2}}$.
- The default probability changes to $\Phi\left(\frac{k_i - \beta_i \bar{m}}{\sqrt{1 - \beta_i^2}}\right)$, the probability of a realization of the standard normal less than or equal to $\frac{k_i - \beta_i \bar{m}}{\sqrt{1 - \beta_i^2}}$.

This gives us the **conditional default probability distribution function**

$$p_i(m) = \mathbf{P}[r_i \le k_i | m] = \Phi\left(\frac{k_i - \beta_i m}{\sqrt{1 - \beta_i^2}}\right), \qquad i = 1, 2, \dots .$$

The conditional default distribution is a normal with a shifted mean and tighter variance. Both parameters β_i and k_i continue to influence the shape of the distribution function. The market factor continues to be a random variable driving default and appears as the argument of the conditional default probability distribution function. Note that this meaning of "conditional" is different from that in the discussion of hazard rates, where it refers to non-default in a prior period. Figure 13.7 shows how the unconditional distributions shifts and tightens when a realization of m is stipulated.

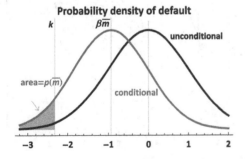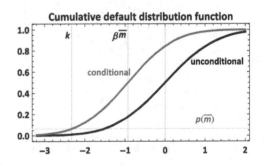

Figure 13.7 Conditional default probability distribution

Density and cumulative probability distribution of firm asset return as a function of idiosyncratic shock. Graph assumes $\beta_i = 0.4$, $k_i = -2.33$ ($\Leftrightarrow \pi_i = 0.01$), and $\bar{m} = -2.33$. The unconditional asset return distribution is a standard normal, while the conditional asset return distribution is $\mathcal{N}(\beta_i \bar{m}, 1 - \beta_i^2) = \mathcal{N}(-0.9305, 8400)$. The shaded area in the density plot and horizontal grid line in the cumulative distribution plot identify $p(\bar{m})$, as in the example.

Example 13.6 Assume a firm has the parameters $\beta_i = 0.4, k_i = -2.33$ (so $\pi_i = 0.01$) and there is a market shock $\bar{m} = -2.33$ (a sharp downturn). Table 13.3 shows the impact of the shock on the return distribution and default probability:

Table 13.3   Impact of a market shock

	Unconditional	*Conditional*	*Change*
Mean return	0	−0.9305	−0.9305
Return variance	1	0.8400	−0.1600
Return std. deviation	1	0.9165	−0.0835
Distance-to-default	2.33	1.3958	−0.9305
(standardized)	2.33	1.5230	−0.8034
Default probability	0.01	0.0639	0.0539

13.2.3   Portfolio Credit Value-at-Risk

The ϵ_i are independent, so once the market factor is realized, the conditional returns and default distributions of two different obligors are independent. Because firms' returns are independent, conditional on a particular value of the market factor, we can use the representative obligor's default probability distribution as the portfolio credit loss distribution. We'll assume the credit portfolio is granular, homogeneous, and completely diversified.[7] Each obligor has a market risk factor loading β and default probability $\pi = \Phi(k)$, and all the pairwise correlation returns are β^2. The loss given default is 100 percent for all.

The conditional default probability distribution function common to all the obligors is then

$$p(m) = \Phi\left(\frac{k - \beta m}{\sqrt{1 - \beta^2}}\right) = \Phi\left[\frac{\Phi^{-1}(\pi) - \beta m}{\sqrt{1 - \beta^2}}\right].$$

The law of large numbers implies that in a highly granular portfolio, idiosyncratic risk disappears. The portfolio credit loss rate is then a function only of the market shock. The fraction x of loans defaulting meaning the loss rate, equals the representative single-firm default probability, conditional on a market shock m:

$$x = p(m) = \Phi\left[\frac{\Phi^{-1}(\pi) - \beta m}{\sqrt{1 - \beta^2}}\right].$$

Default correlation affects the loss distribution through the parameter β. The market shock is a latent factor: we don't have to observe it for it to drive the model. We only have surmise its properties, in this case, that it is a standard normal and independent of all firms' idiosyncratic shocks. This is an important difference from the CAPM in which the market or systematic factor must be observable for it to drive market valuation.

---

[7] The model is also known as the **asymptotic single factor credit risk model** because of its reliance on the assumption of a large number of loans, each a diminishingly small fraction of the portfolio.

The probability of a loss rate x is still conditional on the probability of the corresponding realization of m. We can now derive the unconditional probability distribution of the loss rate from the distribution of m. First, we find the market shock m that leads to a given loss rate x by solving for m as a function of x:

$$m = \frac{\Phi^{-1}(\pi) - \sqrt{1 - \beta^2}\Phi^{-1}(x)}{\beta}. \tag{13.2}$$

In a portfolio, a market shock with a specified probability leads to a conditional default probability for a representative loan. That *probability* is the conditional loss *rate* x of the pool, and the probability of the loss rate is the specified probability of the market shock m that leads to it. A sharply negative market factor m corresponds to a high loss rate x (Figure 13.8).

In the second step, we map the probability of any specific realization of the loss rate x to that of the corresponding market shock m (from equation 13.2). Because m is a standard normal variate,[8]

$$\mathbf{P}[\tilde{m} \le m] = \Phi(m).$$

A high loss rate x corresponds to a sharply negative market factor realization with a low probability:

$$\mathbf{P}[\tilde{x} \le x] = \mathbf{P}[\tilde{m} \ge m] = 1 - \mathbf{P}[\tilde{m} \le m] = 1 - \Phi(m) = \Phi(-m),$$

The unconditional cumulative probability distribution function of x—the probability of a credit loss no worse than x—is

$$\mathbf{P}[\tilde{x} \le x] = \Phi\left[\frac{\sqrt{1 - \beta^2}\Phi^{-1}(x) - \Phi^{-1}(\pi)}{\beta}\right]. \tag{13.3}$$

Its parameters are the representative firm's default probability and correlation. The term inside the brackets is the market factor realization m corresponding to the loss rate x.

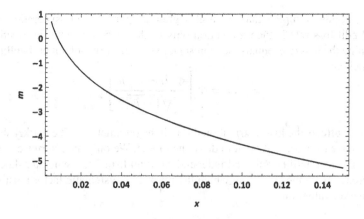

Figure 13.8 Market factor and loss rate

Market factor as a function of loss rate. Default probability $\pi = 0.01$ (1 percent, $k = -2.33$), $\beta = 0.25$.

---

[8] We use the notation $\tilde{x}$ and $\tilde{m}$ to distinguish the random variables from particular realizations x and m.

We can now see what the credit loss distribution looks like for different default probabilities and correlations. The expected loss rate equals the typical portfolio constituent's default probability π. For default probabilities below 50 percent, the median portfolio loss rate—the loss rate that has a 50-50 chance of being exceeded—is at least somewhat lower than the mean default rate.[9] There's a better than even chance of having a loss rate below the typical default probability:

$$\mathbf{P}[\tilde{x} \leq \pi] > 0.5, \quad \forall \pi < 0.5.$$

If the default correlation is very low, the difference between the mean and median loss rate will be small:

$$\lim_{\beta \to 0} \mathbf{P}[\tilde{x} \leq \pi] = 0.5.$$

Figure 13.9 displays some of the patterns in the cumulative probability distribution of credit losses for different values of the default correlation. With a correlation near 1, the portfolio behaves as if it consisted of a single loan or obligor. High correlation induces Bernoulli-like, binary loss behavior in the portfolio, similar to a highly non-granular, uncorrelated credit portfolio. The portfolio is a reverse lottery ticket. The likelihood $\mathbf{P}[\tilde{x} \leq \varepsilon]$ of nearly no loss is near $1 - \pi$, and a near-complete loss $\mathbf{P}[\tilde{x} \leq 1 - \varepsilon]$ is near π, with ε a tiny positive number. The median loss is near zero. Intermediate outcomes have low probabilities. With high correlation, default clusters and surprising "clusters" of non-default are both more likely.

With a correlation near zero, there is a high probability of a portfolio loss rate very close to the typical firm's default probability. Default clusters surprises either way from the portfolio EL are unlikely. Pricing the loan rate and reserving for defaults using EL for guidance is highly reliable. If, in addition, the default probabilities are low, the variation around the portfolio EL will be even tighter.

A moderate correlation permits some credit diversification benefit. With a correlation "in the middle" and a moderate default probability, a range of loss rates would be unsurprising. Default clusters are unusual but have to be taken into account.

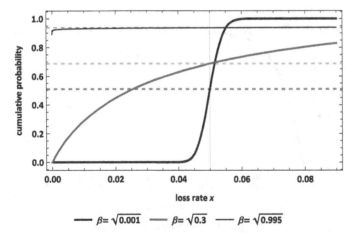

Figure 13.9 Credit loss distribution and default correlation

Granular portfolio; default probability and portfolio expected loss rate 5 percent. Losses expressed as a fraction of portfolio par value. The horizontal dashed grid lines are located at the probability of the portfolio experiencing a loss less than or equal to the expected loss rate of 5 percent.

---

[9] Realistically, only a portfolio of claims on obligors on the brink of bankruptcy would have a default probability in excess of 50 percent.

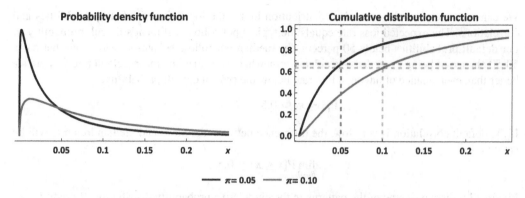

Figure 13.10 Credit loss distribution and default probability

Granular portfolio, $\beta = \sqrt{0.3} = 0.5477$ for all obligors. Losses expressed as a fraction of portfolio par value. The horizontal dashed grid lines are located at the probability of the portfolio experiencing a loss less than or equal to the expected loss rate of 5 percent.

Low default probability induces some of the binary loss behavior of a high-correlation portfolio. If the default probability is quite low, with a moderate default correlation, the loss density will be highly skewed to low loss levels. If the default probability is quite high, with a moderate default correlation, there will be a higher likelihood of surprisingly high portfolio losses but the loss density is more spread out over a range of loss levels (Figure 13.10). The portfolio behaves most like a lottery if default correlation is high and default probability is low.

The loss distribution function permits us to find quantiles of loss corresponding to specific probabilities. Those quantiles, minus EL, are the credit VaR corresponding to a given confidence level. Higher correlation leads to higher VaR, by increasing the likelihood of default clusters. Figure 13.11 illustrates.

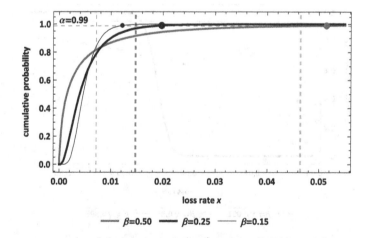

Figure 13.11 Credit Value-at-Risk and default correlation

Granular portfolio; default probability 0.5 percent. Losses expressed as a rate or fraction of portfolio par value. Vertical grid lines indicate credit VaR at 99-percent confidence level for each default correlation assumption. Points mark quantiles of portfolio credit losses for each default correlation assumption.

Further Reading

Lucas (1995) is an introduction to default correlation. Wilson (1998) is a basic introduction to portfolio credit risk models.

The articles in which the single factor or Vasicek model was initially presented are reprinted in Part IV of Vasicek (2015). Kealhofer (2003a and 2003b) provide a summary of the model. Crouhy et al. (2000a) is a survey of commercial portfolio credit risk models.

14

Securitization and Structured Product Risk

14.1 Introduction to Securitization

14.1.1 Function and Design of Securitization

Securitization is the issuance of securities backed by a **collateral pool** of underlying assets, such as mortgages or consumer debt. The securities are typically **tranched**, forming a capital structure of securities ranking their contractual claims on interest, principal, prepayments, or other cash flows from the pool.

Securitizations are distinguished by the type of asset backing them, the liabilities issued, and the way they are structured. Bonds backed by mortgage loans are called **residential** or **commercial mortgage-backed securities** (RMBS and CMBS). Agency MBS are the most common type of RMBS and of securitization generally. Bonds backed by consumer debt are called **asset-backed securities** (ABS). Claims created in **synthetic** credit derivatives form, or from pools of bank or corporate debt, are called **structured credit products**. **Collateralized debt obligations** (CDOs) are a broad category of structured credit products, with collateral pools consisting of bonds, bank loans, or tranches of other securitizations. **Collateralized loan obligations** (CLOs), issued in large volumes in recent years, are backed by bank loans.

Securitization and structured credit carry out several important intermediation functions. They are a means to pool and diversify credit risk similar to banks and investment funds. Investors can own claims on a granular pool of obligors rather than a concentrated credit exposure. As with any credit portfolio, effective risk reduction is limited if default correlation is high.

Securitization facilitates risk transfer, which is the separation of **loan origination** from investment and use of capital with lower transactions costs than outright sale of debts. In the **originate-to-distribute** business model, banks make loans in the expectation of a securitization "exit" from credit risk exposure and use of capital. The banks retain the information-gathering function of selecting borrowers, but the revenue source shifts from net interest margin to fees.

Securitization, finally, serves as a form of risk distribution, by creating securities with different risk-reward characteristics. Structured products can have very different cash flows and risks from the underlying loan or asset pool. They are potentially better suited than the underlying assets to investors' objectives and risk preferences. Some tranches have highly leveraged exposures to the collateral pool and are a means of taking on embedded leverage: other tranches are remote enough from the underlying collateral that their credit risk is very low. We discussed forms of interest rate risk peculiar to MBS, prepayment risk, and convexity risk, in Chapter 10, and will focus on credit risk here.

If longer-term debt back a securitization, the collateral pool will likely consist of a set of existing loans, such as residential mortgages, commercial mortgages, and bank loans. If the collateral is primarily short-term debt, such as credit card receivables and auto loans, it will be set up as a **revolving pool** in which the collateral is replaced by fresh debt of the same type as it is repaid. Some securitizations may even be backed by future cash flows, such as export receivables or remittances from workers abroad. Revolving pools and pools consisting of future flows tend to be highly granular. Pools consisting of commercial mortgages are generally less granular and may even consist of only one or a few loans.

The capital structure of a securitization is the balance sheet of a robot corporation managing its cash flows, assets and liabilities following predetermined rules. A legal entity, the **special purpose vehicle** (SPV) or **entity** (SPE), is formed, which owns the underlying assets and finances their purchase from the originator by issuing debt securities. It is generally a type of trust that has a beneficial ownership interest in the underlying assets. In some cases, the actual assets themselves, such as loans, may be sold into the SPV. More typically, the bank or other sponsor sells claims on the cash flows from the assets, its receivables, into the SPV. Together with the use of a trust entity, this gives the banks some flexibility in replacing assets as they are repaid or default, and to separate fee-earning administration of the assets from the cash flows related to the debt itself. Banks may delegate monitoring of borrowers and the collection of interest and principal from the underlying assets to a third party, the **servicer**, or retain that function in-house. This is particularly important in the case of MBS.

The acquisition by the SPV must follow a **true sale** of the underlying claims. Together with the use of a trust entity, this keeps the SPV **bankruptcy remote**: the sponsor and the SPV are each shielded from the event of the other's bankruptcy. There must also be no **implicit recourse** to or guarantee by the seller of the assets: the SPV's balance sheet must stand on its own.

If the structure is not properly designed, it will carry with it a form of legal risk to the originators and investors that manifested itself during the global financial crisis. Investors may be persuaded, or the structure may be designed so they have recourse to the originator in the event the asset pool experiences a surprisingly high default rate. Before the global financial crisis, a large volume of structured products were originated via similar structures such as structured investment vehicles (SIVs). Legally, they were bankruptcy remote and, therefore, obtained favorable regulatory treatment. But holders of claims on SIVs and similar structures enjoyed implicit recourse. Sponsors, such as Citibank, felt obliged to assume them back to their own balance sheets to minimize reputational and legal risk and suffered substantial losses. They were a factor weakening banks in reality and in the perception of market participants as stress mounted.[1]

14.1.2   Securitization in the United States

US securitization trends over the past few decades put these concepts in context. Figure 14.1 compares securitization issuance with bond market issuance overall. MBS, almost all residential, are by far the largest segment of the securitized debt market. Before the global financial crisis, MBS and ABS issuance had grown to nearly half of total US bond issuance. After the onset of the crisis, total bond issuance remained fairly constant, but securitization's share was replaced by government, agency, and to a lesser extent corporate issuance. MBS remain a large part of the total.

Tranched products have been issued since the early 1980s, introduced in the form of **collateralized mortgage obligations** (CMOs) designed to mitigate prepayment risk. Early on, as seen in Figure 14.2, most ABS issuance was in the auto loan and credit-card receivables segments. Subsequently, the growth was in CDOs and, most recently, CLOs. CDO issuance was high precrisis, but fell off sharply with the onset of the crisis. CDO liabilities are very long-lived, especially those of

---

[1] See Gorton (2008). Appendix B of that paper lists the SIVs assumed onto sponsor balance sheets.

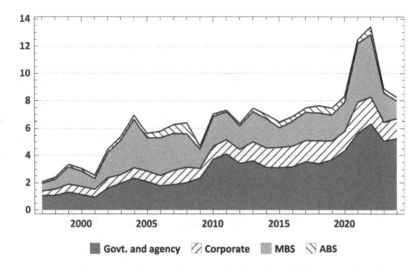

Figure 14.1 US fixed-income securities issuance 1996–2023

$ trillion, annual. *Source*: SIFMA, US Bond Market Issuance and Outstanding.

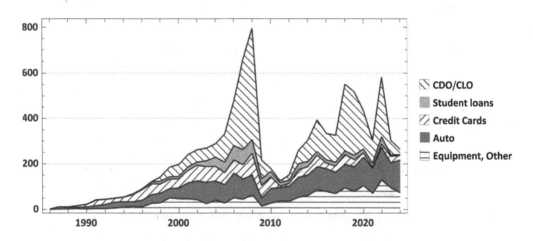

Figure 14.2 US asset-backed securities issuance 1985–2023

CLOs includes CBOs and other CDOs. $ trillion, annual. *Source*: SIFMA, US ABS Issuance and Outstanding.

legacy, precrisis CDOs with credit-troubled collateral, leading to a much smaller decline in the share of CDOs in outstanding ABS (Figure 14.3).

In recent years, a large volume of CLOs collateralized by **leveraged loans**, which are large bank loans to noninvestment-grade firms, has been issued. Leveraged loans are generally floating-rate loans with wide spreads to the index rates. They are **syndicated**, that is, originated by several banks, each bearing the risk only of its own issuance and are intended for sale into a CLO asset pool. Leveraged loans are used to finance mergers and acquisitions, particularly **leveraged buyouts** (LBOs) by private equity firms.

The motivation for issuing ABS and the pitfalls of investing in them are illustrated in Figure 14.4, which compares credit spreads of corporate bonds to those of senior tranches of credit card ABS.

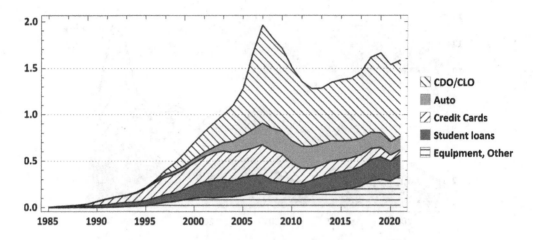

Figure 14.3 US asset-backed securities outstanding 1985–2021

CLOs includes CBOs and other CDOs. $ trillion, annual. *Source*: SIFMA, US ABS Issuance and Outstanding.

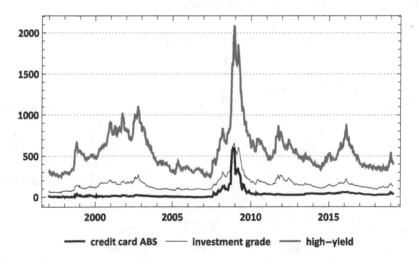

Figure 14.4 US credit spreads 1997–2019

Option-adjusted spreads (OAS) over swaps, in basis points. Credit card ABS: 5-year AAA US credit-card ABS, daily 03Jan1997 to 21Feb2019. Investment grade and high yield: BofA Merrill Lynch US Corporate Master OAS indexes (C0A0 and H0A0). *Sources*: Barclays, FRED.

The spreads on AAA-rated ABS were remarkably tight before the global financial crisis, just a few basis points and well below those of investment-grade corporate bonds. During the crisis, spreads widened drastically, leading to far worse price declines than for corporate issues.

14.2   Securitization Structure

The liabilities of the SPV are generally several debt securities or tranches with clearly defined payment priority. Each tranche is subordinate to the one above it with an equity tranche at the bottom of the stack. Intermediate subordinated tranches are called **mezzanine** bonds, similar to hybrid debt. **Overcollateralization** creates protection for the tranches. Those that are senior to the equity are overcollateralized by the notional value of all tranches subordinated to them. Collateral pools are typically larger than the volume of bonds issued, and loans in the pool itself may also be collateralized, providing additional credit risk protection to all the tranches. If interest or principal payments to the liabilities are missed or collateral pool performance deteriorates, the bonds are said to have suffered a **material impairment** rather than default.

A tranched securitization operates under rules, called the **waterfall**, about how collateral cash flows and default losses are distributed to tranches. Typically, cash flows are distributed top-down, to senior tranches first, then mezzanine, and any residual to the equity. Losses are distributed bottom-up, with the equity written down first and a senior tranche experiencing writedowns only if the tranches subordinate to it have been written down to zero. Exceptions to these typical rules can be written into operating agreements.

The **thickness** of a tranche is its share of total liabilities, that is, the portion of the assets it funds, and can be stated as a set of **attachment** and **detachment points** within the overall liability structure. The attachment point of a tranche is the fraction of the total par value of liabilities subordinate to it. The detachment point of a tranche is the fraction of liabilities to which it is subordinate. The attachment point of one tranche is the detachment point of the next-most junior tranche. The thickness of a tranche equals the difference between its detachment and attachment points.

Defaults of assets in the collateral pool affect tranche returns through writedowns of liabilities and because cash flows to the SPV are reduced by missed interest payments. Nondefaulting loans continue to make interest payments, and there may be recovery on defaulted loans, so pool losses—the default rate of the collateral pool—can be somewhat higher than its attachment point without causing losses to a tranche.[2]

We'll illustrate the structure and risk behavior of a securitization with an extended example. The tranche structure is displayed in the balance sheet of Figure 14.5

Assets	Liabilities
Underlying debt instruments: $100 million of loans Rate: risk-free+750 bps	Equity note $5 million
	Mezzanine debt $15 million Coupon: risk-free+500 bps
	Senior debt $80 million Coupon: risk-free+100 bps

Figure 14.5 Tranche structure of a securitization

---

[2] The fraction of pool losses to which a tranche is *not* exposed and the fraction of pool losses at which it is entirely wiped out are sometimes used as definitions of the attachment and detachment points.

The parameters for the example are:

Risk-free rate (%)	r^f	3.5
Loan interest rate (%)	r_l	11.0
Mezzanine coupon (%)	c_m	8.5
Senior coupon (%)	c_s	4.5
Mezzanine attachment point (% of liabilities)	a_m	5
Senior attachment point (% of liabilities)	a_s	20

The example makes a number of assumptions about market pricing and risk. The underlying loans are 1-year loans with no prepayment option. Principal and interest are due at maturity, so all cash flows occur at initiation and one year in the future. Pool losses and writedowns are recorded at maturity as well. The expected default rate is $\pi = 0.05$ (5 percent), and the expected recovery rate is zero. The liabilities are 1-year par bonds with a single coupon at maturity, similar to a zero-coupon.

The senior bond has a priority claim over mezzanine, and both bonds have a priority claim over the equity. The credit enhancement of the "20–100" senior bond in the example consists of the $5 million equity note plus the $15 million mezzanine debt. The equity note is the credit enhancement of the "5–20" mezzanine bond. All three securities enjoy any overcollateralization of the aggregate liabilities or underlying loans. The structure is similar to typical ABS securitizations of subprime auto loans. Its collateral pool debt is granular and has a short **weighted-average life** (WAL) and a fairly high default rate.

The credit enhancement and coupons of the senior and mezzanine bonds are assumed to be sufficient compensation for credit and other risks, so they can be priced at par on issuance. The "0–5" equity note is also assumed to price at par on issuance. It will then have an expected return of 11.5 percent if the expected default rate of $\pi = 0.05$ is realized.

Cash flows of principal and interest due from the underlying loan obligors to the SPV are contactually stipulated as are those from the SPV to the senior and mezzanine bonds. These cash flows will be realized as long as there is no material impairment of the liabilities. Each loan obligor is obliged to pay $1 + r_l$ times the individual loan principal in one year. The aggregate for the pool is $1 + r_l$ times the total par value of the collateral pool. The SPV is to pay out the par value plus the coupon, $1 + c_s$ or $1 + c_m$ times each bond's principal, in one year (see Table 14.6):

$$(1 - a_s)(1 + c_s) \times \text{total par value of collateral},$$
$$(a_s - a_m)(1 + c_m) \times \text{total par value of collateral}.$$

(14.1)

No contractually stipulated cash flows are due the equity note.

Table 14.1 Contactually stipulated bond payments

	senior	mezzanine
Tranche thickness (% of SPV liabilities)	80	15
Principal and interest due (% of pool principal)	83.600	16.275
Principal and interest due ($)	83 600 000	16 275 000

14.3   Credit Risk Measurement of Securitizations

14.3.1   Securitization Loss Scenarios

The risk analysis of securitization tranches starts from analysis of the underlying collateral pool and is then applied to find the potential losses of each tranche. We begin with a what-if scenario analysis in which we calculate the waterfall and tranche cash flows under credit loss scenarios without assigning probabilities to those scenarios. The baseline is the expected default rate $\pi = 0.05$. We can trace through the cash flow results for each tranche and determine the loss levels that "break" each tranche.

The loan proceeds flowing into the SPV (as a multiple of notional) depend on the default rate:

$$\text{loan proceeds}(x) = (1 - x)(1 + r_l), \qquad 0 \le x \le 1.$$

Because the waterfall begins with the underlying collateral, scenarios can be defined as high or low realized default rates x in the loan pool, for example, x far in excess of π. We then calculate the cash flows to the tranches for any value of x. The senior bond has a priority claim over the mezzanine and equity tranches. Therefore, it receives all the loan proceeds up to its own par value plus coupon payment $(1 - a_s)(1 + c_s)$:

$$\text{senior cash flow}(x) = \min[(1 - x)(1 + r_l), (1 - a_s)(1 + c_s)].$$

The mezzanine bond receives cash flows only if the senior bond is paid its share $(1 - a_s)(1 + c_s)$ in full. If that condition is satisfied, it will receive all post-senior loan proceeds up to its own par value and coupon $(a_s - a_m)(1 + c_m)$:

$$\text{mezzanine cash flow}(x)$$
$$= \max[\min[(1 - x)(1 + r_l) - (1 - a_s)(1 + c_s), (a_s - a_m)(1 + c_m)], 0].$$

The equity note receives the remaining cash flows, if positive, that is, they have not been exhausted by higher-priority cash flows to the senior and mezzanine bonds:

$$\text{equity cash flow}(x)$$
$$= \max[(1 - x)(1 + r_l) - (1 - a_s)(1 + c_s) - (a_s - a_m)(1 + c_m), 0].$$

The scenario results for our example are displayed in Table 14.2.

Table 14.2   Securitization scenario analysis

	x	*senior*	*mezzanine*	*equity*
Baseline cash flow	5.0	83.600	16.275	5.575
Baseline return	5.0	4.50	8.50	11.50
Maximum return	0.0	4.50	8.50	122.50
Stress case return	12.5	4.50	−9.83	−100.00

The baseline cash flow expressed in $ millions. Scenario default rate in loan pool x and returns in percent.

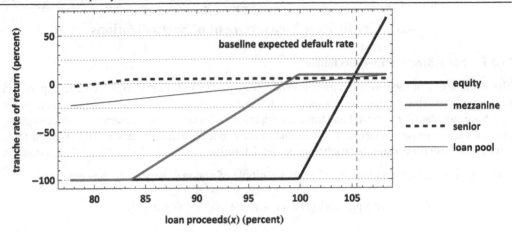

Figure 14.6 Pool and tranche returns in the example.

We can also state the cash flows as tranche returns, measured relative to the tranche thickness or par value:

$$\text{senior return}(x) = \frac{\text{senior cash flow}(x)}{1 - a_s} - 1$$

$$\text{mezzanine return}(x) = \frac{\text{mezzanine cash flow}(x)}{a_s - a_m} - 1$$

$$\text{equity return}(x) = \frac{\text{equity cash flow}(x)}{a_m} - 1.$$

The securitization tranches behave as option portfolios on the underlying loan pool proceeds or credit losses, and the tranche risks can be evaluated using the Merton credit risk model of Chapters 9 and 13. The exercise prices are the loss levels at which the bond tranches suffer material impairment.[3] Figure 14.6 shows tranche returns in the example as a function of the pool default rate. The senior tranche behaves as a portfolio of a short put on the loan pool proceeds and a riskless bond. The mezzanine tranche behaves as a collar—a long put plus a short call at a lower strike—on the loan pool proceeds, and the equity tranche behaves as a long call on the loan pool proceeds.

Consistent with their option-like behavior, the securitization tranches contain embedded leverage. The attachment and detachment points determine the tranche thickness and the extent of this leverage. A tranche suffers losses once its attachment point is breached. The degree of embedded leverage is therefore, governed by two characteristics: how low the tranche's position in the waterfall is and the tranche's thickness. Thin, highly subordinated tranches take proportionally greater losses for any given pool loss rate. In our example, a 10 percent loan default rate barely brings the pool rate of return to zero but leads to a near-total loss on the equity tranche.

The event of material impairment of a bond tranche is defined similarly to the event of default of a plain-vanilla bond: failure to pay principal or interest due. In our example, material impairment—"default" henceforth, to save ink—can occur only at a single 1-year payment date for bond principal and interest. Insolvency may become evident well within one year, for example, if

---

[3] These differ from the attachment and detachment points due to the cash flows from the SPV assets.

realized loan defaults are high. There is no zero recovery event for the tranches, but a small increase in pool losses can drive a thin tranche from a marginal material impairment to complete loss.

A bond tranche with a default-triggering loss level $x°$ defaults if the realized loss rate $x \geq x°$, that is:

$$(1 - x)(1 + r_l) < \begin{cases} (1 - a_s)(1 + c_s) & \Leftrightarrow \quad \text{senior defaults} \\ (1 - a_s)(1 + c_s) + (a_s - a_m)(1 + c_m) & \Leftrightarrow \quad \text{mezzanine defaults} \end{cases}$$

The default-triggering loss level $x°$ for the bond tranches is thus

$$x° = \begin{cases} 1 - \dfrac{(1 - a_s)(1 + c_s)}{1 + r_l} \\ 1 - \dfrac{(1 - a_s)(1 + c_s) + (a_s - a_m)(1 + c_m)}{1 + r_l} \end{cases}$$

$$\text{for the} \begin{cases} \text{senior} \\ \text{mezzanine} \end{cases} \text{tranche,}$$

which in our example take on the values

	Default-triggering loss level	
	senior	mezzanine
$x°$ (%)	24.685	10.023

The equity tranche cannot default, as no payments are contractually owed to it. But it can suffer lower-than-expected or negative returns. The loss level x at which the equity tranche return is zero, with its principal and no more flowing back to it, is found by solving

$$x = 1 - \frac{(1 - a_s)(1 + c_s) + (a_s - a_m)(1 + c_m) + a_m}{1 + r_l}.$$

The equity tranche return is zero if $x = 0.05518$, or 5.518 percent. The loss level at which equity tranche is wiped out (the return is -100 percent) is the x at which the bond tranches are just barely paid in full, with no cash flow to the equity and is identical to the mezzanine default-triggering loss level.

14.3.2   Securitization Risk Modeling

More formal credit portfolio modeling approaches to securitization also proceed from the analysis of the collateral pool, treating the loss rate x as a random variable. They include simulation approaches, generally using **copula models** and specific credit models.[4] The single factor model of the previous chapter is applicable to the credit risk analysis of a securitization if the collateral pool is granular. We can then combine the risk analysis of the loan pool with the securitization waterfall to find the credit loss distribution of each tranche, and explore the impact of changes in collateral default probability and correlation.

To apply the single factor model to our securitization example, we assume the distributions of pool losses and tranche returns depend on a latent market factor. We have given assumptions on the

---

[4] The Gaussian copula model assumes that defaults are driven by asset returns following a multivariate normal distribution with estimated or stipulated parameters.

expected default rate (π) and their correlation to the market factor (β). The baseline parameters in our example are:

$$\pi = 0.05,$$

$$\beta = \sqrt{0.25},$$

The asset correlation among the underlying loans is then $\beta^2 = 0.25$, and the default correlation is

$$\rho = \frac{\Phi_{\beta^2}(k, k) - \pi^2}{\pi(1 - \pi)} = 0.0767,$$

with $k = -1.64485$, the 0.05-quantile of a standard normal. The cumulative distribution function of pool losses (a random variable $\tilde{x}$) in the single factor model is equation 13.3, reproduced here:

$$\mathbf{P}[\tilde{x} \leq x] = \Phi\left[\frac{\sqrt{1 - \beta^2}\Phi^{-1}(x) - \Phi^{-1}(\pi)}{\beta}\right]. \tag{14.2}$$

We can analyze the effect on the credit loss distributions of varying π and β. The model also lends itself to a market risk analysis by assuming the securitization was designed and constructed under these baseline parameters and correspond to the initial market view or expectations about default behavior. Changes in the market values of the tranches are then driven by changes in the market assessment or risk preferences regarding the expected loan default rate and default correlation.

Figure 14.7 displays the estimated credit loss distribution of the loan pool in our example under the baseline and under higher default probability and correlation assumptions. A higher default probability leads to a more dispersed, less kurtotic pool credit loss distribution.

As we saw in Chapter 13, default correlation has a large impact on the probability distribution of collateral pool losses. The loss distribution becomes more skewed with a higher default correlation. There is higher tail risk, with a greater likelihood of default clusters and of very large and very low losses:

	$\beta = \sqrt{0.25}$	$\beta = \sqrt{0.75}$
$\mathbf{P}[\tilde{x} \leq 0.01]$	0.230	0.711
$\mathbf{P}[\tilde{x} \geq 0.25]$	0.017	0.066

Default correlation therefore, has a large impact on the risk of the equity and senior tranches.

To go from collateral pool to tranche risk analysis, start by noting that each scenario or realization x of the pool default rate has a cumulative probability $\mathbf{P}[\tilde{x} \leq x]$ in the model. The waterfall implies specific cash flow consequences of each possible realization of x for each tranche. Together, this gives us the cumulative distribution function of cash flows for each tranche. For example, the cash flow distribution of the senior tranche is the set of pairs

$$\{\text{senior cash flow}(x), \mathbf{P}[\tilde{x} \leq x]\}\ x \in [0,1].$$

An analogous set can be computed for each tranche and can be mapped into the distributions of returns as well as of cash flows for each tranche.

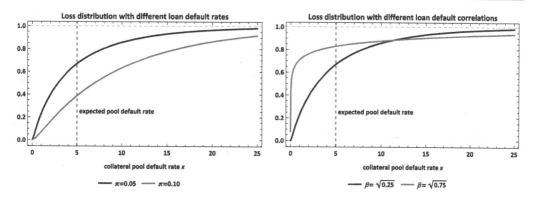

Figure 14.7 Cumulative distribution function of pool losses

Left panel: both plots use baseline parameter $\beta = \sqrt{0.25}$. Right panel: both plots use baseline parameter $\pi = 0.05$.

With the distribution function of cash flows to each tranche, we can find the probability of material impairment of a bond tranche. Above, we calculated the default-triggering loss level for each bond tranche based on its coupon and the waterfall. A tranche with a default-triggering loss level $x°$ defaults if pool losses reach or exceed that level, $x \geq x°$. The probability of a tranche default is

$$\mathbf{P}[\tilde{x} \geq x°] = 1 - \mathbf{P}[\tilde{x} \leq x°] = 1 - \Phi \left[\frac{\sqrt{1 - \beta^2}\Phi^{-1}(x°) - \Phi^{-1}(\pi)}{\beta} \right].$$

Table 14.3 displays a risk analysis of a senior bond, and Figure 14.8 shows the senior bond return distribution function for different combinations of parameters.

A higher pool loss default rate and a higher default correlation are adverse for a senior bond, shifting the return distribution function to more extreme credit losses. The risk of the senior bond is particularly sensitive to default correlation. With correlation very low, the senior bond default probability is low even if the pool default rate is high. A high default correlation induces a higher probability of default clusters that can reach into the senior tranche even if the default probability is low.

Table 14.4 displays the probabilities of a loss and Figure 14.9 the return distribution function of the equity note for different settings of the pool loss distribution parameters. Increasing the default correlation generally lowers the tranche loss probability. At a high correlation, the probability of the equity tranche experiencing a negative return more than triples as the default probability of its constituents increases from 2.5 to 10 percent. But at a low correlation, the same increase in default

Table 14.3 Senior bond default probability

	$\beta = \sqrt{0.05}$	$\beta = \sqrt{0.25}$	$\beta = \sqrt{0.50}$	$\beta = \sqrt{0.75}$
$\pi = 0.025$	0.0000	0.0031	0.0184	0.0309
$\pi = 0.05$	0.0000	0.0177	0.0503	0.0663
$\pi = 0.10$	0.0030	0.0842	0.1297	0.1390

Probability of material impairment, displayed as decimal, for different settings of the pool loss distribution parameters.

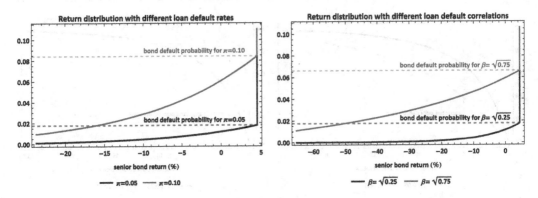

Figure 14.8 Pool default behavior and senior bond returns

Left panel: both plots use baseline parameter $\beta = \sqrt{0.25}$. Right panel: both plots use baseline parameter $\pi = 0.05$.

Table 14.4   Equity tranche: probability of negative return

	$\beta = \sqrt{0.05}$	$\beta = \sqrt{0.25}$	$\beta = \sqrt{0.50}$	$\beta = \sqrt{0.75}$
$\pi = 0.025$	0.0355	0.1241	0.1200	0.0899
$\pi = 0.05$	0.3458	0.3000	0.2328	0.1642
$\pi = 0.10$	0.8903	0.5801	0.4146	0.2884

Probability of a negative return on the equity tranche (cash flow to the equity note lower than its par value), displayed as decimal, for different settings of the pool loss distribution parameters.

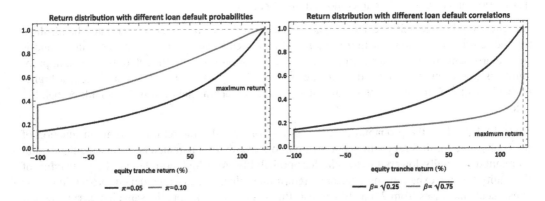

Figure 14.9 Pool default behavior and equity tranche returns

Left panel: both plots use baseline parameter $\beta = \sqrt{0.25}$. Right panel: both plots use baseline parameter $\pi = 0.05$.

probability increases the probability of a negative equity return more than 25-fold, to nearly 90 percent, as a wipe-out of the equity becomes highly likely. The probability of a surprisingly low number of defaults constrains the decline in value when correlation is high.

A higher pool default rate decreases equity returns; its return distribution shifts to the left. But a high default correlation increases equity returns; its return distribution shifts to the right. The equity note has limited downside but unlimited upside. Higher correlation implies a higher likelihood of

Table 14.5 Mezzanine bond default probability

	$\beta = \sqrt{0.05}$	$\beta = \sqrt{0.25}$	$\beta = \sqrt{0.50}$	$\beta = \sqrt{0.75}$
$\pi = 0.025$	0.0007	0.0443	0.0679	0.0638
$\pi = 0.05$	0.0379	0.1418	0.1478	0.1230
$\pi = 0.10$	0.4401	0.3648	0.2973	0.2295

Probability of material impairment, displayed as decimal, for different settings of the pool loss distribution parameters.

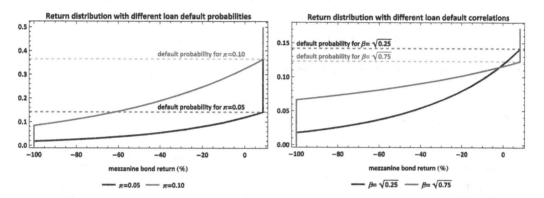

Figure 14.10 Pool default behavior and mezzanine tranche returns

Left panel: both plots use baseline parameter $\beta = \sqrt{0.25}$. Right panel: both plots use baseline parameter $\pi = 0.05$.

very many and of very few defaults. The former doesn't much diminish expected return because the equity tranche's value cannot go below zero, but the latter adds to expected return because it increases the low probability that the equity note emerges relatively unscathed by pool losses. The shape of the return distribution function reflects this lottery-like return behavior by becoming more convex.

For the mezzanine tranche, as for all the tranches, a higher pool default rate decreases return. But the impact of default correlation is more ambiguous than for the senior and equity tranches. The mezzanine will generally benefit less than the equity and suffer less than the senior from higher correlation, but it depends on the mezzanine attachment point and thickness. Table 14.5 displays default probabilities, and Figure 14.10 shows the return distribution function of the mezzanine bond for different combinations of parameters.

14.3.3   Credit Value-at-Risk of Securitizations

We can also estimate the credit VaR of securitization tranches. Quantiles of cash flow, the return to a tranche, and the credit loss can be found from the tranche loss distribution. The credit VaR of a tranche is equal to the credit loss at a specified quantile, minus the expected loss (EL).[5]

Figure 14.11 and Table 14.6 illustrate the calculation of the 1-year credit VaR for the bond tranches, evaluated using the single factor model under the baseline parameter assumptions. At the 99 percent

---

[5] The expected loss of a tranche can be calculated numerically as the integral of the loss probability density function corresponding to equation 14.2 and the cash flow or return to the tranche over the range of possible loss rates.

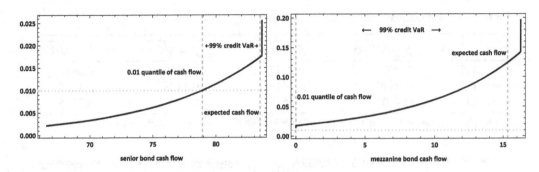

Figure 14.11 Credit Value-at-Risk of bond tranches

Vertical grid lines in each plot placed at the cash flow with cumulative probability 0.01, and at the expected value of cash flow. The distance between the two grid lines is the credit VaR for the tranche. Both plots use baseline parameters $\pi = 0.05$ and $\beta = \sqrt{0.25}$.

Table 14.6 Credit Value-at-Risk of securitization tranches

	Mezzanine bond	*Senior bond*
Expected loss	5.822	0.172
0.01-quantile of cash flow	0.000	94.398
Credit VaR	94.178	5.430

Results for the bond tranches are expressed in percent of the principal and interest due.

confidence level, the senior bond has a small loss relative to the expected loss, but the mezzanine and the equity tranche are wiped out.

14.3.4   Risk Analysis and Structuring of Securitizations

Risk is modeled during underwriting in the process of structuring a securitization. Taking pool credit quality and cash flows into account, it guides the location of the attachment and detachment points, that is, the tranche sizes. Tranching is done with great care to obtain advantageous credit ratings for non-equity tranches.

The senior tranche, in our example and in practice, is critical in the design of a securitization. The senior tranche has the lowest risk and the lowest coupon in the structure. The thicker the senior tranche and the lower its coupon relative to the collateral pool's cash flows, the lower is the overall funding rate at which the entire pool can be financed and the higher are the returns to the junior tranches. Sponsors of the securitization endeavor to finesse this trade-off to obtain the cheapest overall funding of the structure while still being able to place all tranches with investors.

Mezzanine tranches may have a low default probability but very high LGD; if there is a material impairment, it will be severe. The equity is typically issued as an unrated note. The audience for these securities is less risk averse than that for the senior tranches but smaller and more specialized.

For example, suppose it is desired that the senior bond have a default probability no greater than 1 percent given its relatively low coupon. That can be carried out by finding the required attachment point a_s given the pool credit risk parameters. The required attachment point satisfies

$$x^\circ = 1 - \frac{(1 - a_s)(1 + c_s)}{1 + r_l} \quad \text{and}$$

$$0.01 = 1 - \mathbf{P}[\tilde{x} \le x^\circ].$$

In our example, using the baseline parameters, the required attachment point is $a_s = 0.2448$, reducing the senior tranche thickness to $1 - a_s = 0.7552$. The equity and/or mezzanine tranches will need to be somewhat wider. This would reduce the share of relatively cheap senior funding, correspondingly diminish the expected returns and alter the risk-return profile of the two junior tranches in a way that could make them less attractive to a small but risk-friendly audience.

The model risk, and specifically the risk of underestimating tail risk inherent in the credit risk modeling of securitization tranches, has important market risk consequences. The default correlation is the more sensitive but also more difficult-to-estimate parameter. Once securities are brought to market and are on investors' balance sheets or trade in secondary markets, their values can change as the market adjusts its economic and risk assessments. The bonds are often highly convex in the parameters the market is reassessing. Clusters of default may be deemed more likely than initially modeled, fundamentally changing the risk-reward balance of the tranches. High correlation benefits equity and reduces the value of the higher-rated senior bonds. A low correlation implies a higher probability of a steady trickle of defaults reducing the value of equity and increasing the value of senior tranches.

Model risk also affects the assignment of credit ratings to structured products. Rating agencies analyze credit stress scenarios featuring much higher than expected default rates, stipulating default and recovery behavior of the loan pool over time. **Ratings inflation** refers to the assignment by rating agencies of unwarranted high ratings to bonds, particularly securitization tranches. It can be achieved by underestimating collateral pool default probabilities, expected losses, or default correlations, justifying thicker senior tranches.

Ratings inflation of structured products had been linked in the wake of the global financial crisis to the issuer-pays model (see Chapter 9), in which rating agencies are paid by issuers who benefit from having lower-coupon senior bonds as a larger share of liabilities and a lower overall funding cost. Because the senior bonds have low coupons if they can be judged safe, they are considered the key to a successful securitization in the sense that it can be brought to market and sold at low spreads over the risk-free rate. Thickening the senior bond—lowering its attachment point—increases its risk, so potential senior tranche investors will demand a higher coupon and potentially jeopardize its investment-grade rating. Ratings inflation would ease this tension.

Institutional investors have been eager purchasers of highly rated paper with yields even slightly higher than risk-free alternatives, as seen in Figure 14.4, a phenomenon related to reaching for yield (see Chapter 15) and demographics. They have strong motivation to accept an approach to ratings that increases the availability of highly rated bonds while still satisfying regulatory constraints. There is a trade-off between the size of the hard-to-place equity and the eagerly sought AAA bonds. If the investor base for the AAA bonds is motivated to underestimate its risks, the equity is easier to place, enabling the entire structure to come to market. Ratings inflation serves both audiences.

14.4 Credit Correlation Trading

14.4.1   CDS Indexes and Standard Tranches

Credit exposures are frequently traded in the form of **CDS indexes**, which are CDS written on debt securities of groups of companies. The most commonly traded are synthetic, written on benchmark or standardized portfolios of **reference obligations**. The **CDX** investment-grade (IG) and high-yield (HY) indexes include 125 CDS on North American investment grade or 125 high-yield firms, and the **iTraxx** indexes cover European and Asian firms, selected using criteria such as size and credit rating and with equal notional weights. The indexes are updated regularly as the credit markets evolve.

CDS indexes are used by a range of market participants to hedge or establish open positions. The pricing of a CDS index is a measure of the risk-adjusted present value that protection buyers are prepared to make to insure against a future credit loss among the constituent firms in the index. For the investment grade CDX.NA.IG, the standard fixed rate premium is 100 basis points, apart from a market-adjusted up-front payment by the fixed rate or contingent leg to the other at initiation of the contract or at the time of a trade in a CDS index.

Four standard tranches of synthetic CDOs, structured products based on each CDS index, are traded: equity, mezzanine, senior, and super-senior. The attachment points of the CDX.NA.IG standard tranches are 3, 7, and 15 percent of the notional value.

The pricing of the tranches, as well as of the indexes, reflects changing views about credit quality generally and about the specific included firms, risk preferences, hedging demand, and CDS index liquidity. Their values change nonlinearly with default expectations as expressed through the market spread of the index over a risk-free benchmark, observed directly through market price quotations or derived from the points up front and running spread of the index or tranche. The tranche spreads are higher for equity and lower for senior tranches than that of the CDS index.

For each tranche, a delta can be estimated that quantifies the change in spread of the tranche if the index spread widens by 1 basis point, in other words, the ratio of the CS01 of a tranche to that of the index. The convexity of a tranche measures the extent to which the tranche delta increases or decreases as the index spread rises.

Credit convexity is perhaps less familiar than its option- and mortgage-related cousins. The delta and convexity of the tranches are driven by changing market expectations and risk appetites regarding default likelihoods and correlations. Just as a risk-neutral default probability can be inferred from the spreads on debt securities and risk-free rates, an implied risk-neutral default correlation between pairs of firms in the indexes can be inferred from the prices of synthetic CDS index tranches. **Base correlation** is a standard measure defined using a specific model and procedure to match tranche prices to that of the index similar to option-implied volatility. It is not a direct measure of default correlation because at any point in time it will differ across tranches.[6]

The equity tranches display positive convexity: the equity value declines at a declining rate in response to index spread widening. The convexity of the equity tranche is more pronounced when default correlation is viewed as high or markets are more wary of near-simultaneous defaults. The intuition is that you can't beat a dead horse: if you are long credit risk through the equity tranche,

---

[6] The model is most often the Gaussian copula model with known univariate or marginal distributions linked by an unknown correlation. The correlation estimate is the parameter that fits the observed tranche and index prices. The correlations are found tranche by tranche, bootstrapping from the equity tranche.

once you've lost much of your investment due to increases in default rates, you will lose a bit less from the next increase in default rates. The tranche becomes inert.

Because positive convexity indicates a positive exposure to default correlation, traders can express a view that default correlation is likely to increase or that a surprising number of constituent firms is likely to default through a long credit position in the equity tranche. In our example (see Table 14.4), if the default probability doesn't rise too much, a higher default correlation will lower the likelihood of a negative equity tranche return.

More senior tranches display milder negative convexity. A higher default correlation increases the likelihood of a rare cluster of defaults and the likelihood of a material impairment of the senior tranche. Traders can express a view that default correlation is likely to increase through a short credit position in the CDX super-senior tranche. The mezzanine tranches fall somewhere in between with less pronounced positive or negative convexity depending on market conditions and the CDO structure.

14.4.2   The 2005 Auto Industry Credit Crisis and the "London Whale"

Two events involving convexity trading of CDX tranches illustrate the relationships between credit risk parameters and credit pricing. They also illustrate failures of risk management, model risk, the pitfalls of carry trades, and the behavior of liquidity in stressed markets.

The first episode took place in the wake of the surprising credit downgrades of the two largest US auto manufacturers, Ford and General Motors (GM). The auto industry had been troubled, and spreads on its debt securities had been widening for a long time in early 2005. Ford and GM, their captive finance companies, and several auto part manufacturers were constituents of the CDX IG index.

A number of leveraged traders had followed similar strategies in the equity and mezzanine tranches, selling protection on the equity tranche of the index, hedged by buying a larger notional amount of protection on the mezzanine tranche, in the ratio of the modeled deltas of the two tranches. The equity position was long credit risk and the mezzanine short credit risk.

The trade had positive carry: the CDS premium for protection was so much higher for the equity tranche than for the mezzanine that it more than offset the higher notional amount of the latter. The trade also had positive convexity and was long exposure to default correlation. A high default correlation is advantageous to long credit risk positions expressed via equity. If the default probability is low, as is typically the case for investment-grade companies but defaults are expected or feared to cluster, the equity tranche will act as a reverse lottery ticket; it has a small probability of being wiped out entirely but a reasonably high likelihood of surviving largely intact.

A bet on correlation remaining high seemed reasonable with the debt of several firms in the ailing auto sector accounting for some 10 percent of the IG index. The leveraged funds were positioning for their survival and for the equity tranche base correlation to remain high. A decline in correlation would render the equity profit and loss (P&L) more linear and steeply negatively sloped as CS01 rises.

In May 2005, rating agencies downgraded Ford and GM from investment to speculative grade. The spreads of their captive finance companies widened, and two part suppliers, Delphi and Visteon, filed for bankruptcy. The shock triggered the unwinding of the long correlation positions. It became clear that specific firms were defaulting or might be about to, idiosyncratic risk now seemed dominant, and it appeared more likely that the equity tranche could be written down entirely.

Market liquidity played an important role. The equity tranche value and its base correlation plunged. The mezzanine tranche, however, maintained its value, as traders hastening to unravel the long correlation trade attempted to cover their positions by selling protection. The equity tranche spread spiked in line with that of the index as the mezzanine spread rose far less, leading to extreme losses on portfolios thought to have been hedged against credit spread risk.

The second credit convexity event was directly related to large losses experienced by one of the largest too-big-to-fail banks. The London Whale episode originated in a mid-2011 effort by JPMorgan Chase & Company to hedge the long credit exposure of its loan portfolio through positions established by a proprietary credit derivatives trading desk. Market turmoil had set in from the end of July, and credit spreads were widening. Sources of stress included a US political fight over the debt ceiling and a credit downgrade of its debt, the spread of Europe's sovereign debt crisis to Italy, and the Swiss decision to peg the franc to the euro to constrain further appreciation.[7]

The trading desk took a short credit risk position by buying protection on the mezzanine tranche of the then-current iTraxx CDS index series. The equity tranche was thin and inert, with several defaulted and removed names in the index, making the mezzanine behave more like an equity tranche. With a high delta, it was cost-effective as an opportunistic credit hedge compared to buying protection on a CDS index, such as the IG or iTraxx. The bank would have determined the dollar loss in its loan portfolio from spread widening it wished to hedge and bought protection on the notional amount of the mezzanine that would have an offsetting gain.[8]

A further advantage of the mezzanine tranche at this time was that its base correlation was relatively high. That made the mezzanine relatively expensive—analogous to a tight credit spread relative to the index or to senior tranches—and therefore added to its attractiveness as an instrument with which to put on a short credit hedge. The spread and the base correlation continued to rise steadily in the second half of 2011 as the market priced in increased default risk and a higher likelihood of default clusters. Figure 14.12 displays the CDS spreads, mezzanine base correlation, and the applicable hedge ratio for the Whale trades for the on-the-run 5-year iTraxx CDS index.

At the end of 2011, the portfolio's value had risen considerably. The short mezzanine position had behaved like a short position in a high-yield bond acquired at a tight spread that had subsequently widened. The continued rise in the mezzanine tranche base correlation somewhat offset these gains and made the mezzanine more negatively convex. The mezzanine now more closely resembled a reverse lottery ticket that just might evade high credit losses.

A combination of calming markets and a desire to lower regulatory capital requirements prompted JPMorgan to reconsider the portfolio. Market conditions seemed favorable with both the index spread and the mezzanine base correlation having peaked and easing off. The trading desk was aware the positions were quite large relative to trading volumes and that this was becoming widely known among rival trading desks. Rather than unwinding them, additional trades were put on to "hedge-the-hedge," primarily a longer-term, super-senior long credit position with a more linear response to changes in spread and positive convexity. Because the delta of the super-seniors was much smaller than that of the mezzanine, the hedge ratio would have been high, with the notional amount of the supers position 9 or 10 times that of the mezzanine.

---

[7] We describe the Swiss Franc (CHF) episode in Chapter 15.

[8] The portfolio was in fact significantly more complex, involving index and single-name CDS on investment-grade and high-yield names.

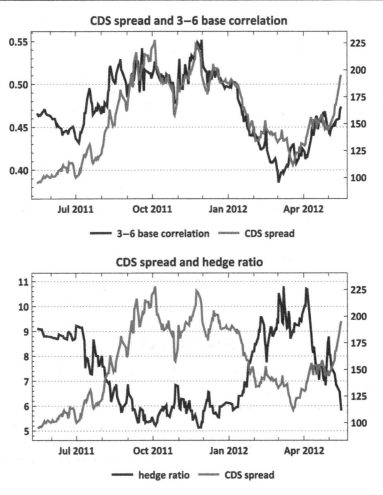

Figure 14.12 Markit iTraxx CDS data 2011–2012

Markit iTraxx Europe Main Series 9, 5-year maturity, expiring June 20, 2013. Upper panel: mezzanine (3–6 percent) tranche base correlation (left axis) and CDS spread (right axis). panel: ratio of delta of super-senior (22–100 percent) to delta of mezzanine (3–6 percent) tranche (left axis) and CDS spread (right axis). Daily, 16May2011 to 16May2012. *Source*: JPMorgan.

The combination of a long protection (short credit) position in the highly negatively convex mezzanine and a large short (long credit) super-senior position gave the portfolio a highly negatively convex P&L profile with respect to changes in the CDS spread. Figure 14.13 is a stylized illustration of the P&L of the "hedged" portfolio. For small changes in the CDS spread, the P&L would be modest, but for larger changes, particularly spread tightening, the losses would be very high.

At this point, the trap the JPMorgan trading desk had set for itself over the preceding months was sprung. The market, having been asked to take the other side, was well aware of its large positions. As long as correlation and the credit spread were falling, losses could be contained. Once the spread began to widen, as it did from mid-March 2012, losses exploded. The speed with which credit spreads widened at times during March and April is evidence of a fire sale. The portfolio was unwound under the worst of liquidity circumstances, at an eventual $6.2 billion loss.

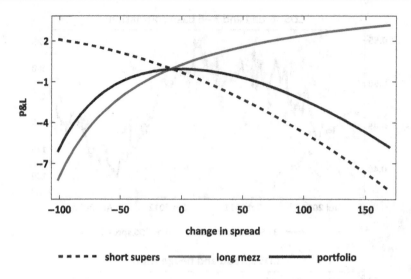

Figure 14.13 Stylized P&L of the Whale portfolio

P&L in $ billions.

Further Reading

Rutledge and Raynes (2010) is an introductory text on securitization. Martin and Sayrak (2022) describes recent trends in CLO issuance.

Gorton and Metrick (2012) and Ashcraft and Schuermann (2008) describe securitization structures and markets before the global financial crisis. Longstaff and Rajan (2008) describe CDX tranches and estimate default correlation and other credit parameters from their market prices. The copula approach is presented in Li (2000). Nickerson and Griffin (2017) find underestimation of default correlation by ratings agencies before the crisis.

The credit convexity events of 2005 are discussed in Packer and Wooldridge (2005), Acharya et al. (2008), and Coudert and Gex (2010). Marthinsen (2018) and Zeissler et al. (2019) recount the Whale episode.

15

Financial Instability and Financial Crises

15.1 Defining Financial Crises

Financial crises are major disturbances involving interruption of credit intermediation, widespread intermediary failures, and significant macroeconomic impact. Funding liquidity is a typical crisis trigger as short-term lenders decline to continue extending credit and assets must be quickly sold at a loss. Market liquidity and market functioning are disordered, with the potential or reality of impairment of payments systems. Asset prices typically display extreme volatility, and many risk asset prices plummet. Economic activity falls rapidly; recession or a depression ensues that is generally unusually long and severe. There is more often than not an international dimension: the crisis affects a number of countries with abrupt changes in exchange rates or capital flows, transmitted via trade and financial channels.

Financial crises are a very old phenomenon, dating back at least to the late medieval era and the origins of deposit banking. Major crises before the Great Depression include:

1343: Collapse of several Florentine banks on the failure of England to repay war-financing debts.
1763: Widespread failures of Dutch and German banks follow the end of the Seven Years' War and war boom.
1825: Bank of England suffers a gold drain, widespread bank failures, and stock and bond price declines following the post-Napoleonic war credit expansion.
1837: Widespread suspension of specie payments by and failures of US banks, and a sharp recession.
1873: Failure of the Jay Cooke & Company bank, followed by widespread bank failures, stock crashes in many countries, and a "Long Depression" lasting until 1893.
1907: Exposure of losses by some banks leads to widespread runs and stock market declines.

The arguably deepest financial crisis in modern history began with the market crash of 1929. Widespread bank failures and a world Great Depression ensued, followed immediately by the worst international conflict in history.

The immediate postwar period was relatively free of global-scale crises though smaller or more local financial stress events occurred frequently, among them:

Collapse of Bretton Woods 1968–1971, at the start of the 1970s stagflation.
Savings and loan (S&L) crisis of early 1980s in United States, following the 1970s inflation and 1980s deflation. It led to the depletion of the federal deposit insurance fund and widespread gambling for resurrection (see Chapter 11) by likely insolvent banks.
1987 stock market crash: a 20 percent decline, the largest in one day in the history of the S&P 500 index, had little lasting effect.
Japan's lost decade had been preceded by a rapid rise in stock and land prices. It began with a sharp drop in land prices in 1989, followed by a protracted recession.
European Monetary System crisis of 1992–1993: speculative attack on fixed exchange rates.

Mexico default on US dollar-denominated debt 1994–1995, following abandonment of an exchange rate peg. It had been precipitated by a sharp rise in US interest rates.

Asian crisis 1997–1998: fixed exchange rate pegs were broken, leading to failures of local banks with heavy short-term foreign exchange borrowing and exposed to wrong-way risk (see Chapter 8). The crisis eventually spread to Russia and Latin America.

Global financial crisis 2008–2011: on a much larger scale than other postwar crises due to extreme leverage, it was set off by a liquidity crunch and initiated a series of disruptions, compounded from 2010 by the European sovereign debt crisis.

Covid-19 2020: extreme supply and demand shocks triggered a liquidity crunch and impairment of market functioning.

Financial crises are not a tightly defined phenomenon nor entirely distinguishable from the broader phenomenon of business fluctuations or variations in the pace of economic activity. Each is a unique historical event, and dating the onset and end of a crisis and classification is difficult. Different features play central roles in different crises. A typical classification, based on triggering events and focal point, is:

Banking crises: widespread bank failures, triggered by market or other events, igniting fears of loan losses. Banking panics are less frequent since the advent of deposit insurance, but runs on demandable liabilities also take other forms, centered on banks or other intermediaries.

Debt crises: an event or fear of large or widespread defaults. **External debt crises** involve claims by foreign residents or in foreign currencies and have been more frequent since the end of the Bretton Woods regime. **Sovereign debt** or **fiscal crises** involve public debt.

Currency crises feature sharp devaluations of local currency, often following the failure of a peg, or balance of payments crises.

Financial crises are rarely purely of one type. Banking crises are often associated with sovereign debt crises because governments are explicit and implicit guarantors of banks via deposit insurance or bailout expectations. A sovereign-bank **doom loop** arises when banks are large holders of sovereign debt, and governments commit to preventing bank failures or losses to their claimants. The mutual exposure of banks and sovereigns weakens both and induces fragility. Banks suffer losses on their sovereign debt, and the bailout commitment brings the solvency of the government into question.

A crisis almost invariably affects credit markets, with a surge in bankruptcies in the private and public sector and an increase in financial firm failures. A **credit crunch**, a sudden contraction of bank lending and pervasive withdrawal of credit, is typical. The supply of credit shifts in; at any lending rate, banks and other creditors are willing to lend only a smaller volume than previously. Because it most often happens when banks have begun experiencing losses, the credit crunch is sometimes referred to as a capital crunch, amplifying the leverage effect.

Figure 15.1 tracks fluctuations in US bank lending. It declines sharply during recessions and during stress events, such as the global financial crisis and the onset of Covid. Loan volume rebounds reliably sharply at the ends of recessions.

15.2   Runs and Liquidity in Financial Crises

Financial crises often lead to or are triggered by concerns about intermediaries' liquidity as well as solvency. A **run** or **panic** is a sudden withdrawal by lenders of short-term credit, coupled with a sudden increase in **liquidity preference**, which is the demand for liquidity related to risk aversion

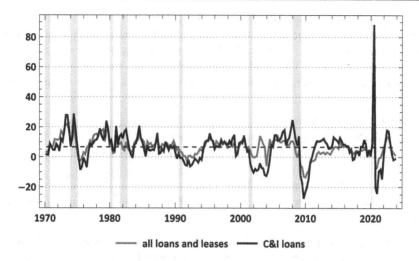

Figure 15.1 Growth rate of US bank lending 1970–2023

Annualized growth rate of all loans and leases in bank credit and of commercial and industrial (C&I) loans, by all US commercial banks, seasonally adjusted, percent, quarterly, Q1 1970 to Q3 2023. The horizontal grid line represents the mean growth rate of all loans over the period. The mean growth rates by loan category are:

Loans and leases in bank credit	6.67
Commercial and industrial loans	5.99

Vertical shading represents NBER recession dates. *Source*: Federal Reserve Board, H.8 data release.

and uncertainty. Originally coined to refer to banks, the term is applied also to demands for the immediate return of other forms of short-term lending, such as repo and money market funds.

Deposits have contractual characteristics that motivate bank runs, that is, simultaneous attempts at withdrawals by many depositors out of fear a bank's liquidity reserves will be depleted. **Par redemption** is the right to redeem deposits on demand in cash, in full, at par, and without delay when the demand is presented. The **sequential service constraint**, or "first-come first-served," obliges banks to satisfy depositors seeking withdrawals in the order in which they present their demands until and unless reserves are depleted. A failure to pay triggers insolvency, so depositors not redeeming ahead of others are compensated out of deposit insurance funds or become unsecured claimants on a bankrupt firm, though senior to other unsecured creditors.

Runs occur when there is extensive maturity and liquidity transformation and a lack of asset and funding diversification on the balance sheet of the intermediary, vulnerabilities to which the commercial banking model is highly susceptible. In simplified models, there are **multiple equilibria**: all can run or all can stay. Fractional-reserve banks are fragile: demand deposits only work in the "good," no-run equilibrium.

These conditions apply also to other intermediaries funded through debt contracts with the redemption features of deposits. Money market mutual funds, like any mutual fund, are in principle run-proof because shares are claims on the assets at their value at the time of redemption. They are rendered susceptible to runs by contractual or regulatory provisions that transform the shares into claims to a par value.

Narrow banking, originally proposed as the Chicago Plan during the Great Depression, would permit banks to create only deposits backed by government-issued money, or equivalently, central bank reserves. It would separate banks' payments and lending functions, eliminate fractional-reserve banking, and require banks to fund their lending with equity or non-runnable forms of debt. A variant on narrow banking, the Vollgeld-Initiative, was rejected by Swiss voters in June 2018. The US firm TNB USA Inc. attempted to create such a bank, motivated by the potential to earn a low-risk spread between deposit funding costs and interest on the reserve balances it would be eligible to hold under the Fed's current operating framework, but its application for an account at the Fed was denied.

Intermediaries other than banks can experience runs as well. Insurance companies issue short-term liabilities, such as GICs, that can be redeemed at short notice. Highly rated General American Life Insurance Co. had funded illiquid investments through agreements permitting its money market fund lenders to redeem with a few days' notice. Liquidity concerns prompted Moody's to downgrade the insurer from A2 to A3 on July 30, 1999. Within a few days, accelerating funding agreement redemptions by money funds forced General American into acquisition by MetLife at a low price.[1]

Runs can be experienced by market-based intermediation as well. It may involve a **flight to quality** or **safety**, a narrowing of the palette of assets that market participants consider safe and liquid. The substitutability between privately created forms of money is abruptly eroded, increasing the demand for cash, the supply of which may be inelastic. In the 2008 "run on repo," the sudden disqualification of large amounts of repo collateral as safe led to a collapse in the volume of short-term lending.

Run risk can be mitigated in a number of ways. On the asset side of an intermediary's balance sheet, it can maintain ample or 100 percent reserves and high-quality loan and debt assets. Depositors, like other providers of funding, can monitor asset quality, and the fragility induced by run risk may motivate depositors to do so. In historical practice, a number of mechanisms, such as deposits contractually permitting temporary or limited **suspension of convertibility** into cash or access to jointly held reserves at clearing houses, have been developed. Ample equity funding can inhibit runs by assuring depositors that the bank is viable. Regulatory measures have included deposit insurance and the lender of last resort function of central banks.[2]

Market Episode: Banks' commercial paper during the global financial crisis

Commercial paper is an important source of short-term financing for banks though its share in US bank funding has declined since the global financial crisis. It enables banks to diversify short-term funding away from deposits at the often low cost of highly rated short-term paper. Banks trade off the lower funding costs of the shortest-term commercial paper against the lower funding liquidity risk of longer-term paper.

Figure 15.2 chronicles the interaction of bank issuers and lenders in the US commercial paper market during the global financial and European debt crises. In 2007, as stress mounted in markets, commercial banks became increasingly anxious about rollover risk. Accepting the somewhat higher cost, they began to term out their paper issuance, roughly doubling the share with maturities greater than two weeks. This came to an abrupt halt when the crisis broke out and lenders would no longer extend credit with maturities beyond a few days. Banks were then forced to take greater funding liquidity risk and the longer-term share dropped.

---

[1] Deborah Lohse, "How General American got fancy in investing, lost its independence," *Wall Street Journal*, Sept. 3, 1999, https://www.wsj.com/articles/SB936310659442544935. See also Foley-Fisher et al. (2015).

[2] See Chapter 18.

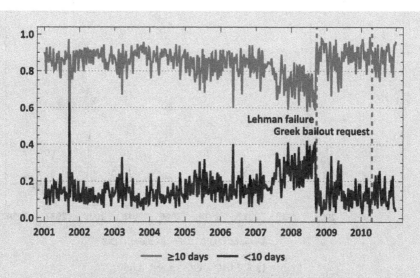

Figure 15.2 AA financial commercial paper 2006–2010

Shares of amount issued of AA financial commercial paper with original maturities of 1–9 days, and maturities of 10 days or more, weekly, 11Jan2006 to 29Dec2010. *Source*: Federal Reserve Board, available at www.federalreserve.gov/releases/cp/.

Solvency and liquidity are conjoined causes of bank failure and difficult to distinguish. If problems arise, such as unanticipated loan credit problems or a decline in the value of banks' securities holdings, depositors may fear insolvency and flee highly leveraged banks. It may not then be possible to sell assets quickly except at a loss. But banks with high capital funding don't typically experience liquidity problems apart from extreme market stress episodes.

Until the recent decline in the volume of interbank lending and the phasing out of LIBOR, the spread between LIBOR and OIS rates—the LOIS spread—had been an important indicator of concerns about solvency of banks during periods of financial stress.[3] To smooth out fluctuations in their own cash balances, banks borrow and lend reserve balances held at central banks in the short-term interbank lending market. Term interbank rates reflect banks' wariness about lending to other banks for longer periods and contain credit and liquidity risk premiums as well as embedding expectations of the path of overnight rates. OIS rates in contrast are influenced primarily by rate expectations rather than risk premiums because the instrument does not involve payment of principal at initiation and have lower credit risk.

The LOIS spread rises sharply in a crisis because banks are eager to term out their funding, but other banks are reluctant to extend credit. Figure 15.3 illustrates the extraordinarily rapid widening of LOIS spreads during the global financial crisis. Less dramatic but still pronounced widening can be seen at other times of significant stress, such as the 2011 US debt ceiling crisis, Covid, and the 2023 banking turmoil. The suddenness of the widening is also evidence against the view that depositors, including other banks, are effective at monitoring bank solvency.[4]

---

[3] See Chapters 6 and 12.
[4] See Chapter 12.

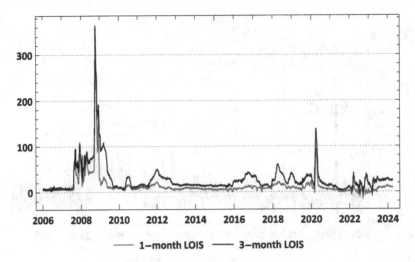

Figure 15.3 LIBOR-OIS spread 2006–2024

1-month and 3-month USD BBA LIBOR minus OIS of like maturity, basis points, daily, 05Jan2006 to 28Mar2024. *Source*: Bloomberg.

The interbank market has become attenuated since 2008, and LOIS has lost relevance with the transition from LIBOR to secured rates as benchmarks. Other unsecured market rates that can be compared to term OIS to discern bank credit risk fears include banks' commercial paper and term CD rates.

Regulators have been unwelcoming of the introduction of new credit risk-sensitive money market benchmarks based on unsecured rates that have been developed by some data providers and exchange operators, citing their low turnover volume and the propensity for these markets to shrivel during crises. SOFR and other nearly risk-free rates are the only benchmarks that can be relied on not to attract negative regulatory scrutiny, compounding the effect of the decline in fed funds trading volume in limiting banks' and other market participants' ability to contract privately to hedge unsecured funding rate risk.

Fire sales and **margin spirals** lie at the intersection of market and funding liquidity. In a fire sale, a seller is obliged to sell assets at a "wrong" low price, measured by how quickly and how far the price has dropped below estimates of fair value. Fire sales are typically triggered by the inability of market participants to roll over the short-term debt funding their portfolios, or by collateral calls that cannot be met immediately using liquid assets, forcing an unwinding of positions. Some market participants may sell higher credit-quality, information-insensitive securities and at least initially avoid selling those more susceptible to suspicion of adverse selection. If some intermediaries still need to raise cash as stocks of more liquid securities are exhausted, less liquid securities are offered, accelerating the effect on prices.

Wrong-way risk can exacerbate fire sales. A prime broker's counterparty exposure to a hedge fund customer and its leverage increase when the hedge fund suffers losses. The prime broker also becomes an additional source of risk to its other counterparties, transmitting selling pressure through the market.

Rehypothecation chains can act as a fire sale mechanism during financial stress. Prime brokers facing liquidity pressures may reduce collateralized securities lending, say, to hedge funds. But it would lose access to rehypothecated collateral it has used to fund that lending. A hedge fund, if it can find an alternative, might choose to reduce borrowing from a troubled prime broker, depriving it of collateral it can rehypothecate.

The hedging response to price changes, for example in option trading, can have a large short-term effect on asset prices. In the so-called Volmageddon episode of February 5, 2018, several exchange-traded products (ETPs) that had taken short positions in CBOE Volatility Index (VIX) futures were forced to cover by buying long VIX exposures, leading to a doubling in the VIX and the collapse of several of the ETPs.[5]

Liquidity contraction often coincides with impairment of market functioning and shrinking markets, as measured by volumes, the depth of order books, or bid-ask spreads. Market makers become less willing or unable to provide liquidity and inventory assets. Markets clear only with wider swings in transacted prices or fail to clear at all. Spreads and basis spreads between interest rate swaps and Treasury securities with similar maturities that are routinely kept narrow by near-arbitrage trades widen.

15.3   Causes of Financial Crises

Economists have studied **business cycles**—the phenomenon of boom and bust—for centuries. The term "cycle" itself has been controversial because it conveys a sense of inevitability and implies they are inherent in a market economy possessing a financial sector. Inevitable or not, mechanisms exist in the economic and financial system that generate **financial imbalances** with lasting effects, primarily monetary factors, low interest rates, and the behavior of exchange rates for smaller countries. Crises aren't evenly distributed across countries, and politically driven governance and regulatory environments also play a role.

15.3.1   Interest Rates, Volatility, and Financial Imbalances

Though hard to verify empirically, interest rates have likely been lower than their natural or equilibrium level for much of the so-called Great Moderation period. Expansive monetary policy operates through financial channels and can induce imbalances rather than inflation. Monetary and credit expansion and low interest rates increase the values of longer-term investments, amplifying returns, and permit governments and private entities to borrow extensively. Business and household debt, particularly reliant on short-term leverage, and fiscal and balance of payments deficits rise. Low rates increase risk-shifting from owners to lenders. Companies that couldn't compete in a higher-return environment can emerge and survive. These path dependency effects are at odds with pure long-run neutrality of money.

The mechanisms are **procyclical**, reinforcing expansions and contractions once initiated. Indicators of financial imbalances include buoyant asset prices, a decline in risk premiums, greater risk-taking, and more optimistic expectations. Evidence that risk premiums are low include tight credit spreads, low implied and realized volatility, rising option trading volumes, and unwarranted confidence of market participants in the low probability of large losses. There may also be an international dimension, such as capital inflows.

Low interest rates change the mix of investments chosen by a range of actors, from households investing more in residential housing to institutional investors increasing allocations to lower-rated securities. They played a key role in the rapid rise in residential and commercial real estate investment before the global financial crisis and in the growth of alternative investments throughout. Imbalances are likely to surface during periods of stable prices and employment but then put an end to stability, a

---

[5] Augustin et al. (2021) describes the episode.

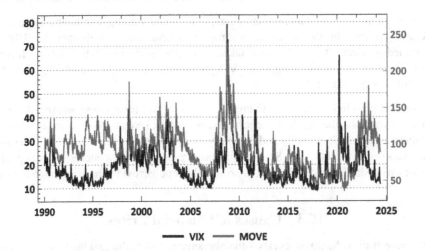

Figure 15.4 Equity- and swaption-implied volatility 1990–2024

CBOE Volatility Index (VIX): weighted average of annual implied volatilities of S&P 500 Index options with approximately 1 month to expiry and a range of strike prices; Merrill Lynch Option Volatility Estimate (MOVE) Index: index of annual implied normal volatilities of at-the-money over-the-counter options with approximately 1 month to expiry on 2- to 30-year US Treasury notes and bonds; weekly, 05Jan1990 to 17May2024. *Source*: Bloomberg.

pattern called the **financial cycle** to distinguish it from the business cycle reflected in macroeconomic variables. When interest rates return closer to their natural level, the effects of these investments don't disappear but require painful and costly reallocation.

The **paradox of volatility** is that volatility is often very low when risk-taking is high. Unusually low volatility can therefore, present a warning signal rather than a sign of calm. Implied volatility reflects the state of expectations and risk preferences. Estimates of realized volatility can be taken as a rough measure of expected volatility.[6] Both have been persistently low for long intervals in recent decades and particularly before the global financial crisis, reflecting the impact of low interest rates, but interrupted by brief episodes of suddenly heightened risk aversion. Figure 15.4 displays the VIX and Merrill Lynch Option Volatility Estimate (MOVE), a widely used index of US fixed-income volatility.

The **variance risk premium** is the difference between implied and realized volatility, and a measure of the reward to supplying protection against volatility (Figure 15.5). It tends to rise when implied and realized volatility are very low and protection against asset price changes is cheap and desirable.[7] The variance risk premium has been lower since the global financial crisis, falling from an average of about 4.4 percent from January 1990 to the onset of the crisis in February 2007, to about 3.3 percent since May 2009. The decline reflects unprecedentedly low rates after the crisis and regular confirmation that implicit public guarantees of private risk-taking will be made good.

Low volatility encourage risk-taking and credit extension and contributes to building financial imbalances. Once a crisis begins, intermediaries hasten to reduce leverage. For example, hedge funds take greater risk when markets are calm. Hedge fund leverage has a negative correlation with the volatility of fund returns but a positive correlation with asset values.[8] This pattern is related to the volatility

---

[6] See Chapter 6.

[7] Occasional sharp negative divergences also occur when realized volatility abruptly rises. Implied volatility spikes even higher, indicating heightened risk aversion but needs a few days to catch up.

[8] See Ang et al. (2011).

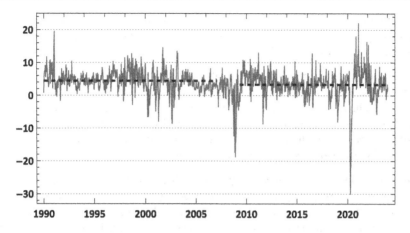

Figure 15.5 Implied and realized volatility 1990–2024

Difference between CBOE Volatility Index (VIX) and estimated realized volatility (EWMA with decay factor $\lambda = 0.94$), in percent at an annual rate, weekly, 03Jan1990 to 10Jan2024. Dashed horizontal grid lines represent pre- and post-crisis mean volatility risk premium estimates. *Data source*: Bloomberg.

asymmetry in asset return behavior (see Chapter 4). A decline in equity prices is associated with a sharp initial rise in already elevated leverage, requiring higher expected future returns and validating lower asset prices.

Financial imbalances may lead to **financial repression**, policy measures through which the government lowers interest rates or diverts investment patterns so as to lower its own cost of borrowing or reduce its debt burden. Federal Reserve policy during and after World War II of capping interest rates and the regulatory treatment until the global financial crisis of some highly indebted European countries' government debt as default-risk free are forms of financial repression. More recently, large-scale central bank purchases of government securities aimed at lowering longer-term interest rates substitute lower-cost reserve funding for bond funding of government spending. US money market funds are large investors in US short-term government debt and in Federal Reserve liabilities. The provision of implicit guarantees to US money funds against runs and lighter regulation of those investing in government rather than privately issued debt also supports a source of government financing.

15.3.2   Long-Term Liabilities and Interest Rates

Institutional investors in many countries, with a large volume of assets under management, face fixed long-term liabilities. These include defined benefit pension funds (or "schemes" in the United Kingdom) and insurance companies, which write long-term life and property-casualty policies and issue annuities, claims that pay specified sums during the lifetime of the beneficiary. Pension liabilities and annuities create payment obligations to policy owners or beneficiaries extending far into the future. Policy premiums and retirement contributions are invested to pay distant future claims.

Insurance and defined benefit plan liabilities are contingent, but their present values can be calculated with considerable confidence using actuarial projections and applying a discount factor. The fixed liabilities define a solvency threshold, with a shortfall potentially leading to inability to pay benefits or claims. Insurance companies are exposed to increases in the numbers of claims or in life expectancy relative to long-term investment returns on policy revenues. A defined benefit plan's ability to pay promised benefits and avoid becoming **underfunded** depends on the returns on accumulated invested funds and on inflows from current employees and sponsors. Both bear the demographic or longevity risk of lengthening expected lifespans and years of service, inflation risk if claims or benefits are indexed, and portfolio investment risk.

As interest rates fell over several decades through 2020, pension funds' and many insurance portfolios' liabilities increased. Low interest rates also increased their duration, amplifying the impact on the liabilities' present value of higher estimated claims or benefits and of further changes in interest rates. Underfunding of pension plans and underpricing of insurance lines relative to future claims are forms of insolvency: though not leading to immediate cash shortfalls, they lead over the longer term to inability to meet pension commitments or claims.

The viability of underfunded defined benefit plans has become a public policy issue. Many private-sector plans have been acquired by insurance companies through **pension risk transfers**, in which an insurance company takes on the plan liabilities and a portfolio of assets and manages them in a separate account, assuming the risks. The process has advanced further in the United States than in the United Kingdom, which is estimated to have on the order of £2 trillion of corporate obligations.

US state and local government defined benefit pension plans are substantially underfunded. The underfunding is estimated at between 25 and 50 percent of liabilities, varying with assumed discount rates and, to a lesser extent, actuarial projections. The estimates in Figure 15.6 show a tug-of-war between increases in pension claims and accumulated returns and fluctuations in the value of liabilities with interest rates and other variables.

15.3.3   Reaching for Yield

Intermediaries and investment managers respond to low interest rates, spread compression, curve flattening, and a low-return environment by seeking additional risk, **reaching** or **searching for yield**. First noted during the Great Moderation, it includes allocation shifts to riskier securities, alternative investments, derivatives strategies, and additional leverage. The bias is toward strategies with lower volatility day-to-day but higher probabilities of extremely adverse outcomes.

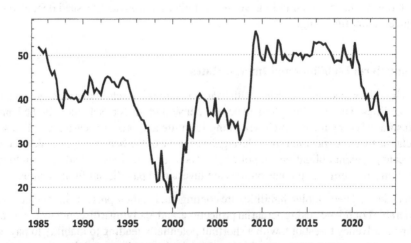

Figure 15.6 Public pension plan underfunding 1975–2023

Ratio of the gap between defined benefit pension plan entitlements (liabilities) and assets to entitlements, in percent, quarterly, Q1 1975 through Q4 2023. *Source*: Federal Reserve Board, Financial Accounts of the United States (Z.1), Table L.120.b, lines 16 and 18.

However, riskier investments increase the dispersion of possible outcomes and the probability of failing to meet required returns.

Insurance companies and defined benefit pension funds are under particular pressure to reach for yield to meet plan obligations or policy claims. Risk taking may also be constrained by regulation, leading institutional investors to engage in higher risk within statutory and regulatory categories. Imposing higher capital requirements on insurance company investments in equity may reduce equity investment in favor of asset types that are not traditionally a large component of institutional portfolios. Managers may extend the duration of their portfolios, use derivatives-based embedded leverage, or invest in alternatives and whole loans.

The increased duration of institutional investors' portfolios contributed to a reversal of the normal relationship between swap and Treasury rates. Swap par rates should be be somewhat higher than Treasury yields with the same maturity to compensate for exposure to counterparty and liquidity risks. Swaps indexed to LIBOR also bear the large-bank credit risk of interbank loans, somewhat diminished in recent years by clearing mandates. Treasurys, in contrast, can be expected to have particularly low rates due to their low risk and high liquidity.

In the past, swap spreads have typically been positive and occasionally quite wide. During a brief period from 1998 to 2001 of US budget surpluses, 30-year bond issuance was suspended, adding to Treasury scarcity. Since the global financial crisis, however, swap rates have fallen closer to or even below Treasury yields, as seen in Figure 15.7. Treasury issuance has increased with federal deficits although much of it in bills rather than notes and bonds. Institutional investors, a large constituent of the market, hedge duration risk in part by receiving fixed on swaps. As duration has increased with low rates and demographic change, the demand to receive fixed in swaps has grown, lowering par rates. Diminished Treasury market liquidity and reduced dealer capacity to hold longer-term securities also play a role.[9]

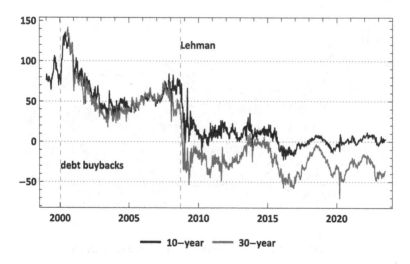

Figure 15.7 Swap spreads 1999–2023

Spread of plain-vanilla interest rate swaps over yield of Treasury of like maturity, basis points, daily, 06Jan1999 to 28Jun2023. *Data source*: Bloomberg.

---

[9] See Chapter 19.

Reaching for yield behaviors include investing in lower credit-quality bonds or seeking out higher-yielding securities with a given credit rating to take advantage of variations in credit quality that are recognized by the market but treated as equivalent under investment mandates or regulation. Institutional investors have also been drawn to smart beta investment strategies, which deviate from the market-value weighted portfolio in a rules-based fashion based on identified risk factors, liquid alternatives, and ETFs that employ high leverage.

The phenomenon has led to the development of new types of securities and investment vehicles, developed in part to accommodate institutional investors facing constraints on risk taking. Among these are CLOs and CDOs and CLO collateral with unusual non-price features. **Cov-lite** loans lack covenants typically present in high-yield loans that limit additional borrowing by the obligor and accounted for 90 percent of overall leveraged loan issuance by 2021. CLOs are very long-lived securities and permit institutional investors to lengthen the duration of portfolios. These trends are also related to ratings inflation and to efforts to increase the size of senior tranches of securitizations through less-conservative assessments of default and default correlation risks.

Figure 15.8 displays the credit risk allocation of US property-casualty insurance companies. These firms have kept approximately the same allocation to investment-grade bonds but, within that, have shifted to lower rated bonds. The allocation to AAA-rated bonds has fallen from about two-thirds to 15 percent. Most of the reallocation is to AA bonds and to the lowest-rated investment-grade bonds. The initial sharp drop in 2008–2009 is due primarily to downgrades of existing bonds early in the global financial crisis and some of the subsequent decrease to the general fall in the volume and availability of the highest rated bonds. With increasing reliance on repo, FHLB advances, and other short-term funding, the turn to riskier assets with lower market liquidity also increases the insurers' funding liquidity risk.[10]

Public defined benefit plans have also increased asset risk. Some alternative asset allocations now exceed one-third and are related to higher leverage. Private equity investment commitments not yet

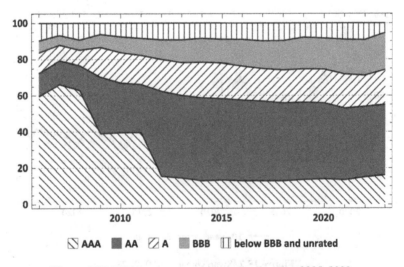

Figure 15.8 US insurance company credit allocation 2005–2022

Credit rating shares (percent of par) of fixed-income investments of US property-casualty insurance companies, annual. *Source*: New England Asset Management.

---

[10] See   https://www.spglobal.com/marketintelligence/en/news-insights/latest-news-headlines/covenant-lite-deals-exceed-90-of-leveraged-loan-issuance-setting-new-high-66935148 and Board of Governors of the Federal Reserve System (2023b), p. 57f. The increased risk taking is similar to that of AIG's life insurance subsidiaries before the crisis Peirce (2014).

subjected to cash calls can be used as margin for stock futures positions. These leveraged exposures to conventional equity markets are treated as "rebalancing." While it is disputable whether this has resulted in higher returns for the pension funds over time, once fees are accounted for, has certainly led to occasional large losses.

US state and local defined benefit plans have also understated the degree of underfunding by over-estimating discount rates and thus, understating the liabilities. As of June 2023, public plans used an average 6.88 percent assumed rate of return as a discount factor compared to the 8.1 percent typical in 2001. Both discount factors were well above measures of the risk-free rate, which would be arguably more appropriate for an actuarially near-certain public-sector liability. A lower underfunding estimate creates leeway for officials to offer higher benefits to public employees in exchange for political support.

Market Episode: The September 2022 UK gilt sell-off

In the United Kingdom, **liability-driven investing** (LDI) is a form of reaching for yield via leveraged exposures. Many private-sector UK defined benefit plans employed LDI strategies creating highly leveraged long-duration, fixed-income positions, in the form of UK gilts financed through repo, and by receiving fixed on swaps.

A plan could, for example, receive fixed on interest rate swaps, pledging part of its assets as collateral with its counterparty. If interest rates fell, its liabilities would grow, but the swap NPV would increase in its favor by a like amount. Alternatively, the plan could use a repo transaction to gain a long exposure to UK gilts. It would not need to use all its assets to gain sufficient exposure to hedge its pension liabilities, but it also creates a short-term vulnerability to margin and collateral calls. With the liabilities hedged, the plan can then use the unpledged bulk of its assets to earn additional return. Some of the LDI strategies were implemented through separate pooled funds serving a number of plans.

On September 23, 2023, following the presentation of a so-called "mini-Budget" that reduced taxes but not government spending and openly anticipated higher future budget deficits, gilt yields rose sharply. This triggered margin calls on repo and swap positions, forcing pension funds and LDI funds to raise cash or unwind positions. The liquidity buffers they could draw on were insufficient or required more time, so funds were forced to sell the gilts that served as collateral for the repo borrowing that financed them or to sell gilts in their portfolios to meet margin calls on interest rate swaps. The selling was on a scale the gilt market was unable to handle quickly. The general impairment of market functioning since the crisis and the post-crisis regulatory changes likely also played a role. Pooled LDI funds came under particular selling pressure because participating plans had weak incentives to provide capital infusions that would benefit all participants.

Gilt yields rose by a record amount over three trading days; the event was a far outlier from a fixed-income risk management standpoint. The Bank of England, which had been raising short-term rates and reducing the size of its balance sheet, introduced a temporary program on September 28 to buy gilts, stabilize the market, and avert pension fund insolvencies.

Even following the unfortunate UK defined benefit plan experience with LDI, US plans have continued to increase leverage strategies.[11] Underfunding has led some funds into investments they

---

[11] Josephine Cumbo, Sun Yu, and Antoine Gara, "US pension funds worth $1.5tn add risk through leverage," *Financial Times*, Jan. 20, 2024, https://www.ft.com/content/623b67f9-090c-457f-a327-dc9f767e327a.

do not fully understand, such as the Allianz Global Investors Structured Alpha strategies disaster (Chapter 7).

15.4   International Financial Imbalances

15.4.1   Rising International Trade and Global Debt

Over the past half century, a large increase in international transactions, including international trade in goods and services (Figure 15.9), has accompanied income growth and the removal of tariffs and other protectionist measures. The integration of labor, service and product markets, and increased international specialization, often summarized as "globalization," establishes production processes or supply chains in which products are created in many stages with inputs in multiple locations.

There has also been a large increase in international financial transactions, apart from trade, in which banks and other residents of one country lend in various currencies to obligors domiciled in another, and the integration of many regions into international financial markets. The increase in cross-border banking activity includes the establishment of bank branches and subsidiaries in other countries.

International transactions are recorded in the **balance of payments**. The **current account balance** is a broad measure of a region's balance of trade and of income received from and paid to the rest of the world. Its net investment flows—acquisition or diminution of the stock of financial assets—are in the **financial account**. The two, apart from statistical discrepancies, offset one another. Regions "pay" for a trade deficit—a surplus of goods and services—by incurring liabilities through capital outflows (or, in the opposite case, acquire foreign assets).

Gross capital flows measure the cross-border acquisition of assets and liabilities. They include changes in **official foreign exchange reserves** and **foreign direct investment**, in which residents of one jurisdiction acquire long-term equity stakes in nonresident firms. Gross flows are often large and dissociated from trade and net flows—large borrowers may also be large lenders—but have a large impact on financial conditions.

Net foreign assets are a measure of international indebtedness and ownership of domestic assets by nonresidents. Cumulative current and financial account balances drive a region's **net international**

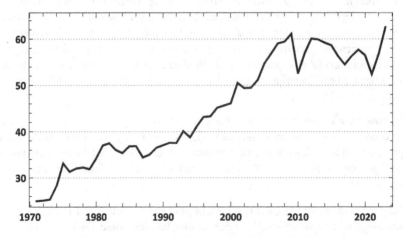

Figure 15.9 World trade relative to GDP 1970–2021

Sum of exports and imports of goods and services as a share of gross domestic product, annual. *Source*: World Bank [NE.TRD.GNFS.ZS].

investment position (NIIP) after valuation changes are also taken into account. Current account surpluses—positive net saving—correspond to increases in NIIP. Valuation changes, due to asset price and exchange rate fluctuations, can be large relative to the current account and even offset it.

Many countries have large and persistent current account surpluses or deficits. The patterns have changed widely over time. During the Bretton Woods era, initial US surpluses were followed by deficits. Since the Great Moderation of the early 1980s, advanced East Asian regions, northern Europe, and oil exporters have had persistent surpluses; the United States and many developing or middle-income countries have had persistent deficits.

Deficit regions typically experience rising foreign debt and a depreciating currency or devaluation pressure.[12] Surplus regions experience rising holdings of foreign assets, including foreign exchange reserves and an appreciating currency. External debt or surpluses create pressure for **external adjustment**, offsetting contractionary or expansionary monetary and fiscal policies.

The adjustments of deficit regions are generally more painful because they must devalue or deflate, so they try to build precautionary reserves, also with contractionary effects. The pressure arises from the **impossible trinity**, or **trilemma**: a country cannot simultaneously maintain a fixed exchange rate, an autonomous monetary policy, and free movement of capital across its borders. A deficit country must accept (i) depreciation of its currency, making its goods and assets relatively cheaper, (ii) adopt a tighter monetary policy than warranted by local conditions to coax capital inflows, or (iii) impose capital controls.

Target zones are a policy in which monetary authorities attempt to limit exchange rate fluctuations by maintaining a formal or informal range. Some countries have opted to give up monetary independence entirely, adopting a **currency board** system, such as the Hong Kong Monetary Authority, in which there is no central bank. The currency board issues domestic currency at a fixed rate to an anchor currency and with 100 percent reserve backing. A country can adopt official or full **dollarization**, using the US dollar for accounts and transactions. In some countries, informal dollarization has taken hold in response to high inflation.

Market Episode: The Swiss franc-euro exchange rate 2011–2015

The exchange rate policy of the Swiss National Bank (SNB) and the evolution of the euro-Swiss franc (EUR-CHF) exchange rate from 2011 to 2015 illustrate the potential volatility of even advanced-economy exchange rates and the trilemma. From the beginning of the global financial crisis, the Swiss franc appreciated steadily against the euro. This was an unsurprising market development, as the Swiss franc, like the US dollar, has long been considered a safe-haven currency.

Franc appreciation accelerated dramatically as the crisis within the European Monetary Union deepened in 2011. On September 6, 2011, the SNB announced a type of target zone, a minimum exchange rate of CHF 1.20 per euro. The SNB stated that it was " … prepared to buy foreign currency in unlimited quantities" to enforce it.[13] In doing so, the SNB lost much of its

---

[12] According to the World Bank's *International Debt Report*, external debt of low- and middle-income countries was 26 percent of GDP in 2021, compared to 22 percent in 2010.

[13] See the SNB announcement at https://www.snb.ch/en/mmr/reference/pre_20110906/source/pre_20110906.en.pdf

ability to determine monetary policy because its management of its balance sheet would now depend on the volume of capital inflows at the minimum exchange rate.

With a monetary policy rate already set below zero, the policy led to a doubling of foreign exchange reserves, from CHF 257.5 billion at the end of 2011 to CHF 510.0 billion at the end of 2014. The SNB announced the abandonment of the minimum exchange rate policy on January 15, 2015. The timing was a surprise, and the exchange rate closed 20.7 percent stronger on the day of the announcement.

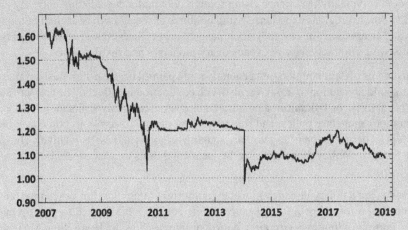

Figure 15.10 Euro-Swiss franc exchange rate 2015–2016

Daily, 30Sep2015 to 30Sep2016. The rate is expressed as the CHF price of €1. *Source*: Bloomberg.

15.4.2   The Role of the US Dollar

Since the emergence of the modern financial system, the pound sterling through the early 20th century and the dollar since have played a central role in international finance. This centrality has a number of dimensions: the volume of foreign exchange trading, the use of the dollar in international trade, its share in the portfolios of investors worldwide, and the influence of US monetary and liquidity conditions on those of the world.

The dollar is by far the most widely traded currency, with daily turnover of about $7.5 trillion. The Bank for International Settlements (BIS) finds that the dollar share has hovered at about 90 percent of total turnover since the 1989 inception of its survey of these largely OTC markets.[14] The dollar is also the most widely used trade invoice currency with about 50 percent of international trade denominated in USD. Trade between countries outside the United States and euro area is most often invoiced in dollars. The legal oil trade, for example, is almost exclusively invoiced in dollars.

US monetary and fiscal policies heavily influence world liquidity and credit. The Federal Reserve acts to an extent as the world's central bank, as its actions heavily influence the level of interest

---

[14] The most recent BIS Triennial Central Bank Survey was conducted in 2022. The market surveyed consists primarily of spot and forward foreign exchange transactions, and foreign exchange swaps.

rates of other currencies. The United States provides money market liquidity through short-term borrowing and lending and influences liquidity conditions worldwide.

US and dollar-denominated assets are in high demand by the rest of the world. US Treasurys are the preferred safe asset, and the United States is more generally the asset provider of choice. European banks, including state-affiliated banks, such as IKB Deutsche Industriebank AG, were major investors in US subprime securitizations before the global financial crisis. Official foreign exchange reserves and **sovereign wealth funds** had at one time been composed predominantly of dollar-denominated assets. Although central banks have been steadily increasing the share of euros and, more recently, emerging-market and middle-income countries' central banks have been increasing their reserve allocations to gold, the dollar remains around 60 percent of aggregate official reserves.

Dollar-denominated debt issuance of private and public non-US residents far exceeds US debt issuance in other currencies, apart from the euro. As seen in Figure 15.11, before the introduction of the euro, nearly all debt issued in foreign currency was dollar-denominated. Since 1999, euro issuance has grown and leveled off.

Borrowers in emerging markets face lower interest rates in dollars than in local currencies. In some, longer-term debt markets are undeveloped so longer-term funding is available only in dollars. Emerging and advanced market economies also issue in dollars to take advantage of the appetite for dollar assets and its dampening effect on rates. Figure 15.12 shows the growth of non-US borrowing in dollars.

The central role first of sterling and later of the dollar, and the confidence that assets denominated in sterling and the dollar are safe, are a result of the greater wealth of the issuing countries and of the high degree of development of financial markets in London and New York. The trust that market participants in all countries have had in the rule of law and its firm anchoring in constitutional governance in the United Kingdom and United States, compared to other countries, play an important part. Property rights and the adjudication of contracts are seen as more secure and less subject to arbitrary change.

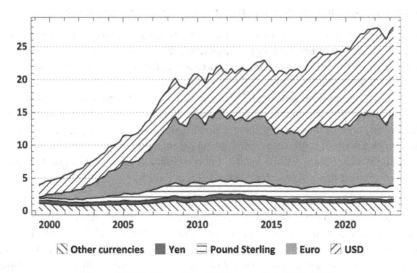

Figure 15.11 International debt securities 1999–2023

Outstanding stock of international debt securities issued outside the local market of the country where the borrower resides, by currency of denomination, trillions of dollars, quarterly, Q1 1999 to Q1 2023. *Source*: BIS debt securities statistics, Table C3.

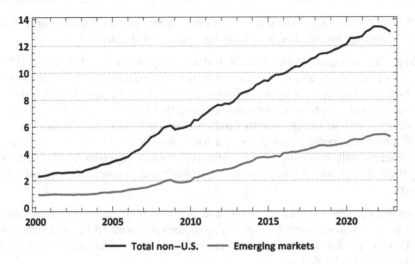

Figure 15.12 US dollar lending abroad 2000–2022

US dollar-denominated credit—bank loans and debt securities—to nonbank borrowers outside the United States, amounts outstanding, trillions of dollars, quarterly, Q1 2000 to Q3 2022. *Source*: BIS Global Liquidity Indicators, Table E2-USD.

The United States has run current account deficits from the 1960s and has been a net international debtor from the 1980s. Foreign-owned US assets (US liabilities), a range of public and private debt issues, and direct portfolio equity investment exceed US-owned foreign assets (foreign liabilities). The US negative NIIP is large, approximately 40 percent of US GDP.

Nonetheless, the United States has an annual net international investment income surplus of about 1 percent of GDP. This US investment income puzzle—the "dark matter"—arises from the fact that low-yield US Treasury debt, considered the premiere safe asset, constitutes a large fraction of US liabilities, but US-owned foreign assets are more heavily weighted to higher-return equity investment. The differential may to some extent be an artifact of US multinational tax arbitrage with income generated partly domestically reported in low-tax jurisdictions outside the United States.

The United States is an exception to many of the patterns seen in international finance and appears exempt from the external adjustment constraints one sees in other countries in a similar external position. Although running large and persistent current account deficits, the US dollar does not come under persistent depreciation pressure. The role of the dollar confers a direct benefit on the United States, referred to as **exorbitant privilege**.[15] During the Bretton Woods era of fixed exchange rates, which ended in the early 1970s, the privilege referred to the ability of the United States to run current account deficits and finance them in large part with dollar reserves of central banks. A country issuing fiat currency reaps a form of **seignorage**, purchasing assets with a costless liability. To the extent the US dollar is sought after by non-US residents, it corresponds to an import of goods in exchange for a perpetual zero-interest receivable, a loan extended indefinitely.

Exorbitant privilege has also been viewed from the financial account perspective as a consequence of the US role as "banker to the world," supplying liquid assets in the form of its own short-term liabilities and investing at long term in illiquid claims on foreign firms. As US investments in exchange for its flows of short-term liabilities have shifted toward higher-return foreign equity and foreign direct investment, the United States has come to be seen as "venture capitalist to the world."

---

[15] A 1965 coinage of then finance minister of France Valery Giscard d'Estaing.

The role of the US dollar in international finance is not inevitable or permanent but anchored in confidence in US financial, legal, and political institutions and policies. Its erosion could be prompted by sustained high levels of US government debt or inflation, perhaps in response to a financial crisis, or other US policies at odds with the dollar's role.

15.4.3   The Cross-Currency Basis

The importance of US dollar funding in the international financial system is reflected in the failure of covered interest rate parity to hold.[16] Differences at a point in time between money market rates and the forward foreign exchange premium they imply should, in frictionless markets, be closed by near-arbitrage. In practice, even taking account of the inevitable small discrepancies attributable to information and transactions costs, the arbitrage is not completed. The forward foreign exchange premium implies higher US rates than actually are prevailing in the money markets but non-U.S. borrowers lack full access to the lower rate.

As a simple illustration, imagine the current USD-EUR spot rate is $1.10, the 1-year forward is $1.1275, and the 1-year euro money market rate is 2 percent. The implied 1-year USD rate is then $\frac{1.1275}{1.10}1.02 - 1 = (1.025)(1.02) - 1$ or 4.55 percent. If the observed 1-year USD rate is only 4.25 percent, there is a basis of 30 basis points.

To arbitrage the basis away would require a large increase in banks' balance sheets. US-domiciled banks, including US and non-US banks, have better access to the depositor public in the United States. But even large non-US banks directly raising dollar funding via local branch offices in the United States do not have the US resident deposit funding base they'd need to support the global demand for USD funding. Large banks also face constraints, regulatory and those imposed by their owners and lenders, on balance sheet expansion that limit the arbitrage required to seamlessly keep departures from covered parity minimal.

In times of stress, the demand for dollar funding skyrockets, and reliance on forward foreign exchange markets to satisfy part of the demand grows as well, leading to a widening of the cross-currency basis even for major crosses against the dollar. In more recent years, it has rarely settled back toward zero. The basis and its fluctuations, for example, the sharp swings at the onset of the pandemic, also reflect impairment of market functioning and the expansion of Federal Reserve currency swaps with foreign central banks.[17]

In another aspect of exorbitant privilege, a negative basis boosts returns on US dollar-based investments in foreign-denominated assets and boosts dollar borrowing costs and lowers dollar returns for foreign-domiciled market participants. The basis makes US dollar funding more expensive for emerging-markets borrowers.

Figure 15.13 displays the USD-EUR cross-currency basis over the past two decades, based on spot (S_t) and three-month forward $\left(F_{t,\frac{1}{4}}\right)$ exchange rates (the USD price of €1), and 3-month Euribor $\left(r^*_{t,\frac{1}{4}}\right)$ and USD LIBOR rates $\left(r_{t,\frac{1}{4}}\right)$.[18] The basis is defined as the difference between a non-US bank's cost of borrowing USD for three months directly from another bank—USD LIBOR—and the cost of instead doing so by borrowing euros, purchasing dollars and committing to selling the dollars

---

[16] See Chapter 6.

[17] See Chapter 20.

[18] These conventions are being adapted to rely on SOFR and its non-US equivalent nearly risk-free rates in place of LIBOR.

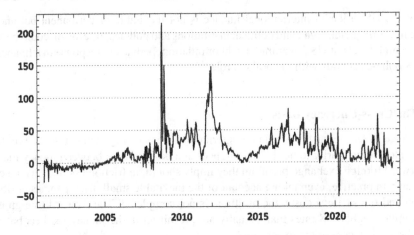

Figure 15.13 EUR-USD cross-currency basis 2001–2023

Spread in basis points between the annual rate for 3-month US dollar funding indirectly via foreign exchange (FX) swaps and directly via LIBOR, daily, 02Jan2001 to 20Mar2023. A *positive* spread indicates LIBOR funding is cheaper and corresponds to a *negative* cross-currency basis swap spread. *Data source*: Bloomberg.

forward for euros to repay the loan. To estimate the basis, we express the forward premium at an annual rate, compute the implied USD lending rate, and subtract the observed USD LIBOR rate:

$$\left(\frac{F_{t,\frac{1}{4}}}{S_t}\right)^4 \left(1 + r^*_{t,\frac{1}{4}}\right) - 1 - r_{t,\frac{1}{4}}.$$

15.4.4 International Financial Imbalances and Stability

International trade and financial markets can transmit or amplify financial shocks through balance of payments channels, valuation of foreign assets, amplification of banks' leveraging and deleveraging, and transmission of monetary policy. International financial flows are correlated with financial conditions. Increases in gross capital flows tend to coincide with growth in credit and leverage and with rising asset prices and risk appetite, indicators of an expansion that may be unsustainable and culminate in a crisis. International capital flows are procyclical; deficit countries borrow more readily and there is greater tolerance of currency mismatch by non-US intermediaries when financial conditions are loose.

US interest rates are important in driving world interest rates so, much of this variation is linked to US monetary and fiscal policies. The expansionary bias in US monetary policy leads to an expansionary bias in the international financial system via the role of the US dollar in global intermediation and a potential misalignment with local macroeconomic conditions (the **dollar cycle**).

Due to its unique role, the United States is partially insulated from changes in the dollar's value. Outside the United States, exchange-rate movements have conflicting effects. Dollar appreciation and associated high US interest rates increase a smaller country's net exports with expansionary macroeconomic and financial effects. But dollar appreciation also leads to financial weakening of domestic firms borrowing in dollars and the non-US banks lending to them. The flip side of the exorbitant privilege is the resulting **original sin**. For an emerging markets obligor with primarily non-dollar revenues, borrowing in dollars creates a currency mismatch and vulnerability to exchange rates that cannot be hedged easily or to a maturity mismatch if local borrowers choose instead to roll over short-term local currency debt.

Rapid depreciation of the local currency may not avert vulnerability to rising US rates but just put a sudden end to the expansion that occurred under accommodative US monetary policy. Markets may force adjustment: regions experiencing persistent current account deficits are vulnerable to **speculative attack** or to a **sudden stop** in capital inflows if their current account deficits are considered unsustainable. Countries with exchange rates pegged to the dollar, or adopting the dollar as a local currency entirely lose monetary independence unless they impose restrictions on capital flows.

Financial imbalances may thus, reduce the trilemma to a dilemma. Variations in smaller countries' interest rates and other determinants of credit conditions may be driven in large part by Federal Reserve policy. Exchange rate swings may be insufficient to compensate for changes in financial conditions and restore independence from the influence of global monetary conditions. The desire to avoid large capital inflows and outflows has led some smaller countries to adopt fixed exchange rates pegged to the dollar, or to **fear of floating**, informal avoidance of large exchange rate changes. Only capital controls—in principle because they are difficult to enforce—will then insulate a country from international transmission.

For this dilemma situation to prevail, there must also be a failure of uncovered interest rate parity. The discrepancy between money-market rates or the forward foreign exchange rate on the one hand and the exchange rate expected in the future on the other can persist for a long time.

The extent of these dislocations provides a good example of the risks of the carry trade (see Chapter 11). In contrast to the cross-currency basis, which presents an arbitrage opportunity that would be continuously eliminated in frictionless, perfectly informed markets, a trader wishing to exploit departures from uncovered interest parity has to take open positions in foreign exchange and money markets and hold them for a period. The gains arrive in the form of carry not entirely offset by exchange rate depreciation.

Example 15.1   Turkish lira carry trade

The ebb and flow of returns on the Turkish lira (TRY) carry trade illustrates the deviations of real-world exchange rate behavior from uncovered parity. It also tracks the efforts of the Central Bank of Turkey (CBRT) to manage domestic interest rates and the exchange rate with high inflation. We compute returns over time from a leveraged carry trade in which a short-term USD borrowing is deployed to buy the equivalent in TRY and deposit it at the 3-month local rate implied by the 3-month foreign exchange premium. For simplicity, we assume that the returns are swept out rather than accumulated and there are no financing constraints so that a negative equity position is met by investing more funds.

Turkey has experienced persistent and at times quite high inflation, and monetary policy has gone through several phases in coping with it while also trying to stabilize exchange rates and keep interest rates as low as feasible. In late February 2001, an attempted exchange rate peg failed, resulting in a roughly 50 percent devaluation within a few days. In the years following, the CBRT focused primarily on inflation, and interest rates were relatively high.

From about 2011, the emphasis shifted to an expansive monetary policy, implemented through a complex set of mechanisms by which the devaluation pressure on TRY resulting from rising inflation and low interest rates could be contained. The CBRT borrowed dollars from commercial banks rather than using central bank reserves, and the government encouraged deposits of domestic currency through guarantees of their value in dollars. This apparatus has become progressively more difficult to maintain in recent years. The volatility of interest rates and the exchange rate has increased, and larger gaps have opened between domestic deposit rates and those implied by foreign exchange swap prices.

We assume the carry trade is implemented through foreign exchange swaps rather than in local markets. To estimate the carry, we use spot and forward rates and the USD LIBOR rate to compute the time-t implied τ-year TRY lending rate as

$$r^*_{t,\tau} = \frac{1}{\tau}\left[\frac{S_t}{F_{t,\tau}}(1 + \tau r_{t,\tau}) - 1\right],$$

with spot (S_t) and forward ($F_{t,\tau}$) exchange rates expressed as the dollar price of TRY.[19] The 3-month swap-implied rate estimate was generally quite close to the domestic 3-month deposit rate until recent years in which Turkish authorities engaged in a concerted effort to keep domestic rates low while restraining exchange rate depreciation.

The carry, in percent at a quarterly rate, can be written as:

$$\frac{1}{4}\left(r^*_{t,\frac{1}{4}} - r_{t,\frac{1}{4}}\right) = \left(\frac{S_t}{F_{t,\frac{1}{4}}} - 1\right)\left(1 + \frac{1}{4}r_{t,\frac{1}{4}}\right).$$

The TRY amount invested is $\frac{1}{S_t}$ times the size of the trade in dollars. The P&L is the dollar value of the carry proceeds, valued at the quarter-end exchange rate. The total return is equal to the carry, valued at the period-end exchange rate:

$$\frac{S_{t+\frac{1}{4}}}{S_t}\left[1 + \frac{1}{4}\left(r^*_{t,\frac{1}{4}} - r_{t,\frac{1}{4}}\right) - 1\right] = \left(\frac{S_{t+\frac{1}{4}}}{F_{t,\frac{1}{4}}} - 1\right)\left(1 + \frac{1}{4}r_{t,\frac{1}{4}}\right).$$

For example, if the carry is 5 percent over the quarter, and the lira depreciates by 25 percent, the quarterly return in dollars is −16 percent. Should the lira appreciate by 4 percent, the return is 9.375 percent.

Figure 15.14 illustrates the returns to the TRY carry trade. The return is decomposed into two parts: the carry return if the exchange rate were unchanged over the quarter and the P&L stemming from the exchange rate change, which can be measured as the difference between the constant-exchange rate carry return and the total return to the trade.

There are some clear patterns over time in the carry returns. During the years in which domestic interest rates were successfully kept relatively low, the returns tended to be negative, with a generous carry more than offset by TRY depreciation. Overall, uncovered interest rate parity is clearly violated. The carry trade is often profitable but at very high risk.

---

[19] The market convention is the reciprocal, TRY per dollar.

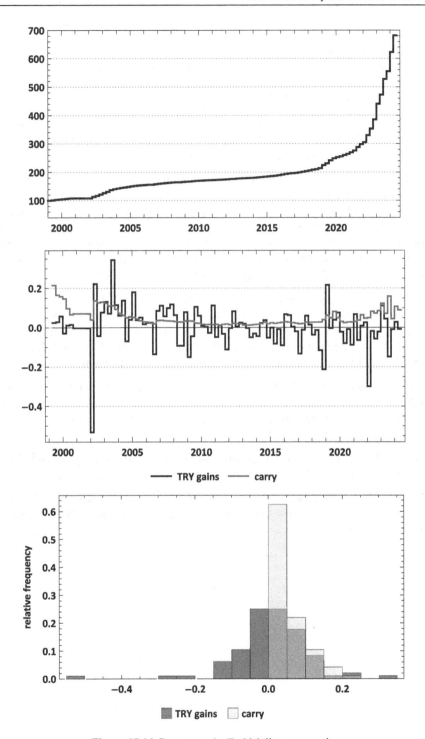

Figure 15.14 Returns to the Turkish lira carry trade

Upper panel: cumulative quarterly returns to the carry trade, per $100 invested. The center panel decomposes the return into the interest rate and exchange-rate fluctuation components, and the bottom panel shows the distribution of returns attributable to the two sources. Quarterly, 31Dec1998 to 30Jun2023. *Data source*: Bloomberg.

Further Reading

Brunnermeier and Reis (2023) is a survey of the study of financial crises and Reinhart and Rogoff (2009) is a history and typology. Frydman and Xu (2023) is a recent literature survey. Claessens et al. (2014) is a collection of survey articles on financial crises. Adrian and Shin (2010a) discuss patterns of leverage during financial crises.

The Diamond-Dybvig model, the baseline approach to understanding bank runs as liquidity events, was initially presented in Diamond and Dybvig (1983). Diamond (2007) is a nontechnical summary. Dowd (1992) provides a critical survey of the bank run literature.

Gorton and Metrick (2012) and Shleifer and Vishny (2011) discuss runs and fire sales in repo and other markets. See Kiyotaki and Moore (2002) on propogation of financial distress across firms. Foley-Fisher et al. (2015) analyze runs on short-term liabilities of insurers by institutional investors. Boyarchenko et al. (2018a) and Hanson et al. (2024) analyze negative swap spreads. Kruttli et al. (2022) discuss the mechanisms by which hedge fund leverage shrinks during financial stress periods. Schrimpf and Sushko (2019) discuss the difficulties raised for banks' funding liquidity risk management by exclusive reliance on nearly risk-free rates as benchmarks.

Rajan (2005) and White (2006) sounded early warnings regarding low interest rates, financial fragility and financial imbalances before the global financial crisis. Becker and Ivashina (2015) discuss reaching for yield and its regulatory incentives. Boon et al. (2018) attempt to empirically identify the impact of regulation on pension fund investment. Novy-Marx and Rauh (2009) and Giesecke and Rauh (2023) estimate the underfunding of US public pension funds.

Cohen et al. (2017) discuss the role of the US dollar in international financial markets. Gourinchas and Rey (2007) analyze the US international investment position. Yeager (1976) and Eichengreen (2019) provide historical introductions to the international financial system. Hertrich and Zimmermann (2017) describe the euro- Swiss franc exchange rate floor experience.

Eichengreen and Hausmann (1999) discuss original sin. Rey (2013 and 2016), and Obstfeld and Zhou (2022) describe the global dollar cycle and its effect on financial conditions.

Du et al. (2018) relate the magnitude of violations of covered interest rate parity to banks' and general funding liquidity liquidity conditions. Gürkaynak et al. (2023) and Setser (2023) discuss Turkey's economic policies.

Part IV: Monetary and Regulatory Policy

16

Overview of Financial Regulation

16.1 Structure of Financial Regulation

Though often represented as a product of design, regulation is governed largely by institutional rather than by functional considerations. Like all institutions, regulation is emergent, the outcome of a long historical evolution involving governments, private financial institutions, and myriad competing interests. Much of this history is shaped by responses to financial and other crises.

16.1.1 Financial Regulatory Authorities

There is a bewildering array of regulations and regulatory authorities, within and across regions. Banks, in particular, are regulated at different levels of government and by different regulatory agencies. Jurisdictions can be nations, or subnational or supranational. Financial regulatory bodies are responsible, within a jurisdiction, for:

- intermediary types, such as banks, insurance companies, securities dealers, investment advisers;
- markets or platforms, such as securities exchanges;
- activities and contract types, such as dispensing investment advice or derivatives.

The United States, where restrictions on the locations as well as on the activities of banks have been the historical norm, has unusually many relatively small, locally focused banks compared to most countries, in addition to larger regional and internationally active banks. A large US bank, broker-dealer, or insurance company bank is typically organized as a holding company, with many subsidiaries of different types, for example, a bank, a securities dealer, and an investment advisor in each of a number of jurisdictions. It is not unusual for such a firm to be regulated by scores or even hundreds of authorities, reflecting its geographical ambit and the scope of its intermediation activities. In Europe, banks have typically engaged in a wide range of activities, the **universal banking** model and, consequently, have simpler holding company and regulatory structures, but more complex internal organization of businesses.

A **dual-banking system** of state and national bank regulation has grown in the United States under the federal system of government. Each bank has a **primary regulator**. Federal regulation includes the **Office of the Comptroller of the Currency** (OCC), the primary regulator for national banks established by the **National Bank Act** (1863). Most US banks, however, are chartered at the state level.

The Federal Reserve, established in 1913, is the primary regulator for **bank** and **financial holding companies** (BHCs and FHCs), state-chartered member banks, and for US offices and branches of foreign banks, or **foreign banking organizations** (FBOs). Member banks of the Federal Reserve System have access to Fed lending facilities. The Fed also regulates **financial market utilities** (FMUs), a recent regulatory designation for payments, clearing, and settlement platforms operated by exchanges.

The **Federal Deposit Insurance Corporation** (FDIC), established in 1933, regulates national and state-chartered banks with insured deposits. It is also the primary regulator for the typically small state-chartered banks that aren't members of the Federal Reserve System. Each state also regulates banks it charters—in New York, for example, through the **New York State Department of Financial Services**—in addition to supervision by the FDIC or Fed.

US regulation classifies commercial banks as a type of **depository institution**. Two other types, non-profit **credit unions**, owned by their depositors and borrowers, and **savings institutions** are small, regional and focus on consumer loans and residential mortgages.

US regulation of nonbank intermediaries is also dispersed among a number of regulators. US stock and bond markets and mutual funds are regulated primarily at the national level by the **Securities and Exchange Commission** (SEC), established in 1934. The SEC also has oversight of broker-dealers and investment advisors. Derivatives exchanges are regulated by the **Commodities Futures Trading Commission** (CFTC), established in 1974. US insurance companies are regulated at the state level in the United States, informally coordinated through the **National Association of Insurance Commissioners** (NAIC), which may choose a lead regulator for an insurer active in several states.

Under a system of **self-regulation**, there are nongovernment advisory organizations with rulemaking power. Substantial regulatory responsibility resides with the **Financial Industry Regulatory Authority** (FINRA) overseeing US broker-dealers, the **Financial Accounting Standards Board** (FASB), and other private nonprofit organizations setting enforceable standards.

In the European Union, the division of responsibility between Europe-wide and national regulatory authorities mirrors in some ways the federal structure of US regulation. Under the **European System of Financial Supervision**, a **Single Supervisory Mechanism** (SSM) coordinates bank regulation across countries. The **European Banking Authority** (EBA) under the ECB, together with national regulators, carry out supervisory responsibilities. The **Markets in Financial Instruments Directive** (MiFID) II, now in a second post-crisis iteration, governs securities regulation in the EU.

International committees set standards for regulation in a number of areas, especially regulatory capital and liquidity standards. Apart from the EU system with its federal structure, international bodies have a purely advisory role. Legally binding statutory and regulatory implementation of their recommendations is carried out by federal or national authorities. International standard setting has been facilitated historically by the **Bank for International Settlements** (BIS), established in 1930 in Basel as part of international efforts to address international financial imbalances and conflicts after World War I. It provides banking services for central banks and hosts a number of international financial committees.

The **Group of Ten** (G10) was established in 1962 to help cope with the international imbalances that eventually brought the Bretton Woods system to an end. It includes finance ministers and central bank governors of 11 countries (Switzerland having joined in 1964). The G10 in 1974 established the **Basel Committee on Banking Supervision** (BCBS) or Basel Committee to set international bank regulatory standards. The **Financial Stability Board** (FSB), established in 2009 and also hosted by the BIS, sets standards focused on financial stability for banks and other firms. Two groups facilitate international coordination for securities and insurance regulators, the **International Organization of Securities Commissions** (IOSCO) and **International Association of Insurance Supervisors** (IAIS).

16.1.2   Law and Regulation

In a jurisdiction governed by the rule of law, regulation requires legal underpinning. In the United States, federal regulation is part of three levels of authorization for administrative law. Legislation underpins the entire regulatory system. Any regulation must be based on or called for by a law. Its promulgation must then follow a procedure, called "notice-and-comment" rulemaking, enshrined in the **Administrative Procedure Act** (APA) of 1946.

Under the APA, following legislation, a regulatory agency first develops a draft rule and publishes it as a **Notice of Proposed Rule in Guidance**. In many instances of US regulation, several regulatory bodies jointly formulate rules pertaining to banks they regulate. A public comment period, typically 60 days, follows. After review, a **Final Rule** is published in the **Federal Register** and incorporated in the **Code of Federal Regulations** (CFR). Federal banking regulations are published in Title 12: Banks and Banking of the CFR.

Administrative guidance documents are less formal, providing more detail on regulatory policies and how they will be enforced than is contained in laws and rules. One vehicle is the Federal Reserve's **Supervision and Regulation Letters**. An example illustrating the potentially large impact on banks' behavior is the *Interagency Guidance on Leveraged Lending* of March 21, 2013, making public the Fed's discouragement and supervisory scrutiny of leveraged loans, which may have been an inhibiting factor on banks' direct funding.[1] Even less defined is informal guidance conveyed through discussion and supervisory visits that shape banks' expectations of how regulations will be interpreted and enforced.

The discretion that regulatory bodies can exercise in implementing rules and retroactively proscribing activities presents legal and compliance risks to financial and nonfinancial firms. Apart from the additional discretion offered by guidance, regulatory agencies do not always adhere strictly to the notice-and-comment process, either by not fully carrying out the notice requirements or even keeping some regulatory criteria confidential. **Regulation by enforcement** has been applied by the SEC to newer financial innovations for which detailed rules do not yet exist and would require time to create, such as cryptocurrencies and crypto exchanges. It has also been applied by the CFPB in areas of consumer finance or on grounds for which rules are unclear or absent. In these cases, regulatory policy is established through the results of litigation.

16.2   Methods of Regulation

Regulation is implemented through a wide range of tools, some with long histories and others introduced following the global financial crisis:

Charters and **scope restrictions** on banks and other intermediaries authorize them to do business and set out permitted and prohibited activities and locations.
On-site supervision and **monitoring** of individual firms.
Minimum capital standards place limits on intermediaries' debt funding.
Liquidity standards require that intermediaries hold a minimum of cash and liquid assets.
Resolution mechanisms for failing financial firms differ from general corporate bankruptcy procedures.
Accounting and **disclosure standards** that differ in key respects from those of nonfinancial firms.
Regulatory stress tests to assess liquidity and capital adequacy in specified adverse scenarios.
Deposit insurance: government guarantees of the par value of deposits in the event of bank failure.
Macroprudential policies: rules intended to promote overall stability of financial system.

A bank **charter** is a licence to conduct banking business in a particular jurisdiction. Chartering is among the oldest forms of regulation; banks have always required authorization distinct from that

---

[1] See https://www.federalreserve.gov/supervisionreg/srletters/sr1303.htm.

of nonfinancial firms. Charters came into use in early modern Europe, each bank required to seek specific approval by a sovereign or legislature. **Free banking** or entry—more precisely, minimal charter requirements and lighter regulation—has historically been atypical but by no means rare. Among the many episodes are the Scottish banking system of the 18th and 19th centuries and the Suffolk system in early 19th-century New England. In the United States today, a national or state banking licence is required to operate a depository institution.

Scope restrictions have been less common in Europe and Canada than in the United States. In the United States, federal and many state restrictions dating back to the 19th century had made **unit banking**—banks with a single branch—the norm. The New Deal Banking Act of 1933 (Glass-Steagall) and **Regulation Q** precluded commercial banks from offering investment banking services and from paying interest on demand deposits. In Europe, universal banking—wider scope of activities and greater geographical diversification—has been the norm.

In the wake of the global financial crisis, there have been new or revived proposals for scope restrictions on banks. The Dodd-Frank Act of 2010 ordained the **Volcker Rule** prohibiting proprietary trading by commercial banks. It proved difficult to formulate because it's hard to distinguish customer from proprietary trades. **Ring-fencing** separates retail from investment banking within UK bank holding companies.

16.2.1   Bank Supervision

Regulation can never be complete; not every circumstance can be foreseen and pre- or proscribed. Supervision—monitoring to enforce compliance with regulations and more generally keep tabs on banks—is intended to fill this gap. It consists of ongoing monitoring, meetings with firms' senior management and in-depth on-site examinations and inspections. Larger banks may have supervisors permanently on-site. "Horizontal" supervision compares multiple firms in the same sector.

The FDIC issues confidential **CAMELS ratings**, assessing banks on a 1 through 5 scale on their capital funding adequacy, asset quality, management and internal controls, earnings, liquidity, and sensitivity to market risk. The Federal Reserve assigns **RFI** and **LFI ratings** to bank holding companies (BHCs) and Large Financial Institutions (LFIs) it supervises.

Supervision includes reporting requirements by intermediaries on their financial condition and activities. In the United States, quarterly Call Reports contain detailed financial statements. Some data from these reports are made available to the public, and summary and statistical data is published in regular reports by regulatory agencies.[2]

US supervisors can respond with a range of actions to intermediaries' activities or policies they deem problematic. Supervisory actions that are not made public include (in increasing order of seriousness), **Matters Requiring Attention** (MRAs), **Matters Requiring Immediate Attention** (MRIAs), and **Memoranda of Understanding** (MOUs). Silicon Valley Bank(SVB), for example, was informed during its period of rapid growth between 2020 and 2022 of a steady stream of MRAs and MRIAs and had 31 still outstanding at the time it failed.[3] Publicly disclosed and more severe actions include formal agreements requiring specific responses if less-formal supervisory actions don't suffice. Agencies can also issue **cease and desist orders** for potential violations of law.

---

[2] Examples in this book include the data presented in Figures 12.2 and 19.1.

[3] These are detailed in the Federal Reserve report [Board of Governors of the Federal Reserve System (2023a)] on its supervision of SVB.

16.2.2   Regulatory Developments of Recent Decades

US bank regulation has undergone many changes in recent decades, prompted initially by technical and financial innovation and later in response to a sequence of crises. US regulatory constraints on bank branching, investment banking, and controls on deposit interest rates became unsustainable by the 1970s. Deposit rate ceilings and inflation accelerated disintermediation, manifested in the introduction and rapid growth of money market funds. Banks' limited geographical and business diversification made them more fragile.

Changes in regulation, collectively mischaracterized as "deregulation," reshaped the financial sector. The **Monetary Control, Garn-St. Germain,** and **Riegle-Neal Acts** (1980, 1982, and 1994) began removing some restrictions. The **Gramm-Leach-Bliley Act** of 1999 permitted financial conglomerates to combine investment and commercial banking but not to own nonfinancial companies. It introduced the FHC registration and broadened the BHC scope to include them. Larger US-domiciled banks are better situated to take advantage of the broader scope of permitted activities and are now generally organized as BHCs.

The **Federal Deposit Insurance Corporation Improvement Act** (FDICIA) of 1991 introduced the **Prompt Corrective Actions** (PCA) framework of FDIC supervision. It sought to put an end to the regulatory forbearance that was thought to have contributed to the severity of the savings and loan (S&L) crisis. By instructing regulators to intervene quickly upon a bank's failure to meet capital standards, it would reduce the likelihood of the FDIC seeing itself obliged to cover deposits at failed banks to avoid panic. The efficacy of this change was tested in subsequent crises, including the March 2023 episode in which all deposits at SVB, insured and uninsured, were covered (see Chapter 20).

Other regulatory developments include changes to securities market rules that made private markets larger and more liquid; at the same time, other rules, such as **Sarbanes-Oxley Act** (2002) added detailed rules on internal controls and disclosures for firms traded in public markets. **Rule 2a7** permitted MMMFs to maintain a par NAV, as long as fluctuations in its investments remain within a range. Exemptions from the automatic stay in bankruptcy and **close-out netting** appeared to reduce counterparty risk. Close-out netting prevents a situation in which the counterparties of a defaulting counterparty must make good on swaps in which the defaulting counterparty had a positive NPV, while lining up for recovery on those in which it had a negative NPV.

The global financial crisis brought a change in direction. The emphasis was on identifying and remedying vulnerabilities in the financial system that were thought to have been neglected. The most important new legislation was the **Dodd-Frank Wall Street Reform and Consumer Protection Act** of 2010, which initiated changes in most areas of financial regulation, removing language requiring ratings and the creation of a **Consumer Financial Protection Bureau** (CFPB). The CFPB has an unusual structure, administratively housed within and financed by the Federal Reserve System but entirely independent of it.

Some credit rating agencies are SEC-recognized **Nationally Recognized Statistical Rating Organizations** (NRSROs), authorized to issue ratings that can be used to satisfy certain regulatory requirements. Since 1936, banks' bond holdings have been restricted to investment-grade rated securities, and since 1975, ratings have helped determine banks' and securities firms' capital requirements. The issuer-pays model is said to induce conflicts of interest with investors, particularly fraught with respect to securitization, and has been a focus of controversy and regulatory changes since the global financial crisis. Under Dodd-Frank, regulatory reliance on ratings has been reduced, and investors have been encouraged to rely more on credit risk models, an effort at odds with more recent efforts to reduce the role of credit and market risk modeling in bank capital regulation.[4]

Regulation of trading and market structure has also evolved. Among the earlier regulatory reforms, the SEC abolished fixed stock trading commissions on May 1, 1975. The SEC's 2005 **Regulation NMS** (Reg NMS) is a still-evolving complex of rules governing the fragmented US stock trading system. Its Trade-Through Rule mandates that customer orders be filled at the best available price among exchanges and platforms subject to it. It mandates the display and reporting of bid, ask, and executed prices, which have a large impact on market structure, including the role of dark pools or ATS. **Clearing mandates** for derivatives under Dodd-Frank transform OTC swaps from contracts between banks into contracts between banks and **central counterparties** (CCPs) or clearing platforms, a type of FMU.

Supervision and detailed reporting are intended to alert public authorities to inadequacies or flaws in the regulatory system. In practice, crises such as the March 2023 bank panic and the SVB failure appear to be the way regulators and the public learn of problems in the banking system.

16.3   Purposes and Efficacy of Financial Regulation

16.3.1   Rationale of Financial Regulation

The stated public policy goals of financial regulation fall broadly into four categories:

Financial stability: Regulation aims to protect the safety and soundness of individual intermediaries, make financial institution failures less frequent, and protect against wider consequences when they occur, such as failure of other banks, dealers, or investment funds.

Monetary policy: Historically, banks and dealers in government bond, commercial paper, and in recent decades, money market funds have been at the core of monetary policy implementation. Central banks have a keen interest in the reliability and predictability of banks responsiveness to central bank actions and their transmission to the wider financial system.

Consumer and investor protection: Regulation seeks to protect the public against losses due to intermediary failures, inadequate information, or fraud. This is one of the key rationales for deposit insurance but also for extensive limitations on the terms of financial contracts, licensing, and regulation of broker-dealers and investments advisers, and mandated disclosures. Investment in private equity and hedge funds and in private companies is restricted for the most part to accredited investors, those with high net worth or income, or working in financial services.

Many limitations on stock market trading are motivated by consumer protection, with retail stock and stock option trading more prevalent over the past half century. Attention has been drawn to this issue by the emergence of social media and, more recently, artificial intelligence. Firms such as Robinhood Securities provide financial services and use algorithmic tools to assess investors' needs and engage their interest.

Efficiency, growth and competitive advantage: Policymakers aim to improve economic outcomes by making the financial system more efficient, fostering competition or economic growth. Intermediaries' monopoly power is said to permit pricing and other business policies that harm consumers and borrowers. Protecting against competition from foreign banks prepared to take higher risk was a motivation in the early stages of development of international capital regulation.

---

[4] See Chapter 19.

Most regulation addresses several concerns. Restrictions on short-selling appeal to financial stability, consumer protection, and efficiency motivations. Fierce hostility to short positioning as a form of market manipulation and fraud has been prevalent since its advent. In the United States, short positioning is generally permitted, but there are restrictions, especially on naked shorts, in which the seller has not borrowed a stock before sale but plans to buy or borrow it in time to deliver it for settlement. The SEC's Regulation SHO limits naked shorting by requiring a broker or dealer to borrow shares or reasonably expect to locate a borrow before filling a short sale order. It also requires exchanges to impose price triggers or circuit breakers to slow declining markets, seen as a financial stability concern and often attributed to widespread short positions (see Chapter 12).

The rationale for the regulation of financial markets and intermediaries overlaps with that of economic regulation in general and rests on limitations of markets and of voluntary cooperation: Market failures or information problems, such as externalities, imperfect competition, limited information, and conflicts of interest, distort financial markets. Private contract cannot mitigate these problems and they therefore require correction by government. Public-sector officials have superior information and are disinterested, dispassionate parties with no stake in the outcomes other than the public good, so regulation will improve outcomes.[5] These assumptions are critically examined in public-choice economics, which treats government and its employees not as disinterested outsiders but as participants in a competitive economic and political process.

In practice, regulation is often more at odds than in harmony with its putative objectives. Financial stability measures have generally failed to anticipate or even accelerated the development of financial imbalances, consumer protections impose costs and restrictions that are especially burdensome for the less well-to-do, and special interests ensure that rules protect them rather than prioritizing efficiency.

16.3.2 Information Problems in Regulation

Similar problems arise in regulation of financial and nonfinancial firms. They can be broadly grouped as limited information and incentives that are at odds with regulation's efficacy. Market participants' different information sets affect credit risk, asset trading, and firm organization. Asymmetric information and principal-agent problems, pitting intermediaries against customers and beneficiaries, are a prominent argument for consumer protection in investment advice and brokerage. Conflicts of interest internal to firms are viewed as an argument for regulation of compensation structures. Management or firm owners have principal-agent conflicts with employees as well as with investors that contribute to management focus on short-term results.

Regulation presumes a thorough understanding of the regulated industry and information about uncertain future events and the ability to ordain changes with predictable results. With the uncertainty inherent in the world, even owners and managers of regulated firms don't have the needed detailed knowledge. Unawareness of that lack compounds the regulatory challenge. Path dependency makes regulation difficult to assess in retrospect because we cannot know how a market or industry would be structured in a different regulatory environment.

Lack of knowledge on the part of regulators is clearly revealed in times of financial stress. No widespread bank panics or failures in recent memory have been anticipated by supervisors and addressed in advance of the event, including the waves of failure during the S&L crisis, the global financial crisis, the European debt crisis of 2011, and the March 2023 bank panic in the United States.

---

[5] See Chapters 3 and 9.

One of myriad examples is FDIC supervision of First Republic Bank, which consistently received high CAMELS ratings of 2 before failing in 2023 (see Chapter 20). Financial crises have generally been initially addressed using emergency lending techniques developed for earlier episodes, leading to a rush to develop tools better suited for the current crisis.

The life insurance subsidiaries of AIG American International Group, Inc. (AIG) conducted large securities lending programs before the 2008 crisis. They lent Treasurys and other high-quality securities in AIG's investment portfolios and invested cash collateral in long-term, credit-risky securities, with a high concentration of subprime residential MBS. The state insurance regulators overseeing AIG appear to have been unaware of the securities lending programs, which contributed heavily to AIG's losses in 2008 and led to a Treasury-Federal Reserve rescue package.[6]

Any substantial rule or change likely leads to at least some **unintended consequences** of which financial regulation presents many instances:

- The 2013 supervisory guidance intended to reduce leveraged lending instead shifted it away from large banks to nonbanks, which are largely financed through banks. Rather than achieve its intended objective, the guidance added a layer of intermediation and risk to the financial system.
- Regulations imposing ratings criteria for investments are intended to protect investors. They contributed to institutional investor demand for highly rated products with at least a narrow spread over Treasury bonds, efforts to increase their volume through securitization, and erosion of ratings standards.
- Efforts to reduce counterparty risk and the risk of contagion and crises through central clearing mandates has led to the creation of large clearing platforms that may prove a locus of greater risk.
- Limits on the fees banks receive from credit card companies for processing payments under the Durbin Amendment to the Dodd-Frank Act have led banks to make low-fee accounts less available. Deposit insurance fees have a similar effect. Although the fees appear to be borne by banks, they are propagated to end-users of banking services.
- Regulation Q ceilings on demand deposit interest rates led to the advent and growth of money market funds.

The problem of regulator ignorance is compounded by the **excessive complexity** and **cost** of financial regulation. Rules are numerous and very long and detailed, making compliance costlier but evasion easier. There has been a major expansion over time in the number and detail of financial as well as nonfinancial regulations. The Dodd-Frank Act, for example, called for the writing of around 400 new rules, requiring many years of formulation and process. Some, such as the Volcker Rule, proved difficult to formulate and took shape over many years, opening the door to intense industry lobbying.

Complex rules provide the appearance of thoroughness but make costly error or irrelevance more likely in a world of uncertainty. A proliferation of rules introduces more potentially binding constraints on action by intermediaries, with an an impact on market functioning. Unintended consequences contribute to a cycle in which regulations fail to achieve their objective, or worsen the problems they are intended to address, and lead instead to the introduction of additional layers of regulation.

An example is the structure of market making in the US stock market, which has emerged from regulatory and technological developments as well as the economies of scale, informational complexity, and changing demands for trading services. Trading stocks has become very quick and cheap, but the industry structure is highly fragmented, with trading platforms, such as exchanges and dark

---

[6] Peirce (2014) details the extent of AIG risk taking through its insurance subsidiaries and lack of supervisory awareness and understanding.

pools that are regulated very differently from one another and a pricing structure involving bid-ask spreads, fees, commissions, and payment for order flow (PFOF). This has led to demands for additional regulation on top of a dense set of existing rules. Rather than relying on the market to develop contractual arrangements that mitigate such conflicts at lower cost to all parties, the SEC has proposed broad rules to limit the use of technology and to prevent brokers from obtaining payment for routing orders to market makers.[7] Any increase in trading costs could be embedded in slightly wider bid-ask spreads, likely at the expense of retail investors. Another example, discussed in Chapter 20, are the effects of capital regulation on market liquidity and the inhibitions on market-making it generates.

Regulated intermediaries must carry out an increasing amount of quantitative modeling, such as the evolution of the Basel capital rules from simple risk weights to internal models. Banks differ greatly in their mix of businesses and therefore, balance sheets, so these models cannot be applied and assessed consistently across regulated banks. At the same time, the rules impose **uniformity** of practice, at odds with innovation and particularly pernicious in risk management because uniformity of intermediaries' balance sheets and businesses contribute to instability and procyclicality.

Complexity is also related to social cost. Compliance with the Sarbanes-Oxley Act's provisions require costly regular audits of internal controls falling especially heavily on smaller firms. It may have contributed to the sharp decline since the late 1990s in the number of publicly traded firms in the United States and the displacement of public markets by private equity funds as owners of newer, smaller firms.

Regulation of consumer finance and the retail financial industry apply **paternalism**, the use of compulsion for the benefit of consumers. Paternalism in regulation stems from the assumption that regulators have superior information to consumers and has more recently been grounded in behavioral economics, where it is referred to as choice architecture or nudging. An example is the requirement that equity research be organizationally separate from investment banking, introduced in 2002 and 2003 via enforcement of an SEC legal action against large investment firms. The rationale was to make such research accessible to retail investors and was informed by and contributed to entrenching, the investment approach that they should aim to "beat the market" in the face of evidence against the efficacy of active management, particularly for retail investors.[8]

16.3.3   Incentives and the Efficacy of Regulation

Regulation is integrated with the larger political system, emerging from a bargaining process among political, bureaucratic, and private interested parties. "Special interests" may be ideal or material. The impact of regulatory changes on some parties is very large, but for most, the social harms or benefits are small and diffuse. Most of the process of formulating legislation and rules is out of the view of the public, which can discern the bargaining only indirectly and to a limited extent.

These asymmetries and information problems make it more likely that regulation will be oriented to benefit particular interests. Politicians aim to gain financial support and votes, and seek regulatory changes that satisfy focused interests and can be presented to the public in a favorable light. They are less concerned with diffuse, longer-term consequences and with the cumulative effect of regulations layered over a long period of time.

---

[7] See the SEC press releases announcing the proposed rules at https://www.sec.gov/news/press-release/2022-225 and https://www.sec.gov/news/press-release/2023-140.

[8] See Chapter 7.

Residential real estate finance, among the largest special interests, includes a range of industries and actual and potential homeowners. In many countries, but particularly in the United States, a wide range of measures have been taken to subsidize debt-financed ownership of residential real estate, including the mandated prepayment option in residential mortgages, government guarantees of mortgage loans by banks and in securitization vehicles, and publicly owned mortgage lenders. Encouragement of home ownership through subsidies and regulation, with a paternalistic public rationale, has led to many households investing in an undiversified, leveraged portfolio consisting largely of a single illiquid nonearning asset with high idiosyncratic risk.

The political economy problems of regulation are generally presented as a conflict between firms and other private interests advocating for market processes, and public interests represented by regulators. This view is inconsistent with the phenomenon of **regulatory capture** and **arbitrage**, financial sector regulators adopting the industry's special-interest viewpoint. Regulation is susceptible to cooptation and adoption by regulators of the regulated firms' point of view. Regulators lack the detailed knowledge needed to compose the texts of rules and often rely on staff of the industries they regulate or on law firms engaged by regulated entities. Rules can be designed to be ineffective or to shield incumbent firms from competition. Reliance on self-regulation in securities markets opens additional vulnerabilities to regulatory capture as well as lack of accountability.

Lack of direct insight contributes to the alignment of interests between regulated firms and regulators. Regulators are seldom motivated solely by concern for the public good. Rather, as has been explored by public-choice economics, regulators are made out of the same crooked timber as the regulated, with the same wide range of motivations. Regulators, supervisors, and industry staff constitute a unitary labor pool, with similar training and skills. Public-sector and industry staff routinely move from one domain to the other, bringing interests as well as knowledge with them.

Regulatory evasion describes market participants' adoption of the form but not the economic nature of a regulated activity. One form is regulatory arbitrage, the effort by a regulated intermediary to satisfy the letter of the regulation in an optimal way. Intermediaries satisfy any constraint on asset risk in the least costly way possible, with the riskiest and highest-yielding assets in a category, e.g., insurance companies satisfying capital rules with the riskiest securities within a regulatory category. The presence of guarantees may further mute any offsetting impact of higher risk.

Multiple regulators introduce the potential for **jurisdiction shopping**, intermediaries changing their legal form or location so as to come under a more desirable set of supervisors. In the United States, banks have some ability to choose between national and state charters. Regulators with overlapping responsibilities also compete with one another for wider authority. For example, public criticism of the Federal Reserve after the global financial crisis led to efforts to narrow their responsibility for smaller banks, which the Fed successfully resisted at the political level as the Dodd-Frank Act was being drafted.[9]

---

[9] As reported for example in https://www.reuters.com/article/us-financial-regulation-hutchison-klobuc/senate-drops-plan-to-take-small-banks-from-fed-idUSTRE64B3YC20100512.

Further Reading

Labonte (2023a) provides a structural overview of US financial regulation. A number of US law and lobbying firms with extensive financial institutions practices publish up-to-date summaries of regulatory matters, such as capital and liquidity standards. Examples include Davis Polk and Mayer Brown. On US bank regulation, see Avraham et al. (2012).

Selgin and White (1994) discuss free banking and other alternatives to the currently prevalent monetary and banking systems. Dowd (2023) describes a number of historical episodes and variants, and Rolnick et al. (2002) focus on the early 19th century in the United States.

Eisenbach et al. (2017) describe on-site supervision, focusing on the New York Fed's oversight of large US banks, and Hirtle and Kovner (2022) survey research findings on its effects.

Fox et al. (2015) describe changes in US stock markets in recent decades and evaluate the regulatory response. Malz (2021) discusses the regulatory approach to investor protection in the context of the GameStop stock volatility episode. See Teles (2013) on regulatory complexity. Omarova (2019) is an example of calls for additional regulation arising from disappointment with the results of existing regulation. Thaler and Sunstein (2003) offer a defense of consumer financial regulation rooted in behavioral economics.

Manski (2011) describes the analytic and regulatory practice of predicting the results of public policy actions far more precisely than possible. Pirrong (2012) illustrates the unintended consequences of the Dodd-Frank changes to OTC derivatives regulation. Calomiris and Haber (2014) provide a historical perspective on the role of political influence in regulation and Morgenson and Rosner (2011) describe its role leading up to the global financial crisis. Stigler (1971) was an early analysis. See Lindsey and Teles (2017) on regulatory capture. Kim et al. (2018) discuss supervisory guidance on leveraged lending.

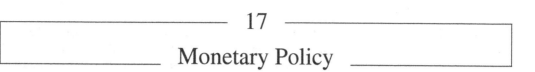

17

Monetary Policy

Monetary policy aims to control inflation and the value of money, or at broader macroeconomic outcomes, by using interest rate and money supply tools to a greater or lesser extent under central bank control. Monetary policy is intertwined closely with regulatory policy and government finance, and overlaps with **fiscal policy**, the use of public spending as a macroeconomic tool.

Monetary policy techniques became fairly standard in modern times, but in recent decades, new tools have responded to the global financial crisis and to the unusually and persistently low level of interest rates. Financial markets and ideas about how interest rates and money affect the economy have also been evolving. To understand current approaches to monetary policy, it's important to review those that were in place in the "normal times" before the crisis.

17.1   The Emergence of Monetary Policy

Central banks have primary responsibility for monetary policy and are involved in policies affecting financial stability, management of foreign exchange reserves, maintaining payment systems, and regulation and supervision of intermediaries and markets. The extent of these responsibilities has varied across jurisdictions and through history.

Central banks are old institutions. There is a long history of Italian and Dutch merchant cities creating semi-public banks to facilitate credit and foreign exchange markets. Among the earliest nation-state central banks are the Sverige Riksbank, founded in 1668, and the Bank of England (1694). These proto-central banks were privately owned and intended to earn a return for its shareholders but had public fiscal obligations. The Bank of England's corporate charter granted it legal privileges, such as exclusive note-issuing rights among City of London banks. Merchants could sell bills—short-term loans they had made in the ordinary course of business—to the Bank for notes and other claims on the Bank widely accepted as money. This made the Bank an attractive lender, while providing means of payment to the economy and centralizing money creation in the Bank.

In return, the Bank carried out its primary intended purpose, which was to support government borrowing by reducing the fragmentation of the government bond market and facilitating uniform long-term and lower-cost issuance, for example, the 3 percent consol—a perpetual annuity—of 1751. The United Kingdom achieved a relatively liquid government bond secondary market by the mid-18th century that contributed to the overall development of its emerging capital markets. Today's central bank functions—monetary, financial stability and regulatory policies, and a leading role in the payments system—emerged as by-products of these developments. A close relationship between long-term government solvency and central bank policies was also established.

For close to two centuries, the Bank's functions as lender of last resort (LOLR) in crises by (see Chapter 18) enhancing market liquidity, providing a uniform and stable means of payment, and setting monetary policy were not firmly anchored in deliberate legislated design. Its position was protected by its legal monopoly of note issuance, and restrictions on most other commercial banks' ability to organize as joint-stock corporations, which have limited liability and continuity advantages compared to partnerships.

The Bank had become the preeminent banker to merchants and other City banks during the 18th century, leading to the birth, or perhaps more accurately discovery of monetary policy. Commercial banks' deposits or reserves at a central bank are part of a bank's overall liquidity reserves, are used to settle payments between banks with minimal delay, and are therefore among the most liquid assets in the financial system. The Bank came to be the primary issuer of liabilities that could serve as liquidity reserves for other commercial banks. Bank rate, the interest rate at which it refinanced merchants' short-term loans, was found to strongly influence lending rates throughout the financial system. The Bank played a stabilizing role in financial crises, such as those of 1797 and after, evolving into its lender of last resort function, an institution banks could rely on to provide them with liquidity and prevent widespread failures during financial crises.

The United Kingdom had gravitated to a gold monetary standard in which the Bank was presumed ready to redeem its notes for gold at a set price, implicitly limiting issuance. Bank failures and the financial panics in 1825 and 1836 had highlighted the tension between limiting note issuance to maintain monetary stability and the need to provide liquidity during stress events. The Peel Bank Charter Act of 1844 formalized the limitations on the Bank's note issuance and separated it from its banking functions. It roughly marks the beginning of the modern approach to central banking in which the central bank consciously influences monetary aggregates and interest rates under its control to achieve macroeconomic objectives.

The Federal Reserve System is one of the last advanced-economy central banks to be established (in 1913). Private liquidity backstop arrangements among commercial banks, in the United States and elsewhere, were in place throughout the 19th century, often effectively carrying out what today are largely central banking functions. The LOLR function was carried out in part via private bank clearinghouses and clearinghouse associations, which were initially established to clear, net, and settle payments between commercial banks. Member banks deposited good collateral with the clearinghouse, which in turn issued certificates, liabilities that were used to settle debts between member banks and circulated as money. The clearinghouses played a key role in crises, for example during the Panic of 1907, addressing depletion of member bank reserves.[1]

The European Central Bank (ECB) was established in 1999 as part of the European Monetary Union (EMU). It conducts a unitary monetary policy on behalf of all member states via the euro to which member states' individual currencies were converted at agreed rates. National central banks share some responsibilities, such as bank supervision and management of foreign exchange reserves. The EMU treaties also provide for unimpeded capital flows between members, a requirement for a unitary money market.

17.2   The Framework of Monetary Policy

The paths or **transmission channels** by which central bank actions affect the economy aren't directly observed, and their outcomes are uncertain. There is deep and long-standing disagreement about the effectiveness of different policy approaches, summarized as **monetary policy frameworks, strategies,** or **regimes**. Historically, such frameworks were more often implicit, but it is increasingly central bank practice to articulate them publicly.

---

[1] An earlier example is the Suffolk Bank in New England, a clearinghouse for banks in the region and a lender of last resort during the banking panic of 1837 (see Chapter 16).

17.2.1   Policy Targets and Instruments

The starting point of a policy framework is the set of objectives or **targets** at which it aims. These may be numerically specified or left somewhat vague to retain flexibility. Past performance and track records are crucial to expectation formation, so **policy rules**—as opposed to **discretion**—together with price stability as the highest priority can serve as a commitment mechanism. A simple rule is to increase a money aggregate by a fixed percentage amount per year. Rules may also take into account macroeconomic variables such as the price level, inflation, or employment. Central bank independence of the political instances is required to make any rule or target regime credible.

Advanced-economy central banks generally practice some form of **inflation targeting**, in which an inflation target is set and central banks measure performance by comparing the target with realized inflation. In the United States, the objectives are enshrined in the **dual mandate** of section 2A of the 1913 Federal Reserve Act, as amended in 1977:[2] " ... maximum employment, stable prices, and moderate long-term interest rates." The ECB has a single primary objective of price stability and a 2 percent inflation rate over the medium term and is thus, not formally concerned with growth employment. Central banks may also engage in **constrained discretion**, informally following a rule but deviating from it on occasion for nonpolitical reasons. An example is the Fed's publication of a *Statement on Longer-Run Goals and Monetary Policy Strategy* since 2012, setting a "goal" rather than a target of 2 percent inflation over the longer run.[3]

Central banks have settled on a typical target rate of inflation of 2 percent because it is low but positive. A target inflation rate of zero, in this view, would be costlier because the imperfect flexibility of price adjustment would force more labor market and output adjustments. A higher target rate would be incompatible with a credible commitment to price stability. The inflation target of 2 percent is intended to accommodate some downward price and wage rigidity while not alarming the public or distorting economic decisions.

In practice, there has been some ambiguity about whether the inflation goal is meant to be an upper limit or longer-term average. Alternative price stability rules open the possibility for a central bank to tolerate transitory above-target inflation in a slump. **Nominal income** or **GDP targeting** tries to capture a price and output objective in one measure and overcome the difficulty of measuring the output gap in real time. **Price level targeting** would permit transitory deviations of inflation from target, so long as they are compensated by subsequent deviations in the other direction.

The Federal Reserve recently reformulated its inflation goal to one that "achieve[s] inflation that averages 2 percent over time," a **flexible average inflation targeting** (FAIT) approach similar to price level targeting in permitting deviations from the target over the medium term.[4] These alternatives address the difficulty experienced of reaching an inflation goal of 2 percent during a disinflationary period with interest rates close to zero, but they carry risks to credibility and of responding too slowly to rising inflation inaccurately perceived as transitory, as occurred during the post-Covid economic recovery.

In pursuing these targets, central banks apply **instruments** or tools that are fully or close to fully under their control, usually the volume and mix of assets and liabilities on its balance sheet or the interest rates at which they buy and sell them. **Intermediate targets** are the money supply, short-term

---

[2] Actually, a triple mandate. See https://www.federalreserve.gov/aboutthefed/fract.htm.

[3] See https://www.federalreserve.gov/monetarypolicy/files/fomc_longerrungoals.pdf. The Fed's measure of inflation is the PCE price index excluding food and energy (see Chapter 4).

[4] The change is formalized in the *Statement on Longer-Run Goals and Monetary Policy Strategy*, which since 2020 has incorporated the average inflation targeting approach.

interest rates, and in smaller countries, foreign exchange rates the central bank influences in pursuit of its objectives:

$$\boxed{\text{Instruments} \longrightarrow \text{Intermediate targets} \longrightarrow \text{Objectives or targets}}$$

They don't fully control any of these variables, which are also affected by market conditions and by fiscal policy, directly or through market responses to government budget decisions.

Control over interest rates, money, and exchange rates is exercised through the central bank's balance sheet, which doesn't exist in isolation. Assets and liabilities of central banks are ultimately those of governments. If the central bank earns a profit on its assets and liabilities, as it usually does, it either transfers those earnings to the government or they accrue to a capital account that is a government asset. The impact of monetary and fiscal policies are thereby related, and financing of government expenditures through taxes, debt, and money issuance are jointly constrained.

17.2.2   Credibility of Monetary Policy

Economic behavior and therefore, the current levels of inflation and output, are driven in large part by expectations of their future values and of future economic policy. Modern monetary frameworks focus on market expectations regarding such variables as future short-term interest rates and inflation. Policy aims for **credibility**, that is consistency of the public's expectations with the central bank's intentions, which minimizes the potential for adverse impact of policy actions on growth or prices. When credibility is weak, policymakers may promise a stable price level to influence price- and wage-setting. If the promise is believed, and inflation restrained, policymakers have an incentive to renege on it to boost output and employment in the short term. If the public expects the central bank to renege, it won't believe the promise to begin with and it can't influence behavior.

Therefore, trend in central banking is away from mystery and toward deliberate management of expectations in a credible and **time consistent** way. Time consistency and credibility prevail when central banks announce or signal a policy path in advance and the public is confident the policy will be adhered to regardless of the short-term political benefits of an easier monetary policy. If successful, it can reduce the overall social cost and risks of monetary policy.

Political time frames are shorter than those over which the effects of economic policies, including monetary and fiscal policies, play out, leading to a bias toward short-term stimulative policies that are not optimal in the longer term. Time consistent monetary policy is supported by central bank independence, the extent to which the central bank can make policy decisions free of political influence. Independence can be established through legislation, appointment processes, and other legal arrangements but is enhanced or undermined over time by norms of political behavior and the evolution of institutions.

Policy attitudes toward inflation have evolved. The costs of inflation, distorting the information content of prices and inducing changes in financial behavior, are well recognized. Reliably stable and low inflation over long periods of time encourages the issuance of longer-term nominal debt, with a benign effect on financial stability. In the 19th century, corporate debt with initial maturities of many decades were not unusual. More recently, before the reemergence of inflation, a number of firms, including The Walt Disney Company, issued such bonds.

Expectations of high inflation became entrenched during the 1970s and, as a result, during the disinflation of the 1980s, there were several periods—"inflation scares"—when long-term interest rates

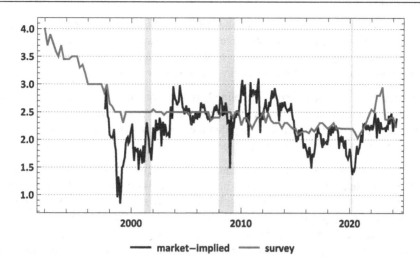

Figure 17.1 Market-implied and survey inflation 1991–2023

Survey of Professional Forecasters median 10-year-ahead annual average inflation forecast, quarterly, Q4 1991–Q4 2023, and 5-year 5-year forward break-even inflation (the inflation rate over future interval implied by yields on nominal and inflation-adjusted bonds of different terms to maturity), month-end, July 1997–Dec. 2023. Vertical shading represents NBER recession dates. *Source*: Bloomberg, Federal Reserve Bank of Philadelphia.

rose sharply as a result of higher inflation expectations and low credibility of the Federal Reserve's commitment to keep inflation low. These episodes inhibited economic growth by obliging the Fed to keep interest rates higher than it otherwise would have, to convince market participants of its determination to achieve lower inflation. In contrast, the disinflation beginning in 2021 appears to have been easier due to the credibility established by the Fed during the 1980s and 1990s. Market-based estimates of inflation (Figure 17.1) were better-anchored and did not exceed 2.5 percent.

The governance of central banks in advanced market economies is designed to ensure independence of the central bank from shorter-term political influence and to enhance credibility. The broad organizational design of the central bank is determined through legislation, in the United States by the Federal Reserve Act. Monetary policy decisions are made by the Federal Open Market Committee (FOMC) with 12 voting members and an additional eight nonvoting participants, all with long appointment terms as insulation from political pressure.

Communication is an important part of a monetary framework. Central banks have in the past been reluctant to spell out their policy plans clearly because if conditions changed and policy were adjusted, it could be perceived as time inconsistent for the sake of short-term political benefit. The FOMC began publicly announcing target rate changes in 1994 as part of a gradual shift toward transparency in an effort to reap the longer-term benefits of time consistency if policy were clearly articulated, viewed as credible, and the public's expectations adapted accordingly. Scheduled communication has opened up, with more rapid release of notes and transcripts following FOMC meetings, and quarterly Fed chair press conferences.

17.2.3 Money Supply Control

High-powered or **base money** refers to assets that serve both as money because they can be used instantly to settle debts and make payments and as unquestionably liquid reserves for a commercial bank. It is typically defined to include cash and deposits at a trusted clearinghouse or the central bank. A central bank is called "the bankers' bank" because its liabilities serve as liquidity reserves and as means of same-day payment for other banks. Reserve balances are counted toward liquid assets that the commercial banks may be required to hold for regulatory purposes.

In a **fiat-money** system, legal tender is defined as cash or currency—government- or central bank-issued coins and banknotes—rather than as an equivalent amount of commodities, such as gold or silver. Forms of high-powered money can then be exchanged for one another but can't be redeemed for any more "ultimate" form of money.

Forms of money issued by governments and central banks, and in a quantity largely under their control, are called **outside money**. In the United States, the **monetary base** is defined by the Federal Reserve as the sum of notes—issued in the past by the US government and the Fed but now only by the latter—in the hands of the public and banks' reserves at the Fed. Base money is usually also outside money. Commercial banks create liquid assets by issuing deposits or immediately redeemable claims. These and other claims on private issuers that are used as money are called **inside money**.

Narrow money or, in the United States **M1**, includes cash and most of the public's deposits in commercial banks. Deposits are easy for the public to use for transactions, usually by writing checks, and banks can easily and quickly clear deposit flows among themselves through the Fed. **Broad money** or, in the United States **M2**, includes forms of money that are less easy to use in transactions, such as savings deposits, or clear more slowly between institutions, such as money market mutual fund shares.

The simplest form of monetary policy in a fiat-money world is **helicopter money**, which is high-powered money issued by the central bank and placed in the hands of public.[5] It is a simple form of expansionary policy and has been proposed as a more stimulative alternative to conventional monetary policy during crises. The liabilities can take the form of non-interest paying notes or reserves. To be effective, it must be permanent and irreversible and seen that way by the public. The helicopter drop must be accompanied by a credible commitment never to repeat it, never to redeem the notes or reserve issuance, and never to raise taxes in the future to offset it.

From the central bank's point of view, no earning asset is created, resulting in a corresponding decline in the central bank's net equity value. From a consolidated, public-sector point of view, the issuance is money-financed fiscal policy, or **overt monetary finance**. The proceeds can finance public spending on goods and services, or transfers to the public, and can boost output in the short term if there are idle resources in the economy. In the long term, it is offset by a temporary increase in inflation and a permanent rise in the price level.

The quantity of inside money is determined in part by market processes in response to changes in the demand for liquid assets and the supply of base money and is therefore, considered an intermediate target rather than instrument of monetary policy. The **velocity of money**, the ratio of a money aggregate to nominal income, is one way of measuring money demand. When market participants desire higher money balances relative to their volume of transactions or the level of their nominal income, velocity falls. This is reliably the case during financial stress and crises when the demand for money or **liquidity preference** sharply increases, and there is abrupt substitution from less to more reliably safe liquid assets.

---

[5] The term "helicopter drop" was introduced by Milton Friedman.

In the contemporary financial system, forms of liquidity have proliferated, processes that began with money market funds and have continued with the growth of short-term wholesale finance (see Chapter 12). The variety of money and close money substitutes has diminished the effectiveness of the volume of high-powered or central bank money as a tool for influencing interest rates and the economy. Since the 1980s, measures of the velocity of money have fluctuated widely, and central banks have turned away from reliance on the money supply. The fluctuations in velocity have been even wider since the global financial and subsequent crises. New forms of liquidity have also contributed to the puzzling coexistence of large volumes of money and other highly liquid assets with strong evidence of tight liquidity in the financial system (see Chapter 20).

17.2.4   Interest Rate Control

A limitation of money supply as an intermediate target is the often weak short-term impact on broad liquidity conditions of the monetary aggregates under central bank control. Central banks have historically more often implemented policy via control over short-term interest rates. Monetary policy operates primarily via a short-term interest-rate target, more effective than the money supply because "it gets in all of the cracks" (Stein 2013). But the rates under central bank control also have an uncertain impact on interest rates generally and their transmission to the economy.

An interest rate control target is accomplished by varying assets and liabilities on the central bank's balance sheet. Before the crisis, the main instrument was market operations, frequent trading of bonds for reserves, banks' deposits at the Fed to control the federal funds rate. Since the crisis, the volume of reserves has been so large that it's no longer a useful way to influence money market rates. Central banks can set **administered rates** they pay on liabilities they issue and now also try to influence longer-term rates through their holdings of bonds.

With these tools, central banks exercise substantial control over overnight and very short-term nominal rates, with weaker control over longer-term rates, reflected in interest rate volatility. Control of short-term rates is strongest in markets in which central bank operate and less so in other money markets as spreads between different money market instruments fluctuate. Prices are less flexible in the short term; at any instant, prices are what they are. Central banks can therefore, also set very short-term real rates. In the longer term, as prices and inflation expectations adjust, central bank control over unobservable longer term real rates fades.

17.2.5   The New Keynesian Framework

Monetary frameworks are based on a model or narrative of how monetary variables affect macroeconomic outcomes. Contemporary frameworks are, for the most part, based on a **new Keynesian synthesis** or **neo-Wicksellian** approach in which the short-term interest rate plays a key role. In Wicksell's original version, there is an equilibrium or **natural real interest rate** that balances the supply and demand of future goods, equates investment and saving, and is consistent with a stable price level. If the short-term rate prevailing in the market is lower or higher than the natural rate, investment will exceed or fall short of saving and prices generally will fall or rise. These changes will continue until equality between the natural and market rates is reestablished.

Prices are not always smoothly flexible, adjusting in continuous response to changes in economic fundamentals. Many contracts fix prices for some period of time. Labor contracts and wages in particular are longer-term and hard to change. As a result, some of the immediate adjustment to change is borne by quantity rather than price adjustments. New Keynesian models combine these elements with the concept of a short-term natural rate of interest, or **r-star** (r^*), to describe how the economy adapts to change and the role central bank policy plays. Figure 3.7 displays estimates of the equilibrium short-term real rate.

A simple model of the economy helps understand how central banks relate instruments to targets and objectives. Its variables include the nominal money-market rate i, the current inflation rate π, and the real rate, the difference $i - E[\pi]$ between nominal interest rates and expected inflation. An output gap variable x represents GDP growth or employment, measured relative to the full, potential, or natural rate of employment of resources and labor.

Two key relationships describe the economy, aggregate demand, in which an increase in the real interest rate depresses output, and aggregate supply or the **short-run Phillips curve**, in which inflation rises with output and expected inflation. The central bank sets the short-term nominal interest rate i, closing up the model and determining together with the other relationships the paths over time of realized—and thus expected—inflation, output, and the real interest rate. The current values of each variable—the state of the economy—depend on the entire expected future path of each variable. Each adjusts gradually over time to shocks, surprises, and news. The financial system—asset prices, risk preferences and credit conditions—is largely absent from the model.

The central bank's strategy is to set i to align short-term market real interest rates with its estimate of the natural rate. If inflation expectations appear to be close to the inflation target and the economy close to its growth potential, then i will be set so the short-term real rate is close to its estimate of r^*. If the economy is far from one or both of these objectives, then i will be set higher or lower so as to bring it back closer.

Price and wage rigidity and other market frictions introduce a short-term trade-off between higher inflation for lower unemployment but not in the longer term. Monetary policy can only influence real variables in the short term. The standard framework is equilibrium-oriented and doesn't have that much to say about how far and for how long policy can drive rates away from the natural rate and neutrality. In the long term, **neutrality of money** prevails. Interest rates and money only influence the price level, with no impact on economic growth and inflation and no lasting alteration of relative prices or of the structure of the economy.

Any framework must have a theory of how monetary policy impacts and influences the economy and attains its inflation and growth goals, that is, the transmission channels connecting i to x, $E[\pi]$, and π. Interest rates influence investment, residential house purchases, and other consumption decisions. If interest rates fall, the US dollar weakens, inducing higher net exports. Equity values rise through the impact of discounting, inducing higher consumption via the **wealth effect**.

The **Taylor rule**, in which the interest rate is raised if inflation or growth exceed their goals, is a policy rule grounded in the new Keynesian framework. A simple example is:

$$i = \underbrace{0.02}_{\text{natural rate}} + \underbrace{0.02}_{\text{target } \pi} + 1.5 \cdot (\pi - \underbrace{0.02}_{\text{target } \pi}) + 0.5 \cdot x.$$

The Taylor rule contains an inflation- and an employment-targeting component. The coefficient on actual compared to target inflation is set above one, instructing the central bank to raise the nominal interest rate above its long-term equilibrium by more than the amount by which inflation exceeds the target, thus also transitorily raising the real above the natural rate. It is a symmetric rule: "lean against the wind" and avoid deviations in either direction equally. If both policy objectives are close to being met and r^* is estimated at a constant 2 percent, then i will be set close to the estimated equilibrium nominal rate of r^* plus target π, or 4 percent. If inflation is running at 3 percent, the policy rate i will be set at 5.5 percent.

Central banks are reluctant to alter policy settings as rapidly as macroeconomic conditions warrant, preferring interest rate smoothing to avoid disruptive large changes in interest rates and roiling financial markets. Evidence of a gap between policymakers' intentions and market expectations of future short-term rates, or about how well- or poorly anchored inflation expectations are, influences policy decisions. Taylor rules may therefore also have an inertial component, with changes in the policy rate depending in part on its current level and adapting more gradually to changing economic data.

Though it hasn't served as an official policy rule, many central banks' actions closely resemble the Taylor rule, so it is viewed descriptively as a **reaction function**. Greater price and output stability from the 1980s on is attributed to adherence to it.[6]

Figure 17.2 shows how realized short-term rates compare with one empirical estimate of the Taylor rule. Such comparisons are highly dependent on the estimates of r^*, and on the price level indexes and the measures of the output gap used, but some overall patterns are clear. The fed funds rate was well below the path recommended by the Taylor rule during the inflationary 1970s and near or above it during the disinflation of the 1980s and 1990s. The fed funds rate was back below the rule's recommendation in the years leading up to the global financial crisis, a gap some economists hold responsible for the expansion that led to it. That gap grew even wider after the onset of the crisis, which may be due in part to a decline in the equilibrium short-term rate below 2 percent and in part to the effective fed funds rate having fallen to zero.

17.2.6   Alternative Approaches to Monetary Policy

A rule or other **nominal anchor** puts a quantitative constraint on a monetary aggregate or price thought to have a stable relationship to the price level generally. A well-functioning nominal anchor

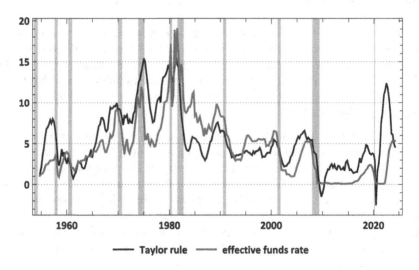

Figure 17.2 Actual and Taylor-rule fed funds rate 1970–2024

Taylor rule $4 + 1.5 \cdot (\pi - 2) + 0.5 \cdot x$, with π measured as the year-over-year change in the PCE deflator and x the difference between actual GDP and the Congressional Budget Office estimate of potential GDP; effective fed funds rate (EFFR), quarter-end. Vertical shading represents NBER recession dates. Percent, quarterly, Q3 1954 to Q3 2023.

---

[6] In practice, central banks employ a variety of quantitative models for forecasting and guidance. The Federal Reserve maintains a large-scale econometric model of the US economy, FRB/US, which has antecedents in older Keynesian approaches.

acts to strengthen expectations of price stability. The **classical gold standard** and its **rules of the game** from 1870 to 1914 called for raising (lowering) rates in response to gold outflows (inflows), but was more asymmetric in practice. The gold standard is a form of **exchange-rate targeting**, used by smaller countries and those for which international trade volumes are large relative to income in which the local exchange rate is fixed or pegged to that of a larger currency with a stable price level.

Monetarism is a broad term for alternatives to the new Keynesian paradigm that focus on money aggregates rather than interest rates as the most effective instruments for implementing monetary policy. A form of it was employed by the Fed from 1979 to 1982 in the earlier stages of its ultimately successful disinflation effort. Some variants of monetarism call for constant money supply growth, encountering the difficulty of choosing a specific aggregate as "the" money supply target in a continuously innovating financial system in which many different assets are substitutable for money. Estimates of the demand for money balances or money velocity vary widely over time as economic conditions change and as firms and households rely on different sets of assets for liquidity. Estimates also diverge for different money aggregates.

Whatever the degree of central bank independence, the central bank and government balance sheets are subaccounts of a unitary public-sector balance sheet that consolidates their assets and liabilities, including illiquid and hard-to-evaluate claims, such as the present value of future tax revenues and legally mandated government pension payments. The Federal Reserve holds a large volume of Treasury bonds that are liabilities of its owner, the federal government, and finances them via liabilities to the banking system, other intermediaries, or the public. In doing so, it indirectly funds part of the consolidated federal government debt at a low average interest rate by issuing base money. The federal debt on Federal Reserve district bank balance sheets if it is expected to remain their indefinitely, has been monetized and transformed into reserve balances, a form of overt monetary finance.

Monetary and fiscal policy are directly connected through this unitary balance sheet. Federal Reserve assets are of fairly long duration and have high yields compared to its liabilities, reserves, and currency bearing zero or low interest rates. Its net earnings, analogous to commercial banks' net interest margin, are added to a capital account representing equity on its balance sheet and remitted to the Treasury once it reaches a certain level. Positive remittances by the Fed add to federal revenues, effectively financing part of federal expenditures through reserve, i.e., money, creation and reducing the federal fiscal deficit. In normal times, this is of only marginal significance but has become more important coming out of an era of low interest rates and with very large central bank holdings of government debt (see Chapter 20).

The **fiscal theory of the price level** views the entire volume of government debt, not only the part issued in the form of high-powered money but also as a relevant aggregate for determining prices. Government budgets must be balanced over the long term, and the price level as well as real yields adjust to the current and expected future fiscal balance. If the volume of debt and budget deficits are expected to grow beyond the potential for offsetting surpluses in the future, the necessity for the government to finance itself will eventually affect monetary policy, a situation known as **fiscal dominance**. The price level will rise, driven not by current issuance of high-powered money but by inflation expectations because monetary policy will eventually be forced to accommodate and monetize the public debt.

17.3   Monetary Operations in Normal Times

Monetary policy operations are the actions a central bank takes to implement policy, and an **operating framework** is the logic informing them. We'll describe here how they worked before the global crisis in contrast to the unconventional approach that followed. Before the crisis, the Fed's balance sheet was much smaller than today (Figure 17.3). Its assets consisted almost entirely of Treasury bills and bonds, with small shares of gold and other holdings.[7] Liabilities consisted primarily of currency. Banks' reserve balances were small in relation.

Like other intermediaries, central banks use the balance sheet to carry out operations: buying or selling, borrowing or lending specific assets. In **open market operations** (OMOs), central banks enter markets at their own initiative to conduct transactions, either via auctions or at a fixed rate they set, aimed at keeping market interest rates close to target. The volume of securities bought or sold may be limited or an unlimited **full allotment**. **Standing facilities** make collateralized borrowing or lending available to eligible counterparties at their initiative and with no limits on volume at administered rates set by the central bank.

In a fractional-reserve banking system, the volume of customer deposits liabilities that commercial banks issue, individually and in aggregate, is a multiple of their reserves. **Reserve requirements**, a regulatory constraint distinct from banks' own liquidity reserve policies, oblige depository institutions to maintain a minimum ratio of reserves to deposits. Until recently, US banks had to hold reserve balances at Federal Reserve district banks equalling 10 percent of average demand deposits over a 2-week **maintenance period**.[8] A bank could maintain additional reserves of liquid assets, such as Treasurys, but could not substitute these for required reserves. Varying reserve requirements have been used as a monetary policy tool, permitting banks to issue greater or smaller quantities of privately created money for a given monetary base. It is currently used mainly by central banks in developing countries, for example, the People's Bank of China (PBC).

If reserves are scarce enough to constrain banks, as was the case up to the global financial crisis, the central bank can influence the broader money supply by varying the volume of reserves it issues. It does so to carry out monetary policy and influence interest rates and economic activity or to meet routine, seasonal, or financial stress-induced fluctuations in the demand for liquidity. The **federal funds market** is the over-the-counter secondary market in reserve balances. In this segment of the money market, banks borrow reserve balances from one another and through brokers, generally overnight. Reserves paid no interest before the crisis but were desired by banks to meet reserve requirements, for clearing and payments, and as part of their liquidity reserve. Banks avoiding the potential cost of shortfalls or overdrafts of reserve balances bought fed funds from banks with higher balances at the Fed than needed. Banks traded off the funds rate against the opportunity cost of maintaining higher zero-interest reserves, so demand to borrow reserves decreased as the fed funds rate rose.

The Fed sets a target fed funds rate, the key short-term rate influencing the general level of money market rates, and indirectly at least, long-term rates as well. It influences the fed funds rate via OMOs, transactions with commercial banks that vary the supply of reserve balances. OMOs add or drain—remove—reserves from the money market, putting downward or upward pressure on the fed funds rate. **Temporary operations** are short-term repo and reverse repo transactions conducted with about two dozen primary dealers to which the Fed initially brings its buy or sell orders. Repo transactions, in which the Fed temporarily lends reserves against Treasury securities as collateral,

---

[7] Debt assets include credit items with foreign central banks and international monetary authorities, which are treated as banking customers. US foreign currency reserves are held by the Treasury.

[8] Reserve balances are held by depository institutions, mainly commercial banks, as well as Federal Home Loan Banks (FHLBs), and government-sponsored enterprises (GSEs), including Fannie Mae and Freddie Mac. But the GSEs and FHLBs are not eligible to receive interest on their reserve balances, a distinction that was to prove important in the aftermath of the crisis.

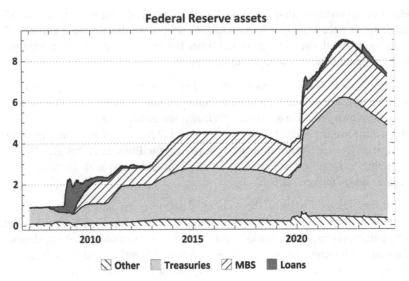

Loans include primary and secondary discount window lending, emergency liquidity facilities, and central bank liquidity swaps. Other assets include gold and unamortized discounts on Treasury and agency securities.

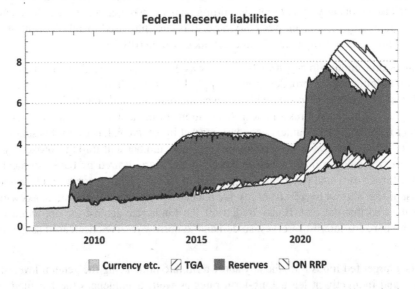

Currency etc. includes reverse repo transactions conducted as an investment service with foreign official and international accounts.

Figure 17.3 Federal Reserve balance sheet 2007–2024

$ trillions, weekly (Wednesday levels), 03Jan2007 to 22May2024. *Source*: Federal Reserve Board, H.4.1 weekly data release (https://www .federalreserve.gov/releases/h41/current/default.htm).

increase reserve balances and put downward pressure on the fed funds rate. Reverse repo transactions do the opposite, snugging up the funds rate.[9]

---

[9] Because not all dealers are banks, there may be additional links in the chain before reserve balances land in the accounts of a bank. The terminology here is also from the point of view of the Fed's dealer counterparty. The dealer repos out the security and is credited—or the bank acting as custodian for the dealer's is credited—with the reserves.

Temporary operations, the most frequent type of OMO before the crisis, were intended to address shorter-term fluctuations in liquidity demand. **Outright operations** via secondary market purchases (adding) and sales (draining) of bonds were less frequent and meant to address seasonal fluctuations and the medium-term growth of reserves, for example, the demand for currency as the economy grows.

The Fed can compare an index of the realized funds rate, the effective fed funds rate (EFFR), to its target as a measure of how successful its operations are. Efficacy can be measured in terms of the liquidity of the fed funds market, how large an OMO and how long it takes to bring the effective fed funds rate back if it strays from the target rate.

Remarkably small operations in the fed funds market sufficed to keep the funds rate close to target before the global financial crisis. The relationship between the funds rate and the volume of reserves was weak. The market cleared close to the target rate with little quantity variation, indicating inelastic bank demand for reserves. Banks tried to keep close to their reserve requirements, but they were seldom binding and not as suitable as a monetary tool as OMOs. OMOs thus shifted a vertical supply curve of fed funds, keeping the funds steady as the relatively inelastic portion of the demand curve shifts with transitory liquidity shortfalls or abundance.

Reserve balances could be low before the crisis in view of strong control over rates. The Fed's approach was to keep the fed funds market tight—a **structural deficiency** of reserves—and supply reserves day-to-day via OMOs as needed to hit the target. This also led banks to borrow funds from one another and encouraged an active fed funds market. With credible policy, the power to influence short-term rates through announcements and signaling regarding current and future policy was high relative to that of OMOs. This approach to monetary operations was implemented in stages in the 1980s and emerged from recognition of the role of expectations and of the power of time consistency and limiting monetary policy discretion to achieve better outcomes.

Figure 17.4 illustrates how OMOs work. In addition to varying reserve balances via OMOs, the Fed maintains a standing facility, the **discount window**. Almost all discount window lending is **primary credit** to banks at a **discount rate** set higher than the target fed funds rate. Although no formal

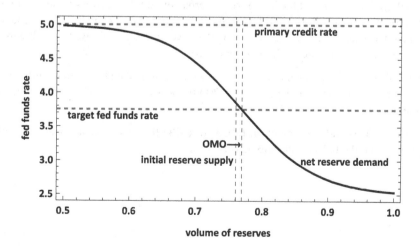

Figure 17.4 Normal monetary operations

Net demand of all depository institutions for reserves. The initial reserve supply permits the funds market to clear above the target rate of 3.75 percent. Following an expansionary OMO, the funds rate falls to 3.75 percent.

limit is set on banks' discount window borrowing by depository institutions, it is avoided because of stigma, that is, the adverse signal it might send about a banks' condition.

This type of operating framework is called a **corridor system**. Before the crisis, corridor systems were typical for central banks in advanced market economies. The discount rate constituted a ceiling on the market fed funds rate. At a high enough funds rate, banks will draw on primary credit, and the demand for fed funds becomes infinitely elastic; no bank will pay a higher rate to borrow more. Reserve balances in the United States were paid no interest, so the floor was effectively equal to zero.

The ECB, until the global financial crisis, conducted broadly similar operations. But its version of a corridor system placed greater reliance on administered rates and standing facilities. The ECB therefore, conducted fewer OMOs to fine-tune overnight rates than the Fed. Most reserves were supplied to banks via regular weekly and monthly tenders—**main** and **longer-term refinancing operations** (MROs and LTROs respectively)—at the policy rate. As in the United States, relatively little fine-tuning was needed to keep the overnight market rate close to the policy rate. A pair of standing facilities stood ready to buy or sell reserves at rates well above and below the policy rate, including a **deposit facility** that provided a floor under the overnight rate.

Further Reading

Grossman (2010) provides an overview of modern commercial and central banking history and of the lender of last resort function. Edvinsson et al. (2018) summarize the histories of the Bank of England and other early central banks. Hetzel (2022) and Mody (2018) are histories of the Federal Reserve and ECB.

Bindseil and Fotia (2021) is an introduction to monetary policy and operations. Federal Reserve Bank of New York (2024) and earlier reports describe Federal Reserve monetary operations in detail. Corsi, Marco and Mudde, Yvo, eds. (2022) and earlier papers describe Eurosystem monetary operations. Reis and Tenreyro (2022) is a recent survey of the definition and potential effects of helicopter money.

Clarida et al. (1999) outline the New Keynesian paradigm within which most developed-country central banks operate today. Goodfriend (1993) discusses inflation scares and central bank credibility. Taylor (1993) first articulated the Taylor rule. Bernanke (2007) describes financial transmission channels of monetary policy. Borio (2021) discusses the difficulty of using the natural rate in monetary policy practice. Clarida (2020) presents the Federal Reserve's flexible average inflation targeting framework, and Levy and Plosser (2022) provide a critique.

Sargent and Wallace (1981) pointed out that long-term government budget deficits must be financed by money creation. Christiano and Fitzgerald (2000) and Cochrane (2022) summarize the fiscal theory of the price level.

Carpenter et al. (2015) and Dawsey et al. (2023) describe the Fed's balance sheet, its relation to monetary policy, and the balance sheet expansion from 2008.

18

_____ Regulation for Financial Stability _____

18.1 The Lender of Last Resort Function

18.1.1 Bagehot's Rule

The Bank of England's (Bank) role in addressing financial crises, like its role in monetary policy, emerged in response to a series of crises during the late 18th and 19th centuries. **Bagehot's Rule**, published in 1873, articulated a Responsibility Doctrine, an idealized description of the Bank's duties in a crisis. The rule distinguished appropriate Bank responses to a surge in presentation of banknotes for gold. In an internal drain, a likely transitory desire for liquidity, the Bank should lend freely and without delay. In an external drain, in which gold flows out to foreign countries, it is more likely due to interest rates lower than is compatible with stable prices. The Bank should then increase rates, reducing reserves. If there is an internal and external drain, likely associated with bank failures and panic, it should lend freely but at a penalty rate.

The responsibility fell to the Bank because its size and central role in money markets gave it "the power of a large holder of money, and no more."[1] Bagehot's Rule provided lending guidelines for the **lender of last resort** (LOLR) function in financial crises that still inform advanced-economy central banks. LOLR financing is to be a backstop to keep it from displacing the private funding on which borrowers should primarily depend and to insure a reversion to normal once the crisis is over. The central bank is to lend on a large scale and without delay, early in an incipient crisis, to solvent firms and against good collateral only and at a penalty rate. Emergency lending is intended to avert a potential widespread systemic risk event.

The LOLR function operates through credibility and expectations as well as the sheer volume of lending. Making LOLR policies clear to the public in advance can reduce their likelihood. The extent to which the precepts are followed in practice is debatable as each is fraught with dilemmas arising from limited information, moral hazard, and unintended consequences.

It may be difficult to set out rules in advance and plan for the unforeseeable. In recent decades, most central bank emergency facilities have been conceived and implemented for the most part thoughtfully but very rapidly. Intervening early carries the risk of false alarms and moral hazard as intermediaries become reliant on likely support. Intervening late carries the risk that panic is already too far advanced. Action that staves off a crisis may appear in retrospect unnecessary. Banks are often reluctant to signal desperation or fragility by borrowing from the central bank at a penalty rate. Central bank lending may exacerbate the problem of stigmatizing, and thus weakening, solvent though temporarily illiquid borrowers.

Foreign-domiciled entities are increasingly important participants in a number of countries' financial markets as borrowers and lenders. Because of the dollar's role in international financial markets, many foreign bank organizations (FBOs) are located in the United States. The Federal

---

[1] Bagehot (1873), p. 118.

Reserve is a lender to FBOs, which make high use of the facilities, as well as to domestic banks and broker-dealers, raising the issue of home-country supervision and responsibility for FBOs in the event of failure.

The lender of last resort function has changed in several important ways since its origins in the 19th century and earlier. The LOLR function has been invoked and applied with increasing frequency since the 1980s and especially since the global financial crisis. Successive crises have been related to known vulnerabilities and followed by reactive public-sector responses. The focus on bank intermediation has widened to support of other segments of the financial industry and market intermediation. The line between liquidity and solvency support and the division of responsibility between central banks and government are blurrier. As its use grows more routine, its character as a last resort has dissipated and LOLR has become part of the overall system of implicit and explicit guarantees of private debt obligations and of the firms issuing them.

18.1.2 Market Maker of Last Resort

Central banks have routinely conducted monetary policy and LOLR functions by lending to banks, which in turn extend credit to other borrowers. The shift from bank to capital-market intermediation (see Chapter 1) has obliged central banks to act as **market maker of last resort**, supporting market liquidity and functioning in assets markets by buying or lending to investors directly rather than acting through banks on a scale or in ways which had little precedent before the global financial crisis. Recent broad-based central bank emergency liquidity programs have extended credit to a wide range of counterparties meeting general criteria rather than vetted individually, part of a loosely defined group of **nonbank financial intermediaries** (NBFIs), encompassing market makers, institutional investors such as insurance companies, clearing platforms, investment funds including hedge funds and money market funds, and securitization vehicles.

The programs respond to drastic spread widening and disappearance of liquidity in asset-backed securities (ABS), commercial paper, municipal bond, and other securities markets due to concerns about the assets' creditworthiness or because highly leveraged investors and market makers can no longer obtain the short-term credit funding their holdings. The central bank lends at a penalty rate and suppresses spreads between liquid assets that are close substitutes in normal times and have risen sharply during stress events.

In recent years, there have been recurrent liquidity stress events in the Treasury and money markets through which the Federal Reserve carries out its monetary operations. Examples are the repo market disturbances in September 2019 and extreme Treasury market volatility at the start of the Covid lockdowns in March 2023. Successful policy implementation requires smooth market functioning, and to maintain it, the Fed took a number of steps structurally similar to monetary operations but aimed at market liquidity conditions and introducing new central bank standing facilities. There are calls for the Federal Reserve to act as an ongoing market maker in Treasury markets rather than intervening sporadically and otherwise acting as a mere participant.[2]

The programs have frequently appeared highly effective, with spreads tightening and prices recovering on small volumes of central bank activity or upon their announcement. In aggregate, Federal Reserve emergency liquidity programs were relatively small compared with the subsequent monetary policy expansion of the Federal Reserve's balance sheet, and some did no transactions at all, having only an announcement effect. Within a month of ECB President Mario Draghi's dramatic

---

[2] See Chapter 20.

July 26, 2012, announcement that it was prepared to do "whatever it takes" to address the European sovereign debt crisis, the euro had risen nearly 10 percent against the dollar, well before the ECB even introduced new liquidity programs.

The post-crisis financial stability focus has emphasized risks posed by NBFIs and the opaque channels through which they obtain funding. Market-based intermediation is considered more procyclical than bank-based intermediation, and regulators as well as the public are concerned that crises can originate in surprising new corners of the financial system. Some NBFIs, however, may use less leverage than banks. Many of the concerns raised, such as the increased volume of leveraged lending or the potential for runs on money funds, are explainable by persistently low interest rates, direct and indirect backstops to the lenders, and the emergence of contractual arrangements and market practices designed to evade regulations.

Some central bank policies may compound problems arising if privately issued short-term liabilities are fragile and runnable rather than safe. Since the crisis, the Federal Reserve has supported its interest rate target by borrowing cash in the repo market from short-term lenders, including nonbanks, through the overnight reverse repurchase agreement (ON RRP) facility. Even before its introduction, Fed officials had expressed concern that short-term lenders might flee to the ON RRP from other short-term assets, such as deposits and commercial paper, putting the central bank into a "borrower of last resort" role during periods of stress. Similar concerns have arisen from proposals to issue central bank digital currencies (CBDCs), which potentially disrupt bank funding if depositors flee banks to CBDCs.

18.1.3   Credit Support and Liquidity Support

Under Bagehot's Rule, the central bank should address panics without putting public funds at more than minimal risk, providing liquidity support only. However, under crisis conditions, solvent intermediaries may not be readily distinguishable from the insolvent. The ambiguity is similar to the difficulty of discerning whether money market spreads, such as LIBOR-OIS (LOIS), are widening because of rising counterparty risk or eroding market liquidity.[3] Programs supporting liquidity may deliberately or inadvertently also provide credit support to borrowers shunned by private lenders.

The dilemma of credit allocation arises out of the difficulty of supporting liquidity large-scale without supporting specific sectors. The Federal Reserve bought large volumes of agency MBS as part of its large-scale bond purchase programs beginning in 2008. The ECB's **targeted longer-term refinancing operations** (TLTROs) offered preferential rates on 3-year loans to banks if they were used to fund loans to nonfinancial businesses and non-mortgage loans to households. The Fed introduced a **Secondary Market Corporate Credit Facility** (SMCCF) making direct purchases of corporate bonds during Covid. Unwinding the large volume of MBS on the Federal Reserve balance sheet through sales or by allowing the securities to mature once the crisis is over is also distortive, keeping mortgage lending rates higher than they would otherwise be.

These actions have been criticized for exposing the central bank to credit risk and for favoring some sectors of the economy over others by extending credit at favorable rates. The central bank and government have a unitary balance sheet, so central bank purchases of government bonds are an exchange of one liability for another. Changes in the value of government bonds cause a gain for either the central bank or government that is offset by a loss for the other. Losses to the central bank from privately issued securities, such as MBS and corporate bonds, are not offset by a gain to an issuing government but to a private issuer that had earlier been able to borrow at a lower rate.

---

[3] See Chapter 15.

Taking credit risk and credit allocation jeopardizes central bank independence and are properly the responsibility of government agencies. The Treasury or finance ministry, as the authority accountable through the democratic process to electoral and legislative oversight, recapitalizes banks or otherwise risks public funds if deemed necessary. Many of the Federal Reserve's emergency liquidity programs have tried to preserve this distinction by having the US Treasury take a first-loss position in the facilities through which they were implemented.

18.2   The Onset of the Global Financial Crisis

The global financial crisis became full-blown in September 2008, but market uneasiness had been building since late 2006 when residential home prices appeared to have peaked[4] and subprime mortgage lenders began reporting losses. Uneasiness turned to alarm in the course of 2007, with a sharp widening of some US banks' credit default swaps (CDS) spreads in February and the collapse in July of two hedge funds operated by Bear Stearns with highly leveraged positions in US subprime mortgage securities. In early August, large-scale unwinding of positions triggered sharp losses for quantitative equity hedge funds. Several German regional *Landesbanken* exposed to US subprime mortgage securities also reported large losses. There was intense market awareness of the exposures and high leverage of large banks in the United States and elsewhere.

The Fed initially addressed the crisis through communication and modifications of its normal operations. On August 10, 2007, it laconically announced that it " ... is providing liquidity to facilitate the orderly functioning of financial markets."[5] Subsequent OMOs were unusual in several respects, conducted several times daily, at nonstandard times including an afternoon operation, in large volumes, and accepting MBS but not Treasury collateral.

Emergency lending programs were introduced in December 2007 and early 2008 to support systemically important intermediaries and infrastructures, the banking system, and thereby indirectly liquidity in Treasury securities markets. The **Term Auction Facility** (TAF) extended credit to banks at longer terms than overnight, addressing the strains in interbank lending markets, while the **Primary Dealer Credit Facility** (PDCF) was opening made discount window lending available to nonbank dealers. Other measures addressed the potential for dysfunction in repo markets.

The crisis impacted the rest of the world as well, primarily through illiquidity in US dollar funding markets. **Currency swap lines** lent dollars to other central banks that they could in turn lend to non-US banks in their jurisdictions. It mitigated the stress on non-US banks lacking direct access to US dollar deposits that normally relied on interbank markets to fund their own dollar lending (see Chapter 15).

With the collapse of Bear Stearns in March 2008, the Fed created the first of the Maiden Lane facilities, special purpose vehicles (SPVs) to finance and house illiquid assets with sunken prices. These later included those of AIG, which failed soon after Lehman Brothers filed for bankruptcy on September 15, 2008, initiating the hot phase of the crisis. The Maiden Lane facilities were intended to prevent wider damage from what it was hoped would remain isolated firm failures by inhibiting fire sales of asset types held also by other fragile intermediaries.

Though the Maiden Lane facilities purchased distressed assets outright. Other programs announced in subsequent months also financed purchases by private investors. Money markets were shrinking

---

[4] For example, the S&P/Case-Shiller US National Home Price Index.

[5] See https://www.federalreserve.gov/newsevents/pressreleases/monetary20070810a.htm.

rapidly, risking disruption of the operations of nonfinancial as well as financial firms and potentially transmitting the turmoil to the real economy. The **Asset-Backed Commercial Paper Money Market Mutual Fund Liquidity Facility** (AMLF) aimed to prevent a run on money market funds, lending to banks buying assets of funds experiencing redemptions. The **Commercial Paper Funding Facility** (CPFF) bought highly rated commercial paper at issue. The **Term Asset-Backed Securities Lending Facility** (TALF) financed purchases of securities in markets that had become highly dependent on wholesale short-term leverage and from which private lenders had withdrawn, lending at long term to a wide range of counterparties including investment funds.

The Fed regarded its immediate response to the Lehman turmoil as an exercise of its LOLR responsibility. Many of the Fed's new facilities were authorized under Section 13(3) of the Federal Reserve Act, which permitted the Fed to lend to nonbanks unable to obtain credit elsewhere under "unusual and exigent circumstances," provided borrowers posted sufficient collateral. US government actions included the Treasury's **Troubled Asset Relief Program** (TARP), authorized after the Lehman bankruptcy. Most of the Federal Reserve lending facilities created after the Lehman filing were structured with TARP funding in a first-loss position, providing the Federal Reserve with security in two forms. The loans themselves were collateralized by the short-term paper or structured products they financed. Write downs of the loans beyond the collateral value would, up to a point, generate losses for the Treasury. The loans, however, were nonrecourse, collateralized only by the securities themselves and not in addition by other assets of the borrowers, so the Fed would have borne any loan losses beyond the TARP equity.

The roles of liquidity and credit in bringing about the crisis are hard to distinguish. Prices of the securities purchased or financed by the Fed generally recovered, and there were no loan losses, consistent with a crisis born of illiquidity rather than insolvency. The recovery of prices does not indicate that the programs were costless as public funds were exposed to risk over a period of time, equivalent to taxpayers having been obliged to purchase at above-market prices credit-risky bonds eventually repaid in full. The sharp widening of LOIS and other spreads closely related to counterparty credit risk indicates deep market concern about credit risk. In any case, had the original lenders financing the troubled assets made the same loans with less leverage, the crisis would have been far less likely or severe.

In the United States, market tensions began to ease more definitively when the results of the **Supervisory Capital Assessment Program** (SCAP), the predecessor of the current stress tests, were announced on May 7, 2009. The markets had been skeptical of the severity of the scenarios, which had not been publicly disclosed in advance, and when the details and results were announced, the shortfalls of equity capital funding were smaller than feared. Markets interpreted the results, together with the earlier announcement of a Treasury backstop funding facility, as implicitly stating that none of the participating banks would be permitted to fail, permitting the banks to raise additional equity more readily. A similar exercise in Europe in 2010 stumbled over the exclusion of sovereign debt in the banking book and was not viewed as credible.

Figure 18.1 provides an illustration of the depth of the market stress, but also of how quickly the markets recovered once reassured that no further major financial institutions were likely to fail. Citigroup was among the large US banks of which investors were wariest in view of their high exposure to short- and long-term subprime residential mortgage securitizations. In the event it failed, its subordinated bonds would be far less likely than its senior bonds to benefit from any public-sector support. The senior-subordinated spread rose to about 1000 basis points by mid-March. The CDS-bond basis, about 500 bps, indicated serious market illiquidity in Citigroup debt markets as well as dealer funding illiquidity. Both spreads had been in low single digits in mid-2006 and tightened rapidly following the SCAP announcement.

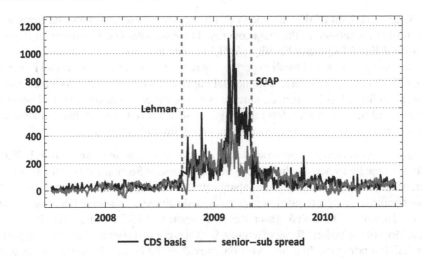

Figure 18.1 Citigroup credit spreads 2007–2010

CDS basis and senior-subordinated bond yield spreads, daily, 02Jul2007 to 02Sep2010, basis points. The senior bond spread over LIBOR (z-spread) is blended from spreads on the 4.7% maturing May 29, 2015 (CUSIP 172967CY5) and the 5.85% maturing August 2, 2016 (CUSIP 172967DQ1). The subordinated bond z-spread is that of the 4.875% issue maturing May 7, 2015. The CDS basis is measured as the spread between the 5-year on-the-run CDS and senior bond spreads, and displayed as a positive number if the cash bond is trading wider than the CDS. Vertical grid lines are placed at the dates of the Lehman bankruptcy filing and the SCAP results announcement. *Source*: Bloomberg.

18.3   Financial Stability Policy

18.3.1   Financial Stability and Monetary Policy

Although central banks share responsibility for financial regulation and crisis policy, there is an ongoing debate about whether and how it should affect the conduct of monetary policy. Financial stability policy focuses on mitigating **systemic risk**, an elusive term for crisis risk used mainly in a regulatory context. It emphasizes interconnectedness, chain-reaction transmission, and contagion via trading and credit relationships. Systemic risk arises from externalities, for example, when the asset risk of one bank increases the risks of others that own the liabilities or one large bank's troubled state impacts public perception of bank safety generally.

Monetary policy is closely related to financial stability, and in one view should not take account only of output and price stability and avoid encouraging high debt and leverage that is likely to lead to a crisis and costly adjustment. The **separation principle**, in contrast, holds that financial stability policies aimed at avoiding crises or addressing market functioning should be separate from monetary policy.

The asset bubble or "lean or clean" controversy in central banking before the global financial crisis was an earlier incarnation. The "clean" camp opposed targeting asset prices via monetary policy as too costly. Real effects of tight monetary policy are hard to offset, for example, long-lasting damage due to loss of labor skills caused by unemployment, and briefly higher inflation will in the long run result merely in a one-off rise in the price level. Monetary policy can and should instead prevent any adverse macroeconomic consequences from the onset of a bear market.[6] The "lean" side was critical of using goods price indexes, with no representation of asset values, as monetary policy

---

[6] The view that central banks should not target asset prices became known as the "Jackson Hole consensus."

targets. It urged an approach to monetary policy cognizant of financial stability concerns, tightening policy in response to financial imbalances, and emphasized the macroeconomic consequences of accommodative monetary policy not only on asset prices but also potentially lasting damage to the real economy.

Including financial stability as a formal or soft mandate of monetary policy would require additional instruments to meet an additional objective.[7] **Macroprudential policy**, which aims to identify and counter systemic risks and imbalances, in contrast to **microprudential policy** focusing on the soundness of individual intermediaries, has been put forward as providing that additional instrument. The term was introduced in 1979 and first appeared in print in 1986 and became a regulatory term of art for proposals responding to the failure to prevent the global financial crisis.

In practice, financial stability is rarely made a formal central bank mandate. Macroprudential has remained a general label for myriad proposed measures to restrain credit expansion, such as constraints on the terms of loans or the underwriting practices of specific types of lenders. The countercyclical capital buffer and other elements of capital funding regulation (see Chapter 19) are among the few areas in which regulatory innovations with a primarily macroprudential rationale have been adopted.

Reliance on formal frameworks for monetary policy, inherently based on simple models, may have contributed to accommodative policy before the global financial crisis. Long-term neutrality of money implies a more limited role for financial stability considerations in its conduct. The new Keynesian paradigm has a limited role for financial transmission mechanisms of monetary policy. Most borrowers lack direct access to capital markets and rely on banks for credit. The **bank lending channel** is the impact of changes in reserves and interest rates on banks' willingness to lend. As the level of economic activity changes, a **financial accelerator** or **credit channel** operating through balance-sheet strength and the value of collateral enables businesses and households to borrow more or less freely from banks or in capital markets.

Neutrality has been questioned by economists pointing out that easy monetary policy can generate misallocation of resources and support levels of debt with long-lasting effects. Conceptually, adding a **risk-taking channel** of transmission reduces the dilemma of financial stability versus an inflation goal by explicitly recognizing the potential future employment costs of a higher likelihood of a financial crisis. The long boom without inflation in the decades following the 1980s disinflation is evidence of a risk-taking channel. Inflation was suppressed by a global savings glut and declining costs accompanying the incorporation of many developing economies into the world trading system and reflected in US current account deficits and the "conundrum" of low long-term rates. This may have led to central banks keeping nominal rates rates low and real interest rates below the natural level and too low for longer-term stability.

Expansionary monetary policy induces leverage and reaching for yield, and the paradox of volatility creates an appearance of short-term stability. Market perception of a "Greenspan put" can lead to complacency and more risk taking. By the same token, declining asset prices and higher volatility can also substitute for increases in policy rates during downturns. Central bank tightening usually has a tightening effect on financial conditions, increasing risk aversion and market volatility, and weighing on asset prices.

Concern about financial stability and precipitating a crisis can serve as a rationale for looser policy and, at the extreme, limit monetary policy in addressing its goal of price stability. **Financial dominance** is a state of affairs in which monetary policy is constrained from tightening policy out of

---

[7] The Tinbergen rule states that the number of instruments in an optimization problem must equal the number of targets.

concern fragile banks may be jeopardized and to avoid political confrontation. It is related to the doom loop in which thinly capitalized domestic banks with large holdings of default-prone government debt make both widespread bank failures and sovereign defaults more likely, and has been a concern in the European Union since its sovereign debt crisis.

Post-crisis, financial stability considerations have arguably had greater influence on the timing of monetary policy actions. Treasury market liquidity stress episodes and responses to them raise additional concerns about the relationship between financial stability and monetary policy. For example, disturbances in repo markets during 2019 led to the Federal Reserve slowing the pace of its asset sales.

18.3.2   Financial Stability Monitoring

The main impact of macroprudential policy to date has been in the creation of new or expanded regulatory financial stability monitoring efforts. In the immediate aftermath of the global financial crisis, there was intense scrutiny of securitization and repo, which together with hedge funds and money market funds were classified as a "shadow banking" system.

New US institutions with a macroprudential orientation include the **Financial Stability Oversight Council** (FSOC), which coordinates financial stability policies vis-à-vis banks, broker-dealers and insurance companies and maintains the **Office of Financial Research** (OFR). The Federal Reserve's **Large Institution Supervision Coordinating Committee** (LISCC), the **European Systemic Risk Board** (ESRB) in Europe, and the **Financial Stability Committee** in the United Kingdom under the Bank of England function primarily as coordinating and monitoring bodies.

A core task of stability regulation as currently conceived is identifying intermediaries, known as **Systemically Important Financial Institutions** (SIFIs) in the United States, that pose systemic risk either through their activities while solvent or their potential failure. The FSB identified 29 **Global Systemically Important Banks** (GSIBs) worldwide as of 2023, eight domiciled in the United States. In the United States and Europe, these new institutions have exhibited tensions arising from the lack of clear and uniform definitions, such as the successful lawsuit over the designation of MetLife as a SIFI.

Macroprudential policy includes monitoring financial conditions, which are said to be loose if credit and leverage are expanding rapidly, volatility is low, and strategies such as basis and carry trades that involve high leverage and tail risk are being executed in large volumes Financial conditions are tight if the opposite is the case. **Financial conditions indexes** developed by private and central bank research departments include interest rates, credit spreads, market valuation metrics, and measures of market volatility. A related set of systemic risk indicators tries to assess the risk of a financial crisis. The normal levels of these indexes and indicators can vary over time, limiting their informativeness.

18.4   The Problem of Public-Sector Guarantees

Financial intermediaries are much more highly leveraged than healthy nonfinancial companies by the nature of their businesses, which consists in "using balance sheet" to intermediate investment or transactions and generating moral hazard that makes intensive monitoring necessary. But by whom? Shareholders, depositors, and other lenders have skin in the game and a direct incentive to monitor, but regulators do not. In the United States and much of the rest of the world, lenders to banks and other financial intermediaries enjoy public guarantees, some explicit but most implicit, that the debts will be repaid, encouraging higher leverage and asset risks. Because the exposure is shared by the public, the guarantees weaken monitoring by lenders.

18.4.1   Deposit Insurance

Deposit insurance is an explicit guarantee instituted in many countries that depositors will be made whole up to specified limits in the event of a bank failure. Its rationale is to protect depositors and avoid runs. It presumes the government guarantor is able to meet the insurance claims, and in some jurisdictions, there is a potential feedback to the solvency of the government guarantor and the risk of a sovereign-bank doom loop.

The drawback of deposit insurance is the moral hazard it generates. With depositors less inclined to run or to monitor, the incentives to excessive risk-taking are greater. Even though deposit insurance is limited to a certain maximum, in practice it is treated as unlimited based on historical experience, most recently the systemic risk exception employed to guarantee all deposits of Silicon Valley Bank (SVB) and Signature Bank (SBNY) in March 2023.

The FDIC practice of resolving failed banks through mergers with healthy ones contributes as well. In a **purchase and assumption** (P&A) **agreement**, part or all of the failed bank's assets and liabilities are acquired by another bank following a bidding process. The FDIC defrays, through the deposit insurance fund, any shortfall for which the acquiring bank must be compensated, and uninsured depositors of the failed bank may not experience losses.

The fraction of US bank failures in which uninsured depositors experienced losses has fallen sharply over time. During the savings and loan (S&L) crisis, uninsured depositors experienced losses in 24 percent of resolutions from 1980 to 1987, and in 14 percent from 1988 to 1991. Many struggling S&L banks increased asset risk during this period and subsequently failed, an example of gambling for redemption (see Chapter 11). In the aftermath of the S&L crisis, from 1992 to 2007, after the passage of FDICIA and with the recent experience of the effects of subsidizing private risk-taking still fresh, the ratio rose to 65 percent. From 2008 to 2022, as P&A agreements became the predominant form of resolution, the fraction of resolutions in which uninsured depositors took losses fell to about 6 percent.

In Europe, deposit insurance remains a set of national deposit guarantee schemes (DGS). Some member states are reluctant to participate in an EU-wide insurance system likely to be used to make depositors whole in other members with weaker banks and viewed as fiscally less sound. The tension between the desire to avoid a sovereign-bank doom loop by providing guarantees at the EU level and the desire to avoid responsibility for other members' banks is similar to that around the Single Resolution Mechanism (see Chapter 19).

18.4.2   Regulation of Money Market Mutual Funds

Money market funds in the United States are regulated by the SEC under Rule 2a-7 of the Investment Company Act of 1940, amended in 1983 following the global financial crisis in 2010 and the March 2020 "dash for cash." Rule 2a-7 restricts the remaining maturity of money fund assets. Originally, the weighted average maturity of a money fund's assets was required to be 90 days or fewer, reduced by post-crisis amendments to 60 days. Securities with a remaining maturity in excess of 1 year are now excluded. The rule also restricts the credit quality of MMMF assets and imposes some granularity by limiting the share of a single issuer in the total.

The SEC defines several categories of MMMF by type of asset and type of investor:[8]

Government funds invest 99.5 percent or more of their assets in cash, government securities, or reverse repo. **Treasury** funds are a subset that hold only US Treasury obligations or repo collateralized by Treasurys.

Prime funds invest in taxable short-term corporate and bank paper, repo, and short-term securitizations called **asset-backed commercial paper** (ABCP).

Tax-exempt funds investing in federally tax-exempt municipal securities are a relatively small and shrinking segment.

The SEC also distinguishes **retail** prime and tax-exempt money funds, owned exclusively by "natural persons," from **institutional** funds.

The most consequential differences between Rule 2a-7 and those governing other investment companies pertain to valuation. Rule 2a-7 enables MMMFs to maintain a **stable net asset value** (NAV) of $1.00 per share at end of day via amortized cost valuation and penny-rounding as long as fluctuations in its asset value remain within a range of 1 percent. Shares in MMMFs maintaining a stable NAV are close substitutes for bank deposits. Both offer par redemption though, in the case of MMMFs, it is end-of-day rather than intraday as well. Therefore, MMMFs are vulnerable to the same run dynamics as banks. Unlike banks, they aren't directly leveraged through debt liabilities though their repo and ABCP assets may have embedded leverage. But suspicion about their asset risk may nonetheless cause runs. If the value of a money fund's assets falls below $0.995 per share, "breaking the buck," par redemption is suspended, the shares lose their substitutability for other forms of money, and a sudden further drop in NAV is likely. No such episode occurred until September 2008, when Reserve Primary Fund, a large fund with a substantial share of its assets in Lehman Brothers commercial paper, broke the buck. In its aftermath, a number of funds received cash contributions from their bank sponsors to avoid a similar fate.

Since 2014, the use of a stable NAV has been restricted to government MMMFs and retail prime and tax-exempt funds. Institutional nongovernment—prime and tax-exempt—funds must use a **floating NAV** approach, applying an amortized or market end-of-day value to its shares. The SEC also now requires nongovernment MMMFs to maintain "liquidity buffers," which are stocks of liquid assets of specified size and composition. Thresholds of these liquidity buffers are linked to another 2014 reform, introducing redemption fees and gates for nongovernment funds. If the buffer falls below 30 percent of total assets, a fund may impose a 2 percent fee on and temporary suspension of redemptions. If the buffer falls below 10 percent, a fund must impose a 1 percent fee on redemptions.

These regulatory changes didn't work as intended during the March 2020 Covid episode in which institutional money funds saw large redemptions. The prospect of gates being imposed may have accelerated withdrawals during that episode. In its aftermath, the rules were amended to eliminate gates and strengthen liquidity requirements on fund assets. Instead, institutional funds will have the option to impose liquidity fees on withdrawals.[9]

18.4.3   Too Big to Fail

The too-big-to-fail (TBTF) problem arises when central banks and governments face a choice between bailing out shareholders or creditors of banks and other intermediaries at public expense,

---

[8] The SEC provides definitions, and the funds report their own categorization on a required Form N-MFP.

[9] The rule amendments are summarized in https://www.sec.gov/files/33-11211-fact-sheet.pdf.

or risking a financial crisis. Market participants are aware of the dilemma, which underpins expectations of support in periods of stress, lowering banks' funding costs and increasing their risk appetites. The dilemma of bailout versus crisis arises when a troubled firm displays negative externalities, such as the impact of its failure on the liquidity and solvency of other banks or on the financial system, so its failure has potential adverse financial stability consequences. At least part of the increase in risk due to higher leverage is then borne by other banks and society as a whole exposed to the risk of a financial crisis.

TBTF is a time consistency problem similar to that which arises in monetary policy, difficult to solve because the credibility of any declaration to do so would be weak. It isn't sufficient to simply declare "no more bailouts," as the cost of a crisis would be large and immediate, while the benefits of ending the TBTF policy would accrue over a long period of time.

18.4.4 Emergence of a Too Big To Fail Policy

Central bank responses to financial crises have become more drastic and accommodative as a policy of supporting troubled financial institutions with public funds to minimize immediate financial stress congealed over the past half century. In 1970, the bankruptcy of the railroad company Penn Central led to the shutdown of the commercial paper market in which it was a large issuer. Fear of insolvencies of other nonfinancial firms depending on commercial paper funding, and of banks which had invested in it, prompted aggressive Fed discount window lending. In 1984, Continental Illinois, a large bank dependent on foreign wholesale money markets as well as deposit funding, was resolved through an infusion of public funds which left all creditors, including uninsured depositors, whole. The TBTF policy was explicitly articulated in subsequent congressional testimony.

The hedge fund Long-Term Capital Management L.P. (LTCM) suffered large losses on highly leveraged long and short US Treasury positions in 1998. A proposal by investor Warren Buffet, a willing hold-to-maturity buyer, to acquire its portfolio at a deep discount was rejected, with the cooperation of the Federal Reserve Bank of New York, in favor of an acquisition by its broker-dealers and counterparties more favorable to them.

The financial crisis of 2007 and after led to an expansion of the TBTF policy in the United States, with the introduction of bank support programs from late 2007 and support for creditors of Bear Stearns, AIG, and Lehman in 2008. Much of the early liquidity support for banks was extended through government-sponsored enterprises (GSEs) that had been designed to subsidize the residential housing market but had evolved to become important lenders of last resort (see Chapter 10). Originally, government-owned, Fannie Mae and Freddie Mac became private owned and publicly traded firms in the decades before the global financial crisis. Their unique corporate charters obliged them to support the US government's residential housing finance policies. The implicit guarantee of their liabilities was fulfilled during the crisis with passage of the **Housing and Economic Recovery Act** (HERA) following the Bear Stearn failure, authorizing a Treasury rescue.

The FHLB system relies on its implicit guarantee to provide subsidized credit to banks and insurance companies when private lenders grow reluctant and has been a linchpin of publicly guaranteed backstop funding of private intermediary risk taking. Banks can borrow freely from FHLBs provided they have, as most do, residential mortgage loans, MBS, and other eligible collateral available to pledge. The extent of borrowing during the crisis was high enough that the FHLB of Seattle, which had extended one-third of its total advances in 2008 to the eventually insolvent Washington Mutual (WaMu), had to be merged with another FHLB. The FHLB System was also used extensively by SVB, Silvergate, and Signature Bank before their collapse as well as by others during the March 2023 episode.[10]

Permitting Lehman's failure and bankruptcy in September was a surprise because the Federal Reserve had assumed a first-loss position in funding Bear Stearns' mortgage-debt book in March. It brought about a market panic that highlighted the short-term costs of not bailing out failing intermediaries. The TBTF policy was further entrenched and extended beyond banks and specific intermediaries to markets with the introduction of liquidity support programs to prevent runs on money market funds and securitization markets.

The Dodd-Frank Act imposed a restriction on Federal Reserve emergency lending authority under Section 13(3), intended to enhance credibility of the no-bailout commitment and address concern about Fed powers. The Fed can lend under 13(3) only in a "program or facility with broad-based eligibility," and cannot aim at "assisting a single and specific company avoid bankruptcy." The Federal Reserve response to Covid raised questions about the effectiveness of these constraints on Section 13(3).

Seemingly unrelated legal and regulatory changes also contribute to the TBTF problem. The exemption from the automatic stay in bankruptcy has been an important factor in the rapid growth of the repo market. By reducing incentives to monitoring of counterparties, the exemption encourages intermediaries to increase reliance on short-term leverage, risk, and to grow in size, contributing to the emergence of TBTF firms.

18.4.5   The Too Big to Fail Subsidy and its Cost

The TBTF creates a subsidy for firms perceived as protected by it, especially large banks, analogous to the default put written by corporate debt investors. The subsidy benefits counterparties and borrowers as well as intermediaries' funding providers. Preferential treatment is given to banks' short-term debt as an asset through lower Basel risk weights and via implicit guarantees of MMMFs, which are key investors in the repo and financial commercial paper markets on which banks rely for funding. The programs to prevent AIG's failure also prevented failures of large broker-dealers that had provided cash collateral to AIG in its securities lending programs or which sought additional collateral on its CDS with AIG.

Several indicators of the presence of a TBTF subsidy are in principle measurable. Ratings agencies report a **ratings uplift**, assigning higher ratings to the largest banks than to otherwise equivalent smaller banks. The overall costs of the TBTF policy and more generally of public-sector reponses to crises are greater than the explicit costs of emergency programs even when these appear to be zero because the emergency loans are repaid with minimal or no loss. Nonetheless, the public has provided a costless default put option to creditors of banks and other intermediaries enjoying the guarantees.

The subsidy affects competitiveness. It reduces banks' default risk, lowering their borrowing costs, encouraging a shift of depositors from smaller to larger banks and a greater willingness to hold uninsured deposits. Larger banks grow larger than economies of scale in banking alone would warrant, reinforcing their TBTF status. Designated SIFIs, GSIBs, and other large banks enjoy lower borrowing costs than smaller banks. Though there is some evidence that the gap had been diminishing

---

[10] Bob Fernandez, "Banks turn to Federal Home Loan Bank funding as system faces review," *Wall Street Journal*, March 31, 2023, https://www.wsj.com/articles/pro-take-banks-turn-to-federal-home-loan-bank-funding-as-system-faces-review-2da1ea70.

since the 2007 crisis, it has remained positive and widened after the March 2023 bank turmoil when deposits flowed from smaller to larger banks. Although the banking system as a whole lost deposits to nonbank forms of short-term lending, the share of large banks in the total grew.

18.4.6   Too Big to Fail and the Regulatory System

Regulatory forbearance is the practice of refraining from supervisory actions out of financial stability considerations. Before the S&L crisis, supervisors observed serious shortcomings in banks' lending practices and avoided actions that might panic a public already alert to their unsound condition. Some failed institutions continued receiving financial support, and consequently continued to take greater asset risk than if it were borne solely by shareholders.[11] A similar mechanism is at work in the phenomenon of zombie lending, which is facilitated by bank supervisors' forbearance from enforcing standards for classifying bank loans as nonperforming or adding to loan-loss reserves.

In jurisdictions with less effective bankruptcy systems, insolvency without effective resolution for nonfinancial firms results in longer periods in which resources are locked up in failing firms, lower recovery rates, and slower recovery from crises. Banks end up with a high volume of nonperforming loans (NPLs), and of legacy loan assets of questionable long-term creditworthiness acquired during economic expansions. The weight of NPLs can turn a bank into a zombie bank, unable both to make new loans or to recoup value from its outstanding loans. Italian banks, for example, had high ratios of NPLs on their balance sheets after the global financial crisis, contributing to low economic growth.

Guarantees are intended to reduce systemic risk but, like other regulatory measures, are subject to political intervention favoring particular interest groups. The immediacy of the costs of permitting bank failures strengthens its political support. For example, large tech industry depositors lobbied intensively to have limitations on deposit insurance lifted during the March 2023 crisis.[12]

The TBTF remains an unsolved public policy dilemma. Current policy approaches to mitigating TBTF focus on two related lines of effort: additional capital requirements for TBTF and large banks generally and changes to resolution mechanisms to enhance the resolvability of large banks and thus enhance the credibility of a no-bailout commitment (see Chapter 19).

Further Reading

Bagehot (1873) is the original presentation of the Rule though it was anticipated by Henry Thornton and other earlier bankers and economists. Capie and Wood (2007) is a collection of source materials and essays on the LOLR function. Madigan and Nelson (2023) discuss the emergency lending programs of recent decades. Grossman and Rockoff (2016) discuss the backward-looking, "always ready for the previous crisis" experience of the LOLR function.

Buiter et al. (2023) discuss the central bank as market maker of last resort. See Ashcraft et al. (2008) and Gissler et al. (2023) on the role of the FHLB System.

The Federal Reserve's emergency liquidity programs beginning in 2007 are described in detail, including terms, counterparties, and maximum usage in Board of Governors of the Federal Reserve System, Office of Inspector General (2010). Goodhart (1999) discusses the difficulty of discerning

---

[11] See Sharma (2022) for evidence from the S&L crisis.
[12] See Chapter 20 below.

between liquidity and solvency in crises. Taylor and Williams (2009) find using market data that counterparty credit risk predominated in the unfolding of the crisis.

Hanson et al. (2011) and Adrian et al. (2015) summarize macroprudential policy and financial stability indicators, and Claessens (2015) surveys their implementation. Malz (2019) is a critical view. Regular financial stability reports of central banks and international organizations are good sources for current data, public-sector concerns and analyses. Examples include those of the Federal Reserve (https://www.federalreserve.gov/publications/financial-stability-report.htm), the BIS, and the International Monetary Fund (https://www.imf.org/en/publications/gfsr). The April 2023 edition of the latter includes extensive discussion of NBFIs.

Schularick and Taylor (2012) document the secular trend in many countries in banks' size and leverage, and in central banks' crisis responses. Greenwood et al. (2022) relate credit growth and high asset returns to the likelihood of subsequent financial crises.

Borio (2014) and Hellwig (2014) discuss the place of financial stability in monetary policy. White (2009) discusses the "lean or clean" debate. Borio and White (2003) raised concerns about a narrow focus of monetary policy on realized inflation before the crisis. Adrian and Shin (2010b) discuss the risk-taking channel of monetary policy. Auer et al. (2022) discuss financial and monetary policy issues related to the possible introduction of CBDCs.

Brunnermeier (2016) and Gros and Shamsfakhr (2021) discuss financial dominance in the context of the European financial crisis and its risk of a doom loop. See Goodfriend (2014b) on central bank credit support and Hooley et al. (2023) for a comparison of experiences across countries.

Calomiris and Kahn (1991) and Calomiris and Jaremski (2023) summarize the debate around the effectiveness of deposit insurance as a financial stability tool. Shibut and de Verges (2020) and Ohlrogge (2023) discuss and present data on the implicit expansion of deposit insurance to uninsured deposits. Kacperczyk and Schnabl (2013) describe the runs on money funds during the global financial crisis. International Organization of Securities Commissions (2020) provides data and surveys public policy approaches to money fund regulation. See also Ennis et al. (2022).

Strahan (2013) and Schich (2018) are surveys of the TBTF problem. See Federal Deposit Insurance Corporation (1997) on the Continental Illinois depositor bailout. Hellwig (2021), Admati and Hellwig (2024a and 2024b) and Cochrane and Seru (2024) argue that the TBTF problem has worsened since the global financial crisis. Federal Reserve Bank of Minneapolis (2017) present a solution to the TBTF problem focusing on much higher equity funding requirements and a tax on leverage applying to nonbanks.

Walter and Weinberg (2002) estimate the magnitude of financial sector guarantees and Santos (2014) estimates the borrowing cost advantage for large banks.

Acharya et al. (2022) and Bellia et al. (2022) estimate the funding advantage and present evidence that the impact of guarantees on bank liability pricing had diminished since the global financial crisis, at least up until the early 2023 bank turmoil.

Lucas (2019) discusses methods of measuring the costs of bailouts using the global financial crisis example. Kelly et al. (2012) estimate their value using option market-implied correlations.

Strahan (2013) presents evidence from Germany that expectations of a bailout increase the likelihood of bank failures, Arteta et al. (2020) find that the presence of guarantees increase large banks' eagerness to take on exposure to tail risk, and Andersen and Jensen (2022) document the effect of a bailout during a 1908 Scandinavian banking crisis on subsequent bank leverage.

Regulation of Capital Funding, Liquidity, and Large Banks

19.1 Historical Background of the Capital Standards

During the international financial instability of the 1960s, foreign banks' international activities were seen as a source of instability in domestic markets. The failure of German Bankhaus Herstatt had caused large losses at some US banks. Central banks and finance ministers grew more concerned about falling bank capital ratios and increased risk, taking. Concerns about competition from highly leveraged foreign banks with lower funding costs also played a role.

A year after its establishment in 1974, the Basel Committee issued a proposal for international regulatory cooperation, the *Report on the Supervision of Banks' Foreign Establishments*, or "Concordat". Since then, the Committee has led international coordination of regulatory standards limiting bank leverage and liquidity risk, beginning with the 1988 **Basel Capital Accord** (the "Accord", or Basel I), an agreement on minimum capital ratios, meaning the share in banks' funding mix of equity and equity-like claims. Statutory implementation is carried out by national authorities.

Initially, the standards focused on credit risk and set out a simple approach to calculating minimum capital ratios, assigning risk weights to different asset types, including off-balance-sheet exposures, and further entrenching agency credit ratings. The 1996 Market Risk Amendment to the Accord allowed the use of banks' own internal models to compute risk weights, and the 2004 Basel II Revised Framework permitted internal modeling of some elements of credit risk measurement.

The global financial crisis, an event the standards had been designed to prevent, revealed a number of gaps and blind spots and spurred a sequence of major revisions "Basel 2.5". The changes, however, have remained within a basic framework enshrining banks as highly leveraged intermediaries, but following a complex set of rules to measure and constrain that leverage in ways thought to enhance stability.

The Basel III revisions, published in 2010 and revised again since, aimed at a number of potentially conflicting objectives only partially met. They called for higher minimum capital funding ratios, especially for large banks, and included more comprehensive treatment of market, counterparty, liquidity and other risks arising from banks' activities in securities and securitization markets that contributed directly to the severity of the crisis and were recognized as having been neglected.

In an effort to reduce regulatory evasion, a set of leverage-based minimums parallel to those based on risk was introduced. A major objective of the post-crisis changes in the Basel standards was higher quality and loss absorbency of capital in an effort to avoid putting public sector resources or senior creditors at risk in unwinding failing intermediaries. The revisions also aimed to reduce variations across banks and jurisdictions in how rules are drafted and interpreted. The new standards hoped to avoid becoming too detailed, complex, and prescriptive in the process.

Covid led to a pause in some implementation dates that had already been incorporated in final rules. Particularly in the United States, the March 2023 bank panic led to additional revisions in regulatory implementation and proposals for higher large-bank capital ratios. US regulators put forward a Notice of Proposed Rule in Guidance to finalize capital regulation in July 2023. Overall, the capital and liquidity standards appear to have reached a relative steady state, and further "Basel IV" or "Basel III endgame" revisions are focused on implementation by specific jurisdictions.

The post-2008 capital standards have had mixed results. The share of funding through equity and highly subordinated debt securities increased materially and brought down the high leverage prevailing before the crisis. The market reaction to investor losses, whether realized or only narrowly averted through public-sector support, would likely have compelled banks to reduce leverage in any case. Although the post-Basel III capital funding ratios are higher, they are likely lower than those which would prevail if banks were obliged to fund their current asset exposures without TBTF and other guarantees.

The capital rules have remained highly complex and likely impose inefficient allocation and administrative costs. As expressed long before the crisis, "Standard government blunderbuss, one-size-fits-all regulations cannot, and should not be expected to match the kind of delicate balancing of interests achievable through private contracting"[1]. The revised capital standards have not prevented large or widespread bank panics, as seen in the series of bank failures beginning in March 2023.

19.2   Bank Accounting Standards and Regulation

The international and US capital standards rely to a large extent on bank accounting, loss and valuation concepts, different in many respects from those of nonfinancial firms. Accounting, regulatory, and tax rules influence the timing of loss recognition and impact lenders' reported income statements and balance sheets. Regulators treat similar positions differently because of their different accounting treatment and motivation. The differences for banks are determined in the United States in part by decisions on **Generally Accepted Accounting Principles** (GAAP) by the Financial Accounting Standards Board (FASB) and similar semi-private organizations in other jurisdictions and internationally. They are intended to make banks' financial statements more informative, but are also subject to lobbying.

19.2.1   Treatment of Losses

Accounting standards and US regulation require banks to estimate a loss reserve, the amount of loans not expected to be collected due to borrower defaults and insolvencies, and report it as a contra asset account on its balance sheet. As loan losses are recognized, they are absorbed by the loss reserve rather than hitting net income; loan assets and the loss reserve are reduced by a **charge-off** or **write down**. The income statement is unaffected unless losses differ from the initial estimate. If losses are expected to be greater than initially estimated, **loss provisioning** by a bank increases the loss reserve. If loans mature without loss, net income will be higher as the reserve is released.

Historically, banks estimated **incurred** or **probable incurred losses**, focusing on likely credit losses, reported in an allowance or reserve for loan and lease losses (ALLL) account. This standard was criticized for tardy recognition of losses, suspected of manipulation to smooth earnings and gain tax advantages, and thought to contribute to procyclicality by obliging banks to increase provisioning during bad times. Regulators in 2016 introduced the **current expected credit losses** (CECL) methodology, based on the bank's forward-looking estimate of loan losses over the entire life of a

---

[1] Miller (1995), p. 488.

debt as determined at the time a loan is extended. An **allowance for credit losses** (ACL) account replaces ALLL.

The CECL standard has been critiqued for reliance on generally inaccurate forecasts of the state of economy over the loan life. By neglecting offsetting revenue from higher spreads compensating for risk in lending rates, it may disincentivize lending to riskier borrowers. If CECL estimates increase provisioning when economic downturns appear more likely, it may also contribute to procyclicality. Large banks have begun implementation, with deadlines extended under the 2020 Coronavirus Aid, Relief, and Economic Security (CARES) Act.

The accounting treatment of banks' securities holdings has also been a focus of regulation. Securities held by banks fall into these accounting categories:

Trading securities are held principally for the purpose of selling in the near term, including market-making inventories, and reported at **fair value**.

Available for sale (AFS) debt securities are held with the intent of selling if the need arises, for example, for liquidity, or opportunistically, and also reported at fair value.

Held to maturity (HTM) debt securities are held as investments and reported at amortized cost tied to purchase price.

Banks also account for unrealized or mark-to-market (MTM) gains and losses stemming from changes in the market or fair values of securities portfolios. For trading securities, MTM fluctuations flow through to reported earnings and net income. For AFS securities, they affect the capital account of the balance sheet through the **accumulated other comprehensive income** (AOCI) account, a component of shareholders' equity. A mark-to-market loss decreases AOCI and equity but doesn't flow to earnings or net income until realized. Gains and losses on HTM securities are not recorded on the balance sheet, but banks make them public in report footnotes. Changes in securities' creditworthiness also affect trading, AFS and HTM securities and are recorded as **other than temporary impairment** (OTTI). It is closely analogous to loss provisioning for bank loans and is reflected in earnings. For a sense of how important these fluctuations can be, Figure 19.1 shows the drastic increase in banks losses following the rapid interest rate hikes of 2022–2023.

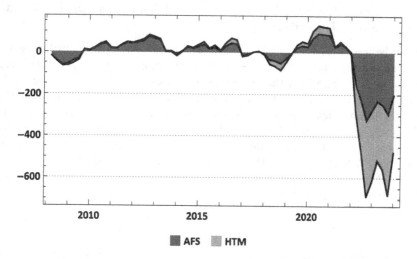

Figure 19.1 Banks' unrealized gains on investment securities 2008–2023

All FDIC-insured institutions, quarterly March 2008 to December 2024 *Source*: FDIC Quarterly Banking Profile, Chart 13.

The credit valuation adjustment (CVA) is an accounting position intended to capture counterparty credit risk (see Chapter 9) and is required for fair-value hedge accounting and by the revised Basel capital standards. CVA is a contra asset account; if a derivatives contract is closed out without loss, the CVA is returned to earnings. The debt valuation adjustment (DVA) has been somewhat controversial because an increase in DVA due to a bank's own credit deterioration leads to a reduction in its net CVA liabilities. The DVA is permitted under accounting but not under Basel capital rules.

19.2.2 The Banking and Trading Books

The capital standards distinguish between a bank's **banking** and **trading books**. Largely aligned with accounting designations, it arises because the capital standards seek to identify the market risk in the banking book and the credit risk in the trading book and to fully capture both.

Banking book assets, the original focus of the Basel framework, are primarily commercial, industrial and residential loans and mortgages with the bulk of assets in most commercial banks. They are valued at par, but with provisions for default loss through the ACL account. The exposures present mostly credit risk and some market, especially interest-rate risk. The banking book also includes illiquid assets, such as unlisted equities and real estate. Securities in the banking book are considered HTM and not marked to market.

The trading book consists of positions held for liquidity, market making, and proprietary trading purposes and hedges of those positions, and it includes trading and AFS securities. They are mostly exposed to market and credit risk.

Shareholders, debt investors, and managers of financial as well as nonfinancial firms are averse to fluctuation in earnings and are only somewhat less averse to fluctuations in AOCI and the book value of equity. Therefore, there is a bias toward classifying securities as HTM rather than AFS and a temptation to opportunistically reclassify securities as market conditions change. A reclassification might avoid reporting a loss or accelerate the reporting of gains. An example from the aftermath of the global financial crisis is Citibank's completion in the first quarter of 2011 of a round-trip transfer of securities from trading to HTM, and then back to the trading portfolio. In doing so, they avoided reporting an initial MTM loss as a reduction of net income followed by a gain when the market value of the securities recovered, smoothing reported earnings.[2]

The distinction between the banking and trading book thus creates an opportunity for regulatory arbitrage. The same asset may have different required capital funding depending on how it is assigned. The Basel Committee's **Fundamental review of the trading book** (FRTB), concluded in 2013, tightened the so-called "boundary" to limit regulatory arbitrage of trading versus banking book assignments. Following these regulatory changes, selling any HTM securities causes the bank's entire HTM portfolio to be irrevocably reclassified as AFS and reported at fair value. Reclassification of AFS securities as HTM still permits banks to avoid marking them to market on their balance sheet and incurring AOCI losses. In 2021, as interest rates began rising sharply, Silicon Valley Bank (SVB) transfered $9.0 billion of securities from AFS to HTM. Banks assiduously shifted bonds into their HTM portfolios in 2022 and 2023.[3]

---

[2] Tracy Alloway, "Citi's Basel-dodging, capital-avoiding, accounting switch," *Financial Times*, April 19, 2011, https://www.ft.com/content/0440dc92-b065-39b5-b405-ba6a47867c6d.

[3] SVB Financial Group (2023), p. 99, and Jonathan Weil, "As interest rates rose, banks did a balance-sheet switcheroo," *Wall Street Journal*, March 29, 2023, https://www.wsj.com/articles/as-interest-rates-rose-banks-did-a-balance-sheet-switcheroo-8e71336f.

19.3   Measuring Risk-Weighted and Adjusted Assets

The Basel III standards set regulatory minimum capital ratios and define in detail the numerator (capital) and denominator (assets). The numerator is the **quantity of capital**, the aggregate volume of specific types of liabilities issued by the bank. The denominator may be either:

Risk-weighted assets (RWA), calculated using detailed weighting systems for broad sources of risk. This denominator is used to compute the **risk-based capital** ratio, intended to provide a risk-sensitive measure that ideally varies accurately with the riskiness of banks' assets and activities. It addresses the disjunction between the size of a bank's balance sheet and the amount of asset risk it faces. A trading book, for example, may include a large volume of low-risk assets. Basel III set more stringent minimum capital ratios to RWA, regarding quality and quantity.

Total or **balance-sheet assets**, adjusted using regulatory definitions. This denominator is used to compute the **leverage-based capital** ratio introduced under Basel III, intended primarily as a backstop or control on risk-based capital, and limit manipulation of risk measures by banks.

Banks must compute the risk- and leverage-based minimum ratios and meet the higher one. If binding, risk-based minimum capital makes lower-risk assets more attractive; if binding, the leverage ratio makes higher-risk assets relatively attractive and disincentivizes lower-risk activities, such as repo and bond market intermediation. The risk-based minimum is typically binding on a bank, but banks are acutely aware of both constraints as they manage their assets and funding.

19.3.1   Risk-Weighted Assets

The Basel standards distinguish broad sources of risk for which RWA are to be computed: credit, market, counterparty or CVA, and operational risk. A bank's total RWA is calculated as a simple sum, with no diversification benefit from combining sources of risk. For each type of risk, there is a simpler or standard approach to computing RWA and a more complex approach based on internal modeling. Larger banks are generally obliged to apply internal models, which are vetted by regulatory bodies and on-site supervisors. Banks using internal models to calculate market risk capital must also calculate it via the standard approach as a control and use the larger of the two.

The **standardized approach** for credit RWA was first introduced in the original 1988 Accord. To apply it, banks essentially look up the weights for their holdings in tables of risk weights by type and credit quality of the assets. Sovereign debt risk weights, for example, depend on the credit rating of the issuer. Risk weights for bank debt are a function of the sovereign rating of the jurisdiction in which the bank is domiciled in a tacit acknowledgement of the potential reliance of bank solvency on the public sector for support. In the United States, the use of ratings is now excluded by the Dodd-Frank Act. Organization for Economic Cooperation and Development (OECD) risk classifications for sovereigns are applied instead.

In the **internal ratings-based** (IRB) **approach**, the bank follows a complex chain of computations to calculate risk weights, rather than looking them up in a table. It is open to banks that meet size and other criteria. In the standardized and IRB approaches, banks apply regulatory weights and parameters, but the IRB approach uses some bank-computed inputs. It has two rungs, distinguished by the set of parameters estimated by the bank:

Foundation IRB: large banks apply an internal estimate of the probability of default (PD).
Advanced IRB: in addition to the PD, very large banks may apply an internal estimate of LGD, exposure at the time of default (EAD), and the maturity of the exposure.

Asset correlation is difficult to reliably estimate empirically, and were banks permitted to provide estimates, the scope for gaming would widen considerably. Therefore, the Basel approach specifies values for the asset correlation and formulas relating the correlation to loan size and PD, higher for larger loans and lower for loans with a higher PD. Correlations range between 0.1 and 0.25, with most near 0.2. Empirical work taking the crisis experience into account finds the Basel correlation parameters may be too low, resulting in lower regulatory capital requirements.

Application of the advanced IRB approach is open only to banks meeting an additional size qualification. In the United States, the advanced IRB approach has been obligatory for **advanced approaches** banks, a regulatory designation for large, internationally active banks with over $250 billion in assets. For banks that qualify, the IRB approach generally reduces RWA and the required capital funding minimum compared to the standard approach.

Requirements for market risk capital are generated primarily in banks' trading books. Market RWA accounts for a smaller portion of total regulatory risk capital than credit risk for most banks but can be substantial for banks with large broker-dealer subsidiaries. Many of the problems exposed by the crisis pertain to market risk, such as underestimation of tail risk and liquidity risk. Several of the 2023 bank failures were largely due to interest rate risk. The revised market risk capital rules also addressed the variability across banks and jurisdictions in how rules for measuring market risk RWA were interpreted at the cost of detailed prescriptive rules and more complexity.

Sources of market risk include:

General market risk arises from shocks to broad risk factors: interest rates, equity, foreign exchange, credit spreads, and commodities.
Default risk or credit-risk exposures are presented by trading book assets such as structured credit products. In earlier states of the standards, it was referred to as **specific risk**, defined as "exposures to specific issuers of debt securities or equities" or other idiosyncratic sources of risk, but the classification was phased out following the FRTB.

Similar to credit risk capital, there are standardized and internal models approaches to calculating market risk capital and a "simplified alternative" to the standardized approach for eligible small banks. The standardized or "building-block" approach treats each risk factor separately. It seeks to capture linear (delta), nonlinear (curvature) sensitivities, and to implied volatility (vega). For delta and vega risks, the standards provide tables of risk weights by type of sensitivity and risk factor. Curvature risk is calculated using scenario analyses of the impact of positive and negative risk factor shocks. Diversification is recognized within risk factors via prescribed correlations but not across risk factors. A **residual risk add-on** (RRAO) of 1 or 0.1 percent of the gross notional of certain assets captures less-common but often important sources of risk, such as the correlation risk of securitizations and the prepayment risk of mortgage-backed securities (MBS).

The internal models approach to calculating market risk capital was formerly based on Value-at-Risk (VaR), but has moved toward expected shortfall following the FRTB. Expected shortfall is computed by each "trading desk" and then aggregated. It is measured at the 97.5 percent confidence level,[4] and based on an instantaneous price shock equivalent to a 10-day move, calculated daily using the worst 250 days of the observation interval. The historical observation period must

---

[4] Under Basel I and 2.5, market risk capital was based on VaR estimated at the 99th percentile, roughly equal to a 97.5 percent expected shortfall if returns follow a normal distribution. A normal parametric 97.5 percent expected shortfall is equal to 1.00492 times a 99 percent VaR.

encompass a minimum of one year of data or a weighted average of 6 months. A range of computational techniques and and models is acceptable; analytical models, Monte Carlo, and historical simulation can be used.

Calculation of expected shortfall includes a liquidity adjustment capturing the time to liquidate positions in stressed market conditions, assumed to be 10–250 days, depending on the risk factor. Liquidity adjustments make the time horizon of the expected shortfall measure a complex weighted average. The **stress capital add-on** is a scenario-based component based on the most severe 12-month stress period of the observation interval. The **default risk capital** (DRC) requirement is applied to credit exposures stemming from debt instruments in the trading book and is a component of market risk capital under both approaches. It employs risk weights by rating under the standard approach or is modeled as a credit portfolio under the internal models approach. Backtesting is required, but because of the inherent difficulty of backtesting expected shortfall (see Chapter 8), the standards rely on VaR backtesting, employing exceedance counts.

The market risk capital requirement under the standardized approach is

$$\text{sensitivities-based capital} + \text{RRAO} + \text{DRC},$$

and under the internal models approach it is

$$\text{expected shortfall} + \text{stressed capital add-on} + \text{DRC}.$$

19.3.2   Leverage Exposure

The Basel III leverage-based capital calls for a minimum **leverage ratio** of aggregate capital funding instruments relative to the **exposure measure** of on- and off-balance-sheet exposures or **adjusted assets**. The denominator includes on-balance-sheet assets, derivative and other off-balance-sheet exposures, based on NPV or option values, plus potential future exposure. It also includes **securities financing transactions** (SFTs)—repo and securities lending—with some netting recognized. Repo netting is generally limited to the same counterparty, settlement platform, or settlement date. For most banks, netting reduces adjusted assets compared to balance-sheet assets, but for some with large derivatives portfolios, adjusted assets may exceed balance-sheet assets.

Since the global financial crisis, regulators have expressed growing discomfort with the capital rules' reliance on risk modeling and wariness of the incentive to reduce RWA and minimum capital requirements through creative use of models and judgment calls about how to apply the detailed guidelines for computing RWA. **RWA density**, the ratio of RWA to adjusted assets, is a measure of the impact of modeling on RWA estimates. A low RWA density may be related to bank's business mix or to RWA manipulation.

19.4   Quality and Quantity of Capital

The required quantity of capital is the volume of liabilities or funding instruments that a bank must issue to be in compliance with the standards. Liabilities eligible to be considered **regulatory capital instruments** are distinguished by the **quality of capital**. The criterion is their **loss absorbency**: can losses be imposed on the liability without jeopardizing the bank or financial stability? The standards set out a hierarchy of loss absorbency and criteria for acceptance of a capital instrument into each category. Loss thresholds are generally set by the standards in accounting terms rather than market values.

19.4.1   Quality of Capital

Tier 1 or **core capital** is intended to cover **going concern** losses the firm is likely to survive. Tier 1 capital instruments should be able to suffer write-downs, even in a crisis or stress event, without jeopardizing the issuing bank or forcing its entry into resolution. Tier 1 has two subcategories: **Common equity Tier 1 capital** (CET1), the most loss-absorbent funding, includes common equity and retained earnings. CET1 is calculated in conformity with accounting standards, but with a number of adjustments. Intangible assets, such as **goodwill** and **Deferred Tax Assets** (DTAs) arising from previous losses are excluded. Larger banks must include AOCI, the cumulative MTM gains or losses on AFS securities, while smaller banks may choose to exclude it. This election became controversial following the bank panic of March 2023 and has been narrowed. Many banks, notably SVB, which opted out of $1.9 billion in losses added to AOCI in 2022, had large unrealized losses on AFS securities, avoiding large diminutions of their regulatory capital.

Additional Tier 1 capital (AT1) includes hybrid securities with equity and debt characteristics, such as **noncumulative perpetual preferred stock** and **contingent capital** or **contingent convertible bonds** ("CoCos"). CoCos have been more widely issued in Europe than by US banks because US tax treatment of their coupons as a deductible interest expense is uncertain. Contingent capital is contractually designed to be written down or converted into common equity when certain triggers are met. Conversion to equity, but not writedown, dilutes existing shareholders, but both contribute to recapitalization. One type of trigger is a reduction in CET1 capital, generally defined as a writedown although market value triggers have also been proposed. Another is a determination by the issuer's regulator that the bank has reached the **point of non-viability** (PoNV).

Tier 2 or **supplementary capital**, which includes certain types of subordinated debt, preferred stock, and loan loss reserves (the ALLL or ACL account) within certain limits, is intended to cover **gone concern** losses, those of a failing firm. Write downs of Tier 2 funding instruments are considered incompatible with the issuer's continued viability. Though going concern capital is about keeping a bank solvent, gone concern capital is about cleaning up the mess if insolvency occurs. Rather than minimizing the PD, Tier 2 capital aims to meet the firm's expected loss given default and protect taxpayers, deposits, and senior unsecured debt in the event of bank failure by making available a volume of junior liabilities to be written off or converted to equity. If the bank fails, these losses are borne by the bank's investors rather than the public.

The concern with the quality of capital reflects the crisis experience. Some funding instruments, such as Trust Preferred Securities (TruPS) in the United States, had been designed to have high loss absorbency but contributed to instability of the issuing banks, rendering them unable to raise capital funding without first reducing TruPS liabilities. Some banks received public support while limiting losses on regulatory capital instruments because officials doubted the capacity of the securities to absorb losses without inducing panic and runs. The public, rather than the banks' investors, bore part of the cost.

19.4.2   Quantity of Capital

The Basel III standards raised the minimum common equity Tier 1 capital ratio from 2 to 4.5 percent. The minimum total Tier 1 capital ratio, including AT1, is 6 percent. Minimum total capital, including Tier 1 and Tier 2, remained at 8 percent under Basel III, unchanged from Basel II.

Under the Basel III standard, the minimum leverage ratio is 3 percent of adjusted assets, to be funded entirely through Tier 1 capital instruments. US bank capital rules for banks generally and large banks in particular are somewhat more stringent than the Basel, FSB, and European Union standards.

Under the PCA framework introduced by the FDICIA in 1991, the FDIC is required to impose a plan to restore capital adequacy to a bank not "adequately capitalized," with a leverage ratio below 4 percent, relative to a generally smaller exposure measure that excludes off-balance-sheet items. Banks not "well capitalized," with a leverage ratio below 5 percent, are restricted from accepting **brokered deposits**, large deposits that are divided up to be eligible for deposit insurance and bought from a large bank through a broker who sells them piecemeal to smaller banks.

The Basel III standards also introduced additional "buffers" that must be met through issuance of CET1. Buffers are mandatory, and compliance requires banks to issue regulatory capital instruments, but they are not labeled risk-based capital requirements. Not meeting these buffers leads to the imposition of restrictions on capital distributions such as dividend payments, and on discretionary bonuses for senior management. The **capital conservation buffer** (CCB) applies to all banks and calls for additional common equity of 2.5 percent of RWA. It is designed to reduce the likelihood that fluctuations in the values of capital instruments bring a bank out of compliance.

A **countercyclical buffer** (CCyB) of 0–2.5 percent, also to be met through CET1 capital funding, is intended to dampen fluctuations in leverage that occur as a result of fluctuations in market sentiment and risk aversion and applied only to large banks. The CCyB is to be set by regulatory authorities within each jurisdiction and varied over time as financial conditions change, increasing, for example, when bank lending is expanding rapidly relative to GDP. In the United States, it is set by the Federal Reserve and has remained at zero to date in contrast to a number of other countries.

In the European Union (EU), capital standards are broadly regulated at the union level but specified and supervised by the member states' regulatory bodies, a process similar to other legislative harmonization efforts in the EU. Some capital rules are uniformly set through a regularly updated **Capital Requirements Regulation** (CRR); a **Capital Requirements Directive** (CRD) sets goals to be implemented by member states. There is a good deal of variation across the EU, particularly in setting capital buffers.

19.4.3   Effectiveness and Market Impact of Capital Regulation

The Basel III capital standards and their implementation have several drawbacks. Perhaps most important is that they likely do not impose on banks an equity funding requirement sufficient to compensate for the market discipline lost through pervasive guarantees of their senior debt and deposit funding. Banks remain highly leveraged if modestly less so than before 2008.

In the absence of a market assessment, determining the appropriate level of capitalization is based on modeling, educated guesswork, and historical comparisons. The standards have grown quite complex, and there is strong evidence that simpler rules would be more effective in preventing bank failures and less susceptible to manipulation for purposes of regulatory evasion.

The design of the rules faces a dilemma: reliance on balance-sheet measures can lead to wildly punitive or permissive standards for banks with different businesses, simple weights can't meet the complexity of large banks' balance sheets, and internal models can be gamed and are susceptible to model risk. A high regulatory leverage ratio is distortive, ignoring the relative risks of different assets and penalizing low-risk activities, such as Treasury repo and covered foreign-exchange arbitrage, that consume a great deal of balance sheet. But the risk-weighting rules incentivize firms to invest in assets with understated risk weights relative to others, increasing overall asset risk relative to any capital ratio. Capital based on RWA can be gamed by selecting the riskiest investments in a risk-weight category, or by adjusting internal models up to the point that would be flagged in supervisory review. Examples before the global financial crisis include low or zero risk weights assigned to senior tranches of subprime mortgage securitizations and sovereign debt of less-creditworthy European countries.

Efforts to constrain subjectivity and gaming of the system may instead lead to different treatment of equivalent risk across banks. The risk-weighting scheme has less efficacy than simple leverage for predicting retroactively which banks would fail in 2008 and 2009, and over the decade preceding the crisis, average RWA of large banks was declining while simple leverage ratios were rising.

Leverage-based capital is one precaution in an effort reduce complexity. Another is to set a floor under the internal model RWA based on the standardised approach RWA. The most recent Basel III standards and their implementation in the United States attempt to address this problem by reducing the scope and incentives for banks to use internal modeling, pushing banks to the more prescriptive standard approaches which in the past have been highly inaccurate in consequential ways. Following the March 2023 bank failure episodes, US regulators have proposed limiting their use further and applying the US version of the international standards to smaller banks. Capital funding adequacy for large banks and financial stability have become more reliant on regulation and less on market discipline even as regulatory authorities are expressing less confidence in the standards.

The rules diminish incentives to market making, reducing market liquidity at times of stress when dealers are called upon to absorb assets being shed by other market participants. For large banks especially, balance sheet has become more costly. Dealers are less eager to engage in market making, and a greater share of market making has gravitated to high-frequency trading firms.

Dealers have also reduced participation in forms of near-arbitrage trading that aim to exploit small price differences, such as US Treasury basis trades. They require large balance-sheet positions and high leverage to attract investors and have become less attractive to banks as a result of capital funding rules that disfavor large but relatively low-risk on-balance-sheet exposures. As the rules have been implemented, dealers have reduced or carefully managed their participation in basis trades, instead indirectly funding such near-arbitrage trades through prime brokerage subsidiaries that extend credit to hedge funds.

Dealers now allocate balance-sheet capacity more carefully among their counterparties. Hedge funds are reliant on dealers to provide precious leverage, and to make good use of the borrowing capacity they have, they have been carrying out a greater share of these near-arbitrage trades. Hedge funds, however, are apt to reduce rather than grow positions during periods of stress and more susceptible to pressure to liquidate positions when spreads widen unexpectedly. Market spreads among near-substitute assets have become wider, more persistent, and prone to suddenly widen drastically.

Negative swap spreads are another example of the effects of regulatory constraints raising the shadow cost of balance sheet for market makers. Market makers paying fixed in interest rate swaps used by insurers and pension funds hedging their liabilities, or by nonfinancial firms transforming fixed into floating rate debt, hedge these positions through offsetting swaps or by taking long positions in Treasurys. With lower rates and larger, higher-duration liabilities, institutional investor demand to receive fixed in swaps shifted higher. This led to a switch in dealer net positions in Treasury securities from short to long just as the regulatory cost of balance sheet increased. If the swap spread is negative, a swap hedged with a long Treasury is a form of carry trade, offering a near-arbitrage opportunity with positive cash flow for the bank. With costlier balance sheet, banks require a wider negative swap spread to do so, driving the two rates persistently and further apart.[5]

---

[5] See also Chapter 15. Data on primary dealers' aggregate net position in Treasury securities are available at https://www.newyorkfed.org/markets/counterparties/primary-dealers-statistics.

Soon after the rules began to be implemented, a number of banks began engaging in **capital relief trades** (CRTs), transactions intended to lower a bank's required capital funding while retaining most of the risk and return of the assets involved. A CRT is a derivative instrument or structured credit product in which the asset pool consists of a set of commercial or real estate loans. The banks sells the first-loss tranche of the exposure to the assets, generally to institutional investors, and retains the more senior tranche. The bank is thereby able to reduce its RWA, while an insurance company gains an exposure to an asset type, say, commercial loans, it could not otherwise readily access. Although the bank retains the default and default correlation risk of a severe deterioration of the underlying credits, it can reduce the risk weight and required capital funding compared to the underlying exposure. The purchaser of the junior exposure takes on the risk of a more moderate deterioration of the credits.

CRTs are structured in different ways, such as credit default swaps or synthetic or cash securitizations. They are also structured differently depending on the jurisdiction of the bank and its particular implementation of Basel III and whether the bank takes the standard or internal models approach to computing capital requirements. The structures take on additional complexity because they are also designed to evade classification as insurance contracts or swaps, which would require conformity to regulation of those financial products. The structure must also avoid being subject to other regulations, such as the Dodd-Frank Act **risk retention** rules, which might require the bank, as a securitization sponsor, to retain a first-loss exposure as well.

19.5 Regulation of Large Banks

Large banks have always received somewhat different treatment from smaller ones due to size and complexity. The regulatory changes since the global financial crisis have focused on capital adequacy for large banks and on how to unwind them without causing wider stress when they fail. The Basel and post-crisis US approach to the financial stability risks presented by large, TBTF banks is to "tailor" by the size of the bank. Some banks are regarded as clearly TBTF because of their size or regulatory designation as an SIFI or GSIB, but large banks are complex and opaque firms and two banks of the same size can differ in their asset risks. Regulators can't be sure in advance which banks are TBTF.

US banks are classified into four categories, broadly distinguished by their size as measured by total assets. Banks particularly reliant on short-term wholesale funding may be assigned to a higher category than based on size alone. The eight largest, the GSIBs, are Category I organizations. They and the Category II organizations are obliged to apply advanced approaches in calculating their risk-based capital requirements. Categories III and IV encompass mid-size and smaller banks.

19.5.1 Regulatory Capital Ratios for Large Banks

The capital standards for large banks are part of the remedy for the consequences of the TBTF guarantee. In the absence of guarantees, banks would likely be obliged by markets to operate with much higher levels of equity funding than in the postwar era generally and especially before the crisis. They would otherwise not be able to obtain debt or deposit funding. In the presence of TBTF and implicit guarantees, they are able to take on far more leverage, and limits on leverage are imposed by regulation rather than lenders.

Minimum capital requirements are higher for large banks. As part of the Basel III framework, a **GSIB surcharge** of between 1 and 3.5 percent CET1 of RWA was introduced for the largest banks.

Calibration of the GSIB surcharge, currently set between 1 and 2.5 percent in different jurisdictions, is based on a **GSIB score** that tries to identify high systemic risk. GSIBs are also subject to higher loss absorbency requirements.

The **supplementary leverage ratio** (SLR) requires banks in Categories I, II, and III to maintain a Tier 1 capital ratio of at least 3 percent. Apart from the Basel GSIB surcharge, GSIBs are required to maintain an **enhanced supplementary leverage ratio** (eSLR) of 2 percent of CET1 capital in addition to the SLR, for a total of 5 percent. Insured bank subsidiaries of GSIBs must maintain an SLR of at least 6 percent to be considered well capitalized. Large banks are required to include a wider range of on- and off-balance-sheet exposures in the denominators of the ratios. The impact of the SLR is primarily on the largest banks, which conduct large volumes of SFTs through dealing subsidiaries. The Federal Reserve scoring system also imposes a higher GSIB surcharge for banks more reliant on short-term wholesale funding (SWTF), which the Basel standards do not directly consider.[6]

In the EU, the CRR sets rules for minimum capital requirements for banks generally, and the ESRB sets standards for additional capital buffers addressing systemically important institutions, including large banks. It has instituted a **systemic risk buffer** (SyRB), which in contrast to the CCyB, is conceived as addressing enduring rather than time-varying systemic risk. Like the CCyB, the SyRB is set individually by member countries depending on the characteristics of its banking sector and can be applied to a subset of bank credit risk exposures.

19.5.2   Bail-in-able Liabilities

Apart from capital rules, large banks are required to fund themselves in ways intended to reduce the potential for drawing on taxpayers or interrupting the flow of credit in the event of insolvency. For smaller and mid-size banks, Tier 2 capital requirements are thought to address these point of non-viability concerns. For large banks, the category of **bail-in-able liabilities** includes other forms of longer-term unsecured subordinated debt that are higher in the bank's capital structure and not considered capital funding instruments. Like Tier 2 capital instruments, they can be written down in the event of failure.

The Basel standards require GSIBs to issue these additional types of debt, **total loss absorbing capacity** (TLAC), to provide an additional buffer against the use of taxpayer funds and address the too-big-to-fail problem. Longer-term TLAC issuance is thought to reduce the probability of triggering runs during crises by making it unnecessary and therefore, less likely in the minds of the public that supervisors might bail in deposits, STWF, or senior secured debt of a failing large bank. In the EU, all banks are required to issue a **minimal amount of equity and bail-in-able liabilities** (MREL), a liability category broadly similar to TLAC. The TLAC issued by the overall bank holding company is required to employ similar triggers to those of AT1 capital instruments, such as a decline in equity value or a determination by the supervisory body.

The TLAC requirement is controversial because it requires additional debt issuance, adding to banks' leverage and to the liabilities that may be perceived as falling under the TBTF guarantee. If a trigger event looks more likely, it might set off market stress. A panic could be focused on the issuer alone or destabilize other banks and financial markets as occurred in several episodes in 2016 in which credit spreads of Deutsche Bank's CoCo bonds widened sharply, with the spread widening also affecting

---

[6] The 2013 Brown-Vitter bill in the US Senate proposed a 15 percent minimum leverage ratio for banks with assets in excess of $500 billion, but found little support.

CoCos issued by other European banks. The experience in 2023 with Credit Suisse's AT1 bonds raised similar concerns, as well as about respect for creditor priority.

TLAC is viewed as a competitive disadvantage for banks with relatively high shares of deposit funding, such as Wells Fargo, as it requires them to shift to costlier funding sources when they enjoy ample access to cheaper ones. It is difficult to measure the requirement because it is related to loss given default. The required issuance volume can depend on a score calculated from a wide range of balance sheet activities and measures.

Under **Pillar III** of the Basel standards, banks are obliged to make public their capital ratios and the data that support them. The Pillar III disclosures help understand the similarities and contrasts among different types of banks. Example 19.1 discusses the capital ratios and their components for three major banks.[7]

Example 19.1   Capital and leverage ratios of major banks

The data in the example were published by Bank of America Corp. (BAC), Morgan Stanley (MS), and Deutsche Bank AG (DB) for 2022.[8] Bank of America is one of the world's largest banks, with operating subsidiaries in many countries and competing in most segments of commercial and investment banking. Deutsche Bank is similar in many respects and has a greater weight of its activities in investment banking, consistent with its European merchant bank origins. It is significantly smaller than Bank of America and suffered severe losses during the global financial and European sovereign debt crises. Morgan Stanley is among the large broker-dealers that became a BHC to gain eligibility for Federal Reserve emergency liquidity programs during the global financial crisis.

Table 19.1 shows how the share of RWA attributed to the major risk categories differs across these firms. All the banks are well above the regulatory minimum ratios. Deutsche, as of 2022, was noteworthy for its low leverage ratio compared to its risk-based capital ratio. It would not meet the FDIC threshold for "well capitalized" although that may be in part due to differences in how the ratio is calculated under EU rules. Its correspondingly low RWA density could reflect a mix of assets that is considered relatively low-risk under the Basel standards or effective use of the rules to lower its estimate of RWA.

Morgan Stanley has a relatively high share of counterparty and market risk capital because its broker-dealer business is a core activity. The two US banks' supplementary leverage exposures are substantially higher than balance sheet or Tier 1 leverage adjusted assets. For both, RWA computed using the standardized is higher than under the advanced approach and sets the binding minimum capital ratios. Note also the substantial share of operational risk for all three firms.

19.5.3   Regulatory Stress Tests

The capital standards are integrated with regulatory stress tests in which larger banks' capital funding ratios under adverse economic scenarios are estimated and reviewed. Regulatory stress tests are primarily a microprudential supervisory tool with no explicit systemic-risk component, such as interactions between firms, but the results arc highly publicized and intended to promote financial stability

---

[7] The Federal Reserve Bank of Kansas City regularly details the capital funding and leverage ratios of very large US and non-US banks and summarizes those of all US banks by size category: https://www.kansascityfed.org/research/bank-capital-analysis/.

[8] More recent Pillar III disclosure have become more complex with the addition of new Basel III endgame items, such as separating securitization exposures in the banking book and equity exposures in the trading book in the presentation.

Table 19.1   Capital and leverage ratios of large banks

	BAC	MS	DB
Assets			
Balance sheet assets	3 053 096	1 180 231	1 336 788
Adjusted assets	2 997 118	1 150 772	1 240 483
Supplementary leverage exposure	3 523 484	1 399 403	NA
Risk-weighted assets			
Credit risk	852 762	252 082	269 338
CVA	127 585	33 556	6 184
Market risk	66 759	50 563	26 131
Operational risk	363 899	102 605	58 349
Total RWA (advanced/internal models)	1 411 005	438 806	360 003
Total RWA (standardized)	1 604 870	447 849	NA
RWA density (%)	47.1	38.1	29.0
Share of total RWA (advanced/internal models, %)			
Credit risk	60.4	57.4	74.8
CVA	9.0	7.6	1.7
Market risk	4.7	11.5	7.3
Operational risk	25.8	23.4	16.2
Capital composition			
Common equity tier 1	180 060	68 670	48 097
Additional tier 1	28 386	8 521	8 518
Tier 1 capital	208 446	77 191	56 616
Tier 2 capital	18 751	9 384	9 531
Total capital	238 773	86 575	66 146
TLAC/MREL	465 451	245 951	123 674
Risk-based capital ratios (%)			
CET1 capital ratio	11.2	15.3	13.4
Tier 1 capital ratio	13.0	17.2	15.7
Total capital ratio	14.9	19.3	18.4
TLAC/MREL ratio	29.0	54.9	34.4
Leverage ratios (%)			
Tier 1 leverage	7.0	6.7	4.6
Supplementary leverage ratio	5.9	5.5	NA

Quarterly Pillar 3 disclosures, BAC and MS Form 10-K reports, Deutsche Bank annual report, Q4 2022. The BAC and MS disclosures reflect CECL transition/phase-in rules. Adjusted assets are used to calculate Basel III Tier I leverage ratios, and are computed somewhat differently under US and EU rules. Currency amounts: US$ mill. for BAC and MS, € mill. for Deutsche.

by strengthening confidence and exposing firms to reputational risks. But they can potentially diminish regulators' credibility if they don't focus on the most pertinent risks or if banks viewed as having inadequate capital funding readily pass.

In the United States, regulatory stress testing began as the ad-hoc SCAP in 2009 during the global financial crisis. Public disclosure of its results proved surprisingly effective in reassuring markets; a similar EU exercise kept results confidential and was less reassuring (see Chapter 18).

Now annual exercises, the **Dodd-Frank stress tests** (DFAST) are applied to about three dozen large BHCs with consolidated assets in excess of $100 billion. The results of the stress tests are incorporated into the **Comprehensive Capital Analysis and Review** (CCAR) process and can lead to imposition of limits on banks' capital distributions via dividends and stock repurchases. The **stress capital buffer** (SCB) of at least 2.5 percent added to the GSIB surcharge is based on stress test results. It was finalized in 2020 and replaces the CCB.

The stress tests have a horizon of several years rather than measuring the results of a one-time shock. The scenarios are made public. A Severely Adverse Stress Scenario is set by the Fed in broad outline in the form of 16 domestic US macroeconomic and financial market variables, such as interest rates and stock and implied volatility indexes. There are a number of additional international variables, e.g., the Global Market Shock Component for larger internationally active banks. A Counterparty Default Component for some banks includes the default of their largest counterparty.

The bank computes the uses and sources of capital over the stress test horizon in accordance with applicable accounting rules. It estimates after-tax net income (or losses), incorporating provisions (realized and estimated future loan losses), MTM or OTTI losses on securities, and taxes under the baseline and adverse scenarios. The capital impact—capital ratios, capital-raising and dividend-payout plans each quarter—is estimated under the entity's baseline capital plan. Net income, but not the capital plan, are computed under stress, that is, there are no unplanned dividend cuts in response to losses. Net income is distributed to shareholders or added to capital. The stress test is intended to reveal if a bank becomes dangerously undercapitalized if it carries out capital distributions as planned under the adverse scenario.

The adverse scenario for interest rates illustrates the challenges of granular regulation of banks' asset risks and the limitations of stress tests focusing on one or a small handful of scenarios. The scenario announced in February 2022 had the US 10-year note yield rising less than 100 bps to 2.6 percent over the subsequent three years, far below the 5 percent high it reached about 18 months later.[9] The failure of SVB in March 2023 was largely due to interest-rate rather than credit risk. SVB was not yet subject to the stress tests in 2022, having only recently grown large enough for its application, but small and large banks suffered heavy MTM and realized losses due to the increase in rates. The increase in rates was unusual, but entirely within the realm of possibilities that would properly have been taken into account in stress testing.

19.5.4   Resolution of Large Banks

> If it were done when 'tis done, then 'twere well
> It were done quickly ...
>
> Shakespeare, *Macbeth* 1.7

Financial firms and contracts are resolved differently from other firms. A court-supervised Chapter 11 process is applied to nonfinancial companies in the United States; bank resolution is generally carried out via the FDIC, together with the Federal Reserve if a larger bank is involved. The typical path is for the FDIC to take control of failed banks late on a Friday after being appointed as receiver by a court. In that capacity, it sells the assets or the entire bank to a solvent bank. The deposit insurance fund covers at least some part of the shortfall between asset value and deposit liabilities, or any liabilities not assumed by a purchaser.

---

[9] The 2022 Stress Test Scenarios are available at https://www.federalreserve.gov/newsevents/pressreleases/files/bcreg20220210a1.pdf.

Broker-dealers, but not their holding companies, are also excluded from Chapter 11 under the **Securities Investor Protection Act** of 1970 (SIPA). Drexel Burnham's bankruptcy in 1990 was of a holding company.

The rationale for an administrative procedure is the potential for disruption of the financial system, given the complexity and interconnectedness of financial intermediaries. The nonfinancial economy is dependent on an uninterrupted flow of credit and the maintenance of clearing and payment systems, which are in large part enmeshed with and operated by banks. Therefore, there is a need to speedily resolve banks, especially large banks. Standard resolutions generally involve lengthy negotiations. The Chapter 11 bankruptcy filing of Lehman Brothers Holdings Inc. took many years to resolve.

There is also a need for predictability in financial resolutions and to limit judicial discretion. The emphasis is on protection of retail customers and taxpayers, and less on the rights of creditors and shareholders. A procedure outside of bankruptcy law exacerbates the TBTF problem, however, by increasing the propensity of regulators to bail out creditors of failing firms.

Assumptions of failed banks' assets and liabilities by solvent banks have become more difficult in recent years. Large banks gain competitive advantage from size and the strength of their TBTF status, which reduce their deposit and general funding costs. They have, nonetheless, become more reluctant to grow by taking on the assets of failed institutions.

In the aftermath of resolution via acquisition, regulators have taken legal actions against the acquiring banks for decisions made by the no-longer extant institution. In 2008, for example, JPMorgan acquired much of the assets of Bear Stearns, and Washington Mutual (WaMu) in its entirety following the largest single bank failure in US history, on an emergency basis, at the behest and with the cooperation of the public sector. Similarly, Bank of America, with regulator encouragement, acquired Countrywide Financial in a more garden-variety acquisition in 2007. Regulators then brought legal actions against JPMorgan and Bank of America for the failed intermediaries' role in residential mortgage markets before the crisis.

A major challenge in the resolution of complex or internationally active financial firms is their holding company structure, which includes operating companies in different lines of business, differently regulated and at different levels within the tree, possibly including foreign subsidiaries, and many issuing liabilities in addition to the parent holding company itself. The post-crisis approach has been to seek a **single point of entry** (SPOE), so resolution is carried out through the top-level holding company, while the subsidiaries are that carry out banking and dealing activities can continue operating. This requires a "clean holding company", keeping short-term debt in the operating subsidiaries.

The SPOE approach to resolution of failing large banks is closely related to the new requirements that banks issue TLAC and othe bail-in-able securities. The overall objective is to mitigate the TBTF problem by making it possible to resolve a failing large bank without imposing costs on the public and without triggering a run on the failing institution, its banking subsidiaries, or other intermediaries and markets. For the approach to succeed, clarity is required about the legal process through which it will be carried out and about which liabilities are bail-inable and their priority. In particular, the regulatory approach seeks to assure investors about the safety from losses and writedowns of deposits and senior unsecured debt. Without that clarity, there can be doubt in a stressed environment about whether resolution without failure is possible and about which liabilities can be considered safe by investors and not susceptible to runs. The alternative, multiple points of entry, has legally independent subsidiaries resolved separately.

An outstanding issue in this area is the absence of a **cross-border resolution regime** to be applied to global intermediaries, especially banks with significant cross-border operations. It introduces a conflict between host and parent countries, because both seek to avoid bearing any taxpayer cost of resolution, and is an issue within the EU and between the the United States and other advanced economies.

In the United States, the SPOE approach had its precedent in the long-standing "source of strength" doctrine, which provides for BHC holding companies to be funded adequately enough that their banking subsidiaries would enjoy unquestioned solvency. This principle appears to have been violated in the failure of SVB, as depositors of the commercial bank subsidiary were made whole above the deposit insurance limit only by imposing a fee on other insured banks, although creditors of the holding company were also made whole.

Post-crisis resolution mechanisms have a wider scope than precrisis, now including nonbank SIFIs and, under the 2008 HERA, US GSEs. In the United States, under Dodd-Frank Act Title II, an as-yet untested **Orderly Liquidation Authority** (OLA) provides for SPOE resolution. The FDIC would take control of the firm's assets, with authorization to use taxpayer funds if needed. Larger intermediaries are required to submit a **living will**, providing a plan for their own orderly resolution should they ever become insolvent.

These mechanisms have been criticized as untested in practice in contrast to a long history of bankruptcy law. Reliance on OLA would seem questionable in the heat of a crisis and policy would lean toward the alternative of a bail-out, further strengthening rather than weakening TBTF. One proposed alternative is the creation of a form of regular bankruptcy adapted to large financial institutions that would incorporate features, such as regulator discretion and speed that the FDIC and the proposed SPOE resolution processes are viewed as having.[10]

In the EU, under the **Bank Recovery and Resolution Directive** (BRRD), a **Single Resolution Board** (SRB) is to implement a **Single Resolution Mechanism** (SRM) in the event of a large bank failure. A **European Stability Mechanism** is tasked with lending to member states experiencing a sovereign debt crisis or financial crisis so they in turn can make emergency loans to or recapitalize their domestic intermediaries. The mechanisms, including funding, have not been tested by large-bank resolutions. The failures of several mid-size banks, such as those of Veneto Banca and Banca Popolare di Vicenza in June 2017, were resolved by national authorities with state, rather than EU aid.

Market Episode: The Failure of Credit Suisse

The failure of Credit Suisse in March 2023 provided a test of some of the new resolution mechanisms as well as of some new types of capital funding instruments. Judging by this sole example of a GSIB failure since the post-crisis reforms, it appears the large banks cannot be dismantled but can only be transferred with public backing to new ownership.

Credit Suisse had been experiencing severe losses for some time, and two large customers and counterparties, Archegos Capital and Greensill, had failed in recent years. Credit Suisse had a capital ratio fully compliant with the Basel III standards even after these losses. Nonetheless, the likelihood of further losses triggered deposit withdrawals in 2023 that reached run-like

---

[10] A US Treasury proposal in 2018 would widen the use of existing bankruptcy law, adding a new Chapter 14 covering banks. This would retain the simplification and directness advantages of SPOE while retaining the predictability and adherence to precedent of a judicial proceeding. See https://home.treasury.gov/sites/default/files/2018-02/OLA_REPORT.pdf.

pace from March 15 on. On the subsequent weekend, Credit Suisse was taken over by the Swiss banking authorities and central bank and sold to UBS Group AG, which received writedowns of the failed bank's equity and other capital instruments as well as public-sector guarantees of losses beyond certain limits. If the run was surprising in view of Credit Suisse's regulatory compliance and relative balance-sheet solidity, it was consistent with the historical experience of runs arising due to a perception of vulnerability and the inherent inability of any fractional-reserve bank to meet a large enough surge in deposit redemption demand.

The acquisition of Credit Suisse by UBS ran counter in several dimensions to the intention of the TBTF reforms that followed the global financial crisis and cast further doubt on SPOE resolution. Credit Suisse's living will played no role in its disposition. Credit Suisse was not resolved but was acquired by a competitor, at odds with the goal of making it possible for a bank of Credit Suisse's size to approach the brink of failure and be resolved without triggering a systemic risk event. Taxpayer funds were put at risk as part of the package to induce UBS, a competing bank, to buy its assets. The Swiss government provided a CHF 9 billion guarantee to UBS covering, in a second-loss position, potential losses on the assets it was assuming, and a CHF 100 billion default guarantee to the Swiss National Bank (SNB) of any liquidity support it might provide to Credit Suisse during the takeover by UBS.[11]

One dimension of Credit Suisse's failue was especially troublesome to investors in AT1 bonds. Once the guarantees had been approved, the Swiss financial market regulator Swiss Financial Market Supervisory Authority (FINMA), backed by a Swiss government emergency decree, determined that a PoNV event had taken place for Credit Suisse and that the value of its AT1 bonds would be written down to zero as part of the UBS takeover. The priority of claims appeared to have been violated as losses were imposed on AT1 bonds without entirely wiping out equity. The decison led to an acceleration of the decline in prices of AT1 bonds generally that had been part of the spring 2023 banking turmoil. The writedown is being litigated by investors disputing the FINMA claim it rightly determined the PoNV trigger had been met.

19.5.5   Regulatory Liquidity Standards for Banks

Regulators and central banks have long been attentive to liquidity. In the United States, liquidity risk is a long-standing element of bank supervision, for example, of the FDIC's CAMELS ratings (see Chapter 18). Indirectly, central bank reserve requirements, intended primarily to control the money supply, also serve to protect banks against losses due to sudden deposit withdrawals.

The motivation of new rules on funding liquidity is to constrain maturity mismatches and prevent runs on wholesale funding sources, such as the 2008 "run on repo." In 2013 and 2014, the Basel Committee put forward a set of standards for minimum liquidity ratios for banks that are being implemented in advanced market economies. The liquidity standards apply to large banks, and more stringent rules apply to the largest banks. US implementation of Basel liquidity standards took place with issuance of a final rule in 2014. The US rules will ultimately apply to any bank with assets exceeding $50 billion with the exception of FBOs.

The Basel liquidity standards rely on two measures, conceptualized as the results of liquidity stress tests with different time horizons. The **liquidity coverage ratio** (LCR) requires banks to hold

---

[11] Both guarantees were terminated by UBS on August 11, 2023.

high-quality liquid assets (HQLA) sufficient to cover cash outflows over a 30-day stress scenario. Its focus is on the tenuousness of short-term funding. Banks in compliance will hold liquid assets in excess of "runable" liabilities. The **net stable funding ratio** (NSFR) requires banks to have a volume of stable funding liabilities—equity and long-term debt—sufficient to cover an entire year of extended stress. Banks in compliance have stable funding in excess of illiquid assets.

To compute the LCR, banks compare the stock of HQLA they hold to an estimate of total net outflows in a short-term liquidity crisis, defined as a 30-day liquidity stress scenario. The rule requires that the ratio

$$\text{LCR} \equiv \frac{\text{stock of HQLA}}{\text{net cash outflows over a 30-day stress period}}$$

exceed 100 percent. The numerator represents liquid assets immediately available to cover the net outflow. An LCR over 100 percent indicates the bank has sufficient liquid assets to survive a severe cash outflow lasting 30 days.

To estimate the net outflow, gross outflows and inflows are estimated. Inflows consist largely of interest and loan repayments from performing borrowers. Outflows encompass sources of a potential short-term liquidity drain lasting 30 calendar days, including:

Maturing funding: deposits and short-term funding secured by illiquid assets or unsecured.
Collateral calls due to credit deterioration or general risk aversion, with counterparties demanding the fullest security within the banks' covenants and agreements.
Commitments and lines of credit drawn by borrowers in anticipation of liquidity stress and lender distress.

The outflows are calculated by applying stress runoff rates to liabilities and off-balance-sheet items maturing or callable within 30 days. For example, the regulatory runoff rate assigned to repo varies between 0 and 100 percent depending on collateral quality. Unsecured wholesale funding and repo secured by lower-quality collateral is assumed to have a high runoff rate.

Overnight deposits are all contractually sight obligations, redeemable on demand or at short term at par, but differ widely in assumed "stickiness," the likelihood of a significant volume of withdrawals during a stress periods. Their assumed stress runoff rates in the LCR outflow calculation distinguishes different purposes and types of depositor. **Operating deposits** are those used by retail depositors as well as nonfinancial and financial firms as money to support day-to-day transactions. Operating deposits are assumed to have low runoff rates, especially insured retail, or core, deposits. Retail deposits are, thus, in effect treated as longer-term debt although they are redeemable. Brokered deposits are not included in core deposits and assumed to have high runoff rates.

Nonoperating deposits are those used by depositors primarily as investments or liquidity reserves, rather than to support transactions. Examples include a substantial portion of the deposits of non-financial firms, held to be more run-prone than operating deposits and assumed to have high stress runoff rates. Nonoperating deposits, like institutional money funds, have little stickiness. Corporate treasurers can readily withdraw such deposits if their liquidity is called into question.

The LCR is intended to disincentivize banks from relying on nonoperating deposits to fund long-term assets, such as commercial and industrial (C&I) lending and securities, rendering such funding sources less attractive to banks. Large uninsured deposits of firms, wealthy households, and brokered deposits nonetheless presented a large funding risk following the massive inflows of 2021. During the 2023 banking turmoil, these deposits proved to be not at all sticky in public perception and in fact.[12]

Total net cash outflows, the denominator of the LCR, is outflows minus inflows, but with the offsetting impact of inflows capped at 75 percent of outflows:

$$\text{total net outflows} = \text{outflows} - \min(\text{inflows}, 0.75 \times \text{outflows}).$$

The cap prevents the denominator of the LCR from becoming small or negative, even if estimated outflows are very large, and reduces the incentive of the bank to overestimate inflows.

HQLA, the numerator of the LCR, is a weighted average value of assets deemed liquid under the rule. The assets included in HQLA are categorized and weighted by degree of liquidity via haircuts:

Level 1 assets include cash, central bank excess reserves (for US banks, in effect, all reserve balances), and sovereign bonds enjoying a zero Basel risk weight and are not subject to haircuts.

Level 2 assets are subject to haircuts and limited to 40 percent of HQLA, thus capping Level 2 at $\frac{2}{3}$ of the Level 1 assets in HQLA.

  Level 2a assets include sovereign debt with nonzero but relatively low Basel risk weights and the "highest-rated" corporate bonds (down to AA-). They are subject to a 15 percent haircut.

  Level 2b assets are subject to higher haircuts and include lower-rated BBB investment-grade corporates, residential mortgage bonds, and publicly traded common equity of nonfinancial firms.

Compliance with LCR does not immunize a bank from runs. There is, however, a trade-off among funding sources. Large banks can rely more on short-term wholesale funding if operating deposits are high. This motivation to offer higher rates on core deposits at least somewhat offsets their size advantage in the deposit market.

> **Example 19.2** For the denominator of the LCR, assume a bank estimates outflows of funding and commitments of $200 billion and inflows of interest and repayments $160 billion in a 30-day stress scenario. The offset from the inflows is capped at 0.75×200 billion, so the net outflow is $50 billion:
>
> $$\text{total net outflows} = \$200 - \min(\$160, 0.75 \times \$200) = \$50.$$
>
> For the numerator of the LCR, assume the bank has Level 1 assets of $30 billion and Level 2a assets of $40 billion. The latter are subject to a 15 percent haircut, so their contribution to HQLA is reduced to $0.85 \times 40 = \$34$ billion. Level 2 assets are further limited to 40 percent of total HQLA, so the eligible portion x of Level 2 assets must satisfy
>
> $$\frac{x}{30+x} \leq 0.4 \quad \Rightarrow \quad x \leq \frac{2}{3} \times 30 = 20.$$
>
> The LCR is 100 percent, exactly meeting the standards' minimum threshold:
>
> $$\frac{\text{stock of HQLA}}{\text{net cash outflows}} = \frac{30+20}{50} = 1.0.$$

---

[12] See Chapter 20.

The focus of the NSFR standard is on the appropriate funding of assets. It requires that assets with longer maturities or lower market liquidity be financed with longer-term or sticky short-term funding, stipulating that the ratio

$$\text{NSFR} = \frac{\text{available stable funding}}{\text{required stable funding}}$$

exceed 100 percent.

Required stable funding is a weighted average of assets, with zero weight on cash, short-term securities, and matched-book reverse repo, and higher weights on less liquid assets. **Available stable funding** is a weighted average of liabilities, with a weight of 100 percent for Tier 1 capital instruments, such as common equity and most Tier 2 capital. Higher weights are given to sticky retail deposits as well as those of small businesses, and a zero weight is assigned to short-term wholesale funding by a broker-dealer.

The two measures in the Basel standards are to some extent equivalent, viewing the firm's balance sheet from different perspectives and somewhat redundant. Consider a firm with this balance sheet:

Assets	Liabilities
HQLA	30-day net outflows
Required stable funding	Available stable funding

If the bank has HQLA at least equal to its runable liabilities, it will necessarily have available stable funding at least as great as that required.

Like the capital standards, the liquidity standards have a significant market impact. Matched books of repo lending and borrowing have become more expensive to fund. The result is to increase the relative demand for HQLA such as T-bills.

Further Reading

Berger et al. (1995) is an overview of the goals of capital requirements and provides some historical perspective on capital ratios of US banks. Admati et al. (2013) and Admati and Hellwig (2024a) clarify the concepts around capital requirements, such as the notion of "holding" capital, and that it is a costly funding source. Walter (1991) and Walker (2019) discuss banks' loss accounting and the debate on CECL.

The current Basel framework's standards are published at https://www.bis.org/basel_framework/. Walter (2019) describes "the Basel capital standards and US implementation. Labonte (2023b) and 2023c are recent summaries of the state of US capital rules. Haldane and Madouros (2012) and Dowd (2014) discuss the complexity of quantitative modeling in capital regulation and the resulting potential, fully realized during the crisis, for ineffectiveness and gaming. Lopez (2004) estimates asset correlations in the single factor credit risk model and compares them with the then-proposed Basel standards. Van Dyk and van Vuuren (2023) estimate asset correlations, including during" the global financial crisis and Covid and find that the prescribed correlations appear too low.

Hirtle and Lehnert (2014) describe Federal Reserve stress tests. Dowd (2015) focuses on Bank of England stress tests and identifies their lack of efficacy in identifying crucial vulnerabilities. Acharya and Steffen (2015) assess the contribution of regulatory arbitrage of capital regulations to the European debt crisis. Doty et al. (2020) describe capital relief trades.

See Calomiris and Herring (2013) on contingent convertible debt. Kupiec and Wallison (2016) and Kupiec (2016) take a critical view of SPOE and TLAC requirements as a mitigant of the TBTF problem. Bologna et al. (2020) analyze the 2016 Deutsche Bank CoCo episodes. Coelho et al. (2023) and Wang (2023) discuss the structure and intended purpose of AT1 funding instruments and the write down of the Credit Suisse AT1 bonds. Fleming and Sarkar (2014) describe the Lehman bankruptcy, and the essays in Jackson et al. (2012) debate the use of bankruptcy to resolve large financial firms.

Cecchetti and Kashyap (2018) use a stylized bank balance sheet to identify the interactions between the impact of the Basel capital and liquidity standards.

20

Monetary Policies Since the Global Financial Crisis

The global financial crisis ushered in a sequence of stress events that have disrupted financial markets and the economy and to which public policies have been forced to respond. The conduct of monetary policy has changed dramatically.

The crisis posed two fundamental policy challenges: its severity, with large intermediaries failing and market functioning impaired, and the low level of interest rates when it began. Since the onset of the crisis, monetary policy in advanced economies has wrestled with a basic problem. With short-term nominal interest rates close to zero or even negative in some currencies, the core of central bank operations is disabled. The central bank cannot drive rates much below the **zero** or **effective lower bound** (ELB), a modestly negative level of rates, limiting the efficacy of conventional monetary policy.[1]

20.1   The Monetary Policy Response to the Global Financial Crisis

Central banks introduced new tools to implement "extraordinary accommodation." At first, variations on existing interest rate tools were employed and, eventually, new types of operation, administered rates, and standing facilities.

20.1.1   Interest on Reserves

Shortly after its earliest intervention in August 2007 (see Chapter 18), expanding open market operations (OMOs) to additional times of day, and acceptance of an unusually high volume of mortgage-backed securities (MBS) rather than Treasurys as collateral, the Fed began lowering rates. The target fed funds rate was brought from 5.25 percent in September 2007 to 2 percent by April 2008. Its balance sheet didn't expand although its composition changed as it acquired nontraditional assets, largely emergency credit to to banks, dealers, and foreign central banks in place of US Treasurys. The Fed was avoiding extremely expansionary monetary policy for the time being, wary of inflation risk and seeking a gradual and orderly deleveraging of the financial system, but the crisis was still deepening. The European Central Bank (ECB), which briefly raised its policy rates in mid-2008 out of concern about inflation, began easing in late 2008.

Following the Lehman Brothers bankruptcy on September 15, 2008, emergency lending was rising so quickly that the Fed was forced to let its balance sheet grow. The corresponding rise in the volume of its reserve liabilities made it impossible to control short-term rates through OMOs alone. To counteract the as-yet unwanted drastic loosening of its monetary stance that would result from a

---

[1] The ELB is slightly negative due to the storage cost of cash. Banks offering negative deposit rates then offer an equally attractive asset.

massive increase in its balance sheet, the Fed began for the first time on October 6, 2008, to pay **interest on reserve balances** (IORB).[2]

IORB remunerated banks for holding a risk-free alternative not only to other money-market lending but also to business and household lending, making reserve balances a more attractive asset, particularly to suddenly risk-averse intermediaries during the crisis. An alternative investment for banks' cash balances would have to pay at least the IORB rate, and rates on alternatives paying more would be bid lower. IORB would effectively set a lower limit or floor on the funds rate and keep it from straying too far from the target rate.

20.1.2   Quantitative Easing

Like conventional monetary policy, **quantitative easing** (QE) is intended to affect the real economy through its effect on interest rates. It calls for the central bank to purchase securities from banks and from the public on a large scale to lower longer-term rates once short-term rates are near the ELB, and leads to a large expansion of the central bank's balance sheet. Introduced by the Federal Reserve at the end of November 2008, it initially focused on MBS and agency debt, but later shifted to Treasurys as well.

The initial rounds ("QE1" and "QE2") of **Large Scale Asset Purchases** (LSAPs) had a pre-announced total volume, subsequently increased. Later iterations extended the duration of the Fed's asset portfolio by reinvesting maturing paper and MBS prepayments in additional MBS and long-term Treasurys and by selling some relatively short-term for longer-term Treasurys.[3] The next iteration ("QE3") had a pre-announced monthly purchase volume of MBS and Treasurys, but no announced total volume or end date. The purchases were "tapered" from 2013 and ended in October 2014, but reinvestment to maintain a constant portfolio size continued until late 2017 when a gradual runoff was permitted. Figure 17.3 shows the growth and changes in composition of the Fed's balance sheet since the onset of the crisis.

The ECB initiated asset purchases in mid-2009, initially focusing on covered bonds, which are debt issued by European banks collateralized by residential mortgage loans. With the onset of the European sovereign debt crisis, the purchase programs expanded to government debt and eventually corporate bonds as well.

Quantitative easing is intended to work primarily through its effect on term premiums, the component of the long-term rate not directly related to the expected path of short-term nominal rates (see Chapter 10). QE lowers the term premium, lowering rates all along the yield curve beyond what was accomplished by cutting the funds rate to zero. QE has a greater effect on longer-term rates, which have larger term premiums. It is also a form of signaling, assuring market participants that accommodative policy will be maintained, keeping the expected path of short-term rates low as well.

Quantitative easing exchanges agency MBS and Treasurys for reserve balances, reducing the volume in the hands of the public. The **portfolio balance channel** views the central bank as thereby creating a tight market for risk-free, long-term, fixed-rate bonds. For quantitative easing to work through the portfolio balance channel, markets must be segmented. Institutional investors, for example, seek a substantial allocation to safe long-term, fixed-rate bonds and are prepared to sacrifice yield

---

[2] IORB had been legislatively authorized in 2006 before the crisis, and its introduction was accelerated in 2008. It has been re-acronymed several times: there were initially distinct rates for required and excess reserves, and reserve requirements themselves were eventually set to zero.

[3] Under the **maturity extension program** (MEP) of 2011–2012.

compared to near substitutes to achieve it. Funneling them onto the central bank balance sheet makes them scarce. Markets bid up the prices of close substitutes, transmitting the effects to other securities markets. QE affects the real economy through wealth effects—assets generally become more valuable—and by widening the gap between the yields on safe and risky assets, encouraging real investment.

Empirical validation of the effectiveness of quantitative easing is elusive because of the many channels though which it might potentially operate. Estimates have found it lowered term premiums but not the expected future path of short-term rates. One objection to the efficacy of the portfolio balance channel is that if the term premium alone is reduced, there will be no impact on investment decisions. Returns on new long-term investment have to exceed the rate implied by the expected path of future short-term rates. Otherwise, firms will arbitrage, responding by substituting long- for short-term debt financing of an unchanged set of investment plans.

The **neo-Fisherian** impediment to effectiveness of quantitative easing invokes the Fisher identity of the nominal rate as the sum of the real rate and expected inflation.[4] An identity in the short term, it is also a long-term relationship stating that higher inflation anchored in expectations, with real rates unchanged, must lead to higher nominal rates. The neo-Fisherian view reverses the causality and states that inflation expectations may be anchored below the central bank's goal because nominal rates are low. Japan's long stagnation near zero nominal interest and inflation rates is seen as a case study, the experience of Turkey in recent years as a counterexample (see Chapter 15). An increase in the nominal policy rate can then, at least over time and counter to the Taylor rule (see Chapter 17), bring inflation higher.

20.1.3   Forward Guidance

With the expected path of short-term rates so crucial to recovery, and by the end of 2008 so close to zero, an important element of policy was **forward guidance**, persuading the public that policy will remain accommodative for the foreseeable future even after it would normally have tightened. It aims to anchor expectations regarding future rates and counteract the public's sense that a policy stance so unusually expansive must be transitory. In a **data-dependent** approach, in contrast, monetary policymakers express less certainty about its future course and state that it will depend more on new information about the economy.

Forward guidance is on a continuum with previous communication policy and has its roots in the shift in recent decades toward commitment, policy transparency, and efforts to avoid time inconsistency. Central banks now intensified their efforts to communicate through public statements and introduced new forms of communication. The Fed began publishing the **Summary of Economic Projections** (SEP) of key policy and macroeconomic variables by Federal Open Market Committee (FOMC) participants from April 2011. The SEP includes projections of the fed funds rate expected to prevail at the end of each of the next three to four years and, in the "longer-term," framed not as intentions but as appropriate policy settings if participants' assessments of future economic conditions prevail.

The projections can be compared with market assessments of future rates to gain insights into market views on future monetary policy. Figure 20.1 displays examples of the "dots plot," a graphical presentation of FOMC participants' fed funds rate projections alongside the term structure of fixed rates on US dollar overnight index swap (OIS) referencing the funds rate (EFFR OIS) on each release date. The OIS rates are risk-neutral, market-adjusted forecasts of future fed funds rates.[5]

---

[4] See Chapter 10.

[5] See Chapter 6.

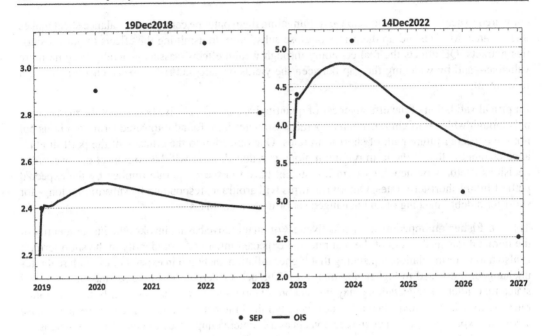

Figure 20.1 The "dots plot"

Points represent median of FOMC participants' projections of future fed funds rate from Summary of Economic Projections (SEP), Dec. 19, 2018, and Dec. 14, 2022. SEP data available at http://www.federalreserve.gov/monetarypolicy/fomccalendars.htm. Solid plot: 4-year forward overnight rates (OIS curves) on the SEP release dates. *Source*: Bloomberg.

At the end of 2018, the markets expected rates to remain much lower than FOMC participants were projecting. The markets may have assessed that inflation would remain well below the Fed's 2 percent goal and that the Fed would, therefore, not raise the funds rate target as much as anticipated. At the end of 2022, in contrast, markets expected rates to remain below the Fed projections for some time but eventually rise a full percentage point higher than the Fed longer-term projections. The markets may have believed that inflation would not return to the 2 percent goal as quickly as the Fed assessed or that real rates would have risen. These gaps may also have reflected risk aversion on the part of market participants eager on the earlier date to hedge against losses that might arise from rates remaining unusually low and on the later date against inflation being surprisingly persistent.

Forward guidance appears to have been effective in influencing interest rate expectations, keeping them lower in the aftermath of the global financial crisis than they otherwise would have been. But the comparison with the dots plot indicates that markets and policymakers adjusted their rate expectations over time. Figure 20.2 shows how the longer-term projections have converged and diverged from those of the market during the decade since their publication began. A substantial divergence between monetary policymakers' stated expectations and those of the market represents a monetary policy as well as a financial stability risk because it implies that policymakers will shift from a declared policy path or that markets are ill-positioned for the currently stated path.

The tension between effective forward guidance and policy flexibility is greater when policy is not governed by a rule. In a changing world, the monetary policymaker projections on which forward guidance is based are likely to prove at least somewhat incorrect, introducing a potential time-consistency problem. Policy responses to surprising new data might be interpreted as weak commitment to the stated long-term goals that untether expectations and undermine policy.

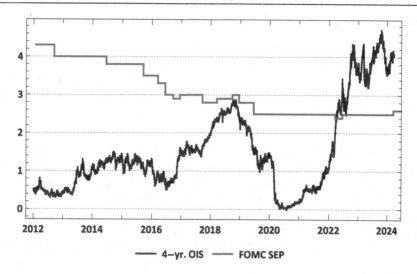

Figure 20.2 Market and FOMC expectations 2012–2024

Median of FOMC participants' projections of longer run fed funds rate from quarterly Summary of Economic Projections (SEP), released quarterly. *Data source*: FRED, series FEDTARMDLR. Fixed rates on 4-year OIS swaps (4-year forward overnight rates), daily, 03Jan2012 to 28Mar2024. *Source*: Bloomberg.

"Odyssean" forward guidance is a commitment to remain consistent with prior guidance—permitting no data dependence—in spite of deviations of actual outcomes from projections. It stands in contrast to the "Delphic" forward guidance associated with more data-dependent communication in normal times. With realized inflation persistently below the 2 percent goal before 2021, Figure 20.2 suggests the Fed was practicing the Odyssean form of forward guidance. If keeping to the announced path in the face of these deviations has relatively low risks or costs in terms of inflation and output goals, then Odyssean forward guidance can minimize those risks and costs by strengthening the commitment and avoiding time inconsistency. If the deviations of actual outcomes from projections are great enough, however, it presents a choice between time consistency and a nonoptimal policy path.

Forward guidance also raises financial stability considerations, a weakness of the separation principle (see Chapter 18). For example, forward guidance through 2021 that the Federal Reserve would not increase the target fed funds range likely added to the readiness of US banks to increase their portfolios of long-term bonds. As seen in Figure 19.1, banks' unrealized losses were very large as of mid-2023—and fatal to Silicon Valley Bank (SVB)—mostly due to interest rate exposure which had seemed low-risk in reliance on forward guidance.

The guidance changed abruptly and the Fed's reliance on forward guidance was tempered in response to the increase in inflation in 2022. The Fed communicated that its decisions on the fed funds rate would depended on data, rather than committing to a long-term path of rates, and has come close to disavowing for now the use of forward guidance.

20.2   Monetary Operations with a Large Balance Sheet

Until the global financial crisis, advanced-economy central banks were in general able to keep overnight rates close to their targets with relatively small OMOs. This changed with the drop in interest rates to the effective lower bound and the dramatic increases in reserves. Since then, central banks have wrestled with a money market which displayed puzzling signs of liquidity and illiquidity.

20.2.1   Quantitative Easing and the Soggy Money Market

Pre-crisis, the fed funds market had large volumes and active participation by US commercial banks borrowing and lending reserves, responding to shortfalls or overestimates of their immediate need for means of payment and settlement with one another. Since the Fed implemented its crisis-era approach to operations, it has wrestled with a soggy fed funds market. Most domestic banks have been content to hold a larger stock of reserves than before the crisis but not for the most part to actively bid for more.

The vast increase in reserve balances issued as the liability counterpart to the assets the Fed acquired was more than interest on reserve balances (IORB) could handle in anchoring rates. The IORB rate was intended as a floor under the fed funds rate, but the funds rate remained generally lower, as seen in Figure 20.3. The main motivation for active fed funds trading, banks' desire to meet end-of-day payment obligations and minimum reserve requirements, had vanished with the increase in reserves. Bank lending did not expand, and most banks were less eager than expected to acquire additional reserves and earn IORB. US banks were not only reluctant to add risky loan assets to their balance sheets. They didn't even wish to add safe reserve balances on which they would earn the positive spread between IORB and the funds rate.

Other participants in the fed funds market include banks in the Federal Home Loan Bank (FHLB) system, which accumulate reserves from mortgage-loan proceeds as commercial banks repay advances that are not immediately reinvested. FHLBs are not eligible to earn IORB and, therefore, are motivated to lend a large part of these reserves. Activities of US branches and offices of foreign banks—foreign banking organizations (FBOs)—and **net interoffice assets** accumulated by foreign banks via FBOs have increased in recent decades. Although these banks lack a natural US deposit base, they participate in US dollar interbank markets, gathering dollar deposits and lending to US as well as non-US residents and entities. They have become an important part of otherwise desiccated interbank and financial commercial paper markets since the 2007 crisis. US-domiciled banks, but not foreign banking organizations (FBOs), are subject to FDIC deposit insurance fees on all assets including reserves. FBOs are therefore more motivated to borrow reserves and earn any IORB-funds spread.

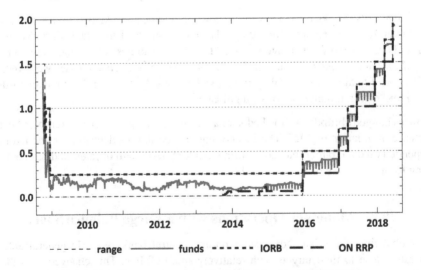

Figure 20.3 Target range and effective fed funds rate 2008–2018

Daily, 09Oct2008 to 29Jun2018. *Data source*: Bloomberg.

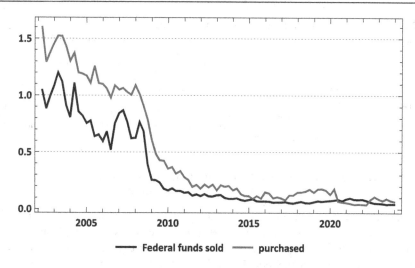

Figure 20.4 Fed funds sold and purchased by banks 2002–2023

As a percentage of total assets of domestic offices of US commercial banks and BHCs. Quarterly, Q1 2002 to Q1 2023. *Source*: Federal Reserve Bank of New York, Quarterly Trends for Consolidated US Banking Organizations.

The funds market became dormant and trading activity shrank drastically, with the bulk of the remaining lending from FHLBs to FBOs. The volume of transactions among banks and between banks and other intermediaries eligible to maintain reserve balances has shrunk to near zero as seen in Figure 20.4. Regular downward spikes in the fund rate also reflect the monthly round trip of reserve balances between FBOs and FHLBs and "window dressing," which is the FBO and general bank practice of trimming the size of balance sheets near month- and quarter-end reporting dates. The abundance of reserves has smothered the short-term interbank lending market. Banks' incentive in an active interbank market to monitor one another's financial condition carefully has also fallen away.

Large banks are generally able to pay lower rates on interest-bearing deposits than smaller banks and are better situated to earn positive net interest on deposit-funded reserves. They hold, but don't trade reserves actively. This incentive, too, is blunted to the extent that capital regulation increases the overall cost of funding reserve balances, which are included in the adjusted asset denominator of the leverage ratio for larger US banks.[6] Eventually, as regulatory changes introduced later on came into force, reserves came to be concentrated on the balance sheets of FBOs and very large US banks.

The funds rate reached the effective lower bound by December 2008. With IORB not effective as an anchor or floor for the funds rate, the Fed, from December 16, 2008, set a target range of 0–25 basis points in place of a point target or level for the fed funds rate. The IORB rate coincided with the upper limit. The funds rate generally stayed within the range but with greater variation day-to-day than before the crisis.

In 2013, it introduced an additional operational tool, the **overnight reverse repurchase agreement**, or repo, (ON RRP) **facility** through which it drains reserves by borrowing from a wide range of intermediaries and not just banks but also money market mutual funds at an administered rate generally equal to the lower limit of the range. With the introduction of new operational tools, the funds rate was eventually stabilized near the middle of the target range. Table 20.1 displays the mean and

---

[6] Apart from a temporary Covid emergency exemption excluding US Treasury securities and reserves from the denominator of the supplementary leverage ratio (SLR).

Table 20.1　Effective versus target fed funds differences

	Mean	Std. dev.
03Jan2000–10Aug2007	0.7	9.9
13Aug2007–31Mar2009	−11.6	27.7
01Apr2009–05Jan2016	−12.3	4.0

Mean and standard deviation of the effective fed funds rate minus the target fed funds rate (until 16Dec2008) or the upper limit of the target range, daily, in basis points. *Data source*: Bloomberg.

standard deviation of the daily difference between the target fed funds rate or upper limit of the target range and the effective fed funds rate before and during the crisis.

The Fed's balance sheet and money market rates are also affected by factors related to fiscal policy and to US Treasury management of its own liquidity. Reserve balances are high and volatile in part because of large variations in the US Treasury's deposit or Treasury General Account (TGA) as tax payments flow in and disbursements out. The TGA is also used by the Treasury to cope with the recurrent debt-limit confrontations with Congress, increasing its balances by issuing additional debt while still well below the limit so that it can draw them down during periods of contention over raising it.

As the TGA fluctuates, with the volume of Federal Reserve assets unchanged, the volume of its other liabilities such as reserves adjust. Variations in the TGA are associated with changes in the issuance of T-bills, flows that affect money markets generally. Higher T-bill supply, for example, increases their yields, making them more attractive to money funds and other investors relative to alternatives such as repo, shifting allocations among them and putting upward pressure on short-term rates generally.

20.2.2　The Ample Reserves Operating Framework

Once the economy began to recover from the crisis, central banks had to consider how to exit from extraordinarily accommodative monetary policies. This involves unwinding the policies themselves and a plan for the conduct of policy in the more normal circumstances of the future. This has proven surprisingly difficult because the crisis expansion in balance sheets has been hard to reverse, new stress events occurred, and money markets are greatly changed, impeding exit and a return to the pre-crisis operating framework.

Fed policymakers are also skeptical of the efficacy of frequent, carefully calibrated, and relatively small OMOs in keeping the funds rate in a narrow range as they had in the past, given the greater size and variability in such Fed balance sheet liabilities as the TGA. The size and difficulty of forecasting fluctuations in the TGA have grown with US federal fiscal deficits and debt. The uptake of facilities with administered rates, such as ON RRP, instead bears some of the burden of adjustment falling on OMOs before the crisis. The TGA is an example of constraints falling short of fiscal dominance that fiscal policy can place on the conduct of monetary policy.

The exit strategy involves the same tools of monetary policy as the accommodative policy itself: the central bank's target short-term interest rate and its control, the size, composition, and financing of its assets, and communication. Reducing the portfolio, or quantitative tightening, can occur with different intensities: (i) reducing regular purchases or tapering, slowing balance sheet growth, (ii) reducing reinvestment of bonds as they mature or pay down, or runoff, gradually shrinking the balance sheet, and (iii) outright sales, accelerating that shrinkage.

Initial communication of the exit strategy was complicated by the "taper tantrum" of May 2013, when long-term rates rose unexpectedly sharply in response to a seemingly anodyne signal that bond purchases could slow. After announcing a shift in December 2013, the Fed began at the beginning of 2014 to reduce the size of its securities purchases. Tapering was complete by October 2014. At the end of 2015, with reinvestment maintaining a steady balance-sheet size, the Fed began "lift-off," raising the target fed funds range in 25 basis point increments. In October 2017, the FOMC initiated a further step toward normalization, with a gradual runoff of assets.

The Fed has issued a series of statements of its exit policy, or balance-sheet normalization, most recently in the first half of 2022.[7] The Fed has remained consistent in viewing the fed funds rate as its main monetary policy tool, planning to gradually reduce the overall size of its balance sheet, and seeking to hold primarily Treasurys rather than agency MBS. Because of the difficulty of reducing its balance sheet without disturbing money markets, it has determined that it will conduct monetary policy with **ample reserves** for the foreseeable future, that is, with a much larger balance sheet relative to, say, the volume of currency or GDP, than in the past. This operating framework is very different from before 2007 and remains reliant on the new crisis-era tools.

Figure 20.5 illustrates the workings of the new approach. The fed funds target remains the policy rate, to be kept in a target range rather than at a point. Banks' net demand for reserves is a function of the fed funds rate. The demand function is flat, and demand is inelastic with respect to the funds rate in two regions. As in the past, the discount rate places a ceiling on the fed funds rate because banks can borrow funds from the Fed at that rate and won't be willing to pay a higher rate in the fed funds market. But the ceiling is in general no longer relevant although the discount rate is now closer to the prevailing funds rate than in the past.[8]

In a scarce reserves regime, the demand curve for reserves flattened at a rate of zero because reserves paid no interest (Figure 17.4). Thus, zero became the de facto lower limit of a corridor system. The

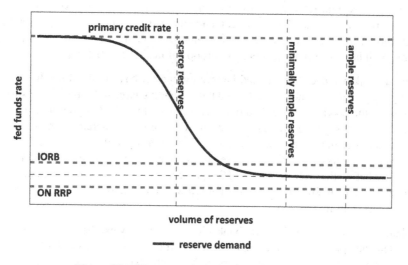

Figure 20.5 Monetary operations with ample reserves

[7] See https://www.federalreserve.gov/newsevents/pressreleases/monetary20220504b.htm.
[8] The demand function is also influenced by the potential for stigma, making banks reluctant to borrow at the discount window.

demand curve is now flat— the elasticity of demand for reserves is near zero—at a positive fed funds rate in the vicinity of the IORB and ON RRP rates at which banks and others can lend funds to the Fed and need not lend to others at a lower rate.

If reserves are scarce, the Fed can move the market funds rate up or down by shifting the supply of reserves by a relatively small amount, particularly if the impact of signaling is strong. In an ample reserves regime, it is no longer possible to use OMOs to keep the effective funds rate in a very narrow range of just a few basis points around the target. Rather, it is constrained by the administered ON RRP and IORB rates to fall within a wider range. Reserve requirements have also been set to zero. The quantity of high-powered money is no longer a focus, let alone an instrument, of Federal Reserve policy.

Maintaining an ample reserves regime entails providing a vertical supply curve of reserves in a flat region of the reserves demand curve even following balance sheet normalization. But the Fed plans to hold "no more securities than necessary for efficient and effective policy implementation" to avoid issuing so large a volume of reserves that the funds rate chronically slips substantially lower than the IORB rate as it has in the past. The long-term size of the balance sheet will be determined by the Fed's estimate of the **minimally ample supply of reserves**, intersecting the demand curve at its inflection point from negatively sloped to flat.

Moderate variations in supply will then have little or no impact on the funds rate. The funds rate will be controlled by infrequent variations of the IORB and ON RRP administered rates rather than by actively operating in the repo market. The IORB rate is viewed as the floor and the ON RRP rate as a supporting level or "subfloor" within a floor system. The range between them will coincide roughly with the target fed funds range.

To maintain a floor system with minimally ample reserves requires an accurate estimate of the demand function for reserves at which the fed funds market is just a bit tight, in order to identify the region in which the elasticity of demand for reserves becomes zero. An over- or underestimate can drastically weaken Federal Reserve control over the fed funds rate. If reserves are less ample than the Fed thinks, relatively small changes in demand can lead to liquidity risk events with effects on asset prices, money markets, market functioning, and the economy. If reserves are more ample, the fed funds rate will have a stronger tendency to droop below the ON RRP rate.

A large central bank balance sheet funded largely by interest-bearing liabilities has fiscal implications. During the global financial crisis, the Fed began funding large holdings of Treasurys and MBS predominantly at the IORB rate. The Fed purchased much of the debt at premiums to its par value, which it recorded in a separate account drawn down as the bonds mature, somewhat offsetting its earnings. With short-term rates near zero and long-term Treasury yields in a range near two percent, its earnings and remittances to Treasury were substantial, rising from between 1 and 2 percent of federal revenues before the crisis to a peak of 3.6 percent in 2011.[9] The increase in interest rates and yield curve inversion from 2021 reversed this pattern with IORB and other expenses substantially in excess of earnings from its assets.

A large balance sheet weakens the central bank's independence by exposing it to political pressures. It may face demands that its asset purchases benefit particular interests, similar to the potential for credit support to favor some economic sectors in the central bank's role as lender of last resort. Its interest payments to banks, the reduction and eventual suspension of remittances to the government, and a negative net equity position may spark public disapproval.

---

[9] See Figure 4 of Congressional Budget Office (2022).

20.2.3   The Impact of Exit on Funding and Market Liquidity

A post-crisis liquidity puzzle has emerged. One rationale for a large central bank balance sheet is that it enhances market liquidity: the volume of reserves is unprecedentedly large, and other liquid assets have become more plentiful. A large central bank balance sheet was thought to reduce the likelihood that liquidity stress events will occur and provide a better starting point for the central bank to respond when they occur because the necessary operating framework is already in place.

To the contrary, the financial system has experienced repeated episodes in which liquidity appeared tight in spite of the growth of the Fed's balance sheet from under \$1 trillion to over \$4 trillion and then to \$8 trillion. **Quantitative tightening** has proven difficult due to the liquidity problems accompanying it, and a large balance sheet and ample reserves regime have been complicated to maintain. The low level of interbank lending dulls price discovery in money and fixed-income markets generally, contributing to market segmentation and otherwise impeding market functioning. The Fed's large stock of high-quality safe assets withdraws them from use in collateral markets.

Large and liquid markets that routinely functioned smoothly in the past have suffered from lack of liquidity. Spreads between different money market rates and basis spreads are wider and more persistent than in the past and prone to sudden widening. This **liquidity paradox** results from the complex chain of consequences of the increase in Federal Reserve assets and liabilities. It coincides with other important developments, particularly major changes in regulation and, more recently, a rapid rise in interest rates, and large inflows of deposits into the banking system followed soon after by large outflows.

Much of the liabilities on the Fed's balance sheet consists of reserve balances, a liquid asset for commercial banks. Before the crisis, reserve balances were desired primarily for liquidity but have since also become an earning asset, especially for larger banks. They are valued as means of settlement of interbank liabilities and as earning assets but also viewed as costly to hold. As with any other asset, they must be financed, likely by deposits or other liquid short-term liabilities, absorbing and offsetting their liquidity. This increases liquidity risk for banks in aggregate, particularly large banks holding the bulk of reserves, which become warier of providing liquidity to the market in any stress period.[10]

Companies, including nonbank financial intermediaries, have in a low interest-rate environment relied more on lines of credit and less on liquid asset holdings to meet their liquidity risk management needs. Banks have incentives not shared by other intermediaries to issue lines of credit. Banks can rely on the capacity for assessing and monitoring creditworthiness used in their core lending business and on central bank liquidity facilities and implicit guarantees during financial stress events in which lines are likely to be heavily drawn upon.[11] The resulting swings in the volume of corporate credit are, therefore, even greater than for loans overall.

In Figure 15.1, showing the growth rate of total and of non-real estate commercial and industrial (C&I) lending by US banks to companies, the volume of banks' C&I loans increases sharply in 2008, reflecting a demand for liquidity by nonfinancial firms drawing at the onset of the crisis on lines of credit previously committed by banks before declining sharply. It swings even more dramatically during Covid in 2020. Larger banks issued substantial volumes of credit lines following the crisis, which do not expand their balance sheets immediately but are a contingent claim on the

---

[10] Banks display a ratchet effect in the management of their liquidity similar to that seen in nonfinancial corporate behavior. Corporations are reluctant to decrease leverage or to finance new projects via equity following losses (see Chapter 11).

[11] See Chapter 12, and Yankov (2020).

banks' liquid assets. Banks can thereby deploy liquidity created through quantitative easing in a way that relies implicitly on a central bank liquidity guarantee in case of crisis.

Regulatory changes also constrain banks' ability to provide liquidity in stress periods. Market-making is a balance-sheet intensive activity relative to its risk. It requires banks and their dealer subsidiaries to maintain large inventories of securities and cash deposits that increase assets and liabilities. Liquidity and leverage-based capital requirements are based on banks' balance sheets rather than risk taking. Regulatory adjustments are made to mitigate the impact on leverage ratios, such as recognition of netting of some matched-book and centrally cleared repo, but they are limited. A large balance sheet potentially also affects a bank's GSIB score.

Large banks are attentive to the potential impact of their response to stressed markets on regulatory ratios. If market-making activities are carried out on a large enough scale, the marginal impact of further increases in Treasury market-making and repo trading on a bank's funding costs and return on equity can be high, especially if they are close to a threshold at which the leverage ratio becomes binding and additional equity funding would be required. With lines of credit already drawn down and short-term borrowing constrained, banks may be averse to using remaining liquidity reserves and stocks of HQLA to finance additional assets, lowering their liquidity ratios.

Recurrent episodes indicate reserves are less ample than the large volume outstanding would suggest including stress in repo markets in 2019, the Treasury market in March 2020, and the bank turmoil of 2023, along with other smaller episodes and an ongoing set of anomalies. Large banks have historically been crucial in maintaining market functioning but did not provide sufficient liquidity during these episodes in spite of substantial holdings of reserves. These experiences may have made the Fed less confident about how precisely it can identify the point at which reserves are minimally ample and more cautious in its quantitative tightening effort than it had been up to 2019. New tools, such as the standing repo facility, have been introduced to help the Fed to respond more quickly if liquidity stresses appear.

20.2.4   Money Markets in September 2019

After the successful lifting of rates since 2015, the operating framework seemed for a time to be working well, with IORB and ON RRP rates stabilizing the funds rate within the target range. The funds rate eventually barely fluctuated at all (see Table 20.1). Repo lending, which is secured, should occur at rates at least a bit below the funds rate as it generally did before the crisis. Reserve balances are claims on the Fed, but fed funds liabilities to other banks are unsecured claims. The repo rate was often higher than the soggy funds rate during the crisis but drew closer to its expected relationship, near and at times somewhat lower than the funds rate. But an anomalous positive spread of repo over the funds rate persistently recurred even during this time of apparent smooth functioning of the framework.

The impact of the conditional liquidity shortage became apparent after the Fed's first round of quantitative tightening, initiated in October 2017 via runoff, permitting its assets to decrease as securities matured. As reinvestment slowed and reserves gradually fell in 2017, however, a contrary problem emerged to that experienced during quantitative easing. The funds rate gradually approached uncomfortably close to the upper limit of the target range, raising the possibility it could evade the Fed's control and breach it.

The Fed has from time to time since 2018 carried out tweaks it refers to as "technical adjustments" to improve control over the fed funds rate, placing the IORB rate lower than the upper limit and the ON RRP slightly higher than the lower limit of the target range. By early 2018, the upward pressure

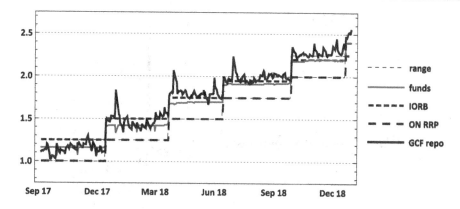

Figure 20.6 Effective fed funds and funds target range in 2018

Effective federal funds rate (EFFR), interest on reserves balances (IORB) rate, General Collateral Financing (GCF) repo rate and target fed funds range, daily 05Sep2017–28Dec2018, in percent at an annual rate. *Data source*: Bloomberg.

on the funds rate was pronounced enough that the FOMC attempted to offset it by lowering the IORB rate, at first to 5, then to 10, 15, and eventually to 20 basis points below it, leaving it just 5 basis points higher than the lower limit.[12] Lowering IORB within the target range should depress the funds rate as well as rates on T-bills, repo, and other money market substitutes. The expectation was that even if arbitrage can't fully coax banks into acquiring reserve balances in the funds market when rates are lower than IORB, it will at least reduce demand and coax them into selling reserves when the funds rate is higher (Figure 20.6).

With the 2018 technical adjustments and stronger demand for reserves, the funds rate traded closer to the center of the range and to IORB rather than somewhat below. The funds rate had some room to exceed IORB while remaining within the range. Even though it appeared that the floor system was now working smoothly, upward pressure on the funds rate was an early sign of a developing liquidity shortage in wholesale money markets that in 2019 would cause serious disruption in the funds and especially the repo market.

Month- and quarter-end pressures had typically depressed the funds rate as banks, especially FBOs, lightened up on funds arbitrage trading near balance-sheet reporting dates for window dressing. But demand for reserves had strengthened enough that the funds rate equalled or exceeded IORB every business day from early 2019 on. The liquidity absorbing function of IORB was now counterproductive. The IORB rate, which was originally intended to act as a floor on rates but didn't and was later intended to dampen upward pressure and act as a ceiling on rates, was now lower than the funds rate, proving ineffective in anchoring rates in loose and tight money markets.

The tightening of money markets led to the March 2019 FOMC decision to halt the slow runoff of assets on its balance sheet that had been in progress since 2017, with announcements that it was ready to resume asset purchases sooner than expected and the resumption of target rate cuts at the end of July. In July and September 2019, the funds rate at times even breached the upper limit. After tightening a bit on September 16, rates on overnight repos spiked hundreds of basis points the next day. Smaller fluctuations in repo rates are not unusual at month-end and other bank balance-sheet

---

[12] The IORB rate has been set to 10 basis below the upper limit since mid-2021.

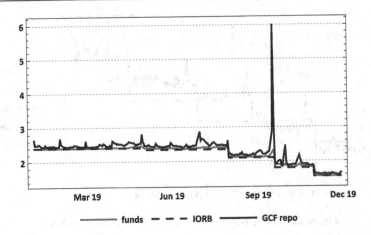

Figure 20.7 Repo market shocks 2019

EFFR, IORB and GCF repo rates, daily 05Sep2018 to 28Feb2020, in percent at an annual rate. *Source*: Bloomberg.

reporting dates, but these were extreme, and occurred in the middle of a month. Trades were recorded at 10 percent, yet banks did not step in to substitute secured repo lending for reserves (Figure 20.7).

Corporate tax payments in mid-September may have increased inflows to the TGA and led to reductions in repo lending by money funds as investors drew down holdings. High Treasury debt issuance at the same time the Fed was reducing its holdings, particularly T-bills, increased the demand for repo borrowing by dealers to finance inventories. These added upward pressure on the repo rate but are unlikely to have been dominant factors because net issuance and tax payments were neither unprecedented nor exceptionally large.

The Fed responded, beginning on September 17, by conducting repo operations on an increasingly aggressive scale. The Fed had not used repos to temporarily add reserves to the banking system since its normal operations before the crisis, and the average daily amount was over 10 times greater than a decade earlier. On October 11, the FOMC committed itself to continuing these operations at least through January 2020. It also announced its intention to initiate outright purchases of Treasury bills until further notice and reiterated its commitment to keep reserves ample.

20.3   The Liquidity Paradox and the Banking Turmoil

20.3.1   The Public-Sector Response to the Covid Pandemic

The onset of Covid in February 2020, its immediate health consequences, and the societal and policy responses to it initiated a series of fresh shocks to the world economic and financial system. Economic activity declined precipitously and goods, services and financial markets experienced severe disruption. In the United States, federal, state, and local governments vastly increased expenditures and undertook administrative and legislative emergency measures. The Federal Reserve undertook emergency lending and monetary policy actions and deferred the implementation dates of some capital and liquidity regulatory standards.

Initial Federal Reserve actions during Covid responded to a renewed liquidity impasse in US Treasury and other financial markets. Treasury yields fell from mid-February 2020 as Covid began spreading in the United States and stock market prices declined sharply in a fairly typical crisis pattern. From early March, however, a range of market participants, particularly hedge funds engaged in Treasury basis trading, sold US Treasurys.[13]

As volatility increased, basis spreads between on- and off-the-run notes and bonds and between futures contracts and cash Treasurys—the Treasury basis—widened drastically. Banks demanded additional margin or declined to extend credit, forcing hedge funds to rapidly reduce their positions in near-arbitrage trades, amplifying funds' typical procyclical response to higher volatility. A similar fire sale had led to the failure of Long-Term Capital Management in 1998, which had engaged in a highly leveraged trade involving on- and off-the-run bonds.

Sellers of US Treasurys included foreign central banks addressing the sharply increased need of non-US banks within their jurisdictions for US dollar funding and fixed-income mutual funds facing large redemptions. Prime and institutional money market mutual funds (MMMFs) saw a large increase in withdrawals, motivated in large part by corporate treasurers' fear of being trapped if fund managers imposed gates or other constraints on redemption as they were empowered by the post-crisis rules to do.

The demand for liquidity skyrocketed just as US Treasurys had rapidly ceased to be a close substitute for cash. Market makers withdrew or reduced the sizes of the trades they were prepared to facilitate. Customers were unable to buy or sell in the quantities or at the pace they sought. It became extremely difficult to trade Treasurys, and yield volatility was extremely high, with yields doubling—from very low levels—over a few trading days in March.[14] The liquidity problems also surfaced in related markets and were severe enough to harm solvent nonfinancial firms unable, for example, to roll commercial paper and other short-term financing of routine operations.

The Fed responded initially by lowering the funds target range, engaging in massive repo operations and with forward guidance, as it had in the global financial crisis. It also resumed outright securities purchases on a large scale, including of agency MBS. By the time the Fed ceased this round of bond purchases—dubbed QE4—in February 2022, the size of its balance sheet had risen to just under $9 trillion, nearly double its size at the end of the previous sequence of Large Scale Asset Purchases (LSAPs) in November 2014. An enduring change to the use of the discount window also emerged from the pandemic response. To encourage banks to borrow at the window in spite of their concern about stigma, the Fed narrowed the spread of the primary credit rate over the fed funds rate, setting it equal to the upper limit of its target fed funds range.

It also made permanent a **Foreign and International Monetary Authorities Repo Facility** (FIMA) that lends US dollars to central banks holding US Treasurys as foreign exchange reserves in custody at the New York Fed. The repo facility for foreign central banks, together with the central bank liquidity swaps in place since 2008, addressed strains in international US dollar money markets that contributed to the liquidity crunch of March 2020.

The Fed revived several emergency liquidity programs used in 2008–2009, addressing money and commercial paper markets and extending credit to primary dealers as well as banks. As in the global financial crisis, these facilities operated under Section 13(3), most had a Treasury first-loss component, and loans were fully collateralized. Also similar to the earlier experience, many of the facilities saw low or zero lending volumes. Their signalling effect, together with the large repo operations and outright purchases, led to the easing of private lending and restoration of market functioning.

---

[13] See Chapters 7 and 19.

[14] The yield of the 10-year note rose from 0.54 percent on March 9 to 1.20 on March 18.

In other respects, the response was adapted to new circumstances: the shutdown of economic activity, the changed nature of the liquidity crunch, the already large size of the Federal Reserve balance sheet, and a large increase in federal government expenditures. The Fed set a new precedent by initiating programs to purchase corporate debt in primary and secondary markets. Such programs had been employed in Europe but not in the United States (see Chapter 18). Purchases of MBS and the revived TALF program also supported credit markets.

In contrast to the experience during the global financial crisis, the government response included large transfers to households and businesses in the form of direct payments or relief from tax and loan payment obligations for households, businesses, and state and local governments, increased health care expenditures, and programs sponsoring loans to businesses that became grants if they documented having maintained their payrolls. The Fed also created a program to refinance banks making government-guaranteed loans to businesses.[15] Estimates of the additional expenditure range from about $4.5 to $6.5 trillion.

The direct payments were in large part initially added to demandable deposit accounts, resulting in a large immediate increase in the money supply and decline in the velocity of money (Figure 20.8). Money balances including deposits rose rapidly, while transactions were declining due to Covid and associated public-health policies. Eventually, as liquidity preference reverted and households had time to adjust, the deposits were reallocated to spending on goods and services, other forms of money, and investments. Figure 12.2 shows the increase in the size of bank balance sheets, sharper and more enduring than during the global financial crisis, and in particular a sharp increase in the volume of deposits.

The influx of deposits created through direct transfers and quantitative easing brought with it a large expansion of banks' market and credit-risky assets. Banks initially deployed the deposits into increased loans and reserves at the Fed but eventually into a large increase in the longer-term securities they held, most of it Treasurys and agency MBS. Though these securities have little credit

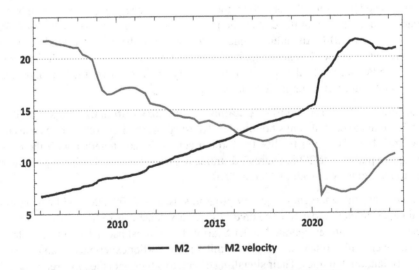

Figure 20.8 M2 money supply and velocity 2006–2024

M2 money stock, $ trillion, monthly, Jan. 2006 to Apr. 2024, and velocity of M2 money stock, quarterly, Q1 2006 to Q1 2024, both seasonally adjusted. *Source*: Federal Reserve H.6 release and Federal Reserve Bank of St. Louis, via FRED.

---

[15] The Paycheck Protection Program Liquidity Facility (PPPLF).

risk and high market liquidity, they are of long duration and have a great deal of interest rate risk. MBS have extension-risk induced negative convexity, becoming longer-duration bonds just as interest rates are rising and bond prices are falling (see Chapter 10). These developments created a new liquidity ratchet exposed during the 2023 bank turmoil.

The rapid growth in US public debt requires much larger primary and secondary debt markets. The September 2019 and March 2020 episodes exposed a surprising vulnerability of expanding Treasury secondary market trading, repo, and other Treasury-related markets to liquidity stresses. In response, the Federal Reserve in July 2021 introduced a domestic **standing repo facility** (SRF) open to primary dealers and banks meeting certain criteria. The minimum SRF bid is set at the upper limit of the Fed's target fed funds range. The SRF has not conducted operations on most days or on a large scale but can be used in size if there is a surge increase in the demand for reserves, so the Fed can respond more smoothly to market stresses such as those of 2019 and 2020. Together with IORB and the ON RRP facility "cushion," the operating framework has come to resemble a narrow corridor system.

Dealers are regulated entities, and the market does not have free entry. When dealers assess that their balance sheets have grown uncomfortably large with inventories of Treasurys, they become reluctant to provide liquidity to the market by buying more from other market participants eager to exit positions. Apart from tasking the Federal Reserve with being a more routine provider of Treasury market liquidity, several proposals have been made to preserve market liquidity and keep primary dealers from protectively shrinking from the market during periods of stress on the understanding that the volume of federal debt as a share of GDP will remain large or continue to grow.

Some proposed mechanisms, under the general heading **all-to-all trading**, would facilitate investors trading more directly with one another as well as with dealers. The Treasury market would more closely resemble the stock market, though both would remain fragmented into differently regulated sectors. Other proposals would have the Federal Reserve more routinely and directly engage in market transactions to enhance liquidity, as distinct from its monetary policy operations, rather than only as market maker of last resort. Eliminating reserve balances from the denominator of the leverage ratio so that it looms less large as a potentially binding constraint has also been proposed.

The SEC has introduced a rule requiring, by 2025, central clearing through the Fixed Income Clearing Corporation (FICC) of much secondary market US Treasury and Treasury repo trading that is currently conducted directly between market participants. The effects of the rule are uncertain, and rapid implementation may be disruptive. But it may also reduce, through netting, the balance sheet and associated leverage ratio constraints on dealers providing Treasury market liquidity during market stress.[16]

20.3.2   The Rise in Interest Rates and the Financial System

Rising interest rates from March 2022 and on were a new source of financial instability. Inflation rose from well below the Fed's 2 percent goal to well over 5 percent in the course of 2021.[17] The Fed responded by increasing the target fed funds range and IORB rate by 5.25 percent in 16 months, a record pace.

In spite of the large stocks of liquid assets outstanding, liquidity grew tight. From mid-2022, the Federal Reserve had capped reinvestment of principal payments on its Treasury and agency MBS securities. Its balance sheet has been gradually shrinking apart from a brief increase during the

---

[16] See the press release at https://www.sec.gov/news/press-release/2023-247.

[17] As measured by the year-over-year change in the core PCE.

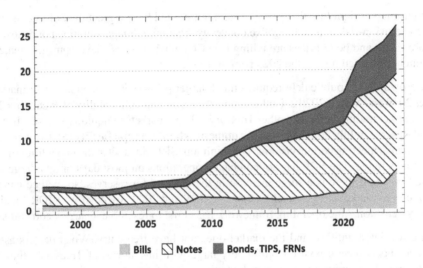

Figure 20.9 US Treasury securities outstanding 1996–2023

$ trillion, annual. *Data source*: SIFMA.

2023 bank turmoil. Bank business customers had been drawing down credit lines. Total gross US Treasury debt issuance and the share of T-bills fell after rising sharply during Covid. The volume of federal debt continued to grow in 2021 and 2022, but that of T-bills, an important money fund asset, declined (Figure 20.9). The Fed's TGA liabilities rose and then fell in 2022 as a matter of Treasury policy in anticipation of reaching the US debt ceiling by early 2023.

Deposit beta is the sensitivity of rates paid on interest-bearing deposits to money market rates and to central bank target rates in particular.[18] Deposit beta varies nonlinearly over time, generally low when rates have been low and rising as money market rates rise and depositors become more sensitive to returns. It is also lower for larger banks, and in regions with less competition between banks.

Banks had rapidly deployed a large inflow of deposits created by pandemic relief policies, in large part by adding to holdings of debt securities, increasing exposure to interest rate risk. The yield curve did not initially flatten with rising rates but remained for a time steeply upward sloping, and deposit betas were unusually low in 2022, so net interest margin (NIM) initially rose for most banks. At the same time, rising long-term rates led to large mark-to-market (MTM) losses on their securities portfolios. By the end of 2022, however, the yield curve had flattened and inverted. Deposit costs and deposit betas rose, especially for midsize and regional banks. The volume of deposits declined as depositors began shifting to money funds and other higher-yielding alternatives, placing funding pressure on bank earnings just as losses were mounting on their securities holdings. Demand for bank loans together with rising short-term rates generated intense competition for funding among banks, and with money funds and other nonbank alternatives. Tightening liquidity was reflected in higher loan-to-deposit ratios, a measure of liquidity risk, and a sharp decline, following a rebound, in stock market margin debt (Figure 12.5).

Banks, apart from the largest ones, have had growing difficulty retaining deposits. The franchise value of a deposit base—the "stickiness" of deposits—has diminished as alternatives have become

---

[18] **Deposit spread beta** is the inverse, the sensitivity of the spread between banks' cost of deposit funding and the central bank target rate to changes in the latter.

commonplace. Smaller and regional banks banks rely to a far greater extent on brokered deposits. Larger banks have an advantage from the stronger public-sector guarantees they enjoy, making them appear a safer repository for uninsured and large deposits.

Competition for funding affected the Federal Reserve's balance sheet. The ON RRP, previously used sparingly to assist in control of interest rates, grew rapidly in the first half of 2023. Reserves must be funded by some liability, and the funding cost of deposits, the natural choice, had been rising particularly for smaller and regional banks, increasing their reluctance to maintain large reserve balances at the Fed. Large banks, in contrast, facing lower deposit beta pressure and deposit spreads, hold the bulk of the declining volume of reserves among domestic US banks.

As bank holdings of reserves and deposits level off or decline and with T-bills less available, investors seeking liquid short-term investments turn to money market funds, which invest in the ON RRP facility and displace banks as holders of Fed liabilities. Discount window borrowing, normally a very small item on the Federal Reserve balance sheet, also became substantial in late 2022.

The 2020–2022 LSAP, together with the rise in interest rates and yield curve inversion affected the Federal Reserve's earnings and altered the path of its remittances to the Treasury. The Fed's balance sheet, following the first three LSAPs, funded long-term assets with short-term liabilities—reserves—and earned positive NIM. It has been described as an unusually large bond market carry trade, bearing some similarities to that of SVB and many other banks in 2021–2023.[19] From 2021, the IORB and ON RRP rates at which most of its portfolio is funded rose sharply, increasing the Fed's interest expenses more than its interest income on a larger balance sheet. Remittances to Treasury have paused for the foreseeable future, and the Fed's negative net income has since the end of 2022 accumulated as a negative liability recorded as a **deferred asset**, analogous to negative net worth, on its balance sheet. The liability, $168.9 billion as of May 15, 2024, can be written down only through future positive net income.[20] The rise in rates has also driven unamortized premiums on the Fed's securities holdings to zero and generated large unrealized losses on the portfolio. As they are realized, they further put off the time when remittances to Treasury can resume.[21]

The reversal in the Fed's net income can have political economy interactions with fiscal policy. As federal debt growth relative to GDP continues and appears increasingly likely to become unsustainable, pressure on the Fed may grow to eliminate IORB, set it to zero, or reinstate minimum reserve requirements at a higher rate relative to deposits than in the past. Were the Fed to do so, it would again earn significant net income it could remit to the Treasury, but acting under fiscal dominance would also erode central bank independence.

20.3.3   The 2023 US Bank Panic

As rates rose, banks' realized and unrealized losses grew. The spring of 2023 saw three of the largest four bank failures in US history, preceded by runs on the banks' deposits. The failure of SVB was the

---

[19] See Goodfriend (2014a). This was an accurate description of the LSAP structure although perhaps conflating the financial risk of a private actor with that of the public sector that can issue money and impose taxes to avoid insolvency in the short term.

[20] See Table 6 of the H.4.1 data release at https://www.federalreserve.gov/releases/h41/20240516/. Estimated net income for 2023 was $-114.3 billion, compared to positive net income of $58.8 billion in 2022 (https://www.federalreserve.gov/newsevents/pressreleases/other20240112a .htm).

[21] See Tables 2 and 4 of Federal Reserve Bank of New York (2024), stating unrealized losses of $948.4 billion, or about 13 percent of the roughly $7.22 trillion securities portfolio, under an interest rate scenario closely resembling conditions in late 2023. The Congressional Budget Office updates its projections at https://www.cbo.gov/system/files/2023-02/58913_Fed_Res_Remittance.pdf.

second-largest in US history (after Washington Mutual in 2008), with assets of $209 billion at the end of 2022, until it was displaced by the failure of First Republic Bank, with $213 billion, over the weekend into May 1. Signature Bank (SBNY) was the fourth-largest ($110 billion).[22] The episode illustrates the interaction of leverage and liquidity in bank stability, the evolution of run dynamics with communication technology, the limitations of regulation and supervision as substitutes for market scrutiny, and the instability induced by long periods of extremely low interest rates.

The bank failures originated in problems on the asset and liability sides of the banks' businesses. Banks had treated forward guidance as credible and underestimated interest rate risk, extending credit and acquiring bonds at low interest rates between 2008 and 2021. Following the rise in rates from 2022, banks owned a large volume of loans and debt securities with unrealized losses. Though loans in the banking book could simply be held at amortized value, securities had to be marked-to-market or the unrealized loss had to be reported publicly.

The increasing prevalence of remote work and online shopping undermined the credit quality of commercial real estate loans, many of which finance office building construction. The fair values of real estate loans are also sensitive to interest rate changes. As a result, many banks announced or were presumed by the markets to have large unrealized losses. Banks' loan loss reserves rose from mid-2022.

On the liability side, many banks were vulnerable to an increase in funding costs and the liquidity risk of reliance on demandable deposits. Much of the large increase in deposits in consequence of Federal Reserve and US government Covid policies were uninsured, and far in excess of transactions balances needed by firms and households. Uninsured deposits accounted for 45.7 percent of the total at US depository institutions at the end of 2021.[23]

The banks that failed in 2023 had concentrated assets and funding. SVB had an unusually large deposit influx stemming from the large increase in tech sector revenues over the preceding few years and tripled in size between 2019 and 2021. Uninsured and interest-bearing deposits that are more susceptible to runs accounted by 2022 for nearly all its funding, and its share of stickier non-interest bearing deposits declined. Signature Bank was reliant on real estate and law firm deposit accounts.

SVB had lent primarily to venture capital and technology firms, which were also the core of its deposit base. Like many US banks, SVB deployed its inflow of deposits, beginning in 2020, to acquire a portfolio of agency MBS, US Treasurys, and other long-term full-faith-and-credit bonds with high interest rate sensitivities. SVB was unusual among US banks for the large share of its assets invested in securities compared to loans and its interest rate market risk. Its portfolio was essentially a carry trade with the thesis that interest rates would remain low for the foreseeable future.

First Republic Bank had a large portfolio of residential real estate loans issued at low interest rates that did not have to be marked to market, but did need to be funded. It was heavily reliant on deposit funding, and its outflow raised the possibility that loans would have to be liquidated at a loss. Silvergate Capital Corp (SI) provided banking services to and had a deposit base centered on the cryptocurrency industry, which was experiencing insolvency and illiquidity of exchanges and stablecoin issuers. It announced its voluntary liquidation on March 8.

---

[22] Chartered in Santa Clara, CA, San Francisco and New York, NY, respectively. The FDIC makes data on US failures available at https://www.fdic.gov/resources/resolutions/bank-failures/.

[23] Table L.110 of the Financial Accounts of the United States (https://www.federalreserve.gov/releases/z1/). The data include FBOs.

In 2021, on-site supervisors had identified several MRAs and MRIAs at SVB, and in 2022 and early 2023 had placed some restrictions on SVB's activities due to its high duration risk and deficient risk management processes, but none that obliged it to immediately address its risk of insolvency as interest-rates began rising. According to SVB's Pillar III disclosure, its risk-based Tier 1 capital ratio was 15.5 percent and and its leverage ratio 8.11 percent at the end of 2022, well above regulatory minimums.[24] While not large enough to be subject to the LCR, it had a substantial stock of US Treasurys that would have gone a considerable way toward meeting a 100 percent minimum LCR. Some elements of the capital rules, such as the exclusion of AOCI from the measurement of Tier 1 capital, permitted banks other than the largest ones to calculate and publicly disclose higher regulatory capital ratios. Many banks would otherwise have had to raise additional equity funding to maintain Tier 1 capital ratios as unrealized losses grew.[25]

Throughout 2022, SVB experienced large unrealized losses on its bond portfolio, and announced large realized losses after liquidating a portion of it to meet deposit redemptions in early 2023. The fair value of its HTM securities had declined by $21.1 billion in 2022, compared to its $16.3 billion book value of equity. The losses and a subsequent failed attempt to raise additional equity capital triggered further redemptions. With concentrated deposits, these readily accelerated into a run on March 10, with $42 billion withdrawn within hours.

SBNY, with assets concentrated in commercial real estate, failed at the same time. A few weeks later, First Republic Bank, with a concentrated uninsured deposit base as well, failed. Large depositors rather than on-site supervisors were reponsible for finally pushing these banks into resolution and might have acted sooner had they not been able to rely on an implicit guarantee of their uninsured deposits. The technology firm Roku disclosed just before SVB's collapse that it had $487 million in uninsured deposits at SVB, over 25 percent of its total cash balances, an example of nonfinancial corporate reliance on implicit guarantees, retrospectively justified by the emergency response to SVB's failure.

The 2023 episode, as was also the case during the 2008 and 2011 crises in the United States and Europe, differed from the standard run model in a crucial respect. They were not indiscriminate but affected only banks that were known to be troubled, overly leveraged, and had serious realized and potential asset losses. Larger banks, although they also had large unrealized losses on their securities portfolios, benefited at least relatively from depositors' turn away from smaller ones.

The FDIC and Federal Reserve actions on the weekend of March 11 and subsequently aimed to resolve the two failed banks, SVB and Signature, and allay public concerns about the safety of the banking system as a whole. Buyers could not be identified immediately, so after being taken into FDIC receivership, the FDIC established bridge banks to hold their assets and liabilities. Although neither bank was large enough to qualify as systemically important or as an advanced approach bank, a "systemic risk" exception was made to the deposit insurance limits to cover their uninsured deposits. First Republic's assets were acquired by JPMorgan Chase in a purchase and assumption agreement with the FDIC. The episode displayed evidence of politicization of the resolution process and has strengthened the implicit guarantee of all uninsured US bank deposits.[26] Public officials subsequently discussed the possibility of raising the deposit insurance coverage limit from $250,000 to as high as $10 million.[27]

---

[24] Available at https://ir.svb.com/financials/Regulatory-Disclosures/default.aspx.
[25] The Fed's proposed capital rule of July 2023 (see Chapter 19) limits the AOCI exclusion.
[26] See, for example, Alan Rappeport et al., "How Washington Decided to Rescue Silicon Valley Bank's Depositors," *New York Times*, March 14, 2023, https://www.nytimes.com/2023/03/14/us/politics/inside-silicon-valley-bank-rescue.html.
[27] https://www.cbsnews.com/news/elizabeth-warren-face-the-nation-transcript-03-19-2023/.

The Federal Reserve initiated several paths of emergency lending to banks. Discount window borrowing conditions were further eased and a new emergency lending program, the **Bank Term Funding Program** (BTFP), was created, extending loans of up to one year secured by Treasurys, agency debt and MBS. The program measures haircuts against the full par value of the collateral, so more than the market value of the collateral can in principle be lent, a further innovation in Federal Reserve lending programs that would be highly unusual in private markets.[28] The Fed also lent to the bridge banks financing the purchase of the defunct bank holding companies' subsidiaries and assets.

The bank failures in the spring of 2023 illustrate the long-noted phenomenon that regulation and supervision are backward-looking and apparently unprepared for the next crisis. New and revised regulations follow each crisis, but it is in the nature of complex rules attempting to comprehensively anticipate future developments that subsequent crises display features for which they are unprepared.

Liquidity conditions eased from the second half of 2023. Demand remained high for safe short-term investments, T-bill issuance increased substantially and TGA liabilities were built up, but the yield curve became somewhat less inverted. The ON RRP facility reverted to lower usage as short-term funding pressure on banks eased, the demand for reserve balances recovered and T-bill yields rose. The Fed felt able to continue the gradual runoff of its portfolio, though emphasizing in its announcements that reserves would remain ample. It has slowed the pace of Treasury securities runoff from May 2, 2024.[29]

Further Reading

Kuttner (2018) summarizes the monetary policy response to the global financial crisis. Bernanke (2020) is a survey of research on the effectiveness of the new monetary policy tools. Krishnamurthy and Vissing-Jorgensen (2011) provide a detailed breakdown of the channels through which quantitative easing operates. Gagnon et al. (2011) find evidence that quantitative easing lowers the term premium, but not the expected path of short-term interest rates, and Stein (2012) questions if quantitative easing can then be effective.

Campbell et al. (2017) discuss Delphic and Odyssean forward guidance. Afonso et al. (2011), Afonso et al. (2020), and Afonso et al. (2023) describe the shrunken fed funds market.

Carpenter et al. (2015) and Dawsey et al. (2023) describe the Fed's balance sheet, its relation to monetary policy, and the balance sheet expansion from 2008. Perli (2024) updates balance sheet developments through early 2024. Borio (2023) and Jordan and Luther (2022) discuss the effects of Federal Reserve balance sheet expansion and subsequent tightening. Greenwood et al. (2016) present the case that ample reserves enhance financial stability. Acharya and Rajan (2022) and Acharya et al. (2024) focus on the liquidity impact.

See Malz (2020) and Afonso et al. (2021) on money market behavior since the global financial crisis and the September 2019 repo market stress.

Duffie (2023) and Golay et al. (2022) discuss Treasury market liquidity and all-to-all trading. Singh and Goel (2019) discuss the impact of collateralized securities markets on monetary policy transmission.

---

[28] The BTFP does however, have a US Treasury backstop and, in contrast to several other Fed lending facilities, has recourse to the borrowing banks' other assets.

[29] See the Implementation Note to the May 1, 2024, FOMC statement at https://www.federalreserve.gov/newsevents/pressreleases/monetary20240501a1.htm.

Vissing-Jorgensen (2021) and Schrimpf et al. (2020) analyze market behavior during the Covid pandemic. O'Hara and Zhou (2023) focus on the disruptions to basis and other trades that operate in part through repo markets. Board of Governors of the Federal Reserve System (2020) and Clarida et al. (2021) summarize the Federal Reserve response to Covid. See also Labonte (2021).

Levin et al. (2022), Federal Reserve Bank of New York (2024) and Congressional Budget Office (2022) provide projections, using different approaches, of the impact of rising interest rates on cash flows and valuation of assets on the Fed's balance sheet and on remittances to the federal government. Calomiris (2023) views fiscal dominance as a likely outcome of current US fiscal policy.

Drechsler et al. (2017) define and estimate deposit betas and Kang-Landsberg et al. (2023) estimate deposit betas during the Fed tightening of 2022. Metrick (2024) analyzes the bank failures of 2023. Board of Governors of the Federal Reserve System (2023a) is the Fed's report on its supervision of SVB and Federal Deposit Insurance Corporation (2023) the FDIC's report on its supervision of First Republic. SVB Financial Group (2023) presents SVB's financial results for the years leading up to its failure.

Appendix

A

Much of the Probability and Statistics You Need

A.1 Probability Distributions and Their Properties

When a well-defined and measurable thing X is uncertain, with a number of ways X could turn out, it defines a **random variable** (r.v.). Each **outcome** or realization has a probability $P[X]$. The function that assigns a probability to each possible outcome of the r.v. X is called a **probability distribution**. One of them is actually going to happen, so probabilities $P[X]$ of all the possible outcomes X add up to exactly 1. If the outcomes can be counted, we have a **discrete probability distribution**. If the possible outcomes lie on a continuum, encompassing all, an interval or a segment of the real numbers, it's a **continuous probability distribution**.

Events are combinations of outcomes, for example, an asset price falling on one day and rising the next or a firm not defaulting this year and also not defaulting next year. Events have probabilities that can be derived from the probability distribution of the outcomes constituting it. Two events A and B are **independent** if they have no outcomes in common. For example, whether a stock price goes up or down today has no bearing on tomorrow's return if successive returns are independent. The probability of both events occurring is $P[A] \cdot P[B]$.

In general, though, there can be some overlap between events rather than independence. If the probability of A depends on whether or not B happens, we can calculate a **conditional probability** of A given that B has occurred, written $P[A|B]$ and calculated as a ratio

$$P[A|B] = \frac{P[A \cap B]}{P[B]},$$

where $A \cap B$ is defined as the event that A and B happen. If A and B are independent, $P[B]$ drops out of the ratio, and $P[A|B] = P[A]$.

For any probability distribution, its **cumulative distribution function** (CDF) gives the probability that the outcome of the r.v. X is less than a particular number. If that number is high enough, X is almost certain to come out no higher, so its CDF takes on a value close to 1. The **probability density function** (PDF) of X gives the probability with which X has a realization between two specific values. Probability distributions are grouped in families that have many properties in common. Within a family, its parameters specify a distribution and a density function.

A.1.1 Moments of a Distribution

Distributions have characteristics by which we can compare and distinguish them. The most important are its **moments**, which summarize the shape of a distribution.

The **expected value** of an r.v. or of a function of the r.v. is the sum of all the possible values it could take on, each weighted by its probability. Each moment of a distribution is an expected value of a power r of the random variable. The **mean** or first moment $\mu_X \equiv \mathbf{E}[X]$ is the expected value of the r.v. itself ($r = 1$) and is a measure of its general size.

Higher moments are measured as the expected value of deviations from the mean (**central moments**) taken to a power $r > 1$. The **variance** or second moment ($r = 2$)

$$\text{Var}(X) \equiv \sigma_X^2 = \mathbf{E}[(X - \mu_X)^2]$$

is a measure of how widely the r.v. varies based on squared deviations from the mean. Its square root, the **standard deviation** σ_X, is expressed in the same units as the r.v. itself.

Skewness and fat tails are measured using higher statistical moments, involving higher powers of the r.v. as well as standardization, dividing by the variance. A **symmetric** probability distribution is one for which there is a value such that outcomes exceeding it by some distance have the same likelihood as outcomes falling short of it by the same distance. Skewness ($r = 3$) measures a distribution's deviations from symmetry. **Kurtosis** ($r = 4$) measures the frequency of extremely large values of either sign.

A.1.2   Quantiles of a Distribution

Quantiles are an inverse way of looking at a probability distribution. Instead of taking a possible outcome of an r.v. and finding the probability that the r.v. has that value or lower as with the CDF, we start with a probability and find an outcome of the r.v. such that the realization will be at that level or lower with the given probability. The α-**quantile** of a continuous random variable X is the realization X° such that the probability of witnessing no more than that level is α:

$$X^\circ \text{ s.t. } \mathbf{P}[X \leq X^\circ] = \alpha.$$

In other words, it is the realization X° with cumulative probability α, the threshold X° below which realizations of X fall with likelihood or frequency α. The **median** is the 0.5 or 50-percent quantile of a distribution, the value of X such that the probability of an outcome above or below it is 0.5. The mean of a distribution with positive skewness, skewed to the right, is higher than its median. The mean of a distribution skewed to the left is lower than its median. The function that maps from the probability α to the r.v. X is the **quantile function** corresponding to the probability distribution.

Quantiles are unambiguously defined for continuous distributions but not always for discrete data. The definition of cumulative probability is asymmetric; the event for which the probability is defined is $X \leq X^\circ$. The distribution function is **right-continuous**, and the quantile function therefore, **left-continuous**. Any outcome of an r.v. has a unique, well-defined cumulative probability, but for some probabilities, several values of the r.v. may fit the definition of the corresponding quantile.

A.2   Important Distributions

> ... the remarkable fact that there exist a few distributions of great universality which occur in a surprisingly great variety of problems. The three principal distributions, with ramifications throughout probability theory, are the binomial distribution, the normal distribution, ... and the Poisson distribution.
>
> Feller, *An Introduction to Probability Theory and Its Applications*[1]

---

[1] Feller (1957), p. 146. Italics omitted.

A.2.1   Binomial Distribution

A **Bernoulli trial** is a random experiment with two possible outcomes, one with a probability π and the other with a probability $1 - \pi$. A fair coin toss is an example of a Bernoulli trial in which the probability of heads or tails is each 50 percent. Another is the event of a particular firm defaulting on its debt, with a likelihood, say, of 1 percent. If we assign the value $Y = 1$ to one of the outcomes of the Bernoulli trial—say, default or an asset price increasing—and the value $Y = 0$ to the other, then Y follows a **Bernoulli distribution** with parameter $\pi = 0.01$. The outcome $Y = 1$ is referred to as a "success" even though it is identified with default or a defective light bulb in a manufacturing process.

Suppose we look at how often a particular outcome occurs in n repeated Bernoulli trials and add up the values of $Y_i, i = 1, \dots, n$. Successive trials are assumed to be independent; the outcome of one trial doesn't affect that of the others. The resulting random variable $X = \sum_{i=1}^{n} Y_i$ is said to follow a **binomial distribution** with parameters π and n. The binomial is a discrete probability distribution, and the probability of obtaining exactly k successes out of n Bernoulli trials with parameter π is

$$P[X = k] = \binom{n}{k} \pi^k (1 - \pi)^{n-k}$$

$$= \frac{n(n-1)\cdots 2 \cdot 1}{[k(k-1)\cdots 2 \cdot 1][(n-k)(n-k-1)\cdots 2 \cdot 1]} \cdot \pi^k (1 - \pi)^{n-k}.$$

We have

$$\mathbf{E}[X] = n\pi$$

$$\mathrm{Var}(X) = n\pi(1 - \pi).$$

A.2.2   Poisson Distribution

The **Poisson distribution**, like the binomial, takes Bernoulli trials as its starting point. The Poisson distribution is a discrete distribution, the mathematical limit of the binomial as the number of trials n grows large, and it represents the fraction of occurrences of the event. It is used to measure the probability of a particular number of relatively rare events occurring over a given time interval when we have a large number of trials and think we can accurately estimate the rate at which successes occur, for example, the number of defaults in a book of small loans over a year.

The probability of obtaining exactly k successes in one period is

$$P[X = k] = \frac{e^{-\lambda} \lambda^k}{k!}.$$

The parameter λ is the rate at which successes are expected to occur in one period, and

$$\mathbf{E}[X] = \mathrm{Var}(X) = \lambda.$$

A.2.3   Normal Distribution

The **normal distribution** is one of the most frequently encountered probability distributions because it fits so many natural and social phenomena well and because it's very useful analytically.

It is denoted $\mathcal{N}(\mu,\sigma^2)$, and its two parameters are its mean μ and variance σ^2. Any outcome corresponding to a real number is possible, so the normal is a continuous distribution. The CDF of a normally distributed random variable X, denoted $\Phi_{\mu,\sigma^2}(x)$, states the probability that it takes on a value no greater than x. It has an S shape, and the corresponding density function has the familiar bell curve shape.

The normal distribution is symmetrical, so its skewness coefficient is zero. A **standardized normal distribution** $\mathcal{N}(0,1)$ is the result of subtracting the mean from a normal variate and dividing by the standard deviation. Its CDF is denoted $\Phi_{0,1}(x) \equiv \Phi(x)$. Standard normal quantiles are $z_\alpha = \Phi^{-1}(\alpha)$.

A.2.4   Multivariate Distributions

A set of n random variables or its realizations can be denoted by vectors, for example, $\mathbf{X} = (X_1, X_2, \dots, X_n)$. **Multivariate probability distributions** describe the joint behavior of several random variables. A bivariate distribution gives the probability with which a pair of random variables $\mathbf{X} = (X_1, X_2)$ falls in a specific region.

Correlation is a strong form of dependence between two or more random variables. Two random variables may be independent, or correlated, or not independent but also not correlated. The **covariance** $\text{Cov}(X, Y)$ of two or more random variables is defined as the expected value of the product of their deviations from the mean:

$$\text{Cov}(X, Y) = \mathbf{E}[(X - \mu_X)(Y - \mu_Y)].$$

Their **correlation coefficient** $\text{Corr}(X, Y)$ is defined as the ratio of the covariance to the standard deviations of the two variables:

$$\text{Corr}(X, Y) = \frac{\text{Cov}(X, Y)}{\sqrt{\text{Var}(X)}\sqrt{\text{Var}(Y)}}.$$

Figure A.1 displays the density function of a pair of jointly standard normally distributed random variables with a correlation coefficient ρ. Its CDF is denoted $\Phi_\rho(\mathbf{x})$ or $\Phi_\rho(x_1, x_2)$.

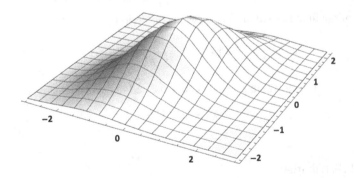

Figure A.1 Bivariate normal density

Density of a bivariate standard (with mean $\mu = 0$ and volatility $\sigma = 1$) normal distribution with correlation coefficient $\rho = 0.5$.

Constant probability **density contours** are sets of points—values of a pair of random variables—with the same density. For a jointly normally distributed pair of variates, they satisfy

$$c = (\mathbf{x} - \boldsymbol{\mu})'\Sigma^{-1}(\mathbf{x} - \boldsymbol{\mu}), \tag{A.1}$$

where the two-dimensional vector $\mathbf{x}$ represents realizations the pair, $\boldsymbol{\mu}$ the mean, and Σ is the 2×2 covariance matrix of the distribution. The $\mathbf{x}$ are the pairs on the "floor" of the bivariate distribution shown in Figure A.1. For a bivariate normal, the constant density contours are ellipsoids; the multivariate normal belongs to the family of **elliptical distributions**. The multivariate normal with pairwise zero correlation and identical variances have circular density contours and belong to the family of **spherical distributions**.

A.3   Stochastic Processes

In finance, we're often focused on how some random phenomenon, such as price or return, behaves over time. A **random** or **stochastic process** describes the state of the random variable over time. It can be thought of as a sequence of random variables, each with an index number that acts as a time stamp. The sequence can be discrete or on a continuum.

Because economic life unfolds over time, stochastic processes are a useful analytical tool. We use it in two ways here: to model the behavior of asset prices over time and to model default as an event that either occurs, or not, at a time in the future. These two applications, market risk and credit risk, are each reasonably well characterized by a particular family of stochastic processes.

A distinct type of correlation is introduced in stochastic processes and time series data. **Autocorrelation** is a measure of dependency in the sequence of realizations of a stochastic process. Analyzing stochastic processes lets us model time dependence, such as return autocorrelation.

A Bernoulli process is a discrete stochastic process, with the outcomes $Y_1, Y_2, \ldots$ of a sequence of Bernoulli trials. If we assign the values -1 and 1 to the outcomes, the result is the **random walk**, an example of discrete stochastic process. The defining properties of a random walk are:

- It is a function of time, starting at time 0 and position or value 0, denoted (0,0).
- It's a discrete process, adding discontinuous increments by jumps up or down in time steps of length Δt.
- The increments have just two possible sizes, $\pm\sqrt{\Delta t}$, occurring with probabilities π and $1 - \pi$.
- Its state or level after t steps is $\sum_\theta^t Y_\theta$.

Therefore, increments can't be zero, so the process can't stay in the same position for two consecutive time steps, though it can return to a position after at least one more step. With the passing of time, a random walk can arrive at many different values, but many different **sample paths** can lead to each value. Viewed from some earlier time, each sample path has the same probability. Figure A.2 shows one sample path of a random walk.

The random walk converges to the continuous **Brownian motion** (or **Wiener** or **diffusion process**) as the intervals between the Bernoulli trials or steps become smaller. The length of the time step Δt and the magnitude of the step size converge to zero. Although it has infinitely many possible paths, there's only one unique Brownian motion. Any random walk, regardless of its positive increment probability π and the size of the time step Δt, converges to the same Brownian motion.

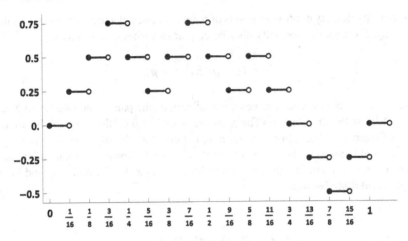

Figure A.2 Sample path of a random walk

Plot shows the first 16 positions of one simulation of a random walk over 1 time unit. The time interval between steps is $\Delta t = \frac{1}{16}$ and the magnitude of the increments is $\sqrt{\Delta t} = \frac{1}{\sqrt{16}} = \frac{1}{4}$. The dots show the value the position takes on at the start of each time interval.

The defining properties of Brownian motion include:

- Its position—the level S_t of the asset price or risk factor—is a function of time t, starting at $S_0 = 0$.
- The **total variation** of a stochastic process is the total distance it moves over a discrete time interval. The total variation of a Brownian motion is infinite. Over even a tiny time interval, any sample path is continuous, with no jumps, but infinitely jagged and thus infinitely long.
- The **quadratic variation** of a stochastic process is the variance of the distance traveled in over a discrete time interval. The quadratic variation of a Brownian motion is finite: Its position after t time units—but uncountably many infinitely small steps—is a normal variate with mean 0 and variance t:

$$S_t \sim \mathcal{N}(0, t).$$

The simple Wiener process has an awkward property for financial analysis: it permits S_t to be negative, which is almost never the case for asset prices. By generalizing Brownian motion and applying it to the logarithm rather than level of the asset price S_t, we arrive at **geometric Brownian motion**. It assumes that tiny increments to the logarithm rather than to the level of S_t itself follow a Brownian motion. A geometric Brownian motion may also scale the variance of S_t by a volatility parameter σ and add to every sample path of S_t a **drift** term, a deterministic increase or trend in the logarithm at a rate μ per unit of time. The drift and volatility may also change over time rather than being constant parameters.

Itô' lemma implies that the level of the asset price S_t then follows a **lognormal distribution**, that is, the logarithmic—continuously compounded—return $r_{t,t+\tau}$ over an interval τ is normally distributed:

$$r_{t,t+\tau} \equiv \ln(S_{t+\tau}) - \ln(S_t) \sim \mathcal{N}\left[\left(\mu - \frac{1}{2}\sigma^2\right)\tau, \sigma^2\tau\right],$$

and therefore

$$\frac{r_{t,t+\tau} - \left(\mu - \frac{1}{2}\sigma^2\right)\tau}{\sigma\sqrt{\tau}} \sim \mathcal{N}(0,1).$$

The normality of log returns implies that the statistical expected value $\mathbf{E}[r_{t,t+\tau}]$ of log returns is

$$\mathbf{E}[r_{t,t+\tau}] = \mathbf{E}[\ln(S_{t+\tau})] - \ln(S_t) = \left(\mu - \frac{1}{2}\sigma^2\right)\tau.$$

But the expected future level of S_t is slightly larger by the **Jensen's inequality term** $\frac{1}{2}\sigma^2\tau$:

$$\mathbf{E}[S_{t+\tau}] = S_t e^{\mu\tau}.$$

With the **jump** or **Poisson process**, we measure the probability with which an event occurs over some time frame. The event is assumed to occur with a probability λ over any tiny time interval. Jump processes are useful in analyzing market return and credit loss behavior. Asset prices may move discontinuously, for example, when fixed exchange rates change or during episodes such as flash crashes. Default occurrences are usefully modeled as Poisson processes.

A.4   Statistical Tests

A.4.1   Samples

Empirical work is usually done with a **random sample** of n observations $X_1, \ldots, X_n$ drawn from a larger **population**, defined to include the totality of some measurable phenomenon that we think has a specific distribution, such as returns of an asset. The observations will all have the distribution of the population they're drawn from. We don't know the parameters of the population distribution, but we draw inferences about them from characteristics of the sample. Sometimes, we make the stronger assumption that the observations are **identically and independently distributed** (i.i.d.).

When we study behavior over time, the observations form a **time series** $X_1, \ldots, X_T$ measured at times $t = 1, \ldots, T$. The behavior of financial time series often displays patterns that are at odds with the i.i.d. assumption, making it potentially a quite strong one. **Simulations** are a type of random sample that is deliberately generated by a computer and can realistically mimic a sample from a particular distribution.

Statistics are numbers computed from the observations in a sample and used in tests or other analyses. **Sample moments** are estimates of the population mean, variance and other moments. For some tests, we need the **order statistics** of a sample, arranging the observations in size order, with the smallest first and largest last. The i-th order statistic is the value of the i-th smallest observation. The position of an observation in the sample's order statistics is its **rank**. The rank of the smallest observation is 1 and that of the largest is n.

A.4.2   Sample Moments

The population mean is estimated by the **sample mean**, the simple average $\bar{X} = \frac{1}{n}\sum_{i=1}^{n} X_i$. The **sample variance** of X is

$$s_X^2 = \frac{1}{n-1}\sum_{i=1}^{n}(X_i - \bar{X})^2.$$

The sample standard deviation is its square root: $s_X = \sqrt{s_X^2}$. Dividing by $n - 1$ rather than n reflects the "loss" of a **degree of freedom** (d.f.) in "using" the same sample information to calculate $\bar{X}$

and makes the estimator s_X^2 **unbiased**: its expected value equals Var(X). Corrections for degrees of freedom are less important in larger samples.

The sample **root mean square** (RMS) is a **raw** moment, the square root of the average of the squared r.v. itself, rather than of its deviations from $\bar{X}$:

$$\text{RMS}_X = \sqrt{\frac{1}{n}\sum_{i=1}^n X_i^2}.$$

The **sample covariance** of a pair of random phenomena X and Y is

$$s_{X,Y} = \frac{1}{n-1}\sum_{i=1}^n (X_i - \bar{X})(Y_i - \bar{Y}),$$

and their **sample correlation** is the ratio

$$r_{X,Y} = \frac{\sum_{i=1}^n (X_i - \bar{X})(Y_i - \bar{Y})}{\sqrt{\sum_{i=1}^n (X_i - \bar{X})^2}\sqrt{\sum_{i=1}^n (Y_i - \bar{Y})^2}} = \frac{s_{X,Y}}{s_X s_Y}.$$

Skewness is measured by the **coefficient of skewness**, the third standardized moment:[2]

$$\frac{\frac{1}{n}\sum_{i=1}^n (X_i - \bar{X})^3}{\left[\frac{1}{n}\sum_{i=1}^n (X_i - \bar{X})^2\right]^{\frac{3}{2}}} = \frac{\sqrt{n}\sum_{i=1}^n (X_i - \bar{X})^3}{\left[\sum_{i=1}^n (X_i - \bar{X})^2\right]^{\frac{3}{2}}}.$$

Kurtosis is measured by the **coefficient of kurtosis**, the fourth standardized moment:[3]

$$\frac{\frac{1}{n}\sum_{i=1}^n (X_i - \bar{X})^4}{\left[\frac{1}{n}\sum_{i=1}^n (X_i - \bar{X})^2\right]^2} = \frac{n\sum_{i=1}^n (X_i - \bar{X})^4}{\left[\sum_{i=1}^n (X_i - \bar{X})^2\right]^2}.$$

The kurtosis of the normal distribution, which is used as a benchmark, is precisely 3, and the **kurtosis excess** is defined as the kurtosis coefficient minus 3.[4]

A.4.3   Quantiles of Samples

Quantiles of empirical distributions, such as a sample from a population or observations of a time series, are less straightforward than those of continuous distributions, and different definitions of quantile can lead to different results. The general definition of the α-quantile of the distribution of a random variable X is

$$X^\circ = \inf\{X | \mathbf{P}[X \leq X^\circ] \geq \alpha\},$$

[2] Defined as the ratio of the 3rd central moment to the $\frac{3}{2}$ power of the 2nd central moment.
[3] Defined as the ratio of the 4th central moment to the square of the 2nd central moment.
[4] These formulas for the higher moments are stated using the number of observations without the correction for degrees of freedom found in some reference works and software.

the *smallest* value $X°$ of X s.t. the cumulative probability of $X°$ is *at least* α. It applies to continuous and discrete distributions, such as samples and simulations.

The definition is consistent with several definitions of the $(1 - \alpha)$-quantile of a discrete data distribution. The most commonly used is the order statistic with rank equal to the **ceiling** $\lceil (1 - \alpha)m \rceil$ of $(1 - \alpha)m$, the smallest integer that is at least $(1 - \alpha)m$. Others include that with rank equal to the **floor** $\lfloor (1 - \alpha)m \rfloor$ of $(1 - \alpha)m$, the largest integer no larger than $(1 - \alpha)m$. We could also interpolate between the $\lfloor (1 - \alpha)m \rfloor$-th and $\lceil (1 - \alpha)m \rceil$-th order statistics. These definitions all lead to $(1 - \alpha)m$ if it is an integer.

A.4.4   Central Limit Theorem

For all its seeming specificity, the normal distribution is remarkably prevalent in actual experience. Much of that has to do with how well it describes phenomena, natural, social, and financial once we start to aggregate them in different ways.

The Bernoulli, binomial, and Poisson distributions are discrete distributions. But the binomial distribution converges to the normal distribution as the number of trials n grows larger, and the Poisson distribution converges to the normal distribution as the parameter λ grows larger.

These convergence result are applications of the **central limit theorem**. Specifically, if we standardize a binomially distributed random variable X by subtracting its mean and dividing by the square root of its variance, we can get its probability distribution arbitrarily close to that of a standard normal variate by increasing n:

$$\mathbf{P} \left[\frac{X - n\pi}{\sqrt{n\pi(1 - \pi)}} \le z \right] \rightarrow \Phi(z) \quad \text{as} \quad n \rightarrow \infty.$$

More generally, if we have a set of i.i.d. random variables, each from the same well-defined distribution that has a mean and a variance, the central limit theorem states the normalized set converges to a standard normal distribution as the set gets larger.[5]

Sampling is a valid way to do empirical research because we think most phenomena obey the **law of large numbers**, which states we can get more confident that the mean of a sample is very close to the population mean by making the sample larger. The larger the sample, the less likely the sample mean is far from the unknown population mean.[6]

A.4.5   Hypotheses

Statistical testing, the idea that if a theory is true, it ought to be reflected in data, relies heavily on the central limit theorem: the distribution of normalized independent variables with the same distribution converges to a normal. The practice of statistical hypothesis testing adheres to the modern methodology of science, developed by Karl Popper in the first half of the 20th century, maintaining that truth can never be proven. Rather, one approaches truth iteratively by **falsification** of erroneous propositions.

---

[5] This is **convergence in distribution**; the distributions become indistinguishable.
[6] This is **convergence in probability**; the probability of a difference becomes very small.

The first step in testing is the precise formulation of a **statistical hypothesis** that is testable with the available data. It is framed as a **null hypothesis** $\mathfrak{H}_0$, a proposition about a distributional characteristic of a population one wants to *disprove*. The null $\mathfrak{H}_0$ is expressed by stipulating a value for a **test statistic**. The data in the sample determines the value of the test statistic. The null $\mathfrak{H}_0$ is rejected or not, depending on its realized value. Nonrejection is taken as confirmation of a theory.

Two kinds of error are encountered in statistical hypothesis testing, and there is generally a trade-off between them:

Type I errors, or "false positives," occur when $\mathfrak{H}_0$ is rejected even though $\mathfrak{H}_0$ is true. The **significance level** of a test is a prespecified, chosen probability of a Type I error, e.g. 0.01 or 0.05.

The *p*-**value** of a realization of a statistical test is the probability, if $\mathfrak{H}_0$ true, of having a test statistic at least as unfavorable to $\mathfrak{H}_0$ as that actually obtained from the data. A small *p*-value means that, if the null were true, it was very unlikely for the test statistic to have had the observed value. It can interpreted as the lowest significance level leading to nonrejection of $\mathfrak{H}_0$, given the realized value of the test statistic.

Type II errors, or "false negatives," occur when one fails to reject $\mathfrak{H}_0$ even though $\mathfrak{H}_0$ is false. The **power** of a test is the probability of a Type II error.

A.4.6   Test Statistics

Certain probability distributions based on the standard normal are used to test whether moments of a population are equal to particular values. These distributions have complicated formulas that, like that of the standard normal, are tabulated or computed on the fly in software.

The **chi-squared** (or χ^2) **distribution** with k degrees of freedom is the distribution of a sum of k squared standard normals. It is used to test hypotheses about the variance of a population and, more generally, hypotheses about distributions.

The χ^2 distribution is also used to plot normal density contours. A density contour, such that realizations **x** of a pair of normally distributed random variables fall within the contour with probability p, is generated by choosing the constant c in equation (A.1) so that

$$c = \chi_2^2(1 - p),$$

where $\chi_2^2(1 - p)$ is the $1 - p$ quantile of the χ^2 distribution with 2 d.f.

The **Student's** t **distribution** with k d.f. is the distribution of the ratio of a standard normal to another r.v., the square root of the ratio of a χ^2 to k, the number of its d.f. All the $k + 1$ standard normals involved in the Student t are assumed independent of one another. The Student's t is used to compare a posited to the estimated mean of a distribution.

A.5   Linear Regression Analysis

In a simple linear regression, we measure the influence of an explanatory variable X—the independent variable—on another, dependent variable Y. We may have a set of observations on the pair $(X_t, Y_t), t = 1, \cdots, T$, drawn from time series, or a cross-section sample of a population (X_i, Y_i), $i = 1, \cdots, n$. We'll focus for concreteness on time series analyses.

The regression assumes a linear relation

$$Y_t = \alpha + \beta X_t + u_t, \qquad t = 1, \dots, T,$$

that holds, not precisely, but with an unobservable error u_t. The model may also assume the u_t are standard normal variates, they are independent of one another over time, and they are independent of the X_t.[7] The X_t in a basic regression model are assumed to be nonstochastic givens as they clearly are when they are time stamps and the regression measures a time trend. The X_i can also be safely treated as nonstochastic when they are elements of a controlled experiment as is very rarely possible in the social sciences.

The least-squares estimates $\hat{\alpha}$ and $\hat{\beta}$ are the values that minimize the variance of the estimated errors $\hat{u}_t = Y_t - \hat{\alpha} - \hat{\beta} X_t$. The estimated $\hat{\beta}$ is the ratio of the covariance of the dependent and independent variables to the variance of X or, equivalently, the correlation coefficient of X and Y times the ratio of Y's standard deviation to that of X. It measures how much in tandem X and Y move around, given how variable Y is relative to X:

$$\hat{\beta} = \frac{\sum_t (X_t - \bar{X})(Y_t - \bar{Y})}{\sum_t (X_t - \bar{X})^2} = \frac{s_{X,Y}}{s_X^2} = r_{X,Y} \frac{s_Y}{s_X}.$$

A high $\hat{\beta}$ reflects some combination of a large-magnitude correlation, close to ± 1 between the dependent and independent variables, and a high variance of the dependent variable compared to the independent variable.

The intercept term $\hat{\alpha}$ is estimated as the part of $\bar{Y}$ that isn't linearly related to $\bar{X}$:

$$\hat{\alpha} = \bar{Y} - \hat{\beta} \bar{X}.$$

If the residuals $\hat{u}_t = Y_t - \hat{\alpha} - \hat{\beta} X_t$ are small, then the estimates will do a lot to "explain" the variation of Y via a linear relationship to X. The sum of squared residuals divided by the d.f. of the estimate

$$s_{\hat{u}}^2 = \frac{1}{T-2} \sum_t \hat{u}_t^2,$$

is an unbiased estimate of the variance σ^2 of the model error term u_i, that is, a measure of the gap between realizations of Y and the extent to which they are explained by a linear relationship to X. It measures the statistical discernment of the model—not the same as truth or accuracy. It has two d.f. because two parameter estimates, $\hat{\alpha}$ and $\hat{\beta}$, are used to compute it. Its square root, $s_{\hat{u}}$, is the **standard error of the regression**.

The (unadjusted) **coefficient of determination** R^2 is a closely related measure, the share of Y's variance that is linearly related to X and captured by the regression:

$$R^2 = \frac{\sum_t (\hat{\alpha} + \hat{\beta} X_t - \bar{Y})^2}{\sum_t (Y_t - \bar{Y})^2} = 1 - \frac{\sum_t \hat{u}_t^2}{\sum_t (Y_t - \bar{Y})^2} = 1 - \frac{T-2}{T-1} \frac{s_{\hat{u}}^2}{s_Y^2}.$$

The R^2 also equals the square of the correlation coefficient between X and Y:

$$R^2 = \hat{\beta}^2 \frac{\sum_t (X_t - \bar{X})^2}{\sum_t (Y_t - \bar{Y})^2} = r_{X,Y}^2.$$

---

[7] Normality is a strong assumption, but the basic model at least assumes the u_{it} are assumed to be independently and identically distributed.

Under the assumptions made regarding the behavior of the u_t, we can state the standard errors of the estimated regression parameters $s_{\hat{\alpha}}$. The square of the standard error of $\hat{\alpha}$, as a function of the standard error of the regression, is

$$s_{\hat{\alpha}}^2 = s_{\hat{u}}^2 \frac{1}{T} \left(1 + \frac{\bar{X}^2}{s_X^2} \right).$$

We can also express $s_{\hat{\alpha}}$ as a function of R^2:

$$s_{\hat{\alpha}}^2 = (1 - R^2) s_Y^2 \frac{1}{T} \frac{T-1}{T-2} \left(1 + \frac{\bar{X}^2}{s_X^2} \right).$$

The square of the standard error of $\hat{\beta}$ is

$$s_{\hat{\beta}}^2 = \frac{s_{\hat{u}}^2}{T s_X^2}.$$

Further Reading

Feller (1957) is a clearly and elegantly written introduction to statistics. Mood et al. (1974) and De-Groot and Schervish (2011) are standard textbooks on probability and statistics. Baxter and Rennie (1996) is an accessible introduction to stochastic processes. Stock and Watson (2015) is an introduction to regression analysis. See also Siegfried (1970).

B
Notation

$\mathbf{P}[x]$ Probability function of a random variable x

$\mathbf{E}[x]$ Expected value of x

$\mathcal{N}(\mu, \sigma)$ Normal distribution with mean μ and standard deviation σ

$\Phi_{\mu,\sigma}(x)$ Cumulative distribution function of a normal distribution with mean μ and standard deviation σ

$\Phi(x)$ Cumulative distribution function of the standard normal distribution

$\phi(x)$ Probability density function of the standard normal distribution

$\Phi_{\rho}(x)$ Cumulative distribution function of the bivariate standard normal distribution with correlation coefficient ρ

C
Abbreviations

ABCP	asset-backed commercial paper
ABS	asset-backed securities
ACH	Automated Clearing House
ACL	allowance for credit losses
AFS	available for sale
ALLL	allowance for loan and lease losses
ALM	asset-liability management
AMLF	Asset-Backed Commercial Paper Money Market Mutual Fund Liquidity Facility
AOCI	accumulated other comprehensive income
APA	Administrative Procedure Act
APT	arbitrage pricing theory
AT1	additional Tier 1 capital
ATM	at-the-money
ATMF	at-the-money forward
BBA	British Bankers' Association
BCBS	Basel Committee on Banking Supervision
BHC	bank holding company
BIS	Bank for International Settlements
bps	basis points
BRRD	Bank Recovery and Resolution Directive
BTFP	Bank Term Funding Program
CAPM	capital asset pricing model
CBDC	central bank digital currency
CBOE	Chicago Board Options Exchange
CBRT	Central Bank of Turkey
CCAR	Comprehensive Capital Analysis and Review
CCP	central counterparty
CCyB	countercyclical buffer
CD	certificate of deposit
CDF	cumulative distribution function
CDO	collateralized debt obligation
CDS	credit default swap
CECL	current expected credit losses
CET1	common equity Tier 1 capital
CFPB	Consumer Financial Protection Bureau
CFR	Code of Federal Regulations
CFTC	Commodities Futures Trading Commission
CLO	collateralized loan obligations
CLS	Continuous Linked Settlement
CHIPS	Clearing House Interbank Payments System

CMBS	commercial mortgage-backed security
CMO	collateralized mortgage obligation
CPFF	Commercial Paper Funding Facility
CRT	capital relief trade
CS01	credit spread01
CUSIP	Committee on Uniform Securities Identification Procedures [number]
CVA	credit valuation adjustment
DFAST	Dodd-Frank stress test
DIP	debtor-in-possession
DVA	debit valuation adjustment
DVP	Delivery-versus-payment
EBA	European Banking Authority
ECB	European Central Bank
EFFR	effective federal funds rate
ELB	effective lower bound
EL	expected loss
ELB	effective lower bound
ES	expected shortfall (conditional value-at-risk)
eSLR	enhanced supplementary leverage ratio
ESRB	European Systemic Risk Board
ETF	exchange-traded fund
ETP	exchange-traded product
EWMA	exponentially weighted moving average
FAIT	flexible average inflation targeting
FASB	Financial Accounting Standards Board
FBO	foreign banking organization
FDIC	Federal Deposit Insurance Corporation
FDICIA	Federal Deposit Insurance Corporation Improvement Act
FHC	financial holding company
FHLB	Federal Home Loan Bank
FIMA	Foreign and International Monetary Authorities Repo Facility
FINRA	Financial Industry Regulatory Authority
FMU	financial market utility
FMV	fair market value
FOMC	Federal Open Market Committee
FRED	Federal Reserve Economic Data
FRN	floating-rate note
FRTB	Fundamental review of the trading book
FSA	Financial Services Authority
FSB	Financial Stability Board
FSOC	Financial Stability Oversight Council
GAAP	Generally Accepted Accounting Principles
GARCH	generalized autoregressive conditional heteroscedasticity
GDP	gross domestic product
GIC	guaranteed investment contracts
GSE	government-sponsored enterprise
GSIB	global systemically important bank
HERA	Housing and Economic Recovery Act
HQLA	high-quality liquid assets

HTM	held to maturity
IAIS	International Association of Insurance Supervisors
ICE	Intercontinental Exchange
IOSCO	International Organization of Securities Commissions
IRR	internal rate of return
ISDA	International Swaps and Derivatives Association
LBO	leveraged buyout
LCR	liquidity coverage ratio
LDI	liability-driven investing
LGD	loss given default
LIBOR	London Interbank Offered Rate
LISCC	Large Institution Supervision Coordinating Committee
LOIS	LIBOR-OIS spread
LOLR	lender of last resort
LSAP	Large Scale Asset Purchase
LTRO	longer-term refinancing operation
MBS	mortgage-backed securities
MiFID	Markets in Financial Instruments Directive
MMMF	money market mutual fund
MOVE	Merrill Lynch Option Volatility Estimate
MOU	Memorandum of Understanding
MRA	Matter Requiring Attention
MREL	minimal amount of equity and bail-in-able liabilities
MRIA	Matter Requiring Immediate Attention
MRO	main refinancing operation
MTM	mark-to-market
NAIC	National Association of Insurance Commissioners
NAV	net asset value
NBER	National Bureau of Economic Research
NBFI	nonbank financial intermediaries
NIIP	net international investment position
NIM	net interest margin
NPL	nonperforming loan
NPV	net present value
NRSRO	Nationally Recognized Statistical Rating Organization
NSFR	net stable funding ratio
NYSE	New York Stock Exchange
OAS	option-adjusted spread
OCC	Office of the Comptroller of the Currency
OIS	overnight index swap
OLA	Orderly Liquidation Authority
ON RRP	overnight reverse repo
OTC	over-the-counter
OTTI	other than temporary impairment
P&L	profit and loss
PCA	Prompt Corrective Action
PDCF	Primary Dealer Credit Facility
PDF	probability density function
PFOF	payment for order flow

PoNV	point of non-viability
RMBS	residential mortgage-backed securities
RMS	root mean square
RoE	return on equity
ROW	rest of world
r.v.	random variable
RWA	risk-weighted assets
SCAP	Supervisory Capital Assessment Program
SCB	stress capital buffer
SEC	Securities and Exchange Commission
SEP	Summary of Economic Projections
SDE	stochastic differential equation
SDF	stochastic discount factor
SFT	securities financing transactions
SIFI	Systemically Important Financial Institution
SIV	Structured Investment Vehicle
SLR	supplementary leverage ratio
SMCCF	Secondary Market Corporate Credit Facility
SOFR	Secured Overnight Financing Rate
SPOE	single point of entry
SRF	standing repo facility
SRM	Single Resolution Mechanism
SSM	Single Supervisory Mechanism
SWF	sovereign wealth fund
SWIFT	Society for Worldwide Interbank Financial Telecommunication
SWTF	short-term wholesale financing
SyRB	systemic risk buffer
TALF	Term Asset-Backed Securities Lending Facility
TAF	Term Auction Facility
TARP	Troubled Asset Relief Program
TBTF	too big to fail
TCE	tangible common equity
TGA	Treasury General Account
TLAC	total loss absorbing capacity
TLTRO	targeted longer-term refinancing operation
TRS	total return swap
VaR	value-at-Risk
VIX	CBOE Volatility Index
WACC	weighted average cost of capital
WAL	weighted-average life
WI	when-issued (Treasury securities)

References

Andrew B. Abel. The equity premium puzzle. *Federal Reserve Bank of Philadelphia Business Review*, **18**(2):3–23, Sep./Oct. 1991. https://fraser.stlouisfed.org/title/5580/item/557660/toc/523719.

Viral V. Acharya and Raghuram Rajan. Liquidity, liquidity everywhere, not a drop to use—why flooding banks with central bank reserves may not expand liquidity. Working Paper 29680, National Bureau of Economic Research, January 2022. http://www.nber.org/papers/w29680.

Viral V. Acharya and Sascha Steffen. The "greatest" carry trade ever? Understanding eurozone bank risks. *Journal of Financial Economics*, **115**(2): 215–236, February 2015. doi: 10.1016/j.jfineco.2014.11.004.

Viral V. Acharya, Stephen M. Schaefer, and Yili Zhang. Liquidity risk and correlation risk: a clinical study of the General Motors and Ford downgrade of May 2005, August 2008. https://ssrn.com/abstract=1074783.

Viral V. Acharya, Deniz Anginer, and A. Joseph Warburton. The end of market discipline? Investor expectations of implicit government guarantees. Discussion Paper 17426, CEPR, July 2022. https://cepr.org/publications/dp17426.

Viral V. Acharya, Matteo Crosignani, Tim Eisert, and Sascha Steffen. Zombie lending: theoretical, international, and historical perspectives. *Annual Review of Financial Economics*, **14**(1):21–38, 2023. doi: 10.1146/annurev-financial-111620-114424.

Viral V. Acharya, Rahul S. Chauhan, Raghuram Rajan, and Sascha Steffen. Liquidity dependence and the waxing and waning of central bank balance sheets. Working Paper 31050, National Bureau of Economic Research, January 2024. http://www.nber.org/papers/w31050.

Anat Admati and Martin Hellwig. *The bankers' new clothes*. Princeton University Press, Princeton, NJ, expanded edition, 2024a.

Anat Admati and Martin Hellwig. The parade of the Bankers' New Clothes continues: 44 flawed claims debunked. Finance Working Paper 951, European Corporate Governance Institute, apr 2024b. https://ssrn.com/abstract=2292229.

Anat R. Admati, Peter M. DeMarzo, Martin F. Hellwig, and Paul Pfleiderer. Fallacies, irrelevant facts, and myths in the discussion of capital regulation: why bank equity is not socially expensive. Research Paper 13-7, Stanford Graduate School of Business, October 2013. https://www.gsb.stanford.edu/faculty-research/working-papers/fallacies-irrelevant-facts-myths-discussion-capital-regulation-why.

Anat R. Admati, Peter M. DeMarzo, Martin F. Hellwig, and Paul Pfleiderer. The leverage ratchet effect. *Journal of Finance*, **73**(1):145–198, February 2018. doi: 10.1111/jofi.12588.

Tobias Adrian and Tommaso Mancini-Griffoli. The rise of digital money. *Annual Review of Financial Economics*, **13**:57–77, 2021. doi: 10.1146/annurev-financial-101620-063859.

Tobias Adrian and Hyun Song Shin. Liquidity and leverage. *Journal of Financial Intermediation*, **19**(3):418–437, July 2010a. doi: 10.1016/j.jfi.2008.12.002.

Tobias Adrian and Hyun Song Shin. Financial intermediaries and monetary economics. In Benjamin M. Friedman and Frank H. Hahn, editors, *The handbook of monetary economics*, volume **3**, pages 601–650. Elsevier, Amsterdam, 2010b. doi: 10.1016/B978-0-444-53238-1.00012-0.

Tobias Adrian, Daniel Covitz, and Nellie Liang. Financial stability monitoring. *Annual Review of Financial Economics*, **7**(1):357–395, 2015. doi: 10.1146/annurev-financial-111914-042008.

Tobias Adrian, Michael Fleming, Or Shachar, and Erik Vogt. Market liquidity after the financial crisis. *Annual Review of Financial Economics*, **9**(1):43–83, 2017. doi: 10.1146/annurev-financial-110716-032325.

Gara Afonso, Anna Kovner, and Antoinette Schoar. Stressed, not frozen: the federal funds market in the financial crisis. *Journal of Finance*, **66**(4): 1109–1139, August 2011. doi: 10.1111/j.1540-6261.2011.01670.x.

Gara Afonso, Marco Cipriani, Gabriele La Spada, and Will Riordan. A new reserves regime? COVID-19 and the Federal Reserve balance sheet. Liberty Street Economics, July 7, 2020. https://libertystreeteconomics.newyorkfed.org/2020/07/a-new-reserves-regime-covid-19-and-the-federal-reserve-balance-sheet.html.

Gara Afonso, Marco Cipriani, Adam Copeland, Anna Kovner, Gabriele La Spada, and Antoine Martin. The market events of mid-September 2019. *Federal Reserve Bank of New York Economic Policy Review*, **27**(2):1–24, August 2021. https://www.newyorkfed.org/medialibrary/media/research/epr/2021/EPR_2021_market-events_afonso.pdf.

Gara Afonso, Gonzalo Cisternas, Brian Gowen, Jason Miu, and Joshua Younger. Who's borrowing and lending in the fed funds market today? Liberty Street Economics, Oct. 10, 2023. https://libertystreeteconomics.newyorkfed.org/2023/10/whos-borrowing-and-lending-in-the-fed-funds-market-today/.

Anna Agapova. Money market mutual funds. In H. Kent Baker, editor, *Mutual funds and exchange-traded funds: building blocks to wealth*, pages 195–214. Oxford University Press, Oxford and New York, 2015. doi: 10.1093/acprof:oso/9780190207434.003.0011.

Jeffery Amato and Eli M. Remolona. The credit spread puzzle. *BIS Quarterly Review*, pages 51–63, December 2003. https://www.bis.org/publ/qtrpdf/r_qt0312e.pdf.

Thomas Barnebeck Andersen and Peter Sandholt Jensen. Too Big to Fail and moral hazard: evidence from an epoch of unregulated commercial banking. *IMF Economic Review*, **70**:808–830, 2022. doi: 10.1057/s41308-022-00167-7.

Torben G. Andersen, Tim Bollerslev, Peter F. Christoffersen, and Francis X. Diebold. Volatility and correlation forecasting. In G. Elliott, C.W.J. Granger, and A. Timmermann, editors, *Handbook of Economic Forecasting*, volume 1, pages 777–878. Elsevier, Amsterdam, 2010. doi: 10.1016/S1574-0706(05)01015-3.

Andrew Ang. *Asset management: a systematic approach to factor investing*. Oxford University Press, New York and Oxford, 2014.

Andrew Ang and Joseph Chen. Asymmetric correlations of equity portfolios. *Journal of Financial Economics*, **63**(3):102–126, March 2006. doi: 10.1016/S0304-405X(02)00068-5.

Andrew Ang, Joseph Chen, and Yuhang Xing. Downside risk. *Review of Financial Studies*, **19**(4):1191–1239, Winter 2006. doi: 10.1093/rfs/hhj035.

Andrew Ang, Sergiy Gorovyy, and Gregory B. van Inwegen. Hedge fund leverage. *Journal of Financial Economics*, **102**(1):102–126, October 2011. doi: 10.1016/j.jfineco.2011.02.020.

Sirio Aramonte. Mind the buybacks, beware of the leverage. *BIS Quarterly Review*, pages 49–59, September 2020. https://www.bis.org/publ/qtrpdf/r_qt2009d.pdf.

Kenneth J. Arrow. Limited knowledge and economic analysis. *American Economic Review*, **64**(1):1–10, March 1973. http://www.jstor.org/stable/1814877.

Carlos Arteta, Mark Carey, Ricardo Correa, and Jason Kotter. Revenge of the steamroller: ABCP as a window on risk choices. *Review of Finance*, **24**(3): 497–528, May 2020. doi: 10.1093/rof/rfz017.

Adam Ashcraft, Morten L. Bech, and W. Scott Frame. The Federal Home Loan Bank System: The lender of next-to-last resort? *Journal of Money, Credit and Banking*, **42**(4):551–583, June 2008. doi: 10.1111/j.1538-4616.2010.00299.x.

Adam B. Ashcraft and Til Schuermann. Understanding the securitization of subprime mortgage credit. *Foundations and Trends in Finance*, **2**(3):191–309, 2008. doi: 10.1561/0500000024.

Clifford S. Asness, John M. Liew, and Robert J. Krail. Do hedge funds hedge? *Journal of Portfolio Management*, **28**(1):6–19, Fall 2001. doi: 10.1111/j.1538-4616.2010.00299.x.

Raphael Auer, Jon Frost, Leonardo Gambacorta, Cyril Monnet, Tara Rice, and Hyun Song Shin. Central bank digital currencies: motives, economic implications, and the research frontier. *Annual Review of Economics*, **14**(1): 697–721, 2022. doi: 10.1146/annurev-economics-051420-020324.

Patrick Augustin, Ing-Haw Cheng, and Ludovic Van den Bergen. Volmageddon and the failure of short volatility products. *Financial Analysts Journal*, **77**(3):35–51, 2021. doi: 10.1080/0015198X.2021.1913040.

Dafna Avraham, Patricia Selvaggi, and James I. Vickery. A structural view of U.S. bank holding companies. *Federal Reserve Bank of New York Economic Policy Review*, **18**(2):65–81, July 2012. https://www.newyorkfed.org/medialibrary/media/research/epr/12v18n2/1207avra.pdf.

Walter Bagehot. *Lombard Street: A description of the Money Market*. Henry S. King & Co., Cambridge, U.K., 3rd edition, 1873. http://files.libertyfund.org/files/128/0184_Bk.pdf.

Laurie Simon Bagwell and John B. Shoven. Cash distributions to shareholders. *Journal of Economic Perspectives*, **3**(3):129–140, September 1989. doi: 10.1257/jep.3.3.129.

Mark Baldassare. *When government fails: the Orange County bankruptcy*. University of California Press, Oakland, CA, 1998. doi: 10.1525/california/9780520214859.001.0001.

Bank of England. Financial Stability Report, December 2010. https://www.bankofengland.co.uk/-/media/boe/files/financial-stability-report/2010/december-2010.pdf.

Nicholas Barberis and Richard Thaler. A survey of behavioral finance. In G.M. Constantinides, M. Harris, and R.M. Stulz, editors, *Handbook of the Economics of Finance*, volume 1B, pages 1053–1128. Elsevier, Amsterdam, 2003. doi: 10.1016/S1574-0102(03)01027-6.

Robert J. Barro. Rare disasters and asset markets in the twentieth century. *Quarterly Journal of Economics*, **121**(3):823–866, August 2006. doi: 10.1162/qjec.121.3.823.

Daniel Barth and Jay Kahn. Basis trades and Treasury market illiquidity. OFR Brief 20-01, Office of Financial Research, 2020. https://www.financialresearch.gov/briefs/2020/07/16/basis-trades-and-treasury-market-illiquidity/.

Daniel Barth, Jay Kahn, and Luke M. Olson. Who participates in cleared repo? OFR Brief 21-01, Office of Financial Research, 2021. https://www.financialresearch.gov/briefs/2021/07/08/who-participates-in-cleared-repo/.

Basel Committee on Banking Supervision. Revisions to the principles for the sound management of operational risk, March 2021. https://www.bis.org/publ/d515.pdf.

Jonathan Barron Baskin and Paul J. Miranti, Jr. *A history of corporate finance*. Cambridge University Press, Cambridge, UK, 1997.

Martin Baxter and Andrew Rennie. *Financial calculus: an introduction to derivative pricing*. Cambridge University Press, Cambridge U.K., 1996.

Bo Becker and Victoria Ivashina. Reaching for yield in the bond market. *Journal of Finance*, **70**(5):1863–1902, October 2015. doi: 10.1111/jofi.12199.

Tanya Styblo Beder. VAR: seductive but dangerous. *Financial Analysts Journal*, **51**(5):12–24, Sep.-Oct. 1995. doi: 10.2469/faj.v51.n5.1932.

Geert Bekaert and Guojun Wu. Asymmetric volatility and risk in equity markets. *Review of Financial Studies*, **13**(1):1–42, January 2000. doi: 10.1093/rfs/13.1.1.

Mario Bellia, Sara Maccaferri, and Sebastian Schich. Limiting too-big-to-fail: market reactions to policy announcements and actions. *Journal of Banking Regulation*, **23**:368–389, December 2022. doi: 10.1057/s41261-021-00176-y.

Allen N. Berger, Richard J. Herring, and Giorgio P. Szegö. The role of capital in financial institutions. *Journal of Banking and Finance*, **19**(3–4):393–430, June 1995. doi: 10.1016/0378-4266(95)00002-X.

Jonathan B. Berk and Richard C. Green. Mutual fund flows and performance in rational markets. *Journal of Political Economy*, **112**(6):1269–1295, December 2004. doi: 10.1086/424739.

Ben S. Bernanke. The financial accelerator and the credit channel, remarks at a Conference on the Credit Channel of Monetary Policy in the Twenty-first Century, Federal Reserve Bank of Atlanta, June 15, 2007, 2007. https://www.federalreserve.gov/newsevents/speech/bernanke20070615a.htm.

Ben S. Bernanke. The new tools of monetary policy. *American Economic Review*, **110**(4):943–83, April 2020. doi: 10.1257/aer.110.4.943.

Hendrik Bessembinder, Michael J. Cooper, and Feng Zhang. Mutual fund performance at long horizons. *Journal of Financial Economics*, **147**(1): 132–158, December 2023. doi: 10.1016/j.jfineco.2022.10.006.

Ulrich Bindseil and Alessio Fotia. *Introduction to central banking*. SpringerBriefs in Quantitative Finance. Springer, New York, 2021. doi: 10.1007/978-3-030-70884-9.

Fischer Black. Noise. *Journal of Finance*, **41**(3):529–543, July 1986. doi: 10.1111/j.1540-6261.1986.tb04513.x.

Fischer Black. Equilibrium exchanges. *Financial Analysts Journal*, **51**(3):23–29, May-Jun. 1995. https://www.jstor.org/stable/4479843.

Fischer Black, Emanuel Derman, and William Toy. A one-factor model of interest rates and its application to Treasury bond options. *Financial Analysts Journal*, **46**(1):33–39, Jan.-Feb. 1990. https://www.jstor.org/stable/4479294.

Olivier J. Blanchard and Mark W. Watson. Bubbles, rational expectations, and financial markets. In Paul Wachtel, editor, *Crisis in the economic and financial structure*, pages 295–315. Lexington Books, Lexington, MA, 1982.

Board of Governors of the Federal Reserve System. Financial Stability Report, May 2020. https://www.federalreserve.gov/publications/files/financial-stability-report-20200515.pdf.

Board of Governors of the Federal Reserve System. Review of the Federal Reserve's supervision and regulation of Silicon Valley Bank, April 2023a. https://www.federalreserve.gov/publications/files/svb-review-20230428.pdf.

Board of Governors of the Federal Reserve System. Financial Stability Report, May 2023b. https://www.federalreserve.gov/publications/files/financial-stability-report-20230508.pdf.

Board of Governors of the Federal Reserve System, Office of Inspector General. The Federal Reserve's Section 13(3) lending facilities to support overall market liquidity: function, status, and risk management, November 2010. http://oig.federalreserve.gov/reports/FRS_Lending_Facilities_Report_final-11-23-10_web.pdf.

Zvi Bodie. On the risk of stocks in the long run. *Financial Analysts Journal*, **51**(3):18–22, June 1995. 10.2469/faj.v51.n3.1901.

Pierluigi Bologna, Arianna Miglietta, and Anatoli Segura. Contagion in the CoCos market? A case study of two stress events. *International Journal of Central Banking*, **16**(6):137–184, December 2020. https://www.ijcb .org/journal/ijcb20q5a4.pdf.

L.N. Boon, M. Brière, and S. Rigot. Regulation and pension fund risk-taking. *Journal of International Money and Finance*, **84**(6):23–41, December 2018. doi: 10.1016/j.jimonfin.2018.01.005.

Claudio Borio. The financial cycle and macroeconomics: what have we learnt? *Journal of Banking and Finance*, **45**(3):182–198, August 2014. doi: 10.1016/j.jbankfin.2013.07.031.

Claudio Borio. Navigating by r*: safe or hazardous? Working Paper 982, Bank for International Settlements, November 2021. https://www.bis.org/publ/work982.pdf.

Claudio Borio. Getting up from the floor. Working Paper 1100, Bank for International Settlements, May 2023. https://www.bis.org/publ/work1100.pdf.

Claudio Borio and William R. White. Whither monetary and financial stability: The implications of evolving policy regimes. In *Monetary policy and uncertainty: adapting to a changing economy*, Jackson Hole Economic Policy Symposium, pages 131–211. Federal Reserve Bank of Kansas City, 2003. https://www .kansascityfed.org/Jackson%20Hole/documents/3431/pdf-Boriowhite2003.pdf.

G.E.P. Box. Robustness in the strategy of scientific model building. In Robert L. Launer and Graham N. Wilkinson, editors, *Robustness in statistics*, pages 201–236. Academic Press, San Diego, 1979. doi: 10.1016/B978-0-12-438150-6.50018-2.

Nina Boyarchenko, Pooja Gupta, Nick Steele, and Jacqueline Yen. Negative swap spreads. *Federal Reserve Bank of New York Economic Policy Review*, **24**(2):1–14, October 2018a. https://www.newyorkfed.org/ medialibrary/media/research/epr/2018/epr_2018_negative-swap-spreads_boyarchenko.pdf.

Nina Boyarchenko, Pooja Gupta, Nick Steele, and Jacqueline Yen. Trends in credit basis spreads. *Federal Reserve Bank of New York Economic Policy Review*, **24**(2):15–37, October 2018b. https://www.newyorkfed .org/medialibrary/media/research/epr/2018/EPR_2018_trends-in-credit-basis-spreads_boyarchenko.pdf.

Aaron Brown. *Financial risk management for dummies*. John Wiley & Sons, Hoboken, NJ, 2016.

Markus K. Brunnermeier. Financial dominance, Twelfth Paolo Baffi Lecture, Bank of Italy, 2016. https://www .bancaditalia.it/pubblicazioni/lezioni-baffi/pblecture-12/Brunnermeier-Baffi-Lecture-2016.pdf.

Markus K. Brunnermeier and Ricardo Reis. *A crash course on crises: macroeconomic concepts for run-ups, collapses, and recoveries*. Princeton University Press, Princeton, NJ, 2023.

Willem Buiter, Stephen Cecchetti, Kathryn Dominguez, and Antonio Sánchez Serrano. Stabilising financial markets: lending and market making as a last resort. Reports of the Advisory Scientific Committee 13, European Systemic Risk Board, January 2023.

Ricardo J. Caballero, Takeo Hoshi, and Anil K. Kashyap. Zombie lending and depressed restructuring in Japan. *American Economic Review*, **98**(5):1943–77, December 2008. doi: 10.1257/aer.98.5.1943.

Ricardo J. Caballero, Emmanuel Farhi, and Pierre-Olivier Gourinchas. The safe assets shortage conundrum. *Journal of Economic Perspectives*, **31**(3):29–46, Summer 2017. doi: 10.1257/jep.31.3.29.

Fang Cai and Sharjil Haque. Private credit: characteristics and risks. FEDS Notes, Board of Governors of the Federal Reserve System, February 2024. https://doi.org/10.17016/2380-7172.3462.

Charles W. Calomiris. Fiscal dominance and the return of zero-interest bank reserve requirements. *Federal Reserve Bank of St. Louis Review*, **105**(4):1–11, Q4 2023. https://research.stlouisfed.org/publications/ review/2023/06/02/fiscal-dominance-and-the-return-of-zero-interest-bank-reserve-requirements.

Charles W. Calomiris and Stephen H. Haber. *Fragile by design: The political origins of banking crises and scarce credit*. Princeton University Press, Princeton, NJ, 2014.

Charles W. Calomiris and Richard J. Herring. How to design a contingent convertible debt requirement that helps solve our Too-Big-to-Fail problem. *Journal of Applied Corporate Finance*, **25**(2):66–89, Spring 2013. doi: 10.1111/jacf.12015.

Charles W. Calomiris and Matthew Jaremski. Deposit insurance: theories and facts. *Annual Review of Financial Economics*, **8**(1):97–120, 2023. doi: 10.1146/annurev-financial-111914-041923.

Charles W. Calomiris and Charles M. Kahn. The role of demandable debt in structuring optimal banking arrangements. *American Economic Review*, **81**(3):497–513, June 1991. http://www.jstor.org/stable/2006515.

Jeffrey R. Campbell, Jonas D. M. Fisher, Alejandro Justiniano, and Leonardo Melosi. Forward guidance and macroeconomic outcomes since the financial crisis. *NBER Macroeconomics Annual*, **31**:283–357, 2017. doi: 10.1086/690242.

John Y. Campbell. *Financial decisions and markets: a course in asset pricing.* Princeton University Press, Princeton, NJ, 2018.

John Y. Campbell, Andrew W. Lo, and A. Craig MacKinlay. *The econometrics of financial markets.* Princeton University Press, Princeton, NJ, 1997.

Eduardo Canabarro and Darrell Duffie. Measuring and marking counterparty risk. In Leo M. Tilman, editor, *Asset/liability management for financial institutions*, pages 122–134. Euromoney Publications, London, 2003.

Forrest H. Capie and Geoffrey E. Wood, editors. *The lender of last resort.* Routledge, London, 2007.

Mark M. Carhart. On persistence in mutual fund performance. *Journal of Finance*, **52**(1):57–82, March 1997. doi: 10.1111/j.1540-6261.1997.tb03808.x.

Seth Carpenter, Jane Ihrig, Elizabeth Klee, Daniel Quinn, and Alexander Boote. The Federal Reserve's balance sheet and earnings: a primer and projections. *International Journal of Central Banking*, **11**(2):237–283, March 2015. https://www.ijcb.org/journal/ijcb15q2a7.pdf.

Fabien Carruzzo, Daniel King, and Stephen D. Zide. Unconventional CDS credit events: Hovnanian Enterprises, April 10 2018. https://www.kramerlevin.com/en/perspectives-search/unconventional-cds-credit-events-hovnanian-enterprises-alert.html.

Stephen Cecchetti and Anil Kashyap. What binds? interactions between bank capital and liquidity regulations. In Philipp Hartmann, Haizhou Huang, and Dirk Schoenmaker, editors, *The changing fortunes of central banking*, pages 192–202. Cambridge University Press, Cambridge, 2018. doi: 10.1017/9781108529549.012.

Alain Chaboud, Dagfinn Rime, and Vladyslav Sushko. The foreign exchange market. In Refet Gürkaynak and Jonathan Wright, editors, *Research handbook of financial markets*, pages 253–275. Edward Elgar Publishing, Cheltenham, UK, 2023.

Donald R. Chambers, Keith Black, and Nelson J. Lacey. *Alternative investments: a primer for investment professionals.* CFA Institute Research Foundation, 2018. https://rpc.cfainstitute.org/-/media/documents/book/rf-publication/2018/rf-v2018-n1-1.pdf.

Somnath Chatterjee. Modelling credit risk. CCBS Handbook 34, Centre for Central Banking Studies, Bank of England, 2015. https://www.bankofengland.co.uk/ccbs/modelling-credit-risk.

Hongyi Chen and Pierre L. Siklos. Central bank digital currency: A review and some macro-financial implications. *Journal of Financial Economics*, **60**: 100985, June 2022. doi: 10.1016/j.jfs.2022.100985.

Lawrence J. Christiano and Terry J. Fitzgerald. Understanding the fiscal theory of the price level. *Federal Reserve Bank of Cleveland Economic Review*, **36**(2):2–37, Q2 2000.

Peter Christoffersen. *Elements of financial risk management.* Academic Press, San Diego, 2nd edition, 2012.

Stijn Claessens. An overview of macroprudential policy tools. *Annual Review of Financial Economics*, **7**:397–422, 2015. doi: 10.1146/annurev-financial-111914-041807.

Stijn Claessens, M. Ayhan Kose, Luc Laeven, and Fabian Valencia, editors. *Financial crises: causes, consequences, and policy responses.* International Monetary Fund, 2014.

Richard Clarida, Jordi Gali, and Mark Gertler. The science of monetary policy: a New Keynesian perspective. *Journal of Economic Literature*, **37**(4): 1661–1707, December 1999. doi: 10.1257/jel.37.4.1661.

Richard H. Clarida. The Federal Reserve's new monetary policy framework: a robust evolution, speech delivered at the Peterson Institute for International Economics, August 31, 2020, November 2020. https://www.federalreserve.gov/newsevents/speech/clarida20200831a.htm.

Richard H. Clarida, Burcu Duygan-Bump, and Chiara Scotti. The COVID-19 crisis and the Federal Reserve's policy response. In Bill English, Kristin Forbes, and Àngel Ubide, editors, *Monetary policy and central banking in the Covid era*, pages 147–169. Centre for Economic Policy Research, 2021. https://cepr.org/publications/books-and-reports/monetary-policy-and-central-banking-covid-era.

R. H. Coase. The lighthouse in economics. *Journal of Law and Economics*, **17**(2):357–376, October 1974. https://www.jstor.org/stable/724895.

John H. Cochrane. *Asset pricing*. Princeton University Press, Princeton, rev. edition, 2005.

John H. Cochrane. Presidential address: discount rates. *Journal of Finance*, **66**(4):1047–1108, August 2011. doi: 10.1111/j.1540-6261.2011.01671.x.

John H. Cochrane. Fiscal histories. *Journal of Economic Perspectives*, **36**(4): 125–46, November 2022. doi: 10.1257/jep.36.4.125.

John H. Cochrane and Amit Seru. Ending bailouts, at last. *Journal of Law, Economics and Policy*, **19**(2):169–193, 2024. https://www.jlep.net/s/Cochrane_Seru-for-PDF.pdf.

Rodrigo Coelho, Jatin Taneja, and Rastko Vrbaski. Upside down: when AT1 instruments absorb losses before equity. FSI Briefs 21, Financial Stability Institute, Bank for International Settlements, 2023. https://www.bis.org/fsi/fsibriefs21.pdf.

Benjamin H. Cohen, Dietrich Domanski, Ingo Fender, and Hyun Song Shin. Global liquidity: A selective review. *Annual Review of Economics*, **9**(1): 587–612, 2017. doi: 10.1146/annurev-economics-063016-104331.

Thomas S. Coleman. *A practical guide to risk management*. Research Foundation of CFA Institute, 2011. https://www.cfainstitute.org/-/media/documents/book/rf-publication/2011/rf-v2011-n3-1-pdf.pdf.

Congressional Budget Office. How the Federal Reserve's quantitative easing affects the federal budget. Report 57519, September 2022. https://www.cbo.gov/system/files/2022-09/57519-balance-sheet.pdf.

Rama Cont. Empirical properties of asset returns: stylized facts and statistical issues. *Quantitative Finance*, **1**(2):223–236, Apr.–June 2001. doi: 10.1080/713665670.

Adam Copeland, Darrell Duffie, Antoine Martin, and Susan McLaughlin. Key mechanics of the U.S. tri-party repo market. *Federal Reserve Bank of New York Economic Policy Review*, **18**(3):17–28, November 2012. https://www.newyorkfed.org/medialibrary/media/research/epr/12v18n3/1210cope.pdf.

Corsi, Marco and Mudde, Yvo, eds. The use of the Eurosystem's monetary policy instruments and its monetary policy implementation framework in 2020 and 2021. Occasional Paper 304, European Central Bank, September 2022.

Virginie Coudert and Mathieu Gex. Contagion inside the credit default swaps market: the case of the GM and Ford crisis in 2005. *Journal of International Financial Markets, Institutions and Money*, **20**(2):109–134, April 2010. doi: 10.1016/j.intfin.2010.01.001.

Joshua Coval and Erik Stafford. The cost of capital for alternative investments. *Journal of Finance*, **70**(1):145–198, February 2018. 10.1111/jofi.12269.

Alfred Cowles, 3rd. Can stock market forecasters forecast? *Econometrica*, **1**(3): 309–324, 1933. http://www.jstor.org/stable/1907042.

K.J. Martijn Cremers, Jon A. Fulkerson, and Timothy B. Riley. Challenging the conventional wisdom on active management: a review of the past 20 years of academic literature on actively managed mutual funds. *Financial Analysts Journal*, **75**(4):8–35, 2019. doi: 10.1080/0015198X.2019.1628555.

Michel Crouhy, Robert Mark, and Dan Galai. A comparative analysis of current credit risk models. *Journal of Banking and Finance*, **24**(1–2):59–117, January 2000a. doi: 10.1016/S0378-4266(99)00053-9.

Michel Crouhy, Robert Mark, and Dan Galai. *Risk management*. McGraw–Hill, New York, 2000b.

Jón Daníelsson. The emperor has no clothes: limits to risk modelling. *Journal of Banking and Finance*, **26**(7):1273–1296, July 2002. doi: 10.1016/S0378-4266(02)00263-7.

Kristopher Dawsey, William B. English, and Brian Sack. The Federal Reserve balance sheet. In Refet Gürkaynak and Jonathan Wright, editors, *Research handbook of financial markets*, pages 6–32. Edward Elgar Publishing, Cheltenham, UK, 2023.

H. DeGroot, Morris and Mark J. Schervish. *Probability and statistics*. Pearson, London, 4th edition, 2011.

Kresimir Demeterfi, Emanuel Derman, Michael Kamal, and Joseph Zou. More than you ever wanted to know about volatility swaps. *Quantitative Strategies Research Notes*, Goldman Sachs and Co., March 1999. https://emanuelderman.com/wp-content/uploads/1999/02/gs-volatility_swaps.pdf.

Emanuel Derman and Michael B. Miller. *The volatility smile*. John Wiley & Sons, Hoboken, NJ, 2016.

David F. DeRosa. *Bursting the bubble: rationality in a seemingly irrational market*. CFA Institute Research Foundation, 2021. https://rpc.cfainstitute.org/-/media/documents/book/rf-publication/2021/rf-derosa-bubbles.pdf.

Douglas W. Diamond. Banks and liquidity creation: a simple exposition of the Diamond-Dybvig model. *Federal Reserve Bank of Richmond Economic Policy Review*, **93**(2):189–200, Spring 2007. https://www .richmondfed.org/publications/research/economic_quarterly/2007/spring/diamond.

Douglas W. Diamond and Philip H. Dybvig. Bank runs, deposit insurance, and liquidity. *Journal of Political Economy*, **91**(3):401–419, June 1983. doi: 10.1086/261155.

Elroy Dimson, Paul Marsh, and Mike Staunton. *Triumph of the optimists: 101 years of global investment returns*. Princeton University Press, Princeton, NJ, 2002.

Curtis A. Doty, Lawrence R. Hamilton, Carol A. Hitselberger, and Matthew F. Kluchenek. Capital relief trades: structuring considerations for synthetic securitizations. *Structured Finance Bulletin*, Mayer Brown, Spring 2020. https://www.mayerbrown.com/-/media/files/perspectives-events/publications/2020/ 02/capital-relief-trades-part-123.pdf.

Kevin Dowd. Models of banking instability: a partial review of the literature. *Journal of Economic Surveys*, **6**(2):107–132, 1992. doi: 10.1111/j.1467-6419.1992.tb00147.x.

Kevin Dowd. *Measuring market risk*. John Wiley & Sons, Hoboken, NJ, 2nd edition, 2005.

Kevin Dowd. Math gone mad: regulatory risk modeling by the Federal Reserve. Policy Analysis 754, Cato Institute, September 2014. https://www.cato.org/policy-analysis/math-gone-mad-regulatory-risk-modeling-federal-reserve.

Kevin Dowd. *No Stress II: the flaws in the Bank of England's stress testing programme*. Adam Smith Institute, London, 2015. https://www.adamsmith.org/research/no-stress-ii-the-flaws-in-the-bank-of-englands-stress-testing-programme.

Kevin Dowd, editor. *The experience of free banking*. Institute of Economic Affairs, London, 2nd edition, 2023. https://iea.org.uk/publications/the-experience-of-free-banking/.

Kevin Dowd. So far, Central Bank Digital Currencies have failed. *Economic Affairs*, **44**(1):71–94, February 2024. doi: 10.1111/ecaf.12621.

Itamar Drechsler, Alexi Savov, and Philipp Schnabl. The deposits channel of monetary policy. *Quarterly Journal of Economics*, **132**(4):1819–1876, November 2017. doi: 10.1093/qje/qjx019.

Wenxin Du, Alexander Tepper, and Adrien Verdelhan. Deviations from covered interest rate parity. *Journal of Finance*, **73**(3):915–957, June 2018. doi: 10.1111/jofi.12620.

Darrell Duffie. Resilience redux in the US Treasury market. In *Structural shifts in the global economy*, Jackson Hole Economic Policy Symposium, pages 131–211, 2023. https://www.kansascityfed.org/Jackson %20Hole/documents/9780/JH-2023BW.pdf.

Rodney Edvinsson, Tor Jacobson, and Daniel Waldenström. *Sveriges Riksbank and the history of central banking*. Cambridge University Press, Cambridge, UK, 2018. doi: 10.1017/9781108140430.

Barry Eichengreen. *Globalizing capital: a history of the international monetary system*. Princeton University Press, Princeton, NJ, 3rd edition, 2019.

Barry Eichengreen and Ricardo Hausmann. Whither monetary and financial stability: The implications of evolving policy regimes. In *New challenges for monetary policy*, Jackson Hole Economic Policy Symposium, pages 329–368. Federal Reserve Bank of Kansas City, 1999. https://www.kansascityfed.org/Jackson %20Hole/documents/3551/1999-S99eich.pdf.

Thomas Eisenbach, Andrew Haughwout, Beverly Hirtle, Anna Kovner, David Lucca, and Matthew Plosser. Supervising large, complex financial institutions: What do supervisors do? *Federal Reserve Bank of New York Economic Policy Review*, **23**(1):57–77, February 2017. https://www.newyorkfed.org/medialibrary/ media/research/epr/2017/EPR_2017_what-do-supervisors-do_eisenbach.pdf.

Robert F. Engle and Andrew J. Patton. What good is a volatility model? *Quantitative Finance*, **1**(2):237–245, Apr.–June 2001. doi: 10.1080/14697680400000028.

Huberto M. Ennis, Jeffrey M. Lacker, and John A. Weinberg. Money market fund reform: dealing with the fundamental problem. Working Paper 22-08R, Federal Reserve Bank of Richmond, June 2022.

Richard M. Ennis. Failure of the endowment model. *Journal of Portfolio Management*, **47**(5):128–143, April 2021. doi: 10.3905/jpm.2021.1.217.

Michael Ewens and Joan Farre-Mensa. The deregulation of the private equity markets and the decline in IPOs. *Review of Financial Studies*, **33**(12): 5463–5509, December 2020. doi: 10.1093/rfs/hhaa053.

Eugene F. Fama. Efficient capital markets: a review of theory and empirical work. *Journal of Finance*, **25**(2):383–417, May 1970. doi: 10.1111/j.1540-6261.1970.tb00518.x.

Eugene F. Fama. Efficient capital markets: II. *Journal of Finance*, **46**(5): 1575–1617, December 1991. doi: 10.1111/j.1540-6261.1991.tb04636.x.

Eugene F. Fama. Two pillars of asset pricing. *American Economic Review*, **104**(6):1467–85, May 2014. doi: 10.1257/aer.104.6.1467.

Eugene F. Fama and Kenneth R. French. The Capital Asset Pricing Model: theory and evidence. *Journal of Economic Perspectives*, **18**(3):25–46, Summer 2004. doi: 10.1257/0895330042162430.

Eugene F. Fama and Kenneth R. French. Luck versus skill in the cross-section of mutual fund returns. *Journal of Finance*, **65**(5):1915–1947, June 2010. doi: 10.1111/j.1540-6261.2010.01598.x.

Federal Deposit Insurance Corporation. Continental Illinois and "Too Big to Fail". In *History of the Eighties: lessons for the future*, volume 1, pages 235–257. Washington, DC, 1997. https://www.fdic.gov/resources/publications/history-eighties/volume-1/index.html.

Federal Deposit Insurance Corporation. FDIC's Supervision of First Republic Bank, September 2023. https://www.fdic.gov/sites/default/files/2024-03/pr23073a.pdf.

Federal Reserve Bank of Minneapolis. The Minneapolis Plan to end Too Big to Fail, December 2017. https://www.minneapolisfed.org/-/media/files/publications/studies/endingtbtf/the-minneapolis-plan/the-minneapolis-plan-to-end-too-big-to-fail-final.pdf.

Federal Reserve Bank of New York. Domestic open market operations during 2023, April 2024. https://www.newyorkfed.org/medialibrary/media/markets/omo/omo2023-pdf.pdf.

William Feller. *An introduction to probability theory and its applications*, volume **1**. John Wiley & Sons, Hoboken, NJ, 2nd edition, 1957.

Matthias Fleckenstein, Francis A. Longstaff, and Hanno Lustig. The TIPS-Treasury bond puzzle. *Journal of Finance*, **69**(5):2151–97, October 2014. doi: https://doi.org/10.1111/jofi.12032. https://onlinelibrary.wiley.com/doi/abs/10.1111/jofi.12032.

Michael J. Fleming. How has Treasury market liquidity evolved in 2023? Liberty Street Economics, Oct. 17, 2023. https://libertystreeteconomics.newyorkfed.org/2023/10/how-has-treasury-market-liquidity-evolved-in-2023/.

Michael J. Fleming and Asani Sarkar. The failure resolution of Lehman Brothers. *Federal Reserve Bank of New York Economic Policy Review*, **20**(2):175–206, December 2014. https://www.newyorkfed.org/medialibrary/media/research/epr/2014/1412flem.pdf.

Nathan C. Foley-Fisher, Borghan Narajabad, and Stephane H. Verani. Self-fulfilling runs: evidence from the U.S. life insurance industry. Finance and Economics Discussion Series 2015-032, Board of Governors of the Federal Reserve System, 2015. https://www.newyorkfed.org/medialibrary/media/research/epr/2014/1412flem.pdf.

Thierry Foucault, Marco Pagano, and Ailsa Roell. *Market liquidity: theory, evidence, and policy*. Oxford University Press, Oxford and New York, 2nd edition, 2023. doi: 10.1093/oso/9780197542064.001.0001.

Merritt B. Fox, Lawrence R. Glosten, and Gabriel V. Rauterberg. The new stock market: sense and nonsense. *Duke Law Journal*, **65**(2):191–277, November 2015. http://www.jstor.org/stable/24692158.

Kenneth R. French. Presidential address: the cost of active investing. *Journal of Finance*, **73**(1): 145–198, February 2018. doi: 10.1111/j.1540-6261.2008.01368.x.

Carola Frydman and Chenzi Xu. Banking crises in historical perspective. *Annual Review of Financial Economics*, **15**(1):265–290, 2023. doi: 10.1146/annurev-financial-100121-114859.

William Fung and David A. Hsieh. A primer on hedge funds. *Journal of Empirical Finance*, **6**(3):309–331, September 1999. doi: 10.1016/S0927-5398(99)00006-7.

Joseph Gagnon, Matthew Raskin, Julie Remache, and Brian Sack. The financial market effects of the Federal Reserve's large-scale asset purchases. *International Journal of Central Banking*, **7**(1):3–43, March 2011. https://www.ijcb.org/journal/ijcb11q1a1.pdf.

Kenneth D. Garbade. The evolution of repo contracting conventions in the 1980s. *Federal Reserve Bank of New York Economic Policy Review*, **12**(1):27–42, May 2006. https://www.newyorkfed.org/medialibrary/media/research/epr/06v12n1/0605garbpdf.pdf.

Peter M. Garber. Famous first bubbles. *Journal of Economic Perspectives*, **4**(2): 35–54, Spring 1990. doi: 10.1257/aer.104.6.1467.

Huseyin Oguz Genc and Soichiro Takagi. A literature review on the design and implementation of central bank digital currencies. *International Journal of Economic Policy Studies*, **18**(1):197–225, February 2024. doi: 10.1007/s42495-023-00125-9.

Mila Getmansky, Peter A. Lee, and Andrew W. Lo. Hedge funds: a dynamic industry in transition. *Annual Review of Financial Economics*, **7**(1):483–577, 2023. doi: 10.1146/annurev-financial-110311-101741.

Oliver Giesecke and Joshua Rauh. Trends in state and local pension funds. *Annual Review of Financial Economics*, **15**:221–238, 2023. doi: 10.1146/annurev-financial-110921-022054.

Gerd Gigerenzer. *Gut feelings: The intelligence of the unconscious*. Viking Press, New York, 2007.

Gerd Gigerenzer. The bias bias in behavioral economics. *Review of Behavioral Economics*, **5**(3–4):303–36, 2018. doi: 10.1561/105.00000092.

Stefan Gissler, Borghan Narajabad, and Daniel K Tarullo. Federal Home Loan Banks and financial stability. *Journal of Financial Regulation*, **9**(1):1–29, March 2023. doi: 10.1093/jfr/fjad002.

William N. Goetzmann. *Money changes everything*. Princeton University Press, Princeton, NJ, 2016.

Ellen Correia Golay, Caren Cox, Michael J. Fleming, Yesol Huh, Frank M. Keane, Kyle Lee, Krista Schwarz, Clara Vega, and Carolyn Windover. All-to-all trading in the U.S. Treasury market. Staff Reports 1036, Federal Reserve Bank of New York, October 2022. https://www.newyorkfed.org/medialibrary/media/research/staff_reports/sr1036.pdf.

Marvin Goodfriend. Interest rate policy and the inflation scare problem: 1979-1992. *Federal Reserve Bank of Richmond Economic Policy Review*, **79**(1):1–24, Winter 1993. https://www.richmondfed.org/publications/research/economic_quarterly/1993/winter/goodfriend.

Marvin Goodfriend. Monetary policy as a carry trade. *Monetary and Economic Studies*, **32**:29–44, November 2014a. http://www.imes.boj.or.jp/research/papers/english/me32-3.pdf.

Marvin Goodfriend. Lessons from a century of FED policy: why monetary and credit policies need rules and boundaries. *Journal of Economic Dynamics and Control*, **49**:112–120, December 2014b. doi: 10.1016/j.jedc.2014.09.005.

Charles A. E. Goodhart. Myths about the Lender of Last Resort. *International Finance*, **2**(3):339–360, March 1999. doi: 10.1111/1468-2362.00033.

Gary Gorton. The development of opacity in U.S. banking. *Yale Journal on Regulation*, **31**(3):825–851, 2014. http://hdl.handle.net/20.500.13051/8211.

Gary B. Gorton. The Panic of 2007. In *Maintaining stability in a changing financial system*, Jackson Hole Economic Policy Symposium, pages 131–262. Federal Reserve Bank of Kansas City, 2008. https://www.kansascityfed.org/Jackson%20Hole/documents/3164/2008-Gorton031209.pdf.

Gary B. Gorton. The history and economics of safe assets. *Annual Review of Economics*, **9**(1): 547–586, 2017. doi: 10.1146/annurev-economics-033017-125810.

Gary B. Gorton and Andrew Metrick. Securitized banking and the run on repo. *Journal of Financial Economics*, **104**(3):425–451, June 2012. doi: 10.1016/j.jfineco.2011.03.016.

Pierre-Olivier Gourinchas and Hélène Rey. From World Banker to World Venture Capitalist: U.S. external adjustment and the exorbitant privilege. In Richard H. Clarida, editor, *G7 current account imbalances: sustainability and adjustment*, pages 11–66. University of Chicago Press, Chicago, 2007. doi: 10.7208/9780226107288-003.

Robin Greenwood, Samuel G. Hanson, and Jeremy C. Stein. The Federal Reserve's balance sheet as a financial-stability tool. In *Designing resilient monetary policy frameworks for the future*, Jackson Hole Economic Policy Symposium, pages 335–97. Federal Reserve Bank of Kansas City, 2016. https://www.kansascityfed.org/documents/7041/steingreenwoodhanson_JH2016.pdf.

Robin Greenwood, Samuel G. Hanson, Andrei Shleifer, and Jakob Ahm Sørensen. Predictable financial crises. *Journal of Finance*, **77**(2):863–921, April 2022. doi: 10.1111/jofi.13105.

Jon Gregory. *Counterparty credit risk and credit value adjustment: A continuing challenge for global financial markets*. John Wiley & Sons, Hoboken, NJ, 2nd edition, 2012.

David Griffiths. CIT—one year on. Weil Restructuring Blog, Dec. 10, 2010. https://restructuring.weil.com/case-overviews/cit-one-year-on/.

Daniel Gros and Farzaneh Shamsfakhr. Financial dominance: not an immediate danger. Monetary dialogue papers, European Union, September 2021. https://www.europarl.europa.eu/thinktank/en/document/IPOL_IDA(2021)695449.

Richard S. Grossman. *Unsettled account: the evolution of banking in the industrialized world since 1800*. Princeton University Press, Princeton, 2010.

Richard S. Grossman and Hugh Rockoff. Fighting the last war: economists on the lender of last resort. In Michael D. Bordo, Øyvind Eitrheim, Marc Flandreau, and Jan F. Qvigstad, editors, *Central banks at a crossroads: what can we learn from history?*, pages 231–279. Cambridge University Press, Cambridge, 2016. doi: 10.1017/CBO9781316570401.

Sanford J. Grossman and Joseph E. Stiglitz. On the impossibility of informationally efficient markets. *American Economic Review*, **70**(3):393–408, June 1980. http://www.jstor.org/stable/1805228.

Refet Gürkaynak, Burçin Kısacıkoğlu, and Sang Seok Lee. Exchange rate and inflation under weak monetary policy: Turkey verifies theory. *Economic Policy*, **38**(115):519–560, July 2023. doi: 10.1093/epolic/eiad020.

Andrew G. Haldane and Vasileios Madouros. The dog and the frisbee. In *The changing policy landscape*, Jackson Hole Economic Policy Symposium, pages 109–159. Federal Reserve Bank of Kansas City, 2012. https://www.kansascityfed.org/Jackson%20Hole/documents/6926/DogFrisbee_Haldane_JH2012.pdf.

Samuel G. Hanson. Mortgage convexity. *Journal of Financial Economics*, **113**(2):270–299, August 2014. doi: 10.1016/j.jfineco.2014.05.002.

Samuel G. Hanson, Anil K. Kashyap, and Jeremy C. Stein. A macroprudential approach to financial regulation. *Journal of Economic Perspectives*, **25**(1): 3–28, March 2011. doi: 10.1257/jep.25.1.3.

Samuel Gregory Hanson, Aytek Malkhozov, and Gyuri Venter. Demand-and-supply imbalance risk and long-term swap spreads. *Journal of Financial Economics*, **154**(2): 103814, 2024. doi: 10.1016/j.jfineco.2024.103814.

Ron Harris. A new understanding of the history of limited liability: an invitation for theoretical reframing. *Journal of Institutional Economics*, **16**(5):643–664, October 2020. doi: 10.1017/S1744137420000181.

Joel Hasbrouck. Securities trading: principles and procedures. online notes, 2023.

Friedrich A. Hayek. The use of knowledge in society. *American Economic Review*, **35**(4):519–30, September 1945. https://www.jstor.org/stable/1809376.

Donald X. He, Jason C. Hsu, and Neil Rue. Option-writing strategies in a low-volatility framework. *Journal of Investing*, **24**(3):116–128, Fall 2015. doi: 10.3905/joi.2015.24.3.116.

Martin Hellwig. Financial stability, monetary policy, banking supervision, and central banking. MPI Collective Goods Preprint 9, Max Planck Institute for Research on Collective Goods, July 2014. https://homepage.coll.mpg.de/pdf_dat/2014_09online.pdf.

Martin Hellwig. Twelve years after the financial crisis—too-big-to-fail is still with us. *Journal of Financial Regulation*, **7**(1):175–187, March 2021. doi: 10.1093/jfr/fjaa012.

Terrence Hendershott, Charles M. Jones, and Albert J. Menkveld. Does algorithmic trading improve liquidity? *Journal of Finance*, **66**(1):1–33, February 2011. doi: 10.1111/j.1540-6261.2010.01624.x.

Markus Hertrich and Heinz Zimmermann. On the credibility of the euro/Swiss franc floor: A financial market perspective. *Journal of Money, Credit and Banking*, **49**(2–3):567–578, Mar.–Apr. 2017. doi: 10.1111/jmcb.12390.

Robert L. Hetzel. *The Federal Reserve: a new history*. University of Chicago Press, Chicago, 2022.

Beverly Hirtle and Anna Kovner. Bank supervision. *Annual Review of Financial Economics*, **14**(1):39–56, 2022. doi: 10.1146/annurev-financial-111620-022516.

Beverly Hirtle and Andreas Lehnert. Supervisory stress tests. Staff Reports 696, Federal Reserve Bank of New York, November 2014. https://www.newyorkfed.org/medialibrary/media/research/staff_reports/sr696.pdf.

John Hooley, Ashraf Khan, Claney Lattie, Istvan Mak, Natalia Salazar, Amanda Sayegh, and Peter Stella. Quasi-fiscal implications of central bank crisis interventions. Working Paper 114, International Monetary Fund, June 2023. https://www.imf.org/en/Publications/WP/Issues/2023/06/02/Quasi-Fiscal-Implications-of-Central-Bank-Crisis-Interventions-534076.

Wenqian Huang and Karamfil Todorov. The post-Libor world: a global view from the BIS derivatives statistics. *BIS Quarterly Review*, pages 19–32, December 2022. https://www.bis.org/publ/qtrpdf/r_qt2212e.pdf.

John C. Hull. *Options, futures and other derivative securities*. Pearson, London, 11th edition, 2022.

John C. Hull. *Risk management and financial institutions*. John Wiley & Sons, Hoboken, NJ, 6th edition, 2023.

Roger G. Ibbotson and James P. Harrington. *Stocks, bonds, bills, and inflation (SBBI): 2021 summary edition*. CFA Institute Research Foundation Books, Chicago, 2021. https://ssrn.com/abstract=3893876.

IHS Markit. CDS Indices Primer, November 2021. https://cdn.ihsmarkit.com/www/pdf/1221/CDS-Indices-Primer---2021.pdf.

Sebastian Infante, Charles Press, and Zack Saravay. Understanding collateral re-use in the US financial system. *AEA Papers and Proceedings*, **110**:482–86, May 2020. doi: 10.1257/pandp.20201099.

International Capital Market Association. Frequently asked questions on repo, January 2019. https://www.icmagroup.org/assets/documents/Regulatory/Repo/Repo-FAQs-January-2019-050221.pdf.

International Capital Market Association. Guide to best practice in the European repo market, November 2023. https://www.icmagroup.org/assets/ERCC-Guide-to-Best-Practice-November-2023-FINAL-2-Nov.pdf.

International Monetary Fund. Tax policy, leverage and macroeconomic stability. Technical report, 2016. https://www.imf.org/external/np/pp/eng/2016/100716.pdf.

International Organization of Securities Commissions. Thematic review on consistency in implementation of money market funds reforms. Final Report 11/20, 2020. https://www.iosco.org/library/pubdocs/pdf/IOSCOPD665.pdf.

Victoria Ivashina and Josh Lerner. *Patient capital: the challenges and promises of long-term investing.* Princeton University Press, Princeton, 2019. doi: doi:10.1515/9780691190037.

Thomas Jackson, Kenneth E. Scott, and John B. Taylor, editors. *Making failure feasible.* Hoover Institution Press, Stanford, CA, 2012. https://www.hoover.org/research/making-failure-feasible.

Jens Carsten Jackwerth. *Option-implied risk-neutral distributions and risk aversion.* Research Foundation of CFA Institute, 2004. https://www.cfainstitute.org/-/media/documents/book/rf-publication/2004/rf-v2004-n1-3925-pdf.

Michael C. Jensen. The performance of mutual funds in the period 1945–1964. *Journal of Finance,* **23**(2):389–416, May 1968. doi: 10.1111/j.1540-6261.1968.tb00815.x.

Jerry L. Jordan and William J. Luther. Central bank independence and the Federal Reserve's new operating regime. *Quarterly Review of Economics and Finance,* **84**:510–515, May 2022. doi: 10.1016/j.qref.2020.10.006.

Philipe Jorion. Lessons from the Orange County bankruptcy. *Journal of Derivatives,* **4**(4):61–66, Summer 1996. doi: 10.3905/jod.1997.407979.

Philipe Jorion. Risk management lessons from Long-Term Capital Management. *European Financial Managemen,* **6**(3):277–300, September 2000. doi: 10.1111/1468-036X.00125.

Marcin Kacperczyk and Philipp Schnabl. The market for "lemons": quality uncertainty and the market mechanism. *Quarterly Journal of Economics,* **128**(3):1073–1122, July 2013. doi: 10.1093/qje/qjt010.

Charles M. Kahn and William Roberds. The CLS bank: a solution to the risks of international payments settlement? *Carnegie-Rochester Conference Series on Public Policy,* **54**(1):191–226, 2001. doi: 10.1016/S0167-2231(01)00047-1.

Charles M. Kahn and William Roberds. Why pay? an introduction to payments economics. *Journal of Financial Intermediation,* **18**(1):1–23, July 2009. doi: 10.1016/j.jfi.2008.09.001.

Daniel Kahneman. Maps of bounded rationality: a perspective on intuitive judgment and choice, Prize Lecture, Royal Swedish Academy of Sciences, December 8, 2002, December 2002. https://www.nobelprize.org/uploads/2018/06/kahnemann-lecture.pdf.

Daniel Kahneman, Jack L. Knetsch, and Richard H. Thaler. Anomalies: the endowment effect, loss aversion, and status quo bias. *Journal of Economic Perspectives,* **5**(1):193–206, March 1991. doi: 10.1257/jep.5.1.193.

Alena Kang-Landsberg, Stephan Luck, and Matthew Plosser. Deposit betas: up, up, and away? Liberty Street Economics, April 11, 2023. https://libertystreeteconomics.newyorkfed.org/2023/04/deposit-betas-up-up-and-away/.

Stephen Kealhofer. Quantifying credit risk I: default prediction. *Financial Analysts Journal,* **59**(1):30–44, Jan.–Feb. 2003a. doi: 10.2469/faj.v59.n1.2501.

Stephen Kealhofer. Quantifying credit risk II: debt valuation. *Financial Analysts Journal,* **59**(3): 78–92, May–June 2003b. doi: 10.2469/faj.v59.n3.2534.

Bryan T. Kelly, Hanno N. Lustig, and Stijn Van Nieuwerburgh. Too-systemic-to-fail: what option markets imply about sector-wide government guarantees. *American Economic Review,* **106**(3):1278–1319, June 2012. doi: 10.1257/aer.20120389.

John Maynard Keynes. The general theory of employment. *Quarterly Journal of Economics,* **51**(2):209–223, February 1937. doi: 10.2307/1882087.

Sooji Kim, Matthew C. Plosser, and João A. C. Santos. Macroprudential policy and the revolving door of risk: lessons from leveraged lending guidance. *Journal of Financial Intermediation,* **34**(3):17–31, April 2018. doi: 10.1016/j.jfi.2018.01.011.

Andrei Kirilenko, Albert S. Kyle, Mehrdad Samadi, and Tugkan Tuzun. The flash crash: high-frequency trading in an electronic market. *Journal of Finance,* **72**(3):967–998, June 2017. doi: 10.1111/jofi.12498.

Israel M. Kirzner. Entrepreneurial discovery and the competitive market process: an Austrian approach. *Journal of Economic Literature,* **35**(1):60–85, March 1997. http://www.jstor.org/stable/2729693.

Richard J. Kish. The dominance of the U.S. 30-year fixed rate residential mortgage. *Journal of Real Estate Practice and Education,* **24**(1):1–16, 2022. doi: 10.1080/15214842.2020.1757357.

Nobuhiro Kiyotaki and John Moore. Balance-sheet contagion. *American Economic Review,* **92**(2):62–66, May 2002. doi: 10.1257/000282802320188989.

Stuart A. Klugman, Harry H. Panjer, and Gordon E. Willmot. *Loss models: from data to decisions.* John Wiley & Sons, Hoboken, NJ, 5th edition, 2019.

Frank H. Knight. *Risk, uncertainty and profit*. Houghton Mifflin Company, Boston, New York, 1921. https://fraser.stlouisfed.org/title/risk-uncertainty-profit-110.

Narayana R. Kocherlakota. Money is memory. *Journal of Economic Theory*, **81**(2):232–251, August 1998. doi: https://doi.org/10.1006/jeth.1997.2357.

Ralph S.J. Koijen, Tobias J. Moskowitz, Lasse Heje Pedersen, and Evert B. Vrugt. Carry. *Journal of Financial Economics*, **127**(2):197–225, February 2018. doi: 10.1016/j.jfineco.2017.11.002.

William S. Krasker. The "peso problem" in testing the efficiency of forward exchange markets. *Journal of Monetary Economics*, **6**(2):269–276, April 1980. doi: 10.1016/0304-3932(80)90031-8.

Arvind Krishnamurthy and Annette Vissing-Jorgensen. The effects of quantitative easing on interest rates: channels and implications for policy. *Brookings Papers on Economic Activity*, (2):215–265, Fall 2011. https://www.brookings.edu/wp-content/uploads/2016/07/2011b_bpea_krishnamurthy.pdf.

Mathias S. Kruttli, Phillip J. Monina, and Sumudu W. Watugala. The life of the counterparty: shock propagation in hedge fund-prime broker credit networks. *Journal of Financial Economics*, **146**(3):965–988, December 2022. doi: 10.1016/j.jfineco.2022.02.002.

Paul Kupiec. Will TLAC regulations fix the G-SIB too-big-to-fail problem? *Journal of Financial Stability*, **24**:158–169, June 2016. doi: 10.1016/j.jfs.2016.04.009.

Paul Kupiec and Peter Wallison. Can the "Single Point of Entry" strategy be used to recapitalize a systemically important failing bank? *Journal of Financial Stability*, **20**:184–197, October 2015. doi: 10.1016/j.jfs.2015.09.007.

Kenneth N. Kuttner. Outside the box: unconventional monetary policy in the great recession and beyond. *Journal of Economic Perspectives*, **32**(4):121–46, November 2018. doi: 10.1257/jep.32.4.121.

Marc Labonte. The Federal Reserve's response to COVID-19: policy issues. CRS Report R46411, U.S. Congressional Research Service, Feb. 8, 2021. https://crsreports.congress.gov/product/pdf/R/R46411/7.

Marc Labonte. Who regulates whom? An overview of the U.S. financial regulatory framework. CRS Report R44918, U.S. Congressional Research Service, Oct. 13, 2023a. https://crsreports.congress.gov/product/pdf/R/R44918.

Marc Labonte. Bank capital requirements: a primer and policy issues. CRS Report R47447, U.S. Congressional Research Service, Mar. 9, 2023b. https://crsreports.congress.gov/product/pdf/R/R47447.

Marc Labonte. Bank capital requirements: Basel III Endgame. CRS Report R47855, U.S. Congressional Research Service, Nov. 30, 2023c. https://crsreports.congress.gov/product/pdf/R/R47855.

Thomas Laubach and John C. Williams. Measuring the natural rate of interest. *Review of Economics and Statistics*, **85**(4):1063–1070, November 2003. doi: 10.1162/003465303772815934.

William Lazonick. The quest for shareholder value: stock repurchases in the US economy. *Recherches Économiques de Louvain*, **74**(4):479–540, 2008. https://www.jstor.org/stable/40724543.

Andrew T. Levin, Brian L. Lu, and William R. Nelson. Quantifying the costs and benefits of quantitative easing. Working Paper 30749, National Bureau of Economic Research, December 2022. http://www.nber.org/papers/w30749.

Ross Levine. Finance and growth: theory and evidence. In Philippe Aghion and Steven N. Durlauf, editors, *Handbook of Economic Growth*, volume **1**, part A, pages 865–934. Elsevier, Amsterdam, 2005. doi: 10.1016/S1574-0684(05)01012-9.

Ross Levine. Finance, growth, and inequality. Working Paper 164, International Monetary Fund, June 2021. https://www.imf.org/en/Publications/WP/Issues/2021/06/11/Finance-Growth-and-Inequality-460698.

Mickey D. Levy and Charles I. Plosser. The murky future of monetary policy. *Federal Reserve Bank of St. Louis Review*, **104**(3):178–88, Q3 2022. doi: 10.20955/r.104.178-88.

David X. Li. On default correlation: a copula function approach. *Journal of Fixed Income*, **9**(4):43–54, Spring 2000. doi: 10.20955/r.104.178-88.

Brink Lindsey and Steven M. Teles. *The captured economy: how the powerful enrich themselves, slow down growth, and increase inequality*. Oxford University Press, Oxford and New York, 2017.

Thomas J. Linsmeier and Neil D. Pearson. Value at risk. *Financial Analysts Journal*, **56**(2):47–67, Mar.–Apr. 2000. doi: 10.2469/faj.v56.n2.2343.

Paul C. Lipson, Bradley K. Sabel, and Frank M. Keane. Securities lending. Staff Reports 555, Federal Reserve Bank of New York, March 2012. https://www.newyorkfed.org/medialibrary/media/research/staff_reports/sr555.pdf.

Xiaoxi Liu and Jinming Xie. Forecasting swap rate volatility with information from swaptions. *Journal of Futures Markets*, **43**(4):455–479, April 2023. doi: 10.1002/fut.22395.

Simon P. Lloyd. Overnight indexed swap-implied interest rate expectations. *Finance Research Letters*, **38**:1–8, January 2023. doi: 10.1016/j.frl.2020.101430.

Andrew W. Lo. Risk management for hedge funds: introduction and overview. *Financial Analysts Journal*, **57**(6):16–33, Nov.–Dec. 2001. doi: 10.2469/faj.v57.n6.2490.

Francis A. Longstaff and Arvind Rajan. An empirical analysis of the pricing of collateralized debt obligations. *Journal of Finance*, **63**(2):529–563, April 2008. 10.1111/j.1540-6261.2008.01330.x.

Jose A. Lopez. The empirical relationship between average asset correlation, firm probability of default, and asset size. *Journal of Financial Intermediation*, **13**(2):265–283, April 2004. doi: 10.1016/S1042-9573(03)00045-7.

Deborah Lucas. Measuring the cost of bailouts. *Annual Review of Financial Economics*, **11**(1):85–108, 2019. doi: 10.1146/annurev-financial-110217-022532.

Douglas J. Lucas. Default correlation and credit analysis. *Journal of Fixed Income*, **4**(4):76–87, Spring 1995. doi: 10.3905/jfi.1995.408124.

Brian F. Madigan and William R. Nelson. Central bank lending. In Refet Gürkaynak and Jonathan Wright, editors, *Research handbook of financial markets*, pages 79–101. Edward Elgar Publishing, Cheltenham, UK, 2023.

Igor Makarov and Antoinette Schoar. Cryptocurrencies and decentralized finance (DeFi). *Brookings Papers on Economic Activity*, pages 141–215, Spring 2022. https://www.brookings.edu/articles/cryptocurrencies-and-decentralized-finance-defi/.

Burton G. Malkiel. The efficient market hypothesis and its critics. *Journal of Economic Perspectives*, **17**(1):59–82, 2003. doi: 10.1257/089533003321164958.

Burton G. Malkiel. *A random walk down Wall Street*. W. W. Norton & Co., New York, 13th edition, 2023.

Burton G. Malkiel and Atanu Saha. Hedge funds: risk and return. *Financial Analysts Journal*, **61**(6):80–88, 2005. doi: 10.2469/faj.v61.n6.2775.

Allan M. Malz. *Financial risk management: models, history, and institutions*. John Wiley & Sons, Hoboken, NJ, 2011.

Allan M. Malz. Implied rate correlations and policy expectations. Economic Letters 2013-32, Federal Reserve Bank of San Francisco, November 2013. http://www.frbsf.org/economic-research/publications/economic-letter/2013/november/implied-rate-correlations-interest-rate-movements-yield-curve-options/el2013-32.pdf.

Allan M. Malz. A simple and reliable way to compute option-based risk-neutral distributions. Staff Reports 677, Federal Reserve Bank of New York, June 2014. https://www.newyorkfed.org/medialibrary/media/research/staff_reports/sr677.pdf.

Allan M. Malz. Macroprudential policy, leverage, and bailouts. *Cato Journal*, **39**(3):499–528, Fall 2019. doi: 10.36009/CJ.39.3.2.

Allan M. Malz. Money market turmoil. *Cato Journal*, **40**(1):47–76, Winter 2020. doi: 10.36009/CJ.40.1.4.

Allan M. Malz. The GameStop episode: what happened and what does it mean? *Journal of Applied Corporate Finance*, **33**(4):87–97, Fall 2021. doi: 10.1111/jacf.12481.

Allan M. Malz, Ernst Schaumburg, Roman Shimonov, and Andreas Strzodka. Convexity event risks in a rising interest rate environment. Liberty Street Economics, Mar. 24, 2014. https://libertystreeteconomics.newyorkfed.org/2014/03/convexity-event-risks-in-a-rising-interest-rate-environment/.

Charles F. Manski. Policy analysis with incredible certitude. *Economic Journal*, **121**(554):F261–F289, August 2011. doi: 10.1111/j.1468-0297.2011.02457.x.

John E. Marthinsen. *Risk takers: uses and abuses of financial derivatives*. Walter de Gruyter, Boston/Berlin, 3rd edition, 2018.

John Martin and Akin Sayrak. Collateralized loan obligations: a primer. *Journal of Applied Corporate Finance*, **34**(3):35–50, Summer 2022. doi: 10.1111/jacf.12514.

Patrick McGuire, Andreas Schrimpf, and Nikola Tarashev. OTC foreign exchange and interest rate derivatives markets through the prism of the Triennial Survey. *BIS Quarterly Review*, pages 15–18, December 2022. https://www.bis.org/publ/qtrpdf/r_qt2212d.pdf.

Michael McLeay, Amar Radia, and Ryland Thomas. Money in the modern economy: an introduction. *Quarterly Bulletin*, pages 4–13, Q1 2014a. https://www.bankofengland.co.uk/quarterly-bulletin/2014/q1/money-in-the-modern-economy-an-introduction.

Michael McLeay, Amar Radia, and Ryland Thomas. Money creation in the modern economy. *Quarterly Bulletin*, pages 14–26, Q1 2014b. https://www.bankofengland.co.uk/quarterly-bulletin/2014/q1/money-creation-in-the-modern-economy.

Alexander J. McNeil, Rüdiger Frey, and Paul Embrechts. *Quantitative risk management: concepts, techniques and tools*. Princeton University Press, Princeton, NJ, revised edition, 2015.

Edward F. McQuarrie. Stocks for the long run? Sometimes yes, sometimes no. *Financial Analysts Journal*, **80**(1):12–28, May–Jun. 2024. doi: 10.1080/0015198X.2023.2268556.

Michael Melvin and Duncan Shand. When carry goes bad: the magnitude, causes, and duration of currency carry unwinds. *Financial Analysts Journal*, **73**(1):121–144, Q1 2017. doi: 10.2469/faj.v73.n1.4.

Lev Menand and Josh Younger. Money and the public debt: Treasury market liquidity as a legal phenomenon. *Columbia Business Law Review*, **2023**(1): 19–47, 2023. doi: https://doi.org/10.52214/cblr.v2023i1.11900.

Robert C. Merton. On estimating the expected return on the market: an exploratory investigation. *Journal of Financial Economics*, **8**(4):323–361, December 1980. doi: 10.1016/0304-405X(80)90007-0.

Robert C. Merton. Financial innovation and the management and regulation of financial institutions. *Journal of Banking and Finance*, **19**(3):461–481, June 1995. doi: 10.1016/0378-4266(94)00133-N.

Andrew Metrick. The failure of Silicon Valley Bank and the Panic of 2023. *Journal of Economic Perspectives*, **38**(1):133–52, February 2024. doi: 10.1257/jep.38.1.133.

Merton H. Miller. Do the M & M propositions apply to banks? *Journal of Banking and Finance*, **19**(3-4):483–489, August 1995. doi: 10.1016/0378-4266(94)00134-O.

Mark Mitchell, Lasse Heje Pedersen, and Todd Pulvino. Slow moving capital. *American Economic Review*, **97**(2):215–220, May 2007. doi: 10.1257/aer.97.2.215.

Franco Modigliani and Merton H. Miller. The cost of capital, corporation finance and the theory of investment. *American Economic Review*, **48**(3):261–297, June 1958. https://www.jstor.org/stable/1809766.

Ashoka Mody. *EuroTragedy: A drama in nine acts*. Oxford University Press, New York and Oxford, 2018.

Alexander M. Mood, Franklin A. Graybill, and Duane C. Boes. *Introduction to the theory of Statistics*. McGraw-Hill Book Company, New York, 3rd edition, 1974.

Gretchen Morgenson and Joshua Rosner. *Reckless endangerment: how outsized ambition, greed, and corruption led to economic armageddon*. Times Books, New York, 2011.

Benjamin Munyan. The repo market. In Refet Gürkaynak and Jonathan Wright, editors, *Research handbook of financial markets*, pages 237–252. Edward Elgar Publishing, Cheltenham, UK, 2023.

Michael Mussa. Empirical regularities in the behavior of exchange rates and theories of the foreign exchange market. *Carnegie-Rochester Conference Series on Public Policy*, **11**:9–57, 1979. doi: 10.1016/0167-2231(79)90034-4.

Stewart C. Myers. Determinants of corporate borrowing. *Journal of Financial Economics*, **5**(2): 147–175, November 1977. doi: 10.1016/0304-405X(77)90015-0.

Stewart C. Myers. Capital structure. *Journal of Economic Perspectives*, **15**(2): 81–102, June 2001. doi: 10.1257/jep.15.2.81.

Salih N. Neftci. *Principles of financial engineering*. Academic Press, San Diego, 2nd edition, 2008.

Jordan Nickerson and John M. Griffin. Debt correlations in the wake of the financial crisis: what are appropriate default correlations for structured products? *Journal of Financial Economics*, **125**(3):454–474, September 2017. doi: 10.1016/j.jfineco.2017.06.011.

Robert Novy-Marx and Joshua D. Rauh. The liabilities and risks of state-sponsored pension plans. *Journal of Economic Perspectives*, **23**(4): 191–210, December 2009. doi: 10.1257/jep.23.4.191.

Maurice Obstfeld and Haonan Zhou. The global dollar cycle. *Brookings Papers on Economic Activity*, (2):361–447, Fall 2022. https://www.brookings.edu/wp-content/uploads/2022/09/BPEA-FA22_WEB_Obstfeld-Zhou.pdf.

Maureen O'Hara and Xing (Alex) Zhou. Things fall apart: Fixed income markets in the COVID-19 crisis. *Annual Review of Financial Economics*, **15**(1):forthcoming, 2023. doi: 10.1146/annurev-financial-110821-020622.

Michael Ohlrogge. Why have uninsured depositors become de facto insured? Technical report, November 2023. https://papers.ssrn.com/sol3/papers.cfm?abstract_id=4624095.

Saule T. Omarova. The "Too Big to Fail" problem. *Minnesota Law Review*, **103**: 2495–2541, 2019. https://scholarship.law.umn.edu/mlr/3290.

Elinor Ostrom. Beyond markets and states: polycentric governance of complex economic systems. *American Economic Review*, **100**(3):641–672, June 2010. doi: 10.1257/aer.100.3.641.

Elinor Ostrom, Christina Chang, Mark Pennington, and Vlad Tarko. *The future of the commons: beyond market failure and government regulation.* Institute of Economic Affairs, London, 2012. https://iea.org.uk/publications/research/the-future-of-the-commons-beyond-market-failure-and-government-regulation.

Frank Packer and Philip D Wooldridge. Overview: repricing in credit markets. *BIS Quarterly Review*, pages 1–14, June 2005. https://www.bis.org/publ/qtrpdf/r_qt0506a.pdf.

Lasse H. Pedersen. Sharpening the arithmetic of active management. *Financial Analysts Journal*, **74**(1):21–36, 2018. doi: 10.2469/faj.v74.n1.4.

Hester Peirce. Securities lending and the untold story in the collapse of AIG. Working Paper 14–12, Mercatus Center at George Mason University, May 2014. http://mercatus.org/sites/default/files/Peirce: SecuritiesLendingAIG_v2.pdf.

Roberto Perli. Balance sheet reduction: progress to date and a look ahead, remarks at 2024 Annual Primary Dealer Meeting, May 8, 2024, 2024. https://www.newyorkfed.org/newsevents/speeches/2024/per240508.

Edmund S. Phelps. Equilibrium: an expectational concept. In *The new Palgrave dictionary of economics*, pages 3857–3860. Palgrave Macmillan, London, UK, 2018. doi: 10.1057/978-1-349-95189-5_334.

Edmund S. Phelps, Hian Teck Hoon, and Gylfi Zoega. *The great economic slowdown.* Palgrave Macmillan, Cham, CH, 2023. doi: 10.1007/978-3-031-31441-4.

Craig Pirrong. Clearing and collateral mandates: a new liquidity trap? *Journal of Applied Corporate Finance*, **24**(1):67–73, Fall 2012. doi: 10.1111/j.1745-6622.2012.00366.x.

Michael Polanyi. *Personal knowledge: towards a post-critical philosophy.* Haper Torchbooks, New York, 1964 [1958].

Ser-Huang Poon and Clive Granger. Forecasting volatility in financial markets: a review. *Journal of Economic Literature*, **41**(2):478–539, June 2003. doi: 10.1257/002205103765762743.

Ser-Huang Poon and Clive Granger. Practical issues in forecasting volatility. *Financial Analysts Journal*, **61**(1):45–56, Jan./Feb. 2005. https://www.jstor.org/stable/4480636.

Eswar Prasad. *The future of money: how the digital revolution is transforming currencies and finance.* The Belknap Press of Harvard University Press, Cambridge, MA, 2021.

Raghuram G. Rajan. Has financial development made the world riskier? In *The Greenspan era: lessons for the future*, Jackson Hole Economic Policy Symposium, pages 313–397. Federal Reserve Bank of Kansas City, 2005. http://www.kansascityfed.org/Publicat/sympos/2005/PDF/Rajan2005.pdf.

Riccardo Rebonato. *Plight of the fortune tellers: why we need to manage financial risk differently.* Princeton University Press, Princeton, NJ, 2007.

Carmen M. Reinhart and Kenneth S. Rogoff. *This time is different: eight centuries of financial folly.* Princeton University Press, Princeton, 2009.

Ricardo Reis and Silvana Tenreyro. Helicopter money: what is it and what does it do? *Annual Review of Economics*, **14**(1):313–335, 2022. doi: 10.1146/annurev-economics-051420-020618.

Hélène Rey. Dilemma not trilemma: The global financial cycle and monetary policy independence. In *Global dimensions of unconventional monetary policy*, Jackson Hole Economic Policy Symposium, pages 285–333. Federal Reserve Bank of Kansas City, 2013. https://www.kansascityfed.org/.publicat/sympos/2013/2013Rey.pdf.

Hélène Rey. International channels of transmission of monetary policy and the Mundellian trilemma. *IMF Economic Review*, **64**(1):6–35, 2016. doi: 10.1057/imfer.2016.4.

Kenneth S. Rogoff, Barbara Rossi, and Paul Schmelzing. Long-run trends in long-maturity real rates, 1311–2022. *American Economic Review*, **114**(8): 2271–2307, August 2024. doi: 10.1257/aer.20221352.

Richard Roll. A critique of the asset pricing theory's tests Part I: On past and potential testability of the theory. *Journal of Financial Economics*, **4**(2): 129–176, March 1977. doi: 10.1016/0304-405X(77)90009-5.

Arthur J. Rolnick, Warren E. Weber, and Bruce D. Smith. Lessons From a Laissez-Faire Payments System: The Suffolk Bank and the Panic of 1837. *Federal Reserve Bank of Minneapolis Quarterly Review*, **26**(4):32–42, Fall 2002. doi: 10.21034/qr.2421.

Joshua V. Rosenberg and Robert F. Engle. Empirical pricing kernels. *Journal of Financial Economics*, **64**(3):341–372, June 2002. doi: 10.1016/S0304-405X(02)00128-9.

Stephen A. Ross. *Neoclassical finance.* Princeton University Press, Princeton, NJ, 2005.

Ann Rutledge and Sylvain Raynes. *Elements of structured finance.* Oxford University Press, Oxford, New York, 2010.

João A. C. Santos. Evidence from the bond market on banks "Too-Big-to-Fail" subsidy. *Federal Reserve Bank of New York Economic Policy Review*, **20**(2): 29–39, December 2014. https://www.newyorkfed.org/medialibrary/media/research/epr/2014/1412sant.pdf.

Thomas J. Sargent and Neil Wallace. Some unpleasant monetarist arithmetic. *Federal Reserve Bank of Minneapolis Quarterly Review*, **5**(3):1–17, Fall 1981. doi: 10.21034/qr.531.

Sebastian Schich. Implicit bank debt guarantees: costs, benefits and risks. *Journal of Economic Surveys*, **32**(5):1257–1291, December 2018. doi: 10.1111/joes.12287.

Andreas Schrimpf and Vladyslav Sushko. Beyond LIBOR: a primer on the new reference rates. *BIS Quarterly Review*, pages 29–52, March 2019. https://www.bis.org/publ/qtrpdf/r_qt1903e.pdf.

Andreas Schrimpf, Hyun Song Shin, and Vladyslav Sushko. Leverage and margin spirals in fixed income markets during the covid-19 crisis. BIS Bulletin 2, Bank for International Settlements, April 2020. https://www.bis.org/publ/bisbull02.pdf.

Moritz Schularick and Alan M. Taylor. Credit booms gone bust: monetary policy, leverage cycles and financial crises, 1870–2008. *American Economic Review*, **102**(2):1029–61, April 2012. doi: 10.1257/aer.102.2.1029.

G. William Schwert. Why does stock market volatility change over time? *Journal of Finance*, **44**(5):1115–1153, December 1989. doi: 10.1111/j.1540-6261.1989.tb02647.x.

G. William Schwert. Stock market volatility. *Financial Analysts Journal*, **46**(1): 23–34, May–Jun. 1990. doi: 10.2469/faj.v46.n3.23.

G. William Schwert. Anomalies and market efficiency. In G.M. Constantinides, M. Harris, and R.M. Stulz, editors, *Handbook of the Economics of Finance*, volume **1B**, pages 939–974. Elsevier, Amsterdam, 2003. doi: https://doi.org/10.1016/S1574-0102(03)01024-0.

George A. Selgin and Lawrence H. White. How would the invisible hand handle money? *Journal of Economic Literature*, **32**(4):1718–1749, December 1994. http://www.jstor.org/stable/2728792.

Brad W. Setser. Turkey's increasing balance sheet risks. Follow the Money, June 6, 2023. https://www.cfr.org/blog/turkeys-increasing-balance-sheet-risks.

Padma Sharma. Government assistance and moral hazard: evidence from the savings and loan crisis. *Federal Reserve Bank of Kansas City Economic Review*, **107**(3):37–53, Q3 2022. doi: 10.18651/ER/v107n3Sharma.

William F. Sharpe. *Portfolio theory and capital markets*. McGraw-Hill, New York, 1970.

William F. Sharpe. The arithmetic of active management. *Financial Analysts Journal*, **47**(1):7–9, Jan.–Feb. 1991. https://www.jstor.org/stable/4479386.

Lynn Shibut and George de Verges. FDIC resolution tasks and approaches: a comparison of the 1980 to 1994 and 2008 to 2013 crises. Staff Studies 2020-05, Federal Deposit Insurance Corporation, July 2020. https://www.fdic.gov/analysis/cfr/staff-studies/2020-05.pdf.

Robert J. Shiller. From efficient markets theory to behavioral finance. *Journal of Economic Perspectives*, **17**(1):83–104, Winter 2003. doi: 10.1257/089533003321164967.

Andrei Shleifer and Lawrence H. Summers. The noise trader approach to finance. *Journal of Economic Perspectives*, **4**(2):19–33, Winter 1990. doi: 10.1257/jep.4.2.19.

Andrei Shleifer and Robert W. Vishny. The limits of arbitrage. *Journal of Finance*, **52**(1):35–55, March 1997. doi: 10.1111/j.1540-6261.1997.tb03807.x.

Andrei Shleifer and Robert W. Vishny. Fire sales in finance and macroeconomics. *Journal of Economic Perspectives*, **25**(1):29–48, Winter 2011. doi: 10.1257/jep.25.1.29.

John B. Shoven. The tax consequences of share repurchases and other non-dividend cash payments to equity owners. *Tax Policy and the Economy*, **1**:29–54, 1987. doi: 10.1086/tpe.1.20061762.

John J. Siegfried. A first lesson in econometrics. *Journal of Political Economy*, **78**(6):1378–1379, July 1970. doi: 10.1086/259717.

Herbert A. Simon. Invariants of human behavior. *Annual Review of Psychology*, **41**(1):1–20, 1990. doi: 10.1146/annurev.ps.41.020190.000245.

Manmohan Singh. *Collateral and financial plumbing*. Risk Books, London, 2014.

Manmohan Singh and Rohit Goel. Pledged collateral market's role in transmission to short-term market rates. Working Paper 106, International Monetary Fund, May 2019.

Manmohan Singh and Miguel A. Segoviano. Counterparty risk in the over-the-counter derivatives market. Working Paper 258, International Monetary Fund, November 2008.

S&P Dow Jones Indices. SPIVA U.S. Scorecard, 2023. https://www.spglobal.com/spdji/en/documents/spiva/spiva-us-year-end-2022.pdf.

Erik Stafford. Replicating private equity with value investing, homemade leverage, and hold-to-maturity accounting. *Review of Financial Studies*, **35**(1):299–342, January 2022. doi: 10.1093/rfs/hhab020.

Jeremy C. Stein. Large-scale asset purchases, speech at the Third Boston University/Boston Fed Conference on Macro-Finance Linkages, November 30, 2012, November 2012. https://www.federalreserve.gov/newsevents/speech/files/stein20121130a.pdf.

Jeremy C. Stein. Overheating in credit markets: origins, measurement, and policy responses, speech at a research symposium sponsored by the Federal Reserve Bank of St. Louis, February 7, 2013, February 2013. https://www.federalreserve.gov/newsevents/speech/stein20130207a.htm.

George J. Stigler. The theory of economic regulation. *Bell Journal of Economics and Management Science*, **2**(1):3–21, Spring 1971. https://doi.org/10.2307/3003160.

James H. Stock and Mark W. Watson. *Introduction to econometrics*. Pearson, Boston, 3rd, updated edition, 2015.

Philip E. Strahan. Too big to fail: causes, consequences, and policy responses. *Annual Review of Financial Economics*, **5**:43–61, 2013. doi: 10.1146/annurev-financial-110112-121025.

Ren M. Stulz. Hedge funds: past, present, and future. *Journal of Economic Perspectives*, **21**(2):175–194, Spring 2007. doi: 10.1257/jep.21.2.175.

Suresh Sundaresan. A review of Mertons model of the firm's capital structure with its wide applications. *Annual Review of Financial Economics*, **5**(1): 21–41, 2013. doi: 10.1146/annurev-financial-110112-120923.

SVB Financial Group. Form 10-K for the fiscal year ended December 31, 2022, 2023. https://ir.svb.com/financials/quarterly-results/.

David F. Swensen. *Pioneering portfolio management: an unconventional approach to institutional investment*. Free Press, New York, rev. edition, 2009.

Nassim Taleb. *Dynamic hedging: managing vanilla and exotic options*. John Wiley & Sons, New York, 1997.

John B. Taylor. Discretion versus policy rules in practice. *Carnegie-Rochester Conference Series on Public Policy*, **39**:195–214, December 1993. doi: 10.1016/0167-2231(93)90009-L.

John B. Taylor and John C. Williams. A black swan in the money market. *American Economic Review: Macroeconomics*, **1**(1):58–83, January 2009. doi: 10.1257/mac.1.1.58.

Steven M. Teles. Kludgeocracy in America. *National Affairs*, (17):97–114, Fall 2013. https://www.nationalaffairs.com/publications/detail/kludgeocracy-in-america.

Richard H. Thaler and Cass R. Sunstein. Libertarian paternalism. *American Economic Review*, **93**(2):175–179, May 2003. doi: 10.1257/000282803321947001.

James Tobin. Liquidity preference as behavior towards risk. *Review of Economic Studies*, **25**(2):65–86, February 1958. https://www.jstor.org/stable/2296205.

James Tobin. Financial intermediaries. In *The new Palgrave dictionary of economics*, pages 3857–3860. Palgrave Macmillan, London, UK, 2018.

Pablo Triana. Credit risk of options: the Berkshire Hathaway case. *Corporate Finance Review*, **19**(4):42–47, Jan/Feb 2015.

Bruce Tuckman. Short-term rate benchmarks: the post-LIBOR regime. *Annual Review of Financial Economics*, **15**(1):473–491, 2023. doi: 10.1146/annurev-financial-110921-015054.

Bruce Tuckman and Angel Serrat. *Fixed income securities: tools for today's markets*. John Wiley & Sons, Hoboken, NJ, 4th edition, 2022.

Anton Van Dyk and Gary van Vuuren. Measurement and calibration of regulatory credit risk asset correlations. *Journal of Risk and Financial Management*, **16**(9):1–19, April 2023. https://www.mdpi.com/1911-8074/16/9/402.

Oldrich Vasicek. *Finance, economics and mathematics*. John Wiley & Sons, New York, 2015.

François R. Velde. Was John Law's System a bubble? The Mississippi Bubble revisited. In Jeremy Atack and Larry Neal, editors, *The origins and development of financial markets and institutions: from the seventeenth century to the present*, pages 99–120. Cambridge University Press, Cambridge, 2009.

James Vickery and Joshua Wright. TBA trading and liquidity in the agency MBS market. *Federal Reserve Bank of New York Economic Policy Review*, **19**(2):1–18, May 2013. https://www.newyorkfed.org/research/epr/2013/1212vick.html.

Annette Vissing-Jorgensen. The Treasury market in spring 2020 and the response of the Federal Reserve. *Journal of Monetary Economics*, **124**(3): 19–47, November 2021. doi: 10.1016/j.jmoneco.2021.10.007.

Michael J. Walker. Benefits and challenges of the "CECL" approach. Supervisory Research and Analysis Notes 19-1, Federal Reserve Bank of Boston, March 2019. https://www.cigionline.org/publications/design-and-governance-financial-stability-regimes-challenge-technical-know-how.

John R. Walter. Loan loss reserves. *Federal Reserve Bank of Richmond Economic Review*, **77**(4):20–30, July 1991. https://www.richmondfed.org/-/media/RichmondFedOrg/publications/research/economic_review/1991/pdf/er770402.pdf.

John R. Walter. U.S. bank capital regulation: history and changes since the financial crisis. *Federal Reserve Bank of Richmond Economic Quarterly*, **105**(1):1–40, Q1 2019. doi: https://doi.org/10.21144/eq1050101.

John R. Walter and John A. Weinberg. How large is the Federal financial safety net? *Cato Journal*, **21**(3):369–393, Winter 2002. https://www.cato.org/sites/cato.org/files/serials/files/cato-journal/2002/1/cj21n3-2.pdf.

Zhenyu Wang. Coco bonds: are they debt or equity? *The ECGI Blog*, April 6, 2023. https://www.ecgi.global/blog/coco-bonds-are-they-debt-or-equity-do-they-help-financial-stability-%E2%80%94-lessons-credit-suisse-nt1.

Lawrence A. Weiss and Karen H. Wruck. Information problems, conficts of interest, and asset stripping: Chapter 11's failure in the case of Eastern Airlines. *Journal of Financial Economics*, **48**(1):55–97, April 1998. doi: 10.1016/S0304-405X(98)00004-X.

William R. White. Is price stability enough? Working Papers 205, Bank for International Settlements, April 2006. https://www.bis.org/publ/work205.pdf.

William R. White. Should monetary policy "lean or clean"? *Central Banking*, **19**(4):32–42, May 2009. https://williamwhite.ca/wp-content/uploads/2010/03/White_Article_CentralBanking.pdf.

Oliver E. Williamson. *The economic institutions of capitalism: firms, markets, relational contracting*. Free Press, New York, 1985.

Thomas C. Wilson. Portfolio credit risk. *Federal Reserve Bank of New York Economic Policy Review*, **4**(3):71–82, October 1998. https://www.newyorkfed.org/research/epr/98v04n3/9810wils.pdf.

Vladimir Yankov. The Liquidity Coverage Ratio and corporate liquidity management. FEDS Notes, Board of Governors of the Federal Reserve System, February 26, 2020. https://doi.org/10.17016/2380-7172.2509.

Leland B. Yeager. *International monetary relations: theory, history, and policy*. Harper and Row, New York, 2nd edition, 1976.

Arwin G. Zeissler, Daisuke Ikeda, and Andrew Metrick. JPMorgan Chase London Whale A: risky business. *Journal of Financial Crises*, **1**(2):40–59, 2019. https://elischolar.library.yale.edu/journal-of-financial-crises/vol1/iss2/2.

Index

Page numbers followed by *f* and *t* refer to figures and tables, respectively.